HP
Certified Systems
Administrator

EXAM
HP0-095

Training Guide and Administrator's Reference

2nd Edition
August 2007

Asghar Ghori

Lightning Source

1246 Heil Quaker Blvd., La Vergne, TN USA 37086
6 Precedent Dr., Rooksley, Milton Keynes, UK MK13-8PR
www.lightningsource.com

Technical Reviewers: Mehmood Khan, Ming Zhao, Asif Zuberi, and Kurt Glasgow
Cover Design: Asif Zuberi
Printers and Distributors: Lightning Source Inc.

Printed in the United States of America and the United Kingdom.

ISBN: 978-1-4243-4231-0

Printed and Distributed by: Lightning Source Inc.

To order additional copies, please contact us.
Lightning Source Inc.
www.lightningsource.com
USA (615) 213-5815 / UK (44) 1908-443555

Preface

Here is the second edition of the book. The objective to update and bring out this edition is based on the fact that HP recently revised the Certified Systems Administrator exam. The new exam HP0-095 (which has replaced HP0-091) covers several additional topics that have made it more comprehensive and broader in terms of scope. This edition of the book reflects the updates and provides a single, comprehensive resource that equips you with enough knowledge to pass the exam. At the same time, the book also furnishes you with procedures to help setup and administer an HP-UX operating system based computing environment effectively and efficiently.

I have put together 672 practice exam questions to help you prepare for the certification exam. My suggestion to you is to take this quiz once you finish studying the entire book along with all installation, configuration, and administration tasks offered. Passing the exam does not mean that you become an expert in the area. You need to do hands-on practice on actual HP-UX systems as much as possible to master the concepts learnt. If a command does not produce desired results, see what messages it generates and try to resolve it. Minor issues, such as wrong path, prevent commands from being executed. Sometimes there are syntax errors in the command construct. HP-UX manual pages prove helpful and useful in comprehending commands and their syntax. There is a whole bunch of commands, options, and configuration files in the operating system. Discussing all of them is not possible within the scope of this book.

There are three areas where you should focus to gain expertise with HP-UX – grasping concepts, mastering step-by-step implementation procedures, and learning commands, configuration files, and service daemons. An excellent understanding of which command involves and updates which files, which daemon provides what services, etc. must also be developed. This way you develop a better overall understanding of what exactly happens in the background when a command is executed. This book provides all that knowledge. Troubleshooting becomes easier when concepts are clear and working knowledge is solid.

I am maintaining *www.getitcertify.com* website where errors encountered in the book, additional exam information, and links to useful resources are made available. I encourage you to visit it.

At the end, I would like to ask you to forward your feedback, negative or positive, to my personal email address *asghar_ghori2002@yahoo.com* about the content, structure, layout, consistency, clarity, and flow of the book. Please also let me know if you come across any errors or mistakes. Improvement is a continuous process and I am sure your feedback will help me bring out a better and improved third edition, as it helped me with this second edition.

Good luck in your endeavors.

Asghar Ghori
August 2007
Toronto, Canada

Acknowledgments

I am grateful to God who enabled me to write and update this book successfully.

I would like to thank my friends, colleagues, students, and peers that supported and encouraged me to write this book. I am also grateful for their tremendous feedback from the first edition of this book that assisted me to come up with a better, updated second edition. I am thankful to all of them for their invariable support, constant encouragement, constructive feedback, and valuable assistance.

Finally, I would like to pay my special thanks to my wife, two daughters, and son, who endured me through the lifecycle of this project and extended their full assistance, support, and love. I would not be able to complete this project without their cooperation and support.

Asghar Ghori

About the Author

Currently working as an independent technical consultant on a large-scale server refresh and infrastructure upgrade project, Asghar Ghori has been in the IT industry for 17+ years. He started his career as a UNIX support engineer working with SCO UNIX and SCO XENIX visiting customers and providing UNIX technical support services. He has worked with various flavors of the UNIX operating system including HP-UX, SUN Solaris, IBM AIX, Microsoft XENIX, AT&T UNIX, SGI's IRIS, ISC UNIX, DYNIX/ptx, Stratus UNIX, etc. He has worked in different capacities, such as UNIX support engineer, UNIX administrator, UNIX specialist, technical lead, solution design lead, and technology consultant serving business and government customers. In addition, he has architected and deployed solutions around HP-UX and Sun Solaris operating system flavors that involved enterprise disk and tape storage subsystems, Storage Area Networks, clustering technologies, such as HP ServiceGuard and Veritas Cluster Server, systems management software, and so on.

Asghar Ghori has been involved in planning, developing, and executing IT infrastructure disaster recovery procedures for multiple large corporations.

Asghar Ghori holds a BS in Engineering, and has delivered and attended numerous training programs. He has been delivering courses on UNIX for the past seven years at local colleges in Toronto, Canada. He teaches UNIX as a sessional faculty at Algoma University. He is HP Certified Systems Administrator (HP0-002, HP0-091, HP0-095), HP Certified Systems Engineer (lab – HP-UX operations), SUN Certified System Administrator (SCSA) for various Solaris versions, IBM Certified Specialist for AIX, Certified Novell Engineer (CNE), EMC Proven Professional Technology Storage/Architect (EMCPA), and holds Project Management Professional (PMP) certification designation.

Conventions Used in this Book

The following typographic and other conventions are used throughout this book:

Arial Italic is used in text paragraphs for file and directory names, commands, daemons, hostnames, usernames, printer names, URLs, and special words or phrases that are emphasized. For example:

> "HP-UX, like other UNIX operating systems, is a *multi-user, multi-tasking, multi-processing, and multi-threading* operating system meaning that a number of users can access an HP-UX machine simultaneously and share its resources."

Arial Bold is used for commands and command line arguments that the user is expected to type at the command prompt. For example:

> $ **ls –lt**

All headings and sub-headings are also bold.

ctrl+x key sequence means that you hold down the *ctrl* key on the keyboard and then press the other key.

Light grey background is used to highlight output generated by commands and shell scripts.

. . . . Dotted lines are used to show the continuation of text in command outputs.

 Indicates additional information.

☞ Indicates a task performed using HP-UX System Administration Manager (SAM).

About this Book

Like the first edition of this book, the second edition also covers three main objectives – to provide a comprehensive resource to individuals, including novice, IT/Non-HP-UX administrators, and HP-UX administrators who intend to take the new HP Certified Systems Administrator exam HP0-095 and pass it; to provide a quick and valuable on-the-job resource to HP-UX administrators, administrators of other UNIX operating systems, IT managers, programmers, and DBAs working in the HP-UX environment; and to provide an easy-to-understand guide to novice and IT/non-HP-UX administrators who intend to learn HP-UX from the beginning.

This book contains 38 chapters and is structured to facilitate readers to grasp concepts, understand implementation procedures, understand basic troubleshooting, learn command syntax, configuration files, and daemons involved. The 38 chapters are divided into three key areas: UNIX Fundamentals, HP-UX System Administration, and HP-UX Network Administration.

1. **UNIX Fundamentals** (chapters 1 to 6 and 23) covers the basics of UNIX. Most information is not specific to a particular UNIX flavor, rather includes general UNIX concepts, file manipulation and security techniques, vi editor, shell and awk programming, basic commands, and other essential topics. Unlike many other similar books, a chapter on shell scripting is presented after covering HP-UX System Administration area. This is done purposely to supply readers with practical examples based on the knowledge they gain from UNIX Fundamentals and HP-UX System Administration chapters.

2. **HP-UX System Administration** (chapters 7 to 22) covers the HP-UX-specific system administration concepts and topics, including system partitioning and HP-UX installation; software and patch management; user and group administration; LVM and VxVM management; file system and swap administration; system shutdown and startup procedures; kernel configuration and reconfiguration techniques; backup and restore functions; printer and print request management, job automation and process control; and system logging and performance monitoring.

3. **HP-UX Network Administration** (chapters 24 to 38) covers HP-UX network administration concepts and topics, such as OSI and TCP/IP reference models; network hardware overview and LAN card administration; IP subnetting and routing techniques; basic network testing and troubleshooting; internet services and sendmail; time synchronization (NTP) and resource sharing (NFS, AutoFS, and CIFS) services; naming (DNS, NIS, and LDAP) and boot services; automated installation techniques and high-availability concepts; and system security and hardening.

Each chapter begins with a list of major topics to be covered in the chapter and ends with a summary. Throughout the book, tables, figures, screen shots, and examples are given for explanation purposes. The output generated because of running commands and shell scripts is highlighted in light grey background to differentiate from surrounding text.

The book includes several appendices, one of which contains 672 practice exam questions. Answers to practice exam questions and tables of commands, important files, and service daemons are included in appendix area as well.

About the HP CSA Exam (HP0-095)

The Certified Systems Administrator certification exam from Hewlett-Packard is designed for UNIX professionals. There is only one exam to pass to get this certification. There are total 78 questions on the exam. Question formats include multiple choice, drag-and-drop, and graphical. A minimum score of 70% is required to pass the exam within 105 minutes. The official exam objectives are given below and are covered in various chapters throughout the book.

Objective 1: HP-UX System Administration

1. Architecture and structure of HP-UX
2. Describe the HP-UX OS architecture
3. Describe the HP-UX processor families
4. Describe the major hardware components found in HP's current systems
5. Describe the features and benefits of HP disk management solutions
6. Describe the significance of basic LVM concepts and structure
7. Describe the significance of basic VxVM concepts and structure

Objective 2: HP-UX user environment, basic commands, and utilities

1. Login and logout of an HP-UX system
2. Determine basic information about a system
3. Execute HP-UX commands from the command line
4. Manage and manipulate files and directories
5. Define and describe the attributes of basic system components
6. Demonstrate the tools and techniques used to identify, monitor, and terminate programs and processes
7. Identify and explain how and when to use advanced shell features
8. Describe and demonstrate how to communicate with system users
9. Describe when and how to access basic network services

Objective 3: HP-UX system administration and operational tasks

1. Boot, reboot, and shutdown an HP-UX system or partition
2. Connect and configure HP-UX hardware
3. Describe, configure, and manage HP-UX device files
4. Configure and manage disks and partitions
5. Maintain file and file system integrity and design
6. Backup and recover data on an HP-UX system
7. Create and manage swap space
8. Create and manage user/group environments
9. Describe print spooling and its use
10. Configure and reconfigure the HP-UX kernel
11. Describe common areas of performance bottlenecks
12. Describe SYS-V IPC services and their use
13. Describe SAM and its use
14. Describe System Startup model and its use
15. Describe chroot and its use
16. Describe /etc/default and its use

17. Monitor system activity and events
18. Implement HP partitioning solutions

Objective 4: HP-UX system network administration tasks

1. Describe MAC addressing and its use
2. Describe IP addressing and its use
3. Describe NIC and its use
4. Enable DHCP for NIC address configuration
5. Check local connectivity to a known neighbor by IP or by MAC address
6. Describe set_parms and its use
7. Describe common network configuration files and their use
8. Describe network monitor utilities and their use
9. Configure and monitor network services
10. Describe the HP CIFS product suite and its use
11. Describe the ONC suite of network services and their use
12. Describe LDAP and its use
13. Describe DNS and its use
14. Describe sendmail and its use as a MTA and MDA
15. Describe NTP and its use

Objective 5: HP-UX installation, upgrade, and recovery tasks

1. Perform an HP-UX installation from local installation media
2. Perform HP-UX software installation from an SD-UX server
3. Configure a SD-UX depot server
4. Install HP-UX patches
5. Describe the features and benefits of Ignite-UX
6. Perform an HP-UX installation from an Ignite-UX Server
7. Install and configure an Ignite-UX server

Objective 6: HP-UX security administration tasks

1. Cite 'users level' security settings
2. Describe trusted system and its use
3. Describe password creation options and their use
4. Describe how to implement system access restrictions
5. Describe common system security concerns
6. Describe ssh and its use
7. Describe PAM and its use
8. Describe available security tools
9. Describe common administrative security tasks
10. Explain how various network architectures/features can affect a system security policy
11. Describe Standard Mode Security Extensions

Objective 7: Describe HP-UX High Availability and Clustering Features

1. Explain Key HA Terms
2. Identify the Risks with SPOF

Visit *www.hp.com/go/certification* for up-to-date and more in-depth information about the CSA exam requirements.

Exam Fee and How to Register for the Exam

The exam fee is US$124. To register for the exam, call Prometric at 1 800 718-3926 or visit *www.2test.com* or *www.prometric.com*. A list of Authorized Prometric Testing Centers (APTCs) can be obtained from these sites as well. You are required to provide your HP student ID when you register for the exam.

HP Student ID

Before registering for the HP CSA HP0-095 certification exam, you must obtain an HP Student ID. This unique identification number is allocated to each HP-UX exam candidate. Visit *www.hp.com/certification/americas/student_id.html* and follow the procedure.

TABLE OF CONTENTS

Preface iii
Acknowledgments iv
About the Author v
Conventions Used in this Book vi
About this Book vii
About the HP CSA Exam (HP0-095) viii

01. Overview of HP-UX Operating Environment 1
   1.1   Introduction 2
      1.1.1   HP-UX System Structure 2
      1.1.2   HP-UX Features 4
   1.2   Logging In and Out 4
      1.2.1   Logging In and Out at the System Console 4
      1.2.2   Logging In and Out Using CDE 5
      1.2.3   Logging In and Out Using *telnet* 6
   1.3   Common Desktop Environment (CDE) 7
      1.3.1   Front Panel 7
      1.3.2   Clock 8
      1.3.3   The Calendar Manager 8
      1.3.4   The File Manager 8
      1.3.5   Personal Applications 9
      1.3.6   The Mail Manager 9
      1.3.7   The Front Panel Lock 9
      1.3.8   Virtual Workspaces 9
      1.3.9   The Exit Button 10
      1.3.10   The Printer Manager 11
      1.3.11   The Style Manager 11
      1.3.12   The Application Manager 11
      1.3.13   Help 11
      1.3.14   The Trash Can 12
   1.4   Common HP-UX Commands 12
      1.4.1   What is the Command Line? 12
      1.4.2   The *ls* Command and its Variations 12
      1.4.3   The *pwd* Command 15
      1.4.4   The *cd* Command 15
      1.4.5   The *tty* and *pty* Commands 16
      1.4.6   The *who* Command 16
      1.4.7   The *w* Command 17
      1.4.8   The *whoami* Command 17
      1.4.9   The *logname* Command 17
      1.4.10   The *id* Command 17
      1.4.11   The *groups* Command 18
      1.4.12   The *uname* Command 18
      1.4.13   The *hostname* Command 18
      1.4.14   The *model* and *getconf* Commands 18
      1.4.15   The *clear* Command 19
      1.4.16   The *date* Command 19

1.4.17   The *cal* Command 19
1.4.18   The *uptime* Command 19
1.4.19   The *banner* Command 20
1.4.20   The *wc* Command 20
1.4.21   The *diff* Command 21
1.4.22   The *which* and *whence* Commands 22
1.4.23   The *whereis* Command 22
1.4.24   The *write* Command 22
1.4.25   The *talk* Command 22
1.4.26   The *wall* Command 23
1.5   Online Help 23
1.5.1   *man* Sections 24
1.5.2   Searching by Keyword 25
Summary 26

02. Working with Files and Directories 27

2.1   File System Tree 28
2.1.1   The Root File System (/) 29
2.1.2   The Kernel File System (*/stand*) 31
2.1.3   The Variable File System (*/var*) 31
2.1.4   The UNIX System Resources File System (*/usr*) 31
2.1.5   The Temporary File System (*/tmp*) 32
2.1.6   The Optional File System (*/opt*) 32
2.1.7   The Home File System (*/home*) 32
2.2   Absolute and Relative Paths 32
2.2.1   Absolute Path 32
2.2.2   Relative Path 33
2.3   File Types 33
2.3.1   Regular Files 33
2.3.2   Directory Files 34
2.3.3   Executable Files 34
2.3.4   Symbolic Link Files 35
2.3.5   Device Files 35
2.3.6   Named Pipe Files 36
2.3.7   Socket Files 36
2.4   File and Directory Operations 37
2.4.1   File Naming Convention 37
2.4.2   Creating Files and Directories 37
2.4.3   Listing Files and Directories 38
2.4.4   Displaying File Contents 39
2.4.5   Copying Files and Directories 45
2.4.6   Moving and Renaming Files and Directories 46
2.4.7   Removing Files and Directories 47
2.4.8   Summary of File and Directory Operations 48
2.5   Searching for Text within Files 48
2.6   Finding Files in the Directory Structure 51
2.7   Sorting File Contents 53
2.8   Linking Files and Directories 55
Summary 56

03. Working with File and Directory Permissions 59
3.1   Determining Access Permissions 60
3.1.1   Permission Classes 60
3.1.2   Permission Types 60
3.1.3   Permission Modes 60
3.2   Changing Access Permissions 62
3.2.1   Using Symbolic Notation 62
3.2.2   Using Octal (or Absolute) Notation 63
3.3   Setting Default Permissions 64
3.3.1   Calculating Default Permissions 65
3.4   Changing File Ownership and Group Membership 66
3.5   Special Permissions 67
3.5.1   The setuid Bit 67
3.5.2   The setgid Bit 68
3.5.3   The Sticky Bit 69
3.6   Access Control List (ACL) 69
3.6.1   Listing ACL Information 70
3.6.2   Changing ACL Information 70
3.6.3   Default ACL 73
Summary 73

04. The vi Editor and Text Processors 75
4.1   The vi Editor 76
4.1.1   Modes of Operation 76
4.1.2   Starting the vi Editor 76
4.1.3   Inserting text 77
4.1.4   Navigating within vi 77
4.1.5   Deleting Text 78
4.1.6   Undoing and Repeating 78
4.1.7   Searching and Replacing Text 79
4.1.8   Copying, Moving, and Pasting Text 79
4.1.9   Changing Text 80
4.1.10   Importing Contents of Another File 80
4.1.11   Customizing vi Edit Sessions 80
4.1.12   Saving and Quitting vi 81
4.1.13   Miscellaneous vi Commands 81
4.2   The Text Processors 81
4.2.1   The awk Processor 82
4.2.2   The sed Processor 85
Summary 88

05. The HP-UX Shells 89
5.1   The Shell 90
5.1.1   Available Shells 90
5.2   POSIX Shell Features 91
5.2.1   Variables 91
5.2.2   Setting, Unsetting, and Viewing Variables 92
5.2.3   Pre-Defined Environment Variables 94
5.2.4   Changing Command Prompt 95
5.2.5   Input, Output, and Error Redirection 95

5.2.6   Filename Completion, Command Line Editing, and Command History 97
5.2.7   Command Aliasing 99
5.2.8   Special Characters 101
5.2.9   Masking Special Meaning of Some Special Characters 102
5.3   Pipes and Filters 103
5.3.1   Pipes 103
5.3.2   The *tee* Filter 104
5.3.3   The *cut* Filter 105
5.3.4   The *pr* Filter 105
5.3.5   The *tr* Filter 107
Summary 107

06. System Processes and Job Control 109
6.1   Understanding Processes 110
6.1.1   Viewing System Processes 110
6.1.2   Process States 112
6.1.3   Process Priority 112
6.2   Signals and Their Use 113
6.3   Managing Jobs in the POSIX Shell 115
6.4   Executing a Command Immune to Hangup Signals 116
Summary 117

07. System Administration and HP-UX Server Hardware 119
7.1   HP-UX System Administration Overview 120
7.1.1   System Administrator Responsibilities 120
7.1.2   System Administrator Resources 120
7.2   System Administration Manager (SAM) 122
7.2.1   Starting SAM 122
7.2.2   SAM Log 125
7.2.3   Restricted SAM Access to Users 126
7.3   Server Hardware Component Overview 127
7.3.1   Slot 127
7.3.2   PCI and PCI-X 128
7.3.3   Interface Card 129
7.3.4   Network Interface Card 129
7.3.5   SCSI Card 129
7.3.6   Multi-function Card 130
7.3.7   Bus 131
7.3.8   Bus Converter 131
7.3.9   Processor/Core 131
7.3.10   Cell Board 131
7.3.11   I/O Chassis 132
7.3.12   Core I/O 132
7.3.13   Power Supply 132
7.3.14   Server Expansion Unit 132
7.3.15   Cabinet 133
7.3.16   Server Complex 133
7.4   HP-UX Servers 134
7.4.1   HP Integrity Series Servers 134
7.4.2   HP 9000 Series Servers 135

7.5   Device Files and Major/Minor Numbers 136
  7.5.1   Physical Device Addressing 137
  7.5.2   Logical Device Files 138
  7.5.3   Major and Minor Numbres 141
  7.5.4   Creating Device Files 142
  7.5.5   Removing Device Files 144
7.6   Viewing Hardware Diagnostic Messages 144
Summary 146

08. HP-UX Partitioning Continuum 147

8.1   Understanding HP-UX Partitioning Continuum 148
  8.1.1   Supported Partitioning Continuum Technologies 148
  8.1.2   Benefits of Partitioning 148
8.2   Introduction to Management Processor (MP) 148
  8.2.1   Setting Serial MP Display Parameters 149
  8.2.2   Setting LAN MP Parameters 149
  8.2.3   Interacting with MP 150
8.3   Hardware Available to Work with Partitioning 151
8.4   Node Partitioning 152
  8.4.1   Creating the Genesis Partition 153
  8.4.2   Creating an nPar 154
  8.4.3   Changing an nPar Name 155
  8.4.4   Adding a Cell to an nPar 155
  8.4.5   Removing a Cell from an nPar 156
  8.4.6   Removing an nPar 156
  8.4.7   Using Partition Manager GUI 156
8.5   Virtual Partitioning 158
  8.5.1   Bound and Unbound Processors 159
  8.5.2   Creating the First vPar 159
  8.5.3   Creating Another vPar 161
  8.5.4   Adding a CPU to a vPar 162
  8.5.5   Removing a Processor from a vPar 163
  8.5.6   Adding an I/O Path to a vPar 163
  8.5.7   Removing an I/O Path from a vPar 163
  8.5.8   Adding Memory to a vPar 164
  8.5.9   Resetting a vPar 164
  8.5.10   Removing a vPar 164
  8.5.11   Rebooting vpmon 164
  8.5.12   Using Virtual Partition Manager GUI 165
8.6   Integrity Virtual Machines Partitioning 165
8.7   Resource Partitioning 166
Summary 167

09. HP-UX Operating Environment Installation 169

9.1   HP-UX Installation 170
  9.1.1   Types of HP-UX OE Software 170
  9.1.2   Planning Installation 171
  9.1.3   Installing HP-UX Using Local Media 172
9.2   Using *set_parms* 178
Summary 179

10. Software Management 181
10.1   Software Distributor Concepts and Components 182
   10.1.1   Software Structure 182
   10.1.2   Commands and Daemons 182
   10.1.3   Installed Product Database 184
   10.1.4   Software Dependencies 184
   10.1.5   Protected Software 184
10.2   Managing Software 184
   10.2.1   Listing Installed Software 184
   10.2.2   Installing Software 187
   10.2.3   Verifying Installed Software 190
   10.2.4   Removing Software 190
10.3   Software Depots 192
   10.3.1   Catalog Files 192
10.4   Managing Software Depots 193
   10.4.1   Copying Software to a Depot 193
   10.4.2   Registering and Unregistering a Depot 195
   10.4.3   Listing Depots 196
   10.4.4   Listing Depot Contents 196
   10.4.5   Verifying Depot Contents 197
   10.4.6   Removing Software from a Depot 198
   10.4.7   Removing a Depot 199
Summary 199

11. Patch Management 201
11.1   Understanding Patch Management 202
   11.1.1   Patch Naming Convention 202
11.2   Patch Attributes 202
   11.2.1   Patch Suppression 203
   11.2.2   Patch Dependency 203
   11.2.3   Patch Rating 204
   11.2.4   Critical and Non-Critical Patches 204
   11.2.5   Patch Status 204
   11.2.6   Patch State 204
   11.2.7   Category Tag 205
   11.2.8   Patch Ancestry 205
11.3   Managing Patches 206
   11.3.1   Listing Installed Patches 206
   11.3.2   Acquiring Individual Patches 207
   11.3.3   Installing Individual Patches 208
   11.3.4   Listing Installed Patch Bundles 210
   11.3.5   Acquiring Patch Bundles 211
   11.3.6   Installing Patch Bundles 212
   11.3.7   Installing Patches from CD/DVD 214
   11.3.8   Installing Patches from Tape 214
   11.3.9   Verifying a Patch and Patch Bundle 214
   11.3.10   Rolling Back (Removing) a Patch 216
   11.3.11   Committing a Patch 216
11.4   Additional Patch Tools 217
   11.4.1   The Patch Assessment Tool 217

11.4.2   The Security Patch Check Tool 219
11.4.3   Introduction to HP-UX Software Assistant (SWA) 220
Summary 220

12. User and Group Account Administration 223

12.1   Why Create Users and Groups 224
12.1.1   User Authentication – The /etc/passwd File 224
12.1.2   User Authentication – The /etc/group File 225
12.1.3   Verifying /etc/passwd and /etc/group File Consistency 227
12.1.4   Locking /etc/passwd File 227
12.2   Managing User Accounts and Passwords 227
12.2.1   Creating a User Account 227
12.2.2   Creating Multiple User Accounts in One Go 231
12.2.3   Modifying a User Account 232
12.2.4   Deactivating and Reactivating a User Account 233
12.2.5   Deleting a User Account 233
12.2.6   Displaying Successful User Login Attempts History 234
12.2.7   Displaying Unsuccessful User Login Attempts History 235
12.2.8   Displaying Currently Logged In Users 235
12.2.9   Displaying and Setting User Limits 235
12.3   Managing Group Accounts 236
12.3.1   Creating a Group Account 236
12.3.2   Modifying a Group Account 236
12.3.3   Deleting a Group Account 237
12.3.4   Assigning Multiple Group Memberships 238
12.4   User Login Process & Initialization Files 238
12.4.1   Initialization Files 239
12.4.2   User Login Process via CDE 242
Summary 243

13. Logical Volume Manager 245

13.1   Disk Partitioning Solutions 246
13.2   The Logical Volume Manager (LVM) Solution 246
13.2.1   LVM Concepts 247
13.2.2   LVM Major and Minor Numbers 250
13.2.3   LVM Data Structure 250
13.3   Managing Volumes Using LVM 251
13.3.1   Identifying Available Disk Devices 251
13.3.2   Creating a Physical Volume 253
13.3.3   Creating and Displaying a Volume Group 254
13.3.4   Creating and Displaying a Logical Volume 256
13.3.5   Extending a Volume Group 259
13.3.6   Extending a Logical Volume 260
13.3.7   Reducing a Logical Volume 261
13.3.8   Removing a Logical Volume 262
13.3.9   Reducing a Volume Group 262
13.3.10   Removing a Volume Group 262
13.3.11   Backing Up and Recovering LVM Configuration 263
13.4   LVM Mirroring 264
13.4.1   Mirroring the Boot Volume Group 264

13.4.2   Mirroring a Non-Boot Volume Group 269
13.4.3   Mirroring and Allocation Policies 270
13.4.4   Extending Mirrors 278
13.4.5   Reducing Mirrors 278
13.4.6   Synchronizing Stale Mirrors 279
13.4.7   Splitting Mirrors 279
13.4.8   Merging Mirrors 280
13.5   The Whole Disk Solution 280
Summary 281

14. Veritas Volume Manager 283
14.1   The Veritas Volume Manager Solution 284
14.1.1   VxVM Concepts and Structure 284
14.1.2   Supported RAID Levels 286
14.1.3   VxVM Interfaces 287
14.1.4   VxVM Commands and Daemons 289
14.2   Managing Volumes Using VxVM 290
14.2.1   Identifying Available Disk Devices 291
14.2.2   Making a Disk Visible to VxVM 291
14.2.3   Initializing a Disk 293
14.2.4   Creating and Displaying a Disk Group 294
14.2.5   Creating and Displaying a Volume 294
14.2.6   Expanding a Disk Group 295
14.2.7   Growing a Volume 295
14.2.8   Shrinking a Volume 295
14.2.9   Removing a Volume 296
14.2.10   Reducing a Disk Group 296
14.2.11   Deporting and Importing a Disk Group 296
14.2.12   Renaming a Disk Group 297
14.2.13   Destroying a Disk Group 297
14.2.14   Converting LVM *vg00* to VxVM *rootdg* 297
14.2.15   Converting LVM non-*vg00* to VxVM non-*rootdg* 298
14.3   VxVM Mirroring 298
14.3.1   Mirroring the Boot Disk Group 299
14.3.2   Mirroring a Non-Boot Disk Group 301
14.3.3   Growing Mirrors 301
14.3.4   Shrinking Mirrors 301
14.4   Comparing LVM and VxVM 301
Summary 302

15. Working with File Systems 303
15.1   File System Concepts 304
15.2   File System Types 304
15.2.1   The High-Performance File System (HFS) 305
15.2.2   The Journaled File System (JFS) 307
15.3   Managing HFS and VxFS File Systems 309
15.3.1   Creating a File System 309
15.3.2   Mounting a File System 312
15.3.3   Viewing Mounted File Systems 313
15.3.4   Creating, Mounting, and Viewing a File System Using SAM 314

15.3.5   Extending a File System 315
15.3.6   Reducing a File System 316
15.3.7   Tuning a JFS File System 317
15.3.8   Defragmenting a JFS File System 317
15.3.9   Unmounting a File System 318
15.3.10   Mounting a File System at System Boot 319
15.3.11   Removing a File System 320
15.4   Repairing a Damaged File System 321
15.5   Managing CDFS and LOFS File Systems 323
15.5.1   Mounting and Unmounting a CDFS File System 323
15.5.2   Mounting and Unmounting a LOFS File System 324
15.6   Monitoring File System Space Utilization 324
15.6.1   Using *bdf* 324
15.6.2   Using *df* 326
15.6.3   Using *du* 327
15.6.4   Using *quot* 328
Summary 328

16. Managing Swap Space 329
16.1   Understanding Swap 330
16.1.1   Swap Space and Demand Paging 331
16.1.2   Device and File System Swap 332
16.1.3   Primary and Secondary Swap 332
16.2   Managing Swap 332
16.2.1   Creating and Enabling a Device Swap 332
16.2.2   Creating and Enabling a File System Swap 334
16.2.3   Enabling Swap Space at System Boot 335
16.2.4   Viewing Swap Utilization 336
16.3   Priority and Best Practices 337
16.4   Related Kernel Parameters 338
Summary 338

17. Shutting Down and Starting Up an HP-UX System 341
17.1   Shuting Down an HP-UX Server 342
17.1.1   Run Control Levels 342
17.1.2   Checking Current and Previous Run Control Levels 342
17.1.3   Changing Run Control Levels 343
17.2   Booting an HP 9000 Server 346
17.2.1   Processor Dependent Code and Boot Console Handler 349
17.2.2   Viewing and Modifying Autoboot and Autosearch Flags 350
17.2.3   Viewing and Setting Primary, HAA, and Alternate Boot Device Paths 351
17.2.4   Booting from Primary, HAA, and Alternate Boot Devices 352
17.2.5   Booting from an Undefined Boot Device 352
17.2.6   Booting to Single User State 353
17.2.7   Booting to LVM and VxVM Maintenance States 354
17.2.8   Booting without Quorum Checking 354
17.2.9   Viewing and Modifying AUTO File Contents 355
17.2.10   Booting from an Alternate Kernel File 355
17.3   Booting an HP Integrity Server 356
17.3.1   Extensible Firmware Interface and Boot Manager 357

17.3.2   Booting Manually versus Automatically 357
17.3.3   Configuring Autoboot and Boot Delay Period 358
17.3.4   Viewing and Setting Primary, HAA, and Alternate Boot Device Paths 359
17.3.5   Booting from an Alternate Boot Device 359
17.3.6   Booting to Single User State 359
17.3.7   Booting to LVM and VxVM Maintenance States 360
17.3.8   Viewing and Modifying AUTO File Contents 360
17.3.9   Booting from an Alternate Kernel File 361
17.4   Initializing HP-UX 362
17.4.1   Kernel Initialization 362
17.4.2   The init Process 362
17.4.3   Building Hardware Device Tree 363
17.4.4   Checking and Activating Volume Groups 363
17.4.5   Starting Up Services 364
17.4.6   Starting and Stopping Services Manually 367
17.4.7   System Startup Log File 367
Summary 369

18. Kernel Reconfiguration Methods 371
18.1   Purpose of Reconfiguring the Kernel 372
18.1.1   Installing or Removing an HP-UX Patch 372
18.1.2   Adding or Removing a Device Driver 372
18.1.3   Adding or Removing a Subsystem 372
18.1.4   Changing the Primary Swap or the Dump Device 372
18.1.5   Modifying a Kernel Parameter 372
18.2   Static and Dynamic Kernel Components 372
18.2.1   Static and Dynamic Kernel Modules 373
18.2.2   Static and Dynamic Kernel Tunable Parameters 373
18.3   Reconfiguring the HP-UX 11iv1 Kernel 373
18.4   Querying, Loading, and Unloading DLKMs 380
18.5   Querying and Modifying DTKPs 382
18.6   Reconfiguring the HP-UX 11iv2 Kernel 383
18.6.1   The *kcweb* Tool 384
18.7   Common Tunable Parameters 386
Summary 387

19. Performing Backup and Restore 389
19.1   Basics of Backup 390
19.1.1   Backup, Restore, and Recovery Functions 390
19.1.2   Types of Backup 390
19.1.3   Levels of Backup 390
19.1.4   Sample Backup Schedule 391
19.1.5   Restore Procedure for the Sample Backup 391
19.2   Managing Backups and Restores 392
19.2.1   Performing Backups Using *fbackup* 392
19.2.2   Performing Restores Using *frecover* 393
19.2.3   *fbackup* and *frecover* via SAM 394
19.2.4   Performing Backups/Restores Using *dump/restore* 395
19.2.5   Performing Backups/Restores Using *vxdump/vxrestore* 396
19.2.6   Using *tar* 397

19.2.7   Using *cpio* 398
19.2.8   Using *dd* 399
19.3   Introduction to HP Data Protector Software 399
Summary 400

20. Print Services Management 401
20.1   Understanding Print Spooler 402
    20.1.1   Print Spooler Directory Hierarchy 402
    20.1.2   Starting and Stopping Print Spooler Daemon 403
20.2   Types of Printer Setups 403
    20.2.1   Local Printer 404
    20.2.2   Remote Printer 404
    20.2.3   Network Printer 405
20.3   Setting Up Printers 405
    20.3.1   Setting Up a Local Printer 406
    20.3.2   Setting Up a Remote Printer 407
    20.3.3   Setting Up a Network Printer 408
20.4   Administering Printers 410
    20.4.1   Setting Default Print Destination 410
    20.4.2   Enabling and Disabling a Printer 411
    20.4.3   Accepting and Rejecting Print Requests 411
    20.4.4   Checking Printer Status 412
    20.4.5   Setting Printer Priority 412
    20.4.6   Setting Printer Fence Level 413
    20.4.7   Removing a Printer 413
20.5   Administering Print Requests 413
    20.5.1   Submitting a Print Request 414
    20.5.2   Listing a Print Request 415
    20.5.3   Modifying a Print Request 415
    20.5.4   Moving a Print Request 415
    20.5.5   Canceling a Print Request 415
Summary 416

21. Job Scheduling and System Logging 417
21.1   What is Job Scheduling? 418
    21.1.1   Starting and Stopping the *cron* Daemon 418
    21.1.2   Controlling User Access 418
    21.1.3   cron Log File 419
21.2   Job Scheduling Using *at* 419
    21.2.1   Setting Up an *at* Job 419
    21.2.2   Listing and Removing *at* Jobs 420
21.3   Job Scheduling Using *crontab* 421
    21.3.1   Syntax of the *crontab* File 421
    21.3.2   Setting Up a *cron* Job 422
    21.3.3   Listing and Removing *cron* Jobs 422
21.4   System Logging 423
    21.4.1   The System Log Configuration File 423
    21.4.2   The System Log File 425
Summary 425

22. Performance Monitoring 427

22.1   Performance Monitoring 428
   22.1.1   Performance Monitoring Tools 428
   22.1.2   Monitoring CPU Performance 429
   22.1.3   Monitoring Physical Memory and Swap Performance 431
   22.1.4   Monitoring Disk Performance 433
   22.1.5   Monitoring System Processes 434
   22.1.6   Monitoring Network Performance 436
22.2   Fixing a Performance Problem 436
Summary 436

23. POSIX Shell Scripting 437

23.1   Shell Scripting 438
23.2   Creating Shell Scripts 438
   23.2.1   Displaying Basic System Information 439
   23.2.2   Executing a Script 440
   23.2.3   Debugging a Shell Script 440
   23.2.4   Using Local Variables 441
   23.2.5   Using Pre-Defined Environment Variables 442
   23.2.6   Setting New Environment Variables 442
   23.2.7   Parsing Command Output 443
   23.2.8   Using Command Line Arguments 444
   23.2.9   Shifting Command Line Arguments 445
   23.2.10   Writing an Interactive Script 446
23.3   Logical Constructs 448
   23.3.1   Exit Codes 448
   23.3.2   What You Can Test 449
   23.3.3   The if-then-fi Construct 450
   23.3.4   The if-then-else-fi Construct 451
   23.3.5   The if-then-elif-fi Construct 452
   23.3.6   The case Construct 454
23.4   Looping Constructs 455
   23.4.1   What You can Test 456
   23.4.2   The for-do-done Loop 457
   23.4.3   The while-do-done Loop 459
   23.4.4   The until-do-done Loop 460
   23.4.5   Controlling Loop Behavior 462
   23.4.6   Ignoring Signals 464
Summary 465

24. Introduction to Networking 467

24.1   What is a Network? 468
24.2   Network Topologies 469
   24.2.1   Bus Topology 469
   24.2.2   Star Topology 470
   24.2.3   Ring Topology 471
   24.2.4   Hybrid Topology 471
24.3   Network Access Methods 472
   24.3.1   CSMA/CD 472
   24.3.2   Token Passing 472

24.3.3   Other Network Access Methods 473
24.4   LAN Cables 473
24.5   Introduction to OSI Reference Model 473
24.5.1   Layer 7: The Application Layer 474
24.5.2   Layer 6: The Presentation Layer 475
24.5.3   Layer 5: The Session Layer 476
24.5.4   Layer 4: The Transport Layer 476
24.5.5   Layer 3: The Network Layer 478
24.5.6   Layer 2: The Data Link Layer 478
24.5.7   Layer 1: The Physical Layer 479
24.5.8   Summary of OSI Layers 479
24.5.9   Encapsulation and De-encapsulation 480
24.5.10   Peer-to-Peer Model 480
24.6   Introduction to TCP/IP 481
24.6.1   TCP/IP Layers 481
24.6.2   MAC Address 482
24.6.3   Address Resolution Protocol (ARP) 482
24.6.4   Reverse Address Resolution Protocol (RARP) 483
24.6.5   Hostname 483
24.6.6   IP Address 484
24.6.7   Network Classes 485
24.6.8   Subnetting 487
24.6.9   Subnet Mask 488
24.6.10   IP Multiplexing 491
24.7   Virtual Private Network 491
Summary 491

25. LAN Card Administration and Routing 493
25.1   LAN Card Administration 494
25.1.1   Configuring a LAN Card/Port 494
25.1.2   Configuring IP Multiplexing 496
25.1.3   Setting a LAN Card/Port to Activate at System Boot 496
25.1.4   Defining an IP Address and Hostname in the /etc/hosts File 498
25.2   Routing 498
25.2.1   Routing Concepts 498
25.2.2   Routing Table 499
25.3   Managing Routes 500
25.3.1   Adding a Route 500
25.3.2   Deleting a Route 502
25.3.3   Flushing Routing Table 502
25.3.4   Setting the Default Route 502
25.4   Enabling DHCP Client Service 503
Summary 504

26. Network Connectivity Troubleshooting and Overview of Network
    Management 507
26.1   Network Connectivity Troubleshooting 508
26.1.1   Using ioscan 508
26.1.2   Using lanscan 509
26.1.3   Using linkloop 510

26.1.4   Using *lanadmin* 511
26.1.5   Using *ping* 514
26.1.6   Using *netstat* 514
26.1.7   Using *traceroute* 516
26.1.8   Using *ndd* 516
26.1.9   Using *nettl* 518
26.2   Overview of Network Management 519
Summary 520

27. Setting Up and Administering Internet Services and Sendmail 521
27.1   The Internet Services 522
27.1.1   Berkeley and ARPA Services 522
27.1.2   The *inetd* Daemon and the */etc/inetd.conf* File 524
27.1.3   Securing *inetd* 526
27.1.4   Enabling *inetd* Connection Logging 527
27.2   Using the Internet Services 528
27.2.1   Establishing Trust Relationship 528
27.2.2   Using Berkeley Services 530
27.2.3   Using ARPA Services 533
27.3   Setting Up Basic Sendmail Functionality 537
27.3.1   Setting Up Sendmail to be Used by Single System Users 538
27.3.2   Setting Up Sendmail in Client/Server Environment 538
27.3.3   Verifying Sendmail Functionality 539
27.3.4   Updating Aliases File 540
Summary 540

28. Setting Up and Administering NTP 541
28.1   NTP Concepts and Components 542
28.1.1   Time Source 542
28.1.2   Stratum Levels 543
28.1.3   NTP Roles 543
28.2   Setting Up NTP 544
28.2.1   Setting Up NTP Server and Peer 544
28.2.2   Setting Up an NTP Client 546
28.2.3   Enabling Authentication 547
28.3   Managing NTP 548
28.3.1   Updating System Clock Manually 548
28.3.2   Querying NTP Servers 548
28.3.3   Tracing Roots of an NTP Server 549
28.4   Troubleshooting Basic Issues 549
Summary 550

29. Setting Up and Administering NFS 551
29.1   Understanding Network File System (NFS) 552
29.1.1   Benefits 552
29.1.2   NFS Versions 553
29.1.3   NFS Daemons, Commands, Configuration Files, and Scripts 553
29.1.4   How NFS Works? 555
29.2   Setting Up NFS 556
29.2.1   Setting Up an NFS Server 556

      29.2.2   Setting Up an NFS Client 559
   29.3   Managing NFS 561
      29.3.1   Viewing Exported and Mounted Resources 562
      29.3.2   Unmounting a Resource 562
      29.3.3   Unexporting a Resource 563
   29.4   Monitoring NFS Activities 563
   29.5   Basic NFS Troubleshooting 564
   Summary 566

30. Setting Up and Administering AutoFS 567

   30.1   Understanding AutoFS 568
      30.1.1   Features and Benefits 568
      30.1.2   How AutoFS Works? 568
      30.1.3   Starting and Stopping AutoFS 569
   30.2   The AutoFS Maps 570
      30.2.1   Setting Up the Master Map 570
      30.2.2   Setting Up the Special Map 571
      30.2.3   Setting Up a Direct Map 572
      30.2.4   Setting Up an Indirect Map 574
      30.2.5   Setting Up AutoFS Maps via SAM 575
   30.3   Accessing Replicated Servers 575
   30.4   Mounting User Home Directories 576
   30.5   Comparing AutoFS and Automounter 576
   Summary 576

31. Setting Up CIFS/9000 579

   31.1   Understanding CIFS/9000 580
      31.1.1   Features of CIFS/9000 580
      31.1.2   Introduction to Samba 580
   31.2   Setting Up CIFS 582
      31.2.1   Setting Up a CIFS Server on HP-UX 582
      31.2.2   Accessing Exported CIFS Share on a Windows System 585
      31.2.3   Accessing a Windows Share on HP-UX 585
   Summary 587

32. Setting Up and Administering NIS 589

   32.1   NIS Concepts and Components 590
      32.1.1   NIS Domain 590
      32.1.2   NIS Maps 590
      32.1.3   NIS Server 591
      32.1.4   NIS Client 592
      32.1.5   NIS Daemons 592
   32.2   Setting Up NIS 593
      32.2.1   Set Up Considerations 593
      32.2.2   Setting Up a Master NIS Server 593
      32.2.3   Setting Up a Slave NIS Server 596
      32.2.4   Setting Up an NIS Client 597
      32.2.5   Configuring /etc/nsswitch.conf File 598
      32.2.6   Testing NIS Master, Slave, and Client Functionality 600

32.3   Managing NIS 601
   32.3.1   Displaying and Searching NIS Maps 601
   32.3.2   Changing a User Password 602
   32.3.3   Updating NIS Maps on the Master Server 602
   32.3.4   Updating NIS Maps on a Slave Server 603
   32.3.5   Manually Binding a Client to Another NIS Server 604
   32.3.6   Using Alternate passwd File 604
32.4   Securing Access to NIS Servers 605
Summary 605

33. Setting Up and Administering DNS 607

33.1   Understanding Name Resolution 608
   33.1.1   Name Resolution Approaches 608
33.2   DNS Concepts and Components 609
   33.2.1   DNS Name Space and Domains 609
   33.2.2   DNS Zones and Zone Files 611
   33.2.3   DNS Roles 611
   33.2.4   BIND Versions 612
   33.2.5   How DNS Works 613
33.3   Setting Up DNS 613
   33.3.1   Setting Up a Master DNS Server 613
   33.3.2   Understanding DNS Boot and Zone Files 615
   33.3.3   Setting Up a Slave DNS Server 621
   33.3.4   Setting Up a Caching-Only DNS Server 622
   33.3.5   Setting Up a DNS Client 622
33.4   Managing DNS 625
   33.4.1   Verifying DNS Functionality 625
   33.4.2   Updating Master, Slave, and Caching-Only DNS Servers 626
Summary 627

34. LDAP Basics 629

34.1   What is LDAP? 630
   34.1.1   Features and Benefits of Using LDAP 630
34.2   LDAP Terminology 631
   34.2.1   Directory 631
   34.2.2   Entry 631
   34.2.3   Attribute 631
   34.2.4   Matching Rule 632
   34.2.5   Object Class 632
   34.2.6   Schema 632
   34.2.7   LDAP Data Interchange Format (LDIF) 632
   34.2.8   Distinguished Name and Relative Distinguished Name 633
   34.2.9   LDAP Roles 633
34.3   Installing Netscape Directory Server Software 634
34.4   Installing an LDAP-UX Client 635
Summary 636

35. Introduction to BootP and TFTP Services 637

35.1   BootP / TFTP Services 638
   35.1.1   How It Works? 638

35.2   Configuring BootP and TFTP 638
    35.2.1   Configuration Files 638
    35.2.2   Adding and Verifying a BootP Client 640
    35.2.3   Adding and Verifying BootP Relay Information 641
Summary 641

36. Using Ignite-UX 643

36.1   Introduction to Ignite-UX 644
    36.1.1   Benefits of Using Ignite-UX 644
36.2   Setting Up an Ignite-UX Server 644
    36.2.1   Installing the Ignite-UX Product 644
    36.2.2   Registered and Anonymous Clients 645
    36.2.3   Setting Up an Ignite-UX Server from the GUI 645
    36.2.4   Setting Up an Ignite-UX Server from the Command Line 651
36.3   Booting Clients and Installing HP-UX OE 655
    36.3.1   Booting and Installing with UI Running on Client Console 655
    36.3.2   Booting and Installing with UI Running on Ignite-UX Server 657
36.4   Cloning (Golden Image) 661
    36.4.1   Creating a Golden Image on Tape 661
    36.4.2   Creating a Golden Image on a Network Directory 662
    36.4.3   Cloning a System Using Golden Image on Tape 663
    36.4.4   Cloning a System Using Golden Image on a Network Directory 663
36.5   System Recovery 664
    36.5.1   Creating and Using Recovery Archives 665
    36.5.2   Creating and Checking Tape Recovery Archive 665
Summary 665

37. Introduction to High Availability and Clustering 667

37.1   Introduction to High Availability 668
    37.1.1   Traditional Network Computing Model 668
    37.1.2   Redundant-Component Network Computing Model 669
    37.1.3   High-Availability Network Computing Model 670
    37.1.4   Ultra High-Availability Network Computing Model 671
37.2   Key HA Terms 672
    37.2.1   Downtime 672
    37.2.2   Uptime 672
    37.2.3   Reliability 672
    37.2.4   Fault Tolerance 672
    37.2.5   Availability 672
    37.2.6   High-Availability 673
    37.2.7   Ultra High-Availability 673
    37.2.8   Cluster 673
    37.2.9   Floating (Virtual) IP Address 673
    37.2.10   Failover 674
    37.2.11   Failback 674
    37.2.12   Primary (Active) Node 674
    37.2.13   Adoptive (Standby or Passive) Node 674
Summary 674

38. Administering HP-UX Security 675

    38.1   Securing an HP-UX System 676

       38.1.1   Setting Password Aging Attributes 676

       38.1.2   Implementing Shadow Password Mechanism 677

       38.1.3   Converting a System to Trusted Mode Security 677

       38.1.4   Implementing Standard Mode Security Extensions 679

    38.2   The Secure Shell 682

       38.2.1   How SSH Encryption Takes Place 683

       38.2.2   Accessing HP-UX Server via SSH 683

       38.2.3   Setting Up Passwordless User Access via ssh 684

    38.3   Pluggable Authentication Module (PAM) 686

    38.4   The *chroot* Jail 688

    38.5   Security Monitoring, Hardening, and Reporting Tools 688

    38.6   Common HP-UX System Hardening Tasks 689

    Summary 690

39. Sample CSA Exam Questions 693

40. Answers to Sample CSA Exam Questions 745

41. Table of HP-UX Commands 749

42. Table of Important HP-UX Files 759

43. Table of HP-UX System Daemons 763

44. Glossary 765

45. Index 775

List of Figures

Figure 1-1 HP-UX System Structure...3
Figure 1-2 CDE Login Screen...5
Figure 1-3 CDE Logout Confirmation Screen...6
Figure 1-4 CDE Front Panel..7
Figure 1-5 CDE Calendar Manager...8
Figure 1-6 CDE File Manager..9
Figure 1-7 CDE Mail Manager...10
Figure 1-8 CDE Style Manager..11
Figure 1-9 CDE Application Manager...11
Figure 2-1 File System Tree..28
Figure 3-1 Permission Settings...61
Figure 3-2 Permission Weights...63
Figure 4-1 *awk* Command Arguments..83
Figure 5-1 The Key Shell..91
Figure 7-1 *www.docs.hp.com*..121
Figure 7-2 *www.itrc.hp.com*..121
Figure 7-3 SAM – GUI Mode..122
Figure 7-4 SAM – TUI Mode...124
Figure 7-5 SAM Log Viewer...125
Figure 7-6 Restricted SAM...126
Figure 7-7 Slots..127
Figure 7-8 PCI Card..128
Figure 7-9 Network Interface Cards..129
Figure 7-10 SCSI Controller Card...130
Figure 7-11 Cell Board..132
Figure 7-12 Server Expansion Unit...133
Figure 7-13 Superdome Server Complex Cabinets...133
Figure 7-14 Server Complex...134
Figure 7-15 HP Superdome and RX7640 Servers...135
Figure 7-16 HP Superdome and RP8420 Servers...136
Figure 7-17 SCSI Hard Drive Naming Convention..139
Figure 7-18 Tape Device File Naming Convention...140
Figure 7-19 SAM – Peripheral Device Administration..143
Figure 8-1 nPar Logical..152
Figure 8-2 Node Partition Manager GUI..157
Figure 8-3 vPar Logical...158
Figure 8-4 Virtual Partition Manager GUI..165
Figure 9-1 HP-UX Installation – Welcome Screen...174
Figure 9-2 HP-UX Installation – User Interface and Media Options...............................175
Figure 9-3 HP-UX Installation – Basic Configuration...175
Figure 9-4 HP-UX Installation – System Configuration..176
Figure 9-5 HP-UX Installation – File System Configuration...177
Figure 9-6 HP-UX Installation – Warning Before Destroying Disk Contents...................178
Figure 10-1 Listing Software...187
Figure 10-2 Software Installation..188
Figure 10-3 *swinstall* Options..189
Figure 10-4 Software Removal..191
Figure 10-5 Copying Software to a Depot..193
Figure 11-1 IT Resource Center Main Screen..207
Figure 11-2 *software.hp.com* Main Page...219
Figure 12-1 User Authentication File – */etc/passwd*...224
Figure 12-2 User Authentication File – */etc/group*..226
Figure 12-3 SAM – User Add..230
Figure 12-4 SAM – User Creation Template..232
Figure 12-5 SAM – Group Administration..237
Figure 13-1 LVM Structure...246
Figure 13-2 SAM – Volume Group Creation...256

Figure 13-3 SAM – Logical Volume Creation 259
Figure 13-4 SAM – Volume Group Extend 260
Figure 13-5 SAM – Logical Volume Extend 261
Figure 13-6 LVM PVG...274
Figure 14-1 Disk under VxVM Control 285
Figure 14-2 VxVM Components..285
Figure 14-3 Veritas Enterprise Administrator GUI 287
Figure 14-4 Veritas Enterprise Administrator – Main Console Screen 288
Figure 15-1 HFS File System Structure 306
Figure 15-2 JFS File System Structure 308
Figure 15-3 SAM – File System Add...314
Figure 16-1 Physical Memory Division 330
Figure 16-2 SAM – Add Device Swap 334
Figure 16-3 SAM – Add File System Swap 335
Figure 17-1 Current and Previous System Run Levels 343
Figure 17-2 System Run Levels..343
Figure 17-3 EFI Boot Manager 357
Figure 18-1 SAM – Kernel Administration Main Screen 376
Figure 18-2 SAM – Kernel Configurable Parameter Administration 377
Figure 18-3 SAM – Kernel Driver Administration 378
Figure 18-4 SAM – Kernel Dump Device Administration 379
Figure 18-5 SAM – Kernel Subsystems Administration 380
Figure 19-1 SAM – Automated Backups 394
Figure 19-2 SAM – Interactive Backup and Restore 395
Figure 20-1 Types of Printer Setups...404
Figure 20-2 SAM – Add Local Printer..407
Figure 20-3 SAM – Add Remote Printer 408
Figure 21-1 Syntax of the crontab File..421
Figure 22-1 GlancePlus GUI...431
Figure 22-2 *gpm* Process List 435
Figure 23-1 Command Line Arguments 444
Figure 24-1 Local Area Network 468
Figure 24-2 Wide Area Network..469
Figure 24-3 Bus Topology..470
Figure 24-4 Star Topology 470
Figure 24-5 Ring Topology 471
Figure 24-6 Hybrid Topology 472
Figure 24-7 The OSI Reference Model...474
Figure 24-8 Encapsulation and De-encapsulation...480
Figure 24-9 TCP/IP Protocol Suite...481
Figure 24-10 Binary to Decimal Conversion 485
Figure 24-11 Class A Address 486
Figure 24-12 Class B Address 486
Figure 24-13 Class C Address 487
Figure 25-1 SAM – LAN Card Configuration 497
Figure 25-2 SAM – Default Gateway 503
Figure 25-3 SAM – DHCP Client Enable/Disable 504
Figure 27-1 SAM – Allow/Deny inetd Services 528
Figure 27-2 SAM – Remote Access...530
Figure 27-3 SAM – Internet Services Allow/Deny 533
Figure 27-4 SAM – Anonymous FTP..536
Figure 28-1 SAM – NTP Server Administration 545
Figure 28-2 SAM – NTP Client Administration 547
Figure 29-1 SAM – Export NFS Resource..559
Figure 29-2 SAM – Mount NFS Resource..561
Figure 30-1 SAM – AutoFS Mount...575
Figure 31-1 Samba GUI..581
Figure 32-1 SAM – NIS Domain Setup 596
Figure 32-2 SAM – NIS Administration 596
Figure 33-1 DNS Hierarchy...610

Figure 33-2 *software.hp.com* Main Page 612
Figure 34-1 LDAP Directory Hierarchy 630
Figure 34-2 *software.hp.com* Main Page 634
Figure 36-1 Ignite-UX – Message When no Clients are Configured 646
Figure 36-2 Ignite-UX – Welcome Screen 646
Figure 36-3 Ignite-UX – Configure Booting IP Addresses 647
Figure 36-4 Ignite-UX – Software Depot Setup 648
Figure 36-5 Ignite-UX – Prompt to Insert the CD/DVD 648
Figure 36-6 Ignite-UX – Prompt for Source Depot Location 649
Figure 36-7 Ignite-UX – Target Depot Location 649
Figure 36-8 Ignite-UX – Server Options 650
Figure 36-9 Ignite-UX – Session Options 650
Figure 36-10 HP-UX Installation – User Interface and Media Options 656
Figure 36-11 HP-UX Installation – Configuration Screen 657
Figure 36-12 HP-UX Installation – Welcome Screen 658
Figure 36-13 HP-UX Installation – User Interface and Media Options 659
Figure 36-14 HP-UX Installation – Installation Clients 660
Figure 36-15 HP-UX Installation – itool Interface 660
Figure 37-1 Traditional Network Computing Model 669
Figure 37-2 Redundant-Component Network Computing Model 670
Figure 37-3 High-Availability Network Computing Model 671
Figure 38-1 PuTTY Interface 684

List of Tables

Table 1-1 *ls* Command Options 13
Table 1-2 *wc* Command Options 20
Table 1-3 Navigating within *man* Pages 24
Table 1-4 *man* Sections 24
Table 2-1 Navigating with *more* 41
Table 2-2 Navigating with *pg* 42
Table 2-3 Summary of File / Directory Operations 48
Table 3-1 Permission Classes 60
Table 3-2 Permission Types 60
Table 3-3 Permission Modes 61
Table 3-4 Octal Permission Notation 63
Table 3-5 ACL Entry Usage 71
Table 4-1 Starting The vi Editor 77
Table 4-2 Inserting Text 77
Table 4-3 Navigating Within vi 78
Table 4-4 Deleting Text 78
Table 4-5 Undoing and Repeating 79
Table 4-6 Searching and Replacing Text 79
Table 4-7 Copying, Moving, and Pasting Text 79
Table 4-8 Changing Text 80
Table 4-9 Importing Contents of Another File 80
Table 4-10 Customizing vi Settings 81
Table 4-11 Saving and Quitting vi 81
Table 4-12 Miscellaneous vi Commands 81
Table 5-1 Setting, Unsetting, and Viewing Variables 92
Table 5-2 Pre-Defined Environment Variables 95
Table 5-3 I/O/E Redirection Symbols 96
Table 5-4 Pre-Defined Command Aliases 100
Table 5-5 Masking Meaning of Some Special Characters 103
Table 5-6 *pr* Command Options 106
Table 6-1 *ps* Command Output Explanation 111
Table 6-2 Some Important Signals 114
Table 6-3 Job Control 115
Table 7-1 SAM Administration Tasks 124
Table 7-2 Navigating Within SAM 124
Table 7-3 SCSI Chart 130
Table 7-4 HP Integrity Server Models 135
Table 7-5 HP 9000 Server Models 136
Table 7-6 Older HP 9000 Server Models 136
Table 7-7 *ioscan* Output Explanation 138
Table 8-1 MP Commands 151
Table 8-2 nPar Administration Commands 152
Table 8-3 vPar Administration Commands 159
Table 8-4 Integrity VM Administration Commands 166
Table 9-1 HP-UX Operating Environment Software Bundles 171
Table 9-2 Sample HP-UX File System Properties 177
Table 10-1 SD-UX Software Structure 182
Table 10-2 SD-UX Commands 183
Table 10-3 SD-UX Daemons 183
Table 11-1 Standard HP-UX Patch Bundles 211
Table 12-1 *useradd* Command Options 228
Table 12-2 SAM – User Add Password Options 231
Table 12-3 Shell Initialization Files 240
Table 13-1 *vgcreate* Command Options 254
Table 13-2 *lvcreate* Command Options 256
Table 14-1 Common VxVM Commands 290
Table 14-2 VxVM Daemons 290

Table 14-3 *vxprint* Command Output Description 293
Table 14-4 LVM / VxVM Terminology Comparison 302
Table 14-5 LVM / VxVM Command Comparison...302
Table 15-1 *newfs* Command Options 311
Table 15-2 *bdf* Command Output Description 325
Table 16-1 *swapon* Options for Device Swap..333
Table 16-2 *swapon* Options for File System Swap..335
Table 16-3 *swapinfo* Command Output Explanation 337
Table 16-4 *swapinfo* Command Options 337
Table 16-5 Swap Kernel Parameters...338
Table 17-1 System Run Levels 342
Table 18-1 HP-UX 11iv2 Kernel Management Commands..384
Table 18-2 Common Kernel Tunable Parameters 386
Table 19-1 Backup Levels 391
Table 19-2 *fbackup* Command Options 392
Table 19-3 *frecover* Command Options 393
Table 19-4 *tar* Command Options..397
Table 19-5 *cpio* Command Options 398
Table 20-1 Print Spooler Directory Hierarchy 403
Table 20-2 Printer Setup Attributes...406
Table 20-3 *lpstat* Command Options 412
Table 20-4 *lp* Command Options 414
Table 21-1 Controlling User Access 419
Table 21-2 *crontab* File Description 422
Table 22-1 Performance Monitoring Tools 429
Table 22-2 *sar* Command Options...429
Table 22-3 *vmstat* Command Output Description 433
Table 22-4 *iostat* Command Output Description..433
Table 23-1 Command Line Arguments Description 445
Table 23-2 Testing Conditions 450
Table 23-3 *let* Operators 456
Table 24-1 TCP vs. UDP 477
Table 24-2 OSI Layer Functions 479
Table 24-3 Subnetting..488
Table 24-4 Subnet Masks for Class C 489
Table 24-5 Subnet Masks for Class B 490
Table 24-6 Subnet Masks for Class C 490
Table 25-1 *netstat* Command Output Description 500
Table 26-1 *ioscan* Command Options 509
Table 26-2 *lanscan* Command Output Description..510
Table 26-3 *lanscan* Command Options 510
Table 26-4 *linkloop* Command Options 510
Table 26-5 *lanadmin* Command Options 513
Table 27-1 Internet Services 524
Table 27-2 Explanation of the */etc/inetd.conf* File Contents 525
Table 28-1 *ntpq* Command Output Description 549
Table 29-1 NFS Daemons 553
Table 29-2 NFS Commands 554
Table 29-3 NFS Configuration and Functional Files...555
Table 29-4 NFS Startup and Shutdown Scripts 555
Table 29-5 *export* and *mount* Command Options 558
Table 30-1 AutoFS Options 569
Table 31-1 CIFS Configuration Parameters 582
Table 32-1 NIS Daemons 592
Table 32-2 Name Service Source Status 599
Table 32-3 Name Service Source Actions...599
Table 32-4 Name Service Source Default Actions 599
Table 33-1 DNS Zone Files 616
Table 33-2 Resource Records Description...620
Table 33-3 Name Service Source Status 623

Table 33-4 Name Service Source Actions 623
Table 33-5 Name Service Source Default Actions 624
Table 33-6 The *etc/resolv.conf* File Description 624
Table 34-1 Common LDAP Attribute Types 632
Table 35-1 */etc/bootptab* Tags 640
Table 36-1 Ignite-UX Bundles...645
Table 36-2 Ignite-UX Server Options..651
Table 36-3 Installation Methods...655
Table 38-1 Per-User Security Attributes 681

## 01

Overview of HP-UX Operating Environment

This chapter covers the following major topics:

- ✓ A brief history of the UNIX operating system
- ✓ Architecture and features of HP-UX
- ✓ How to log in and out
- ✓ Introduction to Common Desktop Environment
- ✓ Command line components and how to build a command
- ✓ General HP-UX commands and how to execute them
- ✓ HP-UX online help

1.1   Introduction

The UNIX operating system is a set of tools created by programmers for programmers at the AT&T Bell laboratories in 1969 when Ken Thompson, Dennis Ritchie, and others developed an early version of the system on a PDP-7 computer in *B* language. The word *UNIX,* spelled "UNICS" and stands for *UNiplexed Information and Computing System,* was derived from another early version of an operating system called *MULTICS* (*MULTiplexed Information and Computing System*). Later, UNIX was re-written in *C* language for portability purposes, among others.

Programmers at the University of California at Berkeley made significant updates to the original source code in the mid 1970's and brought out a new version of the UNIX system called *Berkeley Software Distribution* (BSD) UNIX. BSD UNIX allowed the operating system to function in a networked environment.

At present, there are several flavors of UNIX operating system available from various vendors. Although conceptually and feature-wise UNIX flavors are similar, however, the features and services implemented and used in individual operating system vary.

HP-UX was developed in the early 1980's and the first version was released in 1983. HP-UX was derived from AT&T version of the UNIX system.

1.1.1   HP-UX System Structure

The structure of an HP-UX system comprises of three main components: the *Kernel*, the *Shell*, and the *Hierarchical Directory Structure*. These components are illustrated in Figure 1-1 and explained below.

The HP-UX Kernel

The kernel controls everything inside-out on a machine that runs HP-UX. It controls all associated system hardware including memory, processors, disks, I/O (*Input/Output*), and internal/external devices. It receives instructions from the shell, engages appropriate hardware resources, and acts as instructed.

The Shell

The shell is the interface between a user and the kernel. User provides instructions (commands) to the shell, which are interpreted and passed to the kernel for processing. The shell handles input and output, keeps track of data stored on disks, and communicates with peripheral devices, such as monitors, hard disk drives, tape devices, CD/DVD-ROM drives, printers, modems, and terminals. Chapter 05 "The HP-UX Shells" discusses shells in detail.

The Hierarchical Directory Structure

HP-UX uses a conventional *hierarchical* directory structure, where directories can contain both files and sub-directories. Sub-directories may further contain more files and sub-directories, and so on. A sub-directory (*child directory*) is a directory located under a *parent* directory. That parent directory is a sub-directory of some other higher-level directory. In other words, the UNIX directory structure

---

is similar to an inverted tree where the top is the root of the directory and branches and leaves are sub-directories and files, respectively. The root of the directory is represented by the forward slash (/) character, which is also used to separate directories as shown below:

/home/user1/dir1/subdir1

In this example, *home* sub-directory (child) is located under *root* (/), which is parent directory for *home*. *user1* (child) is located under *home* (parent). Similarly, *dir1* (child) is located under *user1* (parent), and finally *subdir1* (child) is located under *dir1* (parent).

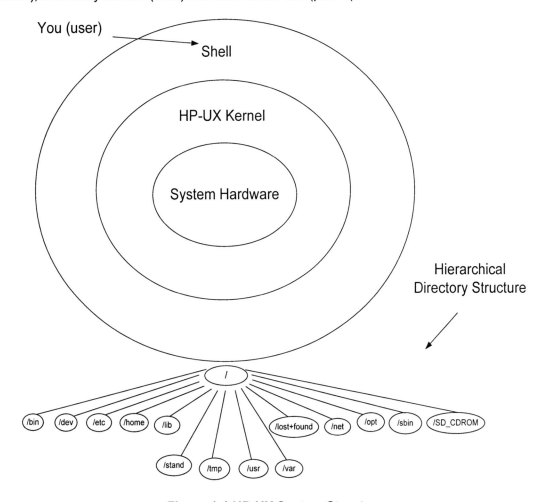

Figure 1-1 HP-UX System Structure

Each directory has a parent directory and a child directory with the exception of the root (/) and the lowest level directories. The root (/) directory has no parent and the lowest level sub-directory has no child.

 The term sub-directory is used for a directory that has a parent directory.

The idea behind the hierarchical directory structure is to keep related information together in a logical fashion. Compare the concept with a file cabinet that has multiple drawers, with each drawer storing multiple file folders.

1.1.2   HP-UX Features

HP-UX, like other UNIX operating systems, is a *multi-user, multi-tasking, multi-processing, and multi-threading* operating system. This means that a number of users can access an HP-UX system simultaneously and share its resources. The system allows each logged in user to run any number of programs concurrently. The kernel is capable of using multiple processors (CPU) installed in the system and breaking large running programs into smaller, more manageable pieces, called *threads*, for increased performance.

 A resource can be a hardware device or a software program or service.

The kernel allows *time-sharing* among running programs. It runs programs in a round-robin fashion to satisfy processing requirements of all running processes on the system.

HP-UX, like most other UNIX systems, is *immune* to viruses and remains up and running in the event a file containing a virus enters the system.

HP-UX is a *file-based* operating system. Hardware devices are accessed through corresponding *device files* that are managed and controlled by the system kernel.

1.2   Logging In and Out

A user must log in to an HP-UX system to use it. The login process identifies a user to the system. There are three common ways of logging in – a textual interface at the system console, a graphical interface called the *Common Desktop Environment* (CDE), and another textual interface called *telnet* from a remote Windows or UNIX system.

1.2.1   Logging In and Out at the System Console

The system console is a serial text terminal (a.k.a. *dumb* or *ASCII* terminal) connected to the serial console port at the back of the system.

Newer HP-UX systems come with a LAN console port too. Connecting a PC or laptop to the LAN console port via a network cable enables you to run a system console session on the Windows machine using, for example, MS Windows Hyper Terminal program.

When a console is connected to the system, login prompt appears by hitting a key on the console keyboard. The default console login prompt looks like:

    GenericSysName [HP Release B.11.11] (see /etc/issue)
    Console Login:

Type in a valid username and associated password to enter the system. Both username and password are case sensitive. Suppose a user account by the name *user1* exists on the system with password *user1234*, messages similar to the following would be displayed when this user logs in:

```
Please wait...checking for disk quotas
(c)Copyright 1983-2000 Hewlett-Packard Co.,  All Rights Reserved.
(c)Copyright 1979, 1980, 1983, 1985-1993 The Regents of the Univ. of California
(c)Copyright 1986-1992 Sun Microsystems, Inc.
(c)Copyright 1985, 1986, 1988 Massachusetts Institute of Technology
(c)Copyright 1989-1993  The Open Software Foundation, Inc.
(c)Copyright 1990 Motorola, Inc.
 (c)Copyright 1988 Carnegie Mellon University
(c)Copyright 1991-2000 Isogon Corporation, All Rights Reserved.


                    RESTRICTED RIGHTS LEGEND
Use, duplication, or disclosure by the U.S. Government is subject to
restrictions as set forth in sub-paragraph (c)(1)(ii) of the Rights in
Technical Data and Computer Software clause in DFARS 252.227-7013.


            Hewlett-Packard Company
            3000 Hanover Street
            Palo Alto, CA 94304 U.S.A.

Rights for non-DOD U.S. Government Departments and Agencies are as set
forth in FAR 52.227-19(c)(1,2).
$
```

The HP-UX command *exit* logs a user out of the login session. Alternatively, the user may press *ctrl+d* key combination to get out.

1.2.2   Logging In and Out Using CDE

The second method of logging in is by using the login screen of the *Common Desktop Environment*, as shown in Figure 1-2. It, too, requires a valid username and password to enter.

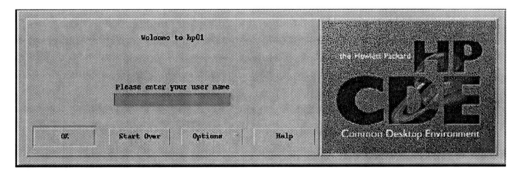

Figure 1-2 CDE Login Screen

In CDE, there is an *Exit* button in the middle of the *Front Panel* bar (see Figure 1-4). Clicking on this button, a user is asked to confirm if he/she really wants to log off (see Figure 1-3). Clicking on OK logs him/her out.

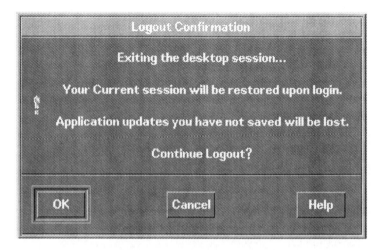

Figure 1-3 CDE Logout Confirmation Screen

1.2.3   Logging In and Out Using *telnet*

The third method to log on is by using the *telnet* command from a Windows or another UNIX system on the network. The *telnet* command requires either an IP address of the HP-UX system or its hostname to be specified. A login prompt similar to the following is displayed by HP-UX when you attempt to access the system (*hp01*, for instance):

$ **telnet hp01**
HP-UX hp01 B.11.11 U 9000/871 (ta)
login:

 Hostname and IP address are explained in Chapter 24 "Introduction to Networking".

Type in the username and hit the *Enter* key. Then type in the password and hit the *Enter* key again.

The HP-UX command *exit* logs a user out of the login session. The user may also press *ctrl+d* to log off.

There are a few other ways of logging in viz., *rlogin* and *ssh*. These will be discussed later in subsequent chapters.

When a user logs in to an HP-UX machine using any of the methods discussed above, the user is placed into a directory, which is referred to as his/her *Home* directory. Each user on an HP-UX system is assigned a home directory where the user normally keeps personal files.

1.3 Common Desktop Environment (CDE)

Common Desktop Environment provides *Graphical User Interface* (GUI) environment to users and has become the standard graphical interface on many UNIX operating system implementations including HP-UX. CDE was developed by a consortium of organizations and UNIX vendors to provide a common graphical environment to UNIX users. With its introduction in vendor UNIX versions, the default, proprietary GUI software that vendors had in their versions of UNIX system were replaced with CDE. As an example, HP-UX's proprietary VUE (*Visual User Environment*) has now been replaced with CDE.

The following sub-sections provide some general information on CDE components.

1.3.1 Front Panel

When you log on using CDE, a bar is displayed at the bottom of the screen. This bar is called the *Front Panel*. It comprises of a set of icons and pop-up menus. The Front Panel contains commonly used applications and tools for managing the working environment. Application icons may be dragged and dropped from the *File Manager* or *Application Manager* to the Front Panel pop-up menus. Similarly, default actions and icons for the pop-ups may be customized. The default CDE Front Panel bar is shown in Figure 1-4.

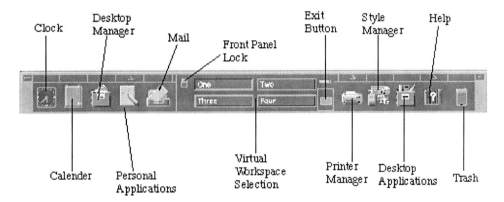

Figure 1-4 CDE Front Panel

The icons on the Front Panel from left to right are:

- ✓ Clock
- ✓ The Calendar Manager
- ✓ The File Manager (a.k.a. Desktop Manager)
- ✓ The Personal Applications (Text Editor and UNIX Terminal)
- ✓ The Mail Manager
- ✓ The Front Panel Lock
- ✓ Virtual Workspaces
- ✓ The Exit Button
- ✓ The Printer Manager
- ✓ The Style Manager

✓ The Application Manager (a.k.a. Desktop Applications Manager)
✓ Help
✓ The Trash can

Each one of these is briefly covered in the following sub-sections.

1.3.2 Clock

The clock displays the current system time in digital and analog form. Click on the arrowhead above it to display more options.

1.3.3 The Calendar Manager

The *Calendar Manager,* Figure 1-5, enables managing, scheduling, and viewing appointments, creating calendars, and interacting with the Mail Manager.

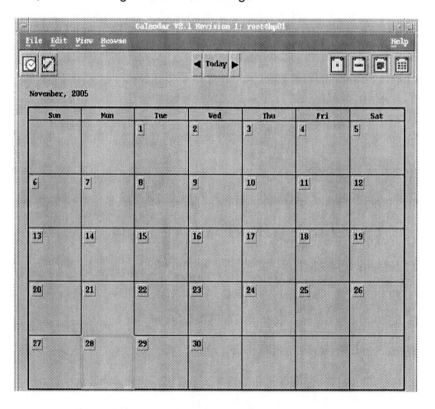

Figure 1-5 CDE Calendar Manager

1.3.4 The File Manager

A standard *File Manager* is included in CDE. The functionality is similar to that of MS Windows' File Manager. You can directly manipulate icons associated with UNIX files, drag-and-drop them, and launch associated applications. Figure 1-6 displays a sample File Manager window.

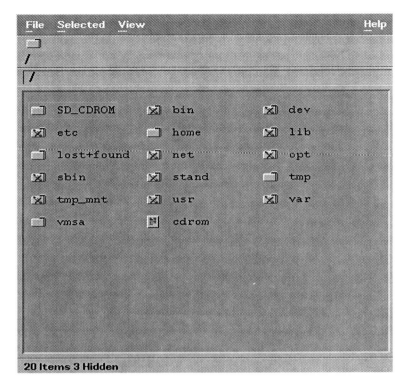

Figure 1-6 CDE File Manager

1.3.5   Personal Applications

Personal Applications include a text editor and an icon to start a UNIX terminal session. The terminal session provides the command prompt where you type in commands. Figure 1-4 shows the location of launching Personal Applications.

1.3.6   The Mail Manager

The *Mail Manager* is used to compose, view, and manage email. You may attach files too. It allows for communication with other applications through the messaging system. A sample Mail Manager window is shown in Figure 1-7.

1.3.7   The Front Panel Lock

Right next to the virtual workspaces area, Figure 1-4, there is a little padlock icon. This icon locks your CDE session to prevent unauthorized users from gaining access to the HP-UX system while you are away. The screen can be unlocked by typing in either your or the *root* user password.

1.3.8   Virtual Workspaces

Virtual Workspaces are located in the middle of the Front Panel bar. By default, there are four buttons, where each button corresponds to an independent virtual workspace. Within each workspace, you can run programs independent of what you are doing in other workspaces. You can add more workspaces by placing the mouse cursor anywhere on the workspace area and right clicking on the mouse button. You can also modify name of a workspace by double clicking on the workspace button to be modified. Each workspace can be customized. See Figure 1-4.

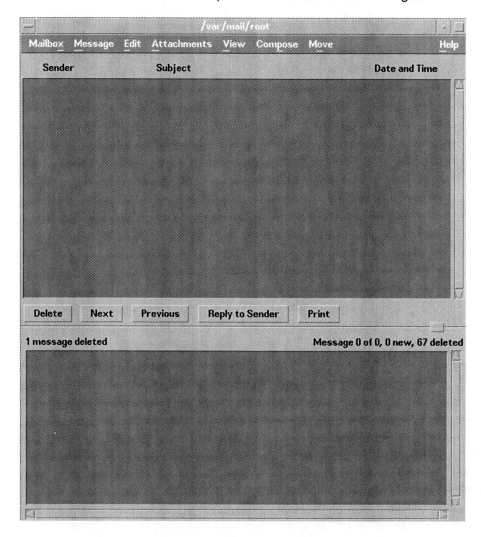

Figure 1-7 CDE Mail Manager

1.3.9   The Exit Button

As mentioned previously, this icon logs you out of HP-UX. Simply click on it and then on *OK* to get out. See Figure 1-4.

1.3.10   The Printer Manager

This is a graphical print job manager for scheduling and managing print jobs on available printers. It also displays information about configured printers. Refer to Figure 1-4.

1.3.11   The Style Manager

The *Style Manager* allows customizing CDE environment. Session color schemes, fonts, background, etc. may be customized as per your requirements. Figure 1-8 shows a sample Style Manager screen.

Figure 1-8 CDE Style Manager

1.3.12   The Application Manager

The *Application Manager* (a.k.a. *Desktop Applications Manager*) allows you to run HP-UX programs, such as the graphical system administration tool called *System Administration Manager (SAM)*. When you double click on the application manager's icon, the application manager window pops up from where you can invoke various tools. Refer to Figure 1-9.

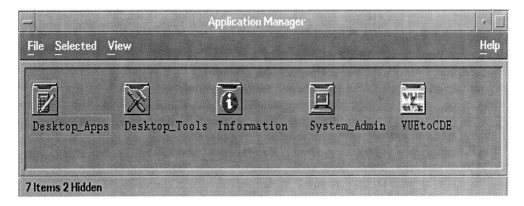

Figure 1-9 CDE Application Manager

1.3.13   Help

Help on CDE and some basic HP-UX tasks and commands is accessible by clicking on the *?* icon. See Figure 1-4 for its location on the Front Panel.

1.3.14   The Trash Can

The *Trash can*, Figure 1-4, is used to dump files and directories that are no longer required. Simply drag and drop a file or directory that you do not need to the trash can.

1.4   Common HP-UX Commands

This section gives an understanding on how commands are formed and describes several common HP-UX commands that you use frequently in routine system administration work.

1.4.1   What is the Command Line?

The *Command Line* refers to the operating system command prompt where a user types commands to execute. The command may or may not have arguments supplied with it. Arguments are used with commands for better, restricted, or enhanced output, or a combination. The basic syntax of a command is:

   $ **command** *argument1 argument2 argument3* ....

where:

   Command: specifies what to do
   Argument: is a file or directory name, text, an option, or something else

You do not always have to supply arguments with every command. Many commands run without an argument specified. Some commands do require that you specify one or more arguments, or specify an exact number of arguments.

The following examples use arguments. The text to the left of the examples tells if and how many arguments are supplied.

   $ **cal** **2005**   (command and argument)
   $ **cal** **10** **2005**   (command and two arguments)
   $ **ls**   (command only)
   $ **ls** –l   (command and argument. The argument is an option)
   $ **ls** *directory_name*   (command and argument)
   $ **ls** –l *directory_name*   (command and two arguments. The first argument is an
                                 option)

1.4.2   The *ls* Command and its Variations

The *ls* (or *lc*) command displays a list of files and directories. It has several options available to it. Some common options are listed in Table 1-1 along with a short description of each.

Option	Description
–a	Lists hidden files. If the name of a file in UNIX starts with a period ".", it is referred to as a hidden file. The *root* user, by default, displays hidden files and it does not require using this option.
–F	Displays file types. For directories it shows (/), for executable files (*), for symbolic links (@), and for text files, it shows nothing.
–l	Displays long listing with detailed file information including file type, permissions, link count, owner, group, size of file, last modification date/time, and filename.
–ld	Displays long listing of the specified directory, but not its contents.
–R	Lists contents of the specified directory and all its sub-directories (recursive listing).
–t	Lists all files sorted by date/time with the latest file first.
–tr	Lists all files sorted by date/time with the oldest file first.

Table 1-1 *ls* Command Options

Following examples help you understand impact of options used with the *ls* command:

To list files in the current directory:

```
$ ls
.profile     dev     lost+found     sbin     usr
.rhosts      etc     mapfile        stand    var
.sw          home    net            tmp      bin
lib          opt     tmp_mnt
```

To list files in the current directory with detailed information:

```
$ ll
total 48
drwxr-xr-x    11    root    sys     1024    Dec 20    06:13    .dt
-r--r--r--     1    bin     bin     1058    Apr 12    14:50    .profile
-rw-r--r--     1    root    root      73    Mar 30    13:53    .rhosts
drwxr-xr-x     6    root    sys       96    Dec 16    07:07    .sw
lr-xr-xr-t     1    root    sys        8    Dec 16    07:36    bin -> /usr/bin
dr-xr-xr-x    17    bin     bin     4096    Mar 30    18:38    dev
dr-xr-xr-x    31    bin     bin     6144    Apr 12    19:22    etc
drwxr-xr-x     9    root    root    1024    Mar 27    20:32    home
lr-xr-xr-t     1    root    sys        8    Dec 16    07:36    lib -> /usr/lib
drwxr-xr-x     2    root    root      96    Dec 16    07:00    lost+found
dr-xr-xr-x     1    root    root     512    Mar 29    05:50    net
dr-xr-xr-x    41    bin     bin     1024    Apr 12    15:46    opt
. . . . . . . .
. . . . . . . .
```

 The *ll* command is equivalent to *ls* –*l*. Try running it and compare results.

To display all files in the current directory with their file types:

```
$ ls -F
.dt/  .sw/     etc/    lost+found/    sbin/     tmp_mnt/
.profile       bin/    home/   net/   stand/    usr/
.rhosts        dev/    lib/    opt/   tmp/      var/
```

 The *ls -F* command is equivalent to *lsf*. Try running it and compare output.

To list all files in the current directory with detailed information and sorted by date/time with the latest file first:

```
$ ls -lt
total 48
drwxrwxrwx  7   bin    bin    1024   Apr 19 15:11   tmp
dr-xr-xr-x  31  bin    bin    6144   Apr 12 19:22   etc
dr-xr-xr-x  41  bin    bin    1024   Apr 12 15:46   opt
-r--r--r--  1   bin    bin    1058   Apr 12 14:50   . profile
dr-xr-xr-x  17  bin    bin    4096   Mar 30 18:38   dev
-rw-r--r--  1   root   root   73     Mar 30 13:53   .rhosts
dr-xr-xr-x  1   root   root   512    Mar 29 05:50   net
drwxr-xr-x  9   root   root   1024   Mar 27 20:32   home
dr-xr-xr-x  4   root   root   96     Feb 27 22:22   tmp_mnt
dr-xr-xr-x  10  bin    bin    024    Jan  3 14:49   stand
drwxr-xr-x  11  root   sys    1024   Dec 20 06:13   .dt
dr-xr-xr-x  25  bin    bin    1024   Dec 17 08:29   var
. . . . . . . .
. . . . . . . .
```

To list all files, including the hidden files, in the current directory with detailed information:

```
$ ls -la
total 52
drwxr-xr-x  16  root   root   1024   Apr 19 15:21   .
drwxr-xr-x  16  root   root   1024   Apr 19 15:21   ..
drwxr-xr-x  11  root   sys    1024   Dec 20 06:13   .dt
-r--r--r--  1   bin    bin    1058   Apr 12 14:50   .profile
-rw-r--r--  1   root   root   73     Mar 30 13:53   .rhosts
drwxr-xr-x  6   root   sys    96     Dec 16 07:07   .sw
lr-xr-xr-t  1   root   sys    8      Dec 16 07:36   bin -> /usr/bin
dr-xr-xr-x  17  bin    bin    4096   Mar 30 18:38   dev
dr-xr-xr-x  31  bin    bin    6144   Apr 12 19:22   etc
drwxr-xr-x  9   root   root   1024   Mar 27 20:32   home
drwxr-xr-x  2   root   root   96     Dec 16 07:00   lost+found
dr-xr-xr-x  41  bin    bin    1024   Apr 12 15:46   opt
. . . . . . . .
. . . . . . . .
```

To list all directory and sub-directory contents recursively for the /etc directory:

$ **ls –R /etc**
    < a very long output will be generated >

 The *ls -R* command is equivalent to *lsr*. Try running it and compare result.

1.4.3   The *pwd* Command

The *pwd* command (*Present Working Directory*) displays a user's current location in the directory tree. The following example shows that *user1* is in the */home/user1* directory:

$ **pwd**
/home/user1

1.4.4   The *cd* Command

The *cd* command (*Change Directory*) is used to move around in the directory tree. Look at the following examples:

To change directory to */usr/bin*:

$ **cd /usr/bin**

To change directory to the home directory of *user1*, do either of the two:

$ **cd**
$ **cd ~**

 The tilde (~) is a special character and does not work in Bourne shell. Refer to Chapter 05 "The HP-UX Shells" for information on shell features.

To go directly from */etc* into *dir1*, which is a sub-directory under *user1's* home directory, perform the following:

$ **cd ~/dir1**

 ~ is used as an abbreviation for absolute pathname to a user's home directory. Refer to Chapter 02 "Working with Files and Directories" to understand what an absolute path is.

To go to the home directory of *user2* from anywhere in the directory structure, use the ~ character and specify the login name of *user2*. Note that there is no space between ~ and *user2*.

$ **cd ~user2**

To go to the root directory, use the forward slash character:

$ **cd** /

To go one directory up to the parent directory, use period twice:

$ **cd** ..

To switch between current and previous directories, repeat the *cd* command with the dash character. Note that the dash character acts as a special character here.

$ **cd** –

– is a special character and does not work in Bourne shell. Refer to Chapter 05 "The HP-UX Shells" for information on shell features.

1.4.5   The *tty* and *pty* Commands

Both commands display *pseudo terminal session* where you are currently logged in.

$ **tty**
/dev/pts/4

1.4.6   The *who* Command

The *who* command displays information about all *currently* logged in users.

$ **who**
user1   pts/3   Feb 25 13:50
user2   Console   Feb 25 13:51   :0

where:

user1	name of the real user
pts/3	the third pseudo terminal session
console	system console screen
Feb 25 13:50	date/time the user logged in
(:0)	the user is logged in via CDE/GUI

When the *who* command is executed with "*am i*" arguments, it shows information only about the user that runs the command. For example:

$ **who am i**
user1   pts/4   Feb 25 13:50   :0

1.4.7   The *w* Command

The *w* command displays information similar to the *who* command but in more detail. It also tells you how long the user has been idle for, his/her CPU utilization, as well as what the user is currently doing. It displays on the first line of the output the current system time, how long the system has been up for, how many users in total are currently logged in, and what the current average load on the system is.

```
$ w
8:01am  up 1 day, 23:17,  1 user,  load average: 0.67, 0.72, 0.95
usertty        login@  idle     JCPU   PCPU   what
root           pts/ta   8:01am                  w
```

 The *uptime* command with –w option displays exact same output. Try running it and compare results

1.4.8   The *whoami* Command

The *whoami* command displays the username of the user who executes this command. The output can be either the current or the effective username. The current username is the name of the user who logs in and runs this command. When this user uses the command *su* to switch to a different user, he/she becomes the effective user.

```
$ whoami
user1
```

1.4.9   The *logname* Command

The *logname* command shows the name of the real user who logs in initially. If that user uses the *su* command to switch to a different user account, the *logname* command, unlike the *whoami* command, still shows the real user name.

```
$ logname
user1
```

1.4.10   The *id* Command

The *id* command displays a user's UID (*User IDentification*), username, GID (*Group IDentification*), group name, and all secondary groups that the user is a member.

```
$ id
uid=101(user1) gid=10(staff)
```

 Each user and group has a corresponding number (called UID and GID, respectively) in UNIX for identification purposes. See Chapter 12 "User and Group Account Administration" for more information".

1.4.11   The *groups* Command

The *groups* command lists all groups the user is a member of.

> **$ groups**
> staff other

The first group listed is the primary group for the user, all others are secondary (or supplementary) groups. Consult Chapter 12 "User and Group Account Administration" for further details.

1.4.12   The *uname* Command

The *uname* command produces basic information about the system. By default, this command displays the operating system name only. Option "–a" can be used to get more information.

> **$ uname**
> HP-UX

> **$ uname –a**
> HP-UX hp01 B.11.11 U 9000/800 2004107371 unlimited-user license

where:

HP-UX	Operating system name
hp01	Hostname
B.11.11	Operating system release
U	Current version level of the operating system
9000/871	Machine hardware and model
2004107371	The system's host id
unlimited-user license	Operating system license level

Try running *uname* with –l, –r, –n, –m, –s, –v, and –i options. These options restrict the *uname* command to display specific information.

1.4.13   The *hostname* Command

The *hostname* command displays your system name.

> **$ hostname**
> hp01

1.4.14   The *model* and *getconf* Commands

The *model* and *getconf* commands display hardware machine model of the system. The following displays output of the two commands when executed on an RP8400 server:

> **$ model**
> 9000/800/S16K-A

```
$ getconf MACHINE_MODEL
9000/800/S16K-A
```

1.4.15   The *clear* Command

The *clear* command clears the terminal screen and places the cursor at the beginning of the screen.

```
$ clear
```

 You must have proper terminal type set in order for this command to produce desired results.

1.4.16   The *date* Command

The *date* command displays current system date and time. You can also use it to modify system date and time.

```
$ date
Sat Nov 19 09:28:51 EST 2005
```

1.4.17   The *cal* Command

The *cal* command displays calendar for the current month.

```
$ cal
         November 2005
 S    M   TU   W   TH   F    S
           1    2    3    4    5
 6    7    8    9   10   11   12
13   14   15   16   17   18   19
20   21   22   23   24   25   26
27   28   29   30
```

1.4.18   The *uptime* Command

The *uptime* command shows a system's current time, how long it has been up for, number of users currently logged in, and average number of processes over the past 1, 5, and 15 minutes. For example, output of the *uptime* command below shows that current system time is 9:19am, system has been up for 1 day, 11 hours and 29 minutes, there is currently one logged in user, and average number of processes over the past 1, 5, and 15 minutes is 0.56, 0.54, and 0.54, respectively.

```
$ uptime
9:19am  up 1 day, 11:29,  1 user,  load average: 0.56, 0.54, 0.54
```

1.4.19   The *banner* Command

The *banner* command prints a banner of text passed to it as an argument. For example, the following command prints a banner of "HP-UX" on the screen:

```
$ banner  HP-UX
#   # #####       #     # #   #
#   # # #   #         #     # # #   #
#   # # #   #         #     # # ##
####  ##### #### #     #   #
#   # # #             #     # # ##
#   # # #             #     # # # #
#   # # #           ####   #   #
```

1.4.20   The *wc* Command

The *wc* command displays number of lines, words, and characters contained in a text file. For example, when you issue the *wc* command on the */etc/profile* file, you will see output similar to the following:

```
$ wc  /etc/profile
129          383      2426      /etc/profile
```

where:

> the 1st column shows the number of lines in */etc/profile* (129 in this example)
> the 2nd column shows the number of words in */etc/profile* (383 in this example)
> the 3rd column shows the number of characters in */etc/profile* (2426 in this example)
> the 4th column shows the file name (*/etc/profile* in this example)

You can use options listed in Table 1-2 to control output of the *wc* command.

Option	Action
–l	Prints line count.
–w	Prints word count.
–c	Prints byte count.
–m	Prints character count.

Table 1-2 *wc* Command Options

The following example displays only the number of lines in */etc/profile*:

```
$ wc  –l  /etc/profile
129   /etc/profile
```

Try running the *wc* command with other three options and view the results.

1.4.21   The *diff* Command

The *diff* command enables a user to find differences between contents of text files and produces line-by-line differences in the output. Two options are commonly used with the *diff* command: –i to ignore letter case and –c to produce a listing of differences divided into three sections.

For example, you have two text files, *testfile1* and *testfile2*, with the following contents:

testfile1	**testfile2**
apple	apple
pear	tomato
mango	guava
tomato	mango
guava	banana

When the –c option is used with the *diff* command, the results are displayed in three sections as follows:

```
$ diff –c  testfile1  testfile2
*** testfile1   Tue Nov 29 16:20:18 2005
--- testfile2   Tue Nov 29 16:20:37 2005
***************
*** 1,5 ****
  apple
- pear
- mango
  tomato
  guava
--- 1,5 ----
  apple
  tomato
  guava
+ mango
+ banana
```

The first section shows file names being compared along with time stamps on them and some fifteen asterisk (*) characters.

The second section tells the number of lines in *testfile1* that differs from *testfile2* and the total number of lines *testfile1* contains. Then actual line entries from *testfile1* are printed. Each line that differs from *testfile2* proceeds by the (–) symbol.

The third section tells the number of lines in *testfile2* that differs from *testfile1* and the total number of lines *testfile2* contains. Then actual line entries from *testfile2* are printed. Each line that differs from *testfile1* precedes by the (+) symbol.

In summary, the result shows that if you remove entries for pear and mango from *testfile1* and append entries for mango and banana to *testfile1*, then both files will become identical.

You can also use the *diff* command to find differences in directory contents. The syntax is the same.

1.4.22 The *which* and *whence* Commands

When the name of a command is specified with either the *which* or the *whence* command, it shows the fully qualified pathname of the command that is executed if run. For example:

$ **which cat**
/usr/bin/cat

$ **whence cat**
/usr/bin/cat

The system returns */usr/bin/cat*, which means that the *cat* command is executed from */usr/bin* directory if you run it without specifying its full path.

1.4.23 The *whereis* Command

When a command name is specified with the *whereis* command, it gives full pathnames of the source, the command, and its manual page sections. For example:

$ **whereis cat**
cat: /sbin/cat /usr/bin/cat /usr/share/man/man1.Z/cat.1

1.4.24 The *write* Command

The *write* command allows you to send a message to another logged in user. It is a uni-directional user communication tool. If you want to send a message to user *user1*, type the following at the terminal screen:

$ **write user1**
How are you, user1?
ctrl+d

The message is displayed on *user1*'s terminal screen as soon as you press the *Enter* key. Press *ctrl+d* to end communication.

 A user must run "*mesg y*" to enable receiving messages from the other party.

1.4.25 The *talk* Command

The *talk* command initiates a screen-oriented two-way communication session between users. The users can be on the same system or on two different systems. When you want to initiate a talk session with *user1* on the same system, type the following at your terminal screen:

$ **talk user1**

User *user1* will see the invite on his screen prompting him to type in the *talk* command with specified arguments. When he enters that, the terminal screens of both of you would split into two and a two-way interactive communication session would establish. Either user who wants to disconnect, would press *ctrl+d*.

 Users must run "*mesg y*" to enable receiving messages from the other party.

1.4.26   The *wall* Command

The *wall* command is used to broadcast a message to either all logged in users on the system or all logged in members of a particular group. Type in a message and press *ctrl+d* to send it.

To broadcast a message to all logged in users, type the *wall* command and hit the *Enter* key. Start typing a message and press *ctrl+d* when finished to broadcast it.

   # **wall**

To broadcast a message to all logged in members of group *dba1*:

   # **wall –g dba1**

To broadcast a message stored in */tmp/message.out* file to all logged in users:

   # **wall –f */tmp/message.out*

1.5   Online Help

While working on an HP-UX system you frequently require help to assist you with understanding a command, its usage, what options are available, and so on. HP-UX offers you online help via manual (or man) pages. The man pages are installed as part of the HP-UX Operating Environment installation. These pages provide detailed information on commands, options available, usage, system configuration files, their syntax, etc.

In order to view help on a command use the *man* command. The following example shows how to check man pages for the *passwd* command.

```
$ man  passwd
passwd(1)                                  passwd(1)
NAME
    passwd - change login password and associated attributes
SYNOPSIS
    passwd [name]
    passwd -r files [-F file] [name]
    passwd -r files [-e [shell]] [-gh] [name]
    passwd -r files -s [-a]
    passwd -r files -s [name]
    passwd -r files [-d|-l] [-f] [-n min] [-w warn] [-x max] name
```

```
        passwd -r nis [-e [shell]] [-gh] [name]
        passwd -r nisplus [-e [shell]] [-gh] [-D domain] [name]
    Standard input
```

While you are in manual pages, some common keys listed in Table 1-3 assist you to navigate through the pages efficiently.

Key	Action
Spacebar or f	Moves forward to the next page.
Enter	Moves forward one line.
b	Moves backward to the previous page.
d	Moves forward half a page.
u	Moves backward half a page.
g	Moves to the beginning of the man pages.
G	Moves to the end of the man pages.
:f	Displays file name being viewed, current line number, percentage of the file precedes the current line, etc.
q	Quits the man pages.
/pattern	Searches forward for the specified pattern.
?pattern	Searches backward for the specified pattern.
n	Finds the next occurrence of the pattern.
N	Finds the previous occurrence of the pattern.
h	Gives help on these and other navigational keys.

Table 1-3 Navigating within *man* Pages

1.5.1   *man* Sections

There are several sections within manual pages. For example, section 1M refers to system administration commands, section 4 refers to man pages on system configuration files, and so on. The default is section 1. A list of key sections is presented in Table 1-4 along with a brief description.

Section	Information
1	User commands.
1M	System administration commands.
2	UNIX and "C" language system calls.
3	"C" language library routines.
4	File formats and conventions for configuration files.
5	Miscellaneous.
7	Device special files.
9	General information and glossary.

Table 1-4 *man* Sections

To look for information on a configuration file */etc/passwd*, do the following:

$ **man 4 passwd**

passwd(4)   passwd(4)
NAME
    passwd - password file, pwd.h
DESCRIPTION
    /etc/passwd contains the following information for each user:

        + login name
        + encrypted password
        + numerical user ID
        + numerical group ID
        + reserved gecos ID
        + initial working directory
        + program to use as shell

    This is an ASCII file. Each field within each user's entry is
    separated from the next by a colon. Each user is separated from the
    next by a newline. This file resides in the /etc directory. It can
    and does have general read permission and can be used, for example, to
    map numerical user IDs to names.

Standard input

1.5.2   Searching by Keyword

Sometimes you need to use a command but you do not know the name of it. HP-UX man pages
allow you to perform keyword search on all available man pages. Use the *–k* option with the *man*
command and specify a keyword. The *man* command lists names of all man pages that contain the
specified keyword. In order to use this *man* command feature, you must run a utility called *catman*
one time on a system to generate a database that enables this feature. The database is created in
/usr/share/lib directory by the name *whatis*.

catman
$ **man –k password**
getspent access secure password entries, for trusted systems only.
keytab (1m)   - A dcecp object that manages server passwords on DCE hosts
pam_dce("5")   - authentication, account, and password management PAM functions for DCE
passwd_export ("1m") - Creates local password and group files
passwd_import ("1m") - Creates registry database entries based on information in UNIX group and
password files
pwd_strengthd ("1m") - The sample Password Management Server
ftpgroups(4)   - group password file for use with the SITE GROUP and SITE GPASS commands.
getpass( )(3C)   - read a password
getprpw(1M)   - display protected password database
getprpwent, getprpwuid, getprpwnam, getprpwaid, setprpwent, endprpwent, putprpwn
am(3)   - manipulate protected password database entries (for trusted systems only).
. . . .
. . . .

When you run *man* to look at manual pages of a command, it looks for help in several man page directories and displays requested information. These directory paths are defined in a variable called MANPATH. Run the following to see all directories where the *man* command searches for help:

$ **echo $MANPATH**

/usr/share/man:/usr/contrib/man:/usr/local/man:/opt/mx/share/man:/opt/upgrade/share/man:/opt/pd/share/man:/opt/pd/share/man:/opt/pd/share/man:/opt/resmon/share/man:/opt/hparray/share/man:/opt/graphics/common/man:/opt/scr/share/man:/usr/dt/share/man:/opt/samba/man:/opt/ignite/share/man:/opt/perf/man:/opt/hpnpl//man:/opt/prm/man:/opt/ssh/share/man

Summary

In this chapter, basics of UNIX operating system were covered. You were provided with an overview of the architecture and components that make up the core of the UNIX system. You looked at some of the common features associated with UNIX. You learned how to enter a system using graphical and textual interfaces, at the system console, and over the network. You studied Common Desktop Environment interface and got an overview of various tools and applications offered by this powerful, graphical application good for novice and experts alike.

You saw how to construct a command; then you executed a number of basic UNIX commands. These commands displayed different type of information including directory path, directory and file listing, directory navigation, user login names, logged in user information, user identification information, basic system and hardware information, basic communication tools, and so on.

Finally, you learned how to access online help on commands and configuration files. You performed keyword search in all available manual pages that listed commands and configuration files whose manual pages contained the keyword.

## 02

Working with Files and Directories

This chapter covers the following major topics:

- ✓ HP-UX directory structure and what it contains
- ✓ Static and dynamic directory types
- ✓ Access files using absolute and relative pathnames
- ✓ Types of files
- ✓ Naming convention for file and directory names
- ✓ Manage and manipulate files and directories including creating, listing, displaying, copying, moving, renaming, and removing them
- ✓ Search for text within files
- ✓ Search for files in the directory system
- ✓ Sort contents of text files
- ✓ Create file and directory links

2.1   File System Tree

HP-UX files are organized in a logical fashion to ease administration. This logical division of files is maintained in hundreds of directories. These directories reside in larger containers called *File Systems*.

The HP-UX file system structure is like an inverted tree with the root of the tree at the top and branches and leaves connected to it toward the bottom. The top-level is referred to as *root* and represented by the forward slash (/) character. This is the point where the entire file system structure ultimately connects to.

There are seven file systems created, by default, when you install HP-UX Operating Environment software on a machine. These are */, /stand, /var, /usr, /tmp, /opt,* and */home*. The main directories under the root and other file systems are shown in Figure 2-1. Some of these directories hold *static* data while others contain *dynamic* (or *variable*) information. The static data refers to file contents that are not usually modified. The dynamic or variable data refers to file contents that are modified when required. Static directories usually contain commands, library routines, kernel files, device files, etc. while dynamic directories hold log files, status files, configuration files, temporary files, etc. A brief description of some of the directories is provided in the following sub-sections.

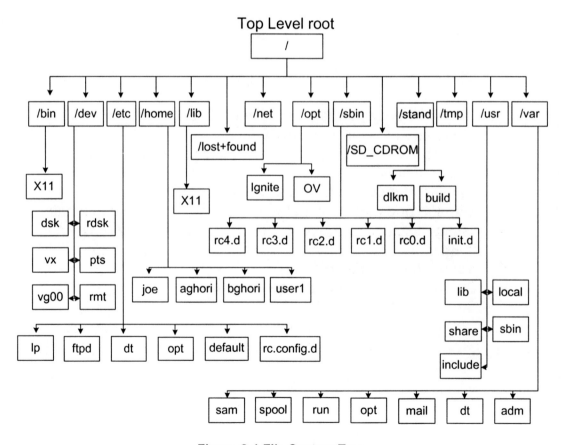

Figure 2-1 File System Tree

2.1.1　The Root File System (/)

The *root* file system contains many higher-level directories, with each holding specific information. Some of the more important directories under the root are:

The Binary Directory (*/bin*)

The *Binary* directory contains user executable commands. This directory is linked to */usr/bin* directory. The */bin* directory holds static data files.

The *X11* sub-directory under */bin* contains X windows related files.

The Devices Directory (*/dev*)

The *Devices* directory contains hardware device files. UNIX kernel communicates with system hardware devices through corresponding device files that are located here.

There are two types of device files: *Character Special Device* files (a.k.a. *Raw Device* files) and *Block Special Device* files. The kernel accesses devices using one or both types of device files.

Character devices are accessed in a serial manner meaning that a stream of bits is transferred during kernel and device communication. Examples of such devices are serial printers, terminals, hard disk devices, etc.

On the other hand, block devices are accessed in a parallel fashion meaning that data is transferred between the kernel and the device in blocks (parallel) when communication between the two happens. Examples of block devices are hard disk devices, CD/DVD-ROM drives, printers, etc.

 Some utilities access hard disk devices as block devices while others access them as character special devices.

Some key sub-directories under */dev* are: *dsk*, *rdsk*, *rmt*, *pts*, and *vg00*. These sub-directories contain block device files for disks including hard disks and CD/DVD-ROM drives (*dsk*), character device files for hard disks and CD/DVD-ROM drives (*rdsk*), tape device files (*rmt*), pseudo terminal session device files (*pts*), and root LVM volume group device files (*vg00*).

The */dev* directory holds static data files.

The Library Directory (*/lib*)

The *Library* directory contains shared library files required by programs. It contains sub-directories that hold script specific library routines. The */lib* directory can also be accessed using */usr/lib* directory path, since both are linked and point to same information.

In Figure 2-1, *X11* sub-directory under */lib* refers to library files used by X Windows system.

The */lib* directory holds static data files.

The System Binary Directory (/sbin)

Most commands required at system boot up are located in the *System Binary* directory. In addition, most commands that require root privileges to run are also located in this directory. This directory does not contain commands intended for regular users (although they still can run a few commands) and hence */sbin* is not included in normal users' default search path.

In Figure 2-1, *init.d, rc0.d, rc1.d, rc2.d, rc3.d,* and *rc4.d* refer to directories where system boot and shutdown scripts are located. The contents of these directories are explained in detail in Chapter 17 "Shutting Down and Starting Up an HP-UX System".

The */sbin* directory holds static data files.

The Etcetera Directory (/etc)

This directory holds most system configuration files. Some of the more popular sub-directories under */etc* are: *rc.config.d, default, opt, dt, ftpd, lp, lvmconf, mail, sam, skel,* and *vx.* These sub-directories contain, in that sequence, configuration files for system startup scripts, system operations and user account defaults, additional software installed on the machine, your CDE desktop environment, file transfer, printers, HP Logical Volume Manager, mail subsystem, System Administration Manager, user profile templates, and Veritas volume manager.

The */etc* directory contains dynamic data files.

The lost+found Directory (/lost+found)

This directory is used to hold files that become *orphan* after a system crash. An *orphan* file is a file that has lost its name. A detailed discussion on orphan files is covered in Chapter 15 "Working with File Systems".

If the *lost+found* directory is deleted, it should be re-created with the *mklost+found* command as follows:

    # mklost+found
    creating slots...
    removing dummy files...
    done

This directory is automatically created in the file system when it is created.

The /net Directory

If AutoFS is used to mount NFS file systems using a special map, all available NFS file systems on the network are mounted beneath */net* directory under their corresponding hostnames. AutoFS and special map are explained in detail in Chapter 30 "Setting Up and Administering AutoFS".

2.1.2   The Kernel File System (*/stand*)

The kernel files are located in the */stand* file system. Files that contain HP-UX kernel code, boot device information, kernel parameter and module information, etc. are stored here.

This directory is only altered when an update to the kernel is required. More information is provided in Chapter 18 "Kernel Reconfiguration Methods".

2.1.3   The Variable File System (*/var*)

/var contains data that frequently change while your system is up and running. Files holding log, status, spool, and other dynamic data are typically located in this file system.

Some common sub-directories under */var* are briefly discussed below.

/var/adm: Most system log files are located here. This directory contains system logs, su logs, user logs, mail logs, etc.

/var/dt: This directory contains CDE related log files.

/var/mail: This is the location for user mailboxes.

/var/opt: For additional software installed in */opt* file system, this directory contains log, status, and other variable data files for that software.

/var/spool: Directories that hold print jobs, cron jobs, email messages, and other queued work before being sent to their proper destination are located here.

/var/tmp: Large temporary files or temporary files that need to exist for extended periods of time than what is allowed in */tmp* are stored here. These files survive across system reboots and are not automatically deleted.

2.1.4   The UNIX System Resources File System (*/usr*)

This file system contains general files related to your system. Usually, this file system occupies more space than others in an HP-UX machine.

Some of the more important sub-directories under */usr* are briefly discussed below.

/usr/sbin: More system administration commands.

/usr/local: System administrators usually keep in this directory commands and tools that they download from the web or obtain elsewhere. These commands and tools are not generally included with the original HP-UX Operating Environment software distribution. In particular, */usr/local/bin* holds executable files, */usr/local/etc* contains their configuration files, and */usr/local/man* holds related man pages.

/usr/include: Header files for the *C* language.

/usr/share: Directory location for man pages, documentation, etc. that may be shared on multi-vendor UNIX platforms with heterogeneous hardware architectures.

/usr/lib: Libraries pertaining to programming sub-routines.

2.1.5   The Temporary File System (*/tmp*)

This file system is a repository for temporary files. Many programs create temporary files as they run. Some programs delete the temporary files that they create after they are finished, while others do not. These files do not survive across system reboots and are removed.

2.1.6   The Optional File System (*/opt*)

This file system typically holds additional software installed on your HP-UX machine. When software is installed in this directory, a sub-directory is created to hold files for that software.

In Figure 2-1, two sub-directories are shown under */opt*. One contains HP OpenView software binaries and the other HP Ignite-UX binaries.

2.1.7   The Home File System (*/home*)

This file system is designed to hold user *home* directories. When a user account is created, it is assigned a home directory where the user keeps personal files. Each home directory is owned by the user the directory is assigned to. No other user usually has access to other user's home directory.

In Figure 2-1, users *joe, aghori, bghori,* and *user1* have their home directories located under */home*.

The directories discussed thus far are HP-UX system related. It is highly recommended that you create separate file systems for data and applications. A detailed discussion on file systems and how to create and use them is covered in Chapter 15 "Working with File Systems".

2.2   Absolute and Relative Paths

A path, like a road map, shows how to get from one place in the directory tree to another. It uniquely identifies a particular file or directory by its absolute or relative location in the directory structure.

At any given time, you are located in one directory within the directory tree, which is referred to as your present (or current) working directory. When you log in to a system, the *current directory* is, by default, set to your home directory. Use the *pwd* command to verify this after you log in.

2.2.1   Absolute Path

An *Absolute Path* (a.k.a. a *Full Path* or *Fully Qualified Path*) points to a file or directory in relation to root (/). An absolute path must always start with the forward slash (/) character. The *pwd* command displays your current location in the tree.

$ pwd
/home/user1/dir1/scripts

This example shows that you are in */home/user1/dir1/scripts* directory. This represents your full path with respect to root (/).

2.2.2   Relative Path

A *Relative Path* points to a file or directory in relation to your current location in the directory tree. A relative path never begins with the forward slash (/) character; it always begins with one of the following three ways:

<u>With a period at the beginning:</u> A period represents the current working directory. For example, you are located in */home/user1/dir1/scripts* directory. If you want to run a script *file1* from this directory, you type:

   ./file1

<u>With a pair of periods at the beginning:</u> A pair of period character represents the parent directory in relation to your current working directory. The parent directory is one-step higher than the current working directory.

To go back one level up to parent directory, type:

   $ cd ..

<u>With a sub-directory name:</u> Let us say you are currently in */home/user1* directory and you want to go to the scripts sub-directory, which is under *dir1* sub-directory. Do the following:

   $ cd dir1/scripts

2.3   File Types

HP-UX supports several different types of files. These file types are described in the following sub-sections.

2.3.1   Regular Files

Regular files may contain text or binary data. These files can be shell scripts or commands. When you do an *ll* on a directory, all line entries for files in the output that begin with " – " (highlighted) represent regular files.

$ ll /bin

```
. . . . . . . .
. . . . . . . .
-r-xr-xr-x     1       bin     bin     16384   Nov 14  2000    whereis
-r-xr-xr-x     1       bin     bin     654     Nov 14  2000    which
-r-xr-xr-x     1       bin     bin     24576   Nov 14  2000    who
```

-r-xr-xr-x	1	bin	bin	12288	Nov 14 2000	whoami
-r-xr-xr-x	1	bin	bin	16384	Nov 14 2000	whois
-r-xr-xr-x	1	bin	bin	16384	Nov 14 2000	write

You can use the *file* command to determine the type of a file. For example, the following shows that */home/user1/.profile* contains ascii text in it:

$ **file /home/user1/.profile**
.profile: ascii text

2.3.2   Directory Files

Directories are logical containers that hold files and sub-directories. When you do an *ll* on the root (/) directory, the output similar to the following is displayed:

$ **ll /**

drwxr-xr-x	5	root	sys	96	Apr 4 2005	.sw
drwxr-xr-x	2	root	sys	96	Apr 4 2005	SD_CDROM
dr-xr-xr-x	14	bin	bin	8192	Nov 16 16:11	dev
dr-xr-xr-x	36	bin	bin	8192	Nov 16 16:17	etc
drwxr-xr-x	5	root	root	96	Nov 24 14:34	home
drwxr-xr-x	2	root	root	96	Mar 29 2005	lost+found
dr-xr-xr-x	1	root	root	512	Nov 16 16:10	net
dr-xr-xr-x	68	bin	bin	8192	Nov 24 14:09	opt
dr-xr-xr-x	13	bin	bin	8192	May 6 2005	sbin
dr-xr-xr-x	11	bin	bin	1024	Nov 16 16:11	stand
drwxrwxrwx	23	bin	bin	8192	Nov 24 16:30	tmp
dr-xr-xr-x	25	bin	bin	8192	Apr 5 2005	usr
dr-xr-xr-x	34	bin	bin	8192	May 20 2005	var

The letter "d" (highlighted) at the beginning of each line entry indicates a directory. Use the *file* command to determine the type. For example:

$ **file /home/user1**
/home/user1:   directory

2.3.3   Executable Files

Executable files could be commands or shell scripts. In other words, any file that can be run is an executable file. A file that has an "x" (highlighted) in the 4th, 7th, or the 10th field in the output of the *ll* command is executable.

$ **ll /bin**

-r-xr-xr-**x**	1	bin	bin	16384	Nov 14 2000	whereis
-r-xr-xr-**x**	1	bin	bin	654	Nov 14 2000	which
-r-xr-xr-**x**	1	bin	bin	24576	Nov 14 2000	who
-r-xr-xr-**x**	1	bin	bin	12288	Nov 14 2000	whoami
-r-xr-xr-**x**	1	bin	bin	16384	Nov 14 2000	whois

| -r-xr-xr-x | 1 | bin | bin | 16384 | Nov 14 2000 | write |

The *file* command can be used to determine the type. For example:

$ file /bin/who
/bin/who: PA-RISC1.1 shared executable dynamically linked

2.3.4   Symbolic Link Files

A *symbolic link* (or *soft link*) is a shortcut to another file or directory. When you do an *ll* on a symbolically linked file or directory, you notice two things. One, the line entry begins with the letter "l" (highlighted), and two, there is an arrow (highlighted) pointing to the linked file or directory. For example:

$ ll /bin
lr-xr-xr-t 1 root   sys   8 Apr 21 2005 /bin -> /usr/bin

The *file* command does not tell you if specified file or directory is linked, rather, it tells you the type based on contents.

$ file /bin
/bin: directory

2.3.5   Device Files

Each piece of hardware in your HP-UX machine has an associated file used by the kernel of the operating system to communicate with it. This type of file is called a *device file*. There are two types of device files: a *character* (or *raw*) special device file and a *block* special device file. The following outputs from the *ll* command display them:

$ ll /dev/dsk
brw-r-----	1	bin	sys	31	0x006000	Apr 21 2005	c0t6d0
brw-r-----	1	bin	sys	31	0x020000	Apr 21 2005	c2t0d0
brw-r-----	1	bin	sys	31	0x034000	Apr 21 2005	c3t4d0

$ ll /dev/rdsk
crw-r-----	1	bin	sys	188	0x006000	Apr 28 2005	c0t6d0
crw-r-----	1	bin	sys	188	0x020000	Apr 28 2005	c2t0d0
crw-r-----	1	bin	sys	188	0x034000	Apr 21 2005	c3t4d0

The first character in each line entry tells you if the file is block or character special. A "b" (highlighted) denotes a block and a "c" (highlighted) stands for character special device file. The *file* command shows their type as follows:

$ file /dev/dsk/c0t6d0
c0t6d0:   block special
$ file /dev/rdsk/c0t6d0
c0t6d0:   character special

2.3.6   Named Pipe Files

A *named pipe* allows two unrelated processes running on the same machine or on two different machines to communicate with each other and exchange data. Named pipes are uni-directional. They are also referred to as *FIFO* because they use *First In First Out* mechanism. Named pipes make *Inter Process Communication* (IPC) possible. The output of the *ll* command shows a "p" (highlighted) as the first character in each line entry that corresponds to a named pipe file.

```
$ ll /etc/opt/resmon/pipe
prw-------  1     root     root     0       Nov 24   14:36   1533300606
prw-------  1     root     root     0       Ap r 21  2005    1573980217
prw-------  1     root     root     0       Apr  21  2005    1652016795
prw-------  1     root     root     0       Apr  28  2005    1761189933
prw-------  1     root     root     0       Nov 24   14:36   1885281202
. . . . . . . .
. . . . . . . .
```

The *file* command shows the type of named pipe file as fifo. See the following example:

```
$ file  /etc/opt/resmon/pipe/1533300606
1533300606:     fifo
```

2.3.7   Socket Files

A *socket* is a named pipe that works in both directions. In other words, a socket is a two-way named pipe. It is also a type of *Inter Process Communication* (IPC). Sockets are used by client/server programs. Notice an "s" (highlighted) as the first character in the output of the *ll* command below for each socket file.

```
$ ll /var/spool/sockets/pwgr
srwxrwxrwx  1     root     mail     0       Nov 24   14:29   client1170
srwxrwxrwx  1     root     root     0       Nov 24   14:29   client1182
srwxrwxrwx  1     root     root     0       Nov 24   14:51   client1283
srwxrwxrwx  1     root     root     0       Nov 24   14:30   client1333
srwxrwxrwx  1     root     root     0       Nov 24   14:30   client1360
. . . . . . . .
. . . . . . . .
```

The *file* command shows the type of socket file as follows:

```
$ file  /var/spool/sockets/pwgr/client1170
client1170:     socket
```

Inter Process Communication allows processes to communicate directly with each other. They tell each other how to act by sharing parts of their virtual memory address space and then reading and writing data stored in that shared virtual memory.

2.4   File and Directory Operations

This section discusses file and directory naming rules and describes various operations on files and directories that users perform. These operations include creating, listing, displaying contents of, copying, moving, renaming, and deleting files and directories.

2.4.1   File Naming Convention

When you create files and directories, you assign them names. There are certain rules, listed below, that you should remember and follow while assigning names. A file or directory name:

- ✓ Can contain a maximum of 255 alphanumeric characters (letters and numbers).
- ✓ Can contain non-alphanumeric characters, such as underscore (_), hyphen (–), space, and period (.).
- ✓ Should not include special characters, such as asterisk (*), question mark (?), tilde (~), ampersand (&), pipe (|), double quotes ("), single back quote ('), single forward quote (`), semi-colon (;), redirection symbols (< and >), dollar sign ($), and so on. These characters hold special meaning to the shell.
- ✓ May or may not have an extension. Some users prefer to use extensions, others do not.

2.4.2   Creating Files and Directories

Files can be created using multiple ways, whereas for creating a directory there is only one command.

Creating Files Using the *touch* Command

The *touch* command creates an empty file. If the file already exists, the time stamp on it is updated with the current system date and time. Do the following as *user1*:

```
$ cd
$ touch  file1
$ ll  file1
-rw-rw-rw-  1 user1    users        0 Nov 25 15:30 file1
```

As shown in the output above, the fifth field is 0 "zero" meaning that *file1* is created with zero bytes. Now, if you run the command again on *file1* you will notice that the time stamp is updated.

```
$ touch  file1
$ ll  file1
-rw-rw-rw-  1 user1    users        0 Nov 26 11:13 file1
```

Creating Files Using the *cat* Command

The *cat* command allows you to create short text files.

```
$ cat  >  newfile
```

When you execute this command, you will see nothing on the screen after pressing the *Enter* key. The system, at this point, expects you to input something. When you are done, press *ctrl+d* to save what you have typed to a file called *newfile*.

Creating Files Using the *vi* Command

This is called the *vi* editor. System users and administrators frequently use the vi editor to create and modify text files.

Refer to Chapter 04 "The vi Editor and Text Processors" for detailed understanding of the vi editor.

Creating Directories Using the *mkdir* Command

The *mkdir* command is used to create directories. In the following example, you create a new directory by the name *scripts1* in *user1*'s home directory (*/home/user1*):

```
$ cd
$ pwd
/home/user1
$ mkdir  scripts1
```

You can create a hierarchy of sub-directories using the *mkdir* command with the –p option. In the following example, *mkdir* creates a directory *scripts2* in *user1*'s home directory. At the same time, it creates a directory *perl* as a sub-directory of *scripts2*, and a sub-directory *perl5* under *perl*.

```
$ mkdir  –p  scripts2/perl/perl5
```

You must have appropriate permissions to create a directory, otherwise, you get an error message complaining about lack of permissions.

2.4.3   Listing Files and Directories

To list files and directories, use the *ls* or *ll* command. For example, when you run the *ll* command in your home directory, it lists your files and directories in there. The following example runs *ll* as *user1* in *user1's* home directory:

```
$ ll
total 608
-rw-rw-rw-   1      user1   users   1089     Feb  4 22:56    file1
-rw-rw-rw-   1      user1   users   2426     Feb  4 22:56    file2
-rw-rw-rw-   1      user1   users   270336   Feb  4 22:57    file3
-rw-rw-rw-   1      user1   users   11       Feb  4 22:57    file4
-rw-rw-rw-   1      user1   users   67       Feb  4 22:57    file5
-rw-rw-rw-   1      user1   users   21       Feb  4 22:57    file6
drwxrwxrwx  2      user1   users   96       Feb  4 22:55    scripts
drwxrwxrwx  2      user1   users   96       Feb  4 22:55    scripts1
drwxrwxrwx  2      user1   users   96       Feb  4 22:55    subdir1
```

Notice that there are nine columns in the output of the *ll* command. These columns contain:

Column 1: The 1st character tells you the type of file. The next 9 characters indicate permissions. File permissions are explained at length in Chapter 03 "Working with File and Directory Permissions".

Column 2: Displays how many links the file or the directory has.

Column 3: Shows owner name of the file or directory.

Column 4: Displays group name that owner of the file or directory belongs to.

Column 5: Gives file size in bytes. For directories, this number reflects number of blocks being used by the directory to hold information about its contents.

Column 6, 7, and 8: List month, day of the month, and time the file or directory was created or last accessed/modified.

Column 9: Name of file or directory.

2.4.4   Displaying File Contents

There are several commands that HP-UX offers to display file contents. Directory contents are simply the files and sub-directories within it. Use the *ll*, the *ls,* or the *lc* command to view directory contents as explained in the "Listing Files and Directories" section earlier.

For files, you can use the *cat, more, pg, head, tail, view, vi,* and *strings* commands. Following sections explain each one of them.

Using the *cat* Command

The *cat* command displays the contents of a text file. In the example below, */home/user1/.profile* is displayed using the *cat* command.

$ **cat /home/user1/.profile**

@(#)B.11.11_LR

Default user .profile file (/usr/bin/sh initialization).

Set up the terminal:
      if ["$TERM" = ""]
      then
            eval ` tset -s -Q -m ':?hp' `
      else
            eval ` tset -s -Q `
      fi
      stty erase "^H" kill "^U" intr "^C" eof "^D"

```
        stty hupcl ixon ixoff
        tabs

# Set up the search paths:
        PATH=$PATH:.

# Set up the shell environment:
        set -u
        trap "echo 'logout'" 0

# Set up the shell variables:
        EDITOR=vi
        export EDITOR
```

Using the *more* Command

The *more* command displays the contents of a long text file one page at a time. In the example below, */etc/profile* is shown with the *more* command. Notice in the last line how *more* shows the percentage of the file being displayed.

```
$ more  /etc/profile
# @(#)B.11.11_LR

# Default (example of) system-wide profile file (/usr/bin/sh initialization).
# This should be kept to the bare minimum every user needs.

# Ignore HUP, INT, QUIT now.

    trap "" 1 2 3

# Set the default paths - Do NOT modify these.
# Modify the variables through /etc/PATH and /etc/MANPATH

        PATH=/usr/bin:/usr/ccs/bin:/usr/contrib/bin
        MANPATH=/usr/share/man:/usr/contrib/man:/usr/local/man

# Insure PATH contains either /usr/bin or /sbin (if /usr/bin is not available).

        if [ ! -d /usr/sbin ]
        then
                PATH=$PATH:/sbin

        else    if [ -r /etc/PATH ]
                then
profile (23%)
```

When viewing a large file with *more*, the keys in Table 2-1 would prove helpful for navigational purposes.

Key	Purpose
spacebar	Scrolls to the next screen.
Enter	Scrolls one line at a time.
b	Moves back one screen.
f	Moves forward one screen.
u	Moves up half a screen.
d	Moves forward half a screen.
h	Displays the help menu.
q	Quits and returns to the shell prompt.
/string	Searches forward for string.
?string	Searches backward for string.
n	Finds the next occurrence of string.
N	Finds the previous occurrence of string.

Table 2-1 Navigating with *more*

 The *more* command is the default when viewing man pages.

Using the *pg* Command

The *pg* command displays the contents of a file page-by-page as does the *more* command. It does not display the percentage, rather it shows the colon (:) character at the bottom of the screen.

```
$ pg  /etc/profile
# @(#)B.11.11_LR
# Default (example of) system-wide profile file (/usr/bin/sh initialization).
# This should be kept to the bare minimum every user needs.
# Ignore HUP, INT, QUIT now.

    trap "" 1 2 3

# Set the default paths - Do NOT modify these.
# Modify the variables through /etc/PATH and /etc/MANPATH

     PATH=/usr/bin:/usr/ccs/bin:/usr/contrib/bin
     MANPATH=/usr/share/man:/usr/contrib/man:/usr/local/man

# Insure PATH contains either /usr/bin or /sbin (if /usr/bin is not available).

     if [ ! -d /usr/sbin ]
     then
          PATH=$PATH:/sbin
     else    if [ -r /etc/PATH ]
          then
:
```

When you navigate contents of a file with *pg*, the keys listed in Table 2-2 would prove helpful. You need to hit the *Enter* key after every command.

Key	Purpose
Enter	Scrolls to the next screen.
l	Displays the next line.
d	Displays half a page.
.	Redisplays the current page.
h	Displays a help menu of more features.
q	Quits and returns to the shell prompt.
+/string/	Searches forward for the string.
$	Moves to the last page.

Table 2-2 Navigating with *pg*

Using the *head* Command

The *head* command displays the first few lines of a text file. By default, the first 10 lines are displayed. The following example displays the first 10 lines from the */etc/profile* file:

$ head /etc/profile

@(#)B.11.11_LR

Default (example of) system-wide profile file (/usr/bin/sh initialization).
This should be kept to the bare minimum every user needs.

Ignore HUP, INT, QUIT now.

    trap "" 1 2 3

To view a different number of lines, specify the number with the *head* command as an argument. The following displays the first three lines from */etc/profile* file. Notice the two empty lines in the output.

$ head −3 /etc/profile

@(#)B.11.11_LR

The following example displays the first fifteen lines from */etc/profile* file:

$ head −15 /etc/profile

@(#)B.11.11_LR

Default (example of) system-wide profile file (/usr/bin/sh initialization).
This should be kept to the bare minimum every user needs.

```
# Ignore HUP, INT, QUIT now.

    trap "" 1 2 3

# Set the default paths - Do NOT modify these.
# Modify the variables through /etc/PATH and /etc/MANPATH

    PATH=/usr/bin:/usr/ccs/bin:/usr/contrib/bin
    MANPATH=/usr/share/man:/usr/contrib/man:/usr/local/man
```

Using the *tail* Command

The *tail* command displays the last few lines of a file. By default, the last 10 lines are displayed. The following example shows the last 10 lines from the */etc/profile* file:

$ tail /etc/profile
```
            echo "Please change the backup tape.\n"
            rm -f /tmp/changetape
      fi

  fi                              # if !VUE

# Leave defaults in user environment.

    trap 1 2 3
```

You can specify with *tail* a numerical value to display different set of lines. The following example displays the last 17 lines from */etc/profile* file:

$ tail −17 /etc/profile
```
      then news -n
        fi

    # Change the backup tape

      if [ -r /tmp/changetape ]
      then    echo "\007\nYou are the first to log in since backup:"
            echo "Please change the backup tape.\n"
            rm -f /tmp/changetape
      fi

  fi                              # if !VUE

# Leave defaults in user environment.

    trap 1 2 3
```

The *tail* command also allows you to view all lines in a text file starting from the specified line number to the end of the file and skips all previous lines. In the following example, the first 101 lines are skipped from */etc/profile* and the remaining are shown:

```
$ tail  +101  /etc/profile
   # Notify if there is mail

        if [ -f /usr/bin/mail ]
        then
                if mail -e
                then   echo "You have mail."
                fi
        fi

   # Notify if there is news

        if [ -f /usr/bin/news ]
        then news -n
        fi

   # Change the backup tape

        if [ -r /tmp/changetape ]
        then   echo "\007\nYou are the first to log in since backup:"
               echo "Please change the backup tape.\n"
               rm -f /tmp/changetape
        fi

  fi                              # if !VUE

   # Leave defaults in user environment.

     trap 1 2 3
```

The *tail* command proves to be very useful when you wish to view a log file while updates to the file are being done. The option that enables this function is –f. The following example shows how to view the HP-UX system log file */var/adm/syslog/syslog.log* in this manner. Try running this command on your system and notice the behavior.

```
$ tail  –f  /var/adm/syslog/syslog.log
```

Using the *view* Command

The *view* command opens a text file as read-only in the *vi* editor. See Chapter 04 "The vi Editor and Text Processors" to get details on the vi editor.

```
$ view  /home/user1/.profile
```

Using the *vi* Command

This is the vi editor. System users and administrators often use the vi editor to create and modify program files. Refer to Chapter 04 "The vi Editor and Text Processors" for detailed information on vi.

Using the *strings* Command

The *strings* command finds and displays legible information embedded within a non-text or binary file. For example, when you run the *strings* command on */usr/bin/cat*, you observe output similar to the following. Although */usr/bin/cat* is a non-text file, it does contain some legible information.

```
$ strings  /usr/bin/cat
$Revision: 92453-07 linker linker crt0.o B.11.16 000601 $
/usr/lib/dld.sl
ERROR: mmap failed for dld
ERROR: mmap failed for TSD
usrvbnte
Usage: cat [-benrstuv] [-|File ...]
cat: Cannot get status on standard output.
cat: Cannot open
cat: Cannot get status on
. . . . . . . .
. . . . . . . .
M-^%c
M-%c
cat: read error
cat: Cannot close the file
cat: Cannot write to output
```

2.4.5   Copying Files and Directories

Copying Files

The *cp* command is used to copy one or more files to either current or another directory. If you want to duplicate a file in the same directory, you must give a different name to the target file. If you want to copy a file to a different directory, you can either use the same file name as the original file has or assign it a different name. Consider the following examples:

To copy *file1* in the same directory by the name *newfile1*:

```
$ cp  file1  newfile1
```

To copy *file1* into another directory called *subdir1* by same name:

```
$ cp  file1  subdir1
```

By default, when you copy a file, the destination is overwritten and a warning message is not generated. In order to avoid such a situation you can use the –i option with the *cp* command, which prompts for confirmation before overwriting.

> $ **cp –i file1 file2**
> overwrite file2? (y/n)

Copying Directories

The *cp* command copies a directory and its contents to another location. You must use the –r (recursive) option to perform this operation. In the following example, *scripts1* directory is copied under *subdir1*:

> $ **cp –r scripts1 subdir1**

You may wish to use the –i option with *cp* command here too.

2.4.6   Moving and Renaming Files and Directories

Moving and Renaming Files

The *mv* command is used to move files around or rename them. The –i option can be specified for user confirmation if the destination file exists. The following example moves *file1* to *subdir1* and prompts for confirmation if a file by the same name exists in *subdir1*:

> $ **mv –i file1 subdir1**
> remove subdir1/file1? (y/n)

To rename *file3* as *file4*, do the following:

> $ **ll file3**
> -rw-rw-rw- 1 user1   users   270336 Feb 4 22:57 file3
> $ **mv file3 file4**
> $ **ll file4**
> -rw-rw-rw- 1 user1   users   270336 Feb 4 22:57 file4

You may want to use the –i option with *mv* command.

Moving and Renaming Directories

To move a directory along with its contents to some other directory location or simply change the name of the directory, use either the *mv or* the *mvdir* command. For example, moving *scripts1* under *scripts2* (*scripts2* must exist), do one of the following:

> $ **mv scripts1 scripts2**
> # **mvdir scripts1 scripts2**

By default, *mvdir* does not have execute permission set for normal users other than *root*. This prevents normal users from running this command. If execute permission is set, a normal user would be able to run it as well. See Chapter 03 "Working with File and Directory Permissions" on how to modify permissions.

To rename *scripts1* as *scripts10* (*scripts10* must not exist), do one of the following:

$ mv scripts1 scripts10
 # mvdir scripts1 scripts10

You may like to use the –i option with *mv* command. This option is not supported with *mvdir*.

2.4.7   Removing Files and Directories

Removing Files

You can remove a file using the *rm* command. The *rm* command deletes one or more specified files at once. The –i option can be used to prevent accidental file removal. The option prompts for confirmation before removing it. The following example prompts for confirmation to delete *file1* and *file2*:

$ rm –i file1 file2
rm: remove file1: (y/n) ? y
rm: remove file2: (y/n) ? y

Removing Directories

You have two commands available to remove directories. Following examples explain them.

To remove an empty directory, use the *rmdir* command:

$ rmdir /home/user1/subdir100

To remove a directory that contains files or sub-directories, or both, use *rm* with –r option:

$ rm –r /home/user1/subdir1

Use the *rm* command with –i option to interactively remove directories and their contents:

$ rm –ir subdir1
directory subdir1: ? (y/n) y
directory subdir1/subdir2: ? (y/n) y
subdir1/subdir2: ? (y/n) y
directory subdir1/subdir3: ? (y/n) y
subdir1/subdir3: ? (y/n) y
subdir1: ? (y/n) y

2.4.8   Summary of File and Directory Operations

Table 2-3 lists commands for file and directory operations you just learnt.

Command to	File	Directory
Create	cat, touch, vi	mkdir
List	ll, ls, lc, and variants	ll, ls, lc, and variants
Display	cat, more, pg, head, tail, view, vi, strings	ll, ls, lc, and variants
Copy	cp	cp
Move	mv	mv, mvdir (*root* only)
Rename	mv	mv, mvdir (*root* only)
Remove	rm	rm −r, rmdir

Table 2-3 Summary of File / Directory Operations

2.5   Searching for Text within Files

HP-UX provides a powerful tool to search the contents of one or more text files for a pattern (also called *Regular Expression* or *Pattern Matching*). A pattern can be a single character, a series of characters, a word, or a sentence. You must enclose in double quotes if the pattern contains one or more white spaces.

The tool is called *grep* and stands for *Global Regular Expression Print*. It searches contents of one or more specified files for a regular expression. If found, it prints, by default, every line containing the expression to the screen without changing the original file contents. Consider the following examples.

To search for the pattern "user1" in the */etc/passwd* file:

$ **grep user1 /etc/passwd**
user1:Gwt8NJlhTltXY:105:20::/home/user1:/sbin/sh

To search for all occurrences of the pattern "root" in both the */etc/passwd* and */etc/group* files:

$ **grep root /etc/passwd /etc/group**
/etc/passwd:root:/af/4dEOdgkpY:0:3::/:/sbin/sh
/etc/group:root::0:root
/etc/group:other::1:root,hpdb
/etc/group:bin::2:root,bin
/etc/group:sys::3:root,uucp
/etc/group:adm::4:root,adm
/etc/group:daemon::5:root,daemon
/etc/group:mail::6:root
/etc/group:lp::7:root,lp
/etc/group:users::20:root

To display, from the specified file list, only the names of those files that contain the pattern "root", use the –l option.

> **$ grep –l root /etc/group /etc/passwd /etc/hosts**
> /etc/group
> /etc/passwd

To search for the pattern "root" in the */etc/group* file along with associated line number(s), use the –n option.

> **$ grep –n root /etc/group**
> 1:root::0:root
> 2:other::1:root,hpdb
> 3:bin::2:root,bin
> 4:sys::3:root,uucp
> 5:adm::4:root,adm
> 6:daemon::5:root,daemon
> 7:mail::6:root
> 8:lp::7:root,lp
> 11:users::20:root

To search for the pattern "root" in the */etc/group* file and do not show the lines in the output that contain this pattern. In other words, show only the lines that do not include the pattern "root". Use the –v option.

> **$ grep –v root /etc/group**
> tty::10:
> nuucp::11:nuucp
> nogroup:*:-2:
> ids::101:
> smbnull::102:

To search for all lines in the */etc/passwd* file that begin with the pattern "root". The POSIX shell treats the caret (^) sign as a special character which marks the beginning of a line or word. This is useful, for instance, if you want to know whether there are more than one users by that name.

> **$ grep ^root /etc/passwd**
> root:nTdJmqERsWwbg:0:3::/:/usr/bin/sh

To list all lines from the */etc/passwd* file that end with the pattern "sh". The POSIX shell treats the dollar ($) sign as a special character which marks the end of a line or word. This is useful, for example, to determine which users using the POSIX shell and which ones the Bourne shell.

> **$ grep sh$ /etc/passwd**
> root:nTdJmqERsWwbg:0:3::/:/usr/bin/sh
> daemon:*:1:5::/:/sbin/sh
> bin:*:2:2::/usr/bin:/sbin/sh
> adm:*:4:4::/var/adm:/sbin/sh
> lp:*:9:7::/var/spool/lp:/sbin/sh

```
hpdb:*:27:1:ALLBASE:/:/sbin/sh
ids:*:101:101:IDS/9000 Administrator:/home/ids:/sbin/sh
smbnull:*:102:102:DO NOT USE OR DELETE - needed by Samba:/home/smbnull:/sbin/sh
user1:hRefSO6p0MNNI:103:20::/home/user1:/usr/bin/sh
```

To search for all empty lines in the */etc/passwd* file, do the following:

$ grep ^$ /etc/passwd

To search for all lines in the */etc/passwd* file that contain only the pattern "root":

$ grep ^root$ /etc/passwd

To search for all lines in the */etc/passwd* file that contain the pattern "root". The –i option used with the *grep* command here ignores letter case. This is useful to determine if there are *root* user accounts with a combination of lowercase and uppercase letters.

$ grep –i root /etc/passwd
```
root:nTdJmqERsWwbg:0:3::/:/usr/bin/sh
```

To print all lines from the output of the *ll* command that contain either "bin" or "root" pattern:

$ ll | grep –E 'bin | root'

-rw-------	1	root	sys	0	Nov 19 09:50	.ICEauthority
-rw-------	1	root	sys	69	Nov 19 08:51	.TTauthority
-rw-rw-rw-	1	root	sys	10442	Jul 4 2005	.WindU
-rw-------	1	root	sys	49	Nov 19 08:51	.Xauthority
drwxr-xr-x	11	root	sys	8192	Nov 19 09:23	.dt
-rwxr-xr-x	1	root	sys	5451	Nov 19 08:51	.dtprofile
-r--r--r--	1	bin	bin	1089	Oct 29 2005	.profile
-rw-rw-rw-	1	root	sys	31	Apr 13 15:33	.rhosts
-rw-------	1	root	sys	6642	May 10 10:45	.sh_history
. . . .						
. . . .						

> *grep* –E is same as the old *egrep* (extended grep) command, which still exists in HP-UX for backward compatibility.

To print all lines from the */stand/system* file that contain the character " * ". Note that with the –F option, " * " is treated as a regular character and not as a wildcard character.

$ grep –F '*' /stand/system
```
****************************************
* Source: /ux/core/kern/filesets.info/CORE-KRN/generic
* @(#)B.11.11_LR
*
****************************************
```

```
* Additional drivers required in every machine-type to create a complete
* system file during cold install.  This list is every driver that the
* master.d/ files do not force on the system or is not identifiable by
* ioscan.
* Other CPU-type specific files can exist for their special cases.
* see create_sysfile (1m).
*****************************************
*
* Drivers/Subsystems
. . . . . . . .
. . . . . . . .
```

grep –F is same as the old *fgrep* (fast or fixed grep) command, which still exists in HP-UX for backward compatibility.

2.6   Finding Files in the Directory Structure

Sometimes you need to find one or more files or directories in the file system structure based on a criteria. To enable you to perform this function, HP-UX offers a command called *find*. The *find* command recursively searches the directory tree, finds files that match the specified criteria, and optionally performs an action. This powerful command can be customized to look for files in a number of ways. The search criteria may include searching for files by name, size, ownership, group membership, last access or modification time, permissions, file type, inode number, and so forth. Here is the command syntax.

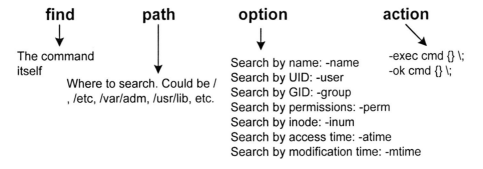

find

The command itself

path

Where to search. Could be /
, /etc, /var/adm, /usr/lib, etc.

option

Search by name: -name
Search by UID: -user
Search by GID: -group
Search by permissions: -perm
Search by inode: -inum
Search by access time: -atime
Search by modification time: -mtime

action

-exec cmd {} \;
-ok cmd {} \;

When the *find* command is executed, files that match the criteria defined with the command are located and the full path to each file is displayed on the screen. Let us look at a few examples.

To search for *file2* in *user1*'s home directory /home/*user1*.

```
$ cd
$ find  . –name  file2 –print
./file2
./subdir6/subdir54/subdir20/subdir1/file2
```

–print is optional. The *find* command, by default, displays results on the screen. You do not have to specify this option.

To search for files and directories in */dev* directory that begin with "vg". Run this command as *root*.

> **# find /dev –name vg***
> /dev/vg00
> /dev/vg01
> /dev/vg02

The character (*) is used as a wildcard character. It means any files or directories that begin with the pattern "vg" followed by any characters.

To find files larger than 1000 blocks in size (one block equals 512 bytes) in *user1's* home directory:

> **$ find ~ –size +1000**

Here ' ~ ' called 'tilde', represents user's home directory. See Chapter 05 "The HP-UX Shells" for details.

To find files in */home* owned by *user1*. Run it as *root*.

> **# find /home –user user1**

To find files in */etc/rc.config.d* directory that were modified more than 120 days ago. Run this command as *root*.

> **# find /etc/rc.config.d –mtime +120**

To find files in */etc/rc.config.d* directory that have not been accessed in the last 90 days. Run this command as *root*.

> **# find /etc/rc.config.d –atime –90**

To search for character special files in */dev* directory with permissions 700. Run this command as *root*.

> **# find /dev/rdsk –type c –perm 700**

In the above example, two criteria are defined. Files that match both criteria are displayed. The criteria are to look for files that are character special having read/write/execute permissions for the file owner, and no permissions to any other users.

To search for symbolic link files in */usr* directory with permissions 777. Run this command as *root*.

> **# find /usr –type l –perm 777**

To search for core files in the entire directory tree and delete them as found without prompting for confirmation. Run this command as *root*.

find / –name core –exec rm {} \;

 The last few characters "{} \;" are part of the syntax and must be defined that way.

To search for core files in the entire directory tree and prompt to delete them as found. Run this command as *root*.

find / –name core –ok rm {} \;

2.7　Sorting File Contents

Sorting allows you to arrange columns of text in an specified order. The *sort* command is used for this purpose. It sorts contents of a file and prints the result on the screen. You can specify multiple files for sort. Also, you can sort file contents in either alphabetic (default) or numeric order.

Let us look at a few examples to understand the usage of *sort*.

Consider a file, *file10*, in *user1*'s home directory with the following text in two columns. The first column contains alphabets and the second contains numbers.

Maryland 667
Mississippi 662
Pennsylvania 445
Missouri 975
Florida 772
Montana 406
Massachusetts 339

To sort this file alphabetically:

$ **sort file10**
Florida 772
Maryland 667
Massachusetts 339
Mississippi 662
Missouri 975
Montana 406
Pennsylvania 445

To sort this file numerically, use the –n option and specify the column number:

```
$ sort -n +1 file10
```
Massachusetts **339**
Montana **406**
Pennsylvania **445**
Mississippi **662**
Maryland **667**
Florida **772**
Missouri **975**

To sort *file10* numerically (–n option) but in reverse order (–r option):

```
$ sort -rn +1 file10
```
Missouri **975**
Florida **772**
Maryland **667**
Mississippi **662**
Pennsylvania **445**
Montana **406**
Massachusetts **339**

To sort the output of the *ll* command run on *user1*'s home directory:

```
$ ll | sort
```

-rw-rw-rw-	1	user1	users	11	Feb 4 22:57	file4
-rw-rw-rw-	1	user1	users	21	Feb 4 22:57	file6
-rw-rw-rw-	1	user1	users	67	Feb 4 22:57	file5
-rw-rw-rw-	1	user1	users	1089	Feb 4 22:56	file1
-rw-rw-rw-	1	user1	users	2426	Feb 4 22:56	file2
-rw-rw-rw-	1	user1	users	270336	Feb 4 22:57	file3
drwxrwxrwx	2	user1	users	96	Feb 4 22:55	scripts
drwxrwxrwx	2	user1	users	96	Feb 4 22:55	scripts1
drwxrwxrwx	2	user1	users	96	Feb 4 22:55	subdir1
drwxrwxrwx	2	user1	users	96	Feb 4 22:55	subdir2
total 608						

To sort on the 5th column (month column) the output of the *ll* command run on */etc/skel* directory:

```
$ ll -a /etc/skel | sort +5M
```
total 80

dr-xr-xr-x	31	bin	bin	8192	**May** 8 13:37	..
drwxrwxr-x	2	root	sys	96	**Jun** 11 2005	.
-r--r--r--	1	bin	bin	334	**Nov** 14 2000	.login
-r--r--r--	1	bin	bin	347	**Nov** 14 2000	.exrc
-r--r--r--	1	bin	bin	439	**Nov** 14 2000	.profile
-r--r--r--	1	bin	bin	832	**Nov** 14 2000	.cshrc

By default, output of *sort* is displayed on the screen. If you like to save the output into a file, you may redirect it using –o option. The example below saves output in */tmp/sort.out* and does not display it on the screen.

HP Certified Systems Administrator

$ ll /etc/skel | sort +5M –o /tmp/sort.out

To sort on the 5th and then on the 6th column, do the following. This is an example of multi-level sorting.

```
$ ll –a /etc/skel | sort +5M +6n
total 80
dr-xr-xr-x    31    bin     bin     8192    May  8 13:37    ..
drwxrwxr-x    2     root    sys     96      Jun 11 2005     .
-r--r--r--    1     bin     bin     334     Nov 14 2000     .login
-r--r--r--    1     bin     bin     347     Nov 14 2000     .exrc
-r--r--r--    1     bin     bin     439     Nov 14 2000     .profile
-r--r--r--    1     bin     bin     832     Nov 14 2000     .cshrc
```

There are numerous other options available with the *sort* command. Try them to build a better understanding. Refer to the man pages of *sort*.

2.8   Linking Files and Directories

Each file in HP-UX has a unique number assigned to it at the time it is created. This number is referred to as its inode (*index node)* number. All file attributes, such as the name, type, size, permissions, ownership, group membership, last access/modification time, etc. are maintained in that inode. In addition, the inode points to the exact location in the directory structure where the data for the file sits. See Chapter 15 "Working with File Systems" for details on inodes.

Linking files (or directories) means you have more than one file (or directory) name pointing to the same physical data location in the directory tree.

There are two types of links: *Symbolic* (or *Soft*) link and *Hard* link.

Symbolic Link

A *Symbolic* link makes it possible to associate one file with another file. It is similar to a "shortcut" in MS Windows where actual file resides somewhere else but you may have multiple "shortcuts" or "pointers" with different names pointing to that file. This means accessing the file via actual file name or any of the shortcuts yields identical result. A symbolic link is also referred to as *Soft* Link.

A symbolic link can cross file system boundaries and can be used to link directories.

To create a soft link for *file1* as *file10* in the same directory, use the *ln* command with –s option:

```
$ cd /home/user1
$ ln –s file1 file10
```

where:

file1 is an existing file
file10 is symbolically linked to *file1*

After you have created this link, do an *ll with –i option*. Notice the letter "l" as the first character in the second column of the output. Also notice an arrow pointing from the linked file to the original file. This indicates that *file10* is nothing but a pointer to *file1*. The –i option displays associated inode numbers in the first column.

```
$ ll –i
48 -rwxr--r--          1       user1   users   101     May 10 12:13    file1
49 lrwxrwxrwx          1       user1   users   5       May 10 12:13    file10 -> file1
```

If you remove the original file (*file1* in the example), the link (*file10*) still stays there but pointing to something that does not exist.

Hard Link

A *Hard* link associates two or more files with a single inode number. This allows the files to share same permissions, ownership, time stamp, and file contents. Changes made to any of the files are reflected on the other linked files. All files will actually contain identical data.

A hard link cannot cross file system boundaries and cannot be used to link directories.

The following example uses the *ln* command and creates a hard link for *file2* located under */home/user1* directory to *file20* in the same directory. *file20* does not currently exist, it will be created.

```
$ cd  /home/user1
$ ln  file2  file20
```

After creating the link, do an *ll* with –i option.

```
$ ll –i
18 -rw-rw-rw-          2       user1   users   412     Nov 25 15:38    file2
18 -rw-rw-rw-          2       user1   users   412     Nov 25 15:38    file20
```

Look at the first and the third columns. The first column indicates that both files have identical inode numbers and the third column tells you that each file has two hard links. *file2* points to *file20*, and vice versa. If you remove the original file (*file2* in the example), you still have access to the data through the linked file (*file20*).

Summary

In this chapter, you got an overview of the HP-UX file system structure and significant higher level sub-directories. Those sub-directories consisted of either static or variable files, which were logically grouped into further lower level sub-directories. The files and sub-directories were accessed using path relative to either the top-most directory of the file system structure or your current location in the tree.

You learned about different types of files and a set of rules to adhere to when creating files or directories. You looked at several file and directory manipulation tools, such as creating, listing, displaying, copying, moving, renaming, and removing them.

Searching for text within files and searching for files within the directory structure using specified criteria provided you with an understanding and explanation of tools required to perform such tasks.

Finally, you studied how to sort in ascending or descending order contents of a text file or output generated by executing a command. The last topic discussed creating soft and hard links between files and between directories.

HP Certified Systems Administrator

## 03

Working with File and Directory Permissions

This chapter covers the following major topics:

- ✓ File and directory permissions assigned to owners, members of owner's group, and others
- ✓ Types of permissions based on read, write, and execute requirements
- ✓ Modes of permissions based on adding, revoking, or assigning permissions
- ✓ Modify file and directory permissions using symbolic and octal notations
- ✓ Set default permissions on files & directories
- ✓ Change a user's primary group for the time being
- ✓ Modify ownership and group membership on files and directories
- ✓ Configure special permissions on executable files and directories by setting setuid, setgid, and sticky bits
- ✓ Extended file and directory permissions using Access Control List (ACL)

3.1   Determining Access Permissions

In HP-UX, permissions are set on files and directories to prevent access by unauthorized users. Users on the system are grouped into three distinct categories. Each user category is then assigned required permissions. The following sub-sections elaborate on file and directory permissions.

3.1.1   Permission Classes

Users on the system are categorized into three distinct classes for the purpose of maintaining file security through permissions. These classes are described in Table 3-1.

Permission Class	Description
User (u)	Owner of file or directory. Usually the person who creates a file or directory is the owner of it.
Group (g)	A set of users that need identical access to files and directories that they share. You create and maintain group information in the */etc/group* file and assign users to groups according to shared file access requirements.
Others (o)	All other users that have access to the system except the owner and group members. Also called *public*.

Table 3-1 Permission Classes

3.1.2   Permission Types

Permissions control who can do what to a file or directory. There are four types of permissions as defined in Table 3-2.

Permission Type	Symbol	File	Directory
Read	r	Displays file contents or copies contents to another file.	Displays contents with the *ll* command.
Write	w	Modifies file contents.	Creates, removes, or renames files and sub-directories.
Execute	x	Executes a file.	"*cd*" into the directory.
Access Denied	-	None.	None.

Table 3-2 Permission Types

3.1.3   Permission Modes

A permission mode relates a permission type to a permission class. Table 3-3 shows various permission modes.

Permission Mode	Description
Add permissions (+)	Gives specified permission(s).
Revoke permissions (-)	Removes specified permission(s).
Assign permissions (=)	Gives specified permission(s) to owner, group members, and public in one go.

Table 3-3 Permission Modes

The output of the *ll* command lists files and directories along with their type and permission settings. This information is shown in the first column of the command's output where 10 characters are displayed. The first character indicates the type of file: d for directory, – for regular file, l for symbolic link, c for character special device file, b for block special device file, n for named pipe, s for socket, and so on. The next nine characters – three groups of three characters – show read (r), write (w), execute (x), or none (-) permissions for the three user classes: user, group, and others, respectively.

Figure 3-1 illustrates the *ll* command output and its various components.

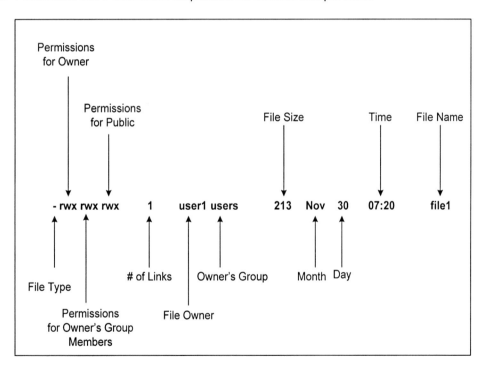

Figure 3-1 Permission Settings

From Figure 3-1, it is obvious who the owner (3rd column) of the file is and which group (4th column) the owner belongs to.

3.2   Changing Access Permissions

The *chmod* command is used either by file owner or *root* to change file permissions. This command can modify permissions specified in one of two methods: *Symbolic* or *Octal*.

The symbolic notation uses combination of letters and symbols to add, revoke, or assign permissions to each class of users, whereas the octal notation, also known as the *Absolute* notation, uses numbers for that purpose.

3.2.1   Using Symbolic Notation

The symbolic notation denotes the permission class, type, and mode.

The following examples and their explanation provide an understanding on how to set file permissions. It works in an identical fashion on directories.

For the purpose of explanation, say you have a file called *file1* with read permission to the owner, group members, and others. This file is owned by *user1* who is going to be doing the permission modifications.

   -r--r--r--   1 user1   users   0 Nov 30 07:20 file1

To modify permissions on *file1* to add execute permission for *owner*:

   $ chmod u+x file1
   -r-xr--r--   1 user1   users   0 Nov 30 07:20 file1

To modify permissions on *file1* to add write permission for *owner*:

   $ chmod u+w file1
   -rwxr--r--   1 user1   users   0 Nov 30 07:20 file1

To modify permissions on *file1* to add write permission for group members and public:

   $ chmod go+w file1
   -rwxrw-rw-   1 user1   users   0 Nov 30 07:20 file1

To modify permissions on *file1* to remove write permission for public:

   $ chmod o-w file1
   -rwxrw-r--   1 user1   users   0 Nov 30 07:20 file1

To modify permissions on *file1* to assign read, write, and execute permissions to all three user categories:

   $ chmod a=rwx file1
   -rwxrwxrwx   1 user1   users   0 Nov 30 07:20 file1

3.2.2   Using Octal (or Absolute) Notation

Octal notation uses a three-digit numbering system that ranges from 0 to 7 to specify permissions for the three user classes. Octal values are given in Table 3-4.

Octal Value	Binary Notation	Symbolic Notation	Explanation
0	000	---	No permissions.
1	001	--x	Execute permissions only.
2	010	-w-	Write permissions only.
3	011	-wx	Write and execute permissions.
4	100	r--	Read permissions only.
5	101	r-x	Read and execute permissions.
6	110	rw-	Read and write permissions.
7	111	rwx	Read, write, and execute permissions.

Table 3-4 Octal Permission Notation

From Table 3-4, it is obvious that each "1" corresponds to an "r", a "w", or an "x", and each "0" corresponds to the "-" character for no permission at that level. Figure 3-2 shows weights associated with each digit location in the 3-digit octal numbering model. The right-most location has weight 1, the middle location has weight 2, and the left-most location has weight 4. When you assign a permission of 6, for example, it would correspond to the two left-most digit locations. Similarly, a permission of 2 would mean only the middle digit location.

Figure 3-2 Permission Weights

The following examples and their explanation provide an understanding on how to set file permissions using octal method. It works in an identical fashion on directories.

For the purpose of explanation, say you have a file called *file2* with read permission to the owner, group members, and others. This file is owned by *user1* and permission modifications in the following examples are going to be done by *user1*.

    -r--r--r-- 1 user1   users   0 Nov 30 07:23 file2

The current permissions on *file2* in the octal notation is 444, where each digit represents one class of users. The first 4 is for file owner, the second 4 is for owner's group members, and the third 4 is for everyone else.

To modify permissions on *file2* to add execute permission for the file owner:

```
$ cd
$ chmod  644  file2
-rw-r--r--  1 user1    users       0 Nov 30 07:20 file2
```

To modify permissions on *file2* to add write permission for the owner:

```
$ chmod  744  file2
-rwxr--r--  1 user1    users       0 Nov 30 07:20 file2
```

To modify permissions on *file2* to add write permission for group members and others:

```
$ chmod  766  file2
-rwxrw-rw-  1 user1    users       0 Nov 30 07:20 file2
```

To modify permissions on *file2* to revoke write permission from public users:

```
$ chmod  764  file2
-rwxrw-r--  1 user1    users       0 Nov 30 07:20 file2
```

To modify permissions on *file2* to assign read, write, and execute permissions to all three user categories:

```
$ chmod  777  file2
-rwxrwxrwx  1 user1    users       0 Nov 30 07:20 file2
```

3.3   Setting Default Permissions

When you create a file or directory, the system assigns *default permissions* to it. The default permissions are calculated based on the umask (**user mask**) permission value subtracted from a pre-defined value called *initial* permissions.

The umask value is a three-digit value that refers to read/write/execute permissions for owner, group, and other. Its purpose is to set default permissions on new files and directories. In HP-UX, the default umask value is set to 022. To display the current value, use the *umask* command without any options.

```
$ umask
022
```

To display the umask value in symbolic notation, run *umask* with the –S option:

```
$ umask  –S
u=rwx,g=rx,o=rx
```

The umask value is shown differently in different shells. In Bourne shell, it is shown as 0022, in the POSIX and Korn shells, it is shown as 022, and in the C shell, as 22.

The initial permission values pre-defined in HP-UX are 666 (or rw-rw-rw-) for files and 777 (or rwxrwxrwx) for directories.

3.3.1   Calculating Default Permissions

Here is how you would calculate default permission values for files:

```
Initial Permissions        666
umask                    – 022   (subtract)
========================
Default Permissions        644
```

This indicates that when a file is created it will have read and write permissions assigned to owner and read-only permission to owner's group members, and public.

To determine default values on a directory, use the initial value of 777. Here is how to calculate default permission values for directories:

```
Initial Permissions        777
umask                    – 022   (subtract)
========================
Default Permissions        755
```

This indicates that when a directory is created it will have read, write, and execute permissions assigned to owner and read and write permissions to owner's group members, and public.

Now, if you wish to have different default permissions set when you create a file or directory, you need to modify umask. First determine what default values you need. For example, you want all your new files and directories to have 640 and 750 permissions, respectively. Run *umask* and set the value to 027 as follows:

```
$ umask  027
```

The new umask value gets in effect right away. Make a note that the new umask is applied only to those files and directories created after the umask is changed. The existing files and directories will have absolutely no effect. Create a file by the name *file10* and a directory by the name *dir10* as *user1* under */home/user1* to test the effect of the change.

```
$ touch  file10
$ ll  file10
-rw-r-----  1 user1     users        0 May 18 15:01 file10
$ mkdir  dir10
$ ll –d  dir10
drwxr-x---  2 user1     users       96 May 18 15:01 dir10
```

The above examples show that new files and directories are created with different permissions. The files have (666 – 027 = 640) and directories (777 – 027 = 750).

When umask is set to a new value at the command line, it gets lost as soon as you log off. In order to retain the new setting, you must place it in one of the shell initialization files. Customizing your shell initialization files is covered in Chapter 12 "User and Group Account Administration".

3.4   Changing File Ownership and Group Membership

In HP-UX, every file and directory has an owner associated with it. By default, the creator becomes the owner. The ownership can be altered, if required, and allocated to some other user.

Similarly, every user is a member of one or more groups. A group is a collection of users that have same privileges on a file or directory. By default, the owner's group is assigned to a file or directory.

For example, below is an output from the *ll* command on *file1*:

$ ll file1
-rw-r--r-- 1 **user1**   **users**   0 Nov 30 14:04 file1

This output indicates that the owner of *file1* is *user1* who belongs to group *users*.

To alter ownership or group membership, use the *chown* and *chgrp* commands. Consider the following examples.

To change ownership from *user1* to *user2*. You must be either the file owner or *root* to make this modification.

$ **chown user2 file1**
$ ll file1
-rwxr--r-- 1 **user2**   users   101 May 18 15:09 file1

To change group membership from *users* to *other*. You must be either *user2* or *root* to make this modification.

chgrp other file1
ll file1
-rwxr--r-- 1 user2   **other**   101 May 18 15:09 file1

To modify both ownership and group membership in one go, use the *chown* command. You must be either *user2* or *root* to successfully issue the following command.

$ **chown user1:users file1**
$ ll file1
-rwxr--r-- 1 **user1**   **users**   101 May 18 15:09 file1

To modify all files and sub-directories under *dir1* to be owned by *user2* and group *users,* use the –R (recursive) option with the *chown* command.

$ **chown –R user2:users dir1**

3.5 Special Permissions

There are three special types of permissions available in HP-UX for executable files and directories. These permissions may be assigned if required. These are:

- ✓ The setuid (*set user identification*) bit
- ✓ The setgid (*set group identification*) bit
- ✓ The sticky bit

Let us discuss them one by one.

3.5.1 The setuid Bit

The *setuid* bit is set on executable files at the file owner level. Having this bit enabled, the file is executed by other users with exact same privileges that the owner of the file has on it. For example, the *su* command is owned by *root* with group membership set to *bin*. This command has setuid bit enabled on it. See the highlighted "s" in the owner's permission class below.

```
$ ll /usr/bin/su
-r-sr-xr-x  1 root    bin      24576 Nov 14  2000 /usr/bin/su
```

When a normal user executes this command, it runs as if *root* (the owner) is running it, and hence the user is able to run it and gets the desired result.

> The *su* (*switch user*) command allows a user to switch to some other user's account provided the switching user knows the password of the user he/she is trying to switch to.

Now, let us remove the setuid bit from *su* and replace it with an "x". You must be either *root* or the file owner to do so.

```
# chmod  555  /usr/bin/su
-r-xr-xr-x  1 root    bin      24576 Nov 14  2000 /usr/bin/su
```

Still the file is executable, but when a normal user runs it, he/she will be running it as himself/herself and not as *root*. Here is what is going to happen when *user1* tries to *su* into *user2* and enters a valid password.

```
$ su – user2
Password:
su: Invalid ID
```

user1 sees the "Invalid ID" message even though he/she entered correct login credentials.

To set setuid bit back on *su* or on some other file, run the *chmod* command as follows:

> **# chmod 4555 /usr/bin/su**
> **# ll /usr/bin/su**
> -r-s**r**-xr-x 1 root   bin   24576 Nov 14 2000 /usr/bin/su

When digit 4 is used with the *chmod* command in this manner, it sets the setuid bit on the file.

Alternatively, you can use the symbolic notation to get exact same results:

> **# chmod u+s /usr/bin/su**

To search for all files in the system that have setuid bit set on them, use the *find* command:

> **# find / −perm −4000**

3.5.2   The setgid Bit

The *setgid* bit is set at the group level. When this bit is set on an executable file, that file is executed by other users with exact same privileges that the group members have on it. For example, the *write* command is owned by *bin* with group membership set to *bin*. This command has setgid bit enabled on it, which is represented by the character "s" in the group permissions as follows:

> **$ ll /usr/bin/write**
> -r-xr-**s**r-x 1 bin   bin   16384 Nov 14 2000 /usr/bin/write

When a regular user executes this command, it runs as if *bin* is running it, and hence the user is able to run it successfully and gets the desired result.

To set setgid bit on an executable file, run the *chmod* command. Let us set the setgid bit on */home/user1/file1*. Do it as *root*.

> **# chmod 2555 /home/user1/file1**
> **# ll**
> -r-xr-**s**r-x 1 user1   user1   101 May 18 15:09 file1

When digit 2 is used with the *chmod* command in this manner, it sets the setgid bit on the file.

Alternatively, you can use the symbolic notation to get exact same results:

> **# chmod g+s /home/user1/file1**

To search for all files in the system that have setgid bit set on them, use the *find* command:

> **# find / −perm −2000**

You may want to setup setgid bit on a shared directory accessed by users of a group. This allows the group members to be able to create files in the directory but the files created will not have group

---

membership of the creator's group, rather they will have group membership of the group which the directory belongs to.

To set setgid bit on a shared directory, issue the *chmod* command the same way as you did when you enabled setgid on files, as discussed above.

3.5.3   The Sticky Bit

The *Sticky* bit is set on public writable directories to protect files and sub-directories of individual users from being deleted by other users. This is typically done on */tmp* and /var/tmp directories in HP-UX. Normally, all users are allowed to create and delete files and sub-directories in */tmp* and */var/tmp*. With default permissions, any user can remove any other user's files and sub-directories.

Here is how you would set sticky bit on */tmp* and */var/tmp*:

    # chmod 1777 /tmp
    # chmod 1777 /var/tmp

When digit 1 is used with the *chmod* command in this manner, it sets sticky bit on the specified directory.

Alternatively, you can use the symbolic notation to do exactly the same:

    # chmod o+t /tmp
    # chmod o+t /var/tmp

After setting up sticky bits on the directories above, do an *ll* and you will notice the character "t" in other's permissions. This indicates that sticky bit is enabled.

    # ll –ld /tmp /var/tmp
    drwxrwxrwt 6 bin   bin   8192 Nov 30 15:30 tmp
    drwxrwxrwt 4 bin   bin   6144 Nov 30 15:30 var/tmp

To search for all directories in the system that have sticky bit set, use *find* command:

    # find / –type d –perm –1000

3.6   Access Control List (ACL)

Access Control List provides an extended set of permissions on files and directories. These permissions are on top of the standard UNIX file and directory permissions discussed earlier in this chapter. The ACL allows you to define permissions for specific users or groups. You can use either octal or symbolic notation to setup ACL.

There are five commands available to work with ACL. These are *ls, lsacl, getacl, setacl, and chacl*. The *ls, lsacl,* and *getacl* commands display permission information, while the *setacl and chacl* commands are used to set, modify, substitute, or delete ACL entries.

There are two disk-based file systems used in HP-UX: HFS and JFS. In newer implementations, all but the */stand* file system (that contains kernel related files) are JFS. From the above commands, *lsacl* and *chacl* work only with HFS. In this section, you are going to cover the *getacl* and *setacl* commands that work with JFS since that is the type of file system you will be dealing with most of the time. The *ls* command works with both types of file systems and is covered here as well. See Chapter 15 "Working with File Systems" for details on file systems.

3.6.1   Listing ACL Information

You have two ways (*ll* and *getacl* commands) to determine if a file or directory has ACL set on it. The *ll* command only displays whether or not a file or directory has ACL on it. If it displays a (+) sign right next to permissions, that would indicate that ACL is set.

> **$ ll file1**
> -rw-r--r-- 1 user1   users   0 Nov 30 14:04 file1

The *getacl* command provides details, as shown below:

> **$ getacl file1**
> # file: file1
> # owner: user1
> # group: users
> user::rw-
> group::r--
> class:r--
> other:r--

This information indicates that currently there is no ACL set on *file1*. It shows that file owner is *user1* having read and write permissions, the file owner belongs to *users* group that has read-only permission, and everyone else has read-only permission on *file1* too.

3.6.2   Changing ACL Information

Let us set ACL on *file1* with the *setacl* command and then perform modify, substitute, and delete functions to understand the behavior in greater detail.

Before you begin, look at Table 3-5 to see how ACL entries are used with the *setacl* command.

Suppose you have *user1*, *user2*, *user3*, and *user4* as members of *users* group and you have *file1* owned by *user1* with 644 permissions. Currently, as you can see, *file1* has no ACL set on it.

> -rw-r--r-- 1 user1   users   0 Nov 30 14:04 file1

To allocate read/write/execute permissions to a specific user, *user2*, use *setacl* as follows:

> **$ setacl –m u:user2:7 file1**

ACL Entry	Description
u[ser]::perm	Standard UNIX permissions for file or directory owner.
g[roup]::perm	Standard UNIX permissions for group members, which the file or directory owner belongs.
o[ther]:perm	Standard UNIX permissions for public.
c[lass]:perm	Maximum permissions a specific user or a specific group can have on a file or directory. If this is set to, for example, rw-, then no specific user or group can have more than read/write permissions.
u[ser]:UID:perm (or u[ser]:username:perm)	Permissions assigned to a specific user. The user must exist in /etc/passwd file.
g[roup]:GID:perm (or g[roup]:groupname:perm)	Permissions assigned to a specific group. The group must exist in /etc/group file.
d[efault]:u:perm	Default standard UNIX permissions for the owner set at the directory level.
d[efault]:u::perm	Default permissions for a specific user set at the directory level.
d[efault]:g:perm	Default standard UNIX permissions for owner's group members set at the directory level.
d[efault]:g::perm	Default permissions for a specific group set at the directory level.
d[efault]:o:perm	Default permissions for public set at the directory level.
d[efault]:c:perm	Maximum default permissions a user or group can have when the user or a group member creates a file in a directory where default ACL is set.

Table 3-5 ACL Entry Usage

The *ll* command will report:

```
$ ll
-rw-rwxr--+  1 user1    users         0 Nov 30 14:04 file1
```

Notice the (+) sign appeared next to permissions column. This indicates that *file1* has now ACL set on it.

The *getacl* command will report:

```
$ getacl  file1
# file: file1
# owner: user1
# group: users
user::rw-
user:user2:rwx
group::r--
class:rwx
other:r--
```

Notice a line added for *user2* showing rwx (7) permissions. Also notice that the entry *class* is now changed to rwx (it was r-- initially). The value of *class* determines the maximum permissions assigned to a specific user or group. In this case, the maximum permissions allocated to *user2* is rwx, hence *class* changed to rwx as well.

To modify these entries to have *user4* read/write permissions on *file1* as well, do the following:

> **$ setacl –m u:user4:rw file1**

The *getacl* command reports:

> **$ getacl file1**
> # file: file1
> # owner: user1
> # group: users
> user::rw-
> user:**user2**:rwx
> user:**user4**:rw-
> group::r--
> class:rwx
> other:r--

To delete the ACL entries for *user2*, use the –d option with *setacl* as follows:

> **$ setacl –d u:user2 file1**
> **$ getacl file1**
> # file: file1
> # owner: user1
> # group: users
> user::rw-
> user:user4:rw-
> group::r--
> class:rw-
> other:r—

Note that the maximum permissions are now reduced to read/write since that is what the maximum is for a specific user or group defined by *class*.

To substitute entire ACL for *file1* to have rwx for the owner, rw for the group, r-- for other, and rwx for *user3*, use the –s option with *setacl* as follows:

> **$ setacl –s u::rwx,g::rw,o:r,u:user3:rwx file1**
> **$ getacl file1**
> # file: file1
> # owner: user1
> # group: users
> user::rwx
> user:**user3**:rwx
> group::rw-

HP Certified Systems Administrator

class:rwx
other:r--

The above command in octal notation would be:

$ **setacl –s u::7,g::6,o:4,u:user3:7 file1**

3.6.3 Default ACL

Sometimes it is imperative for several users belonging to different groups to share directory contents. They want to have permissions setup on a shared directory in such a way that when files and sub-directories are created underneath, they inherit parent directory permissions. This way they do not have to modify permissions on each new file and sub-directory after its creation. Setting default ACL on a directory fulfills this requirement.

Default ACL can be described as the maximum discretionary permissions that can be allocated on files and directories. It is setup only on directories.

You must set default ACL entries at the user, group, and other level, and ACL mask before you define a default ACL entry for additional users or groups.

Summary

In this chapter, you learned about file and directory permissions assigned to their owners, members of the group that the owner belonged to, and other users on the system. You looked at types and modes of permissions and how to modify those using symbolic and octal notations.

You studied how default permissions could be setup for new files and directories and the role of umask value in determining new default permissions.

Then you saw how a user could alter his/her primary group membership temporarily and how a user or root could modify ownership and group membership on files and directories.

Finally, you learned about setting special permissions on executable files and directories and setting extended permissions on files and directories using Access Control List.

HP Certified Systems Administrator

## 04

The vi Editor and Text Processors

This chapter covers the following major topics:

- ✓ Modes of operation for the vi editor
- ✓ Start and quit the vi Editor
- ✓ Navigate within vi
- ✓ Manipulate text
- ✓ Save modifications
- ✓ Customize vi settings
- ✓ Manipulate columns of text via the awk text processor
- ✓ Manipulate rows of text via the sed text processor

4.1   The vi Editor

The vi editor is an interactive *visual* text editor tool that enables a user to create and modify text files. It was written by Bill Joy in the mid 1970s. All text editing with the vi editor takes place in a buffer (a small chunk of memory used to hold updates being done to the file). Changes can either be written to the disk or discarded.

It is essential for system administrators to master the vi editor skills. Following sections provide details on how to work and interact with vi.

4.1.1   Modes of Operation

The vi editor has three basic modes of operation:

- ✓ Command mode
- ✓ Edit mode
- ✓ Last line mode

Command Mode

The *Command* mode is the default mode of vi. When you start the vi editor, it places you into this mode. While in the command mode, you can carry out various tasks on text including copy, cut, paste, move, remove, replace, change, search, etc. in addition to performing navigational tasks. This mode is also known as the *Escape* mode as the *Esc* key is pressed to enter it.

Input Mode

In *Input* mode, anything you type at the keyboard is entered into the file as text. Commands cannot be run in this mode. The input mode is also called the *Edit* mode or the *Insert* mode. To go back to the command mode, simply press the *Esc* key.

Last Line Mode

While in the command mode, you may carry out advanced editing tasks on text by pressing the colon (:) character. This places you at the beginning of the last line of the screen, and hence referred to as the *Last Line* mode. This mode is considered a special type of command mode.

4.1.2   Starting the vi Editor

You can start vi in one of the ways described in Table 4-1.

Method	Description
vi	Starts vi and opens up an empty screen for you to enter text. You can save or discard the text entered later as you wish.
vi *existing_file*	Starts vi and loads the specified file for editing or viewing.
vi *new_file*	Starts vi and creates the specified file when saved.

Table 4-1 Starting The vi Editor

4.1.3   Inserting text

To start entering text, type one of the commands described in Table 4-2 from the command mode to switch to the edit mode.

Command	Action
i (lowercase)	Allows you to insert text before the current cursor position.
I (uppercase)	Allows you to insert text at the beginning of the current line.
a (lowercase)	Allows you to append text after the current cursor position.
A (uppercase)	Allows you to append text at the end of the current line.
o (lowercase)	Opens up a new line below the current line and allows you to insert text.
O (uppercase)	Opens up a new line above the current line and allows you to insert text.

Table 4-2 Inserting Text

When you are done with inserting text, press the *Esc* key to return to the command mode.

4.1.4   Navigating within vi

Table 4-3 elaborates key sequences that control cursor movement while you are in the vi editor. You must be in the command mode to move around.

Command	Action
h, left arrow, backspace, or ctrl-h	Moves left (backward) one character.
j or down arrow	Moves down one line.
k or up arrow	Moves up one line.
l, right arrow, or spacebar	Moves right (forward) one character.
W or w	Moves forward one word.
B or b	Moves backward one word.
E or e	Moves forward to the last character of the next word.
M	Moves to the line in the middle of the page.
$	Moves to the end of the current line.
0 (zero) or ^	Moves to the beginning of the current line.
Enter	Moves down to the beginning of the next line.

ctrl+f	Moves forward to the next page (scrolls down).
ctrl+d	Moves forward one-half page (scrolls down).
ctrl+b	Moves backward to the previous page (scrolls up).
ctrl+u	Moves backward one-half page (scrolls up).
G or]]	Moves to the last line of the file.
(	Moves backward to the beginning of the current sentence.
)	Moves forward to the beginning of the next sentence.
{	Moves backward to the beginning of the preceding paragraph.
}	Moves forward to the beginning of the next paragraph.
1G or [[or :1	Moves to the first line of the file.
:11 or 11G	Moves to the specified line number (such as line number 11).
ctrl+g	Tells you what line number you are at.

Table 4-3 Navigating Within vi

4.1.5   Deleting Text

Commands listed in Table 4-4 are available to perform delete operations. You must be in the command mode to accomplish these tasks.

Command	Action
x (lowercase)	Deletes a character at the current cursor position. You may type a digit before this command to delete that many characters. For example, 2x would remove two characters, 3x would remove 3 characters, and so on.
X (uppercase)	Deletes a character before the current cursor location. You may type a digit before this command to delete that many characters. For example, 2X would remove two characters, 3X would remove 3 characters, and so on.
dw	Deletes a word or part of the word to the right of the current cursor location. You may type a digit before this command to delete that many words. For example, 2w would remove two words, 3w would remove 3 words, and so on.
dd	Deletes the current line. You may type a digit before this command to delete that many lines. For example, 2dd would remove two lines, 3dd would remove 3 lines, and so on.
D	Deletes at the current cursor position to the end of the current line.
:6,12d	Deletes lines 6 through 12.

Table 4-4 Deleting Text

4.1.6   Undoing and Repeating

Table 4-5 explains commands available to undo the last change you did and repeat the last command you ran. You must be in the command mode to perform the tasks.

Command	Action
u (lowercase)	Undoes the last command.
U (uppercase)	Undoes all changes at the current line.
:u	Undoes the previous last line mode command.
. (dot)	Repeats the last command you ran.

Table 4-5 Undoing and Repeating

4.1.7 Searching and Replacing Text

Search and replace text functions are performed using commands mentioned in Table 4-6. You must be in command mode to do these tasks.

Command	Action
/string	Searches forward for string.
?string	Searches backward for string.
n (lowercase)	Finds next occurrence of string. This would only work if you have run either a forward or a backward string search.
N (uppercase)	Finds previous occurrence of string. This would only work if you have run either a forward or a backward string search.
:%s/old/new	Searches and replaces the first occurrence of *old* with *new*. For example, to replace first occurrence of "profile" with "Profile", you would use ":%s/profile/Profile".
:%s/old/new/g	Searches and replaces all occurrences of *old* with *new*. For example, to replace all occurrences of "profile" with "Profile" in the file, you would use ":%s/profile/Profile/g".

Table 4-6 Searching and Replacing Text

4.1.8 Copying, Moving, and Pasting Text

The *co* command writes copied text into a temporary buffer. The *P* or *p* command reads text from the temporary buffer and writes it into current file at the specified location. You can also do move and copy functions from the last line mode. See Table 4-7 for further information.

Command	Action
yy (lowercase)	Yanks the current line into buffer. You may specify a digit before this command to yank that many lines. For example, 2yy yanks two lines, 3yy yanks three lines, and so on.
p (lowercase)	Pastes yanked line below the current line.
P (uppercase)	Pastes yanked line above the current line.
:1,3co5	Copies lines 1 through 3 and pastes them after line 5.
:4,6m8	Moves lines 4 through 6 after line 8.

Table 4-7 Copying, Moving, and Pasting Text

4.1.9   Changing Text

To change text, use commands given in Table 4-8 below. Some of these commands take you to the edit mode. To return to the command mode, press the *Esc* key.

Command	Action
cw	Changes a word (or part of a word) at the current cursor location to the end of the current word.
C (uppercase)	Changes at the current cursor position to the end of the current line.
r (lowercase)	Replaces character at the current cursor location with the character entered following this command.
R (uppercase)	Overwrites or replaces text on the current line.
s (lowercase)	Substitutes a string for character(s).
S (uppercase) or cc	Substitutes an entire line.
J (uppercase)	Joins the current line and the line below it.
xp	Switches position of the character at the current cursor position with the character to the right of it.
~ (tilde)	Changes letter case (uppercase to lowercase, and vice versa) at the current cursor location.

Table 4-8 Changing Text

4.1.10   Importing Contents of Another File

While working in vi you may want to insert contents of some other file. The vi editor allows you to do that. You must be at the last line mode to accomplish this. See Table 4-9 below.

Command	Action
:r file2	Reads *file2* and inserts its contents below the current line.

Table 4-9 Importing Contents of Another File

4.1.11   Customizing vi Edit Sessions

The vi editor supports settings to customize edit sessions to display line numbers, invisible characters, and so on. Use the *set* command to control these options. Consult Table 4-10 below.

Command	Action
:set nu	Shows line numbers.
:set nonu	Hides line numbers.
:set ic	Ignores letter case when carrying out searches.
:set noic	Does not ignore letter case when carrying out searches.
:set list	Displays invisible characters, such as *tab* and *End Of Line* (EOL).
:set nolist	Hides invisible characters, such as *tab* and *EOL*.
:set showmode	Displays current mode of operation.

Command	Action
:set noshowmode	Hides mode of operation.
:set	Displays current vi variable settings.
:set all	Displays all available vi variables and their current settings.

Table 4-10 Customizing vi Settings

4.1.12   Saving and Quitting vi

When you are done with your modifications, you would want to either save them or just discard them. Commands listed in Table 4-11 would help you.

Command	Action
:w	Writes changes into currently-opened file without quitting vi.
:w file3	Writes changes into a new file called *file3*.
:w!	Writes changes into currently-opened file even if file owner does not have write permission on the file.
:wq or :x or ZZ	Writes changes to currently-opened file and quits vi.
:wq! or :x!	Writes changes into currently-opened file and quits vi even if file owner does not have write permission on the file.
:q	Quits vi if no modifications were made.
:q!	Quits vi if modifications were made but you do not wish to save them.

Table 4-11 Saving and Quitting vi

4.1.13   Miscellaneous vi Commands

Table 4-12 describes some additional commands available to perform specific tasks within vi.

Command	Action
ctrl+l or ctrl+r	Refreshes the vi screen, if proper terminal type is set.
:sh	Exits vi editor session temporarily. Type *exit* or *ctrl+d* to come back.
:!cmd	Executes the specified command without quitting vi. You would type the command preceded by the ! character in the last line mode.

Table 4-12 Miscellaneous vi Commands

4.2   The Text Processors

The HP-UX Operating Environment supports two famous text processors to perform functions on rows and columns of text. These are known as *awk* and *sed*. These text processors can work on input taken either from a specified file or from the output of a command, such as *ll*. Neither text processor makes any modifications to files provided as input. They only read input files and display results on the screen. If you wish to save the result, you must use output redirection (See Chapter

05 "The HP-UX Shells" on how to use output redirection). Let us take a look at both and understand them with the help of examples.

4.2.1   The *awk* Processor

The name *awk* was derived from the first initial of the last names of those who developed it: Alfred **A**ho, Peter **W**einberger, and Brian **K**enigham.

awk works on columns of text to change data and generate reports. It scans a file or input provided one line at a time. It starts from the first line and searches for lines matching a specified pattern enclosed in quotes and curly braces. Finally, it performs selected actions on those lines.

In order to explain the behavior of the *awk* utility, create a file by running the *ll* command and redirect its output to a file called *ls.out*. Then use this file as input to the *awk* command and examine results displayed on the screen. Before doing that, let us see how *awk* interprets columns. In other words how *awk* differentiates between columns. Let us run the *ll* command as *user1* on *user1's* home directory */home/user1*.

```
$ cd
$ ll
total 608
-rw-rw-rw-  1       user1   users   1089     Feb  4 22:56    file1
-rw-rw-rw-  1       user1   users   2426     Feb  4 22:56    file2
-rw-rw-rw-  1       user1   users   270336   Feb  4 22:57    file3
-rw-rw-rw-  1       user1   users   11       Feb  4 22:57    file4
-rw-rw-rw-  1       user1   users   988      Feb  4 23:26    ll.out
drwxrwxrwx  2       user1   users   96       Feb  4 22:55    scripts
drwxrwxrwx  2       user1   users   96       Feb  4 22:55    scripts1
drwxrwxrwx  2       user1   users   96       Feb  4 22:55    subdir1
drwxrwxrwx  2       user1   users   96       Feb  4 22:55    subdir2
drwxrwxrwx  2       user1   users   96       Feb  4 22:55    subdir3
drwxrwxrwx  2       user1   users   96       Feb  4 22:55    subdir4
```

awk automatically breaks a line into columns and assigns a variable name to each one of them. A white space, such as a tab, is used as a default delimiter between columns to separate them.

Each line from the output of the *ll* command contains nine columns of text. Figure 4-1 shows how *awk* represents each column with respect to its position.

Here, $1 represents the first column, $2 represents the second column, $3 represents the third column, and so on. All columns are collectively represented by $0. The following examples help you develop an understanding on the usage of *awk*.

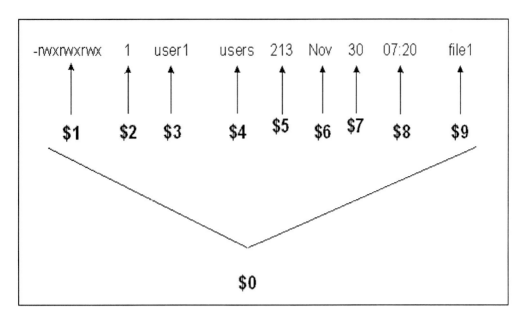

Figure 4-1 *awk* **Command Arguments**

Let us save the output of the *ll* command into a file called *ll.out* as *user1*.

$ ll > ll.out

To display only the file name (column 9), file size (column 5), and file owner (column 3), use the following *awk* command. Note a space between variables. The output will not contain any spaces between columns. It will be printed as one single string of characters.

```
$ awk '{print $9 $5 $3}' ll.out
file11089user1
file22426user1
file3270336user1
file411user1
ll.out988user1
scripts96user1
scripts196user1
subdir196user1
subdir296user1
subdir396user1
subdir496user1
```

awk requires that you enclose the pattern in quotes and curly braces. The print function within curly braces is part of the syntax. The above output does not contain any spaces between columns.

To place a single space between columns in the output, use a comma between variables:

```
$ awk '{print $9, $5, $3}' ll.out
file1 1089 user1
file2 2426 user1
file3 270336 user1
file4 11 user1
ll.out 988 user1
scripts 96 user1
scripts1 96 user1
subdir1 96 user1
subdir2 96 user1
subdir3 96 user1
subdir4 96 user1
```

To provide for exact alignment between columns, insert a tab or two:

```
$ awk '{print $9 "   " $5 "      " $3}' ll.out
file1      1089     user1
file2      2426     user1
file3      270336   user1
file4      11       user1
ll.out     988      user1
scripts    96       user1
scripts1   96       user1
subdir1    96       user1
subdir2    96       user1
subdir3    96       user1
subdir4    96       user1
```

To rearrange columns to display file owner first, then file size, and then file name:

```
$ awk '{print $3,$5,$9}' ll.out
user1 1089 file1
user1 2426 file2
user1 270336 file3
user1 11 file4
user1 988 ll.out
user1 96 scripts
user1 96 scripts1
user1 96 subdir1
user1 96 subdir2
user1 96 subdir3
user1 96 subdir4
```

To add text between columns:

```
$ awk '{print $9,"was last modified/accessed on",$6,$7,"at",$8}' ll.out
file1 was last modified/accessed on Feb 4 at 22:56
file2 was last modified/accessed on Feb 4 at 22:56
file3 was last modified/accessed on Feb 4 at 22:57
file4 was last modified/accessed on Feb 4 at 22:57
ll.out was last modified/accessed on Feb 4 at 23:26
scripts was last modified/accessed on Feb 4 at 22:55
scripts1 was last modified/accessed on Feb 4 at 22:55
subdir1 was last modified/accessed on Feb 4 at 22:55
subdir2 was last modified/accessed on Feb 4 at 22:55
subdir3 was last modified/accessed on Feb 4 at 22:55
subdir4 was last modified/accessed on Feb 4 at 22:55
```

Note that when inserting text between columns, each text insert must be enclosed in double quotes and all but the last text inserted must be followed by a comma.

4.2.2   The *sed* Processor

Unlike *awk* that works on columns of text, the *sed* (*stream editor*) text processor works on rows of text. Following examples help understand the working of *sed*.

To search */etc/group* file for all lines containing the word "root" and remove them. Again it is not going to remove anything from the specified file. Let us first see what */etc/group* file contains.

```
$ cat  /etc/group
root::0:root
other::1:root,hpdb
bin::2:root,bin
sys::3:root,uucp
adm::4:root,adm
daemon::5:root,daemon
mail::6:root
lp::7:root,lp
tty::10:
nuucp::11:nuucp
users::20:root
nogroup:*:-2:
ids::101:
smbnull::102:
```

Now run *sed* to get the desired result:

```
$ sed  '/root/d'  /etc/group
tty::10:
nuucp::11:nuucp
nogroup:*:-2:
```

```
ids::101:
smbnull::102:
```

/root/d is enclosed in single quotes. The first forward slash tells *sed* to search for the following pattern and the second forward slash deletes that pattern from the output.

To remove all lines from the output of the *ll* command containing digit "3":

```
$ ll | sed '/3/d'
total 624
-rw-rw-rw-   1      user1   users   1089   Feb  4 22:56      file1
-rw-rw-rw-   1      user1   users   2426   Feb  4 22:56      file2
-rw-rw-rw-   1      user1   users   11     Feb  4 22:57      file4
drwxrwxrwx 2        user1   users   96     Feb  4 22:55      scripts
drwxrwxrwx 2        user1   users   96     Feb  4 22:55      scripts1
drwxrwxrwx 2        user1   users   96     Feb  4 22:55      subdir1
drwxrwxrwx 2        user1   users   96     Feb  4 22:55      subdir2
drwxrwxrwx 2        user1   users   96     Feb  4 22:55      subdir4
```

To print all lines in duplicate that contain the pattern "root" from */etc/group* file. All other lines to be printed one time. Use the "p" option.

```
$ sed '/root/p' /etc/group
root::0:root
root::0:root
other::1:root,hpdb
other::1:root,hpdb
bin::2:root,bin
bin::2:root,bin
sys::3:root,uucp
sys::3:root,uucp
adm::4:root,adm
adm::4:root,adm
daemon::5:root,daemon
daemon::5:root,daemon
mail::6:root
mail::6:root
lp::7:root,lp
lp::7:root,lp
tty::10:
nuucp::11:nuucp
users::20:root
users::20:root
nogroup:*:-2:
ids::101:
smbnull::102:
```

To print only those lines that contain the pattern "root" in */etc/group* file. Ignore all other lines. Use the –n option.

```
$ sed –n '/root/p' /etc/group
```
root::0:root
other::1:root,hpdb
bin::2:root,bin
sys::3:root,uucp
adm::4:root,adm
daemon::5:root,daemon
mail::6:root
lp::7:root,lp
users::20:root

To append character string "HPUX" at the end of every line in the output of the *ll* command. In the following command, "s" is used for substitute and "$" represents end of line. Run the command as *user1* on *user1's* home directory */home/user1*.

```
$ ll | sed 's/$/ HPUX/'
```
total 624 HPUX

-rw-rw-rw-	1	user1	users	1089	Feb 4 22:56	file1 HPUX
-rw-rw-rw-	1	user1	users	2426	Feb 4 22:56	file2 HPUX
-rw-rw-rw-	1	user1	users	70336	Feb 4 22:57	file3 HPUX
-rw-rw-rw-	1	user1	users	11	Feb 4 22:57	file4 HPUX
-rw-rw-rw-	1	user1	users	988	Feb 4 23:26	ll.out HPUX
drwxrwxrwx	2	user1	users	96	Feb 4 22:55	scripts HPUX
drwxrwxrwx	2	user1	users	96	Feb 4 22:55	scripts1 HPUX
drwxrwxrwx	2	user1	users	96	Feb 4 22:55	subdir1 HPUX
drwxrwxrwx	2	user1	users	96	Feb 4 22:55	subdir2 HPUX
drwxrwxrwx	2	user1	users	96	Feb 4 22:55	subdir3 HPUX
drwxrwxrwx	2	user1	users	96	Feb 4 22:55	subdir4 HPUX

To perform two edits on */etc/group* file where the first edit replaces all occurrences of *root* with *ROOT* and the second edit replaces *daemon* with USERS.

```
$ sed –e 's/root/ROOT/g' –e 's/daemon/USERS/g' /etc/group
```
ROOT::0:ROOT
other::1:ROOT,hpdb
bin::2:ROOT,bin
sys::3:ROOT,uucp
adm::4:ROOT,adm
USERS::5:ROOT,USERS
mail::6:ROOT
lp::7:ROOT,lp
tty::10:
nuucp::11:nuucp
users::20:ROOT
nogroup:*:-2:
ids::101:
smbnull::102:

Summary

Chapter 04 talked about the vi editor and text processors. You learned various vi editor operating modes and methods of starting it. Once you were in vi, you studied how to navigate within vi, insert and delete text, undo and repeat previous commands, change text, search and replace text, copy, move, and paste text, import contents from another file, customize vi settings, save modifications, and exit out of it.

You also learned how to manipulate columns and rows of text using the *awk* and *sed* text processors. You saw several examples that explained the usage in detail.

## 05

The HP-UX Shells

This chapter covers the following major topics:

- ✓ HP-UX shells
- ✓ Features associated with the POSIX shell
- ✓ Local and environment variables
- ✓ Setting and unsetting variables
- ✓ Viewing variable values
- ✓ Modifying command prompt
- ✓ Getting input from alternate source and sending output and error messages to alternate destinations
- ✓ Filename completion, command line editing, command history, and command aliasing
- ✓ Special characters and masking special meaning of some of those
- ✓ Pipes and filters including |, tee, cut, tr, and pr

5.1   The Shell

In the UNIX world, the shell is referred to as a command interpreter. It accepts instructions or input from users or scripts, interprets it, and passes the instructions on to the HP-UX kernel to process it. The HP-UX kernel utilizes all hardware and software components required to process the instructions. When it finishes, it sends the results back to the shell to exhibit, by default, on the terminal display. The shell also produces appropriate error messages, if generated. In short, the shell operates as an interface between a user and HP-UX kernel.

The shell provides many services, such as I/O redirection, filename expansion, pattern matching, environment variables, job control, command line editing, command aliasing, command history, quoting mechanisms, conditional execution, flow control, writing shell scripts, and so on.

The shell is easily changeable providing a user with flexibility to choose a command interpreter at any time.

5.1.1   Available Shells

There are five shells available in HP-UX Operating Environment: the *Bourne* shell, the *Korn* shell, the *POSIX* shell, the *C* shell, and the *Key* shell. These are explained below.

The Bourne Shell

Written by Steve Bourne for the very earliest versions of AT&T UNIX, the Bourne shell is widely available but being phased out in HP-UX in favor of the more powerful and versatile POSIX shell. The Bourne shell has the $ prompt and it resides in */usr/old/bin/sh* file. The Bourne shell is the default shell for the *root* user. A restricted version of the Bourne shell, located in */usr/bin/rsh*, is also available that restricts a user of the shell to his/her home directory. The user cannot *cd* out of the directory.

The Korn Shell

The Korn shell is a superset of the Bourne shell and very close to the POSIX shell in terms of features. It provides features that you need to use often. The Korn shell is not standardized and there are differences among various vendor versions. The Korn shell was created by David Korn at the AT&T labs and its prompt is $. It resides in */usr/bin/ksh* file. A restricted version of the Korn shell, located in */usr/bin/rksh*, is also available that limits a user of the shell to his/her home directory. The user cannot *cd* out of the directory.

The POSIX Shell

The *Portable Operating System Interface eXchange* (POSIX) shell is similar to the Korn shell in terms of features and is a superset of the Bourne shell. Its prompt is also $. It is located in */usr/bin/sh* file. The POSIX shell is expected to be available on most common UNIX versions and will eventually replace the Bourne shell in newer HP-UX Operating Environment releases. The POSIX shell is the default shell for users. A restricted version of the POSIX shell, located in */usr/bin/rsh*, is also available that limits a user of the shell to his/her home directory. The user cannot *cd* out of the directory.

The C Shell

The C shell is mainly used by developers. It provides a programming interface similar to the C language. It offers many Bourne and Korn shell functions in addition to numerous other features. This shell was created by Bill Joy at the University of California at Berkeley for early BSD UNIX releases. The prompt for the C shell is % and it resides in /usr/bin/csh file.

The Key Shell

The Key shell is an extension to the Korn shell. It presents an interactive interface to users where a softkey menu appears at the bottom of the screen. It provides context-sensitive help as you type commands at the prompt.

It is invoked by typing *keysh* at the command prompt. It loads a menu displayed at the bottom of the screen, as shown in Figure 5-1. You may want to assign this shell to a user so whenever he/she logs in, this shell is invoked directly for the user.

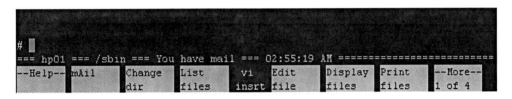

Figure 5-1 The Key Shell

5.2   POSIX Shell Features

The POSIX shell offers scores of features discussed at length in this chapter.

5.2.1   Variables

A variable is a temporary storage of data in memory. Variables contain information used for customizing the shell environment. Their values are used by many system and application processes to function properly. The shell allows you to store values into variables.

Variables are of two types: *Local* and *Environment*.

Local Variables

A local variable is private to the shell it is created in and its value cannot be used by processes that are not started in that shell. This brings the concept of *current* shell and *sub*-shell (or *child* shell). The current shell is where you execute programs from, whereas a sub-shell is created by a running program.

Environment Variables

The value of an environment variable, however, is passed from current shell to sub-shell. In other words, the value stored in an environment variable is passed from parent process to child process.

The environment variable is also called *Global* variable. When you log into a system, some variables are set automatically for you through system and user initialization files. You may also set variables in shell scripts or at the command line as per your requirement.

5.2.2 Setting, Unsetting, and Viewing Variables

To set, unset, or view shell variables, consult Table 5-1, which sets two example variables: *V1* and *V2*. It is recommended to use uppercase letters in variable names to distinguish them from the names of any commands or programs that you might have on your system.

Action	Local Variable	Environment Variable
Setting a variable	Syntax: V1=value Examples: **$ V1=college** **$ V2="I am using HP-UX"**	Syntax: V1=value; export V1 OR export V1=value Examples: **$ V1=college; export V1** **$ V2="I am using HP-UX"; export V2** OR **$ export V1=college** **$ export V2="I am using HP-UX"**
Displaying variable values	**$ print $V1** OR **$ echo $V1**	
Listing set variables	**$ set** **$ env** **$ export**	
Unsetting a variable	**$ unset V1**	

Table 5-1 Setting, Unsetting, and Viewing Variables

To set a local variable, V1, to contain the value *college*, simply define it as shown in Table 5-1. Note that there must not be any spaces either before or after the equal (=) sign. To make V1 a global variable, use the *export* command. Another example sets a variable, V2, containing a series of space-separated words. Make sure to enclose them in double quotes.

To display the value of a variable, use either the *print* or the *echo* command.

The *set* command lists current values for all shell variables including local and environment variables. The *export* and *env* commands list only environment variables.

```
$ set
COLUMNS=80
EDITOR=vi
ERASE=^H
```

ERRNO=9
FCEDIT=/usr/bin/ed
HISTFILE=/.sh_history
HISTSIZE=1000
HOME=/
IFS='

'
LINENO=1
LINES=25
LOGNAME=root
MAIL=/var/mail/root
MAILCHECK=600
MANPATH=/usr/share/man/%L:/usr/share/man:/usr/contrib/man/%L:/usr/contrib/man:/usr/local/man/%L:/u
sr/local/man:/opt/mx/share/man:/opt/upgrade/share/man/%L:/opt/upgrade/share/man:/opt/pd/share/man/%
L:/opt/pd/share/man:/opt/pd/share/man/%L:/opt/pd/share/man:/opt/pd/share/man/%L:/opt/pd/share/man:/o
pt/hparray/share/man/%L:/opt/hparray/share/man:/opt/graphics/common/man:/usr/dt/share/man:/opt/samb
a/man:/opt/gnome/man:/opt/perf/man/%L:/opt/perf/man:/opt/prm/man/%L:/opt/prm/man:/opt/wlm/share/ma
n/%L:/opt/wlm/share/man:/opt/ignite/share/man/%L:/opt/ignite/share/man:/opt/wbem/share/man:/opt/ssh/s
hare/man:/opt/hpnpl
//man:/opt/resmon/share/man/%L:/opt/resmon/share/man
OPTARG
OPTIND=1
PATH=/usr/sbin:/usr/bin:/usr/ccs/bin:/usr/contrib/bin:/opt/hparray/bin:/opt/nettladm/bin:/opt/upgrade/bin:/op
t/resmon/bin:/opt/pd/bin:/usr/bin/X11:/usr/contrib/bin/X11:/opt/graphics/common/bin:/opt/gnome/bin:/opt/pe
rf/bin:/opt/mozilla:/opt/prm/bin:/opt/mx/bin:/opt/wlm/bin:/opt/ignite/bin:/usr/sbin/diag/contrib:/opt/wbem/bin:/
opt/wbem/sbin:/opt/hpnpl//bin:/opt/OV/bin/OpC:/opt/OV/bin:/sbin:/
PPID=13703
PS1='<hp02:$PWD>
$ '
PS2='> '
PS3='#? '
PS4='+ '
PWD=/
RANDOM=21440
SECONDS=515
SHELL=/usr/bin/sh
TERM=ansi
TZ=EST5EDT
V1=college
V2='I am using HP-UX'
_=set

$ **env**
_=/usr/bin/env
MANPATH=/usr/share/man/%L:/usr/share/man:/usr/contrib/man/%L:/usr/contrib/man:/usr/local/man/%L:/u
sr/local/man:/opt/mx/share/man:/opt/upgrade/share/man/%L:/opt/upgrade/share/man:/opt/pd/share/man/%
L:/opt/pd/share/man:/opt/pd/share/man/%L:/opt/pd/share/man:/opt/pd/share/man/%L:/opt/pd/share/man:/o
pt/hparray/share/man/%L:/opt/hparray/share/man:/opt/graphics/common/man:/usr/dt/share/man:/opt/samb
a/man:/opt/gnome/man:/opt/perf/man/%L:/opt/perf/man:/opt/prm/man/%L:/opt/prm/man:/opt/wlm/share/ma

n/%L:/opt/wlm/share/man:/opt/ignite/share/man/%L:/opt/ignite/share/man:/opt/wbem/share/man:/opt/ssh/share/man:/opt/hpnpl
//man:/opt/mqm/man:/opt/resmon/share/man/%L:/opt/resmon/share/manPATH=/usr/sbin:/usr/bin:/usr/ccs/bin:/usr/contrib/bin:/opt/hparray/bin:/opt/nettladm/bin:/opt/upgrade/bin:/opt/resmon/bin:/opt/pd:/usr/bin/X11:/usr/contrib/bin/X11:/opt/graphics/common/bin:/opt/gnome/bin:/opt/perf/bin:/opt/mozilla:/opt/prm/bin:/opt/mx/bin:/opt/wlm/bin:/opt/ignite/bin:/usr/sbin/diag/contrib:/opt/wbem/bin:/opt/wbem/sbin:/opt/hpnpl//bin:/opt/OV/bin/OpC:/opt/OV/bin:/sbin:/
V1=college
V2=I am using HP-UX
COLUMNS=80
EDITOR=vi
HISTFILE=/.sh_history
LOGNAME=root
MAIL=/var/mail/root
ERASE=^H
PS1=<hp02:$PWD>
$
SHELL=/usr/bin/sh
HISTSIZE=1000
HOME=/
TERM=ansi
PWD=/
TZ=EST5EDT
LINES=25

Finally, to unset a variable, use the *unset* command and specify the variable name. It will remove the variable.

5.2.3   Pre-Defined Environment Variables

Some environment variables are defined by the shell when you log into the system. You may define more environment variables if and when you need them. Some of the more commonly used environment variables are EDITOR, HOME, LOGNAME, PATH, PWD, PS1, PS2, SHELL, TERM, MAIL, TZ, DISPLAY, HISTFILE, and HISTSIZE. Here is a brief description of each one of these in Table 5-2.

Variable	Description
EDITOR	Defines default editor. It is usually set to the vi editor.
HOME	Contains home directory path.
LOGNAME	Stores login name.
PATH	Defines a colon separated list of directories to be searched when a user executes a command.
PWD	Stores current directory location.
PS1	Defines primary command prompt. For root, it is # (by default).
PS2	Defines secondary command prompt. By default it is >.
SHELL	Holds fully qualified pathname of primary shell.
TERM	Holds terminal type value.
MAIL	Contains path to user mail directory. For *user1* it would be */var/mail/user1*.

TZ	Contains timezone value including offset from *Universal Time Coordinated* (UTC).
DISPLAY	Stores hostname or IP address to display graphics.
HISTFILE	Defines file name where shell stores a history of all commands as you execute them.
HISTSIZE	Defines maximum size for HISTFILE to grow to.

Table 5-2 Pre-Defined Environment Variables

5.2.4   Changing Command Prompt

You know that the primary command prompt for user *root* is the # sign. Also for the POSIX, Korn, and Bourne shell users, the primary command prompt is the $ sign and that for the C shell is the % sign. It is a good idea to customize primary command prompt so it displays useful information, such as who you are, which system you are currently logged on to, and your current location in the directory tree. The following example shows how to modify *user1*'s primary command prompt from the default $ sign to the one below:

$ **export PS1="< $LOGNAME@`hostname`:\$PWD > "**

user1's command prompt will now look like:

< user1@hp01:/home/user1 >

This example shows how to modify a user's primary command prompt to include information from different sources.

When *user1* moves around in the directory tree, the value of the pre-defined environment variable, PWD, will reflect the directory location in his/her prompt. This is called *Variable Substitution*. For example, if he/she moves to */usr/bin*, the prompt will change to:

< user1@hp01:/usr/bin >

Also, in this example the value of another pre-defined environment variable, LOGNAME, is used to display user's login name.

Running the command *hostname* and assigning its output to a variable is an example of a shell feature called *Command Substitution*. Note that the command the output of which you want to assign to a variable must be enclosed in single forward quotes.

5.2.5   Input, Output, and Error Redirection

Many programs in HP-UX read input from the keyboard and write output to the terminal window where the program was run from. If any errors are encountered, they are displayed on the terminal window too. This is the default behavior. What if you do not wish to take input from the keyboard or write the output to the terminal window? The POSIX shell allows you to redirect input, output, and error messages. Programs or commands will read input from something other than the keyboard and send output and errors to something other than the terminal window.

The default (or the standard) locations for input, output, and error are referred to as *stdin*, *stdout*, and *stderr*, respectively. Table 5-3 demonstrates that each one of the three has an association with a symbol and a digit. These symbols and digits are usually used at the command line and in shell scripts for redirection purposes.

File Descriptor	Symbol	Associated Digit	Description
stdin	<	0	Standard input
stdout	>	1	Standard output
stderr	>	2	Standard error

Table 5-3 I/O/E Redirection Symbols

The following text explains how redirection of input, output, and error is done.

Redirecting Standard Input

Through input redirection, you can instruct a command to read required information from an alternate source, such as a file, instead of the keyboard. For example, to have the *mailx* command send contents of *file1* to *user2*, do the following:

$ cd
$ mailx user2 < file1

In order for *mailx* to work properly, you have to have sendmail configured and running. See Chapter 27 "Setting Up and Administering Internet Services and Sendmail" on how to configure and use Sendmail.

Redirecting Standard Output

Through output redirection, you can send the output generated by a command to an alternate destination, such as a file, instead of sending it to the terminal window. For example, to direct the *sort* command to send the sorted output of *file1* to a file called *sort.out,* do the following. This overwrites any contents *sort.out* file already has. If *sort.out* does not exist, it will be created.

$ sort file1 > sort.out

To direct the *sort* command to append output to *sort.out* file and does not overwrite existing contents, use the >> symbols:

$ sort file1 >> sort.out

Redirecting Standard Error

Through error redirection, you can send any error messages generated to an alternate destination, such as a file, instead of sending them to the terminal window. For example, to direct the *find* command to send any error messages generated to */dev/null*, do the following. The */dev/null* file is a special system file used to discard data.

```
$ find / –name core –print 2> /dev/null
```

When this command is executed, it searches for all occurrences of files by the name *core* in the entire root directory tree. Error messages will be generated when a directory where the user does not have access to is accessed with normal user privileges. These error messages will be discarded and sent to garbage.

Redirecting both Standard Output and Error

To redirect both stdout and stderr to the same file called *testfile1*, do the following:

```
$ ls /etc /cdr 1> testfile1 2>&1
```

This example will produce a listing of the */etc* directory and saves the result in *testfile1*. At the same time, it will generate an error message complaining about non-existence of */cdr* directory. This error message will also be sent to the same file and saved. In this example, 1 represents stdout and 2 represents stderr.

5.2.6 Filename Completion, Command Line Editing, and Command History

Filename Completion or *Filename Expansion* is a POSIX shell feature whereby typing a partial filename at the command line and then hitting the *Esc* key twice, completes a filename if there are no other possibilities. If there exists multiple possibilities, it will complete up to the point they have in common.

Command Line Editing allows you to edit a line of text right at the command prompt. When you are at the command prompt, press the *Esc+k* key combination to bring to the prompt the last command you executed. If you press the letter "k" repeatedly, it scrolls you backward to previous commands in reverse chronological order. The letter "j" scrolls you forward through the command history in chronological order. When you get the desired command, you may wish to edit it right at the command prompt using the vi editor commands (refer to Chapter 04 "The vi Editor and Text Processors" to learn about the vi editor commands). If you do not wish to edit or you are done with your editing, simply press the *Enter* key to execute it.

Command History, or simply *History*, keeps a log of all commands that you run at the command prompt. The shell stores command history in a file located, by default, in user's home directory. You may retrieve these commands, modify them at the command line, and re-run them using the command line editing feature.

There are three variables that enable the features you just learnt. These variables are listed below along with sample values.

```
HISTFILE=~/.sh_history
HISTSIZE=1000
EDITOR=vi
```

The HISTFILE variable tells the POSIX shell to store all commands run by a user at the command prompt in *.sh_history* file in that user's home directory. This file is created automatically if it does not exist. Each command, along with options and arguments, is stored on a separate line. You may later retrieve any of them to edit and re-run.

The HISTSIZE variable controls the maximum number of commands that can be stored in HISTFILE. The default is 128. In the example above, you modified it to 1000.

The EDITOR variable defines what text editor to use. If this variable is not set, issue the following to be able to use the filename expansion, command line editing, and command history features:

> $ **set −o vi**

The three variables discussed are usually defined in user initialization files. Refer to Chapter 12 "User and Group Account Administration" on how to define variables in user initialization files to customize the behavior.

HP-UX provides the *history* command to display previously executed commands. This command gets history information from *.sh_history* file. By default, the last 16 entries are displayed.

> $ **history**
> 488   vi mailservs
> 489   /sbin/init.d/sendmail stop
> 490   /sbin/init.d/sendmail start
> 491   ps -eaf|grep send
> 492   kill -9 17388 17366
> 493   clear
> 494   ps -eaf|grep send
> 495   mailx user1 < /etc/profile
> 496   pwd
> 497   more mails*
> 498   cd
> 499   clear
> 500   exit
> 501   clear
> 502   history
> 503   su - user1

Let us use some of the *history* command options to alter its behavior.

To display the command history without line numbers:

> $ **history −n**

To display this command and 25 commands preceding it:

> $ **history −25**

To display command history in reverse order:

$ **history −r**

To display all commands between the most recent occurrence of one command and the most recent occurrence of another command. For example, to list all commands between the most recent occurrences of *mv* and *cp*.

$ **history mv cp**

To re-execute a command by its line number in history. For example, to run a command that exists on line number 38 in the history file, do the following:

$ **r 38**

To re-execute the most recent occurrence of a command that starts with a particular letter or series of letters. For example, to run the most recent occurrence of the command that starts with "ch" in the history file, do the following:

$ **r ch**

To repeat the most recent occurrence of a command beginning with letters "ch", perform a simple edit, and execute the modified command:

$ **chown user1 file1**
$ **r file1=file2**

5.2.7   Command Aliasing

A *Command Alias*, or simply, an *Alias*, allows you to create shortcuts for lengthy commands. When an alias is run, the POSIX shell executes the corresponding command. This saves you time typing the same command repeatedly.

The POSIX shell contains several pre-defined aliases, which you can view by running the *alias* command. Any new aliases that you have defined are also displayed.

```
$ alias
autoload='typeset -fu'
command='command '
functions='typeset -f'
history='fc -l'
integer='typeset -i'
local=typeset
nohup='nohup '
r='fc -e -'
stop='kill -STOP'
suspend='kill -STOP $$'
type='whence -v'
```

These aliases are explained in Table 5-4 below.

Alias	Value	Definition
autoload	"typeset –fu"	Defines how to load a function automatically.
command	"command"	Executes a command.
functions	"typeset –f"	Displays defined functions.
history	"fc –l"	Lists command history.
integer	"typeset –i"	Displays integer variables.
local	"typeset"	Defines a local attribute for variables and functions.
nohup	"nohup"	Keeps background jobs running even if you log off.
r	"fc –e –"	Re-executes the last command.
stop	"kill –STOP"	Suspends a job.
suspend	"kill –STOP $$"	Suspends the current job.
type	"whence –v"	Tells how it is interpreted if used as a command name.

Table 5-4 Pre-Defined Command Aliases

To work with aliases, two commands are available: *alias* and *unalias*. The *alias* command displays and sets an alias while the *unalias* command unsets it. Let us look at a few examples.

To abbreviate the *find* command, create an alias "f". You can use either single quotes or double quotes to enclose multiple words.

$ alias f="find / –name core –exec rm {} \;"

You must not leave any spaces before and after the = sign.

Now, when you type an "f" at the command prompt and hit the *Enter* key, the shell replaces the alias "f" with what is stored in it. Basically, you created a shortcut to that lengthy command.

Sometimes you create an alias by a name that matches the name of a system command. In this situation, the shell gives the alias precedence over the command. This means the shell will run the alias and not the command. For example, you are aware that the *rm* command deletes a file without giving any warning. To prevent accidental deletion of files with *rm*, you may wish to create an alias by the same name.

$ alias rm="rm –i"
$ rm file1
file1: ? (y/n)

When you execute *rm* now, the shell runs what you have stored in the rm alias, and not the command *rm*. If you wish to run the *rm* command, run it with a preceding \ character as follows:

$ \rm file1

To unset an alias, use the *unalias* command:

$ unalias f

$ unalias rm

5.2.8   Special Characters

Special characters are the symbols on your keyboard that possess special meaning to the shell. These characters are also loosely referred to as *Metacharacters* or *Wildcard* characters. Some of these, such as dash (–), tilde (~), and redirection symbols (< >) have been discussed in previous sections. In this section, you will be presented with four other special characters: asterisk (*), question mark (?), square brackets ([ ]), and semicolon (;).

The Asterisk (*) Character

The *asterisk* (*) character matches zero to unlimited number of characters. It does not match the leading period (.) character in a hidden file. See the following examples to understand its usage.

To list names of all files that start with letters "fi" followed by any characters:

> $ ls fi*
> file1.txt file2.txt file3.txt file4 file5 file6

To list names of all files that start with letter "d". You will notice in the output that contents of *dir1* and *dir2* sub-directories are also listed.

> $ ls d*
> date1 date2 date3
> dir1:
> scripts1 scripts2
> dir2:
> newfile1 newfile2 newfile3 newfile4

To list names of all files that end with the digit "4":

> $ ls *4
> file4

To list names of all files that have a period (.) followed by letters "txt" at the end:

> $ ls *.txt
> file1.txt file2.txt file3.txt

The Question Mark (?) Character

The *question mark* (?) character matches exactly one character. It does not match the leading period (.) character in a hidden file. See the following example to understand its usage.

To list all files that begin with characters "file" followed by one single character:

```
$ ls  file?
file4  file5  file6
```

The Square Bracket ([ ]) Characters

The *square brackets* ([ ]) can be used to match either a set of characters or a range of characters for a single character position.

When you specify a set of characters, order is not important. Hence, [xyz], [yxz], [xzy], and [yxz] are treated alike. The following example encloses two characters within square brackets. The output will include all files and directories that start with either of the two characters followed by any number of characters.

```
$ ls  [cf]*
car1  car2  file1.txt  file2.txt  file3.txt  file4  file5  file6  fruit  fruit2
```

A range of characters must be specified in proper order, such as [a-z] or [0-9]. The following example matches all file and directory names that begin with any alphabet between "a" and "f":

```
$ ls  [a–f]*
alpha1  beta2  car1  car2  data1  data2  echo.txt  file1  file.1  file.3  file2  file4

dir1:
fruit  trees
dir2:
scripts  bourne  korn
```

The Semicolon (;) Character

The *semicolon* (;) character separates commands. It enables you to enter multiple commands on a single command line. The following example shows three commands: *cd*, *ls*, and *date* separated by semicolon. The three commands will be executed in the order they are specified.

```
$ cd; ls  fil*; date
file1.txt  file2.txt  file3.txt  file4  file5  file6
Fri Dec  9 16:50:10 EST 2005
```

5.2.9   Masking Special Meaning of Some Special Characters

Sometimes you are in a situation where you want the shell to treat a special character as a regular character. There are three special characters that disable the meaning of other special characters when properly used with them. These characters are described with examples in Table 5-5.

HP Certified Systems Administrator

Special Character	Description	Example
\	Ignores the meaning of the special character following it.	A file is created by the name " * " and now you want to remove it with the *rm* command. Specify the \ character to mask the special meaning of the special character " * ". If you do not, *rm* will remove all files in that directory. **$ rm ***
'	Ignores the meaning of all enclosed special characters.	**$ echo '$LOGNAME'** $LOGNAME **$ echo '\\'** \
"	Ignores the meaning of all but three special characters: \, $, and '. These special characters retain their special meaning if used within double quotes.	**$ echo "$SHELL"** /usr/bin/sh **$ echo "\\$PWD"** $PWD **$ echo "\\"** ^c > "

Table 5-5 Masking Meaning of Some Special Characters

5.3   Pipes and Filters

This section talks about pipes and filters often used at the command line and in shell scripts.

5.3.1   Pipes

The pipe, represented by the (|) character and resides with the (\ ) character on the keyboard, is a special character that sends output of one command as input to another command.

The following example uses the *ll* command to display contents of the */etc* directory. The output is piped to the *more* command, which displays the listing one screen at a time.

```
$ ll /etc | more
total 1920
-r--r--r--    1      bin     bin     717     Apr 12 16:13    MANPATH
-rw-r--r--    1      root    sys     481     Aug 24 2005     PATH
-r--r--r--    1      bin     bin     112     Jun 11 2005     SHLIB_PATH
drwxr-xr-x    2      bin     bin     96      May 3 23:07     SnmpAgent.d
-r--r--r--    1      bin     bin     21      Mar 30 12:14    TIMEZONE
drwxr-xr-x    7      root    sys     8192    Jun 11 2005     X11
```

The HP-UX Shells

drwxr-xr-x	2	bin	bin	96	Jun 11 2005	acct
lrwxr-xr-x	1	root	sys	17	Jun 11 2005	aliases -> /etc/mail/aliases
lr-sr-xr-t	1	root	sys	13	Jun 11 2005	arp -> /usr/sbin/arp
drwxr-xr-x	3	bin	bin	96	Jun 11 2005	asx
drwxr-xr-x	3	bin	bin	96	Jun 11 2005	atm
dr-xr-xr-x	2	bin	bin	96	Jun 11 2005	atmrev
-r--r--r--	1	bin	bin	8974	Nov 14 2000	audeventstab
lr-xr-xr-t	1	root	sys	17	Jun 11 2005	audomon -> /usr/sbin/audomon
-rw-r--r--	1	root	root	25	Jun 11 2005	auto_master
-rw-r--r--	1	root	root	44	May 3 23:05	auto_parms.log
-rw-r--r--	1	root	sys	219	May 3 21:55	auto_parms.log.old
lrwxr-xr-x	1	root	sys	16	Jun 11 2005	backup -> /usr/sbin/ba

--more—

. . . .

. . . .

To count number of lines in the output of the *w* command, do the following. The output is piped as input to the *nl* command, which counts number of lines.

```
$ who | nl
     1  root    pts/0    May 12 10:16
     2  root    pts/1    May 12 11:17
```

The following example creates a pipeline whereby the output of the *ll* command is sent to the first *grep* command, which filters out all lines that do not contain the pattern *root*, then the new output is further sent to the second *grep* command that filters out all lines that do not contain the pattern *may*. Finally, the output is numbered and displayed on the screen. A structure like this with multiple pipes is referred to as a *Pipeline*.

```
$ ll /etc | grep root | grep –i may | nl
```

1	-rw-r--r--	1	root	root	44	May 3 23:05	auto_parms.log
2	-rw-r--r--	1	root	sys	219	May 3 21:55	auto_parms.log.old
3	-rw-rw-rw-	1	root	sys	58	May 1 15:46	exports
4	-rw-r--r--	1	root	sys	27	May 3 23:06	ifconfig.muxids
5	-rw-r--r--	1	root	sys	3856	May 3 23:05	ioconfig
6	drwxr-xr-x	2	root	root	8192	May 8 13:37	lvmconf
7	-rw-------	1	root	sys	3122	May 8 13:37	lvmtab
8	-rw-r--r--	1	root	root	294	May 8 13:37	mnttab
9	-rw-r--r--	1	root	sys	813	May 10 18:18	passwd
10	-rw-r--r--	1	root	root	22965	May 3 23:08	rc.log

5.3.2   The *tee* Filter

The *tee* filter is used to send output to more than one destinations. If used with pipe, the *tee* command can send one copy of the output to a file and second copy to the screen (or another program).

HP Certified Systems Administrator

In the following example, the output from the *ll* command is counted and captured in a file called *ll.out* under */tmp* directory. The output is displayed on the screen at the same time too.

```
$ ll /etc | nl | tee /tmp/ll.out
```

Once the execution of this command is complete, *cat* the */tmp/ll.out* file. You will notice that the file contains exact same information that was displayed on the screen when you executed the command.

If you specify the –a option with the *tee* command, the output gets appended to the file, rather than overwriting existing contents.

```
$ date | tee –a /tmp/ll.out
```

5.3.3   The *cut* Filter

The *cut* filter extracts selected columns from a line. The default column separator used is white space, such as a tab. The following example command cuts out columns 1 and 4 from the */etc/group* file as specified with the –f option. The colon character is used as a field separator.

```
$ cut –d : –f 1,4 /etc/group
root:root
other:root,hpdb
bin:root,bin
sys:root,uucp
adm:root,adm
daemon:root,daemon
mail:root
lp:root,lp
tty:
nuucp:nuucp
users:root
nogroup:
ids:
smbnull:
dba:oraids
```

5.3.4   The *pr* Filter

The *pr* filter is used to format and display the contents of a text file. Its output may be piped to a printer if one is configured.

By default, the *pr* command prints file name, time stamp on it, page number, and file contents. For example, to display the contents of */etc/group file*:

$ pr /etc/group

May 10 18:18 2006 /etc/group Page 1

root::0:root
other::1:root,hpdb
bin::2:root,bin
sys::3:root,uucp
adm::4:root,adm
daemon::5:root,daemon
mail::6:root
lp::7:root,lp
tty::10:
nuucp::11:nuucp
users::20:
nogroup:*:-2:
ids::101:
smbnull::102:
dba::201:

Options listed in Table 5-6 are available with the *pr* command for enhanced readability.

Option	Purpose
+page	Begins printing from the specified page number: **$ pr +2 /etc/group**
–column	Prints the file in multiple columns. **$ pr –2 /etc/group**
–d	Prints with double line spacing. **$ pr –d /etc/group**
–l lines	Changes page length (default is 66 lines): **$ pr –l 20 /etc/group**
–m	Prints specified files side-by-side in separate columns: **$ pr –m /etc/group /etc/passwd /etc/hosts**
–h header	Replaces filename.
–t	Does not print the filename and time stamp on it.
–n	Assigns a number to each line in the output.

Table 5-6 *pr* Command Options

HP Certified Systems Administrator

The following example prints the /etc/group file in two columns with double spacing between lines, the header title "My PR Command Test", and the page length not more than 20 lines. Run this command on your system to view the results.

$ **pr** **−2dh** **"My PR Command Test"** **−l 20 /etc/group**

5.3.5   The *tr* Filter

The *tr* filter translates specified input characters and displays the output on the screen. Following are a few examples.

To remove all but one space between columns in the output of the *w* command. Note that there is a single space between double quotes in the command below.

```
$ w | tr −s '' ''
2:28am up 12 days, 4:38, 1 user, load average: 0.50, 0.52, 0.53
usertty      login@  idle     JCPU   PCPU   what
user1        pts/ta  2:28am                  tr -s
```

To remove all digits from the output of the *w* command, use the −d option.

```
$ w | tr −d '[0-9]'
 :am up  days, :,  user, load average: ., ., .
usertty      login@  idle     JCPU   PCPU   what
userpts/ta   :am                      tr -d [-]
```

To display all letters in uppercase:

```
$ w | tr '[a-z]' '[A-Z]'
2:31AM  UP 12 DAYS, 4:41,    1 USER, LOAD  AVERAGE: 0.52, 0.52, 0.53
USER    TTY          LOGIN@        IDLE   JCPU   PCPU   WHAT
USER1   PTS/TA                     2:28AM                TR [A-Z] [A-Z]
```

Summary

Chapter 05 discussed shells and shell features in detail. You looked at shells available in HP-UX; features of the POSIX shells including setting, unsetting, and displaying contents of local and environment variables, modifying command prompt to display useful information, getting input from non-default sources, sending output and error messages to alternate destinations, defining and undefining shortcuts to lengthy commands; and setting required variables to enable filename completion, command line editing, and command history features.

You learned about special characters and how to mask special meanings of some of them.

Finally, you studied the use of the pipe (|) character and the commands – *tee, cut, tr,* and *pr* – for use as filters.

06

System Processes and Job Control

This chapter covers the following major topics:

- ✓ Understand system and user executed processes
- ✓ Display processes and check their states
- ✓ What signals are and how to use them
- ✓ What is a nice value and how to start a process with a non-default nice value
- ✓ How to modify nice value of a running process
- ✓ Manage jobs in the POSIX shell
- ✓ Run a command immune to hang-up signals

6.1 Understanding Processes

A process is created in memory when a program or command is executed in HP-UX. A unique identification number, known as *Process IDentification* (PID), is allocated to it. This identification number is used by the kernel to manage the process until the program or command it is associated with is complete. When a user logs in to an HP-UX system, shell is started, which is a process. Similarly, when a user executes a command or opens up an application, a process is created. Thus, a process is any program that runs on the system.

At system boot up, several processes are started. Many of these sit in memory and wait for an event to trigger a request to use their service. These background system processes are called *daemons* and are critical to system functionality. Daemons are also processes.

6.1.1 Viewing System Processes

There are two commands commonly used to view currently running processes. These are *ps* (*process status*) and *top*.

When the *ps* command is executed without any options or arguments, only processes specific to the terminal the *ps* command is run from are displayed.

```
$ ps
PID        TTY     TIME    COMMAND
21938      pts/ta  0:00    ps
21924      pts/ta  0:00    sh
21923      pts/ta  0:00    telnetd
```

This output has four columns: PID of the process in the first column, terminal the process belongs to in the second column, cumulative time the process is given by the system CPU in the third column, and actual command or program being executed in the last column.

Two options –e (**every**) and –f (**full**) are popularly used to generate detailed information on every process running in the system. There are other options available too. Check the *ps* command man pages for detailed information.

```
# ps -ef
UID     PID     PPID    C    STIME       TTY      TIME    COMMAND
root    0       0       0    15:03:30    ?        0:02    swapper
root    8       0       0    15:03:31    ?        0:00    supsched
root    9       0       0    15:03:31    ?        0:00    strmem
root    10      0       0    15:03:31    ?        0:00    strweld
root    11      0       0    15:03:31    ?        0:00    strfreebd
root    2       0       0    15:03:31    ?        0:00    vhand
root    3       0       0    15:03:31    ?        0:51    statdaemon
root    1       0       0    15:03:32    ?        0:01    init
root    18947   18919   8    06:45:56    pts/ta   0:00    ps -ef
. . . . . . . .
. . . . . . . .
```

The above output shows more in depth information about running processes. Table 6-1 describes content type of each column.

Title Heading	Description
UID	User ID of process owner.
PID	Process ID of process.
PPID	Process ID of parent process.
C	Process Priority.
STIME	Process start time.
TTY	Terminal where process was started. Console represents system console. ? indicates a daemon running in the background.
TIME	Cumulative execution time for process.
COMMAND	Command or process name.

Table 6-1 *ps* Command Output Explanation

Notice there are scores of daemon processes running in the background that have association with no terminal. Also notice PID and PPID numbers. The smaller the number, the earlier it is started. The process with PID 0 is started first at system boot, followed by the process with PID 1 and so on. Each PID has a PPID in the 3rd column, which tells that that process is started by the process having that PPID. Owner of each process is also shown along with the command or program name.

Information on each running process is kept and maintained in a process table, which the *ps* and other commands read to display output.

The other command to view process information is the *top* command. It displays additional information including CPU and memory utilization. A sample output from a running top session is shown below:

```
$ top
System: hp01                        Thu Dec 29 10:14:40 2005
Load averages: 0.52, 0.53, 0.53
127 processes: 105 sleeping, 22 running
Cpu states:
CPU  LOAD  USER  NICE   SYS  IDLE   BLOCK SWAIT  INTR  SSYS
0    0.03  0.0%  0.0%  0.0% 100.0%  0.0%  0.0%   0.0%  0.0%
1    1.00  0.0%  0.0%  0.0% 100.0%  0.0%  0.0%   0.0%  0.0%

---  ----  - - - - - -  -----
avg  0.52  0.0%  0.0%  0.0% 100.0%  0.0%  0.0%   0.0%  0.0%

Memory: 100144K (55512K) real, 350304K (248828K) virtual, 758248K free  Page# 1/11
CPU TTY  PID USER PRI NI SIZE   RES   STATE  TIME %WCPU %CPU CMD
1    ?  1474  root 152 20 4900K 6916K run    6:57  1.15  1.15 prm3d
0    ?    34  root 152 20    0K  336K run    0:52  0.36  0.36 vxfsd
1    ?   993  root 152 20 1596K 1944K run    0:02  0.23  0.23 dmisp
1    ?  1772  root 152 20 1076K 1956K run    0:02  0.10  0.10 samd
```

Press *ctrl+c* to quit.

6.1.2   Process States

After a process is started, it does not run continuously. It may be in a non-running condition for a while or waiting for some other process to feed it with information so it continues its execution. There are five process states: *running*, *sleeping*, *waiting*, *stopped*, and *zombie*.

The running state determines that the process is currently being executed by system CPU.

The sleeping state shows that the process is currently waiting for user input or input from another process.

The waiting state means that the process received input it has been waiting for and now it is ready to continue its execution as soon as its turn arrives.

The stopped state indicates that the process is currently halted. The process is not going to run even when its turn comes unless it is sent a signal to continue its execution.

The zombie state determines that the process is dead. A zombie process exists in process table just as any other process entry but takes up no resources. The entry for zombie is retained until the parent process permits it to die. A zombie process is also called a *defunct* process.

6.1.3   Process Priority

Process priority is determined using the *nice* value. The system assigns a nice value to a process when it is initiated to establish priority.

There are total 40 nice values with 0 having the highest priority. Most system-started processes use default nice value of 20. A child process started by a parent process inherits the parent's nice value.

Use the *ps* command and specify the –l option to determine nice values of running processes. See associated nice values for each process under the "NI" column in the following example:

 # ps –efl
F S UID PID PPID C PRI **NI** ADDR SZ WCHAN STIME TTY TIME COMD

A different priority may be assigned to a program or command at the time it is executed. For example, to run *sam* with lower priority, execute as follows:

 # nice –2 sam

The value assigned with the *nice* command is relative to the default nice value of 20. The number – 2 is added to 20, which means the specified program will run at a lower priority since its nice value is 22.

To run the same program at a higher priority with nice value 18, use a pair of dash characters as follows:

 # nice --2 sam

HP Certified Systems Administrator

Programs running in background using the & sign gets the default nice value of 24. To run *sam* in background with nice value 10:

nice −14 sam &

To alter nice value of a running program, use the *renice* command. To change the nice value of the running *sam* program from 10 to 15, specify its PID (24854) with the *renice* command as follows:

renice −n 5 24854
24854: old priority -10, new priority 5

Add 20 to −10 to get the previous nice value, which was +10. The new priority is actually 25 (20 + 5) but the system shows 5.

To alter nice values of all processes owned by members of a particular group, use the –g option with the *renice* command. Similarly, to alter nice values of all processes owned by a particular user, use the –u option with the *renice* command. Check *renice* command's man pages on the usage.

6.2   Signals and Their Use

An HP-UX system runs several processes simultaneously. Sometimes it is necessary to pass a notification to a process alerting it of an event. A user or the system uses signals to pass that notification to a process. A signal contains a signal number and is used to control processes.

There are a number of signals available for use but most of the time you deal with only a few. Each signal is associated with a unique number, a name, and an action. A list of available signals can be displayed with the *kill* command using the –l option.

kill −l

1) HUP	16) USR1	31) RESERVED
2) INT	17) USR2	32) DIL
3) QUIT	18) CHLD	33) XCPU
4) ILL	19) PWR	34) XFSZ
5) TRAP	20) VTALRM	35) bad trap
6) IOT	21) PROF	36) bad trap
7) EMT	22) POLL	37) RTMIN
8) FPE	23) WINCH	38) RTMIN+1
9) KILL	24) STOP	39) RTMIN+2
10) BUS	25) TSTP	40) RTMIN+3
11) SEGV	26) CONT	41) RTMAX-3
12) SYS	27) TTIN	42) RTMAX-2
13) PIPE	28) TTOU	43) RTMAX-1
14) ALRM	29) URG	44) RTMAX
15) TERM	30) LOST	

Table 6-2 describes signals that are more oftenly used.

Signal Number	Signal Name	Action	Response
1	SIGHUP	*Hang UP* signal causes a phone line or terminal connection to be dropped. Also used to force a running daemon to re-read its configuration file.	Exit
2	SIGINT	*INTerrupt* signal issued from keyboard, usually by ^c.	Exit
9	SIGKILL	*KILLs* a process abruptly by force.	Exit
15	SIGTERM	Sends a process a soft *TERMi*nation signal to stop it in an orderly fashion. This signal is default.	Exit

Table 6-2 Some Important Signals

To pass a signal to a process use the *kill* command. Usually, the *kill* command is used to terminate a process. Ordinary users can kill processes they own while the *root* user can kill any process. The syntax of the *kill* command to kill a single process is:

kill PID
kill –s <signal name or signal number> PID

The syntax of the *kill* command to kill multiple processes is:

kill PID PID PID ....
kill –s <signal name or signal number> PID PID PID ....

The older usages were:

kill –s<signal name or signal number> PID
kill –<signal name or signal number> PID PID PID ....

Obtain signal names and associated numbers from the output of the *kill* command with –l option. These names or numbers are then used with the *kill* command to send appropriate signals to processes. Let us look at a few examples.

To pass a signal to a process, first use the *ps* command to determine PID of the process. For example, to soft terminate the printing daemon, *lpsched*, with PID 1230, do the following:

 # ps –ef | grep lp
lp **1230**   1 0 Dec 23 ?   0:08 /usr/sbin/lpsched
 # kill 1230

You can also terminate process 1230 using any one of the following methods:

 # kill –s 15 1230
 # kill –15 1230
 # kill –s SIGTERM 1230
 # kill –SIGTERM 1230

Using the *kill* command without specifying a signal name or number sends default signal of 15 to the process. This signal usually causes the process to terminate.

Some processes ignore signal 15. These processes might be waiting for an input from some source so that they continue processing. The processes that do not respond to SIGTERM can be terminated by force using signal 9 as follows:

$ kill –s 9 PID

6.3   Managing Jobs in the POSIX Shell

A job is a process started by a user and controlled by the terminal where it is run from. It is assigned a PID by the system and a job ID by the POSIX shell at the time it is started.

When a job begins, it ties up the terminal window where it is started from until finished. The POSIX shell provides a feature that enables you to run a job in the background. This way the terminal window is freed up right away and you can run other programs from the command prompt.

The POSIX shell allows running scores of jobs simultaneously including copying large amount of data and running application programs in the background.

Jobs running in the background can be brought to foreground, taken back to background, suspended, or stopped. The management of several jobs within a shell environment is called *Job Control*.

There are certain commands pertaining to job control and are listed in Table 6-3.

Command	Description
jobs	Displays currently running jobs.
bg %*job_ID*	Places a job in the background.
fg %*Job_ID*	Places a job in the foreground.
ctrl+z	Suspends a job running in the foreground.
stop %*job_ID*	Stops a background job.

Table 6-3 Job Control

To run a job in the background type the command followed by the ampersand (&) character.

The example below runs three commands in the background: *top*, *glance*, and *vi*. When these commands are executed, the shell will display job IDs enclosed in square brackets and associated PIDs. The job IDs allow you to control the actual jobs. The PIDs are used by the kernel to manage the jobs.

$ **top &**
[1] 4635
$ **glance &**
[2] 4696

```
$ vi  file1  &
[3]   4767
```

To view all running jobs, type the *jobs* command as follows:

```
# jobs
[1] – Stopped top &
[2] – Stopped glance &
[3] + Running vi file1 &
```

To bring job ID 1 to the foreground, do the following:

```
# fg  %1
```

Before going to the next example, set an *stty* command option, susp as follows:

```
# stty  susp  ^z
```

To suspend job ID 1 and sends it to the background again, press ^z followed by the following command to get the command prompt back:

```
# bg  %1
```

To stop job ID 3, do the following:

```
# stop  %3
```

When a job finishes, a message is displayed indicating that the background job has been completed.

```
[3] + Done vi file1 &
```

6.4   Executing a Command Immune to Hangup Signals

In HP-UX, when a command, or for that matter program or process, is executed it ties itself to the terminal session where it is executed from. While the command is running, if a user terminates the terminal session, the command also gets terminated with the terminal session.

To protect commands that need to run for extended periods of time from being terminated when the terminal sessions they were invoked from are terminated, use the *nohup* command to execute them. The *nohup* command causes the specified command to continue to run even after the user who executed it logs off and the terminal session is closed.

For example, to copy */opt/data1* directory containing several gigabytes of data to */opt/data2*, issue the *cp* command as follows. Specify, as well, the ampersand (&) character as shown.

```
# nohup  cp  –rp  /opt/data1  /opt/data2  &
```

The above command will continue to run even if the user who initiated it logs off or his/her terminal session dies.

Summary

You studied about processes in this chapter. A good understanding of what user and system processes are running on the system is vital for performance and general system administration. You learned how to display processes and about the five process states.

Next, you looked at signals and understood what they did when passed to processes via the *kill* command.

You studied nice values and how they were used to compute priority for a given process. You may either execute a process or command with the default nice value or assign one when you run it. You can always modify nice value of a process at any time in future while the process is still running.

Finally, you learned how to manage background jobs and run commands immune to hang-up signals.

HP Certified Systems Administrator

## 07

System Administration and HP-UX Server Hardware

This chapter covers the following major topics:

- ✓ Responsibilities of the HP-UX system administrator in HP-UX-based computing environment
- ✓ Help resources available to the HP-UX system administrator
- ✓ System Administration Manager (SAM) and how to use it
- ✓ Overview of hardware components found in HP servers that run HP-UX
- ✓ Overview of HP Integrity and HP 9000 series servers
- ✓ Device files, physical and logical addressing, and major and minor numbers
- ✓ Create and remove device files
- ✓ View hardware diagnostic messages

7.1 HP-UX System Administration Overview

System administration is a series of management tasks that a person, normally referred to as System Administrator, is responsible to carry out on a routine basis. The computing environment where the system administrator works may comprise one or several networked HP-UX systems. Administration on standalone HP-UX machines is typically referred to as system administration, whereas administration of services that involve more than one HP-UX systems is usually referred to as network administration. In the HP-UX world, the term HP-UX System Administrator is commonly used for an individual that performs both system and network administration tasks on HP-UX systems.

7.1.1 System Administrator Responsibilities

The HP-UX system administrator is responsible for installing, configuring, and supporting servers running HP-UX Operating Environment software in a networked environment. This includes management of hardware and hardware integration, server partitioning and OE installation, software and patches, users and groups, LVM and VxVM, file systems and swap spaces, system shutdown and startup, kernel and backups, printing and scheduling, logging and performance, network cards and routing, internet services and sendmail, time and resource sharing, naming and boot services, automated installation and system recovery, high availability and clustering, security and server hardening, and so on.

The system administrator requires data center access and *root* user privileges to configure and support an HP-UX operating system environment.

7.1.2 System Administrator Resources

There are certain tools and resources available to the HP-UX system administrator to help perform system and network administration tasks effectively and efficiently. Some of the key ones are:

- ✓ *System Administration Manager* (SAM) – used to perform a number of day to day tasks. SAM runs in both *Graphical User Interface* (GUI) and *Textual User Interface* (TUI) modes. SAM is described in the next section.

- ✓ Online *man* pages – typically loaded on the system as part of the HP-UX Operating Environment software installation. See Chapter 01 "Overview of HP-UX Operating Environment" on usage and details.

- ✓ *www.docs.hp.com* – contains documentation on current and previous HP-UX Operating Environment and Operating System versions and releases, server and workstation hardware, and so on. Visit this site to access up-to-date technical information. Figure 7-1 shows portion of the main web page.

- ✓ *www.itrc.hp.com* – HP's *Information Technology Resource Center* (ITRC) that provides detailed maintenance and support information on HP software and hardware products including technical knowledge base and patch management. Figure 7-2 displays portion of the main ITRC web page.

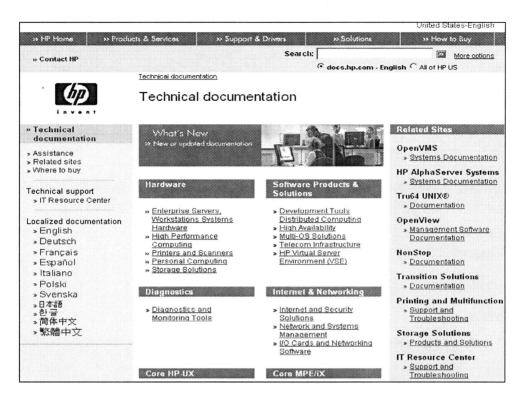

Figure 7-1 *www.docs.hp.com*

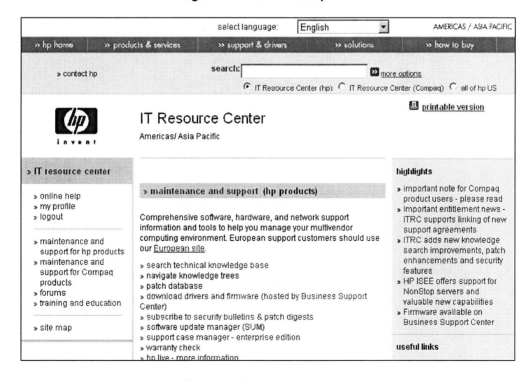

Figure 7-2 *www.itrc.hp.com*

7.2 System Administration Manager (SAM)

The *System Administration Manager* is a menu-driven program that enables a system administrator to perform system and network administration tasks without the knowledge of HP-UX Operating Environment software commands. SAM runs in both GUI and TUI modes and provides identical functionality in both.

7.2.1 Starting SAM

To start SAM in graphical mode, the DISPLAY variable must be set correctly. For example, if *hp01* is the hostname and is properly defined in the */etc/hosts* file, then do the following:

    # DISPLAY=hp01:0.0
    # export DISPLAY

Now run SAM as follows:

    # sam

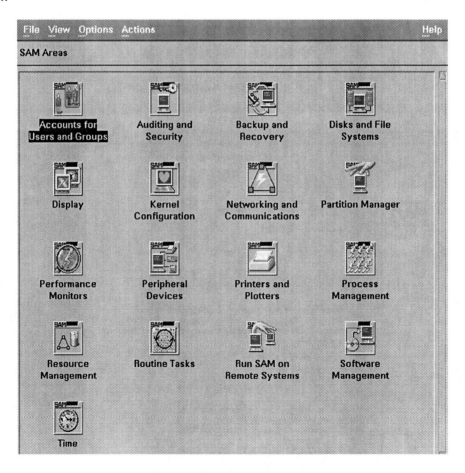

Figure 7-3 SAM – GUI Mode

The main SAM window pops up as displayed in Figure 7-3 which contains three major sections:

- ✓ The *Menu Bar* at the top provides pull-down menus. The pull-down menus vary from screen to screen. Click on a menu item to view available options.
- ✓ The *Status Bar* beneath the *Menu Bar* identifies where you are within SAM. It changes as you move around within SAM.
- ✓ Icons in the large window represent tools to carry out administration tasks. There are total 17 icons on the main SAM screen. When you double-click on an icon, SAM takes you further down where it presents a list of sub-items available in that category. By double-clicking on an item at that level, SAM enables you to perform administration tasks on it. Table 7-1 lists and explains the 17 administration categories and tasks you can perform in each one of them.

Item	Function
Accounts for Users and Groups	Allows you to perform user and group account management tasks including creating, viewing, modifying, and removing users and groups, activating and deactivating users, and setting password aging attributes on user accounts.
Auditing and Security	Allows you to perform auditing and security management tasks including converting system to trusted security mode, unconverting system from trusted security mode, turning auditing on or off, setting global system security policies, and viewing audit logs.
Backup and Recovery	Allows you to perform backup and restore tasks, such as carrying out interactive and automated backups, doing restores, and listing backed up files on the media.
Disks and File Systems	Allows you to administer disk devices, file systems, LVM, VxVM, and swap.
Display	Allows you to configure and manage X server and monitor.
Kernel Configuration	Allows you to modify kernel configuration by tuning kernel parameters. and adding, changing, or removing kernel modules, dump device, device drivers, and subsystems.
Networking and Communications	Allows you to perform network-related configuration tasks on NFS, AutoFS, NIS, NIS+, DNS, and LAN cards.
Partition Manager	Allows you to perform node partitioning tasks.
Performance Monitors	Allows you to list, view, and manage performance of CPU, memory, swap, disk, and I/O.
Peripheral Devices	Allows you to configure and manage peripheral devices, such as I/O cards, terminals, modems, tape drives, monitors, UPS, etc.
Printers and Plotters	Allows you to define and administer local, remote, and network printers.
Process Management	Allows you to manage processes and schedule cron jobs.
Resource Management	Allows you to configure and manage *Event Monitoring Service* (EMS), which is used to monitor system resources.
Routine Tasks	Allows you to trim log files, remove un-needed files, shutdown system, and so on.
Run SAM on Remote Systems	Allows you to run SAM on other HP-UX systems.

Software Management	Allows you to perform software management tasks including listing, installing, copying, viewing, and removing software.
Time	Allows you to setup and administer NTP and local system clock.

Table 7-1 SAM Administration Tasks

When SAM is started, it checks whether or not the DISPLAY variable is set correctly. If the variable is not set or not set correctly, SAM senses it and gets itself automatically started in TUI mode. SAM runs in text mode on character (non-graphics) terminals as well. Figure 7-4 shows SAM's text interface.

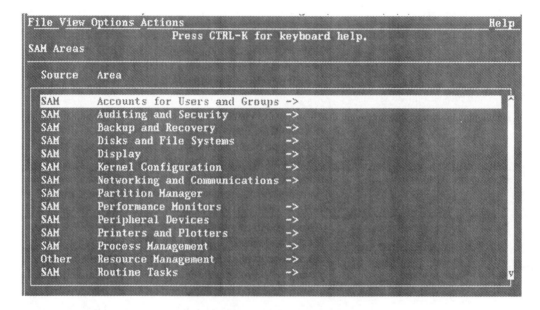

Figure 7-4 SAM – TUI Mode

Use keyboard in text mode for navigation purposes. Table 7-2 lists and explains common navigational keys.

Key	Action
Up and down arrows	Move up and down through the list.
Left and right arrows	Move to the menu item you wish to open.
Tab	Moves forward to control buttons and to Menu Bar.
Shift tab	Moves backward to control buttons.
Spacebar	Highlights a choice.
Enter	Chooses an item.

Table 7-2 Navigating Within SAM

7.2.2   SAM Log

SAM logs all actions and activities performed in the */var/sam/log/samlog* file. If you wish to see SAM activities, you can call SAM viewer by clicking on *Actions* in the *Menu* bar at the top and then selecting *View SAM Log*. Figure 7-5 shows a sample SAM log view in graphical mode.

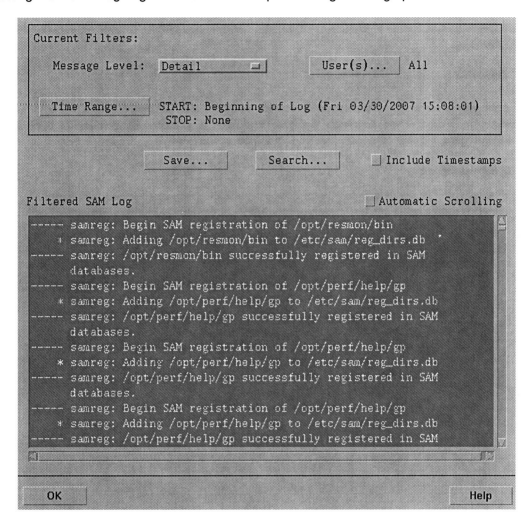

Figure 7-5 SAM Log Viewer

You do not have to be in SAM to view the log. You may view it by running the following command at the command prompt. It will produce same results.

/usr/sam/bin/samlog_viewer

7.2.3   Restricted SAM Access to Users

By default, normal system users cannot execute SAM. It requires *root* privileges to run. However, you can allow normal users or groups of users to run SAM and preform one or more administration tasks without becoming *root*. This gives *Restricted SAM Access* to normal users. As *root*, execute *sam* with –r option to start SAM in restricted builder mode. Highlight a user and administrative functionality that you wish to enable for the user. Then go to *Actions → Enable* to activate the functionality.

   # **sam –r**

Suppose you allocate *user1* access to *Accounts for Users and Groups* administration tasks. *user1* can now run SAM and see *Accounts for Users and Groups* functionality enabled for him/her, as shown in Figure 7-6. No other function will be visible to the user.

   $ **/usr/sbin/sam**

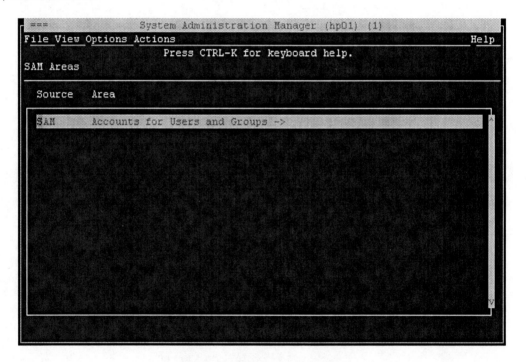

Figure 7-6 Restricted SAM

Although SAM offers ease of management, it is preferable to use command line as much as possible to understand what really happens behind the scenes when you execute a command. A clear and solid understanding of concepts, commands, command syntax, configuration files, and daemon processes is critical to successful system administration as well as troubleshooting. In addition, good working knowledge of step-by-step task implementation is necessary to setup and manage a service. Throughout this book, emphasis is put on how to perform tasks from the command line.

7.3 Server Hardware Component Overview

This section talks about hardware components found in HP servers that run HP-UX Operating Environment software.

7.3.1 Slot

A *Slot* (a.k.a *I/O Slot*) is a receptacle for installing an interface card. Figure 7-7 shows a system board with multiple I/O slots.

Figure 7-7 Slots

In HP-UX 11iv1, the *rad* command displays configuration and status information of PCI slots on selected servers. Run this command with –q option.

rad –q

Slot	Path Num	Bus	Max Spd	Spd	Pwr	Occu	Susp Mode	Driver(s) Capable	Max	Mode
2	0/4/0	32	N/A	33	On	Yes	No	Yes	N/A	N/A
6	0/2/0	16	N/A	33	On	Yes	No	Yes	N/A	N/A
9	1/4/0	160	N/A	33	On	Yes	No	Yes	N/A	N/A
11	1/8/0	192	N/A	33	On	Yes	No	Yes	N/A	N/A

The output indicates that there are 4 PCI slots in the system. It shows each slot's number, hardware path, bus number, maximum and current speeds, power status, occupied or not occupied status, suspended or not suspended status, driver configured or not configured status, and so on.

In HP-UX 11iv2, use *olrad* command instead.

 # olrad −q

Slot	Path	Bus Num	Max Spd	Spd	Pwr	Occu	Susp	Driver(s) Capable OLAR Mode	OLD	Max	Mode
3	0/7/1	35	266	266	On	Yes	No	Yes	N/A	PCI-X	PCI-X
4	0/3/1	15	266	266	On	Yes	No	Yes	N/A	PCI-X	PCI-X
5	0/6/1	30	133	133	On	Yes	No	Yes	N/A	PCI-X	PCI-X
6	0/2/1	10	133	133	Off	No	N/A	N/A	N/A	PCI-X	PCI-X
7	0/5/1	21	66	66	Off	No	N/A	N/A	N/A	PCI-X	PCI-X
8	0/5/2	21	66	66	Off	No	N/A	N/A	N/A	PCI-X	PCI-X
9	0/1/1	1	66	66	Off	No	N/A	N/A	N/A	PCI-X	PCI-X
10	0/1/2	1	66	66	Off	No	N/A	N/A	N/A	PCI-X	PCI-X

The output indicates that there are 8 PCI-X slots in the system. It shows each slot's number, hardware path, bus number, maximum and current speeds, power status, occupied or not occupied status, suspended or not suspended status, whether or not slot supports adding and replacing an interface card online, slot type (PCI or PCI-X), and so on.

7.3.2   PCI and PCI-X

PCI stands for *Peripheral Component Interconnect* and PCI-X stands for *PCI eXtended*. The PCI or PCI-X technology includes a slot, an interface adapter that goes into the slot, and the electronic circuitry that connects the slot to the system or cell board. HP-UX systems come with a mix of both PCI and PCI-X slots, and I/O cards that fit into them.

PCI provides a shared data path between CPUs and I/O adapters. It runs at 33MHz and 66MHz speeds and supports both 32-bit and 64-bit data paths. Figure 7-8 shows picture of a PCI card.

Figure 7-8 PCI Card

PCI-X is an enhanced version of PCI and is backward compatible to it. PCI-X runs at 133MHz and 266MHz speeds and supports both 32-bit and 64-bit data paths, but 64-bit are more common. The 64-bit PCI-X slots and PCI-X adapters are longer in size than their PCI counterparts and are almost twice as fast.

Both PCI and PCI-X cards can be installed and removed using HP-UX OLA/R (*OnLine Addition / Replacement*) functionality while the machine is up and running.

The OLA/R function can be performed either through SAM or the *rad* (or *olrad*) command. Some administrators perfer SAM since it performs critical resource analysis too that tells the administrator of any potential impact due to replacing a particular card. The *rad* and *olrad* commands do not do that. They simply do the job quietly.

To perform an OLA/R function on a card, use the *rad* (or *olrad*) ommand with proper options. Check man pages for detailed information.

To use SAM for an OLA/R task, follow steps below:

☞ Go to SAM → Peripheral Devices → Cards. Choose a card to replace and go to Actions. Here you will see "Analyze Critical Resources", "Remove", "Create Device Files", and "Show Device Files" options. Do the "Analyze Critical Resources" on the card first before you "Remove" it.

7.3.3   Interface Card

An *Interface Card* is either integrated onto the system board or plugs into one of the system slots. It enables the system to communicate with external hardware devices. Different types of interface cards are available to connect fibre channel, SCSI, LAN, and other types of external devices. Interface cards are also referred to as *Host Adapters, Device Adapters*, and *Controller Cards*. Figures 7-8 through 7-10 show different types of interface cards.

7.3.4   Network Interface Card

Each system or device that you want to connect to the network requires to have a **Network Interface Card** (NIC) installed. The network card can be built-in to the system board or it can be a separate card installed in one of the system slots. NICs are also known as *LAN Cards* and *LAN Adapters*. Multiport LAN cards are also available that give you 2 or 4 ports on a single physical card. LAN cards enable your system to send and receive data to and from other systems on the network. You must have proper software driver installed in order to use them. Figure 7-9 shows pictures of 1-port and 4-port LAN cards.

Figure 7-9 Network Interface Cards

7.3.5   SCSI Card

Small Computer System Interface (SCSI) was developed in 1986 and has since been widely used in computer systems. SCSI is an I/O bus technology controlled by a set of protocols. It allows

---

several peripheral devices (including hard drives, tape drives, CD or DVD ROM drives) to be connected to a single SCSI controller card – also called SCSI *Host Bus Adapter* (HBA). Figure 7-10 shows picture of a SCSI HBA.

Figure 7-10 SCSI Controller Card

Many types of SCSI cards are available that differ based on factors, such as bandwidth, data transfer speed, and pin count on the connector. Table 7-3 lists various SCSI types.

Most HP servers today come standard with an Ultra160 SCSI port.

When working with SCSI devices and SCSI interface cards, make sure that the two are of same type. For example, an Ultra3 SCSI DVD-ROM requires that the HBA it is connected to is also Ultra3 SCSI.

Type	Bus Width	Max Data Transfer Rate
SCSI	8 bit	5 MB/second
Wide SCSI	16 bit	10 MB/second
Fast SCSI	8 bit	10 MB/second
Fast Wide SCSI	16 bit	20 MB/second
Ultra SCSI	8 bit	20 MB/second
Ultra Wide SCSI	16 bit	40 MB/second
Ultra2 SCSI	8 bit	40 MB/second
Wide Ultra2 SCSI	16 bit	80 MB/second
Ultra160 (Ultra 3)	16 bit	160 MB/second
Ultra320	16 bit	320 MB/second

Table 7-3 SCSI Chart

7.3.6   Multi-function Card

A multi-function card is a card that has the capability built in to it to perform more than one functions concurrently. Such cards are commonly used in servers to save on slots. Some examples of multi-function cards include:

- ✓ Cards with both LAN (Ethernet) and SCSI ports
- ✓ Cards with both LAN and Fibre Channel (FC) ports
- ✓ Cards with both SCSI and FC ports
- ✓ Cards with both LAN and modem ports
- ✓ Cards with LAN console, serial console, and SCSI ports. These cards are also referred to as *Core I/O* cards.

7.3.7   Bus

All hardware components, such as processors, memory, and interface cards in a system communicate with one another through electrical circuits, called *Buses*. Data flows between processor and memory, between memory and disk, between memory and interface cards, and so on. Busses can be internal or external. Internal busses facilitate data movement within the system while external buses allow external devices to become part of the system through interface adapters.

7.3.8   Bus Converter

In an HP-UX system there are different types of hardware components installed. Some are very fast, others are slower or too slow. When a higher speed component talks to a slower speed component or device, a *Bus Converter* is used to facilitate data transmission. A bus converter is represented by the forward slash (/) character in the hardware path of a device.

7.3.9   Processor/Core

HP-UX OE software runs on two types of hardware architectures – Integrity and 9000.

The Integrity server family is based on 64-bit *Itanium2* processors (formerly known as IA-64 and previous generation was called *Itanium* processors). The Itanium2 processors are based on the *Explicitly Parallel Instruction Computing* (EPIC) technology. Most of the current Itanium2 processors are dual-cored meaning that a single processor module chip has two independent processors on it that share the chip connections to the system (or cell) board.

The 9000 server family is based on 64-bit *Precision-Architecture Reduced Instruction Set Computing* (PA-RISC) processors. Most of the current PA-RISC processors are also dual-cored.

7.3.10   Cell Board

A *Cell Board*, or simply a *Cell*, holds processors and memory. The newer cell boards support up to 4 dual-core processor modules and 128GB of memory per cell board. The largest HP-UX server complex supports up to 16 cell boards and 2TB of memory. Figure 7-11 shows picture of a cell board.

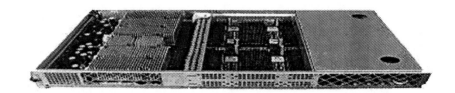

Figure 7-11 Cell Board

Each cell board can be connected to one I/O chassis at a time, which cannot be shared with another cell board.

7.3.11   I/O Chassis

I/O Chassis (or *I/O Card Cage*) holds a set of 12 PCI and PCI-X slots for HP Superdome and RP/RX84xx servers. I/O chassis for RP/RX74xx servers holds 8 PCI and PCI-X slots. It has its own power supplies. You can add more slots to a server in multiples of 12 or 8 depending on the server model. One cell board handles up to 12 (or 8) PCI slots. If you need additional 12 (or 8) PCI slots in a node partition (nPar), you need to add a cell board and an I/O chassis to the partition. Detailed discussion on node partitions is covered in Chapter 08 "HP-UX Partitioning Continuum".

Each node partition must have at least one I/O chassis, which must contain a core I/O card.

7.3.12   Core I/O

Each server, or an nPar within a server complex, must have a unique card called *Core I/O* card installed. This card always sits in slot 0 and has one serial and one LAN port for MP/console access into the server or nPar. This card also has a SCSI port. The cell board whose I/O chassis contains the core I/O card is referred to as the *Core Cell*.

7.3.13   Power Supply

There are two types of power supplies in large and mid-range servers – *System Power Supplies* and *PCI Power Supplies*. System power supplies provide power to the entire system while PCI power supplies provide power to I/O chassis. All servers that run HP-UX come standard with at least two power supplies for redundancy purpose.

Entry-level servers come with power supplies that support the entire machine.

7.3.14   Server Expansion Unit

Mid-range servers (rp84xx) can hold up to two cell boards and two I/O chassis units within the server. For growing requirements, you may need to add a pair of cell boards and I/O chassis units. These additional components are installed in a hardware unit external to the server. This hardware unit is referred to as the *Server Expansion Unit* (SEU). Once installed, the SEU becomes an integral part of the server. Figure 7-12 shows picture of an SEU.

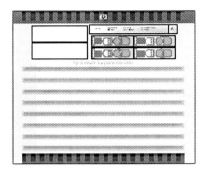

Figure 7-12 Server Expansion Unit

An SEU comes with its own power supplies and fan units. It has room to accommodate additional hard drives, tape drives, and CD/DVD-ROM drives besides cell boards and I/O chassis.

7.3.15   Cabinet

The term *Cabinet* is typically used with Superdome servers. Superdomes are the largest HP servers with support for up to 16 cell boards and 16 I/O chassis units in addition to power supplies, fans, and other hardware components. The base Superdome server fits into one cabinet space but a fully loaded one requires one additional cabinet. Figure 7-13 shows two cabinets of a Superdome server complex.

Figure 7-13 Superdome Server Complex Cabinets

Mid-range and entry-level servers do not employ the term *Cabinet* since they are small enough to fit in one cabinet.

7.3.16   Server Complex

A *Server Complex* is a complete physical hardware box including cell boards, power system, node partitions, I/O chassis, server expansion unit, one or more cabinets, and so on. Figure 7-14 displays picture of a mid-range server complex.

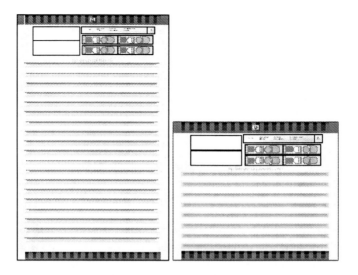

Figure 7-14 Server Complex

7.4   HP-UX Servers

There are two types of HP servers that run HP-UX. These are divided into two series – Integrity and 9000. The following sub-sections provide overview of both.

7.4.1   HP Integrity Series Servers

The Integrity series servers are powered by Intel *Itanium2* processors and are capable of running multiple HP-UX 11iv2 and 11iv3, MS Windows 2003, and Linux operating system instances concurrently in separate nPars and vPars within a single server complex.

nPar (*node partition*) and vPar (*virtual partition*) are server partitioning techniques available on mid-range and high-end HP-UX servers. Both are covered in detail in Chapter 08 "HP-UX Partitioning Continuum".

There are several server sizes available under the Integrity series and are classified into entry-level, mid-range, and high-end. The servers are grouped based on factors, such as maximum number of processors, maximum amount of memory, maximum number of PCI slots, etc. that they support. Table 7-4 provides summarized information. Visit *www.hp.com* for latest and more accurate information.

Server	Max Processors / Cores	Max Memory	Max PCI Slots	Internal Disk	Cell Board	nPar	vPar	Server Expansion Unit
rx1620	2/2	16GB	2	2 Disks	N/A	N/A	N/A	No
rx2620	2/4	32GB	4	3 Disks	N/A	N/A	N/A	No
rx2660	2/4	32GB	3	8 Disks	N/A	N/A	N/A	No
rx3600	2/4	96GB	8	8 Disks	N/A	N/A	N/A	No
rx4640	4/8	128GB	6	2 Disks	N/A	N/A	N/A	No

rx6600	4/8	192GB	8	16 Disks	N/A	N/A	N/A	No
rx7620	16	128GB	15	4 Disks	2	2	N/A	No
rx7640	8/16	128GB	15	4 Disks	2	2	N/A	No
rx8620	32	256GB	16	8 Disks	4	4	N/A	Yes
rx8640	16/32	256GB	16	8 Disks	4	4	N/A	Yes
Superdome	64/128	2TB	192	No Disks	16	16	N/A	Yes

Table 7-4 HP Integrity Server Models

Figure 7-15 displays front views of Superdome and rx7640 servers.

Figure 7-15 HP Superdome and RX7640 Servers

7.4.2   HP 9000 Series Servers

The 9000 series servers, on the other hand, are powered by PA-RISC processors. This server series supports all versions of HP-UX Operating Environment software that have been out there so far. The 9000 servers may be divided into nPars and vPars where you can run multiple, independent instances of HP-UX 11i OE v1, v2, and v3.

There are several server sizes available under the 9000 series and are classified into entry-level, mid-range and high-end. The servers are grouped based on factors, such as number of processors, amount of memory, number of PCI I/O slots, etc. that they support. Table 7-5 provides summarized information. Visit *www.hp.com* for latest and more accurate information.

Server	Max Processors / Cores	Max Memory	Max PCI Slots	Internal Disk	Cell Board	nPar	vPar	Server Expansion Unit
rp3410	1/2	6GB	2	3 Disks	N/A	N/A	N/A	No
rp3440	2/4	32GB	4	3 Disks	N/A	N/A	N/A	No
rp4410	2/4	128GB	6	2 Disks	N/A	N/A	N/A	No
rp4440	4/8	128GB	6	2 Disks	N/A	N/A	N/A	No
rp7420	8/16	128GB	15	4 Disks	2	2	16	No
rp7440	8/16	128GB	15	4 Disks	2	2	16	No
rp8420	16/32	256GB	32	8 Disks	4	4	32	Yes

rp8440	16/32	256GB	32	8 Disks	4	4	32	Yes
Superdome	64/128	2TB	192	No Disks	16	16	128	Yes

Table 7-5 HP 9000 Server Models

Figure 7-16 displays front views of Superdome and rp8420 servers.

Figure 7-16 HP Superdome and RP8420 Servers

For your reference, some older HP-UX server models are listed in Table 7-6 below:

Server	Max Processors	Max Memory	Max PCI Slots	Cell Board	nPar	vPar	Server Expansion Unit
rp24x0	2	8GB	4	N/A	N/A	N/A	No
rp54x0 (L class)	4	16GB	11	N/A	N/A	4	No
rp7400 (N class)	8	32GB	12	N/A	N/A	8	No
rp7410	8	32GB	15	2	2	8	No
rp8400	16	64GB	16	4	4	16	Yes

Table 7-6 Older HP 9000 Server Models

Additionally, A, D, E, F, G, H, K, R, T, and V class servers were also available. To obtain technical information about old server models visit *www.docs.hp.com* or *www.itrc.hp.com*.

7.5 Device Files and Major/Minor Numbers

Device files are of two types: physical and logical. Following sub-sections explain their basics and how to view and manage them.

HP Certified Systems Administrator

7.5.1   Physical Device Addressing

Each hardware component in an HP-UX system has a physical location where it can be reached at by the kernel when it requires to talk to it. This location is called *Hardware Address* or *Physical Address*. An HP-UX command, *ioscan*, allows you to view devices and associated addresses of all available devices on your machine. A sample *ioscan* –f (*full*) output is shown below:

```
# ioscan –f
Class    I   H/W Path   Driver        S/W State  H/W Type      Description
===========================================================
. . . . . . . .
. . . . . . . .
target   0  8/8.4       tgt           CLAIMED    DEVICE
disk     0  8/8.4.0     sdisk         CLAIMED    DEVICE        SEAGATE ST39173WC
target   1  8/8.7       tgt           CLAIMED    DEVICE
ctl      0  8/8.7.0     sctl          CLAIMED    DEVICE        Initiator
target   2  8/8.12      tgt           CLAIMED    DEVICE
disk     1  8/8.12.0    sdisk         CLAIMED    DEVICE        SEAGATE ST39173WC
ext_bus  1  8/12        c720          CLAIMED    INTERFACE     GSC add-on Fast/Wide SCSI
Interface
target   3  8/12.0      tgt           CLAIMED    DEVICE
disk     2  8/12.0.0    sdisk         CLAIMED    DEVICE        SEAGATE ST39173WC
target   4  8/12.4      tgt           CLAIMED    DEVICE
disk     3  8/12.4.0    sdisk         CLAIMED    DEVICE        SEAGATE ST39173WC
target   5  8/12.6      tgt           CLAIMED    DEVICE
ctl      1  8/12.6.0    sctl          CLAIMED    DEVICE        Initiator
target   6  8/12.12     tgt           CLAIMED    DEVICE
disk     4  8/12.12.0   sdisk         CLAIMED    DEVICE        SEAGATE ST39173WC
ba       2  8/16        bus_adapter   CLAIMED    BUS_NEXUS     Core I/O Adapter
ext_bus  3  8/16/0      Centlf        CLAIMED    INTERFACE     Built-in Parallel Interface
tty      0  8/16/4      asio0         CLAIMED    INTERFACE     Built-in RS-232C
ext_bus  2  8/16/5      c720          CLAIMED    INTERFACE     Built-in SCSI
target   7  8/16/5.0    tgt           CLAIMED    DEVICE
tape     0  8/16/5.0.0  stape         CLAIMED    DEVICE        HP  C1533A
target   8  8/16/5.2    tgt           CLAIMED    DEVICE
disk     5  8/16/5.2.0  sdisk         CLAIMED    DEVICE        TOSHIBA CD-ROM XM-5701TA
target   9  8/16/5.7    tgt           CLAIMED    DEVICE
. . . . . . . .
. . . . . . . .
```

There are seven columns in the above output. Table 7-7 explains them:

Column	Explanation
Class	Category of device. Examples are disk, printer, tape, lan, processor, memory, etc.
Instance	A unique number associated with the device or interface adapter within a class.

H/W Path	Hardware or physical path is a series of digits separated by slash (/) and period (.) characters. Slash represents a bus converter. A hardware path indicates the location of a hardware component on the path to the physical device.
Driver	Software driver that controls hardware. For example, sdisk is for SCSI disk and CD/DVD drive, and stape is for SCSI tape device.
S/W State	Software state is either CLAIMED or UNCLAIMED. CLAIMED means the driver for the device is successfully bound to it. UNCLAIMED means no driver is available for the device.
Hardware Type	An identifier for the hardware component.
Description	A short description.

Table 7-7 *ioscan* Output Explanation

The bold text in the *ioscan* output above shows details about the hard disks, the CD-ROM drive, and the tape drive installed in the system. The output indicates that there are total 5 SCSI hard drives; two on 8/8 hardware busses and three on 8/12. Their SCSI IDs are 4, 12, 0, 4, and 12, respectively. SCSI IDs are explained in the next section.

The tape device at 8/16/5.0.0 hardware address is on a different bus and using SCSI ID 0. The CD-ROM drive is on the same bus too but using SCSI ID 2.

Try running the *ioscan* command with following switches:

# ioscan	Scans entire system and lists all hardware found.
# ioscan –f	Shows full listing of all system hardware components.
# ioscan –fH 8/12.0.0	Searches for all devices at the specified hardware address.
# ioscan –fn	Scans entire system and displays logical device files too.
# ioscan –fnk	Same as "*ioscan* –fn" but does not rescan the system. Instead, it brings information from the running kernel, which is much quicker.
# ioscan –fnkCdisk	Searches for devices of the specified class. In this example, *ioscan* searches for all disk devices.

7.5.2   Logical Device Files

It is a little tedious to work with hardware device files. As a system administrator you would probably prefer to use a different approach that uses logical device naming convention. Logical device files are mere pointers to their associated hardware device addresses but simpler to manipulate. The following sub-sections explain logical naming scheme used with different device types.

Disk Device Files

Run the *ioscan* command as follows to list all disk devices installed:

```
# ioscan –fnkCdisk
Class   I H/W Path   Driver   S/W State H/W Type  Description
=============================================================
disk    0 8/8.4.0   sdisk     CLAIMED  DEVICE    SEAGATE ST39173WC
```

```
                /dev/dsk/c0t4d0   /dev/rdsk/c0t4d0
disk    1 8/8.12.0   sdisk     CLAIMED  DEVICE    SEAGATE ST39173WC
                /dev/dsk/c0t12d0  /dev/rdsk/c0t12d0
disk    2 8/12.0.0   sdisk     CLAIMED  DEVICE    SEAGATE ST39173WC
                /dev/dsk/c1t0d0   /dev/rdsk/c1t0d0
disk    3 8/12.4.0   sdisk     CLAIMED  DEVICE    SEAGATE ST39173WC
                /dev/dsk/c1t4d0   /dev/rdsk/c1t4d0
disk    4 8/12.12.0  sdisk     CLAIMED  DEVICE    SEAGATE ST39173WC
                /dev/dsk/c1t12d0  /dev/rdsk/c1t12d0
disk    5 8/16/5.2.0 sdisk     CLAIMED  DEVICE    TOSHIBA CD-ROM XM-5701TA
                /dev/dsk/c2t2d0   /dev/rdsk/c2t2d0
```

From this output it is evident that there are five hard drives and one CD-ROM drive installed at different hardware addresses. Each disk device has an associated logical device name and follows convention illustrated in Figure 7-17.

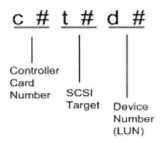

Figure 7-17 SCSI Hard Drive Naming Convention

In this device convention, "c#" identifies SCSI adapter number, "t#" identifies SCSI target ID, and "d#" identifies SCSI disk device number (also called *Logical Unit Number* – LUN) on the SCSI target.

The *ioscan* command output above indicates that the first two hard drives are connected to SCSI controller card number 0 (c0) having target SCSI IDs 4 and 12, respectively. The SCSI disk device number is always 0 if there is no other device sharing the target ID.

Similarly, the next three hard drives are attached to SCSI card number 1 (c1) at SCSI target IDs 0, 4, and 12, in that order.

The last disk shown is the CD-ROM drive with device file *c2t2d0* and placed on a different SCSI controller card.

 Each SCSI disk must have a unique address on the SCSI bus otherwise conflicts will occur.

You can use the *lssf* command to view device characteristics. The following examples show attributes of */dev/rdsk/c0t4d0* and */dev/dsk/c2t2d0*:

 # lssf /dev/rdsk/c0t4d0
sdisk card instance 0 SCSI target 4 SCSI LUN 0 section 0 at address 8/8.4.0 /dev/rdsk/c0t4d0

---

lssf /dev/dsk/c2t2d0

sdisk card instance 2 SCSI target 2 SCSI LUN 0 section 0 at address 8/16/5.2.0 /dev/dsk/c2t2d0

Tape Drive Device Files

Tape devices are located in the */dev/rmt* directory. The first tape drive installed in a system is represented by the digit 0, followed by 1 for the next one, 2 for the third, and so on. The following *ioscan* command shows that there is only one tape drive in the system but with multiple logical device files pointing to it:

```
# ioscan –fnkCtape
tape      0 8/16/5.0.0  stape    CLAIMED   DEVICE     HP    C1533A
/dev/rmt/0m                       /dev/rmt/c2t0d0BESTn
/dev/rmt/0mb                      /dev/rmt/c2t0d0BESTnb
/dev/rmt/0mn                      /dev/rmt/c2t0d0DDS
/dev/rmt/0mnb                     /dev/rmt/c2t0d0DDSb
/dev/rmt/c2t0d0BEST              /dev/rmt/c2t0d0DDSn
/dev/rmt/c2t0d0BESTb             /dev/rmt/c2t0d0DDSnb
```

Naming convention illustrated in Figure 7-18 is followed for tape device files.

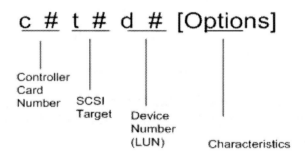

Figure 7-18 Tape Device File Naming Convention

This convention is same as used with disks with the exception that it includes one or more options with it. For example:

/dev/rmt/c2t0d0BEST refers to the first tape drive and uses medium compression. It is hard linked to */dev/rmt/0m* and */dev/rmt/c2t0d0DDS*.

/dev/rmt/c2t0d0BESTb is same as above but uses Berkeley-style behavior. It is hard linked to */dev/rmt/0mb* and */dev/rmt/c2t0d0DDSb*.

/dev/rmt/c2t0d0BESTn is same as the first one but does not rewind the tape after a backup is finished. It is hard linked to */dev/rmt/0mn* and */dev/rmt/c2t0d0DDSn*.

/dev/rmt/c2t0d0BESTnb is same as the previous one but uses Berkeley-style behavior. It is hard linked to */dev/rmt/0mnb* and */dev/rmt/c2t0d0DDSnb*.

DDS (*Digital Data Storage*) is a format of storing data on 4mm DAT (*Digital Audio Tape*) media. DAT media requires DAT drives. The first generation of DAT drives was referred to as DDS1 and was able to store up to 4GB of data on a single tape in compressed mode. The second, third, and fourth generations were referred to as DDS2 (8GB), DDS3 (24GB), and DDS4 (40GB). The fifth and sixth generations are called DAT72 (72GB) and DAT160 (160GB).

Terminal and Modem Device Files

Device files for terminals and modems are located under the */dev* directory and identify serial port they are connected to. For example, a D370 server has two built-in serial ports with following device files:

/dev/tty0p0 and /dev/tty1p0

If you connect a serial multi-port concentrator or a multiplexer to the first serial port, the device files on these devices will be:

/dev/tty0p0 – device file for the terminal on the first MUX at port #0
/dev/tty0p1 – device file for the terminal on the first MUX at port #1
/dev/tty0p2 – device file for the terminal on the first MUX at port #2
/dev/tty0p3 – device file for the terminal on the first MUX at port #3
.... and so on

Typical modem device files look like */dev/cua0p0, /dev/cu10p0*, and */dev/ttyd0p0*.

7.5.3   Major and Minor Numbres

Every hardware device in a server has an associated device driver loaded in the HP-UX kernel. Some of the hardware devices are SCSI drives, printers, terminals, tape drives, modems, etc. The kernel talks to hardware devices through their respective device drivers. Each device driver has a unique number called *Major* number by which kernel recognizes its type.

Furthermore, there may be more than one devices controlled by a single device driver. For example, SCSI device driver controls all SCSI hard disks, CD-ROM, and DVD-ROM drives. Since there may be numerous devices of the same type controlled by one single device driver, the kernel assigns another unique number called *Minor* number to each individual device within that device driver category. In summary, major number points to the device driver whereas minor number points to an individual device controlled by that device driver.

The major and minor numbers can be viewed using the *ll* command as follows:

```
# ll /dev/vg00
crw-r-----   1     root    sys     64    0x000000    Dec 16 07:01    group
brw-r-----   1     root    sys     64    0x000001    Dec 16 07:01    lvol1
brw-r-----   1     root    sys     64    0x000002    Dec 16 07:01    lvol2
brw-r-----   1     root    sys     64    0x000003    Dec 16 07:01    lvol3
brw-r-----   1     root    sys     64    0x000004    Dec 16 07:01    lvol4
brw-r-----   1     root    sys     64    0x000005    Dec 16 07:01    lvol5
```

brw-r-----	1	root	sys	64	0x000006	Dec 16 07:01	lvol6
brw-r-----	1	root	sys	64	0x000007	Dec 16 07:01	lvol7
brw-r-----	1	root	sys	64	0x000008	Dec 16 07:01	lvol8
crw-r-----	1	root	sys	64	0x000001	Dec 16 07:01	rlvol1
crw-r-----	1	root	sys	64	0x000002	Dec 16 07:01	rlvol2
crw-r-----	1	root	sys	64	0x000003	Dec 16 07:01	rlvol3
crw-r-----	1	root	sys	64	0x000004	Dec 16 07:01	rlvol4
crw-r-----	1	root	sys	64	0x000005	Dec 16 07:01	rlvol5
crw-r-----	1	root	sys	64	0x000006	Dec 16 07:01	rlvol6
crw-r-----	1	root	sys	64	0x000007	Dec 16 07:01	rlvol7
crw-r-----	1	root	sys	64	0x000008	Dec 16 07:01	rlvol8

Column 5 shows major numbers and column 6 shows minor numbers. Notice that major number 64 always represents the device driver for LVM. All minor numbers are unique. The output shows both block and character special device files.

Another HP-UX command that allows you to view major numbers for both character and block devices is the *lsdev* command.

```
# lsdev
Character   Block   Driver      Class
    0        -1     cn          pseudo
    1        -1     asio0       tty
    2        -1     devkrs      pseudo
    3        -1     mm          pseudo
    4        -1     lpr0        unknown
    5        -1     td          fc
    6        -1     btlan       lan
    7        -1     ip          pseudo
    8        -1     arp         pseudo
   10        -1     rawip       pseudo
   11        -1     tcp         pseudo
  . . . . . . . .
  . . . . . . . .
```

The first column lists major numbers associated with character devices, the second column shows major numbers associated with block devices, the third column displays device driver used to control the devices, and the last column signifies the device class. -1 in either the first or the second column indicates that a major number does not exist for that device.

7.5.4   Creating Device Files

All system hardware is scanned with the *ioscan* command and device files are created by the *insf* command during HP-UX installation process. All device information is then stored in the */etc/ioconfig* file. Each time the system is rebooted, the *ioinit* (*i/o init*ialization) command calls the *insf* command, which automatically creates device files for any new devices it finds and updates */etc/ioconfig*. Similarly, it automatically removes device files for any devices it does not find and

---

HP Certified Systems Administrator

updates */etc/ioconfig*. This automatic process of creation and deletion of device information is called *Autoconfiguration*.

Sometimes it becomes necessary to create device files manually. You may use SAM or command line for this purpose. If you prefer to use SAM, follow the procedure below.

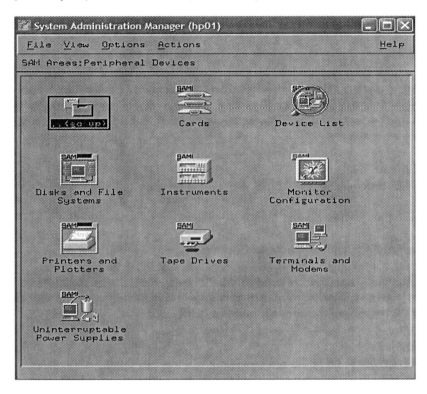

Figure 7-19 SAM – Peripheral Device Administration

☞ Go to SAM → Peripheral Devices. Select the type of device and go to Actions → Add the device file(s). See Figure 7-19.

At the command prompt, you have three commands available: *insf*, *mksf*, and *mknod*. Let us see how these commands are used to create device files.

Creating Device Files with the *insf* Command

The *insf* (*install special file*) command creates device files under the */dev* directory for new devices that it finds. The following shows various examples.

To create device files for all existing and new devices:

    # insf –e

To create device files for all devices of class "disk" only:

    # insf –C disk

To create device files for a specific device located at hardware address 8/8.4.0:

    # insf –H 8/8.4.0 –e

Creating Device Files with the *mksf* Command

The *mksf* (*make special file*) command may be used to create device files for devices seen by the *ioscan* command but missing device files. The following example shows how to create a character special tape device file for the tape device located at 8/16/5.0.0 address with instance number 0 and hardware class type "tape":

    # cd /dev/rmt
    # mksf –C tape –H 8/16/5.0.0 –I 0
    # ll
    crw-rw-rw- 1 bin   bin   205 0x020000 Dec 18 03:47 c2t0d0BEST

Creating Device Files with the *mknod* Command

The *mknod* command can also be used to create device files. It requires that you supply major and minor device numbers. The following example shows how to create a character device file called *group* with major number 64 and minor number 0x010000:

    # cd /dev
    # mknod group c 64 0x010000
    # ll group
    crw-rw-rw- 1 bin   bin   64 0x010000 Dec 18 03:53 group

7.5.5   Removing Device Files

Use the *rmsf* (*remove special file*) command to remove any device files that you no longer need. For example, to remove all device files that refer to tape device at hardware address 8/16/5.0.0, do the following:

    # rmsf –H 8/16/5.0.0

7.6   Viewing Hardware Diagnostic Messages

The *dmesg* (*diagnostic messages*) command gathers recent diagnostics messages from a log file and displays them on the screen. This information may prove helpful in your troubleshooting efforts.

---

dmesg

. . . .

. . . .

8/12.6 tgt

8/12.6.0 sctl

8/12.12 tgt

8/12.12.0 sdisk

8/16 bus_adapter

8/16/4 asio0

8/16/5 c720

8/16/5.0 tgt

8/16/5.0.0 stape

8/16/5.2 tgt

8/16/5.2.0 sdisk

8/16/5.7 tgt

8/16/5.7.0 sctl

8/16/6 lan2

8/16/0 Centlf

8/16/7 ps2

8/20 bus_adapter

8/20/5 eisa

8/20/2 asio0

10 ccio

32 processor

34 processor

49 memory

btlan: Initializing 10/100BASE-TX card at 8/0/1/0....

System Console is on the Built-In Serial Interface
Entering cifs_init...
Initialization finished successfully... slot is 9
Logical volume 64, 0x3 configured as ROOT
Logical volume 64, 0x2 configured as SWAP
Logical volume 64, 0x2 configured as DUMP
  Swap device table: (start & size given in 512-byte blocks)
    entry 0 - major is 64, minor is 0x2; start = 0, size = 4194304
  Dump device table: (start & size given in 1-Kbyte blocks)
    entry 00000000 - major is 31, minor is 0x4000; start = 310112, size = 2097152
Starting the STREAMS daemons-phase 1
Create STCP device files
Starting the STREAMS daemons-phase 2
  $Revision: vmunix: vw: -proj   selectors: CUPI80_BL2000_1108 -c 'Vw for CUPI80_BL2000_1108
build' -- cupi80_bl2000_1108 'CUPI80_BL2000_1108' Wed Nov 8 19:05:38 PST 2000 $
Memory Information:
  physical page size = 4096 bytes, logical page size = 4096 bytes
  Physical: 1048576 Kbytes, lockable: 759292 Kbytes, available: 880216 Kbytes

Summary

In this chapter, you learned about the responsibilities of a system administrator in an HP-UX-based computing environment. You looked at available resources to seek help when required. The System Administration Manager is a very powerful tool that makes your life easy as an administrator and can be used to perform a number of tasks without getting into underlying details. You were provided information on how to use it. You also looked at how SAM could be configured to delegate to normal users tasks that only superuser could otherwise perform.

The next set of topics covered in detail HP server hardware components including slot, PCI and PCI-X card, interface card, network card, SCSI card, bus, bus converter, processor/core, cell board, I/O chassis, core I/O, power supply, server expansion unit, cabinet, and server complex. You were presented with HP-UX's online addition/replacement functionality. You looked at HP's Integrity and 9000 server families.

You learned about device files and how to view, create, and remove them. You understood the concept of major and minor numbers. Finally, you saw how to display hardware diagnostic messages.

## 08

HP-UX Partitioning Continuum

This chapter covers the following major topics:

- ✓ Understanding HP-UX partitioning continuum
- ✓ Benefits of partitioning
- ✓ Introduction to Management Processor
- ✓ Node partitioning – concepts, creating, modifying, and removing
- ✓ Virtual partitioning – concepts, creating, modifying, and removing
- ✓ Virtual Machines partitioning – concepts
- ✓ Resource partitioning – concepts

8.1 Understanding HP-UX Partitioning Continuum

HP-UX 11i Operating Environment software offers *Partitioning Continuum* technologies. These technologies enable you to logically divide a server complex into several smaller computers, with each allotted dedicated (or shared) hardware resources and run an independent HP-UX 11i OE instance. Each of these virtual computers can be used to run a unique application completely independent of applications running in other virtual computers.

8.1.1 Supported Partitioning Continuum Technologies

Currently, the following four partitioning techniques are available:

1. **Node Partitioning** – used on both HP Integrity and HP 9000 cell-based servers.
2. **Virtual Partitioning** – used on both HP Integrity and HP 9000 mid-range and high-end servers.
3. **Virtual Machines Partitioning** – used on HP Integrity servers only.
4. **Resource Partitioning** – used on both HP Integrity and HP 9000 servers via HP *Process Resource Manager* (PRM) and *Work Load Manager* (WLM) software.

8.1.2 Benefits of Partitioning

Partitioning continuum technologies offer several benefits, such as:

- ✓ Better system hardware resource utilization.
- ✓ Online allocation, deallocation, and administration of hardware resources.
- ✓ Separate, independent OE instance in each partition.
- ✓ Different patch level in each partition.
- ✓ Dissimilar kernel in each partition.
- ✓ Unique application in each partition with complete isolation from other applications.
- ✓ Software fault isolation.

Note that not all partitioning techniques offer all these benefits. Most are associated mainly with the first three. The fourth – resource partitioning – supports only a subset.

This chapter covers the first two partitioning techniques – node and virtual partitioning – at length; the rest are briefly touched upon.

Before getting into the details of partitioning, let us study something called *Management Processor*.

8.2 Introduction to Management Processor (MP)

The *Management Processor* (MP) is part of all new HP Integrity and 9000 series servers. It is a small hardware module that is installed in servers for system management purposes. It has its own processor and can be rebooted independent of the server in which it is installed without impacting the server operation. Through MP, you can access a server complex and perform tasks, such as:

- ✓ Access server or node partition (nPar) console.
- ✓ Access virtual partition (vPar) console.
- ✓ Power off, reset, and send *Transfer Of Control* (TOC) signal to the system or nPar.

✓ Send event notification.
✓ View and log console messages, system events, and error messages.
✓ View updated cell board and nPar status.
✓ View cell configuration information.
✓ View updated boot information through *Virtual Front Panel* (VFP).
✓ Display environment parameters, such as electrical power and cooling.
✓ View and modify LAN MP TCP/IP settings for over the network telnet access.

On older server models, MP is called *Guardian Service Processor* (GSP). MP can be accessed via serial or Ethernet port. Both ports are part of the MP module and dedicated for MP access. For local MP access, you can physically connect any serial display device to the serial MP port. On some server models, this port is referred to as *Console/Remote/UPS*. For remote, over the network MP access, you need to configure TCP/IP parameters on the LAN MP port. You also need to ensure that proper network connectivity is in place to access the MP remotely using the configured IP address.

At this point, it is important to highlight the differences between LAN MP port and other network ports available in the server or nPar. Although both require configuring TCP/IP parameters, the LAN MP port is dedicated for MP operations and console access. It is available even if the server is down. In contrast, other network ports provide access into the server or nPar and only when the server or nPar is up and in functional state. Users and applications employ these network ports.

8.2.1   Setting Serial MP Display Parameters

It is important to set correct parameter values on the serial console device to allow text and menus to be displayed correctly and navigated properly.

Follow the steps below to perform key console settings on an HP dumb terminal device.

✓ Connect the HP dumb console terminal to the serial MP/console port on the system.
✓ Power it on.
✓ Press *User / System* key located in the middle of the top row on the console keyboard.
✓ Press F4 to select *Remote Mode*. Make sure that the asterisk (*) character appears beside it.
✓ Press F8 to go to *Config Keys* and then F3 for *Datacomm Config*. Set *BaudRate* to "9600", *Parity/DataBits* to "None/8", *RecvPace* to "Xon/Xoff", and *XmitPace* to "None". Press F1 to save when done.
✓ Press F8 again to go to *Config Keys* and then F5 for *Terminal Config*. Set *Datacomm/ExtDev* to "Serial (1) / Serial (2)", *Terminal Id* "70096", *Keyboard* "USASCII", *Language* "ENGLISH", *LocalEcho* "off", and *CapsLock* to "off".

This completes the setup of the display terminal and now it should work well.

8.2.2   Setting LAN MP Parameters

If you wish to access MP over the network as well, you need to connect a display terminal device to the serial MP port and log in to MP (follow procedure in the next sub-section on how to log in to MP). Go to the command mode by typing *cm* at the MP prompt (refer to Table 8-1 on various commands and options available at the MP level). Execute the *lc* command to set appropriate network parameters, such as IP address, subnet mask, default gateway, and MP hostname. Execute the *xd* command when done to reset and restart MP.

This completes the setup of LAN MP port. You should now be able to access the server or nPar remotely from over the network via this interface.

8.2.3   Interacting with MP

MP is accessed via user accounts. Up to 32 user accounts can be defined, with each user may be set to have different level of access to server complex and MP commands. There exists one powerful pre-configured user called *Admin* with full access to entire server complex. Other user accounts that you may wish to create can have operator or nPar-specific access.

 MP user accounts have nothing to do with HP-UX user accounts.

To access MP via serial port, type in "Admin" as username and "Admin" as password at the MP login prompt. The MP> main menu will appear.

For over the network access, supply the LAN MP IP address with the *telnet* command to get the MP login prompt. Enter the username and password, as above, to get the MP> prompt.

The following sample is taken from an rp8400 server:

```
MP login: Admin
MP password: *****

          Welcome to the

          Rp8400 Management Processor

(c) Copyright 1995-2002 Hewlett-Packard Co., All Rights Reserved.

          Version 4.20

   MP MAIN MENU:

      CO: Consoles
      VFP: Virtual Front Panel (partition status)
      CM: Command Menu
      CL: Console Logs
      SL: Show chassis Logs
      HE: Help
      X: Exit Connection

   MP:>
```

If you are already connected and logged in to the MP, you need to press *ctrl+b* to get the MP prompt

The main menu options are CO, VFP, CM, CL, SL, HE, and X. Table 8-1 describes them.

MP Option	Description
CO	Takes you to the console of the connected system or nPar.
VFP	Displays diagnostic state of the system or nPar as it boots up.
CM	Displays available commands. You can run commands when you get in to the CM sub-menu. Some of the key commands are: bo – Boots up a system or an nPar. cc – Initiates a complex configuration. cp – Displays which cell is assigned to which nPar. dc – Resets parameters to factory defaults. dl – Disables LAN MP/console access. el – Enables LAN MP/console access. lc – Configures network parameters for LAN MP port. ls – Displays network parameters for LAN MP port. ma – Returns to the main menu. pe – Powers a system or nPar on or off. ps – Displays hardware and power configuration information. rr – Resets a system or an nPar for reconfiguration. rs – Resets a system or an nPar. so – Creates and manages MP user accounts and controls security. tc – Sends a TOC to a system or nPar. xd – Reboots MP. Also used to run MP diagnostics.
CL	Displays console logging information.
SL	Displays hardware chassis logging information.
HE	Displays help.
X	Exits out of MP.

Table 8-1 MP Commands

At times, it is necessary to press *ctrl+E+c+f* to gain access to the console.

8.3   Hardware Available to Work with Partitioning

In the next two sections, node and virtual partitioning techniques are discussed. In order to explain various administrative operations, example commands are executed on an RP8400 server and output of some of them displayed here. Note that most tasks can be performed on Integrity machines the way they are performed on 9000 systems. The RP8400 server has the following hardware configuration:

Hardware model: HP 9000 RP8400   Number of cabinets: 1
Number of server expansion units: 1   Number of cell boards: 4
Number of processors: 16 (4 on each cell board)   Memory on each cell board: 8GB
Total amount of memory: 32GB   Number of I/O chassis: 4

Number of I/O slots: 32 (8 in each I/O chassis)   Maximum nPars this server supports: 4
Maximum vPars this server supports: 16

Let us now examine the two more commonly employed partitioning techniques – node partitioning and virtual partitioning – under HP-UX Operating Environment software.

8.4   Node Partitioning

Node partitioning is a hardware partitioning technique used to divide a cell-based mid-range or high-end server into several smaller computers called *node partitions* (nPars). Each nPar can then be used as a separate, independent, standalone server running HP-UX OE instance with its own dedicated processors, memory, and I/O chassis. Depending on the hardware model, a server complex may be divided into as many electrically-separated nPars as the total number of cell boards in the complex. The minimum number of nPars that can be created in a server complex is 2 and the maximum in the largest server complex is 16. Each nPar must have (at least) one core I/O card installed in slot 0 of its I/O chassis. Figure 8-1 shows a logical nPar running two applications.

One or more cell boards with core I/O card
One or more I/O chassis
Boot disks
Applications 1 and 2
Patch level June 2003

Figure 8-1 nPar Logical

In the following sub-sections, nPar administration tasks, such as creating the genesis partition, creating an nPar, changing an nPar name, adding a cell to an nPar, removing a cell from an nPar, and removing an nPar, are explained. You can issue commands to perform these operations from any of the nPars within the server complex. Alternatively, you can use the GUI software called *Partition Manager* to perform these tasks.

Some of the nPar administration commands are given in Table 8-2.

nPar Command	Description
parcreate	Creates the genesis partition and an nPar.
parmodify	Modifies an nPar including: ✓ Adding and removing cell boards, I/O chassis, and so on. ✓ Setting primary, alternate, and HAA boot paths. ✓ Changing an nPar name.
parremove	Removes an nPar.
parstatus	Displays status information of one or more nPars.

Table 8-2 nPar Administration Commands

8.4.1   Creating the Genesis Partition

The first nPar created in a server complex is always referred to as the *Genesis Partition*. It is a single-cell partition built via MP. Once created, you can load the HP-UX 11i OE into it.

To create the genesis partition, go to MP → CM → CC → and choose option G. Pick a cell that contains processors and memory, and must be connected to an I/O chassis with a core I/O card installed. When done, use the *bo* MP command to boot the nPar. Insert the HP-UX 11i DVD installation media in the drive and follow the procedure outlined in Chapter 09 "HP-UX Operating Environment Installation" to install the OE in the nPar.

After the installation is over, log in to the genesis partition, and issue the *parstatus* command to check the status and resources available in it.

```
# parstatus  –w
The local partition number is 0.
# parstatus  –Vp0
[Partition]
Partition Number          : 0
Partition Name            : Partition 0
Status                    : active
IP address                : 0.0.0.0
Primary Boot Path         : 0/0/0/2/0.6.0
Alternate Boot Path       : 0/0/0/3/0.6.0
HA Alternate Boot Path    : 0/0/0/0/0.0.0
PDC Revision              : 17.8
IODCH Version             : 5E40
CPU Speed                 : 750 MHz
Core Cell                 : cab0,cell0
```

```
[Cell]
                           CPU     Memory                              Use
                           OK/     (GB)                       Core     On
          Hardware  Actual Deconf/ OK/                        Cell     Next  Par
          Location  Usage  Max     Deconf  Connected To       Capable  Boot  Num
          ========  ====== ======  ======  ===============    ======   ====  ===
          cab0,cell0 active core 4/0/4  8.0/ 0.0 cab0,bay0,chassis0 yes       yes   0
```

```
[Chassis]
                          Core  Connected    Par
Hardware Location  Usage  IO    To           Num
===============    =====  ====  =========    ====
cab0,bay0,chassis0 active yes   cab0,cell0   0
```

By default, the genesis partition is called "Partition 0".

As you can see from the output that there are 4 processors in the genesis partition and 8GB of memory. It also shows the primary and alternate boot disk paths.

8.4.2   Creating an nPar

Once the genesis partition is formed, you can make additional nPars using unused cell boards and I/O chassis in the server complex.
Let us create a single cell nPar called *test_npar*. Log in to the genesis partition and perform the following steps:

1.   Identify what cell board is available. Run the *parstatus* command:

     # partstatus –AC
     Cell 1 is available.
     Cell 2 is available.
     Cell 3 is available.

2.   Determine which I/O chassis is free. Do the following:

     # parstatus –AI
     I/O chassis 1 is available.
     I/O chassis 2 is available.
     I/O chassis 3 is available.

3.   Execute the *parcreate* command to create *test_npar*. Use cell board 1 and I/O chassis 1. Specify nPar name with the –P option and cell number to include with the –c option. Values following each colon character are "base" (for cell type), "y" (to include the cell in next boot), and "ri" (reuse interleave – to reuse memory after a failure). Since these are default values, they are not exhibited in the following command line:

     # parcreate –P test_npar –c1:::
     Partition Created. The partition number is: 1

4.   Define primary (–b option) boot disk using the *parmodify* command. If you wish to use alternate boot disk as well, define it using the –t option.

     # parmodify –p1 –b 1/0/0/2/0.6.0 –t 1/0/0/3/0.6.0

5.   Verify that the nPar is created successfully. Use the *parstatus* command.

     # parstatus –Vp1
     [Partition]
     Partition Number   : 1
     Partition Name   : test_npar
     Status   : active
     IP address   : 0.0.0.0
     Primary Boot Path   : 1/0/0/2/0.6.0
     Alternate Boot Path   : 1/0/0/3/0.6.0
     HA Alternate Boot Path   : 0/0/0/0/0.0.0
     PDC Revision   : 17.8
     IODCH Version   : 5E40
     CPU Speed   : 750 MHz
     Core Cell   : cab0,cell1
     [Cell]

Hardware Location	Actual Usage	CPU OK/ Deconf/ Max	Memory (GB) OK/ Deconf	Connected To	Core Cell Capable	Use On Next Boot	Par Num
cab0,cell1 [Chassis]	active core	4/0/4	8.0/ 0.0	cab0,bay0,chassis1	yes	yes	1

Hardware Location	Usage	Core IO	Connected To	Par Num
cab0,bay0,chassis1	active	yes	cab0,cell1	1

This nPar also has 4 processors and 8GB of memory.

```
# parstatus –P
```
[Partition]

Par Num	Status	# of Cells	# of I/O Chassis	Core cell	Partition Name (first 30 chars)
0	active	1	1	cab0,cell0	Partition 0
1	active	1	1	cab0,cell1	test_npar

You need to install the HP-UX 11i OE in the new nPar now. Use the *bo* MP command to boot the nPar. Make sure that you have the HP-UX 11i DVD installation media in the drive. Follow the HP-UX 11i OE installation procedure outlined in Chapter 09 "HP-UX Operating Environment Installation" to install the OE in the nPar.

8.4.3   Changing an nPar Name

To change the first (genesis) nPar name from *Partition 0* to *prod_npar*, use the *parmodify* command. Verify results with *parstatus* after the operation is complete.

```
# parmodify –p0 –P prod_npar
# parstatus –P
```
[Partition]

Par Num	Status	# of Cells	# of I/O Chassis	Core cell	Partition Name (first 30 chars)
0	active	1	1	cab0,cell0	**prod_npar**
1	active	1	1	cab0,cell1	test_npar

8.4.4   Adding a Cell to an nPar

To add a cell to an active nPar (say *test_npar*), use the *parmodify* command. Specify partition number with –p option and cell number with –a option. Make sure that the cell (cell 2 in this case) is available. The –B option activates the nPar after it is rebooted. You must reboot the nPar for reconfig (option –R with the *shutdown* command) before the modification takes place.

```
# parmodify –p1 –a2::y: –B
```
In order to activate any cell that has been newly added, reboot the partition with the -R option.
Command succeeded.
```
# shutdown –Ry now
```

When the nPar is back up, execute *parstatus* and verify added hardware.

```
# parstatus –P
[Partition]
Par              # of      # of I/O
Num Status       Cells     Chassis    Core cell     Partition Name (first 30 chars)
===  =====       ====      ======     =======       ========================
 0   active       1          1        cab0,cell0    prod_npar
 1   active       2          2        cab0,cell1    test_npar
```

To add a cell to an inactive nPar, you have two options. If you wish to boot up the nPar and activate it after the modification is done, use the *parmodify* command as above. Do not specify –B option if you do not wish to boot and activate the nPar.

8.4.5   Removing a Cell from an nPar

To remove an active cell from an active nPar, use –d option with *parmodify* and specify the cell number (cell 2 in this case). You must reboot the nPar for reconfig (–R option with *shutdown*) for the changes to take effect.

```
# parmodify –p1 –d2 –B
command succeded
# shutdown –Ry now
```

To remove an inactive cell from an active or inactive nPar, use –d option and specify the cell number to delete. No need to specify –B option and no need to reboot.

```
# parmodify –p1 –d2
```

8.4.6   Removing an nPar

To remove an active nPar, run *parremove* from the nPar you wish to delete and supply –F option. This operation unassigns all cells from the nPar and destroys its partition definition. You must then shutdown and halt the nPar for the changes to take effect.

```
# parremove –Fp1
Use "shutdown -R -H" to shutdown the partition.
The partition deletion will be effective only after the shutdown.
# shutdown –RH now
```

To remove an inactive nPar, run *parremove,* as above, from an active nPar and specify the partition number of the nPar you wish to delete. No need to use –F option and no need to shutdown the inactive/deleted partition since it is already down.

8.4.7   Using Partition Manager GUI

The *Partition Manager* software is loaded as part of the HP-UX 11i OE installation on supported servers. You can run it either in graphical or textual mode via SAM as follows:

☞ Go to SAM → Partition Manager.

You can run it in graphical mode using a browser or *parmgr* command as well. The browser interface requires that you have Apache web server setup, and up and running.

To start partition manager using the browser interface, set the variable WEBADMIN to 1 in the */etc/rc.config.d/webadmin* file and execute associated startup script.

```
# vi /etc/rc.config.d/webadmin
WEBADMIN=1
# /sbin/init.d/webadmin  start
/usr/obam/server/bin/apachectl start: httpd started
```

The default port number is 1188. If the system or nPar name is *hp10*, for instance, you would type the following URL in the browser to run it:

http://hp10:1188/parmgr

The *parmgr* command enables you to run partition manager from the command prompt. Figure 8-2 exhibits partition manager GUI.

```
# /opt/parmgr/bin/parmgr
```

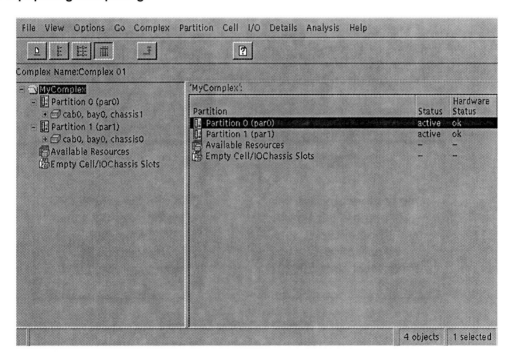

Figure 8-2 Node Partition Manager GUI

From the two graphical interfaces you can create, view, modify, and remove nPars, among other nPar administrative activities.

8.5   Virtual Partitioning

Virtual partitioning is a software partitioning technique used to divide a server or an nPar into several virtual, smaller computers called *Virtual Partitions* (vPars). Each vPar can then be used as a separate, independent, standalone server running HP-UX OE instance with its own processor(s), memory, and I/O slot(s). The number of vPars that can be created in a server or an nPar is equal to the number of processors you have in the server or nPar. In other words, each vPar requires at least one processor to be created. The minimum number of vPars that can be defined in a server complex is 2 and the maximum in the largest server complex is 128. Figure 8-3 exhibits a server/nPar running two applications. This server/nPar is divided into two vPars, each with different patch level and running different applications.

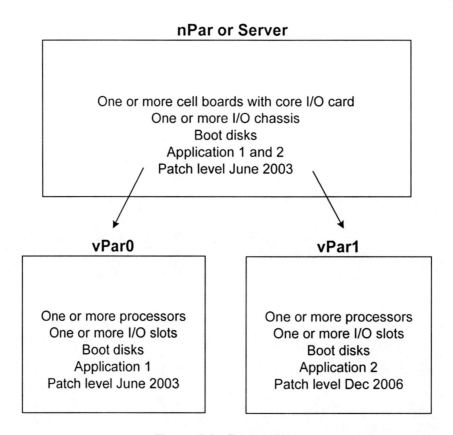

Figure 8-3 vPar Logical

When vPars are created, a software piece called *vpmon* is enabled, which sits between the server firmware and HP-UX OE instances running in vPars. When a vPar boots up, vpmon looks into the vPar database, */stand/vpdb*, and loads the OE in the vPar. It uses the boot disks defined for the vPar and assigns the hardware components configured for it.

In the following sub-sections, vPar administration tasks, such as creating a vPar, adding a processor to a vPar, removing a processor from a vPar, adding an I/O path to a vPar, removing an I/O path from a vPar, adding memory to a vPar, resetting a vPar, and removing a vPar, are explained. You can issue commands to carry out these operations from any of the vPars within the server complex. Alternatively, you can use the GUI software called *Virtual Partition Manager* to accomplish these tasks.

Some of the more common vPar administration commands you are going to be interacting with are given in Table 8-3.

vPar Command	Description
vparboot	Boots a vPar.
vparcreate	Creates a vPar.
vparmodify	Modifies a vPar including adding and removing processors, I/O paths, memory, and so on.
vparremove	Removes a vPar.
vparreset	Resets a vPar.
vparstatus	Displays status information of one or more vPars.

Table 8-3 vPar Administration Commands

You can create vPars on either a supported server (not already node-partitioned) or in an nPar. Make sure that you have VPARMGR and T1335AC software installed. Issue the *swlist* command as follows to check whether or not the two software components are loaded:

```
# swlist | grep  VPARMGR
VPARMGR            B.11.11.01.02     Virtual Partition Manager - HP-UX
# swlist | grep  T1335AC
T1335AC            A.02.02.00        HP-UX Virtual Partitions
```

Install them using the *swinstall* command if they are not already loaded. Consult Chapter 10 "Software Management" on how to install software.

8.5.1   Bound and Unbound Processors

When working with vPars, you can assign processors as either *bound* or *unbound*.

A processor assigned to a vPar to handle both normal processing as well as I/O interrupts is referred to as a bound processor. Every vPar must be assigned at least one bound processor. A processor should be allocated as a bound processor to a vPar if the vPar runs applications which require both processor and I/O horsepower. A processor can be added online to a vPar as a bound processor, however, a bound processor cannot be removed online from a vPar.

An *unbound* processor, on the contrary, is either not assigned to a vPar, or assigned, but does not handle the vPar's I/O interrupts. A processor should be allocated as an unbound processor to a vPar if the application running in the vPar is processor-intensive but not I/O-intensive. An unbound processor can be added to or removed from a vPar online.

8.5.2   Creating the First vPar

To understand vPar operations, let us assume that an nPar, containing 2 cell boards with 8 processors, 16GB of memory, and 2 I/O chassis, is available in the RP8400. The hardware addresses of the processors are 41, 45, 101, 109, 141, 145, 201, and 209. Use the *vparcreate* command to create a vPar called *test_vpar0* with 1 processor bound to it and 1 unbound. Set the minimum and maximum limit on the number of processors this vpar can get to 1 and 2, respectively. Allocate 8GB of memory and define hardware I/O paths 1/0/0/2 and 1/0/0/3. Use 1/0/0/2/0.6.0 as primary boot disk. With –B option, specify that the vPar, at each reboot, is going to search automatically for the bootable devices and boot from the one it finds first. When the following is executed, all the configuration information gets stored in the vPar database located in */stand/vpdb* file. If this file does not exist, it will be created.

> # **vparcreate –p test_vpar0 –a cpu::2 –a cpu:::1:2 –a cpu:41 –a mem::8192 –a \\
> io:1/0/0/2 –a io:1/0/0/3 –a io:1/0/0/2/0.6.0:BOOT –B search –B auto**

The options used with *vparcreate* are explained below:

> –p → vPar name.
> –a cpu::2 → number of processors to be allocated.
> –a cpu:::1:2 → minimum and maximum limits on processor allocation.
> –a cpu:41 → hardware address of the processor to be bound. If not explicitly defined, the processor will be assigned as unbound.
> –a mem::8192 → amount of memory, in MBs, to be allocated.
> –a 1/0/0/2 → all devices physically located on the path will become available to this vPar.
> –a 1/0/0/2/0.6.0:BOOT → primary boot path.
> –B search → automatic search for the boot device at boot time is enabled.
> –B auto → autoboot is enabled.

The last three functions can also be performed using the *setboot* command, the *vparmodify* command, or commands at the BCH or EFI menu. Detailed discussion on BCH and EFI is covered in Chapter 17 "Shutting Down and Starting Up an HP-UX System".

Modify the AUTO file on the primary boot path (*/dev/rdsk/c0t6d0* in our case) on the server or nPar in which you created the vPar. Use the *mkboot* command. This is done to make the system aware that vPars are implemented and make sure that the system loads vpmon first at next system reboot before it starts loading the HP-UX kernel.

On HP 9000 servers, do the following:

> # **mkboot –a "hpux /stand/vpmon –a" /dev/rdsk/c0t6d0**

On HP Integrify servers, do the following:

> # **mkboot –a "boot vpmon –a" /dev/rdsk/c0t6d0**

This creates a vPar within the nPar with 2 out of 8 processors and 8GB out of 16GB memory allocated to it. Now each time you reboot this nPar, it will come up as a vPar.

To manually boot *test_vpar0*, go to the nPar console, press *ctrl+a* to get the *Virtual Console* monitor MON> prompt, and run the *vparload* command as follows:

> MON> **vparload –p test_vpar0**

Alternatively, you can boot the vPar from ISL prompt (in case of HP 9000 server):

HP Certified Systems Administrator

ISL> **hpux /stand/vpmon vparload –p test_vpar0**

Once *test_vpar0* is up and functional, run *vparstatus* to view status information.

```
# vparstatus
[Virtual Partition]
                                              Boot
Virtual Partition Name  State   Attributes  Kernel Path    Opts
======================  =====   =======     ===========    ====
test_vpar0              Up      Dyn,Auto    /stand/vmunix

[Virtual Partition Resource Summary]
                                CPU       Num      Memory (MB)
                        CPU     Bound/    IO       # Ranges/
Virtual Partition Name  Min/Max Unbound  devs   Total MB  Total MB
======================  ======= =======  ====   ================
test_vpar0              1/  2   1   1    8       0/   0    8192
```

Under Attributes column, two values – Dyn and Auto – are shown. "Dyn" means dynamic hardware configuration changes are allowed for the vPar and "Auto" indicates that the vPar is auto-bootable.

Run *vparstatus* again to display the information in a different way.

```
# vparstatus –vp test_vpar0
[Virtual Partition Details]
Name:            test_vpar0
State:           Up
Attributes:      Dynamic,Autoboot
Kernel Path:     /stand/vmunix
Boot Opts:

[CPU Details]
Min/Max:         1/2
Bound by User [Path]:
Bound by Monitor [Path]:  41
Unbound [Path]:  45

[IO Details]
   1.0.0.2
   1.0.0.3
   1.0.0.2.0.6.0  BOOT

 [Memory Details]
Specified [Base  /Range]:
      (bytes) (MB)
Total Memory (MB):  8192
```

8.5.3   Creating Another vPar

At this point, you may wish to create another vPar using some or all available resources. Execute *vparcreate* command as follows from *test_vpar0* to create *test_vpar1*:

```
# vparcreate –p test_vpar1 –a cpu::2 –a cpu:::1:2 –a cpu:101 –a mem::8192 –a \
io:2.0.0.2 –a io:2.0.0.3 –a io:2/0/0/2/0.6.0:BOOT –a io:2/0/0/3/0.6.0:ALTBOOT \
–B search –B auto
```

This creates *test_vpar1* within the nPar. Note that this command sets up primary as well as alternate boot disk paths.

You now need to install HP-UX 11i OE in *test_vpar1*. Make sure that you include vPar software when you install the OE. Shutdown *test_vpar0*, go to the BCH prompt, and install HP-UX 11i OE on one of the boot disks assigned to *test_vpar1*. Use the DVD drive available to the nPar. When installation is complete, go to the virtual monitor prompt and boot *test_vpar0*.

```
MON> vparload –p test_vpar0
```

Log on to *test_vpar0* when it is up and execute the *mkboot* command to modify the AUTO file contents on *test_vpar1*'s boot disks.

```
# mkboot –a "hpux /stand/vpmon –a" /dev/rdsk/c2t6d0
# mkboot –a "hpux /stand/vpmon –a" /dev/rdsk/c3t6d0
```

Now run *vparboot* from *test_vpar0* to bring *test_vpar1* up.

```
# vparboot –p test_vpar1
```

When *test_vpar1* is up, use *vparstatus* to verify the configuration and hardware allocation.

8.5.4   Adding a CPU to a vPar

The *test_vpar0* vPar currently has 1 bound (hw path 41) and 1 unbound (hw path 45) processors. In order to add a bound processor, you need to first increase the maximum processor allocation limit to at least 3 from current 2, and then add the processor. This operation requires that *test_vpar0* is down. Do the following on *test_vpar0*:

```
# shutdown –hy now
```

Log on to *test_vpar1* and execute the *vparmodify* command as follows. The first command increases the maximum limit to 3, the second adds the processor at hw path 101 as bound, and the third boots up *test_vpar0*.

```
# vparmodify –p test_vpar0 –m cpu:::1:3
# vparmodify –p test_vpar0 –a cpu:141
# vparboot –p test_vpar0
```

When *test_vpar0* is back up, run *vparstatus* with –vp options to verify the modifications.

To add a processor as unbound, you do not need to shutdown *test_vpar0*. First, increase the processor limit to 4 (since you now have 3 processors assigned) and then add a processor. When the hardware path of a processor is not explicitly defined, *vparmodify* adds the processor as unbound.

```
# vparmodify  –p  test_vpar0  –m  cpu:::1:4
```

Now add a processor. Do either of the following two. Both produces the same result. The first command increases the total count of processors to 4 (from current 3) and the second simply adds one processor.

```
# vparmodify  –p  test_vpar0  –m  cpu::4
# vparmodify  –p  test_vpar0  –a  cpu::1
```

8.5.5   Removing a Processor from a vPar

At this point, you have four processors assigned to *test_vpar0* (2 bound and 2 unbound). To remove the bound processor (141) from *test_vpar0*, shut it down.

```
# shutdown  –hy  now
```

Run *vparmodify* on *test_vpar1* and specify the affected vPar name with –p option. Use –d to furnish the hardware path of the bound processor to be removed.

```
# vparmodify  –p  test_vpar0  –d  cpu:141
# vparboot  –p  test_vpar0
```

To remove an unbound processor, do one of the following on *test_vpar0*:

```
# vparmodify  –p  test_vpar0  –m  cpu::2
# vparmodify  –p  test_vpar0  –d  cpu::1
```

This reduces the total number of processors in *test_vpar0* from current 3 to 2. No need to shutdown.

Check the results using *vparstatus* with –vp options.

8.5.6   Adding an I/O Path to a vPar

To add an I/O path to *test_vpar0*, shut it down, and execute the following on *test_vpar1*. When done, boot *test_vpar0* from *test_vpar1*. Check the results using *vparstatus* with –vp options.

```
# vparmodify  –p  test_vpar0  –a  io:3.0.0.3
# vparboot  –p  test_vpar0
```

8.5.7   Removing an I/O Path from a vPar

To remove an allocated I/O path from *test_vpar0*, shut it down and execute the following on *test_vpar1*. When done, boot it up from *test_vpar1*. Verify the results using *vparstatus* with –vp options.

```
# vparmodify  –p  test_vpar0  –d  io:3.0.0.3
# vparboot  –p  test_vpar0
```

8.5.8   Adding Memory to a vPar

To allocate additional 4GB of memory to *test_vpar0*, shut it down and execute the following on *test_vpar1*. When done, boot it up from *test_vpar1*. Check the results using *vparstatus* with –vp options.

```
# vparmodify –p test_vpar0 –a mem::4096
# vparboot –p test_vpar0
```

8.5.9   Resetting a vPar

A hung vPar can be reset from another running vPar. Use the *vparreset* command on *test_vpar1* to reset *test_vpar0* (assuming it is hung).

```
# vparreset –p test_vpar0
```

8.5.10   Removing a vPar

A vPar can be removed from another running vPar. All resources allocated to it becomes free. Use the *vparremove* command to remove *test_vpar0*. Run the command on *test_vpar1*.

```
# vparremove –p test_vpar0
```

8.5.11   Rebooting vpmon

Sometimes it becomes necessary to stop and restart vpmon to perform maintenance tasks on the server or nPar that houses vPars. Follow the steps below to reboot vpmon.

1. Shut down all vPars. Go to the MON> prompt and verify. You should see the following:

    ```
    MON> test_vpar0 has halted.
    MON> test_vpar1 has halted.
    ```

2. Power off the server or nPar (if necessary).
3. Perform the maintenance task.
4. Power on the server or nPar (if necessary).
5. Interact with BCH or EFI as appropriate.
6. Execute the *bo* command from the BCH prompt. On Integrity servers, perform the boot via EFI Boot Manager. See Chapter 17 "Shutting Down and Starting Up an HP-UX System" for details.

    Main Menu: Enter command or menu > **bo**

7. Interact with ISL and type the following:

    ISL> **hpux /stand/vpmon**

8. Press *ctrl+a* to go to MON> prompt and execute the following to boot all vPars:

    MON> **vparload –all**

HP Certified Systems Administrator

8.5.12 Using Virtual Partition Manager GUI

Virtual Partition Manager GUI allows you to create, view, modify, reset, and remove vPars, among other vPar administration functions. To start the GUI, run the *vparmgr* command as follows. Figure 8-4 displays the main screen.

/opt/parmgr/bin/vparmgr

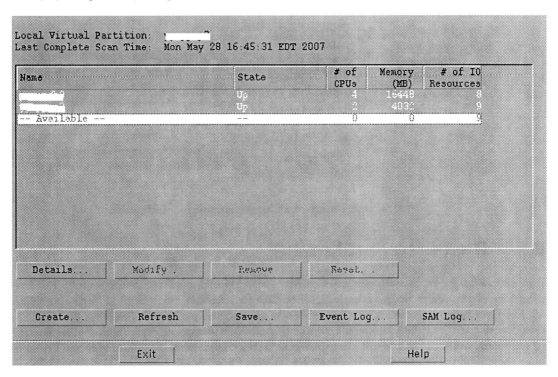

Figure 8-4 Virtual Partition Manager GUI

8.6 Integrity Virtual Machines Partitioning

Integrity Virtual Machines (Integrity VM) is a software product designed to work on HP Integrity servers and nPars. With this software product, you can divide a server or an nPar running HP-UX 11iv2 or HP-UX 11iv3 OE into hundreds of *Virtual Machines* (VM) that run on top of the underlying HP-UX OE. Each virtual machine can be configured to run its own fully loaded, operational *Guest* operating system instance, such as HP-UX 11iv2, HP-UX 11iv3, MS Windows 2003, or Linux, in an isolated environment. Application failures on one virtual machine do not affect other virtual machines.

Integrity VM virtualizes physical resources – processor, memory, and I/O devices – and allows you to allocate these resources as virtual resources to virtual machines dynamically and on as-needed basis. Users logged on to virtual machines get the feeling as if they are on separate, dedicated, physical systems. Virtual machines can be created using either command line or GUI, and can be managed centrally from one VM console.

Integrity VM is similar to VMWare software, which provides comparable functionality on top of MS Windows based Intel x86 architecture computers.

Table 8-4 lists and describes some key commands pertaining to virtual machines.

Command	Description
hpvmclone	Clones virtual machines.
hpvmcollect	Collects virtual machines statistics.
hpvmcreate	Creates virtual machines.
hpvminfo	Displays information about virtual machines host.
hpvmmodify	Modifies virtual machines.
hpvmnet	Creates and modifies virtual networks.
hpvmremove	Removes virtual machines.
hpvmresources	Stipulates storage and network devices used by VMs.
hpvmstart	Starts virtual machines.
hpvmstatus	Displays guest status information.
hpvmstop	Stops virtual machines.

Table 8-4 Integrity VM Administration Commands

8.7   Resource Partitioning

Resource Partitioning technique is intended for resource and workload management on servers, nPars, or vPars, which typically run several applications concurrently. Each of these applications may require varying amount of hardware resources, such as processor, memory, and disk I/O, to operate well. Unlike nPars and vPars, resource partitions are not independent, standalone servers or partitions, rather, they work at the process and application level and allow you to allocate to applications resources they need. This way applications are guaranteed to have dedicated resources available to them at all times.

Resource partitioning can be implemented using two software products called *Process Resource Manager* (PRM) and *WorkLoad Manager* (WLM).

PRM is a manual resource management tool. With this tool, groups, called *PRM Groups*, are created and processes and users are assigned to them. Required reources are then allocated to these groups. Two benefits are achieved with this approach. One, processes are guaranteed dedicated resources, and two, no processes or users that are part of the PRM group can use system resources other than what they are assigned. PRM can be configured using either commands or HP system management homepage.

WLM, on the other hand, is an automatic resource management tool used to monitor resources periodically and adjusts them automatically to keep up with changing application needs. With this tool, groups, called *Workload Groups*, are created and applications and user processes are assigned to them. Required resources are then allocated to these groups. This product is useful in an environment where system load, resource utilization, or resource needs, change frequently and automatic adjustments are necessary. WLM can be configured using commands, configuration wizard, or GUI.

Summary

In this chapter, you learned about various partitioning options available in HP-UX operating environment software. You learned their concepts. You performed tasks to create and manage node and virtual partitions. You studied management processor concepts and how to access it, locally and remotely, and use it. You saw how a dumb console terminal could be setup to display correct text and menus.

Finally, you were presented with a brief introduction on Integrity virtual machines and resource partitioning techniques.

## 09

HP-UX Operating Environment Installation

This chapter covers the following major topics:

- ✓ Types of HP-UX Operating Environment software bundles
- ✓ Plan HP-UX installation
- ✓ HP-UX installation using local DVD drive
- ✓ System configuration using the set_parms command

9.1   HP-UX Installation

In the first six chapters, you read basics of HP-UX. The next two chapters followed gave you enough understanding of HP-UX system administration, HP hardware, and partitioning techniques. I am positive that you would have spent enough time practising the material read.

This chapter explains how to perform a fresh installation of HP-UX operating environment software on a server or partition. A server or partition that already has the HP-UX system software installed but an older version may be upgraded to a higher version. The upgrade gives you an opportunity to preserve any or all information that the OS disk already contain. An operating system is like the soul in a body (computer hardware), without which the computer hardware cannot operate.

The HP-UX installation procedure requires that you plan ahead of time as to what configuration you need on your server or partition. Configuration items, such as what disk you want the operating environment software to be loaded on, disk management software to be used, types and sizes of file systems, locale information, and so on, need to be identified before starting the OE load.

9.1.1   Types of HP-UX OE Software

The HP-UX Operating Environment software runs on HP 9000 and HP Integrity server families. Currently, the latest version of HP-UX OE is 11.31 and is commonly known as HP-UX 11iv3. Also available are HP-UX OE 11.23 (11iv2) and HP-UX OE 11.11 (11iv1). HP 9000 server family supports all three versions, whereas HP Integrity server family supports 11iv2 and 11iv3 only. One good thing to note is that the later versions are backward compatible.

The three OEs are available in five bundles of which three are more popular. The three bundles are *Foundation Operating Environment* (FOE), *Enterprise Operating Environment* (EOE), and *Mission-Critical Operating Environment* (MCOE). Depending on what the business and application needs are, you can decide which OE bundle to go for. Table 9-1 lists which OE includes what components. For latest and more accurate information, visit *www.hp.com*.

Component	FOE	EOE	MCOE
Core HP-UX Operating System including Networking, CDE, SD-UX, LVM, PERL, NFS, Online Diagnostics, etc.	Yes	Yes	Yes
Ignite-UX	Yes	Yes	Yes
Host Intrusion Detection System	Yes	Yes	Yes
Java RTE, JDK, JPI, and OOB Tuning Tools	Yes	Yes	Yes
CIFS Client & Server	Yes	Yes	Yes
IP Filter	Yes	Yes	Yes
OpenSSL	Yes	Yes	Yes
Secure Shell	Yes	Yes	Yes
LDAP-UX Integration	Yes	Yes	Yes
Base Veritas File System and Volume Manager	Yes	Yes	Yes
Pluggable Authentication Module (PAM) Kerberos	Yes	Yes	Yes
Netscape Directory Server	Yes	Yes	Yes
Red Hat Directory Server	Yes	Yes	Yes
Mozilla Web Browser	Yes	Yes	Yes
HP-UX Web Server Suite	Yes	Yes	Yes

Internet Express	Yes	Yes	Yes
EMS Framework	Yes	Yes	Yes
Software Package Builder	Yes	Yes	Yes
Partitioning Providers and Management Tools	Yes	Yes	Yes
Trial gWLM Agent	Yes	Yes	Yes
System Insight Manager	Yes	Yes	Yes
System Management Homepage – Web-Based System Management Tool	Yes	Yes	Yes
iCAP and PPU Enablement	Yes	Yes	Yes
Install Time Security (11iv2 and 11iv3)	Yes	Yes	Yes
Security Patch Check (11iv2 and 11iv3)	Yes	Yes	Yes
Bastille (11iv2 and 11iv3)	Yes	Yes	Yes
Distributed Systems Administration Utilities (11iv2 and 11iv3)	Yes	Yes	Yes
IPSec (11iv3)	Yes	Yes	Yes
PCI OL* (11iv3)	Yes	Yes	Yes
Native MultiPathing (11iv3)	Yes	Yes	Yes
Online JFS	-	Yes	Yes
MirrorDisk/UX	-	Yes	Yes
Process Resource Manager (PRM)	-	Yes	Yes
GlancePlus Pak	-	Yes	Yes
Event Monitoring Services (EMS)	-	Yes	Yes
HA Monitors	-	Yes	Yes
ServiceGuard	-	-	Yes
ServiceGuard NFS and Enterprise Cluster Master (ECM) Toolkits	-	-	Yes
ServiceGuard Provider and Cluster Object Manager (11iv3)	-	-	Yes
WorkLoad Manager (WLM) and WLM Toolkit	-	-	Yes

Table 9-1 HP-UX Operating Environment Software Bundles

Beginning version 11.11, HP-UX is made available as OE bundles. Previous versions 11.0 and earlier were referred to as operating systems. Operating environment includes operating system as the core product, which acts as the most essential and critical component. Operating system comprises of core HP-UX functionality while an operating environment includes additional components and functionalities, such as Online JFS, MirrorDisk/UX, GlancePlus, ServiceGuard, and so on. These components were separately purchasable with 11.0 and earlier versions.

The other two OE bundles – *Minimum Technical Operating Environment* (MTOE) and *Technical Computing Operating Environment* (TCOE) – are designed to run specialized software applications for engineering, architectural, and technical use. Most features available in EOE are included in them in addition to graphics and advanced math functions.

9.1.2   Planning Installation

Installation of HP-UX 11i OE on a server or partition requires that you have, at the minimum, the following information handy. You will need this information during the OE load to define system configuration.

- ✓ Type of OE to load (FOE, EOE, MCOE, MTOE, or TCOE)
- ✓ What hard disk to use if there are more than one
- ✓ Amount of primary swap space
- ✓ Disk management approach (whole disk, LVM, or VxVM)
- ✓ Sizes of file systems
- ✓ Type of file systems (HFS or VxFS)
- ✓ Size and location of dump device (default is the swap space)
- ✓ Hostname (unique 8 character alphanumeric string used to identify the server or partition)
- ✓ IP address (unique 32-bit or 128-bit address)
- ✓ Subnet mask
- ✓ Root password
- ✓ Date/Time
- ✓ Time Zone
- ✓ Language
- ✓ Keyboard type
- ✓ Any additional software to load

9.1.3   Installing HP-UX Using Local Media

Let us perform an installation of HP-UX 11i OE using local DVD drive. The install procedure on HP 9000 servers and nPars is same. Likewise, the install procedure on HP Integrity architecture servers and nPars is same.

Here is the sequence of steps you will need to follow to install HP-UX on an HP 9000 server. There are a few differences in the way you install HP-UX on the two hardware platforms. The differences are highlighted. Let's get started.

1. Power the server on. In case of an nPar just created, log on to MP and go into command mode. Execute the *pe* command to power the nPar on.
2. Insert the HP-UX 11i DVD into the drive.
3. This step is specific to HP 9000 servers and nPars. After the power-on self-test on the hardware is finished executing, you will be given 10 seconds within which you need to press any key to stop the autoboot process and interact with *Boot Console Handler* (BCH) menu. BCH is explained in Chapter 17 "Shutting Down and Starting Up an HP-UX System".

Processor is booting from first available device.

To discontinue, press any key within 10 seconds.

Boot terminated.

------ Main Menu ---

Command	Description
--------------	---------------
BOot [PRI|ALT|<path>]	Boot from specified path
PAth [PRI|ALT|CON|KEY] [<path>]	Display or modify a path
SEArch [DIsplay|IPL] [<path>]	Search for boot devices

```
COnfiguration [<command>]                Access Configuration menu/commands
INformation [<command>]                  Access Information menu/commands
SERvice [<command>]                      Access Service menu/commands

DIsplay                                  Redisplay the current menu
HElp [<menu>|<command>]                  Display help for menu or command
RESET                                    Restart the system
-------
Main Menu: Enter command >
```

To proceed with installation on HP 9000 server or nPar, jump to step 5.

4. This step is specific to Integrity servers and nPars. Stop the autoboot process by pressing any key within 10 seconds. Select *EFI Shell.* EFI stands for *Extensible Firmware Interface* and is equivalent to BCH on HP 9000 servers. From the *EFI Shell*, issue the **map** command to list all available devices. Select the device name that points to the DVD drive, such as *Shell> fs1:*, and hit the *Enter* key to get to the *fs1:\>* prompt. At this prompt, type **install** and press the *Enter* key.

5. Search for bootable devices by running *search* or *sea* at the BCH main menu prompt.

```
Main Menu: Enter command > sea
Searching for potential boot device(s)...
This may take several minutes.
To discontinue search, press any key (termination may not be immediate).

Path Number   Device Path (dec)        Device Type
-------------- -----------------------  ----------------
PO            8/8.4                     Random access media
P1            8/8.12                    Random access media
P2            8/12.0                    Random access media
P3            8/12.4                    Random access media
P4            8/12.12                   Random access media
P5            8/16/5.2                  Random access media
P6            8/16/5.0                  Sequential access media
P7            8/16/6.0                  LAN Module

Main Menu: Enter command >
```

6. Boot from the DVD using the listed path number. In your case here, the path is p5. Alternatively, you can specify the device path with the *boot* command. The commands at this level can be abbreviated, such as for *boot,* you can use *bo*. At the next prompt *Interact with IPL*, say *n*.

```
Main Menu: Enter command > bo  p5
Interact with IPL (Y, N, or Cancel)?> n

Booting...
Boot IO Dependent Code (IODC) revision 1
```

HARD Booted.

ISL Revision A.00.43 Apr 12, 2000

ISL booting hpux (;0):INSTALL

Boot
: disk(8/16/5.2.0.0.0.0.0;0):INSTALL
8541668 + 1052672 + 707072 start 0x14ebe8
. . . .
. . . .

From this point on, installation procedure is same on both HP 9000 and HP Integrity servers/nPars.

7. Select *Install HP-UX* and press the *Enter* key at the initial welcome screen as demonstrated
    in Figure 9-1. This screen also displays hardware inventory of the server or nPar. It displays
    total number of hard disk drives, CD/DVDs, tape devices, LAN cards, memory, number of
    CPUs, etc.

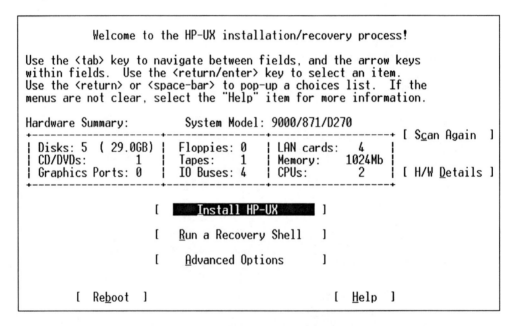

Figure 9-1 HP-UX Installation – Welcome Screen

8. Next, the system displays *User Interface and Media Options* window, as shown in Figure 9-2.
    Select *Media Only Installation* under *Source Location Options* to install from the CD/DVD.
    Under *User Interface Options* choose *Advanced Installation*. This option enables you to
    customize the installation. The *Guided Installation* option provides limited choices and the *No
    User Interface* choice takes all system defaults, which we do not want. Use the *tab* key to
    navigate and the *spacebar* key to select an option. Select OK and hit the *Enter* key, when
    done.

```
┌─────────────────────────────────────────────────────────────────────┐
│                  ▐User Interface and Media Options▌                   │
│                                                                       │
│   This screen lets you pick from options that will determine if an    │
│   Ignite-UX server is used, and your user interface preference.       │
│                                                                       │
│   Source Location Options:                                            │
│      [ * ]  Media only installation                                   │
│      [   ]  Media with Network enabled (allows use of SD depots)      │
│      [   ]  Ignite-UX server based installation                       │
│                                                                       │
│   User Interface Options:                                             │
│      [   ]  Guided Installation   (recommended for basic installs)    │
│      [ * ]  Advanced Installation (recommended for disk and filesystem management) │
│      [   ]  No user interface - use all the defaults and go           │
│                                                                       │
│                                                                       │
│   Hint: If you need to make LVM size changes, or want to set the      │
│         final networking parameters during the install, you will      │
│         need to use the Advanced mode (or remote graphical interface).│
│                                                                       │
│                                                                       │
│   [   ▐OK▌   ]              [ Cancel ]                  [  Help  ]     │
└─────────────────────────────────────────────────────────────────────┘
```

Figure 9-2 HP-UX Installation – User Interface and Media Options

9. Next appears the screen shown in Figure 9-3, which provides you with an opportunity to customize the installation. There are five sub-screens at this level: Basic, Software, System, File System, and Advanced. Use the *tab* key on the keyboard to navigate.

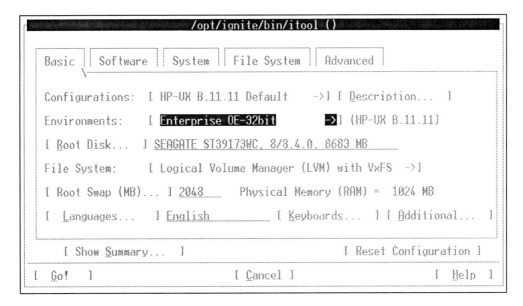

Figure 9-3 HP-UX Installation – Basic Configuration

10. On the "Basic" sub-screen, you hang on to *HP-UX B.11.11 Default* Configurations choice. Next, choose an appropriate HP-UX 11i OE that you wish to install. If you have inserted the

MCOE media, the choices here would include Foundation, Enterprise, and Mission-Critical. Further down, you will see the disk that the installation process has picked up, by default, to install the OE on. This default disk is chosen based on the hardware scan performed in step 7. If you wish to use this disk, then go to next selection "File System", otherwise highlight *Root Disk* and press *Enter* to select an alternate disk, if available, from the list. The *File System* option allows you to select the disk management and file system type that you want to have on the system. You are provided with three choices, use the one that says *Logical Volume Manager (LVM) with VxFS*. This combination is more commonly used on HP-UX (*Veritas Volume Manager with VxFS* is also available now with EOE and MCOE). The "Basic" sub-screen also shows amount of physical memory available on the server or assigned to nPar, and the swap space. The swap space is, by default, twice the size of physical memory, which the installation procedure picks up by itself. A detailed discussion on swap is given in Chapter 16 "Managing Swap Space". The *Language*, *Keyboard*, and *Additional* options are left to default values for English language and US keyboard layout. See Figure 9-3.

11. On the next sub-screen "Software", select and include any additional software product, such as Ignite-UX that you wish to load as part of the OE install.

12. Now move on to the third sub-screen "System", which looks similar to the one shown in Figure 9-4.

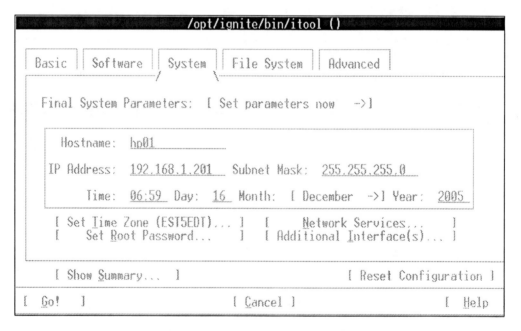

Figure 9-4 HP-UX Installation – System Configuration

Choose *Set parameters now* for "Final System Parameters" option. Then type in hostname, IP address, and subnet mask for this server or nPar. The date/time is usually shown correctly, otherwise, you can modify it. You need to go in to *Set Time Zone* and choose an appropriate time zone. For example, EST5EDT is US/Canada Eastern Time zone. Next, go to *Set Root Password* and type in a password for the *root* user account. Skip *Network Services* and *Additional Interface(s)* options.

If you do not wish to perform step 12 at this point, you can choose "Set parameters later" for "Final System Parameters" option. This will force execute the *set_parms* command when you boot the server or nPar the first time after it has been installed. The *set_parms* command is explained later in this chapter.

13. Next, go to the "File System" sub-screen using the *tab* key. The screen looks similar to the one shown below in Figure 9-5.

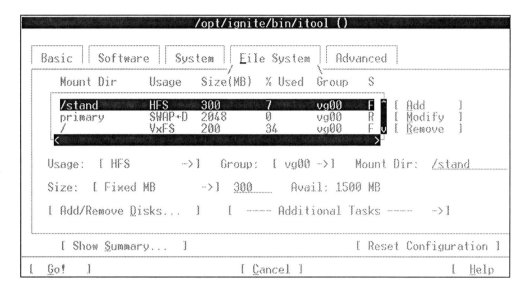

Figure 9-5 HP-UX Installation – File System Configuration

On this sub-screen you can add or remove file systems and modify their properties. Specify file system parameters as per your requirements. You may use sample file system properties given in Table 9-2 on a 9GB hard drive. Use large sizes on bigger disk drives. Use the *tab* key to move around. Leave *Add/Remove Disks* and *Additional Tasks* to defaults.

File System	Usage (FS Type)	Group	Mount Dir	Size (Fixed MB)
/stand	HFS	vg00	/stand	300 MB
Primary swap	VxFS	vg00	N/A	2048 MB
/	VxFS	vg00	/	500 MB
/home	VxFS	vg00	/home	600 MB
/tmp	VxFS	vg00	/tmp	600 MB
/usr	VxFS	vg00	/usr	1500 MB
/var	VxFS	vg00	/var	1500 MB
/opt	VxFS	vg00	/opt	1500 MB

Table 9-2 Sample HP-UX File System Properties

14. Leave to defaults selections on the next sub-screen "Advanced". This sub-screen allows you to specify any pre-install or post-install script, or both, to run before and/or after the install process.

15. Next, tab to "Show Summary" option and hit *Enter* to view a summary of how your system will be configured based on the choices you have made. Verify your selections and hit the OK button. You will see the message on your screen similar to the one shown in Figure 9-6.

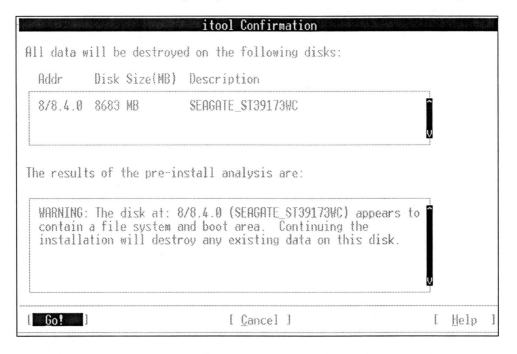

Figure 9-6 HP-UX Installation – Warning Before Destroying Disk Contents

16. Highlight the Go! button and press *Enter* to continue the install. The install process will not prompt you for any further information. Within an hour or so, depending on the system speed, you will see a login prompt on the system console. You should also be able to log in to the system over the network using the *telnet* or *ssh* command.
17. Eject the DVD. You are done with the installation.

9.2   Using *set_parms*

As mentioned in the note in step 12 of the installation process in the previous section, if *Set Parameters Later* under *Final System Parameters* option was chosen, the system would run the *set_parms* command with the argument "initial" during the first system boot up. It would display the following:

Welcome to HP-UX!

Before using your system, you will need to answer a few questions.

The first question is whether you plan to use this system on a network.

Answer "yes" if you have connected the system to a network and are ready to link with a network.

HP Certified Systems Administrator

Answer "no" if you:

* Plan to set up this system as a standalone (no networking).
* Want to use the system now as a standalone and connect to a network later.

Are you ready to link this system to a network?

Press [y] for yes or [n] for no, then press [Enter]

You would follow steps to configure system parameters given below. You would enter a y for yes and an n for no, as appropriate, when a question was asked.

✓ Hostname.
✓ Physical location of the system, such as option 1 for North America.
✓ Time zone for the location, such as option 3 for "Eastern Standard/Daylight" time zone.
✓ System date and time.
✓ IP address.
✓ Subnet mask and gateway IP address.
✓ DNS domain name and DNS server name or IP address for DNS client setup, if appropriate.
✓ NIS domain name and NIS server name or IP address for NIS client setup, if appropriate.

Summary

You got from this chapter enough knowledge to differentiate among various HP-UX Operating Environment software bundles that are more commonly used in the industry. You studied requirements to install HP-UX and learned how to perform an HP-UX Operating Environment software installation using a local installation media. Finally, you looked at the *set_parms* utility that allowed you to do initial system configuration.

HP Certified Systems Administrator

## 10

Software Management

This chapter covers the following major topics:

- ✓ Software Distributor concepts and components including Installed Product Database
- ✓ Software dependencies and protected software
- ✓ Administer software including listing, installing, verifying, and removing them
- ✓ Software depot concepts and components including catalog files
- ✓ Administer software depots including copying software to a depot, registering and unregistering depot software, listing depots, listing and verifying depot contents, removing depot software, and removing a depot

10.1 Software Distributor Concepts and Components

HP-UX provides a rich set of tools to administer software centrally in a multi-system HP-UX environment. This set of tools is called the *Software Distributor for HP-UX* (SD-UX). It enables you to install and manage software on local and remote HP-UX machines. When an HP-UX system is setup as an SD-UX server, its resources become available to be accessed by other HP-UX systems on the network.

SD-UX is a client/server functionality and only available in multi-user mode.

10.1.1 Software Structure

SD-UX commands work on software objects that make up applications or HP-UX OE software components. There are four such objects. Table 10-1 lists and describes them.

Object	Description
Fileset	A fileset contains files and control scripts that make up a product. A fileset can be part of a single product or included in other bundles or subproducts at the same time. A fileset is the lowest level of object managed by SD-UX.
Subproduct	A subproduct is a collection of filesets or other subproducts, or both, and control scripts.
Product	A product is a grouping of filesets in a logical fashion. A product is packaged and distributed for installation as a single entity. It can exist within a bundle or as a single, separate entity.
Bundle	A bundle consists of groups of filesets or products, or both, packaged together for a specific purpose. A bundle resides in a software depot and managed by SD-UX commands as a single entity.

Table 10-1 SD-UX Software Structure

10.1.2 Commands and Daemons

Several commands are included in SD-UX to perform various software management functions. All these commands have similar syntax and options. Table 10-2 provides a list of most of them along with a short description of each. The table also lists the log file name for each command.

Command	Description	Log File
swinstall	Installs or updates software. Runs in both GUI and TUI modes.	/var/adm/sw/swinstall.log
swlist	Lists installed software, software in a registered depot, or software on media. Runs in both GUI and TUI modes.	N/A
swcopy	Copies software from one depot to another. Runs in both GUI and TUI modes.	/var/adm/sw/swcopy.log
swremove	Removes installed software, software in a depot, or an entire depot. Runs in both GUI and TUI modes.	/var/adm/sw/swremove.log

swpackage	Creates software packages, which can then be used as a source for other SD-UX commands.	/var/adm/sw/swpackage.log
swconfig	Configures, reconfigures, or unconfigures software.	/var/adm/sw/swconfig.log
swverify	Verifies the integrity of installed software by comparing IPD information with the files actually installed. Also used to verify depot contents.	/var/adm/sw/swverify.log
swmodify	Modifies the IPD and catalog files that contain information about the software on the system or in depot.	/var/adm/sw/swmodify.log
swreg	Registers or unregisters a depot. Registering makes a depot manageable by SD-UX commands.	/var/adm/sw/swreg.log

Table 10-2 SD-UX Commands

Table 10-3 provides a list of the SD-UX daemons along with a short description of each.

Daemon	Description	Log File
swagentd	Server daemon used by *swagent*.	/var/adm/sw/swagentd.log
swagent	SD-UX agent that communicates with *swagentd*. Whenever an SD-UX command is executed, *swagent* is started, which then communicates with *swagentd* to get the task done.	/var/adm/sw/swagent.log

Table 10-3 SD-UX Daemons

Although *swagentd* gets started automatically when a system boots up to run level 2, you can manually stop, start, or restart it, if you need to.

To stop *swagentd*, do either of the following:

 # /usr/sbin/swagentd −k
 # /sbin/init.d/swagentd stop
The swagentd daemon is stopped.

To start *swagentd*, do the following:

 # /sbin/init.d/swagentd start

To restart a running *swagentd*, do the following:

 # swagentd −r

10.1.3   Installed Product Database

The *Installed Product Database* (IPD) is a set of files and sub-directories located under the */var/adm/sw/products* directory and contains detailed information on all software products currently installed on the system. This information includes software product name, description, readme file, copyright information, revision information, operating system name/release/version, hardware machine type, vendor information, software state, and part number. The IPD is maintained by the SD-UX utilities.

When install, configure, copy, and delete operations are performed on software using the *swinstall*, *swconfig*, *swcopy*, and *swremove* commands, respectively, the IPD is updated automatically. The *swlist* and *swverify* commands use IPD to list and verify installed software.

To control multiple simultaneous read/write access to software objects, a file called *swlock* in the */var/adm/sw/products* directory is created when the *swagent* client process is started. This file is created to prevent HP-UX to run more than one instance of the software agent to avoid any inconsistencies to occur in the IPD.

10.1.4   Software Dependencies

Software installation of a product requires certain files or products to be present, or available, in order for a successful installation of the software product. Similarly, many software products require certain files or products to be present in order for them to be able to run properly. This is called *Software Dependency* where a software depends on other software to install or run in a proper manner. When you use the *swconfig*, *swcopy*, *swinstall*, *swremove*, or *swverify* commands, they normally automatically select additional software to meet dependency requirements.

10.1.5   Protected Software

Some software products require that a codeword and customer ID be provided to be installed or copied. These software are known as *Protected Software*. This approach restricts the software to be installed to a specific customer environment only.

The *swinstall* and *swcopy* commands prompt to input codewords and customer ID when installing and copying a protected software.

10.2   Managing Software

This section talks about software management tasks including listing installed software, installing new software, verifying installed software, and removing installed software.

10.2.1   Listing Installed Software

Information about software installed on a machine is stored in the IPD. To see what software is installed, use the *swlist* command. This command reads the IPD and displays requested information.

To display all software bundles currently installed on a machine, run *swlist* without any arguments.

```
# swlist
# Initializing...
# Contacting target "hp01"...
#
# Target:  hp01:/
#
#
# Bundle(s):
#
```

BUNDLE11i	B.11.11.0102.2	Required Patch Bundle for HP-UX 11i, February 2001
Base-VXVM	B.03.20.1	Base VERITAS Volume Manager 3.2 for HP-UX
CDE-English	B.11.11	English CDE Environment
FDDI-00	B.11.11.02	PCI FDDI;Supptd HW=A3739A/A3739B;SW=J3626AA
FibrChanl-00	B.11.11.09	PCI/HSC FibreChannel;Supptd

HW=A6684A,A6685A,A5158A,A6795A

GigEther-00	B.11.11.14	PCI/HSC GigEther;Supptd

HW=A4926A/A4929A/A4924A/A4925A;SW=J1642AA

HPUX11i-OE-Ent	B.11.11.0203	HP-UX Enterprise Operating Environment Component
HPUXBase32	B.11.11	HP-UX 32-bit Base OS
HPUXBaseAux	B.11.11.0203	HP-UX Base OS Auxiliary
HWEnable11i	B.11.11.0203.5	Hardware Enablement Patches for HP-UX 11i, March 2002
OnlineDiag	B.11.11.06.09	HPUX 11.11 Support Tools Bundle, Mar 2002
perl	B.5.6.1.C	Perl Programming Language

To display all products currently installed on a machine, run *swlist* with –l option and specify product as an argument.

```
# swlist  –l  product
# Initializing...
# Contacting target "hp01"...
#
# Target:  hp01:/
#
```

Accounting	B.11.11	Accounting
ApacheStrong	1.3.19.23	HP Apache-based Web Server with Strong (128bit) Encryption
. . . .		
. . . .		
VUEtoCDE	B.11.11	HP VUE to CDE Migration Tools
X11	B.11.11	HP-UX X Window Software
Xserver	B.11.11	HP-UX X Server
. . . .		
. . . .		

To display all sub-products currently installed on a machine, run *swlist* with –l option and specify subproduct as an argument.

```
# swlist  –l  subproduct
# Initializing...
# Contacting target "hp01"...
#
# Target:  hp01:/
#

# 100BT-EISA-FMT            B.11.11.01      EISA 100BT/9000 formatter product.
  100BT-EISA-FMT.MinimumRuntime            Minimum Runtime Configuration  100BT-EISA-
FMT.Runtime      Runtime Configuration
# 100BT-EISA-KRN            B.11.11.01      EISA 100BT/9000 kernel products.
  100BT-EISA-KRN.MinimumRuntime            Minimum Runtime Configuration
  100BT-EISA-KRN.Runtime                   Runtime Configuration
# 100BT-EISA-RUN            B.11.11.01      EISA 100BT/9000 command products.
  100BT-EISA-RUN.MinimumRuntime            Minimum Runtime Configuration
  100BT-EISA-RUN.Runtime                   Runtime Configuration
  ATM2HSC                   K.11.11.30      HP-HSC ATM Physical Driver for ATM/9000 LINK
  ATM2PCI                   K.11.11.30      PCI ATM Physical Driver for ATM/9000 LINK
  . . . . . . . .
  . . . . . . .
```

To display all filesets installed on a system, run *swlist* with –l option and specify fileset as an argument.

```
# swlist  –l  fileset
# Initializing...
# Contacting target "hp01"...
#
# Target:  hp01:/
#
# 100BT-EISA-FMT                     B.11.11.01      EISA 100BT/9000 formatter product.
  100BT-EISA-FMT.100BT-FORMAT        B.11.11.01      EISA 100BT/9000 formatter library
# 100BT-EISA-KRN                     B.11.11.01      EISA 100BT/9000 kernel products.
  100BT-EISA-KRN.100BT-KRN           B.11.11.01      EISA 100BT/9000 kernel library
# 100BT-EISA-RUN                     B.11.11.01      EISA 100BT/9000 command products.
  100BT-EISA-RUN.100BT-INIT          B.11.11.01      EISA 100BT/9000 master file.
  100BT-EISA-RUN.100BT-RUN           B.11.11.01      EISA 100BT/9000 command libraries
  . . . . . . . .
  . . . . . . . .
```

To run *swlist* in GUI or TUI mode, use –i option. If DISPLAY environment variable is properly set, *swlist* will start in graphical mode, otherwise, it will come up in textual mode.

```
# swlist  –i
```

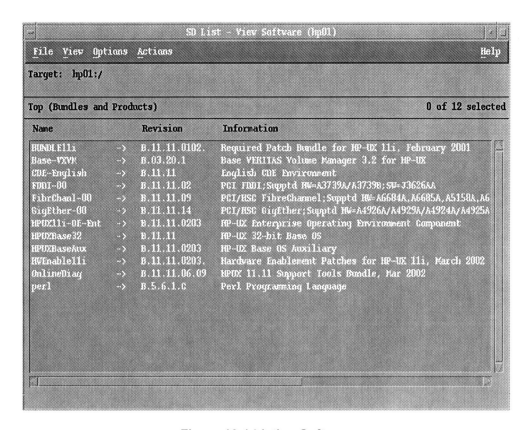

Figure 10-1 Listing Software

10.2.2   Installing Software

Software install is performed using the *swinstall* command, which can be run in either GUI or TUI mode depending on whether or not the DISPLAY environment variable is properly set. This command can also be run without getting into graphical or textual mode by supplying proper parameters at the command line.

The *swinstall* command requires the hostname and a full path to the location where the software to be installed resides. If codeword and customer ID are required, *swinstall* prompts you to enter that information. The command validates the input supplied and goes through various phases. It performs a number of checks, such as if the software is already installed, enough disk space is available, and dependencies are met, during these phases. If no errors are encountered, it displays a message and seeks your input to proceed, among other choices. It goes ahead and install the software when you press the OK button. The command generates messages as it proceeds and logs them. It updates and rebuilds the kernel, if required. When the installation is finished, a message is displayed on the screen. If the kernel is rebuilt, the server or partition reboots automatically, otherwise, you can simply exit out of the *swinstall* interface.

To start *swinstall* in GUI or TUI mode, run *swinstall*. A sample *swinstall* screen is shown in Figure 10-2.

---

swinstall

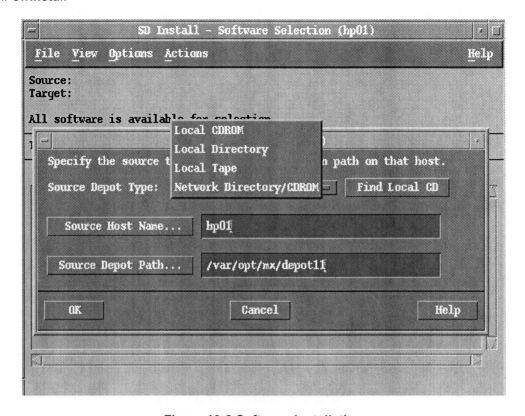

Figure 10-2 Software Installation

One of the main menu choices displayed is "Options". Choose "Change Options" from "Options". Modify any options if necessary before proceeding with software installation. Figure 10-3 displays available options.

Let us take a look at a few examples to understand various scenrios of software installation.

To install software called *AgentConfig* located in */var/opt/mx/depot11* directory with all default options, execute *swinstall* with –s switch as follows:

swinstall –s /var/opt/mx/depot11

When you execute this command, it brings up GUI or TUI and displays all software available to be loaded in the specified depot. Highlight *AgentConfig* and select "Install" from "Actions". An analysis will be done to check whether or not the software is already installed, enough disk space is available, and so on. When the command comes back after the analysis, click on the OK button to get the software installed.

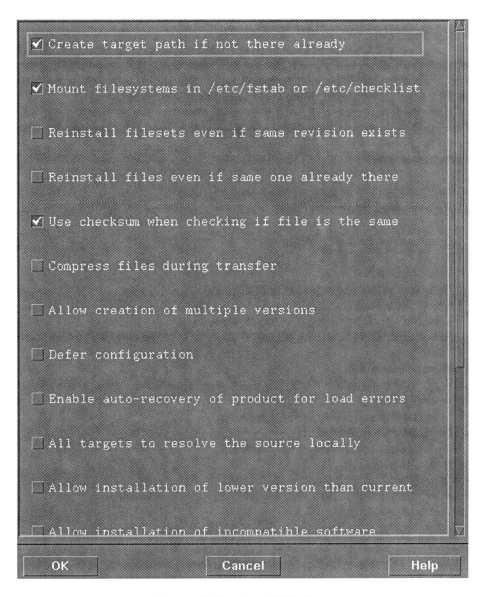

Figure 10-3 *swinstall* **Options**

To install another software called *CMSConfig* located on a remote machine, *hp02*, in */var/opt/mx/depot11* directory with all default options, execute the following:

swinstall –s hp02:/var/opt/mx/depot11

To install *AgentConfig* without invoking the graphical or textual interface, execute the following:

swinstall –s /var/opt/mx/depot11 AgentConfig

There are numerous options available to *swinstall*. Refer to man pages for detailed information.

10.2.3   Verifying Installed Software

Once software is installed, verify it with the *swverify* command. This command checks all files and associated attributes against the information stored in IPD about the software to ensure that the software is installed successfully. If any issues are found, it reports them.

To verify the perl package, do the following. The –v option is used for verbose purposes.

```
# swverify  –v  perl

=======  12/19/05 17:06:09 EST  BEGIN swverify SESSION
        (non-interactive) (jobid=hp01-0006)

    * Session started for user "root@hp01".

    * Beginning Selection
    * Target connection succeeded for "hp01:/".
    * Software selections:
        perl,r=B.5.6.1.C,a=HP-UX_B.11.11_32/64,v=HP
        Perl5.PERL-RUN,l=/,r=B.5.6.1.C,a=HP-UX_B.11.11_32/64,v=HP,fr=B.5.6.1.C,fa=HP-
UX_B.11.00_32/64
    * Selection succeeded.

    * Beginning Analysis
    * Session selections have been saved in the file
    "/.sw/sessions/swverify.last".
    * The analysis phase succeeded for "hp01:/".
    * Verification succeeded.

=======  12/19/05 17:06:38 EST  END swverify SESSION (non-interactive)
        (jobid=hp01-0006)
```

 More information may be found in the agent logfile by running the command: "swjob -a log hp01-0006 @ hp01:/".

There are numerous options available with *swverify*. Refer to man pages for more information.

10.2.4   Removing Software

The *swremove* command is used to remove installed software from a machine. The command unconfigures the software before it proceeds with removal. It is invoked in GUI or TUI mode depending on whether or not the DISPLAY environment variable is set.

Start *swremove* and highlight the software to remove from *Software Selection* window. See Figure 10-4. Go to *Actions* and select *Remove*. The command performs an analysis on the software and then proceeds with removing it.

```
# swremove
```

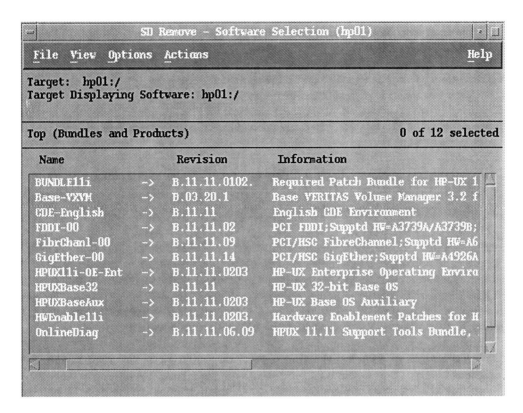

Figure 10-4 Software Removal

To remove *AgentConfig* without invoking the graphical or textual interface, execute the following:

 # swremove AgentConfig
```
======= 06/04/07 23:17:37 EDT  BEGIN swremove SESSION
    (non-interactive) (jobid=hp01-0037)

  * Session started for user "root@hp01".

  * Beginning Selection
  * Target connection succeeded for "hp01:/".
  * Software selections:
      AgentConfig.SCR-CONFIG,l=/,a=HP-UX_B.11.00_32/64,v=HP
      AgentConfig.SD-CONFIG,l=/,a=HP-UX_B.11.00_32/64,v=HP
  * Selection succeeded.

  * Beginning Analysis
  * Session selections have been saved in the file
    "/.sw/sessions/swremove.last".
  * The analysis phase succeeded for "hp01:/".
  * Analysis succeeded.

  * Beginning Execution
```

* The execution phase succeeded for "hp01:/".
* Execution succeeded.

NOTE: More information may be found in the agent logfile using the
command "swjob -a log hp01-0037 @ hp01:/".

======= 06/04/07 23:17:41 EDT END swremove SESSION (non-interactive)
(jobid=hp01-0037)

There are numerous options available with the command. Refer to man pages for more information.

10.3   Software Depots

A depot is a location that holds software products in installable format. The location may be a directory, a CD/DVD drive, a tape drive, and so on. A directory depot is created to copy installable software in it, whereas a CD/DVD or tape depot is used for software distribution purposes.

The process of setting up a directory depot is to copy the software to the directory using the *swcopy* command. A directory depot sitting on a server offers several advantages:

✓   The server acts as a central software repository. You need to manage software only on one system.
✓   You can have as many depots on a server as you wish. Application depots, patch depots, etc. can be put on the server.
✓   When required software needs to be installed on a client machine, invoke *swinstall* on the client and perform a pull install of the software.
✓   Installation of one software can be done on multiple servers simultaneously.
✓   Having software in depots eliminates (or at least reduces) loading and unloading of CD/DVD and tape.

A tape depot is created using the *swpackage* command. A tape depot can be accessed by only one user at a time.

10.3.1   Catalog Files

Catalog files hold depot description and software information located in depots. These are equivalent to IPD. Catalog files are stored in the catalog directory that resides in the same directory as the depot software.

When a depot is created, these files are created and placed in the depot directory. When a depot is modified, these files are updated automatically. When a depot is removed, these files are deleted too.

10.4   Managing Software Depots

Managing software depots involve copying software to a depot, registering a depot, unregistering a depot, listing depots, listing software in a depot, verifying depot contents, removing software from a depot, and removing depots. The following sub-sections elaborate these depot management tasks.

10.4.1   Copying Software to a Depot

Use the *swcopy* command to copy software to a directory depot. Note that there is a difference between copying software and installing it. Copying software copies an entire image of the software to a depot to be used for installation purposes later, while installing software puts files in different directory locations for execution purposes. Simply copying software to a directory using the *cp* command and then trying to install that software does not work. The *swcopy* command maintains the software structure.

To start *swcopy* in GUI or TUI mode, type in the command at the prompt and hit the *Enter* key, as shown in Figure 10-5.

> # **swcopy**

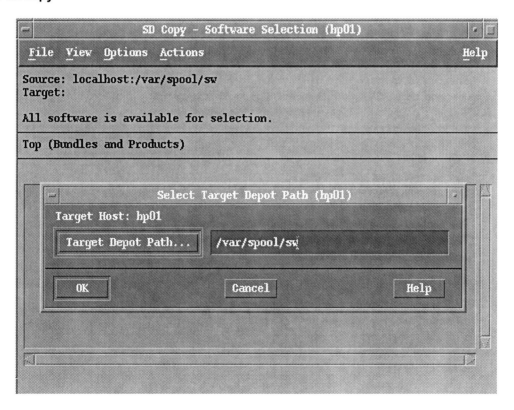

Figure 10-5 Copying Software to a Depot

A *Software Selection* window pops up with a *Select Target Depot Path* dialog box superimposed. The *Target Depot Path*, by default, displays the default target depot, which is */var/spool/sw*. If you want the software to be copied to this location, click on OK to proceed with analysis and copy process, otherwise specify an alternate location.

The following examples show various software copy tasks performed at the command line without invoking GUI or TUI.

To copy software *AgentConfig* from a local depot */var/opt/mx/depot11* to a local depot */depots/depot1*:

> # **swcopy −s /var/opt/mx/depot11 AgentConfig @ /depots/depot1**

> ======= 06/04/07 23:29:47 EDT BEGIN swcopy SESSION (non-interactive)
>   (jobid=hp01-0044)

>   * Session started for user "root@hp01".

>   * Beginning Selection
>   * "hp01:/depots/depot2": This target does not exist and will be
>   created.
>   * Source connection succeeded for "hp01:/var/opt/mx/depot11".
>   * Source: /var/opt/mx/depot11
>   * Targets: hp01:/depots/depot2
>   * Software selections:
>   AgentConfig.SCR-CONFIG,a=HP-UX_B.11.00_32/64,v=HP
>   AgentConfig.SD-CONFIG,a=HP-UX_B.11.00_32/64,v=HP
>   * Selection succeeded.

>   * Beginning Analysis and Execution
>   * Session selections have been saved in the file
>   "/.sw/sessions/swcopy.last".
>   * The analysis phase succeeded for "hp01:/depots/depot2".
>   * The execution phase succeeded for "hp01:/depots/depot2".
>   * Analysis and Execution succeeded.

>   NOTE: More information may be found in the agent logfile using the
>   command "swjob -a log hp01-0044 @ hp01:/depots/depot2".

>   ======= 06/04/07 23:29:48 EDT END swcopy SESSION (non-interactive)
>   (jobid=hp01-0044)

To copy software *perl* located on a local CD-ROM to a depot at */depots/depot2* on your local machine:

> # **swcopy −s /SD_CDROM perl @ /depots/depot2**

To copy all software on a local CD-ROM to a depot at */depots/depot3* on your local machine:

># swcopy −s /SD_CDROM '*' @ /depots/depot3

To copy all software on a local CD-ROM to a depot at */depots/depot1* on *hp02* server:

># swcopy −s /SD_CDROM '*' @ hp02:/depots/depot1

To copy all software from a tape drive at */dev/rmt/0* to */var/spool/sw* on the local system:

># swcopy −s /dev/rmt/0m *

10.4.2   Registering and Unregistering a Depot

To use software located in a depot, the depot must be registered. If *swcopy* is used to copy software, there is no need to register it as it automatically takes care of this. Downloaded software from HP's website or software obtained elsewhere must be registered prior to use. The *swreg* command performs registering and unregistering of depots.

To register a depot located at */depot/depot4*, do either of the following:

```
# swreg −l depot /depot/depot4
# swreg −l depot @ /depot/depot4
======= 12/20/05 10:59:59 EST  BEGIN swreg SESSION (non-interactive)

     * Session started for user "root@hp01".
     * Beginning Selection
     * Targets:         hp01
     * Objects:         /depot/depot4
     * Selection succeeded.
======= 12/20/05 10:59:59 EST  END swreg SESSION (non-interactive)
```

To unregister the same depot, do either of the following:

```
# swreg −ul depot /depot/depot4
# swreg −ul depot @ /depot/depot4
======= 12/20/05 11:01:41 EST  BEGIN swreg SESSION (non-interactive)

     * Session started for user "root@hp01".
     * Beginning Selection
     * Targets:         hp01
     * Objects:         /depot/depot4
     * Selection succeeded.
======= 12/20/05 11:01:41 EST  END swreg SESSION (non-interactive)
```

10.4.3   Listing Depots

Depots are registered with the *swreg* command. When software is copied into depots with *swcopy*, they get registered automatically. If you wish to list what depots are registered and available, you can use the *swlist* command.

To list all depots currently registered on the local system. The following output shows that there are four registered depots: */var/opt/mx/depot11*, */home/GOLDQPK11i/depot*, */SD_CDROM*, and */var/spool/sw*:

> **# swlist –l depot**
> # Initializing...
> # Target "hp01" has the following depot(s):
>   /var/opt/mx/depot11
>   /home/GOLDQPK11i/depot
>   /var/spool/sw

To list all depots registered on a remote machine *hp02*:

> **# swlist –l depot @ hp02**
> # Initializing...
> # Target "hp02" has the following depot(s)
>   /var/opt/mx/depot11
>   /home/GOLDQPK11i/depot

10.4.4   Listing Depot Contents

The previous sub-section shows how to list what depots are available. If you wish to view what software are available within registered depots, you can use *swlist* in the following manner.

To list software residing in a depot on local machine. The output below shows that *AgentConfig* and *CMSConfig* are two registered software in */var/opt/mx/depot11* depot.

> **# swlist –l product –d @ /var/opt/mx/depot11**
> # Initializing...
> # Contacting target "hp01"...
> #
> # Target: hp01:/var/opt/mx/depot11
> #
>   AgentConfig   ServiceControl Agent Config
>   CMSConfig   SCMgr CMS Configuration

To list software products residing in */var/opt/mx/depot11* depot on remote machine *hp02*:

> **# swlist –l product –d @ hp02:/var/opt/mx/depot11**
> # Initializing...
> # Contacting target "hp02"...
> #

```
# Target: hp02:/var/opt/mx/depot11
#
  AgentConfig             ServiceControl Agent Config
  CMSConfig               SCMgr CMS Configuration
```

To list software on local tape drive depot located at */dev/rmt/0*:

 # swlist −d @ /dev/rmt/0

10.4.5   Verifying Depot Contents

The *swverify* command is used to verify software sitting in a depot. It verifies dependencies, reports missing files, and checks file attributes including permissions, file type, size, checksum, mtime, and major/minor attributes.

To verify all software in */var/opt/mx/depot11* depot on the local machine:

 # swverify −d * @ /var/opt/mx/depot11

```
======= 12/20/05 11:43:48 EST  BEGIN swverify SESSION
       (non-interactive) (jobid=hp01-0059)

    * Session started for user "root@hp01".

    * Beginning Selection
    * Target connection succeeded for
      "hp01:/var/opt/mx/depot11".
    * Software selections:
        AgentConfig.SD-CONFIG,a=HP-UX_B.11.00_32/64,v=HP
        CMSConfig.PRM-CMS-Tools,a=HP-UX_B.11.00_32/64,v=HP,fr=C.02.01,fa=HP-
UX_B.11.00_32/64
        CMSConfig.WLMB-CMS-Tools,a=HP-UX_B.11.00_32/64,v=HP,fr=A.02.01,fa=HP-
UX_B.11.00_32/64
    * Selection succeeded.
    * Beginning Analysis
    * Session selections have been saved in the file
      "/home/root/.sw/sessions/swverify.last".
    * The analysis phase succeeded for
      "hp01:/var/opt/mx/depot11".
    * Verification succeeded.
======= 12/20/05 11:43:49 EST  END swverify SESSION (non-interactive)
       (jobid=hp01-0059)
```

More information may be found in the agent logfile using the command "*swjob -a log hp01-0059 @hp01:/var/opt/mx/depot11*" after the *swverify* task is finished.

10.4.6   Removing Software from a Depot

The *swremove* command is used to remove one or more software from a depot.

To remove *AgentConfig* from the depot at */var/opt/mx/depot11* on the local machine:

```
# swremove –d AgentConfig @ /var/opt/mx/depot11
======= 05/23/06 11:19:22 EDT  BEGIN swremove SESSION
      (non-interactive) (jobid=hp01-0048)


   * Session started for user "root@hp01".

   * Beginning Selection
   * Target connection succeeded for "hp01:/var/opt/mx/depot11".
   * Software selections:
      AgentConfig.SCR-CONFIG,a=HP-UX_B.11.00_32/64,v=HP
      AgentConfig.SD-CONFIG,a=HP-UX_B.11.00_32/64,v=HP
   * Selection succeeded.

   * Beginning Analysis
   * Session selections have been saved in the file
     "/.sw/sessions/swremove.last".
   * The analysis phase succeeded for "hp01:/var/opt/mx/depot11".
   * Analysis succeeded.

   * Beginning Execution
   * The execution phase succeeded for "hp01:/var/opt/mx/depot11".
   * Execution succeeded.

NOTE:   More information may be found in the agent logfile using the
        command "swjob -a log hp01-0048 @ hp01:/var/opt/mx/depot11".

======= 05/23/06 11:19:25 EDT  END swremove SESSION (non-interactive)
      (jobid=hp01-0048)
```

To remove *app1* from the default depot on the local machine:

```
# swremove –d app1
```

To remove all software from the default depot on a remote machine *hp02*:

```
# swremove –d @ hp02
```

To remove *AgnetConfig* from the depot at */var/opt/mx/depot11* on the remote machine *hp02*:

```
# swremove –d AgentConfig @ hp02:/var/opt/mx/depot11
```

10.4.7 Removing a Depot

When all software in a depot are removed, the depot automatically gets unregistered and considered removed although the directory where it resided still exists.

To remove all software located in */var/opt/mx/depot11* depot and unregister it, do the following:

 # swremove –d * @ /var/opt/mx/depot11

```
======= 05/23/06 11:21:11 EDT  BEGIN swremove SESSION
      (non-interactive) (jobid=hp02-0049)

    * Session started for user "root@hp02".

    * Beginning Selection
    * Target connection succeeded for "hp02:/var/opt/mx/depot11".
    * Software selections:
         CMSConfig.PRM-CMS-Tools,a=HP-UX_B.11.00_32/64,v=HP,fr=C.02.00.02,fa=HP-
UX_B.11.00_32/64
         CMSConfig.WLMB-CMS-Tools,a=HP-UX_B.11.00_32/64,v=HP,fr=A.02.00,fa=HP-
UX_B.11.00_32/64
    * Selection succeeded.

    * Beginning Analysis
    * Session selections have been saved in the file
      "/.sw/sessions/swremove.last".
    * The analysis phase succeeded for "hp02:/var/opt/mx/depot11".
    * Analysis succeeded.

    * Beginning Execution
    * The execution phase succeeded for "hp02:/var/opt/mx/depot11".
    * Execution succeeded.

NOTE:    More information may be found in the agent logfile using the
      command "swjob -a log hp02-0049 @ hp02:/var/opt/mx/depot11".

======= 05/23/06 11:21:13 EDT  END swremove SESSION (non-interactive)
      (jobid=hp02-0049)
```

To remove all software located on the remote machine, *hp02*, in */var/opt/mx/depot11* depot and unregister it, do the following:

 # swremove –d * @ hp02:/var/opt/mx/depot11

Summary

This chapter discussed software management in HP-UX. You learned concepts and components involved including Installed Product Database, dependencies, protection on some software, and catalog files. You performed tasks on software and software depots, such as listing installed software, depots, and depot contents; installing software from local media and depot; copying software to a depot; registering and unregistering depot software; verifying installed software and depot contents; removing an installed software and software from a depot; and removing a depot.

HP Certified Systems Administrator

## 11

Patch Management

This chapter covers the following major topics:

- ✓ Why do we need patches
- ✓ Understand HP-UX patch naming scheme
- ✓ Patch attributes – suppression, dependency, ratings, critical and non-critical, status, states, category tags, and ancestry
- ✓ List installed patches and patch bundles
- ✓ Acquire and install patch bundles and individual patches
- ✓ Install patches from CD/DVD and tape
- ✓ Verify patches and patch bundles
- ✓ Roll back (remove) and commit patches
- ✓ Patch assessment and security patch check tools
- ✓ HP-UX Software Assistant (SWA) tool

11.1   Understanding Patch Management

Patch management is carried out to reduce the risk of potential problems arising out of system crashes, panics, memory leaks, data corruption, application failures, and security breaches. Some patches also deliver new functionality and features, enable new hardware, and update firmware levels. Having proper patches installed ensures:

- ✓ Smooth system operation
- ✓ Optimum performance
- ✓ Enhanced system security
- ✓ Better reliability and higher availability
- ✓ Latest system enhancements and functionality
- ✓ Less patches to install if a problem is encountered
- ✓ Less time required to troubleshoot a problem

Patch management involves tasks, such as acquiring, installing, updating, verifying, testing, listing, copying, committing, and removing patches.

11.1.1   Patch Naming Convention

Each HP-UX patch has a unique patch identification string and fall under one of four categories:

- ✓ Common patches identified by CO. These are general HP-UX patches and do not usually require a system reboot after an installation.
- ✓ Kernel patches identified by KL. These patches modify and update HP-UX kernel and related structure and almost always require a system reboot after an installation.
- ✓ Network patches identified by NE. These patches relate to HP-UX network components and may or may not require a system reboot after an installation.
- ✓ Subsystem patches identified by SS. These patches relate to HP-UX subsystems other than general, kernel, and networking, and may or may not require a system reboot after an installation.

HP-UX patches have the syntax: PHXX_#####, where P stands for Patch, H stands for HP-UX, XX corresponds to one of the four categories mentioned above, and ##### is a unique four or five character numeric string. Usually, the higher this number is the more recently released the patch is.

Patches are installed and managed via the SD-UX commands that you learned in Chapter 10 "Software Management".

11.2   Patch Attributes

Before jumping into managing patches, you need to understand patch attributes, an understanding of which helps you while working with acquiring, downloading, installing, and managing patches.

11.2.1   Patch Suppression

When a new patch comes out, it replaces and supersedes any earlier patches that have been out there for the same reasons. The new patch fixes any bugs in previous versions of that patch or addresses any other unknown issues in that patch. This is called *Patch Suppression*.

To view what patches a given patch has superseded, you can view patch details or associated readme file. Location of both is provided later in this chapter. For patches already installed on your system, execute the following command to display this information:

```
# swlist –l  patch  –x  show_superseded_patches=true
# Initializing...
# Contacting target "hp02"...
#
# Target:  hp02:/

# 100BT-EISA-FMT                    B.11.11.01        EISA 100BT/9000 formatter product.
# 100BT-EISA-FMT.100BT-FORMAT       B.11.11.01        EISA 100BT/9000 formatter library
# 100BT-EISA-KRN                    B.11.11.01        EISA 100BT/9000 kernel products.
# 100BT-EISA-KRN.100BT-KRN          B.11.11.01        EISA 100BT/9000 kernel library
# 100BT-EISA-RUN                    B.11.11.01        EISA 100BT/9000 command products.
# 100BT-EISA-RUN.100BT-INIT         B.11.11.01        EISA 100BT/9000 master file.
# 100BT-EISA-RUN.100BT-RUN          B.11.11.01        EISA 100BT/9000 command libraries
. . . . . . . .
. . . . . . . .
```

You may wish to run the *show_patches* utility that displays the output in a formatted way.

```
# show_patches
```

11.2.2   Patch Dependency

A patch that depends on one or more other patches in order to be installed or run correctly is said to have dependency on those other patches.

HP-UX patches are cumulative. A patch automatically satisfies all the dependencies that all of its superseded patches satisfy.

There are three common dependency types:

- ✓ Patch Dependencies – Patches required for proper operation.
- ✓ Hardware Dependencies – Patches for specific system hardware models.
- ✓ Other Dependencies – Various dependencies needed only under specific circumstances.

11.2.3   Patch Rating

Every HP-UX patch has a quality rating between 1 and 3 indicated by corresponding number of the asterisk (*) characters. When a patch is newly released, it gets a 1 star rating, which means the patch is not well tested in the customer environment and there might be side effects when putting it on a system. As time passes, this rating may be increased to 2 or 3 stars to show higher confidence in the patch.

Each patch is displayed with a corresponding quality rating in the ITRC patch database located at *http://www2.itrc.hp.com/service/patch/mainPage.do*.

11.2.4   Critical and Non-Critical Patches

HP-UX patches are either critical or non-critical. This information can be viewed under the Critical field on the patch details page or in the patch readme file.

A patch is considered critical if it provides a fix for a critical problem, such as system panic, process abort, and so on. Other patches are considered non-critical.

11.2.5   Patch Status

Each patch has an associated status that identifies if the patch is for general use or special. Moreover, it tells if the patch has any warnings associated with it.

11.2.6   Patch State

An installed patch on your system is in one of four states: *applied, committed, superseded,* or *committed/superseded*. This represents the current state of the patch.

The "applied" state tells you that the patch is currently active on the system. The "committed" state indicates that the patch cannot be removed from the system since the files it replaced are no longer available. The "superseded" state states that the patch is superseded by another installed patch. The "committed/superseded" state means the patch is committed and superseded by another installed patch.

Do the following to determine current patch states of installed patches:

```
# swlist −l  fileset  −a  patch_state  *,c=patch
# Initializing...
# Contacting target "hp02"...
#
# Target:  hp02:/
#
# PHCO_22958
  PHCO_22958.FIRST-BOOT          applied
# PHCO_23263
  PHCO_23263.ADMN-ENG-A-MAN      applied
  PHCO_23263.ARRAY-MGMT          applied
```

```
# PHCO_23774
   PHCO_23774.CORE-ENG-A-MAN       applied
   PHCO_23774.SYS-ADMIN            applied
. . . . . . . .
. . . . . . . .
```

11.2.7   Category Tag

A category tag associated with a given patch helps you determine the patch category it falls under. Some of the category tags are *hardware enablement* (provides support for new hardware), *enhancement* (provides added feature), *special release* (developed for a specific situation), *critical* (fixes a critical issue), *firmware* (provides firmware update), and so on.

The patch category for a patch can be determined by viewing the patch details page or the patch's readme file. For installed patches, you can view this information using *swlist* as follows:

```
# swlist –l fileset –a category_tag *,c=patch
# Initializing...
# Contacting target "hp02"...
#
# Target:  hp02:/
#
# PHCO_22958                      patch   defect_repair  hardware_enablement general_release
   PHCO_22958.FIRST-BOOT          patch
# PHCO_23263                      patch   hardware_enablement defect_repair  enhancement
general_release critical
   PHCO_23263.ADMN-ENG-A-MAN      patch
   PHCO_23263.ARRAY-MGMT          patch
# PHCO_23774                      patch   hardware_enablement defect_repair  general_release
manual_dependencies
   PHCO_23774.CORE-ENG-A-MAN      patch
   PHCO_23774.SYS-ADMIN           patch
. . . . . . . .
. . . . . . . .
```

11.2.8   Patch Ancestry

The ancestor of a patch is the original software component that the patch modified. Ancestry impacts patch installation as well as removal. To determine ancestors of all installed patches, do the following:

```
# swlist –l fileset –a ancestor *,c=patch
# Initializing...
# Contacting target "hp02"...
#
# Target:  hp02:/
#
# PHCO_22958
```

```
   PHCO_22958.FIRST-BOOT           SystemAdmin.FIRST-BOOT,fr=B.11.11,v=HP
 # PHCO_23263
   PHCO_23263.ADMN-ENG-A-MAN       OS-Core.ADMN-ENG-A-MAN,fr=B.11.11,v=HP
   PHCO_23263.ARRAY-MGMT OS-Core.ARRAY-MGMT,fr=B.11.11,v=HP
 # PHCO_23774
   PHCO_23774.CORE-ENG-A-MAN       OS-Core.CORE-ENG-A-MAN,fr=B.11.11,v=HP
   PHCO_23774.SYS-ADMIN            OS-Core.SYS-ADMIN,fr=B.11.11,v=HP

 . . . . . . . .
 . . . . . . . .
```

11.3   Managing Patches

Patches are available as individual patches as well as in bundles. A patch bundle is a collection of patches. You can install specific patches to your system according to your needs or apply an entire bundle. Most administrators prefer applying patch bundles as opposed to applying individual patches for ease of management.

In the following sub-sections, you are going to see how individual patches are listed, acquired, installed, verified, rolled back, and committed. Similarly, you will see how patch bundles are listed, acquired, and installed.

11.3.1   Listing Installed Patches

Listing installed patches displays all individual patches currently installed on the system. Use the *swlist* command as follows to list them:

```
# swlist  –l  patch
# Initializing...
# Contacting target "hp02"...
#
# Target:  hp02:/
#
# 100BT-EISA-FMT                  B.11.11.01     EISA 100BT/9000 formatter product.
# 100BT-EISA-FMT.100BT-FORMAT     B.11.11.01     EISA 100BT/9000 formatter library
# 100BT-EISA-KRN                  B.11.11.01     EISA 100BT/9000 kernel products.
# 100BT-EISA-KRN.100BT-KRN        B.11.11.01     EISA 100BT/9000 kernel library
# 100BT-EISA-RUN                  B.11.11.01     EISA 100BT/9000 command products.
# 100BT-EISA-RUN.100BT-INIT       B.11.11.01     EISA 100BT/9000 master file.
# 100BT-EISA-RUN.100BT-RUN        B.11.11.01     EISA 100BT/9000 command libraries
 . . . . . . . .
 . . . . . . . .
```

Alternatively, you can use the *show_patches* command to display patches:

```
# show_patches
   Active                Patch
   Patch                 Description
   ------------------    ----------------------------------------
```

PHCO_23263	HP AutoRAID Manager cumulative patch
PHCO_23370	lint(1) library patch
PHCO_23463	sysdef(1) patch
PHCO_23492	Kernsymtab Patch
PHCO_23702	cumulative header file patch for prot.h
PHCO_23909	cu(1) patch
PHCO_23920	sfd(1M) patch
PHCO_24396	/etc/default/tz patch
PHCO_24440	cumulative cpio(1) patch
PHCO_24456	st(1m) shared tape administration
PHCO_24477	sar(1m) patch
PHCO_24846	ttsyncd(1M) cumulative patch
PHCO_25130	vPar manpage cumulative patch
PHCO_25831	SCSI Ultra160 driver Online Addition script
PHCO_25841	Add Rock Ridge extension to mount_cdfs(1M)
PHCO_25918	sort(1) cumulative patch.
PHCO_25979	vmstat(1) cumulative patch

. . . .
. . . .

11.3.2   Acquiring Individual Patches

Individual patches may be obtained from either of the following two sites:

✓   IT Resource Center (ITRC) site at *www.itrc.hp.com.*
✓   ITRC ftp site at *ftp://ftp.itrc.hp.com.*

Obtain patches from *www.itrc.hp.com.* Figure 11-1 shows the main ITRC web page. Obtaining patches from this site using the procedure mentioned below is recommended. It automatically selects dependent patches as well.

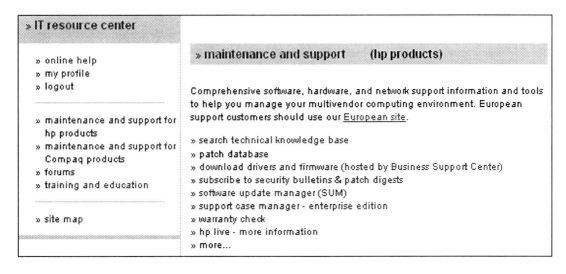

Figure 11-1 IT Resource Center Main Screen

1. Go to *www.itrc.hp.com*.
2. Under "maintenance and support for hp products", click on "find individual patches".
3. Go to "HP-UX".
4. Choose appropriate hardware and HP-UX OE level.
5. You have three search options. Choose one of them:

    ✓ Select "Search by Patch IDs" and specify a patch ID in the window next to it.
    ✓ Select "Search by Keyword" if you do not know the exact patch ID you are looking for and wish to search for the patch based on some matching description.
    ✓ Select "Browse Patch List" to list all available patches and choose the one you need.

6. Review patch information once you find the desired patch. Choose the one that is recommended by checking the box next to it.
7. Click on the patch name to review details about it.
8. Click on "add to selected patch list". If the patch has a warning associated with it, the patch warning page will appear.
9. You may see some more patches automatically added to the download list. These are automatically chosen and are required to satisfy dependencies. Download all of them.
10. Click on "download selected" and then choose one of the three available file formats: zip, gzip, or tar.
11. Choose a download server and format.
12. Click on "download" to get patches.

To acquire individual patches from *ftp://ftp.itrc.hp.com*, follow the steps below. This method does not automatically select dependent patches.

1. Click on "hp-ux_patches".
2. Click on "s700_800".
3. Click on "11.X".
4. All available patches are listed here. Choose the one that you need and download it. Also download corresponding text file.

You may download patches from *ftp://ftp.itrc.hp.com* by running the *ftp* command at the command line as well. Login as *anonymous* user and supply your email as password. This method does not automatically select any dependent patches.

11.3.3   Installing Individual Patches

Follow the procedure below if you have downloaded a patch from the ITRC website. Suppose the downloaded patch is *PHCO_23651.xxx* (where xxx identifies zip, gzip, or tar format).

1. Move the patch to the directory where you like it unpacked.

    ```
    # mkdir /depot/patches
    # mv PHCO_23651.xxx /depot/patches
    # cd /depot/patches
    ```

2. Do one of the following depending on the format of the patch file:

If the patch is in zip format:

unzip PHCO_23651.zip

If the patch is in gzip format:

gunzip PHCO_23651.tgz | tar xvf –

If the patch is in tar format:

tar –xvf PHCO_23651.tar

3. You will notice some files generated after unpacking the patch file. A readme file that contains details about the patch, a *create_depot_hp-ux_11* script, and a file with *.depot* extension. The *.depot* file is the file that holds the actual patch software.

4. Execute the *create_depot_hp-ux_11* script. This script performs unshar function (using the *sh* command) on the patch and then *swcopy* and *swverify* operations. It creates a directory called *depot* where it *swcopy* the patch depot.

```
# ./create_depot_hp-ux_11
DEPOT: /softdepot/depot
BUNDLE: BUNDLE
TITLE: Patch Bundle
UNSHAR: y
PSF: depot.psf
Expanding patch shar files...
x - PHCO_23651.text
x - PHCO_23651.depot [compressed]
x - PHCO_24189.text
x - PHCO_24189.depot [compressed]
x - PHKL_18543.text
x - PHKL_18543.depot [compressed]
. . . . . . . .
. . . . . . . .
===== 01/15/06 14:41:38 EDT  BEGIN swcopy SESSION (non-interactive)
      (jobid=hp02-012)

   * Session started for user "root@hp02".

   * Beginning Selection
   * "hp02:/softdepot/depot":  This target does not exist and will be created.
   * Source:            /softdepot/PHCO_23651.depot
   * Targets:           hp01:/softdepot/depot
   * Software selections:
       PHCO_23651.VXFS-BASE-RUN,r=1.0,a=HP-UX_B.11.00_32/64,v=HP,fr=1.0,fa=HP-
UX_B.11.00_32/64
. . . . . . . .
. . . . . . . .
```

5. Install the patch with *swinstall*. The system reboots automatically, if necessary.

    # swinstall −s /depot/patches/depot

If the patch was downloaded using one of the ftp methods, follow the steps below to install it.

Suppose the downloaded patch, after unpacking, is *hpux_800_11.11.depot*.

1. Move this depot file to the directory where you want to register it.

    # mkdir /depot/patch_depot
    # mv hpux_800_11.11.depot /depot/patch_depot
    # cd /depot/patch_depot

2. Register the depot as follows:

    # swreg −l depot /depot/patch_depot/hpux_800_11.11.depot

3. Install the patch with the *swinstall* command. The system reboots automatically, if necessary.

    # swinstall −s /depot/patch_depot/hpux_800_11.11.depot

11.3.4 Listing Installed Patch Bundles

Listing installed patch bundles displays all patch bundles currently installed on the system. Use the *swlist* command as follows to list them:

```
# swlist
# Initializing...
# Contacting target "hp02"...
#
# Target: hp02:/
#
# Bundle(s):
#
  100BaseT-00     B.11.11.01       EISA 100BaseT;Supptd W=A4308B;SW=J2780BA
  100BaseT-01     B.11.11.01       HP-PB 100BaseT;Supptd HW=A3495A;SW=J2759BA
  ATM-00          K.11.11.30       PCI ATM;Supptd HW=A5483A/
A5513A/A5515A/J3557A;SW=J3572AA/J3572BA
  ATM-01          K.11.11.30       HSC ATM;Supptd HW=J2468A/
J2469A/J2499A/J3420B/J3573A;SW=J2806CA
  B5725AA         B.4.2.110        HP-UX Installation Utilities (Ignite-UX)
  B9901AA         A.03.05.05       HP IPFilter 3.5alpha5
  BUNDLE11i       B.11.11.0102.2   Required Patch Bundle for HP-UX 11i, February 2001
  Base-VXVM       B.03.50.5        Base VERITAS Volume Manager Bundle 3.5 for HP-UX
  CDE-English     B.11.11          English CDE Environment
  FEATURE11-11    B.11.11.0209.5   Feature Enablement Patches for HP-UX 11i, Sept 2002
```

```
FibrChanl-00        B.11.11.09      PCI/HSC FibreChannel;Supptd
HW=A6684A,A6685A,A5158A,A6795A
GigEther-00         B.11.11.14      PCI/HSC GigEther;Supptd
HW=A4926A/A4929A/A4924A/A4925A;SW=J1642AA
HPUX11i-OE-MC    B.11.11.0303  HP-UX Mission Critical Operating Environment Component
HPUXBase32          B.11.11             HP-UX 32-bit Base OS
HPUXBaseAux        B.11.11.0303        HP-UX Base OS Auxiliary
HWEnable11i         B.11.11.0303.4 Hardware Enablement Patches for HP-UX 11i, March 2003
. . . . . . . .
. . . . . . . .
```

11.3.5 Acquiring Patch Bundles

Patch depots may be obtained from one of the following four sources:

- ✓ IT Resource Center (ITRC) site at *www.itrc.hp.com*.
- ✓ ITRC ftp site at *ftp://ftp.itrc.hp.com*.
- ✓ Software depot site at *software.hp.com*.
- ✓ HP Support Plus CD/DVD.

You may download standard HP-UX patch bundles that provide recommended set of system patches. Table 11-1 lists standard bundles available for various HP-UX OE versions.

Patch Bundles for HP-UX 11i v1 and v2	Description
BUNDLE11i	Includes base patches required to be loaded on your system.
GOLDQPK11i (on 11iv2w it is called QPK1123)	Consists of two sub-bundles – GOLDBASE11i and GOLDAPPS11i. The former contains defect fixes for core OS and the latter for non-core OS.
Feature11i (11iv2 only)	Consists of feature enablement patches and core defect fixes uncovered by new product features.
HWEnable11i	Contains Hardware Enablement patches.

Table 11-1 Standard HP-UX Patch Bundles

Apply the first three bundles on new system installs. You should apply updated bundles periodically to keep the patch level current. If you are adding new hardware to a system for which support is not already in the OE, then you need to install Hardware Enablement patch bundle as well. If you are unsure which bundles to load, installing all of them for respective OE version is not a bad idea.

Obtain patch bundles from *www.itrc.hp.com*. Follow the procedure below:

1. Go to *www.itrc.hp.com*.
2. Under "maintenance and support for hp products", click on "standard patch bundles – find patch bundles".
3. Go to "HP-UX patch bundles".
4. Click on a release name based on your OE version.
5. Click on a bundle to download and then on "add to selected patch list".

---

6. Click on "download selected" and then on "Expand to view additional download options".
7. Choose one of the file formats – zip, gzip, or tar – to download the depot in.
8. Click on "download" to get the bundle.

This method automatically selects and downloads dependent patches as well.

You can also acquire patch bundles from *ftp://ftp.itrc.hp.com* using a web browser. With this method you will have to determine and download dependent patches manually.

1. Go to "patch_bundles".
2. Go to "hp-ux". You will see several directories there. Hardware Enablement patches are located in the HWE directory, Quality patches in the QUALITYPACK directory, and Bundle11i and Feature11i in the SPECIAL directory.
3. Go to the desired directory and download the required bundle. Also download corresponding text file.

You may also download patch bundles by running the *ftp* command at the command line as well. Login as *anonymous* user and supply your email as password. This method does not automatically select any dependent patches.

11.3.6   Installing Patch Bundles

If you have downloaded a patch bundle using the ITRC website, follow the steps below to install it. Suppose the downloaded bundle name is *hpux_800_11.11.xxx* (where xxx is zip, gzip, or tar).

1. Move the bundle file to the directory where you want it unpacked.

   # mkdir /depot/patch_depot
   # mv hpux_800_11.11.xxx /depot/patch_depot
   # cd /depot/patch_depot

2. Do one of the following depending on the format of the bundle file:

   If the bundle is in zip format:

   # unzip hpux_800_11.11.zip

   If the bundle is in gzip format:

   # gunzip hpux_800_11.11.tgz | tar xvf –

   If the bundle is in tar format:

   # tar xvf hpux_800_11.11.tar

   You will notice some files generated after unpacking the bundle. A readme file that contains details about the bundle, a *create_depot_hp-ux_11* script, and a file with *.depot* extension. The *.depot* file is the file that holds the actual patch bundle software.

3. Execute the *create_depot_hp-ux_11* script. This script performs unshar function (using the *sh* command) on all the patches included in the bundle and then *swcopy* and *swverify* operations. It creates a directory called *depot* where it copies the depot contents.

```
# ./create_depot_hp-ux_11
DEPOT: /softdepot/depot
BUNDLE: BUNDLE
TITLE: Patch Bundle
UNSHAR: y
PSF: depot.psf
Expanding patch shar files...
x - PHCO_33142.text
x - PHCO_33142.depot [non-ascii]
x - PHCO_33327.text
x - PHCO_33327.depot [non-ascii]
x - PHCO_34196.text
x - PHCO_34196.depot [non-ascii]
. . . . . . . .
. . . . . . . .
======= 02/16/06 15:02:22 EDT  END swverify SESSION (non-interactive)
       (jobid=hp02-0154)
```

4. Install the bundle using *swinstall*. The system reboots automatically, if necessary.

   # **swinstall –s /depot/patch_depot/depot**

If you have downloaded a patch bundle using the ftp method, follow the steps below to install it.

Suppose the downloaded bundle name is *hpux_800_11.11.depot*.

1. Move the depot file to the directory where you wish to register it.

   # **mkdir /depot/patch_depot**
   # **mv hpux_800_11.11.depot /depot/patch_depot**
   # **cd /depot/patch_depot**

2. Register the depot as follows:

   # **swreg –l depot /depot/patch_depot/hpux_800_11.11.depot**

3. Install the bundle with the *swinstall* command. The system reboots automatically, if necessary.

   # **swinstall –s /depot/patch_depot/hpux_800_11.11.depot**

11.3.7　Installing Patches from CD/DVD

To install patches located on CD or DVD, you need to mount the CD/DVD and then register a desired depot in it using the *swreg* command. The following example assumes that the CD/DVD is mounted on */SD_CDROM* directory on your local machine:

> **# swreg –l depot /SD_CDROM**
> **# swinstall –s /SD_CDROM**

It is a good idea to *swcopy* all bundles from a CD/DVD to a directory depot so you do not have to mount, unmount, and remount CD/DVD repeatedly.

11.3.8　Installing Patches from Tape

The following example assumes that the device file for tape is */dev/rmt/0*:

> **# swinstall –s /dev/rmt/0**

It is a good idea to *swcopy* all bundles from a tape to a directory depot so you do not have to load and unload the tape again and again.

11.3.9　Verifying a Patch and Patch Bundle

After completing installation of a patch or patch bundle, you may wish to verify if the patch or patch bundle is installed successfully. Use the *swverify* command for this purpose.

To verify an individual patch, specify its name with *swverify*:

> **# swverify PHKL_25506**
>
> ======= 05/23/06 11:46:46 EDT BEGIN swverify SESSION
>   (non-interactive) (jobid=hp02-0050)
>
>   * Session started for user "root@hp02".
>
>   * Beginning Selection
>   * Target connection succeeded for "hp02:/".
> . . . .
> . . . .
>   * Selection succeeded.
>
>   * Beginning Analysis
>   * Session selections have been saved in the file
>   "/.sw/sessions/swverify.last".
>   * The analysis phase succeeded for "hp02:/".
>   * Verification succeeded.

NOTE: More information may be found in the agent logfile using the
command "swjob -a log hp02-0050 @ hp02:/".

======= 05/23/06 11:46:56 EDT END swverify SESSION (non-interactive)
(jobid=hp02-0050)

To verify a patch bundle, specify its name with *swverify*:

swverify BUNDLE11i

======= 05/23/06 11:48:44 EDT BEGIN swverify SESSION
(non-interactive) (jobid=hp02-0051)

  * Session started for user "root@hp02".

  * Beginning Selection
  * Target connection succeeded for "hp02:/".
. . . .
. . . .
  * Selection succeeded.

  * Beginning Analysis
  * Session selections have been saved in the file
  "/.sw/sessions/swverify.last".
  * The analysis phase succeeded for "hp02:/".
  * Verification succeeded.

NOTE: More information may be found in the agent logfile using the
command "swjob -a log hp02-0051 @ hp02:/".

======= 05/23/06 11:48:57 EDT END swverify SESSION (non-interactive)
(jobid=hp02-0051)

Also, you can run the *check_patches* command anytime or after you have installed patches to find if
there are any issues. This command creates a report and stores it in */tmp/check_patches.report* file
for your review.

check_patches
Obtaining information on installed patches
Checking installed version of /usr/sbin/swconfig
Checking for invalid patches
Checking object module checksums for active patch fileset   757 of   757
Checking patch filesets for active patch   396 of   396
Checking state for patch fileset   892 of   892
Checking patch_state for patch fileset   892 of   892
Running swverify on all patch filesets, this may take several minutes
RESULT: No problems found, review /tmp/check_patches.report for details.

11.3.10   Rolling Back (Removing) a Patch

Sometimes, after applying a patch you realize that the patch is not the one that you wanted or that the patch did not fix the problem for which you installed it. In this situation you may want to remove it and restore the system to its pre-patched state. This process is known as *Patch Rollback*. By default, when a patch is installed, the files it replaces are saved. If you specifically tell the *swinstall* utility at the time of patch installation not to save the files being replaced, then a rollback is not possible.

The *swremove* command is used to rollback a patch. Basically it removes the specified patch and restores original files. To rollback/remove PHCO_25870, do the following:

 # swremove PHCO_25870

```
======= 05/23/06 11:54:08 EDT  BEGIN swremove SESSION
        (non-interactive) (jobid=hp02-0053)

    * Session started for user "root@hp02".

    * Beginning Selection
. . . . . . . .
. . . . . . . .
    * Beginning Analysis
    * Session selections have been saved in the file
      "/.sw/sessions/swremove.last".
    * The analysis phase succeeded for "hp02:/".
    * Analysis succeeded.

    * Beginning Execution
    * The execution phase succeeded for "hp02:/".
    * Execution succeeded.

NOTE:   More information may be found in the agent logfile using the
        command "swjob -a log hp02-0053 @ hp02:/".

======= 05/23/06 11:55:34 EDT  END swremove SESSION (non-interactive)
        (jobid=hp02-0053)
```

11.3.11   Committing a Patch

By default, as you know, when a patch is installed, all files it replaces are saved. If you ever want to remove those saved files to claim disk space, you will need to commit the patch. After a patch is committed, you cannot roll it back.

Execute the *swmodify* command to commit a patch. To commit PHKL_25506, do the following:

 # swmodify −x patch_commit=true PHKL_25506

To commit all superseded patches and remove files associted with them, you can use the *cleanup* command. With –c option, you can specify the number of times the patches have been superseded. The command saves log information in */var/adm/cleanup.log* file.

```
# cleanup  –c  1
### Cleanup program started at 03/16/07  12:21:08
Commit patches superseded at least 1 time(s) on 'hp02'.
All information has been logged to /var/adm/cleanup.log.
### Cleanup program completed at 03/16/07  12:21:08
```

The following patches superseded at least 1 time(s) can be committed:

Superseded	# Times Superseded	Disk Space in /var/adm/sw/save	Superseded By
PHCO_34668	1	16384 bytes	PHCO_35989
PHNE_32477	1	7864320 bytes	PHNE_34293
PHSS_33326	1	9306112 bytes	PHSS_34101

```
WARNING: When a patch is committed, the files saved to /var/adm/sw/save
         during the installation of the patch are removed.  If
         these saved files are not present, then the patch cannot
         be removed from the system via swremove(1M).
. . . . . . . .
. . . . . . . .
Would you still like to commit these patches? y
Committing patches superseded at least 1 time(s) ...done.
All information has been logged to /var/adm/cleanup.log.
### Cleanup program completed at 03/16/07  12:21:25
```

The *cleanup* utility can also be used to remove superseded patches from a patch depot. Execute the following on a patch depot */depot/patch_depot*:

```
# cleanup  –d  /depot/patch_depot
```

11.4   Additional Patch Tools

This section describes two additional patch management approaches using the *Patch Assessment* and *Security Patch Check* tools. These tools analyze your system and reports on what patches you need to obtain and put on the system.

11.4.1   The Patch Assessment Tool

The *Patch Assessment Tool* allows you to create custom patch bundle for your system. The tool helps analyze and select missing patches. Note that the patch assessment tool has replaced the *Custom Patch Manager* (CPM) tool. To access patch assessment tool, follow steps below:

1. Go to *http://itrc.hp.com*.
2. Under "maintenance and support for hp products", click on "patch database".

3. Click on "run a patch assessment".
4. Click on "upload new system information".
5. Download the *swainv* script.
6. Add execute permission to the *swainv* script.
7. Execute *swainv* on the HP-UX system on which you want to perform the assessment. This script collects current patch information from the machine and puts it in a file called *inventory.xml*.

> **# ./swainv.txt**
>
> Copyright (c) Hewlett-Packard 2005-2006. All rights reserved.
>
> ./swainv.txt revision: 3.28
>
> This script lists the patches, products, bundles, and filesets found
> in a system or depot and packages the information in a file for transfer
> to the ITRC or the Response Center.
>
> *   Listing filesets
> *   Listing products
> *   Listing bundles
> *   Inventory written to ./inventory.xml
>
> **# ll inventory.xml**
>
> -rw-rw-rw- 1 root   sys   242659 Jun 8 20:48 inventory.xml

8. Click on "browse" and select the *inventory.xml* file.
9. Click on "submit" to upload the file.
10. You will see three options on the next screen – create a new assessment profile, import an exported assessment profile, or choose hprecommended. Many administrators prefer to use "hprecommended" profile. Otherwise, you may select one of the other two options. If you wish to create a new assessment profile, click on "create a new assessment profile" and fill out a form. If you have previously created a profile and is sitting on your system, click on "import an exported assessment profile" and upload the profile.
11. For this example, choose "hprecommended".
12. Click on "display candidate patches". This generates the patch assessment result and displays patches recommended for your system.
13. Review patches on the list and place a check mark by the ones you need and click on "add to selected patch list". Alternatively, you can click on "select all" and then on "add to selected patch list" to choose all patches.
14. Additional patches needed to satisfy dependencies for the selected patches appear on the next page automatically.
15. Click on "download selected".
16. Choose a file format – zip, gzip, or tar – and click on "download" to download all patches as a single bundle in the specified format.

Follow the patch bundle installation method discussed earlier to install the downloaded bundle on the system.

11.4.2 The Security Patch Check Tool

The *Security Patch Check Tool* analyzes a system or a software depot and compares patches on it to a copy of the security catalog. The tool generates a report listing the patches and actions recommended.

This tool is available at *http://software.hp.com* under "Security and manageability". See Figure 11-2.

Figure 11-2 *software.hp.com* **Main Page**

Download the tool and install it using the *swinstall* command as follows:

swinstall –s /tmp/SecPatchCk_B.02.02.depot

If your HP-UX system has access to the internet, execute the following command that will automatically download the security catalog off the ITRC website and compare security related patches on your system against a list of patches in the security catalog:

/opt/sec_mgmt/spc/bin/security_patch_check –d –r

If your HP-UX system does not have access to the internet, you will need to download the security catalog off *ftp://ftp.itrc.hp.com/export/patches/security_catalog2.gz*, put it in */tmp* directory, uncompress it, and execute *security_patch_check* script as follows:

```
# gunzip /tmp/security_catalog2.gz
# /opt/sec_mgmt/spc/bin/security_patch_check –d –c /tmp/security_catalog2

. . . . . . . .

. . . . . . . .
*** BEGINNING OF SECURITY PATCH CHECK REPORT ***
Report generated by: /opt/sec_mgmt/spc/bin/security_patch_check.pl, run as root

Analyzed localhost (HP-UX 11.11) from ymxppap0
Security catalog: /tmp/security_catalog2
Security catalog created on: Tue May 23 01:32:18 2006
Time of analysis: Tue May 23 12:53:20 2006

List of recommended actions for most secure system:

# Recommended    Bull Cnt Spec Reboot PDep Description
-----------------------------------------------------------------------------
1 Ignite-UX     111r2 1st man ?    ?   check /etc/passwd on trusted systems ignited from old images
2 MANUAL_ACTION 150   1st man ?    ?   check swacl settings
. . . . . . . .

. . . . . . . .
19 OS-Core      304   1st man ?    ?   unpack patches using the new procedure.
20 OBAM         1047  1st man ?    ?   disable the OBAM web administration interface
-----------------------------------------------------------------------------
*** END OF REPORT ***
NOTE:   Security bulletins can be found ordered by Document ID at
http://www.itrc.hp.com/service/cki/secBullArchive.do
```

A report similar to the above will be generated and recommended actions will be provided. Follow the recommendations to obtain patches and apply them on your system.

11.4.3   Introduction to HP-UX Software Assistant (SWA)

Beginning year 2007, both patch assessment and security patch check tools are made part of a new product release called "HP-UX Software Assistant". This product is available at *software.hp.com* under "security and manageability". Once installed, you can use the *swa* command, among others, to perform fuctions that you would otherwise perform using the patch assessment and security patch check tools.

Summary

Patches are installed on a system to fix existing problems and reduce the risk of potential problems. Patches may also bring new functionality to your system. Enabling new hardware and update system firmware are also typically done via patches. You built in this chapter an understanding of standard HP patch naming convention. You understood patch attributes, such as suppression, dependency, ratings, state, status, category tags, ancestry, and critical and non-critical.

You saw how individual patches and patch bundles could be downloaded using different methods and applied to a system. You also saw how to list, verify, roll back, and commit patches.

Finally, you looked at patch assessment and security patch check tools. The former enabled you to create custom patch bundle for your system and the latter used for analyzing whether or not required security patches were installed on your system. An introduction to HP-UX Software Assistant tool was provided at the end to give you a high-level overview of what this new product contained and provided.

HP Certified Systems Administrator

## 12

User and Group Account Administration

This chapter covers the following major topics:

- ✓ Understand /etc/passwd and /etc/group user authentication files
- ✓ Verify /etc/passwd and /etc/group file consistency
- ✓ Lock /etc/passwd file while editing
- ✓ Create, modify, deactivate, reactivate, and delete user accounts
- ✓ Display successful and unsuccessful user login attempts history
- ✓ Display currently logged in users
- ✓ Display and set user limits
- ✓ Create, modify, and delete group accounts
- ✓ Assign a user membership to multiple groups
- ✓ User login process & initialization files

12.1 Why Create Users and Groups

In order for an authorized person to gain access to an HP-UX system, you choose a unique user name (a.k.a. login name) for the individual and create a user account for him/her on the system.. This user is assigned membership to one or more groups. Members of the same group have same access rights on files and directories. Other users, or members of other groups, may or may not be given access to those files.

User account information is stored in two files – /etc/passwd and /etc/group. These files are updated when a user account is created, modified, or removed. The same files are referenced when a user attempts to log in to a system, and hence referred to as user authentication files. The following sub-sections discuss the files.

12.1.1   User Authentication – The /etc/passwd File

The /etc/passwd file contains vital user login information. Each line entry in the file contains information about one user account. Each field is separated from the other by the colon (:) character. A sample entry from /etc/passwd file is displayed in Figure 12-1. Notice that there are a total of seven fields in the row.

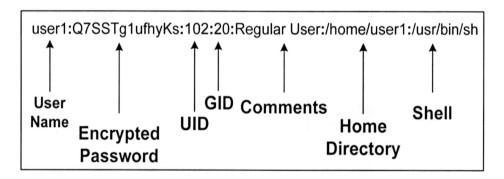

Figure 12-1 User Authentication File – /etc/passwd

Here is what information is stored in each field:

- ✓ The first field contains login name that a user uses to log in to the system. It should not be more than eight characters in length and must start with an alphabet.
- ✓ The second field contains 13 alphanumeric characters. These characters hold a user password in encrypted form. If this field is empty, it indicates that there is no password assigned to the user.
- ✓ The third field holds a unique number between 0 and approximately 2 billion. This number is known as *User ID* (UID). User ID 0 is reserved for the *root* user, UIDs between 1 and 99 are reserved for system accounts, and UIDs 100 and up are typically used for all other users..
- ✓ The fourth field holds a number referred to as *Group ID* (GID). This number corresponds with a group entry in the /etc/group file. At a time, a user can be a member of one group, which must already be defined in the /etc/group file. The GID defined in this field represents a user's primary group.

✓ The fifth field is optional. It contains general comments about a user that may include user's full name, telephone number, location, and organization. This information is displayed when you use commands, such as *finger*.
✓ The sixth field defines absolute path to the user home directory. A home directory is the place where a user is placed when he or she logs in. A user uses the home directory to store personal files.
✓ The last field contains absolute path of the shell file that the user is going to use after he/she logs in. Common shells are Bourne (*/sbin/sh*), Korn (*/usr/bin/ksh*), POSIX (*/usr/bin/sh*), and C (*/usr/bin/csh*).

A sample */etc/passwd* file is shown below:

```
# cat /etc/passwd
root:/af/4dEOdgkpY:0:3::/:/sbin/sh
daemon:*:1:5::/:/sbin/sh
bin:*:2:2::/usr/bin:/sbin/sh
sys:*:3:3::/:
adm:*:4:4::/var/adm:/sbin/sh
uucp:*:5:3::/var/spool/uucppublic:/usr/lbin/uucp/uucico
lp:*:9:7::/var/spool/lp:/sbin/sh
nuucp:*:11:11::/var/spool/uucppublic:/usr/lbin/uucp/uucico
hpdb:*:27:1:ALLBASE:/:/sbin/sh
nobody:*:-2:-2::/:
www:*:30:1::/:
webadmin:*:40:1::/usr/obam/server/nologindir:/usr/bin/false
smbnull:*:101:101:DO NOT USE OR DELETE - needed by Samba:/home/smbnull:/sbin/sh
opc_op:*:777:77:OpC default operator:/home/opc_op:/usr/bin/ksh
```

All these user accounts are standard and created automatically when HP-UX is installed.

 Permissions on */etc/passwd* should be 444 and it must be owned by the *root* user.

12.1.2   User Authentication – The */etc/group* File

The */etc/group* file contains group information. Each row in the file contains one group entry. Each user is assigned at least one group, which is referred to as his/her primary group. Each field in the file is separated from the other by the colon (:) character. A sample entry from */etc/group* file is exhibited in Figure 12-2. Notice that there are a total of four fields.

Here is what information is stored in each field:

✓ The first field contains a unique group name. It should not be more than eight characters in length and must start with an alphabet.
✓ The second field is not typically used and is left blank. However, it may contain an encrypted group-level password (copied and pasted from */etc/passwd* file). You may wish to implement this on a group if you want non-members to be able to change their group membership to this

---

group using the *newgrp* command. The non-members must enter the correct password to accomplish this.

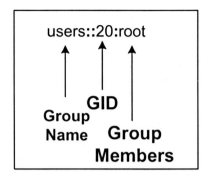

Figure 12-2 User Authentication File – */etc/group*

- ✓ The third field defines the GID, which is placed in the GID field of the */etc/passwd* file. Normally, groups are created with GIDs starting with 100. Several users can be members of one single group. Similarly, one user can be a member of several groups.
- ✓ The last field holds usernames that belong to the group. Note that a user's primary group is defined in the */etc/passwd* file and not here.

A sample */etc/group* file is shown below:

 # cat /etc/group
root::0:root
other::1:root,hpdb
bin::2:root,bin
sys::3:root,uucp
adm::4:root,adm
daemon::5:root,daemon
mail::6:root
lp::7:root,lp
tty::10:
nuucp::11:nuucp
users::20:root
nogroup:*:-2:
smbnull::101:
opcgrp::77:

All these group accounts are standard and created automatically when HP-UX is installed.

 Permissions on the */etc/group* file should be 444 and it must be owned by the *bin* user.

12.1.3 Verifying */etc/passwd* and */etc/group* File Consistency

To verify that the information, the */etc/passwd* file contains, is valid, use the *pwck* command. This command checks and validates total number of fields in each line, login names, UIDs, GIDs, and existence of login directory and shell. It reports any inconsistencies it finds.

To verify that the information, the */etc/group* file contains, is valid, use the *grpck* command. This command checks and validates total number of fields in each line and whether a user belonging to a group in this file is missing from the */etc/passwd* file.

12.1.4 Locking */etc/passwd* File

Although it is not recommended but sometimes you need to manually modify the */etc/passwd* file. You normally use the vi editor to do so. What happens if another user tries to change his/her password while you are editing the file. The password is modified successfully for the user and the */etc/passwd* file is updated to reflect the change, but this change is lost when you save the file later.

To prevent such an unwanted situation from happening, use the *vipw* command to edit */etc/passwd*. This command copies */etc/passwd* to a temporary file called */etc/ptmp* and disables write access to */etc/passwd*. When another user attempts to change his/her password while you are editing the file, he/she is denied permission to change the password. When you quit *vipw*, some automatic checks are performed on */etc/ptmp* to validate contents. If no errors are encountered, this file is moved back to */etc/passwd*, otherwise, */etc/passwd* remains unchanged. The other user should now be able to change his/her password.

12.2 Managing User Accounts and Passwords

Managing user accounts and passwords involve creating, assigning passwords to, modifying, deactivating, reactivating, and deleting user accounts. You have two methods available to manage them: command line and SAM.

12.2.1 Creating a User Account

Use the *useradd* command to create a user account. This command adds entries to the */etc/passwd* file and optionally to the */etc/group* file. It creates a home directory for the user and copies default user initialization files from the skeleton directory (*/etc/skel*) into the user's home directory. The syntax of the command is:

```
useradd  [–u <uid> [–o]]  [–g <group>]  [–G <group>[,<group...>]]  [–d <dir>]  [–s <shell>] \
[–c <comment>]  [–m [–k <skel dir>]]  [–f <inactive>]  [–e <expire>]  <login>
```

Table 12-1 explains options and arguments.

Let us take a look at a few examples to understand the behavior of the command.

Option / Argument	Description
–u uid	Indicates a unique user ID. If this option is not specified, the last UID used in the */etc/passwd* file is incremented by one and assigned to this user account.
–o	Means that the new user can share the UID specified with the –u option and being used by another user. When more than one users have the same UID, both get identical rights on each other's files. This should only be done in specific situations.
–g group	Denotes the primary group. If this option is not mentioned, the default group ID (20 for *users* group) is assigned.
–G group, group….	Specifies membership to up to 20 supplementary groups. If this option is not specified, no supplementary groups are added.
–d dir	Defines absolute path to the user home directory.
–s shell	Defines absolute path to the shell file.
–c comment	Defines useful comments or remarks.
–m	Creates home directory if it does not already exist.
–k skel dir	Specifies location of the skeleton directory (default is */etc/skel*), which contains user initialization template files. When a user account is created, files located in this directory are copied to the user's home directory. Four files are available in this directory by default: *.profile* (for Bourne, Korn, and POSIX shell users) *.login* and *.cshrc* (for C shell users) *.exrc* (shell startup configuration script) You may modify these files if you wish to or add more files to this directory so when a new user is created, he/she gets updated files as well as additional files. Existing user home directories will not be affected by this change.
–f inactive	Denotes maximum days of user inactivity before the user account is declared invalid.
–e expire	Specifies a date after which this account is disabled.
login	Specifies a login name to be assigned to this new user account.

Table 12-1 *useradd* Command Options

To create an account for user *aghori* with home directory */home/aghori*, shell */usr/bin/sh*, UID 101, and membership of *users* group, do the following. Also make sure that the default initialization scripts from the skeleton directory are copied.

 # useradd –u 101 –g users –m –d /home/aghori –s /usr/bin/sh aghori

Create an initial password for *aghori* by running the *passwd* command as follows:

 # passwd aghori
Changing password for aghori
New password:
Re-enter new password:
Passwd successfully changed

This two step procedure completes a new user account creation process.

A password protects a user account from unauthorized access into a UNIX system. It is a user's responsibility to change his/her password periodically. The following password setting requirements apply:

✓ Must be six to eight characters in length.
✓ Must start with a letter.
✓ Must contain at least one lowercase letter and one numeric or special character.
✓ Must differ from the login username.
✓ Must differ from the previous password by at least three characters.
✓ Can contain spaces and periods.

 These requirements do not apply to *root* user password. In fact, *root* can have any or no password.

To modify a user's password, issue the *passwd* command. The following shows how user *aghori* can change his password from the command line:

1. Enter the *passwd* command and hit *Enter*.
2. Type current password and hit *Enter*.
3. Type new password and hit *Enter*.
4. Retype new password to verify and hit *Enter*.

The *root* user has the privilege to change the password of any user on the system including its own. Also, when *root* changes a password, it is not prompted to enter the current user password.

To create an account for user *bghori* with all defaults, do the following. The default values for this user will be *users* (primary group), */home/bghori* (home directory), */sbin/sh* (shell), and no comments. Initialization files will be copied from */etc/skel* as well. When no UID is specified, the command automatically takes the next available from the */etc/passwd* file.

 # useradd bghori

To verify:

 # grep bghori /etc/passwd
bghori:*:102:20::/home/bghori:/sbin/sh

Create an initial password for user *bghori* with the *passwd* command.

In this example you have used user defaults. These defaults are defined in the */etc/default/useradd* file. You can either view the file contents with the *cat* command or do the following to view the default values:

 # useradd –D
GROUPID   20
BASEDIR   /home
SKEL   /etc/skel
SHELL   /sbin/sh
INACTIVE   -1
EXPIRE

You may wish to modify these defaults. For example, do the following to change default base directory to */usr/home* so when new user accounts are created, their home directories are created in there:

 # useradd –D –b /usr/home

This modification is reflected in the */etc/default/useradd* file too.

Let us use SAM to create a user account.

☞ Go to SAM → Accounts for Users and Groups → Users → Actions → Add. A blank form pops up as illustrated in Figure 12-3.

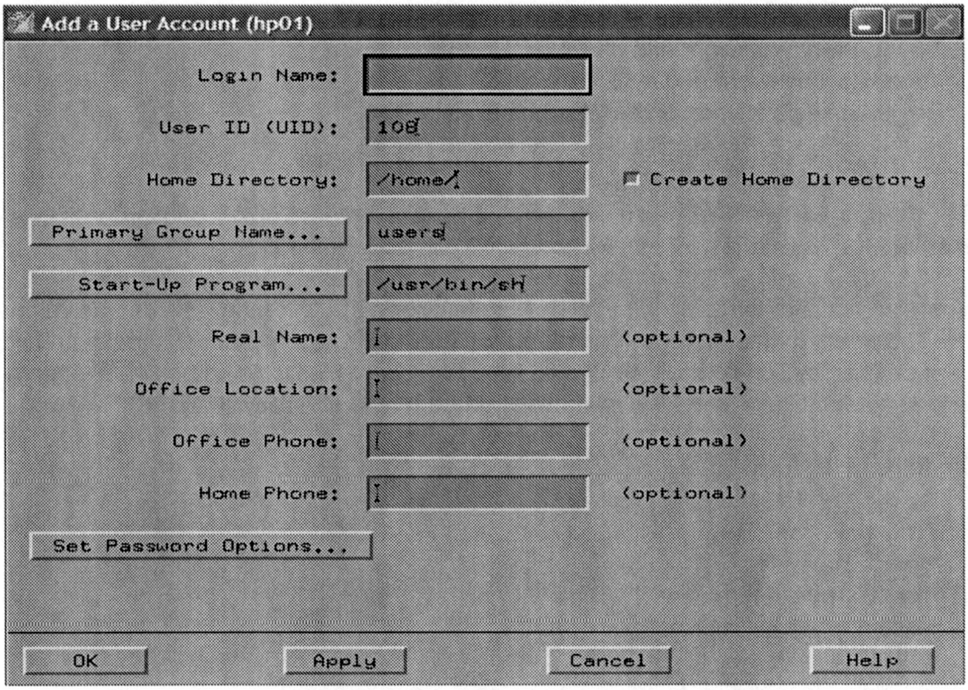

Figure 12-3 SAM – User Add

You need to input user information, such as login name, UID, home directory, primary group name, shell, password options, etc. In "Set Password Options", there are four sub-options. You need to choose one of them. The first one is default. Table 12-2 provides short description of each one of these.

Password Set Option	Description
No restrictions	This is the default option. You assign a password and communicate to the user. The user, at his/her will, may change the password later.
Force password change at next login	You assign an initial password and communicate to the user. The user must change it at first log in attempt.
Allow only superuser to change password	You assign a password and communicate to the user. Whenever the user wants his/her password change, only you, as a system administrator, can change it.
Enable password aging	You assign a password and communicate to the user. With this option, you need to set additional parameters, such as minimum time required between password changes, and so on. Refer to Chapter 38 "Administering HP-UX Security" for details.

Table 12-2 SAM – User Add Password Options

When you are done filling out the form, press OK. This will create a new user account based on the information you provided.

12.2.2 Creating Multiple User Accounts in One Go

You can add multiple user accounts with similar requirements in one shot. You need to create a template in SAM. This template can then be used for this purpose.

☞Go to SAM → Accounts for Users and Groups → Users → Actions → User Templates → Create. See Figure 12-4. Supply a template title and description. Most other fields are the same as on the *Add User* form. You have four options for UID generation, if you do not wish to specify one for each new individual user. These are "first available", "first available greater than one", "first available within range", and "prompt for it". You may also want to go to "Password Specifications" to modify any password aging options. Press OK when you are done.

To use the template to create user accounts, do the following:

☞Go to SAM → Accounts for Users and Groups → Users → Actions → User Templates → Select. See Figure 12-4. Highlight a template title you want to use and press OK. The selected template takes effect right away and is used for all new user adds until you unselect it from SAM → Accounts for Users and Groups → Users → Actions → User Templates → Unselect.

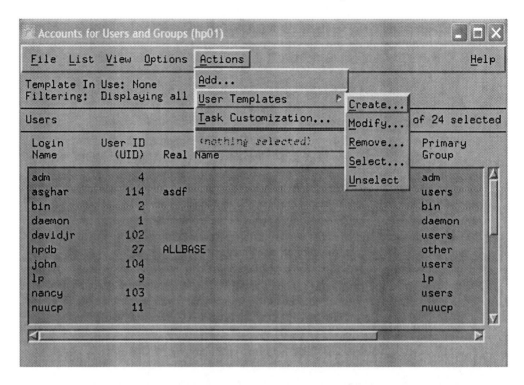

Figure 12-4 SAM – User Creation Template

12.2.3   Modifying a User Account

You can modify a user account with the *usermod* command. The syntax of the command is given below. Notice that options and arguments this command takes are identical with what *useradd* command takes, except with the "–l new logname" argument.

usermod [[–u <uid> [[–o]] [[–g <group>] [[–G <group>[,<group...>]] [[–d <dir> [[–m]] \
[[–s <shell>] [[–c <comment>] [[–f <inactive>] [[–e <expire>] [[–l <new logname>] \ <login>

Let us look at a couple of examples.

To modify user *aghori*'s login name to *aghori1*, home directory from */home/aghori* to */home/aghori1*, login shell from */usr/bin/sh* to */usr/bin/csh*, do the following:

usermod –m –d /home/aghori1 –s /usr/bin/csh –l aghori1 aghori

To verify:

grep aghori /etc/passwd
aghori1:fEncR9gl/GKQE:101:20::/home/aghori1:/usr/bin/csh

To modify user *bghori*'s UID and primary group using SAM, do the following:

HP Certified Systems Administrator

☞Go to SAM → Accounts for Users and Groups → Users. Highlight user *bghori* from the list and go to Actions → Modify. Make appropriate changes and press the OK button.

12.2.4 Deactivating and Reactivating a User Account

When you deactivate a user account, the user is unable to log in. Execute the *passwd* command to deactivate a user account. Notice that the asterisk character " * " appears in the password field.

```
# passwd –l  aghori1
# grep  aghori1  /etc/passwd
aghori1:*:101:20::/home/aghori1:/usr/bin/csh
```

Unless the *root* user runs the *passwd* command again with –d option or supply a new password to the user account to activate it, the account remains deactivated.

To deactivate a user account through SAM, follow the steps:

☞Go to SAM → Accounts for Users and Groups → Users. Highlight a user you want to deactivate and go to Actions → Deactivate.

To reactivate the user account through SAM, follow the steps:

☞Go to SAM → Accounts for Users and Groups → Users. Highlight the user you want to reactivate and go to Actions → Reactivate.

12.2.5 Deleting a User Account

To remove a user from the system, use the *userdel* command. For example, to delete user *bghori* including her home directory, do the following:

```
# userdel  –r  bghori
```

Do not specify the –r option if you do not want to remove user *bghori*'s home directory.

To remove a user account through SAM, follow the steps:

☞Go to SAM → Accounts for Users and Groups → Users. Highlight a user account you wish to remove and go to Actions → Remove.

When a remove operation is performed by SAM on a user account, it looks into the */etc/sam* directory for the existence and contents of a file called *rmuser.excl*. If the name of the user being removed matches with an entry in this file, SAM will not be able to delete that user. The default file is shown below:

```
# cat  /etc/sam/rmuser.excl
root
daemon
bin
sys
adm
uucp
lp
nuucp
hpdb
nobody
www
```

You may wish to modify this file to protect a user from being deleted.

12.2.6   Displaying Successful User Login Attempts History

The *last* command reports on successful user login attempts history and system reboots by looking into the */var/adm/wtmp* file. This file keeps a record of all login and logout activities including login time, duration a user stays logged in, and tty on which a user session takes place. Consider the following examples.

To list all login and logout activities, type the *last* command without any arguments.

```
# last
root          pts/0          Fri Dec 23 14:26        -         16:18  (01:52)
root          pts/ta         Fri Dec 23 12:28        -         13:06  (00:38)
root          pts/0          Thu Dec 22 15:45        -         16:29  (00:44)
root          pts/1          Thu Dec 22 14:54        still logged in
root          pts/ta         Thu Dec 22 13:56        -         14:28  (00:32)
root          pts/0          Mon Dec 19 12:20        -         12:20  (00:00)
root          pts/0          Mon Dec 19 12:19        -         12:20  (00:00)
reboot        system boot    Mon Dec 19 10:10        still logged in
root          pts/ta         Sun Dec 18 01:25        -         01:25  (00:00)
root          pts/ta         Sat  Dec 17 22:19       -         01:25  (03:06)
root          pts/0          Sat  Dec 17 12:06       -         12:07  (00:00)
reboot        system boot    Sat  Dec 17 08:28       -         10:10  (2+01:42)

wtmp begins Sat Dec 17 08:28
```

To list only system reboot information, do the following:

```
# last  reboot
reboot        system boot    Mon Dec 19 10:10        still logged in
reboot        system boot    Sat Dec 17 08:28        -         10:10 (2+01:42)

wtmp begins Sat Dec 17 08:28
```

HP Certified Systems Administrator

12.2.7 Displaying Unsuccessful User Login Attempts History

The *lastb* command reports on unsuccessful user login attempts history by looking into the */var/adm/btmp* file. This file keeps a record of all unsuccessful login attempt activities including login name, time, and tty on which an attempt is made. The *lastb* command produces the same results as the "last –f /var/adm/btmp" command. Consider the following example:

```
# lastb       (or # last –f /var/adm/btmp)
user1         pts/ta    Thu Dec 22 13:56
user1         pts/ta    Thu Dec 22 13:56

btmp begins Thu Dec 22 13:56
```

12.2.8 Displaying Currently Logged In Users

The *who* command looks into the */etc/utmp* file, which keeps a record of all currently logged in users, and lists them on the screen.

```
# who
root          pts/0     Dec 23 16:57
root          pts/1     Dec 22 14:54
```

12.2.9 Displaying and Setting User Limits

ulimit is used to display and set user process resource limits. When executed with –a option, it reports default limits for a user. Limits are categorized as either *soft* or *hard*. With the *ulimit* command, you can change the soft limits up to the maximum set by hard limits. The hard limits can be set only by *root*.

```
# ulimit –a
time(seconds)         unlimited
file(blocks)          unlimited
data(kbytes)          262144
stack(kbytes)         8192
memory (kbytes)       unlimited
coredump(blocks)      4194303
nofiles(descriptors)  60
```

To change the maximum file size from unlimited to 1KB, for instance, that a user can create, do the following:

```
# ulimit –f 1
```

Now try to create a file larger than 1KB in size. The system will not allow you to do that.

12.3 Managing Group Accounts

Managing group accounts involve creating, modifying, and deleting groups. You have two methods available to manage them: command line and SAM.

12.3.1 Creating a Group Account

Use the *groupadd* command to create a new group account. The syntax of the command is:

>   groupadd [–g gid [–o]] group

To create a new group called *dba* and assign it GID 101, do the following:

>   # groupadd –g 101 dba

To verify:

>   # grep dba /etc/group
>   dba::101:

The –o option may be specified to use a GID that is already in use by some other group account. When more than one groups share a GID, group members get identical rights on one another's files. This should be done only in specific situations.

Let us use SAM to create a new group called *sysadmin*. Follow the steps:

☞ Go to SAM → Accounts for Users and Groups → Groups → Actions → Add. Enter required information and hit the OK button. Consult Figure 12-5.

12.3.2 Modifying a Group Account

You can modify a group account with the *groupmod* command. The syntax of the command is given below. Notice that options and arguments this command takes are identical with what the *groupadd* command takes, except with the "–n name" argument which is used to modify group name.

>   groupmod [–g <gid> [–o]] [–n <name>] <group>

To modify group *dba* to *dba1* and GID to 201, do the following:

>   # groupmod –g 201 –n dba1 dba

To verify:

>   # grep dba /etc/group
>   dba1::201:

To do the same change using SAM:

☞Go to SAM → Accounts for Users and Groups → Groups. Highlight group *dba* from the list and go to Actions → Modify. Make appropriate changes and hit the OK button. See Figure 12-5.

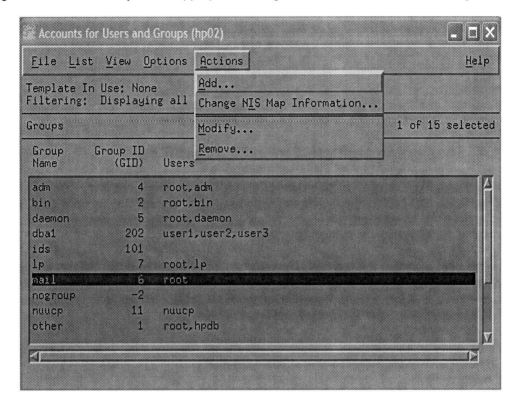

Figure 12-5 SAM – Group Administration

12.3.3 Deleting a Group Account

To delete a group account from the system use the *groupdel* command. For example, to delete group dba1, perform the following:

 # groupdel dba1

To do the same action using SAM:

☞Go to SAM → Accounts for Users and Groups → Groups. Highlight the group *dba1* from the list and go to Actions → Remove. Consult Figure 12-5.

When a remove operation is performed by SAM on a group account, it looks into the */etc/sam* directory for the existence and contents of a file called *rmgroup.excl*. If the name of the group being removed matches with an entry in this file, SAM will not be able to delete that group. The default file is shown below:

```
# cat /etc/sam/rmgroup.excl
root
other
bin
sys
adm
daemon
mail
lp
nogroup
```

You may wish to modify this file to protect a group from being deleted.

12.3.4   Assigning Multiple Group Memberships

A user can be a member of up to 20 groups at a time. One of the groups is considered primary and is defined in the GID field for the user in the /etc/passwd file. The primary group is also the default group for the user. All other groups are considered secondary (or supplementary) and a user entry is defined in the /etc/group file in the fourth field.

A user can alter his or her primary group membership temporarily by using the *newgrp* command. The *id* command can be used by the user anytime to view his/her primary and secondary group memberships. Let us say you are logged in as *aghori1* with UID 101 and primary group *users* with GID 20. You are also a member of *dba1* and *other* groups.

```
$ id
uid=101(aghori1) gid=20(users) groups=1(other),201(dba1)
$ newgrp  dba1
$ id
uid=101(aghori1) gid=201(dba1) groups=20(users),1(other)
```

The *id* command above shows your identification information including associated UID and GIDs. After running *newgrp*, the primary group is changed to *dba1*, which is reflected in the second output of the *id* command.

This change is temporary. You have two options to revert to your original primary group setting: log off and log back in or simply run the *newgrp* command without any options or arguments.

```
$ newgrp
$ id
uid=101(aghori1) gid=20(users) groups=1(other),201(dba1)
```

To permanently change primary group membership, you need to modify the /etc/passwd file.

12.4 User Login Process & Initialization Files

The user login process starts when you are presented with the login prompt and you attempt to log in to the system. The default login prompt you get when you are at the system console is similar to:

HP Certified Systems Administrator

```
GenericSysName [HP Release B.11.11] (see /etc/issue)
console login:
```

This login prompt message is stored in a text file called */etc/issue*. You can modify the text in the file to suit your needs.

The default login prompt you get when you *telnet* to an HP-UX system, *hp01* for example, is similar to:

```
HP-UX hp01 B.11.11 U 9000/800 (ta)
login:
```

When you type in your username, the system prompts you for password. You enter a password. The system tries to match the username entered with an entry in the */etc/passwd* file. If it finds a match, it tries to validate the password you entered by comparing it with the corresponding encrypted password entry for the user in the */etc/passwd* file. If the password is validated, the system lets you in. If either the username or the password is incorrect or invalid, you are denied access into the system.

Upon successful user authentication, contents of two files are displayed on the screen. These files are */etc/copyright* and */etc/motd*.

The */etc/copyright* file displays copyright information and the */etc/motd* (*Message Of The Day*) file, if exists, displays its contents. You can put informational or warning messages in */etc/motd*. Sample */etc/copyright* file is displayed below:

 # cat /etc/copyright
```
(c)Copyright 1983-2000 Hewlett-Packard Co.,  All Rights Reserved.
(c)Copyright 1979, 1980, 1983, 1985-1993 The Regents of the Univ. of California
(c)Copyright 1980, 1984, 1986 Novell, Inc.
. . . . . . . .
. . . . . . . .
Rights for non-DOD U.S. Government Departments and Agencies are as set
forth in FAR 52.227-19(c)(1,2).
```

12.4.1   Initialization Files

In Chapter 05 "The HP-UX Shells" you used local and environment variables. You modified default command prompt and added some useful information to it. You created shortcuts using aliases. In other words you modified your default shell environment to customize according to your needs. The changes you made were lost when you logged off the system. What if you wanted to make those changes permanent so each time you logged in they were there for you?

Modifications to the default shell environment can be stored in files called *Initialization* files. These are text files and executed after you are authenticated by the system and before getting the command prompt. Initialization files are of two types: *system-wide* and *per-user*.

The system-wide initialization files define general environment variables required by all or most users of the system. These files are maintained by the system administrator and can be modified to define any additional environment variables and customization needed by all system users. By default, these files define environment variables, such as PATH, MANPATH, TZ, and TERM by sourcing */etc/PATH*, */etc/MANPATH*, */etc/TIMEZONE*, and */usr/share/lib/terminfo/** files, respectively. Sample */etc/PATH*, */etc/MANPATH*, and */etc/TIMEZONE* files are shown below:

cat /etc/PATH
/usr/bin:/usr/ccs/bin:/usr/contrib/bin:/opt/ipf/bin:/opt/mx/bin:/opt/hparray/bin:/opt/nettladm/bin:/opt/upgrade/
bin:/opt/fcms/bin:/opt/resmon/bin:/opt/pd/bin:/opt/ignite/bin:/usr/bin/X11:/usr/contrib/bin/X11:/opt/graphics/c
ommon/bin:/opt/scr/bin:/opt/perf/bin:/opt/netscape:/var/opt/netscape/servers/shared/bin:/var/opt/netscape/
servers/bin/slapd/server:/var/opt/netscape/servers/bin:/opt/perl/bin:/opt/prm/bin:/usr/sbin/diag/contrib:/opt/
wlm/bin:

cat /etc/MANPATH
/usr/share/man/%L:/usr/share/man:/usr/contrib/man/%L:/usr/contrib/man:/usr/local/man/%L:/usr/local/man:
/opt/ipf/man:/opt/mx/share/man:/opt/upgrade/share/man/%L:/opt/upgrade/share/man:/opt/resmon/share/m
an:/opt/hatmmon/share/man:/opt/pd/share/man/%L:/opt/pd/share/man:/opt/pd/share/man/%L:/opt/pd/shar
e/man:/opt/pd/share/man/%L:/opt/pd/share/man:/opt/ignite/share/man/%L:/opt/ignite/share/man:/opt/hparr
ay/share/man/%L:/opt/hparray/share/man:/opt/graphics/common/man:/opt/scr/share/man:/usr/dt/share/ma
n:/opt/samba/man:/opt/perf/man/%L:/opt/perf/man:/opt/perl/man:/opt/prm/man/%L:/opt/prm/man:/opt/wlm/
share/man/%L:/opt/wlm/share/man:/opt/ldapux/share/man:/opt/ldapux/ypldapd/man

cat /etc/TIMEZONE
TZ=EST5EDT
export TZ

The per-user initialization files override or modify system defaults set by system-wide initialization files. These files may be customized by individual users to suit their needs.

You may wish to create additional per-user initialization files in your home directory to define additional environment variables or set additional shell properties.

Table 12-3 lists various initialization files for the POSIX, Korn, Bourne, and C shells.

Shell	System-Wide	Per-User	When new shell is invoked
POSIX	/etc/profile	$HOME/.profile $HOME/.shrc	$HOME/.shrc
Korn	/etc/profile	$HOME/.profile $HOME/.kshrc	$HOME/.kshrc
Bourne	/etc/profile	$HOME/.profile	-
C	/etc/csh.login	$HOME/.login $HOME/.cshrc	$HOME/.cshrc

Table 12-3 Shell Initialization Files

HP Certified Systems Administrator

Table 12-3 shows that */etc/profile* is the system-wide initialization file for the POSIX, Korn, and Bourne shell users, and */etc/csh.login* is the system-wide initialization file for the C shell users. Sample */etc/profile* and */etc/csh.login* files are displayed below:

 # cat /etc/profile

```
. . . . . . . .
. . . . . . . .
# Ignore HUP, INT, QUIT now.

      trap "" 1 2 3

# Set the default paths - Do NOT modify these.
# Modify the variables through /etc/PATH and /etc/MANPATH

      PATH=/usr/bin:/usr/ccs/bin:/usr/contrib/bin
      MANPATH=/usr/share/man:/usr/contrib/man:/usr/local/man
. . . . . . . .
. . . . . . . .
```

 # cat /etc/csh.login

```
. . . . . . . .
. . . . . . . .
      # default path for all users.
      set path=(/usr/bin /usr/ccs/bin /usr/contrib/bin)

      if ( -r /etc/PATH ) then

            # Insure that $PATH includes /usr/bin . If /usr/bin is
            # present in /etc/PATH then $PATH is set to the contents
            # of /etc/PATH.  Otherwise, add the contents of /etc/PATH
            # to the end of the default $PATH definition above.

            grep -q -e '^/usr/bin$' -e '^/usr/bin:' -e ':/usr/bin:'\
                  -e ':/usr/bin$' /etc/PATH

            if ( $status ) then
                  set path=($path `tr ":" " " </etc/PATH `)
            else
                  set path=(`tr ":" " " </etc/PATH `)
            endif
      endif
. . . . . . . .
. . . . . . . .
```

The per-user initialization files for POSIX, Korn, and Bourne shell users is *.profile*. Moreover, POSIX and Korn shell users may also have additional login files called *.shrc* and *.kshrc*, respectively, which are executed only when a new shell is invoked. The per-user initialization files for C shell users are *.login* and *.cshrc*. Sample *.profile*, *.login*, and *.cshrc* files are shown below:

---

cat $HOME/.profile

. . . .
. . . .
```
        stty erase "^H" kill "^U" intr "^C" eof "^D"
        stty hupcl ixon ixoff
        tabs
# Set up the search paths:
        PATH=$PATH:.
# Set up the shell environment:
        set -u
        trap "echo 'logout'" 0
# Set up the shell variables:
        EDITOR=vi
        export EDITOR
```

cat $HOME/.login

. . . .
. . . .
```
#set up the terminal
eval `tset -s -Q -m ':?hp' `
stty erase "^H" kill "^U" intr "^C" eof "^D" susp "^Z" hupcl ixon ixoff tostop
tabs
# Set up shell environment:
set noclobber
set history=20
```

cat $HOME/.cshrc

. . . .
. . . .
```
# (For security, this default is a minimal set.)
        set path=( $path )


# Set up C shell environment:
        if ( $?prompt ) then        # shell is interactive.
            set history=20          # previous commands to remember.
            set savehist=20         # number to save across sessions.
```
. . . .
. . . .

12.4.2   User Login Process via CDE

Two files are referenced for initialization when you log in via CDE. These files are *Xconfig* and *Xstartup* and are located in the */usr/dt/config* directory. You may copy the two files to */etc/dt/config* directory if you wish to customize them.

The first file is sourced by the */usr/dt/bin/dtlogin* command that is responsible for displaying the CDE login screen and validating user names and passwords.

The second file is a system-wide script that runs to set DISPLAY, HOME, PATH, USER, SHELL, and TZ environment variables.

Summary

In this chapter, you started off with building an understanding of *etc/passwd* and *etc/group* files. You looked at what the files contain, the syntax, and how to verify consistency. You looked at a way to lock the *etc/passwd* file while editing so nobody else can gain write access to it until you release the lock.

You studied user management including creating, modifying, deactivating, reactivating, and deleting them. You learned about a few simple tools that allowed you to view history of successful and unsuccessful user login attempts, display currently logged in users, and view and display user limits. Likewise, you studied group management including creating, modifying, and deleting group accounts, and assigning multiple group memberships to a user.

Finally, you learned what happened when a user entered a valid username and correct password; contents of what files were displayed, what initialization files were involved, and so on.

13

Logical Volume Manager

This chapter covers the following major topics:

✓ LVM concepts, components, and structure
✓ Manage disks using LVM including creating a physical volume, creating and displaying a volume group, creating and displaying a logical volume, extending a volume group, extending a logical volume, reducing a logical volume, removing a logical volume, reducing and removing a volume group, and backing up and recovering LVM configuration
✓ LVM mirroring concepts and requirements
✓ LVM mirroring of boot and non-boot volume groups – creating, extending, reducing, synchronizing, splitting, and merging mirrored logical volumes
✓ Mirroring and allocation policies
✓ Whole disk solution

13.1   Disk Partitioning Solutions

Data is stored on disk drives that are logically divided into partitions. A partition can exist on an entire single disk or it can span multiple disks. Each partition may contain a file system, a raw data space, a swap space, or a dump space.

A file system holds files and directories, a raw data space is used by databases and some other applications, a swap space supplements physical memory on a system, and a dump space stores memory image after a system is crashed.

The HP-UX OE software offers three solutions for creating and managing disk partitions on a system. These are referred to as the *Logical Volume Manager* (LVM) solution, the *Veritas Volume Manager* (VxVM) solution, and the *Whole Disk* solution. All three can be used concurrently on an HP-UX system but cannot co-exist on the same physical disk.

In this chapter, LVM and the whole disk solutions are covered. LVM is covered at length while whole disk is only touched upon since it is not commonly used anymore. The next chapter discusses VxVM in detail.

13.2   The Logical Volume Manager (LVM) Solution

The LVM solution is widely used on HP-UX systems to manage disk storage. It enables you to accumulate spaces taken from one or more disks (called *physical volumes*) to form a large logical container (called *volume group*), which can then be divided into partitions (called *logical volumes*). Figure 13-1 demonstrates LVM components.

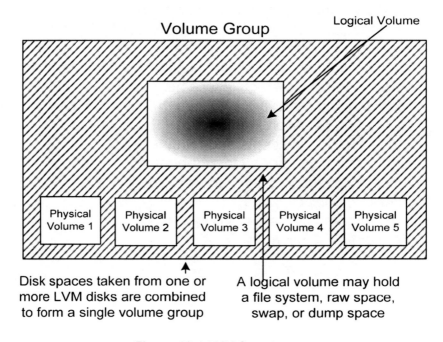

Figure 13-1 LVM Structure

LVM offers the following features and benefits:

- ✓ Supports RAID 0, RAID 1, and RAID 0+1. RAID stands for *Redundant Array of Independent Disks*. Chapter 14 "Veritas Volume Manager" describes various RAID levels.
- ✓ Supports online resizing of logical volumes
- ✓ Supports disk I/O on redundant (multiple) paths to disks (called *Physical Volume Links* or *Alternate Links*)
- ✓ Supports up to 3 mirrored copies of a logical volume

13.2.1   LVM Concepts

Physical Volume

When a disk is brought under LVM control, it is known as a *Physical Volume* (PV). This process initializes the disk and creates LVM data structures on it. A disk must first be initialized before it can be used in a volume group.

A disk in HP-UX has two device files associated with it. These are block and character device files. When the disk is converted into a physical volume, it continues to use the same device naming convention that it used outside the LVM control. A block device file, such as */dev/dsk/c1t0d0,* has a corresponding character device file, */dev/rdsk/c1t0d0*. Notice an "r" that makes the difference.

Volume Group

A *Volume Group* (VG) is created when at least one physical volume is added to it. The maximum number of physical volumes supported in a volume group is 255. The space from all physical volumes in a volume group is summed up to form a large pool of storage, which is then used to build one or more partitions called *Logical Volumes*. The default naming convention for volume groups is *vg00, vg01, vg02,* and so on. However, you may use any naming scheme you wish. For example, a volume group can be called *vgora102, vgtuxedo, vgweb*, and so on.

Each volume group has a sub-directory under */dev* that corresponds to the volume group's name and contains a *group* device file for the volume group and device files for all logical volumes within that volume group. For example, */dev/vg01* is the sub-directory for *vg01*, */dev/vg02* is the sub-directory for *vg02*, and so on. The following shows the *group* device file for the *vg00* volume group:

```
# ll /dev/vg00
crw-r-----  1 root    sys     64 0x000000 Dec 16 07:01 group
```

On every HP-UX system that uses LVM solution for disk management, the *vg00* volume group is considered special. This volume group contains the boot disk and logical volumes that normally contain the entire HP-UX OE software. This volume group is also referred to as the "root" volume group.

You can create as many as 10 volume groups on an HP-UX system by default, with each containing different application software. This default can be raised or lowered by modifying a kernel parameter *maxvgs*. Modifying a kernel parameter is discussed in Chapter 18 "Kernel Reconfiguration Methods".

Physical Extent

When a volume group is created, the physical volume added to it is divided into several smaller pieces known as *Physical Extents* (PEs). An extent is the smallest allocatable unit of space in LVM. When you create a volume group, you can either define the size of the PE or leave it to the default value, which is 4MB. This means a 4GB disk would contain approximately 1000 PEs. The smallest PE size can be 1MB and the largest 256MB.

All physical volumes in a volume group must use the same PE size. You cannot have some physical volumes set to one PE size while others using different.

The following command displays physical extent size used in *vg00* volume group:

```
# vgdisplay  vg00
--- Volume groups ---
VG Name                   /dev/vg00
VG Write Access           read/write
VG Status                 available
Max LV                    255
Cur LV                    8
Open LV                   8
Max PV                    16
Cur PV                    1
Act PV                    1
Max PE per PV             2500
VGDA                      2
PE Size (Mbytes)          4
Total PE                  2169
Alloc PE                  2169
Free PE                   0
Total PVG                 0
Total Spare PVs           0
Total Spare PVs in use    0
```

Logical Volume

A volume group contains a pool of space taken from one or more physical volumes added to the volume group. This volume group space is divided into one or more partitions called *Logical Volumes* (LVs).

A logical volume can be increased or decreased in size and can use space taken from multiple physical volumes inside the volume group. The minimum number of logical volumes that can be created in a volume group is 0 and the maximum 255.

The default naming convention for logical volumes is *lvol1, lvol2, lvol3*, and so on. However, you may use any naming scheme you wish. For example, a logical volume can be called *system, undo, table*, and so on. The following demonstrates device files for logical volumes in the *vg00* volume group. Notice that each logical volume has a block and a corresponding character device file.

ll /dev/vg00

brw-r-----	1	root	sys	64	0x000001	Dec 19 10:10	lvol1
brw-r-----	1	root	sys	64	0x000002	Dec 16 07:01	lvol2
brw-r-----	1	root	sys	64	0x000003	Dec 16 07:01	lvol3
brw-r-----	1	root	sys	64	0x000004	Dec 16 07:01	lvol4
brw-r-----	1	root	sys	64	0x000005	Dec 16 07:01	lvol5
brw-r-----	1	root	sys	64	0x000006	Dec 16 07:01	lvol6
brw-r-----	1	root	sys	64	0x000007	Dec 16 07:01	lvol7
brw-r-----	1	root	sys	64	0x000008	Dec 16 07:01	lvol8
crw-r-----	1	root	sys	64	0x000001	Dec 16 07:01	rlvol1
crw-r-----	1	root	sys	64	0x000002	Dec 16 07:01	rlvol2
crw-r-----	1	root	sys	64	0x000003	Dec 16 07:01	rlvol3
crw-r-----	1	root	sys	64	0x000004	Dec 16 07:01	rlvol4
crw-r-----	1	root	sys	64	0x000005	Dec 16 07:01	rlvol5
crw-r-----	1	root	sys	64	0x000006	Dec 16 07:01	rlvol6
crw-r-----	1	root	sys	64	0x000007	Dec 16 07:01	rlvol7
crw-r-----	1	root	sys	64	0x000008	Dec 16 07:01	rlvol8

Logical Extent

A logical volume is made up of extents called *Logical Extents* (LEs). Logical extents point to physical extents. The larger a logical volume size is, the more LEs it would contain.

The PE and LE sizes are usually kept the same within a volume group. However, a logical extent can be smaller or larger than a physical extent. The default size for an LE is 4MB. The following command displays information about */dev/vg00/lvol1* logical volume. The output does not indicate the LE size, however, you can divide the logical volume size by the Current LE count to get the LE size (which comes to 4MB in this example).

lvdisplay /dev/vg00/lvol1

```
--- Logical volumes ---
LV Name                     /dev/vg00/lvol1
VG Name                     /dev/vg00
LV Permission               read/write
LV Status                   available/syncd
Mirror copies               0
Consistency Recovery        MWC
Schedule                    parallel
LV Size (Mbytes)            300
Current LE                  75
Allocated PE                75
Stripes                     0
Stripe Size (Kbytes)        0
Bad block                   off
Allocation                  strict
IO Timeout (Seconds)        default
```

13.2.2   LVM Major and Minor Numbers

When a volume group and a logical volume are created, their block and character device files are created as well. These device files have major and minor numbers associated with them.

The standard major number used by LVM is 64. The minor numbers may be assigned as follows:

    0x000000, 0x000001, 0x000002, and so on
    0x010000, 0x010001, 0x010002, and so on
    0x020000, 0x020001, 0x020002, and so on

The "0x" in a minor number indicates that the number is hexadecimal, the next two digits are unique to a volume group's *group* file and hence to the volume group itself, and the last two digits represent unique logical volume device file number within the volume group. 00 always represents the *group* file, 01 represents the first logical volume, 02 represents the second logical volume, and so on.

For example:

    0x000000 represents the first volume group's *group* file.
    0x000001 represents the first volume group's first logical volume device file.
    0x000002 represents the first volume group's second logical volume device file.
    . . . .
    . . . .
    0x010000 represents the second volume group's *group* file.
    0x010001 represents the second volume group's first logical volume device file.
    0x010002 represents the second volume group's second logical volume device file.
    . . . .
    . . . .

The following depicts major and minor numbers for logical volumes and the *group* file in *vg00*. Notice that both block and character device files for a logical volume has identical minor number.

```
# ll /dev/vg00
crw-r-----   1    root   sys   64   0x000000   Dec 16 07:01   group
brw-r-----   1    root   sys   64   0x000001   Dec 19 10:10   lvol1
brw-r-----   1    root   sys   64   0x000002   Dec 16 07:01   lvol2
. . . . . . . .
. . . . . . . .
crw-r-----   1    root   sys   64   0x000001   Dec 16 07:01   rlvol1
crw-r-----   1    root   sys   64   0x000002   Dec 16 07:01   rlvol2
. . . . . . . .
. . . . . . . .
```

13.2.3   LVM Data Structure

LVM reserves some area at the beginning of a disk when the disk is initialized to become a physical volume. Additional structural components are added when the physical volume is included in a volume group and logical volumes are created. The following data structure components are essential:

PVRA – *Physical Volume Reserved Area* holds LVM information specific to the entire volume group of which the physical volume is part of. It also holds a copy of VGRA.

VGRA – *Volume Group Reserved Area* contains both VGSA and VGDA. It also maintains a mapping for LEs and PEs. This area is created by the *vgcreate* command.

VGSA – *Volume Group Status Area* contains quorum information for the volume group.

VGDA – *Volume Group Descriptor Area* contains information that the device driver needs to configure the volume group for LVM.

BDRA – *Boot Disk Reserved Area* is created only on a bootable disk. This area is created when a disk is initialized using the *pvcreate* command with –B option.

BBRA – *Bad Block Relocation Area* is created at the time a logical volume is formed. It contains information specific to the recovery of any bad block generated on the physical volume.

The remaining disk space of a physical volume is divided into PEs where typically file systems, raw partitions, and swap space reside.

13.3   Managing Volumes Using LVM

Managing volumes using LVM involves several tasks, such as identifying available disk devices, creating a physical volume, creating and displaying a volume group, creating and displaying a logical volume, extending a volume group, extending a logical volume, reducing a logical volume, removing a logical volume, reducing a volume group, removing a volume group, and backing up and recovering LVM configuration.

13.3.1   Identifying Available Disk Devices

Before starting to work with LVM, figure out what disks are available on the system that you can use. Execute the *ioscan* command to identify disks and device files, and then use the *diskinfo* command to determine disk sizes. Here is how you can do it:

```
# ioscan –fnkCdisk
Class   I H/W Path   Driver    S/W State H/W Type  Description
=====================================================================
disk    0 8/8.4.0   sdisk     CLAIMED  DEVICE   SEAGATE ST39173WC
              /dev/dsk/c0t4d0   /dev/rdsk/c0t4d0
disk    1 8/8.12.0  sdisk     CLAIMED  DEVICE   SEAGATE ST39173WC
              /dev/dsk/c0t12d0  /dev/rdsk/c0t12d0
disk    2 8/12.0.0  sdisk     CLAIMED  DEVICE   SEAGATE ST39173WC
              /dev/dsk/c1t0d0   /dev/rdsk/c1t0d0
```

```
disk    3 8/12.4.0  sdisk    CLAIMED  DEVICE    SEAGATE ST39173WC
              /dev/dsk/c1t4d0  /dev/rdsk/c1t4d0
disk    4 8/12.12.0 sdisk    CLAIMED  DEVICE    SEAGATE ST39173WC
              /dev/dsk/c1t12d0  /dev/rdsk/c1t12d0
disk    5 8/16/5.2.0 sdisk    CLAIMED  DEVICE    TOSHIBA CD-ROM XM-5701TA
              /dev/dsk/c2t2d0  /dev/rdsk/c2t2d0
```

The *ioscan* output shows that there are five hard drives and one CD-ROM drive in the system. You can also view them using SAM as follows:

☞ Go to SAM → Disks and File Systems → Disk Devices. SAM also displays disk sizes and usage information.

One of these hard drives is already in use as the boot disk by the HP-UX OE. Do a *setboot* command and find out which one it is.

 # setboot
Primary bootpath : 8/8.4.0
Alternate bootpath : 8/16/5.0.0

Autoboot is ON (enabled)
Autosearch is ON (enabled)

The *setboot* command notifies that the primary boot disk is installed at hardware address 8/8.4.0, which corresponds to the disk at */dev/dsk/c0t4d0* (see *ioscan* output above). Leaving this disk out, you have four disks – *c0t12d0, c1t0d0, c1t4d0* and *c1t12d0* – available to play with. Issue the *diskinfo* command on the four disk device files to determine their sizes.

 # diskinfo /dev/rdsk/c0t12d0
SCSI describe of /dev/rdsk/c0t12d0:
        vendor: SEAGATE
        product id: ST39173WC
        type: direct access
        size: **8891556 Kbytes**
        bytes per sector: 512

 # diskinfo /dev/rdsk/c1t0d0
SCSI describe of /dev/rdsk/c1t0d0:
        vendor: SEAGATE
        product id: ST39173WC
        type: direct access
        size: **8891556 Kbytes**
        bytes per sector: 512

 # diskinfo /dev/rdsk/c1t4d0
SCSI describe of /dev/rdsk/c1t4d0:
        vendor: SEAGATE
        product id: ST39173WC

```
                type:              direct access
                size:              8891556 Kbytes
                bytes per sector:  512
```

diskinfo /dev/rdsk/c1t12d0
SCSI describe of /dev/rdsk/c1t12d0:
```
                vendor:            SEAGATE
                product id:        ST39173WC
                type:              direct access
                size:              8891556 Kbytes
                bytes per sector:  512
```

And the disk that contains the HP-UX OE has the following size:

diskinfo /dev/rdsk/c0t4d0
SCSI describe of /dev/rdsk/c0t4d0:
```
                vendor:            SEAGATE
                product id:        ST39173WC
                type:              direct access
                size:              8891556 Kbytes
                bytes per sector:  512
```

So you have total 5 x 9GB disks of which 4 are available to you to work with.

13.3.2   Creating a Physical Volume

A disk must be initialized using the *pvcreate* command before it can be used in LVM. The disk is then added to a volume group, as a physical volume, to create logical volumes.

Occasionally, a utility called *mediainit* is run to format a disk and verify its integrity before bringing it under LVM control. This command wipes out everything from the disk. Run it on raw disk device as follows:

mediainit /dev/rdsk/c1t0d0

Now, execute *pvcreate* to reserve space for LVM data structures and create other necessary structures. The command must be run on the raw disk device, such as */dev/rdsk/c1t0d0*.

pvcreate /dev/rdsk/c1t0d0
Physical volume "/dev/rdsk/c1t0d0" has been successfully created.

If the disk was used previously in another volume group, specify the –f option with *pvcreate* to force create new LVM structures on it.

pvcreate –f /dev/rdsk/c1t0d0
Physical volume "/dev/rdsk/c1t0d0" has been successfully created.

13.3.3   Creating and Displaying a Volume Group

The next step is to create a volume group. Creating a volume group requires that you first setup a directory and a *group* file. Follow the steps below to create a volume group *vg01*.

```
# mkdir /dev/vg01
# cd /dev/vg01
# mknod group c 64 0x010000
# ll
crw-rw-rw- 1 root     sys      64 0x010000 Dec 25 09:01 group
```

In the above sequence of activities, a *vg01* directory under */dev* is created that houses the volume group control device file *group*.

The *mknod* command creates the *group* file as a character special device file with LVM major number 64 and minor number 0x010000.

Now, create *vg01* volume group using the *vgcreate* command and specify the */dev/dsk/c1t0d0* physical volume block device file to add to the volume group.

```
# vgcreate vg01 /dev/dsk/c1t0d0
Increased the number of physical extents per physical volume to 2170.
Volume group "/dev/vg01" has been successfully created.
Volume Group configuration for /dev/vg01 has been saved in /etc/lvmconf/vg01.conf
```

There are certain options available with *vgcreate* that you can use if you need to modify certain properties of the volume group. Some of them are described in Table 13-1.

Option	Description
–e MaxPhysicalExtents	Limits maximum number of PEs that can be created on a physical volume (default is 1016).
–l MaxLogicalVolumes	Limits maximum number of LVs that can be created in a volume group (default is 255).
–p MaxPhysicalVolumes	Limits maximum number of PVs that can be added to a volume group (default is 16).
–s PhysicalExtentSize	Assigns the PE size, in MBs, to be used in a volume group (default is 4MB).

Table 13-1 *vgcreate* Command Options

To view what *vgcreate* has done, execute the *vgdisplay* command. Run this command with and without the –v option. With –v, it reports details.

```
# vgdisplay –v vg01
--- Volume groups ---
VG Name                  /dev/vg01
VG Write Access          read/write
VG Status                available
```

Max LV	255
Cur LV	0
Open LV	0
Max PV	16
Cur PV	1
Act PV	1
Max PE per PV	2170
VGDA	2
PE Size (Mbytes)	4
Total PE	2170
Alloc PE	0
Free PE	2170
Total PVG	0
Total Spare PVs	0
Total Spare PVs in use	0
--- Physical volumes ---	
PV Name	/dev/dsk/c1t0d0
PV Status	available
Total PE	2170
Free PE	2170
Autoswitch	On

The *vgdisplay* command shows that there is one physical volume in the volume group with 2170 PEs, each of size 4MB. Currently, none of the PEs are allocated and no logical volume exists. The last portion from the output under "Physical volumes" displays information about the physical volume contained in *vg01*.

You can also view detailed information about a physical volume using the *pvdisplay* command. Run this command with and without the –v option on */dev/dsk/c1t0d0*.

 # pvdisplay /dev/dsk/c1t0d0

--- Physical volumes ---	
PV Name	/dev/dsk/c1t0d0
VG Name	/dev/vg01
PV Status	available
Allocatable	yes
VGDA	2
Cur LV	0
PE Size (Mbytes)	4
Total PE	2170
Free PE	2170
Allocated PE	0
Stale PE	0
IO Timeout (Seconds)	default
Autoswitch	on

You can use SAM too to create a volume group. Follow the steps below:

Go to SAM → Disks and File Systems → Volume Groups → Actions → Create. Fill out the form with required information and hit the OK button. See Figure 13-2.

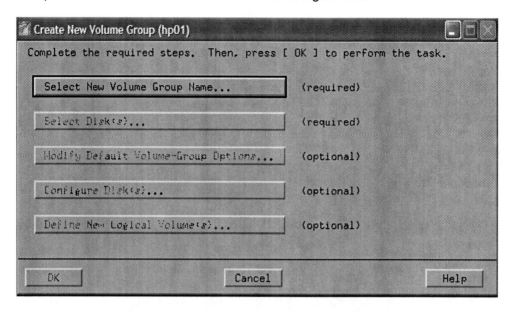

Figure 13-2 SAM – Volume Group Creation

13.3.4   Creating and Displaying a Logical Volume

At this point, you have a pool of storage space available within *vg01* that you can use to construct logical volumes. Create a logical volume with all default values using the *lvcreate* command in *vg01* as follows:

 # lvcreate vg01
Logical volume "/dev/vg01/lvol1" has been successfully created with
character device "/dev/vg01/rlvol1".
Volume Group configuration for /dev/vg01 has been saved in /etc/lvmconf/vg01.conf

When *lvcreate* is executed this way, it takes several defaults. Table 13-2 shows some options that you can define with the command. The table also highlights the default values.

Option	Description
–L LogicalVolumeSize	Specifies logical volume size in MBs (default is 0MB).
–l LogicalExtentsNumber	Assigns logical volume size in LEs (default is 0).
–n LogicalVolumeName	Denotes logical volume name (default is *lvol1*, *lvol2*, *lvol3*, and so on).

Table 13-2 *lvcreate* Command Options

Run the *vgdisplay* command as follows to see what *lvcreate* has performed:

vgdisplay –v vg01
--- Volume groups ---

VG Name	/dev/vg01
VG Write Access	read/write
VG Status	available
Max LV	255
Cur LV	1
Open LV	1
Max PV	16
Cur PV	1
Act PV	1
Max PE per PV	2170
VGDA	2
PE Size (Mbytes)	4
Total PE	2170
Alloc PE	0
Free PE	2170
Total PVG	0
Total Spare PVs	0
Total Spare PVs in use	0

   --- Logical volumes ---

LV Name	/dev/vg01/lvol1
LV Status	available/syncd
LV Size (Mbytes)	0
Current LE	0
Allocated PE	0
Used PV	0

   --- Physical volumes ---

PV Name	/dev/dsk/c1t0d0
PV Status	available
Total PE	2170
Free PE	2170
Autoswitch	On

Notice the change in the output of the *vgdisplay* command before and after the logical volume is created. The logical volume constructed above has used all defaults. It is created with 0 bytes in size using the default naming convention.

Now, allocate 1000MB to *lvol1* as follows:

lvextend –L 1000 /dev/vg01/lvol1
Logical volume "/dev/vg01/lvol1" has been successfully extended.
Volume Group configuration for /dev/vg01 has been saved in /etc/lvmconf/vg01.conf

The size can be specified in LEs too. Since the default LE size is 4MB, the 1000MB *lvol1* requires 250 LEs. The following command does exactly what the above has accomplished:

 # lvextend –l 250 /dev/vg01/lvol1
Logical volume "/dev/vg01/lvol1" has been successfully extended.
Volume Group configuration for /dev/vg01 has been saved in /etc/lvmconf/vg01.conf

This way a logical volume is setup in two steps. In step one, it was created, and in step two, it was given required space.

The following example does both in one go. It creates a logical volume, *lvol2*, and, at the same time, allocates space to it. You can use either of the following. Both will produce identical output.

 # lvcreate –L 2000 vg01
 # lvcreate –l 500 vg01

Use the *vgdisplay* or the *lvdisplay* command in verbose mode and check the *lvol2* information.

Another example below creates a 3150MB *lvdata1* logical volume in *vg01*.

 # lvcreate –L 3150 –n lvdata1 vg01
Warning: rounding up logical volume size to extent boundary at size "3152" MB.
Logical volume "/dev/vg01/lvdata1" has been successfully created with
character device "/dev/vg01/rlvdata1".
Logical volume "/dev/vg01/lvdata1" has been successfully extended.
Volume Group configuration for /dev/vg01 has been saved in /etc/lvmconf/vg01.conf

Notice that since 3150 (LV size in MBs) is not a multiple of 4 (LE/PE default size), the *lvcreate* command rounded it up to the nearest higher number, which is 3152.

To display *lvdata1* logical volume information, use the *lvdisplay* command.

 # lvdisplay /dev/vg01/lvdata1
--- Logical volumes ---
LV Name	/dev/vg01/lvdata1
VG Name	/dev/vg01
LV Permission	read/write
LV Status	available/syncd
Mirror copies	0
Consistency Recovery	MWC
Schedule	parallel
LV Size (Mbytes)	3152
Current LE	788
Allocated PE	788
Stripes	0
Stripe Size (Kbytes)	0
Bad block	on
Allocation	strict
IO Timeout (Seconds)	default

Also try *vgdisplay* with –v option to check the logical volume information.

SAM can be used, as well, for this purpose. Follow the steps below:

☞ Go to SAM → Disks and File Systems → Logical Volumes → Actions → Create. See Figure 13-3. Fill out the form with required information and click on the OK button.

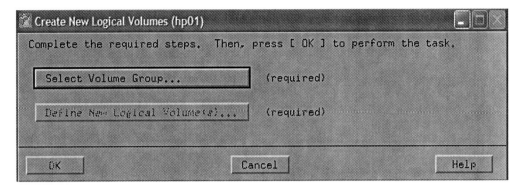

Figure 13-3 SAM – Logical Volume Creation

At this stage, you may want to view the contents of a file called */etc/lvmtab* (***lvm tab**le) that maintains a list of all volume groups on the system together with what physical volumes each of them contains. You must use the *strings* command to view this file.

strings /etc/lvmtab
/dev/vg00
/dev/dsk/c0t4d0
/dev/vg01
/dev/dsk/c1t0d0

As you can see, there are two volume groups, with each containing a single physical volume. This file is created when the first disk on the system is pvcreated.

13.3.5   Extending a Volume Group

Extending a volume group adds one or more physical volumes to it. When you created *vg01*, you added one physical volume, */dev/dsk/c1t0d0,* to it. The following example adds to *vg01* another disk */dev/dsk/c1t4d0*. Run *pvcreate* and then *vgextend* to achieve this.

pvcreate /dev/rdsk/c1t4d0
vgextend vg01 /dev/dsk/c1t4d0
Volume group "vg01" has been successfully extended.
Volume Group configuration for /dev/vg01 has been saved in /etc/lvmconf/vg01.conf

Do a *vgdisplay* with –v to see the updated *vg01* volume group information.

Let us use SAM to extend a volume group. Follow the steps below:

☞ Go to SAM → Disks and File Systems → Volume Groups (highlight a volume group from the list) → Actions → Extend. See Figure 13-4. Input required information and press the OK button.

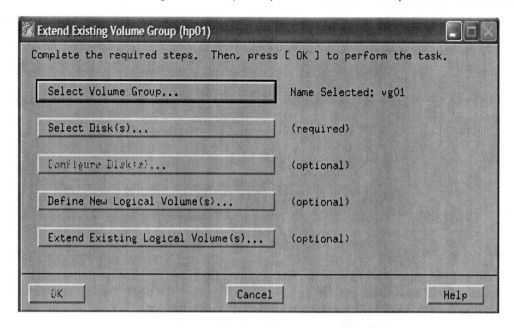

Figure 13-4 SAM – Volume Group Extend

13.3.6   Extending a Logical Volume

Extending a logical volume increases the logical volume in size. You created three logical volumes above: *lvol1*, *lvol2*, and *lvdata1* with sizes 1000MB, 2000MB, and 3150MB, respectively. The following example extends *lvol1* to 3500MB. Use the *lvextend* command to perform this activity. You can specify the size in either MBs or LEs. Both of the following will generate identical output:

    # **lvextend** –L 3500 /dev/vg01/lvol1
    # **lvextend** –l 875 /dev/vg01/lvol1

When a logical volume is extended, it occupies additional space from wherever it finds on the physical volume(s). This is referred to as RAID 0.

You can use SAM too to extend a logical volume. Follow the steps below:

☞ Go to SAM → Disks and File Systems → Logical Volumes (highlight a logical volume from the list) → Actions → Increase Size (Specify the size), as shown in Figure 13-5, and hit the OK button.

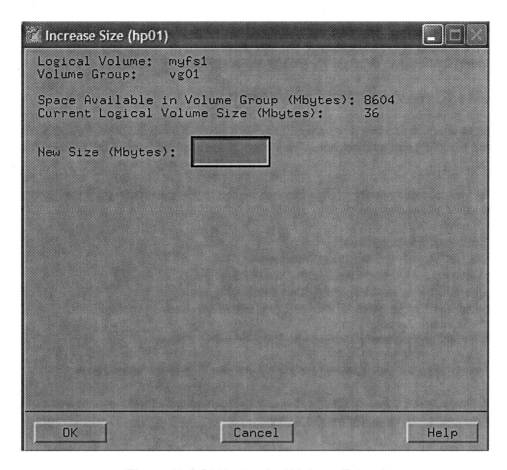

Figure 13-5 SAM – Logical Volume Extend

13.3.7   Reducing a Logical Volume

Reducing a logical volume is to decrease the logical volume in size. Currently, *lvol1* logical volume is 3500MB. The following example reduces it to 500MB. Use the *lvreduce* command to perform this activity. You can specify the size in either MBs or LEs. Both of the following will produce one and the same output:

lvreduce –L 500 /dev/vg01/lvol1
lvreduce –l 125 /dev/vg01/lvol1
Warning: The Logical Volume has a file system larger than the reduced size.
Reducing the Logical Volume will cause file system corruption.
When a logical volume is reduced useful data might get lost;
do you really want the command to proceed (y/n) : y
Logical volume "/dev/vg01/lvol1" has been successfully reduced.
Volume Group configuration for /dev/vg01 has been saved in /etc/lvmconf/vg01.conf

There is some risk involved when you reduce a logical volume size. You might end up losing critical data. Do a backup of the file system in the logical volume before reducing its size. See Chapter 19 "Performing Backup and Restore" for details on how to perform backups.

13.3.8   Removing a Logical Volume

To remove a logical volume, first unmount the file system, if mounted, in it. A detailed discussion on creating, mounting, and unmounting a file system is covered in Chapter 15 "Working with File Systems".

Use the *lvremove* command as follows to remove *lvol1*. You need to confirm the removal by inputting a "y" when prompted.

> **# lvremove /dev/vg01/lvol1**
> The logical volume "/dev/vg01/lvol1" is not empty;
> do you really want to delete the logical volume (y/n) : y
> Logical volume "/dev/vg01/lvol1" has been successfully removed.
> Volume Group configuration for /dev/vg01 has been saved in /etc/lvmconf/vg01.conf

The command gives a warning message. Proceed with caution.

SAM can be used, as well, to remove a logical volume. Follow the steps below:

☞ Go to SAM → Disks and File Systems → Logical Volumes (highlight a logical volume from the list) → Actions → Remove. Hit the OK button.

13.3.9   Reducing a Volume Group

Reducing a volume group removes one or more physical volumes from it. Currently, *vg01* includes two physical volumes: */dev/dsk/c1t0d0* and */dev/dsk/c1t4d0*. Use *vgreduce* to remove */dev/dsk/c1t4d0* from it. The physical volume must not be in use.

> **# vgreduce vg01 /dev/dsk/c1t4d0**
> Volume group "vg01" has been successfully reduced.
> Volume Group configuration for /dev/vg01 has been saved in /etc/lvmconf/vg01.conf

Issue the *vgdisplay* command with –v option to see the updated *vg01* volume group configuration information.

13.3.10   Removing a Volume Group

To remove a volume group, you have two options: one, remove all logical volumes from the volume group and then remove it, and two, use the command *vgexport* and blow away the volume group including all logical volumes within it. Examples of both are given below.

Presently, you have two logical volumes, *lvol2* and *lvdata1*, remaining in *vg01*. With the first method, use the *lvremove* command and remove both logical volumes. Next, use the *vgremove* command as follows to remove *vg01*:

```
# vgremove  vg01
Volume group "vg01" has been successfully removed.
```

The other method requires that you run the following two commands. Note that *vg01* must not be in use. The *vgchange* command with "-a n" deactivates *vg01* and *vgexport* blows it away.

```
# vgchange  -a  n  vg01
# vgexport  vg01
```

Remember to proceed with caution whenever you perform reduce and remove operations.

Let us see how SAM can be utilized to perform a volume group removal operation. Follow the steps below:

☞ Go to SAM → Disks and File Systems → Volume Group (highlight a volume group from the list) → Actions → Remove. Hit the OK button.

13.3.11   Backing Up and Recovering LVM Configuration

LVM structural information pertaining to a volume group, including physical and logical volumes within it, is stored automatically in the */etc/lvmconf* directory, by default, when the volume group is created. The file name where the information is stored corresponds to the volume group's name. Later, whenever a modification is performed using LVM commands, such as *vgextend*, *vgreduce*, *lvcreate*, *lvextend*, *lvreduce*, *lvremove*, *lvsplit*, *lvmerge*, *lvchange*, *lvlnboot*, *lvrmboot*, *pvmove*, or *pvchange* that alters the volume group's structure, an LVM utility called *vgcfgbackup* is executed automatically which updates the configuration file and saves a copy of it with a *.old* extension. Each volume group, including *vg00*, on the system has an associated configuration file in */etc/lvmconf*.

Currently, you have only *vg00* volume group. When you do an *ll* on the */etc/lvmconf* directory, you are going to see something similar to the following:

```
# ll /etc/lvmconf
total 1216
----------    1     root    sys    0        Jan  7  10:49   lvm_lock
-rw-------    1     root    sys    199680   Jan 27  10:44   vg00.conf
-rw-------    1     root    sys    199680   Jan 27  10:41   vg00.conf.old
```

You can run *vgcfgbackup* manually if you wish to. Here is how it works. The following example command backs up *vg01* configuration information, assuming that the volume group exists:

```
# vgcfgbackup  vg01
Volume Group configuration for /dev/vg01 has been saved in /etc/lvmconf/vg01.conf
```

The saved configuration information can be used to recover corrupted or lost LVM structures of the volume group. The *vgcfgbackup* command partners with the *vgcfgrestore* command, which offers the functionality of restoring LVM configuration. Here is how it works. The following example command demonstrates how *vg01* configuration information can be restored to the */dev/dsk/c1t0d0* physical volume:

vgcfgrestore –n vg01 /dev/rdsk/c1t0d0
Volume Group configuration has been restored to /dev/rdsk/c1t0d0

13.4   LVM Mirroring

LVM supports replication of data on up to two additional physical volumes for high availability purposes. This is known as *Mirroring*. With mirroring configuration, if one of the physical volumes fails, there is no service interruption and users continue to access data on the remaining physical volume(s). LVM mirroring is performed at the logical volume level. A logical volume that may have in it a file system, a raw database partition, or a device swap, can be mirrored. One important point to note here is that mirroring does not protect against data loss or corruption; it only protects against disk failures.

In order to perform LVM mirroring, the following is required:

✓   You must have HP-UX MirrorDisk/UX software installed on the system. MirrorDisk/UX is part of HP-UX 11i Enterprise and Mission-Critical OEs.
✓   It is very important to have a minimum of two separate physical volumes, with each connected to a separate physical controller card. If this requirement is not met, you can still do the mirroring but will not be able to get true benefits of it.
✓   The physical volumes must be part of a single volume group.
✓   You have to have a logical volume available for mirroring or create one for this purpose.
✓   The target logical volume must be the same size or larger than the source logical volume.

13.4.1   Mirroring the Boot Volume Group

In this sub-section, you are going to create a two-way mirror of all the logical volumes that reside in *vg00* volume group. A two-way mirror refers to using two physical volumes, a three-way mirror refers to using three physical volumes, and so on. Mirroring is also referred to as RAID 1.

This sub-section contains references to shutting down and booting up the system, modifying boot paths, and some pre-boot level tasks. Refer to Chapter 17 "Shutting Down and Starting Up an HP-UX System" for details.

Here is the procedure. Make sure requirements for mirroring identified earlier are met. From previous sections, you know that *vg00* resides on *c0t4d0* and contains eight logical volumes – *lvol1* through *lvol8*. For the purpose of this demonstration, let us use *c1t4d0* disk, which is available, resides on a separate physical controller card, and is of the same size as *c0t4d0*.

1.   Bring *c1t4d0* under LVM control. Run *pvcreate* on it. Don't forget to specify the –B option. This creates BDRA on the disk.

    # pvcreate –fB /dev/rdsk/c1t4d0

2.   Extend *vg00* to include the physical volume in it. Run *vgextend*.

    # vgextend vg00 /dev/dsk/c1t4d0

---

3. Copy boot utilities to BDRA of *c1t4d0*. Use the *mkboot* command.

   # **mkboot /dev/rdsk/c1t4d0**

4. Copy AUTO file to boot LIF area. Enclose contents to be written within quotes. This file is read at boot time to determine the HP-UX kernel file name and directory location. The –lq options force the boot process to ignore quorum checking and boot the system or partition, even if the other physical volume(s) included in the mirrored configuration, becomes defective.

   # **mkboot –a "hpux –lq(;0)/stand/vmunix" /dev/rdsk/c1t4d0**

5. Mirror all eight logical volumes. The –m option with the *lvextend* command specifies the number of mirrors that you want (1 indicates a two-way mirror, 2 indicates a three-way mirror, and so on). Each logical volume is replicated on to *c1t4d0* physical volume. The output from the first instance of the *lvextend* command is displayed. It will be very similar for the remaining logical volumes. Depending on a logical volume size, it may take long to synchronize mirrors.

   # **lvextend –m 1 /dev/vg00/lvol1 /dev/dsk/c1t4d0**
   The newly allocated mirrors are now being synchronized. This operation will
   take some time. Please wait ....
   Logical volume "/dev/vg00/lvol1" has been successfully extended.

   Volume Group configuration for /dev/vg00 has been saved in /etc/lvmconf/vg00.conf
   # **lvextend –m 1 /dev/vg00/lvol2 /dev/dsk/c1t4d0**
   # **lvextend –m 1 /dev/vg00/lvol3 /dev/dsk/c1t4d0**
   # **lvextend –m 1 /dev/vg00/lvol4 /dev/dsk/c1t4d0**
   # **lvextend –m 1 /dev/vg00/lvol5 /dev/dsk/c1t4d0**
   # **lvextend –m 1 /dev/vg00/lvol6 /dev/dsk/c1t4d0**
   # **lvextend –m 1 /dev/vg00/lvol7 /dev/dsk/c1t4d0**
   # **lvextend –m 1 /dev/vg00/lvol8 /dev/dsk/c1t4d0**

At this stage, you may wish to run the *vgdisplay* command in verbose mode to view how the configuration of the volume group looks like. Notice that the number of **Allocated PE** is twice as many as the number of **Current LE**. Also the number of **Used PV** are **2**. This shows that each LV resides on a different PV and occupying exact number of PEs on both. The **available/syncd** status confirms that both mirrors are in sync.

   # **vgdisplay –v vg00**
   . . . .
   . . . .
     --- Logical volumes ---
     LV Name   /dev/vg00/lvol1
     LV Status   **available/syncd**
     LV Size (Mbytes)   300
     Current LE   **75**
     Allocated PE   **150**
     Used PV   **2**

. . . .

. . . .
    LV Name   /dev/vg00/lvol8

LV Name	/dev/vg00/lvol8
LV Status	**available/syncd**
LV Size (Mbytes)	2428
Current LE	**607**
Allocated PE	**1214**
Used PV	**2**

  --- Physical volumes ---

PV Name	/dev/dsk/c0t4d0
PV Status	available
Total PE	2169
Free PE	0
Autoswitch	On

PV Name	/dev/dsk/c1t4d0
PV Status	available
Total PE	2169
Free PE	0
Autoswitch	On

Let us also issue the *lvdisplay* command on one of the mirrored logical volumes, */dev/vg00/lvol1*, and see how PEs are allocated on the two physical volumes.

 # lvdisplay –v /dev/vg00/lvol1

--- Logical volumes ---

LV Name	/dev/vg00/lvol1
VG Name	/dev/vg00
LV Permission	read/write
LV Status	available/syncd
Mirror copies	1
Consistency Recovery	MWC
Schedule	parallel
LV Size (Mbytes)	300
Current LE	75
Allocated PE	150
Stripes	0
Stripe Size (Kbytes)	0
Bad block	off
Allocation	strict
IO Timeout (Seconds)	default

  --- Distribution of logical volume ---

PV Name	LE on PV	PE on PV
/dev/dsk/c0t4d0	75	75
/dev/dsk/c1t4d0	75	75

  --- Logical extents ---

```
LE      PV1                     PE1    Status 1  PV2           PE2    Status 2
00000 /dev/dsk/c0t4d0   00000 current  /dev/dsk/c1t4d0  00000 current
00001 /dev/dsk/c0t4d0   00001 current  /dev/dsk/c1t4d0  00001 current
00002 /dev/dsk/c0t4d0   00002 current  /dev/dsk/c1t4d0  00002 current
00003 /dev/dsk/c0t4d0   00003 current  /dev/dsk/c1t4d0  00003 current
. . . . . . . .
. . . . . . . .
```

6. Run the *lvlnboot* command to update *vg00* configuration information.

   # lvlnboot –R vg00
   Volume Group configuration for /dev/vg00 has been saved in /etc/lvmconf/vg00.conf

7. All the mirrored logical volumes are set to have *Mirror **W**rite **C**ache* (MWC) enabled. MWC forces logical volumes to synchronize quickly by synching only the stale (out of sync) physical extents. This feature is very useful when your system or a logical volume crashes and recovery of the stale extents takes place. The synchronization and resynchronization processes are time consuming and generate plenty of I/O activities on the mirrored disks. The only logical volume you do not need to have this feature enabled is the primary swap area. Although it does not cause any harm to leave MWC enabled on *lvol2*, disabling it improves overall system recovery time after a system crash. Use the *lvdisplay* command to view the setting of *Consistency Recovery* for */dev/vg00/lvol2*.

   # lvdisplay /dev/vg00/lvol2
   --- Logical volumes ---
   LV Name   /dev/vg00/lvol2
   VG Name   /dev/vg00
   LV Permission   read/write
   LV Status   available/syncd
   Mirror copies   1
   Consistency Recovery   **MWC**
   Schedule   parallel
   LV Size (Mbytes)   2048
   Current LE   512
   Allocated PE   1024
   Stripes   0
   Stripe Size (Kbytes)   0
   Bad block   off
   Allocation   strict
   IO Timeout (Seconds)   default

   In order to disable MWC on the primary swap partition, you need to close (stop) the logical volume. The only way to close the primary swap volume and disable MWC is to shut down the system or partition and go into the LVM maintenance mode. Here are the steps:

   # shutdown –ry now
   . . . .
   . . . .
   Processor is booting from first available device.

To discontinue, press any key within 10 seconds.

Boot terminated.

Main Menu: Enter command or menu > **bo pri**
Interact with IPL (Y, N, or Cancel) ?> **y**

. . . .

. . . .

ISL> **hpux −lm**

8. When you are in LVM maintenance mode, you need to activate *vg00* first before doing anything on it. The −a option with "y" as an argument specifies to activate the volume group and −s option prevents any synchronization from taking place on any logical volumes.

   # **vgchange −a y −s vg00**
   Activated volume group
   Volume group "/dev/vg00" has been successfully changed.

9. Execute the *lvchange* command to disable MWC on *lvol2*. The −M option with "n" as an argument turns MWC off and −c with an "n" ensures deactivation of mirror consistency recoveries for this logical volume at subsequent *vg00* activations.

   # **lvchange −M n −c n /dev/vg00/lvol2**
   Logical volume "/dev/vg00/lvol2" has been successfully changed.
   Volume Group configuration for /dev/vg00 has been saved in /etc/lvmconf/vg00.conf

   Run *lvdisplay* command on *lvol2* to verify the change.

   # **lvdisplay /dev/vg00/lvol2**
   --- Logical volumes ---
LV Name	/dev/vg00/lvol2
VG Name	/dev/vg00
LV Permission	read/write
LV Status	available/syncd
Mirror copies	1
Consistency Recovery	**NONE**
Schedule	parallel
LV Size (Mbytes)	2048
Current LE	512
Allocated PE	1024
Stripes	0
Stripe Size (Kbytes)	0
Bad block	off
Allocation	strict
IO Timeout (Seconds)	default

10. Reboot the system to normal mode.

reboot

11. Once you are back into multiuser mode, you need to configure the path to the mirrored boot disk as an alternate boot path. This ensures that your system is going to boot from this disk if the primary boot disk is not available. Issue the *setboot* command and use the hardware address of the alternate boot disk. You can determine the hardware address using the *ioscan* command.

    # setboot −a 8/12.4.0

12. Verify to make sure the primary and alternate boot paths are set properly. Use the *lvlnboot* command.

    ```
    # lvlnboot  −v
    Boot Definitions for Volume Group /dev/vg00:
    Physical Volumes belonging in Root Volume Group:
            /dev/dsk/c0t4d0 (8/8.4.0) -- Boot Disk
            /dev/dsk/c1t4d0 (8/12.4.0) -- Boot Disk
    Boot: lvol1     on:     /dev/dsk/c0t4d0
            /dev/dsk/c1t4d0
    Root: lvol3     on:     /dev/dsk/c0t4d0
            /dev/dsk/c1t4d0
    Swap: lvol2     on:     /dev/dsk/c0t4d0
            /dev/dsk/c1t4d0
    Dump: lvol2     on:     /dev/dsk/c0t4d0, 0
    ```

13. At this point, update the AUTO file on the primary boot disk as well to specify ignoring quorum check at boot time in case the alternate boot disk is unavailable. Do the following on *c0t4d0*:

    # mkboot −a "hpux −lq(;0)/stand/vmunix" /dev/rdsk/c0t4d0

    Verify that the correct label has been applied to the AUTO file.

    ```
    # lifcp /dev/rdsk/c0t4d0:AUTO −
    hpux −lq(;0)/stand/vmunix
    ```

    Your system attempts (as always) to boot using the primary boot disk and then the alternate (if primary is unavailable).

This completes *vg00* mirroring setup and verification.

13.4.2   Mirroring a Non-Boot Volume Group

In this sub-section, you are going to create a two-way mirror of all the logical volumes that reside in a non-boot volume group, such as *vg02*.

Let us assume that you already have the *vg02* volume group, which exists on *c0t12d0* physical volume and contains *lvol1* and *lvol2* logical volumes in it. Also assume that you have a spare disk,

---

c1t12d0, available, residing on a separate physical controller card, and is no less than the size of *c0t12d0*. Here is the procedure to mirror both logical volumes within *vg02* non-boot volume group.

1. Bring *c1t12d0* under LVM control. Run *pvcreate* on it.

    # pvcreate –f /dev/rdsk/c1t12d0

2. Extend *vg02* to include the physical volume in it. Run *vgextend*.

    # vgextend vg01 /dev/dsk/c1t12d0

3. Mirror both logical volumes.

    # lvextend –m 1 /dev/vg01/lvol1 /dev/dsk/c1t12d0
    # lvextend –m 1 /dev/vg01/lvol2 /dev/dsk/c1t12d0

    Use the *vgdisplay* and *lvdisplay* commands to verify.

This completes the mirroring procedure for a non-boot volume group.

13.4.3   Mirroring and Allocation Policies

When you mirror a logical volume, a few policies are available that allow you to better control as to which specific physical volume(s) to be used to allocate physical extents on. There are three such policies and are referred to as *Allocation Policies*. These are:

✓   Strict Allocation Policy
✓   PVG-Strict Allocation Policy
✓   Distributed Allocation Policy

Strict Allocation Policy

By default, when you create a logical volume, *Strict Allocation Policy* is enforced on it. This means that the logical volume, if mirrored later, will not allow the physical volume it resides on to have a mirror copy of itself on that physical volume. In other words, the mirror of the logical volume must be created on a separate physical volume. In contrast, if strict allocation policy is not enforced, both mirrors can reside on the same physical volume. Although, the latter configuration is supported but is highly undesirable and defeats the purpose of mirroring.

Before proceeding further, let us remove the *vg02* volume group and create another volume group, *vg03,* containing only *c0t12d0*. Then, create *lvol1* logical volume of size 2000MB in *vg03* as follows:

    # lvcreate –L 2000 vg03

To validate if strict policy is enforced automatically on the logical volume, do an *lvdisplay* on it and check the value of "Allocation".

lvdisplay /dev/vg03/lvol1
```
--- Logical volumes ---
LV Name                   /dev/vg03/lvol1
VG Name                   /dev/vg03
LV Permission             read/write
LV Status                 available/syncd
Mirror copies             0
Consistency Recovery      MWC
Schedule                  parallel
LV Size (Mbytes)          2000
Current LE                500
Allocated PE              500
Stripes                   0
Stripe Size (Kbytes)      0
Bad block                 on
Allocation                strict
IO Timeout (Seconds)      default
```

Now, let us try to mirror this logical volume using the *lvextend* command and see what happens.

lvextend –m 1 /dev/vg03/lvol1
lvextend: Not enough free physical extents available.
Logical volume "/dev/vg03/lvol1" could not be extended.
Failure possibly caused by strict allocation policy

This is what you are going to see if you try to mirror a logical volume on the same physical volume with strict allocation policy enabled.

Let us now create a mirrored logical volume, *lvol2,* with strict allocation policy disabled (-s n). You will notice that the system will allow both the logical volume and its mirror to share the *c0t12d0* physical volume.

lvcreate –L 1000 –m 1 –s n vg03
Logical volume "/dev/vg03/lvol2" has been successfully created with character device "/dev/vg03/rlvol2".
Logical volume "/dev/vg03/lvol2" has been successfully extended.
Volume Group configuration for /dev/vg03 has been saved in /etc/lvmconf/vg03.conf

Use the *lvdisplay* command to view what *lvcreate* has done. The output indicates that both copies of the logical volume reside on the same physical volume.

lvdisplay –v /dev/vg03/lvol2
```
--- Logical volumes ---
LV Name                   /dev/vg03/lvol2
VG Name                   /dev/vg03
LV Permission             read/write
LV Status                 available/syncd
Mirror copies             1
Consistency Recovery      MWC
Schedule                  parallel
```

LV Size (Mbytes)	1000
Current LE	250
Allocated PE	500
Stripes	0
Stripe Size (Kbytes)	0
Bad block	on
Allocation	**non-strict**
IO Timeout (Seconds)	default

--- Distribution of logical volume ---

PV Name	LE on PV	PE on PV
/dev/dsk/c0t12d0	**250**	**500**

--- Logical extents ---

LE	PV1	PE1	Status 1	PV2	PE2	Status 2
00000	/dev/dsk/c0t12d0	00200	current	/dev/dsk/c0t12d0	00250	current
00001	/dev/dsk/c0t12d0	00201	current	/dev/dsk/c0t12d0	00251	current
00002	/dev/dsk/c0t12d0	00202	current	/dev/dsk/c0t12d0	00252	current
00003	/dev/dsk/c0t12d0	00203	current	/dev/dsk/c0t12d0	00253	current
00004	/dev/dsk/c0t12d0	00204	current	/dev/dsk/c0t12d0	00254	current
00005	/dev/dsk/c0t12d0	00205	current	/dev/dsk/c0t12d0	00255	current
00006	/dev/dsk/c0t12d0	00206	current	/dev/dsk/c0t12d0	00256	current
00007	/dev/dsk/c0t12d0	00207	current	/dev/dsk/c0t12d0	00257	current

. . . .
. . . .

Let us *pvcreate* an additional disk, *c1t12d0*, *vgextend* it into *vg03*, and create a logical volume, *lvol3*, with strict allocation enabled.

pvcreate /dev/rdsk/c1t12d0
Physical volume "/dev/rdsk/c1t12d0" has been successfully created.
vgextend vg03 /dev/dsk/c1t12d0
Volume group "vg03" has been successfully extended.
Volume Group configuration for /dev/vg03 has been saved in /etc/lvmconf/vg03.conf
lvcreate –L 2000 –m 1 vg03
Logical volume "/dev/vg03/lvol3" has been successfully created with
character device "/dev/vg03/rlvol3".
Logical volume "/dev/vg03/lvol3" has been successfully extended.
Volume Group configuration for /dev/vg03 has been saved in /etc/lvmconf/vg03.conf

Use *lvdisplay* to view the properties of */dev/vg03/lvol3*. The output indicates that each copy of the logical volume is on a separate physical volume.

lvdisplay –v /dev/vg03/lvol3
--- Logical volumes ---

LV Name	/dev/vg03/lvol3
VG Name	/dev/vg03
LV Permission	read/write
LV Status	available/syncd

Mirror copies	**1**
Consistency Recovery	MWC
Schedule	parallel
LV Size (Mbytes)	2000
Current LE	500
Allocated PE	1000
Stripes	0
Stripe Size (Kbytes)	0
Bad block	on
Allocation	**strict**
IO Timeout (Seconds) default	

```
--- Distribution of logical volume ---
PV Name              LE on PV          PE on PV
/dev/dsk/c0t12d0     500               500
/dev/dsk/c1t12d0     500               500

--- Logical extents ---
LE    PV1                PE1    Status 1  PV2               PE2    Status 2
00000 /dev/dsk/c0t12d0   00400  current   /dev/dsk/c1t12d0  00000  current
00001 /dev/dsk/c0t12d0   00401  current   /dev/dsk/c1t12d0  00001  current
00002 /dev/dsk/c0t12d0   00402  current   /dev/dsk/c1t12d0  00002  current
00003 /dev/dsk/c0t12d0   00403  current   /dev/dsk/c1t12d0  00003  current
00004 /dev/dsk/c0t12d0   00404  current   /dev/dsk/c1t12d0  00004  current
00005 /dev/dsk/c0t12d0   00405  current   /dev/dsk/c1t12d0  00005  current
00006 /dev/dsk/c0t12d0   00406  current   /dev/dsk/c1t12d0  00006  current
00007 /dev/dsk/c0t12d0   00407  current   /dev/dsk/c1t12d0  00007  current
. . . . . . . .
. . . . . . . .
```

PVG-Strict Allocation Policy

The *Physical Volume Group (PVG) Strict Allocation Policy* is preferred when working with a large number of physical volumes within a single volume group.

PVG is a group of physical volumes defined within a volume group. When you plan to setup a two-way mirror, for instance, for a number of logical volumes, you can create two PVGs (PVG0 and PVG1) in the volume group. See Figure 13-6. Suppose you have a group of 3 physical volumes (4GB each) connected to *c2* controller card and another group of 3 physical volumes (4GB each) connected to *c3* controller card. All 6 physical volumes reside within a single volume group *vgweb*. You need to define the PVGs in the */etc/lvmpvg* file. This file does not exist by default, but can be created manually. When using the PVG-strict policy, one copy of the logical volume will reside in PVG0 and the other in PVG1. This way an automatic separation of mirrors takes place and you do not need to worry about as to which physical volume to be used for mirror, and so on.

The following demonstrates how you can have the two PVGs defined in */etc/lvmpvg* for *vgweb* volume group with physical volumes – c2t0d0, c2t1d0, c2t2d0, c3t0d0, c3t1d0, and c3t2d0 – reside on *c2* and *c3* controllers:

```
# vi  /etc/lvmpvg
VG      /dev/vgweb
PVG     PVG0
/dev/dsk/c2t0d0
/dev/dsk/c2t1d0
/dev/dsk/c2t2d0
PVG     PVG1
/dev/dsk/c3t0d0
/dev/dsk/c3t1d0
/dev/dsk/c3t2d0
```

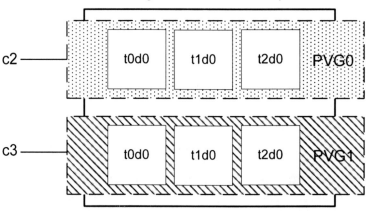

Figure 13-6 LVM PVG

Here is the *vgdisplay* output on *vgweb* after defining PVGs in */etc/lvmpvg* file:

```
# vgdisplay  –v  vgweb
--- Volume groups ---
VG Name                 /dev/vgweb
VG Write Access         read/write
VG Status               available
Max LV                  255
Cur LV                  0
Open LV                 0
Max PV                  16
Cur PV                  6
Act PV                  6
Max PE per PV           1023
VGDA                    12
PE Size (Mbytes)        4
Total PE                6138
Alloc PE                0
Free PE                 6138
Total PVG               2
Total Spare PVs         0
Total Spare PVs in use  0
```

```
--- Physical volumes ---
PV Name                 /dev/dsk/c2t0d0
PV Status               available
Total PE                1023
Free PE                 1023
Autoswitch              On

PV Name                 /dev/dsk/c2t1d0
PV Status               available
Total PE                1023
Free PE                 1023
Autoswitch              On

PV Name                 /dev/dsk/c2t2d0
PV Status               available
Total PE                1023
Free PE                 1023
Autoswitch              On

PV Name                 /dev/dsk/c3t0d0
PV Status               available
Total PE                1023
Free PE                 1023
Autoswitch              On

PV Name                 /dev/dsk/c3t1d0
PV Status               available
Total PE                1023
Free PE                 1023
Autoswitch              On

PV Name                 /dev/dsk/c3t2d0
PV Status               available
Total PE                1023
Free PE                 1023
Autoswitch              On

--- Physical volume groups ---
PVG Name        PVG0
PV Name         /dev/dsk/c2t0d0
PV Name         /dev/dsk/c2t1d0
PV Name         /dev/dsk/c2t2d0

PVG Name        PVG1
PV Name         /dev/dsk/c3t0d0
PV Name         /dev/dsk/c3t1d0
PV Name         /dev/dsk/c3t2d0
```

Let us create *lvol1* mirrored logical volume of size 2000MB in *vgweb*. The "–s g" option forces the *lvcreate* command to use the PVG-strict policy.

 # lvcreate –L 2000 –m 1 –s g vgweb
Logical volume "/dev/vgweb/lvol1" has been successfully created with
character device "/dev/vgweb/rlvol1".
Logical volume "/dev/vgweb/lvol1" has been successfully extended.
Volume Group configuration for /dev/vgweb has been saved in /etc/lvmconf/vgweb.conf

Use *lvdisplay* to view the properties of *lvol1*. The output indicates that each copy of the logical volume is on a separate physical volume within different PVGs.

 # lvdisplay –v /dev/vgweb/lvol1
--- Logical volumes ---

LV Name	/dev/vgweb/lvol1
VG Name	/dev/vgweb
LV Permission	read/write
LV Status	available/syncd
Mirror copies	1
Consistency Recovery	MWC
Schedule	parallel
LV Size (Mbytes)	2000
Current LE	500
Allocated PE	1000
Stripes	0
Stripe Size (Kbytes)	0
Bad block	on
Allocation	**PVG-strict**
IO Timeout (Seconds)	default

--- Distribution of logical volume ---

PV Name	LE on PV	PE on PV
/dev/dsk/c2t0d0	**500**	**500**
/dev/dsk/c3t0d0	**500**	**500**

--- Logical extents ---

LE	PV1	PE1	Status 1	PV2	PE2	Status 2
00000	/dev/dsk/c2t0d0	00000	current	/dev/dsk/c3t0d0	00000	current
00001	/dev/dsk/c2t0d0	00001	current	/dev/dsk/c3t0d0	00001	current
00002	/dev/dsk/c2t0d0	00002	current	/dev/dsk/c3t0d0	00002	current
00003	/dev/dsk/c2t0d0	00003	current	/dev/dsk/c3t0d0	00003	current
00004	/dev/dsk/c2t0d0	00004	current	/dev/dsk/c3t0d0	00004	current
00005	/dev/dsk/c2t0d0	00005	current	/dev/dsk/c3t0d0	00005	current
00006	/dev/dsk/c2t0d0	00006	current	/dev/dsk/c3t0d0	00006	current
00007	/dev/dsk/c2t0d0	00007	current	/dev/dsk/c3t0d0	00007	current

. . . .
. . . .

Distributed Allocation Policy

With *Distributed Allocation Policy* used, physical extents are allocated in a round-robin fashion on a series of available physical volumes within a PVG. These physical extents are then mirrored on the physical volumes that reside in the other PVG in the round-robin fashion. This means that the first free PE is allocated from the first available PV, the second free PE is allocated from the second available PV, the third free PE is allocated from the third available PV, and so on. This policy only works with PVG-strict and is disabled by default. The default behavior uses all free physical extents on the first available physical volume before it starts allocating on the next physical volume. This type of mirroring setup is referred to as RAID 0+1. The */etc/lvmpvg* file is referenced to obtain the list of available physical volumes within each PVG.

Let us create *lvol2* mirrored logical volume of size 2000MB in *vgweb*. The "–s g" option forces the *lvcreate* to use physical extents from both PVGs and "–D y" option enables the distributed allocation policy on the logical volume.

```
# lvcreate –L 2000 –m 1 –D y –s g vgweb
Logical volume "/dev/vgweb/lvol2" has been successfully created with
character device "/dev/vgweb/rlvol2".
Logical volume "/dev/vgweb/lvol2" has been successfully extended.
Volume Group configuration for /dev/vgweb has been saved in /etc/lvmconf/vgweb.conf
```

Use the *lvdisplay* command to view the properties of */dev/vgweb/lvol2*. Notice that the allocation policy used is PVG-strict/distributed. The output also indicates that physical extents are taken in round-robin fashion from each of the three physical volumes in the PVGs.

```
# lvdisplay –v /dev/vgweb/lvol2
--- Logical volumes ---
LV Name                   /dev/vgweb/lvol2
VG Name                   /dev/vgweb
LV Permission             read/write
LV Status                 available/syncd
Mirror copies             1
Consistency Recovery      MWC
Schedule                  parallel
LV Size (Mbytes)          2000
Current LE                500
Allocated PE              1000
Stripes                   0
Stripe Size (Kbytes)      0
Bad block                 on
Allocation                PVG-strict/distributed
IO Timeout (Seconds)      default
   --- Distribution of logical volume ---
   PV Name          LE on PV        PE on PV
   /dev/dsk/c2t0d0  167             167
   /dev/dsk/c2t1d0  167             167
   /dev/dsk/c2t2d0  166             166
   /dev/dsk/c3t0d0  167             167
   /dev/dsk/c3t1d0  167             167
```

/dev/dsk/c3t2d0	166		166		

--- Logical extents ---

LE	PV1	PE1	Status 1	PV2	PE2	Status 2
00000	/dev/dsk/c2t0d0	00500	current	/dev/dsk/c3t0d0	00500	current
00001	/dev/dsk/c2t1d0	00000	current	/dev/dsk/c3t1d0	00000	current
00002	/dev/dsk/c2t2d0	00000	current	/dev/dsk/c3t2d0	00000	current
00003	/dev/dsk/c2t0d0	00501	current	/dev/dsk/c3t0d0	00501	current
00004	/dev/dsk/c2t1d0	00001	current	/dev/dsk/c3t1d0	00001	current
00005	/dev/dsk/c2t2d0	00001	current	/dev/dsk/c3t2d0	00001	current
00006	/dev/dsk/c2t0d0	00502	current	/dev/dsk/c3t0d0	00502	current
00007	/dev/dsk/c2t1d0	00002	current	/dev/dsk/c3t1d0	00002	current
00008	/dev/dsk/c2t2d0	00002	current	/dev/dsk/c3t2d0	00002	current
00009	/dev/dsk/c2t0d0	00503	current	/dev/dsk/c3t0d0	00503	current
00010	/dev/dsk/c2t1d0	00003	current	/dev/dsk/c3t1d0	00003	current
00011	/dev/dsk/c2t2d0	00003	current	/dev/dsk/c3t2d0	00003	current
00012	/dev/dsk/c2t0d0	00504	current	/dev/dsk/c3t0d0	00504	current
00013	/dev/dsk/c2t1d0	00004	current	/dev/dsk/c3t1d0	00004	current
00014	/dev/dsk/c2t2d0	00004	current	/dev/dsk/c3t2d0	00004	current

. . . .
. . . .

13.4.4 Extending Mirrors

Extending a mirrored logical volume increases the logical volume in size. Let us extend
/dev/vgweb/lvol1 logical volume from 2000MB to 4000MB with the lvextend command. You can
specify the size in either MBs or LEs.

lvextend –L 4000 /dev/vgweb/lvol1

Although the size is increased by 2000MB, the number of PEs allocated is double the number of
LEs. In mirrored configuration, LVM takes exact number of PEs from each physical volume. For
instance, 2000MB is equal to 500 PEs per physical volume totaling 1000 PEs on both.

Run vgdisplay in verbose mode on vgweb and check for the number of allocated PE, current LE,
and used PV information to validate.

13.4.5 Reducing Mirrors

Reducing a mirrored logical volume decreases the logical volume in size. Currently,
/dev/vgweb/lvol1 is 4000MB. The following example reduces it to 1000MB with the lvreduce
command. You can specify the size in either MBs or LEs.

lvreduce –L 1000 /dev/vgweb/lvol1
Warning: The Logical Volume has a file system larger than the reduced size.
Reducing the Logical Volume will cause file system corruption.
When a logical volume is reduced useful data might get lost;
do you really want the command to proceed (y/n) : y
Logical volume "/dev/vgweb/lvol1" has been successfully reduced.

Volume Group configuration for /dev/vgweb has been saved in /etc/lvmconf/vgweb.conf

Run *vgdisplay* in verbose mode on *vgweb* and check for the number of allocated PE, current LE, and used PV information to validate.

13.4.6 Synchronizing Stale Mirrors

Mirrored logical volumes in a volume group are automatically synchronized when the volume group is activated. This is the default behavior. Sometimes, they get out of sync because of the reason, such as intermittent problems with one of the mirrored disks. The *vgdisplay* command shows their status as available/stale.

LVM offers two commands to synchronize stale logical volumes. These commands are *lvsync* and *vgsync*. The *lvsync* command synchronizes a single logical volume while *vgsync* synchronizes all stale logical volumes in the volume group. For example:

To synchronize the */dev/vgweb/lvol1* logical volume, run *lvsync* as follows:

> # **lvsync   /dev/vgweb/lvol1**
> Resynchronized logical volume "/dev/vgweb/lvol1".

To synchronize all logical volumes within *vgweb*, run *vgsync* as follows:

> # **vgsync   vgweb**
> Resynchronized logical volume "/dev/vgweb/lvol1".
> Resynchronized logical volume "/dev/vgweb/lvol2".
> Resynchronized volume group "vgweb".

13.4.7 Splitting Mirrors

Splitting a two-way mirrored logical volume creates two logical volumes out of it; one stays as the primary logical volume and the other becomes the detached or secondary copy of it. At this stage, you need to decide what you want to do with the detached copy. You may wish to perform an online backup of it, remove it if not needed, and so on.

Here are examples on how to split mirrors.

To split */dev/vgweb/lvol1* and assign it the default suffix "b", use the *lvsplit* command as follows:

> # **lvsplit   /dev/vgweb/lvol1**
> Logical volume "/dev/vgweb/lvol1b" has been successfully created with character device "/dev/vgweb/rlvol1b".
> Logical volume "/dev/vgweb/lvol1" has been successfully split.
> Volume Group configuration for /dev/vgweb has been saved in /etc/lvmconf/vgweb.conf

To split */dev/vgweb/lvol2* and assign it the suffix "mir", use the *lvsplit* command as follows:

```
# lvsplit –s  mir  /dev/vgweb/lvol2
```
Logical volume "/dev/vgweb/lvol2mir" has been successfully created with character device
"/dev/vgweb/rlvol2mir".
Logical volume "/dev/vgweb/lvol2" has been successfully split.
Volume Group configuration for /dev/vgweb has been saved in /etc/lvmconf/vgweb.conf

13.4.8 Merging Mirrors

If you split the mirrors temporarily, you can merge the secondary copy back with the primary at a
later time. Merging mirrors synchronizes the detached copy with the primary.

Here are examples on how to merge the two secondary copies back to their respective primary
copies.

To merge /dev/vgweb/lvol1b and /dev/vgweb/lvol2mir back, use the lvmerge command as follows:

```
# lvmerge  /dev/vgweb/lvol1b  /dev/vgweb/lvol1
```
Logical volume "/dev/vgweb/lvol1b" has been successfully merged with logical volume "/dev/vgweb/lvol1".
Logical volume "/dev/vgweb/lvol1b" has been successfully removed.
Volume Group configuration for /dev/vgweb has been saved in /etc/lvmconf/vgweb.conf

```
# lvmerge  /dev/vgweb/lvol2mir  /dev/vgweb/lvol2
```
Logical volume "/dev/vgweb/lvol2mir" has been successfully merged with logical volume
"/dev/vgweb/lvol2".
Logical volume "/dev/vgweb/lvol2mir" has been successfully removed.
Volume Group configuration for /dev/vgweb has been saved in /etc/lvmconf/vgweb.conf

13.5   The Whole Disk Solution

The whole disk solution is no longer used by a vast majority of system administrators because of
scores of limitations it has. Some of the major disadvantages with using the whole disk solution are:

- ✓ Cannot create a partition larger than the size of a single physical disk.
- ✓ Cannot have more than one file systems per physical disk.
- ✓ Cannot increase or decrease a file system size on the fly.

Using this solution, you can partition your disk in one of the following five ways only:

- ✓ An entire physical disk is used for a single file system only.
- ✓ An entire disk is used for a single swap partition only.
- ✓ An entire disk is used for a single raw partition only.
- ✓ An entire disk can have one file system and one swap space only.
- ✓ An entire disk can have the root file system (along with boot area) and one swap space only.

These limitations make the whole disk solution impractical for today's data storage requirements.

Summary

In this chapter, you looked at features and benefits associated with two HP disk management solutions: LVM and whole disk. You learned concepts, components, and structure of LVM in detail.

Next, you learned how to manage LVM disks including listing available disks, finding their sizes, converting them into physical volumes, creating, displaying, extending, reducing, and removing volume groups, and creating, extending, reducing, removing, and displaying logical volumes. You looked at how to backup LVM configuration information and restore it when needed.

Finally, in the sections that followed, you studied requirements for mirroring. You performed mirroring of boot and non-boot volume groups that covered creating, extending, reducing, synchronizing, splitting, and merging mirrored logical volumes. You looked at various allocation policies that you might want to use when mirroring logical volumes.

## 14

Veritas Volume Manager

This chapter covers the following major topics:

✓ Features and benefits of VxVM solution
✓ VxVM concepts, components, and structure
✓ VxVM administration interfaces
✓ Manage disks using VxVM including initializing a disk, creating and displaying a disk group, creating and displaying a volume, expanding a disk group, growing a volume, shrinking a volume, removing a volume, reducing a disk group, deporting and importing a disk group, renaming and destroying a disk group, converting vg00 to rootdg, and converting and unconverting non-boot volume group to and from VxVM
✓ VxVM mirroring concepts and requirements
✓ VxVM mirroring of boot and non-boot disk groups – creating, growing, and shrinking mirrored volumes
✓ LVM and VxVM comparison of terminology and commands

14.1 The Veritas Volume Manager Solution

The Veritas Volume Manager (VxVM) software product is implemented in HP-UX Operating Environment software as of HP-UX 11.0 version. There are a number of advantages to using this disk management solution. It provides more flexibility and features as compared to the other two – LVM and Whole Disk – solutions. VxVM is becoming increasingly popular as a preferred choice for disk management on HP-UX platform.

Veritas Volume Manager offers the following benefits:

- ✓ Supports RAID 0, RAID 1, RAID 5, RAID 0+1, and RAID 1+0
- ✓ Supports online resizing of volumes
- ✓ Supports online data migration from one disk to another
- ✓ Supports online relayout of volumes
- ✓ Supports hot relocation of data from failed disk to spare disk
- ✓ Supports disk I/O on redundant paths to disks (*Dynamic Multi Pathing* - DMP)
- ✓ Supports load balancing of disk I/O on redundant paths to disks via DMP
- ✓ Supports up to 32 mirrored copies of data
- ✓ Includes Java-based GUI for administration
- ✓ Is supported on HP-UX and several other UNIX platforms, and on Linux and Windows

14.1.1 VxVM Concepts and Structure

Veritas Volume Manager is basically a software driver and a collection of tools. It fits itself between the disk driver (SCSI, Fibre Channel, EIDE, SATA) that controls hard drives on the system and the HP-UX kernel. Once a disk is brought under VxVM control, all communication between the disk and the HP-UX kernel takes place through the VxVM driver. VxVM allows you to create a large pool of storage space using disk spaces taken from one or more disks.

When a disk is brought under VxVM control, it is referred to as a *VM Disk* and is assigned a *Disk Media* (DM) name. There are two methods for bringing a disk under VxVM control: *Initialization* and *Encapsulation*. The initialization process wipes out everything from a disk and divides it into two regions – the *Public* region and the *Private* region. On the contrary, the encapsulation process also divides a disk into public and private regions, however, it does not remove any information from the disk, rather, it preserves all existing file system structures and data. See Figure 14-1.

The private region is a very small space (just a few MBs) where VxVM metadata information pertaining to the disk is kept. The metadata includes structural information, such as the disk group the disk belongs to, the volumes and plexes it is fully or partially used in, and so forth. The public region represents all remaining space on the VM disk. This space is used to create volumes that may contain file systems, swap spaces, or raw partitions.

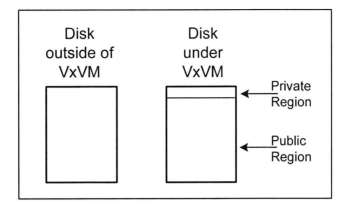

Figure 14-1 Disk under VxVM Control

There are five fundamental logical components of the VxVM structure. These components are also called *Virtual Objects*. These objects are displayed in Figure 14-2 and explained below.

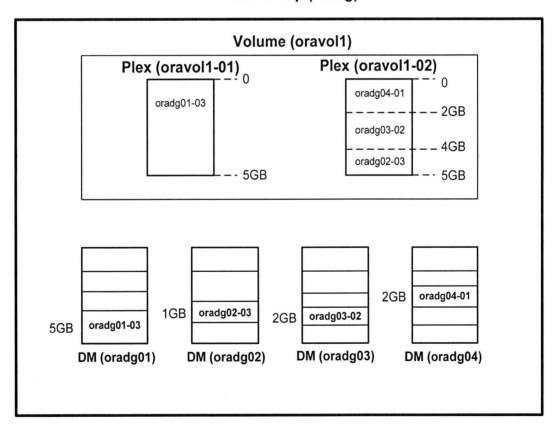

Figure 14-2 VxVM Components

Disk Group

A disk group is a logical container that houses all VxVM components including volume, plex, disk, and subdisk. These components cannot be used outside of the disk group that contains them. A disk group works as a single entity. You can have as many disk groups on your system as you want. In Figure 14-2, a disk group, *oradg*, and what it contains is shown. The concept of disk group is similar to the concept of volume group in LVM.

Volume

A volume is a logical object wherein you can create a file system, a raw space, a swap area, or a dump space. When a volume is created, both block and character device files are created. A volume consists of one or more plexes. In Figure 14-2, a single volume, *oravol1*, is shown containing two plexes. Device files for the volume are created in */dev/vx/dsk/oradg* and */dev/vx/rdsk/oradg* directories. VxVM volume is equivalent to LVM logical volume.

Plex

A plex comprises of one or more subdisks. It represents one copy of data inside a volume. A volume can have more than one plexes, with each containing a mirrored copy of the data. In Figure 14-2, two plexes, *oravol1-01* and *oravol1-02*, are shown that form a single volume. The two plexes are mirrored and, therefore, contain identical data. A plex can be thought of as a logical volume in LVM.

Disk

A physical disk brought under VxVM control using initialization or encapsulation process is known as a *VM Disk* or simply a *Disk*. In Figure 14-2, four VM disks (*oradg01, oradg02, oradg03,* and *oradg04*) are illustrated. Within a disk group, a disk is referred to as a *Disk Medium* (DM). A VM disk or DM is equivalent in concept to the physical volume in LVM.

Subdisk

A *Subdisk* is a logical, contiguous chunk of disk space taken from one of the VM disks inside a disk group. It is the smallest unit of space allocation in VxVM. Subdisks are used to build plexes.

In Figure 14-2, subdisks are shown taken from DMs. A 5GB subdisk, for instance, is taken from *oradg01* DM. The subdisk naming convention is *oradg01-01, oradg01-02, oradg01-03*, and so on for each subsequent subdisk taken from *oradg01*. Follow the same naming convention for subdisks from other DMs. A subdisk is equivalent to LVM's physical extent.

The naming convention demonstrated here is for example purpose only. In fact, you can assign any name to your disk group, volume, plex, and disk.

14.1.2 Supported RAID Levels

VxVM supports the following software RAID levels:

✓ RAID 0 (concatenation) – allows you to add subdisks one after the other in such a way that a single large plex is formed. Subdisks can be taken from multiple VM disks. A major disadvantage is that if one of the subdisks fails, the entire plex and, therefore, the entire volume, stops working.

✓ RAID 0 (striping) – allows you to organize subdisks in a manner that improves data write performance. A major disadvantage is that if one of the subdisks fails, the entire plex and, therefore, the entire volume, stops working.

✓ RAID 1 (mirroring) – facilitates mirroring of two or more plexes. If all but one plexes fail, the system and users continue to function normally.

✓ RAID 5 (striping with parity) – adds an additional plex to RAID 0 striped plex. RAID 5 survives a single plex failure.

✓ RAID 0+1 (mirror-stripe) – enhanced RAID level that enables you to mirror a striped volume. It is also referred to as a *Layered* volume.

✓ RAID 1+0 (stripe-mirror) – enhanced RAID level that enables you to stripe a mirrored volume. It is also referred to as a *Layered* volume.

14.1.3   VxVM Interfaces

Veritas Volume Manager offers three interfaces for disk management – a GUI tool called *Veritas Enterprise Administrator* (VEA) (formerly called *Volume Manager Storage Administrator* (VMSA), a text-based menu-driven program called *vxdiskadm*, and a bunch of command line utilities.

Veritas Enterprise Administrator GUI

You can manage all VxVM objects from VEA GUI. To run VEA, do the following:

   # **/opt/VRTS/bin/vea**

The GUI prompts you to enter username and password. Figure 14-3 shows the authentication screen.

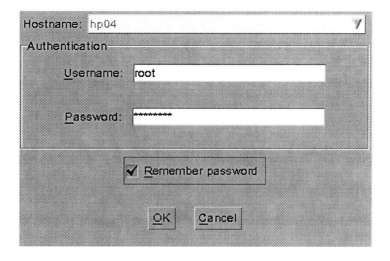

Figure 14-3 Veritas Enterprise Administrator GUI

Supply the correct username and password to get in. Figure 14-4 shows the main console screen.

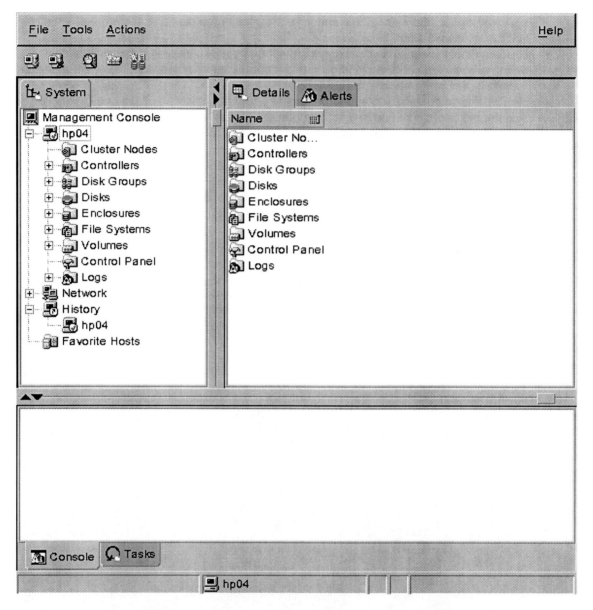

Figure 14-4 Veritas Enterprise Administrator – Main Console Screen

Veritas Disk Administrator Program

This is a menu-driven program and runs in non-GUI mode. Execute the *vxdiskadm* command to bring up the menu.

vxdiskadm

Volume Manager Support Operations
Menu: VolumeManager/Disk

1   Add or initialize one or more disks
2   Remove a disk
3   Remove a disk for replacement
4   Replace a failed or removed disk
5   Mirror volumes on a disk
6   Move volumes from a disk
7   Enable access to (import) a disk group
8   Remove access to (deport) a disk group
9   Enable (online) a disk device
10   Disable (offline) a disk device
11   Mark a disk as a spare for a disk group
12   Turn off the spare flag on a disk
13   Remove (deport) and destroy a disk group
14   Unrelocate subdisks back to a disk
15   Exclude a disk from hot-relocation use
16   Make a disk available for hot-relocation use
17   Prevent multipathing/Suppress devices from VxVM's view
18   Allow multipathing/Unsuppress devices from VxVM's view
19   List currently suppressed/non-multipathed devices
20   Change the disk naming scheme
list List disk information

?   Display help about menu
??   Display help about the menuing system
q   Exit from menus

Select an operation to perform:

Note that the menu description at the top changes as you choose items from the list.

14.1.4   VxVM Commands and Daemons

The latest version of VxVM on HP-UX platform at the writing of this book is 5.0. In versions 3.5 and older, the first item required to be done after the software install was to execute a utility called *vxinstall* to create a disk group called *rootdg*. That was mandatory. The *rootdg* disk group was typically created to house boot disks. Beginning version 4.0, this has no longer been a requirement. In fact, you can create a disk group to house boot disks at any time and by any name.

Tables 14-1 and 14-2 list and explain some common VxVM commands and daemons.

VxVM Command	Description
vea	Java-based GUI to perform VxVM administration tasks on one or more systems.
vxassist	Performs volume management tasks.
vxcp_lvmroot	Converts LVM *vg00* into VxVM *rootdg*.
vxdctl	Manages the *vxconfigd* daemon.
vxdg	Performs disk group management tasks.
vxdisk	Performs disk management tasks.

vxdiskadm	Menu driven program to perform VxVM administration tasks.
vxdisksetup	Brings a disk under VxVM control by initializing it to have private and public regions.
vxdiskunsetup	Removes a disk from VxVM control by removing private and public regions.
vxdmpadm	Performs DMP administration tasks.
vxedit	Creates, modifies, and removes VxVM records.
vxinfo	Displays information on volume usability.
vxinstall	Sets up VxVM initially and creates *rootdg*.
vxlicense	Administers VxVM licenses.
vxmake	Creates records for volumes, plexes, and subdisks.
vxplex	Performs operations on plexes and/or volumes.
vxprint	Displays VxVM configuration.
vxrecover	Performs operations specific to volume recovery.
vxrelayout	Changes a volume's layout.
vxresize	Resizes a volume.
vxrootmir	Performs root disk group mirroring.
vxtask	Performs basic administration tasks on running VxVM operations.
vxunreloc	Un-relocates a subdisk back to original VM disk.
vxvmboot	Sets volumes to be root, boot, dump, or primary swap.
vxvmconvert	Converts LVM non-*vg00* into VxVM non-*rootdg*.
vxvol	Performs volume-related operations, such as starting volumes, stopping volumes, changing volume characteristics, etc.

Table 14-1 Common VxVM Commands

VxVM Daemon	Description
vxconfigd	Configuration daemon. Must be running in order to carry out any configuration modifications. To check the status, use *vxdctl* as follows: # **vxdctl mode** Execute "**vxdctl enable**" if the mode reported is disabled.
vxiod	Starts, stops, and reports on VxVM kernel I/O daemons.
vxnotify	Displays VxVM configuration events.
vxrelocd	Monitors disks for failures and relocates failed disks.

Table 14-2 VxVM Daemons

14.2 Managing Volumes Using VxVM

Managing volumes using VxVM involves several tasks, such as identifying available disk devices, making a disk visible to VxVM, initializing a disk, creating and displaying a disk group, creating and displaying a volume, expanding a disk group, growing a volume, shrinking a volume, removing a volume, reducing a disk group, deporting and importing a disk group, renaming a disk group, destroying a disk group, converting LVM *vg00* to VxVM *rootdg*, and converting LVM non-*vg00* to VxVM non-*rootdg*.

In order to do disk management using VxVM, you can use whichever interface you like. VEA is easy to use and so does *vxdiskadm*. However, in the remaining sections of this chapter, all example operations are performed using commands.

14.2.1 Identifying Available Disk Devices

Before starting to work with VxVM, figure out what disks are available on the system that you can use. Execute the *ioscan* command to identify disks and device files, and then use the *diskinfo* command to determine disk sizes. Here is how you can do it:

```
# ioscan –fnkCdisk
Class        I       H/W Path        Driver  S/W State     H/W Type    Description
==================================================================================
disk         0       0/0/2/0.0.0.0   sdisk   CLAIMED       DEVICE      TEAC DV-28E-N
             /dev/dsk/c0t0d0   /dev/rdsk/c0t0d0
disk         1       0/1/1/0.0.0     sdisk   CLAIMED       DEVICE      HP 36.4GST336754LC
             /dev/dsk/c2t0d0   /dev/rdsk/c2t0d0
disk         2       0/1/1/0.1.0     sdisk   CLAIMED       DEVICE      HP 36.4GST336754LC
             /dev/dsk/c2t1d0   /dev/rdsk/c2t1d0
disk         3       0/1/1/0.2.0     sdisk   CLAIMED       DEVICE      HP 36.4GST336754LC
             /dev/dsk/c2t2d0   /dev/rdsk/c2t2d0
```

This *ioscan* output is from an HP RP3440 server. It shows that there are three hard drives and one DVD-ROM drive in the system. One of these hard drives is already in use as a boot disk by HP-UX. Do a *setboot* command and find which one it is.

```
# setboot
Primary bootpath    : 0/1/1/0.0.0
Alternate bootpath :

Autoboot is ON (enabled)
Autosearch is ON (enabled)
```

The *setboot* command reports that the primary boot disk is installed at hardware address 0/1/1/0.0.0, which corresponds to the disk at */dev/dsk/c2t0d0*. Leaving this disk out, you have two disks – *c2t1d0* and *c2t2d0* – available to play with. The output also indicates that each disk is 36GB in size.

14.2.2 Making a Disk Visible to VxVM

Before a disk can be used in VxVM, the VxVM driver must be able to see it. You need to run the *vxdctl* command as follows to force VxVM to look for any disks that have been recently added to the system:

```
# vxdctl  enable
```

Next, execute the *vxdisk* command to see if the disks are available and seen by VxVM. Initialized and encapsulated disks will have the status "online", while disks not under VxVM control will have "online invalid" status.

vxdisk list

DEVICE	TYPE	DISK	GROUP	STATUS
c2t0d0	simple	rootdisk01	rootdg	online
c2t1d0	simple	-	-	online invalid
c2t2d0	simple	-	-	online invalid

This shows that *c2t0d0* with DM name *rootdisk01* is under VxVM control. The disk is part of the *rootdg* disk group, which was created when HP-UX was installed. Run the *bdf* command and check what file systems exist on it. Notice the device files.

bdf

Filesystem	Kbytes	used	avail	%used	Mounted
on					
/dev/vx/dsk/rootdg/rootvol	1024000	143208	873968	14%	/
/dev/vx/dsk/rootdg/standvol	491952	42720	400032	10%	/stand
/dev/vx/dsk/rootdg/varvol	5120000	3061248	2042904	60%	/var
/dev/vx/dsk/rootdg/usrvol	3072000	1319800	1738536	43%	/usr
/dev/vx/dsk/rootdg/tmpvol	2048000	584272	1452352	29%	/tmp
/dev/vx/dsk/rootdg/optvol	5120000	3066880	2037104	60%	/opt
/dev/vx/dsk/rootdg/homevol	3072000	2224864	840696	73%	/home

Also execute the *vxprint* command to view details of *rootdg* and objects within it.

vxprint
Disk group: rootdg

TY NAME	ASSOC	KSTATE	LENGTH	PLOFFS	STATE	TUTIL0	PUTIL0
dg rootdg	rootdg	-	-	-	-	-	-
dm rootdisk01	c2t0d0	-	35561582	-	-	-	-
v homevol	fsgen	ENABLED	3072000	-	ACTIVE	-	-
pl homevol-01	homevol	ENABLED	3072000	-	ACTIVE	-	-
sd rootdisk01-04	homevol-01	ENABLED	3072000	0	-	-	-
v optvol	fsgen	ENABLED	5120000	-	ACTIVE	-	-
pl optvol-01	optvol	ENABLED	5120000	-	ACTIVE	-	-
sd rootdisk01-05	optvol-01	ENABLED	5120000	0	-	-	-
v rootvol	root	ENABLED	1024000	-	ACTIVE	-	-
pl rootvol-01	rootvol	ENABLED	1024000	-	ACTIVE	-	-
sd rootdisk01-03	rootvol-01	ENABLED	1024000	0	-	-	-
v standvol	fsgen	ENABLED	512000	-	ACTIVE	-	-
pl standvol-01	standvol	ENABLED	512000	-	ACTIVE	-	-
sd rootdisk01-01	standvol-01	ENABLED	512000	0	-	-	-
v swapvol	swap	ENABLED	8388608	-	ACTIVE	-	-
pl swapvol-01	swapvol	ENABLED	8388608	-	ACTIVE	-	-

sd rootdisk01-02	swapvol-01	ENABLED	8388608	0	-	-	-	
v tmpvol	fsgen	ENABLED	2048000	-	ACTIVE	-	-	
pl tmpvol-01	tmpvol	ENABLED	2048000	-	ACTIVE	-	-	
sd rootdisk01-06	tmpvol-01	ENABLED	2048000	0	-	-	-	
v usrvol	fsgen	ENABLED	3072000	-	ACTIVE	-	-	
pl usrvol-01	usrvol	ENABLED	3072000	-	ACTIVE	-	-	
sd rootdisk01-07	usrvol-01	ENABLED	3072000	0	-	-	-	
v varvol	fsgen	ENABLED	5120000	-	ACTIVE	-	-	
pl varvol-01	varvol	ENABLED	5120000	-	ACTIVE	-	-	
sd rootdisk01-08	varvol-01	ENABLED	5120000	0	-	-	-	

where:

dg stands for disk group
dm stands for disk medium
v stands for volume
pl stands for plex
sd stands for subdisk

Table 14-3 explains the columns in the *vxprint* output.

Column	Description
TY	Object type.
NAME	Object name.
ASSOC	Object association. "fsgen" is file system, "swap" is swap device, etc.
KSTATE	Object state. "-" for disk group, disk, and subdisk.
LENGTH	Object size in blocks.
PLOFFS	Plex association offset. "-" for disk group, volume, plex, and disk.
STATE	Object status. "-" for subdisk.
TUTIL0	Set as a lockout mechanism.
PUTIL0	Can be set to prevent associations of plex and subdisk records.

Table 14-3 *vxprint* Command Output Description

14.2.3   Initializing a Disk

A disk must be initialized using the *vxdisksetup* command to be used in VxVM. This command wipes out any information that exists on the disk and creates private and public regions on it. The command must be run on *Disk Access* (DA) record. A DA record is the logical device name without */dev/dsk* and */dev/rdsk*. Issue the command on *c2t1d0* disk as follows:

vxdisksetup −i c2t1d0

14.2.4 Creating and Displaying a Disk Group

The next step is to create a disk group. Let us construct a disk group, *oradg,* containing *c2t1d0* disk with DM name *oradg01*. Do as follows:

vxdg init oradg oradg01=c2t1d0

To view the result, execute the *vxdisk* command as follows:

vxdisk list

DEVICE	TYPE	DISK	GROUP	STATUS
c2t0d0	simple	rootdisk01	rootdg	online
c2t1d0	**simple**	**oradg01**	**oradg**	**online**
c2t2d0	simple	-	-	online invalid

Notice that the status of the disk is changed to "online". Also, under DISK and GROUP columns, the DM and associated disk group names are displayed.

You can check the status of the disk group by running the *vxdg* command as follows:

vxdg list

NAME	STATE	ID
rootdg	enabled	1177803668.1325.hp01
oradg	**enabled**	**1178631866.1416.hp01**

The output shows that *oradg* disk group is created and enabled.

14.2.5 Creating and Displaying a Volume

At this stage, you have storage space available to construct volumes. Create a 10GB concatenated volume called *system* in *oradg* disk group. Use the *vxassist* command as follows:

vxassist –g oradg make system 10g

To check what *vxassist* has done, use the *vxprint* command:

vxprint
Disk group: rootdg
. . . .
. . . .
Disk group: oradg

TY	NAME	ASSOC	KSTATE	LENGTH	PLOFFS	STATE	TUTIL0	PUTIL0
dg	oradg	oradg	-	-	-	-	-	-
dm	oradg01	c2t1d0	-	35561582	-	-	-	-
v	system	fsgen	ENABLED	10240000	-	ACTIVE	-	-

```
pl   system-01      system       ENABLED  10240000  -        ACTIVE   -      -
sd   oradg01-01     system-01    ENABLED  10240000  0        -        -      -
```

The output indicates that a disk group, *oradg*, is available and contains a volume *system*, a plex *system-01*, and a subdisk *oradg01-01*. The status of the virtual objects within *oradg* is active and enabled.

Using the *vxassist* command, you can create RAID 0 striped, RAID 5, RAID 0+1, and RAID 1+0 volumes as well. Note that striped and RAID 5 volumes require at least 2 and 3 disks, respectively. Higher number of disks may be needed for RAID 0+1 and 1+0.

14.2.6   Expanding a Disk Group

Expanding a disk group adds one or more disks to it to satisfy additional storage requirements. When you created *oradg* you added one disk, *c2t1d0*, to it. The following command adds to the disk group another disk, *c2t2d0*. Run *vxdisksetup* and then *vxdg* as follows to achieve this:

```
# vxdisksetup –i  c2t2d0
# vxdg –g  oradg  adddisk  oradg02=c2t2d0
```

Again run *vxprint* and *vxdisk* commands to see updated *oradg* disk group information.

14.2.7   Growing a Volume

Growing a volume increases the volume in size. The following command grows the *system* volume to 12GB from 10GB. Use either *vxassist* or *vxresize* command to perform this activity.

With *vxassist*, do one of the following:

```
# vxassist –g  oradg  growby  system  2g       (specify how much to add)
# vxassist –g  oradg  growto  system  12g      (specify how much in total you want)
```

With *vxresize*, do the following:

```
# vxresize –g  oradg  system  12g
```

The difference between the two commands from the volume resizing perspective is that the *vxassist* command only grows the specified volume. You have to increase the size of the file system later that the volume contains using the *fsadm* command. On the contrary, *vxresize* takes care of both.

Run *vxprint* command to verify the new size.

14.2.8   Shrinking a Volume

Shrinking a volume decreases the volume in size. The following command shrinks the *system* volume to 8GB from 12GB. Use either *vxassist* or *vxresize* command to perform this activity.

With *vxassist*, do one of the following:

> # **vxassist –g oradg shrinkby system 4g**   (specify how much to shrink)
> # **vxassist –g oradg shrinkto system 8g**   (specify how much in total you want)

With *vxresize*, do the following:

> # **vxresize –g oradg system 8g**

There is some risk involved when you shrink a volume size. You might end up losing critical data. Do a backup of the file system in the volume before shrinking its size. See Chapter 19 "Performing Backup and Restore" for details on how to perform backups.

Run *vxprint* command to verify the new size.

14.2.9   Removing a Volume

To remove a logical volume, first unmount the file system, if mounted, in it. A detailed discussion on creating, mounting, and unmounting a file system is covered in Chapter 15 "Working with File Systems".

The following command removes the *system* volume:

> # **vxassist –g oradg remove volume system**

14.2.10   Reducing a Disk Group

Reducing a disk group removes one or more DMs from it. Currently, *oradg* contains *oradg01* and *oradg02*. Use *vxdg* to remove a DM from disk group. The DM must not be in use. The following command removes *oradg02* from *oradg*:

> # **vxdg –g oradg rmdisk oradg02**

Run *vxprint* and *vxdisk* to see the updated *oradg* disk group information.

14.2.11   Deporting and Importing a Disk Group

Ususally, in a clustered environment or at the time of migrating data from one machine to another, this feature of VxVM is employed. A disk group that contains disks shared between two or more systems, can be made available to only one system at a time. In order to give the control of the disk group along with its objects to another machine that shares the disks that the disk group contains, you can *deport* the disk group from the existing machine and *import* it on the other machine. VxVM automatically reads the private regions on the disks on the other machine to determine their identity. Use the *vxdg* command for deport and import operations.

> # **vxdg deport oradg**
> # **vxdg import oradg**

You need to ensure that no volumes of the disk group are in use when you perform the deport operation.

The deport task does not remove any data or VxVM information from the disks in the disk group; it simply makes the disk group inaccessible to the system.

To view all imported as well as deported disk groups, use the *vxdisk* command as follows:

```
# vxdisk -o alldgs list
DEVICE      TYPE   DISK        GROUP        STATUS
c2t0d0      simple rootdisk02   rootdg       online
c2t1d0      simple -            (oradg)      online
c2t2d0      simple -            -            online
```

All deported disk groups are displayed in parentheses.

14.2.12   Renaming a Disk Group

At the time when you deport or import a disk group, you can rename it. Repeat the deport operation and change the disk group name from *oradg* to *oracledg*. Similarly, change the name from *oracledg* to *oraclebindg* when importing it on the other machine.

```
# vxdg -n oracledg deport oradg
# vxdg -n oraclebindg import oracledg
```

14.2.13   Destroying a Disk Group

Destroying a disk group removes the disk group along with any volumes and other objects within it from the VxVM configuration. You must unmount any file systems that reside in the disk group prior to destroying it. Use *vxdg* to destroy *oraclebindg* disk group as follows:

```
# vxdg destroy oraclebindg
```

Execute *vxprint* and *vxdisk* commands to verify the results.

Remember to proceed with caution whenever you perform reduce and destroy operations.

14.2.14   Converting LVM *vg00* to VxVM *rootdg*

This section assumes that you chose LVM when you installed HP-UX OE software on your system. In order to convert from *vg00* volume group to *rootdg* disk group, you need to execute the *vxcp_lvmroot* command. Specify with the command the disk that contains *vg00* and the disk to be used for *rootdg,* in that order.

```
# /etc/vx/bin/vxcp_lvmroot -v -p c2t0d0 c2t1d0
vxcp_lvmroot 23:01: Gathering information on LVM root volume group vg00
vxcp_lvmroot 23:01: Checking specified disk(s) for usability
vxcp_lvmroot 23:01: Starting up VxVM
```

```
vxcp_lvmroot 23:03: Preparing disk c2t1d0 as a VxVM root disk
vxcp_lvmroot 23:04: Adding disk c2t1d0 to rootdg as DM rootdisk01
vxcp_lvmroot 23:05: Preparing disk c2t0d0 as a VxVM disk
vxcp_lvmroot 23:06: Adding disk c2t0d0 to rootdg as DM rootaux01
vxcp_lvmroot 23:06: Copying /dev/vg00/lvol1 (hfs) to /dev/vx/dsk/rootdg/standvol
vxcp_lvmroot 23:07: Cloning /dev/vg00/lvol2 (swap) to /dev/vx/dsk/rootdg/swapvol
vxcp_lvmroot 23:07: Copying /dev/vg00/lvol3 (vxfs) to /dev/vx/dsk/rootdg/rootvol
vxcp_lvmroot 23:09: Copying /dev/vg00/lvol4 (vxfs) to /dev/vx/dsk/rootdg/tmpvol
vxcp_lvmroot 23:09: Copying /dev/vg00/lvol5 (vxfs) to /dev/vx/dsk/rootdg/homevol
vxcp_lvmroot 23:09: Copying /dev/vg00/lvol6 (vxfs) to /dev/vx/dsk/rootdg/optvol
vxcp_lvmroot 23:14: Copying /dev/vg00/lvol7 (vxfs) to /dev/vx/dsk/rootdg/usrvol
vxcp_lvmroot 00:42: Copying /dev/vg00/lvol8 (vxfs) to /dev/vx/dsk/rootdg/varvol
vxcp_lvmroot 00:50: Setting up disk c2t1d0 as a boot disk
vxcp_lvmroot 00:51: Installing fstab and fixing dev nodes on new root FS
vxcp_lvmroot 00:51: Installing bootconf & rootconf files in new stand FS
vxcp_lvmroot 00:51: Disk c2t1d0 is now a VxVM rootable boot disk
```

The output demonstrates that the command performed several actions, such as initializing the target disk, creating *rootdg*, copying data to new volumes, setting the new disk as primary boot device, and updating */etc/fstab*, */stand/bootconf*, and */stand/rootconf* files.

14.2.15   Converting LVM non-*vg00* to VxVM non-*rootdg*

In order to convert a non-*vg00* volume group to VxVM, or vice versa, you need to execute the *vxvmconvert* command. This commands presents you with a menu and guides you through the process of conversion. It prompts you to answer various questions. Choose option 2 to convert a volume group into a disk group, and option 3, for the reverse operation.

 # vxvmconvert

```
Volume Manager Support Operations
Menu: VolumeManager/LVM_Conversion

1              Analyze LVM Volume Groups for Conversion
2              Convert LVM Volume Groups to VxVM
3              Roll back from VxVM to LVM
list           List disk information
listvg         List LVM Volume Group information

?              Display help about menu
??             Display help about the menuing system
q              Exit from menus

Select an operation to perform:
```

14.3   VxVM Mirroring

VxVM supports replication of data on up to thirty one additional plexes for high availability purposes. This is known as *Mirroring*. With mirroring configuration, if one of the DMs fails, there is no service interruption and users continue to access data on the remaining DM(s). VxVM mirroring is performed at the plex level. A plex that may have in it a file system, a raw database partition, or a device swap, can be mirrored. One important point to note here is that mirroring does not protect against data loss or corruption; it only protects against disk failures.

In order to perform VxVM mirroring, the following is required:

✓ You must have the HP-UX MirrorDisk/UX product installed on your system. MirrorDisk/UX is part of HP-UX 11i Enterprise and Mission-Critical OEs. A valid license may need to be entered before using the mirroring feature.
✓ It is very important to have a minimum of two separate DMs, with each connected to a separate physical controller card. If this requirement is not met, you will not be able to get true benefits of mirroring.
✓ The DMs must be part of a single disk group.
✓ You have to have a volume available for mirroring or create a new one for this purpose.
✓ The target plex must be the same size or larger than the source plex.

14.3.1   Mirroring the Boot Disk Group

In this sub-section, you are going to create a two-way mirror of all the volumes that reside in *rootdg* disk group. A two-way mirror refers to using two plexes, a three-way mirror refers to using three plexes, and so on. Mirroring is also referred to as RAID 1.

Here is the procedure. Make sure requirements for mirroring identified above are met. From the output of *vxprint* and *vxdisk* commands, you know that *rootdg* currently resides on *c2t1d0* and contains eight volumes – *homevol, optvol, rootvol, standvol, swaplvol, tmpvol, usrvol,* and *varvol*. For the purpose of this demonstration, let us use *c2t0d0* disk, which is available and is of the same size as *c2t1d0*. To create mirror of all the volumes in *rootdg*, use the *vxrootmir* command with –v and –b options. The –v option displays verbose output and –b option forces the command to call *setboot* command and define the specified disk as the alternate boot disk. The *vxrootmir* command also updates AUTO file on the alternate boot disk.

Execute *vxrootmir* on *c2t0d0* as follows:

```
# vxrootmir –v –b c2t0d0
vxrootmir: 3:01: Gathering information on the current VxVM root configuration
vxrootmir: 3:01: Checking specified disk(s) for usability
vxrootmir: 3:01: Preparing disk c2t0d0 as a VxVM disk
vxrootmir: 3:01: Adding disk c2t0d0 to rootdg as rootdisk02
vxrootmir: 3:01: Mirroring only volumes required for root mirror boot
vxrootmir: 3:01: Mirroring volume standvol
vxrootmir: 3:02: Mirroring volume swapvol
vxrootmir: 3:02: Mirroring volume rootvol
vxrootmir: 3:01: Mirroring volume usrvol
vxrootmir: 3:02: Mirroring volume varvol
vxrootmir: 3:02: Mirroring volume optvol
vxrootmir: 3:01: Mirroring volume homevol
vxrootmir: 3:02: Mirroring volume tmpvol
vxrootmir: 3:03: Current setboot values:
vxrootmir: 3:03: Primary:    0/1/1/0.1.0
vxrootmir: 3:03: Alternate:  0/1/1/0.0.0
vxrootmir: 3:03: Making c2t0d0 (0/1/1/0.0.0) the alternate boot disk
vxrootmir: 3:03: Disk c2t0d0 is now a mirrored root disk
```

Execute *vxprint*, *vxdisk*, and *setboot* commands to verify that mirroring has been completed successfully.

vxprint
Disk group: rootdg

TY NAME	ASSOC	KSTATE	LENGTH	PLOFFS	STATE	TUTIL0	PUTIL0
dg rootdg	rootdg	-	-	-	-	-	-
dm rootdisk01	c2t1d0	-	35561582	-	-	-	-
dm rootdisk02	c2t0d0	-	35561582	-	-	-	-
v homevol	fsgen	ENABLED	3072000	-	ACTIVE	-	-
pl homevol-01	homevol	ENABLED	3072000	-	ACTIVE	-	-
sd rootdisk01-04	homevol-01	ENABLED	3072000	0	-	-	-
pl homevol-02	homevol	ENABLED	3072000	-	ACTIVE	-	-
sd rootdisk02-04	homevol-02	ENABLED	3072000	0	-	-	-
v optvol	fsgen	ENABLED	5120000	-	ACTIVE	-	-
pl optvol-01	optvol	ENABLED	5120000	-	ACTIVE	-	-
sd rootdisk01-05	optvol-01	ENABLED	5120000	0	-	-	-
pl optvol-02	optvol	ENABLED	5120000	-	ACTIVE	-	-
sd rootdisk02-05	optvol-02	ENABLED	5120000	0	-	-	-
v rootvol	root	ENABLED	1024000	-	ACTIVE	-	-
pl rootvol-01	rootvol	ENABLED	1024000	-	ACTIVE	-	-
sd rootdisk01-03	rootvol-01	ENABLED	1024000	0	-	-	-
pl rootvol-02	rootvol	ENABLED	1024000	-	ACTIVE	-	-
sd rootdisk02-03	rootvol-02	ENABLED	1024000	0	-	-	-

. . . .
. . . .

This output indicates that each volume now contains two plexes which are taken from two separate disks.

vxdisk list

DEVICE	TYPE	DISK	GROUP	STATUS
c2t1d0	simple	rootdisk01	rootdg	online
c2t0d0	**simple**	**rootdisk02**	**rootdg**	**online**

setboot
Primary bootpath   : 0/1/1/0.1.0
Alternate bootpath : **0/1/1/0.0.0**

Autoboot is ON (enabled)
Autosearch is ON (enabled)

HP Certified Systems Administrator

In order to make certain that the alternate boot disk boots up the system if primary is unavailable, go to the system console, shutdown and reboot the system, interact with BCH (or EFI), and boot the system using the alternate boot disk path (refer to Chapter 17 "Shutting Down and Starting Up an HP-UX System" for details on pre-boot administration tasks). If the system boots up fine that means you have the *rootdg* mirroring setup correctly. Now your system always attempts to boot from the primary boot disk and then the secondary (if primary is unavailable).

This completes *rootdg* mirroring setup and verification.

14.3.2   Mirroring a Non-Boot Disk Group

Mirroring of volumes that reside in a non-boot disk group is done on a per volume basis. This means that each volume is individually mirrored. Let us assume that a disk group, *testdg*, exists and has a volume, *system,* in it. Also assume that a spare disk, *c2t3d0*, is available. After initializing the disk and expanding the disk group to include the new disk, do the following:

> # **vxassist –g testdg mirror system c2t3d0**

Use *vxprint* to verify. This completes the mirroring procedure for a non-boot disk group.

14.3.3   Growing Mirrors

Growing a mirrored volume increases the volume in size. It adds specified space to each plex that resides within the volume. Use the *vxassist* or *vxresize* command to grow the size of a mirrored volume the same way you grew a non-mirrored volume earlier in this chapter. When you are done, run *vxprint* to validate.

14.3.4   Shrinking Mirrors

Shrinking a mirrored volume decreases the volume in size. It subtracts specified space from each plex that resides within the volume. Use the *vxassist* or *vxresize* command to shrink the size of a mirrored volume the same way you shrunk a non-mirrored volume earlier in this chapter. When you are done, run *vxprint* to validate.

14.4 Comparing LVM and VxVM

Both LVM and VxVM provide logical disk management functionality. Table 14-4 compares the terms used in LVM with VxVM.

LVM	VxVM
Physical volume	VM disk (or disk medium)
Logical volume	Volume
Volume group	Disk group
Physical extent	Subdisk
Mirror or logical extent	Plex (2nd copy of data)
PV link	Dynamic multipathing
Mirror write cache	Dirty region log

PVRA/BDRA/VGRA	Private region
Unused PEs	Free space

Table 14-4 LVM / VxVM Terminology Comparison

Table 14-5 compares LVM and VxVM commands to perform similar tasks.

LVM	VxVM
pvchange	vxdisk and vxedit
pvcreate	vxdisksetup
pvdisplay	vxdisk
pvmove	vxevac and vxsd
pvremove	vxdiskunsetup
vgchange, vgcreate, vgexport, vgextend, vgimport, vgremove	vxdg
vgdisplay	vxdg and vxprint
vgextend	vxdiskadd
vgreduce	vxdiskrm
vgscan	vxinfo and vxprint
vgsync	vxrecover
lvchange	vxedit or vxvol
lvcreate, lvextend, lvmerge, lvreduce, lvsplit,	vxassist
lvlnboot	No single equivalent command
lvremove	vxedit and vxassist
lvsync	vxrecover and vxvol
No equivalent	vxplex
No equivalent	vxsd and vxmend

Table 14-5 LVM / VxVM Command Comparison

Summary

You looked at features and benefits associated with the Veritas Volume Manager solution for disk management in this chapter. You learned concepts, components, and structure of VxVM and various administration interfaces available to manage disk storage.

You learned how to manage VxVM objects specifically tasks pertaining to disks, disk groups, plexes, and volumes. You understood the procedure for converting LVM volume groups to VxVM disk groups, and vice versa.

Next, you studied requirements for mirroring. You performed mirroring of boot and non-boot volume groups.

Finally, you were presented with a comparison between LVM and VxVM terminology and commands.

## 15

Working with File Systems

This chapter covers the following major topics:

✓   File system concepts
✓   Supported file system types in HP-UX
✓   Structure and components of High-Performance File System (HFS)
✓   Structure and components of Journaled File System (VxFS)
✓   Manage file systems including creating, mounting, viewing, extending, reducing, tuning, defragmenting, unmounting, and removing them
✓   Mount file systems automatically at each system boot
✓   Check and repair HFS and VxFS file system structures
✓   Mount and unmount CDFS and LOFS file systems
✓   Use tools, such as bdf, df, du, and quot to monitor file system space utilization

15.1   File System Concepts

A file system is a logical container used to hold files and directories. Each file system is created in a separate volume. A typical HP-UX machine usually has numerous file systems. The following list shows file systems that *vg00* volume group or *rootdg* disk group normally contains and are created, by default, at the time of HP-UX Operating Environment software installation.

vg00 Logical Volume	*rootdg* Volume Group	File System Type	Mount Point
/dev/vg00/lvol1	/dev/vx/dsk/rootdg/standvol	HFS	/stand
/dev/vg00/lvol3	/dev/vx/dsk/rootdg/rootvol	VxFS	/
/dev/vg00/lvol4	/dev/vx/dsk/rootdg/homevol	VxFS	/home
/dev/vg00/lvol5	/dev/vx/dsk/rootdg/optvol	VxFS	/opt
/dev/vg00/lvol6	/dev/vx/dsk/rootdg/tmpvol	VxFS	/tmp
/dev/vg00/lvol7	/dev/vx/dsk/rootdg/usrvol	VxFS	/usr
/dev/vg00/lvol8	/dev/vx/dsk/rootdg/varvol	VxFS	/var

As you can see that each HP-UX file system is constructed in a separate volume and holds a unique type of information. / (root) and */stand* are special file systems without which an HP-UX system cannot boot up. Notice that */stand* is an HFS type file system. In fact, it must be HFS. All other file systems can be either HFS or VxFS.

You may create as many file systems with different types in an HP-UX system as you require. There is no limit. Storing similar data in separate file systems versus storing all data in a single file system offers advantages, such as:

- ✓ You can make a file system accessible or inaccessible to users independent of other file systems. This hides or unhides information contained within that file system.
- ✓ You can perform file system repair activities on individual file systems.
- ✓ You can optimize each file system independently.
- ✓ You can grow or shrink the size of a file system independently.

15.2   File System Types

There are several different types of file systems that HP-UX supports. Some of the key ones are:

- ✓ *High-Performance File System* (HFS)
- ✓ *Veritas File System* (VxFS) [a.k.a. *Journaled File System* (JFS)]
- ✓ *CD-ROM File System* (CDFS)
- ✓ *LOopback File System (LOFS)*
- ✓ *Network File System* (NFS)
- ✓ *Auto File System* (AutoFS)
- ✓ *Common Internet File System* (CIFS)
- ✓ *Cache File System* (CacheFS)

The *fstyp* command displays a list of all supported file systems:

```
# fstyp –l
hfs
nfs
cdfs
nfs3
ffs
vxfs
autofs
cachefs
lofs
cifs
pipefs
```

This chapter covers HFS, VxFS, CDFS, and LOFS file system types. NFS is covered in Chapter 29 "Setting Up and Administering NFS", AutoFS in Chapter 30 "Setting Up and Administering AutoFS", and CIFS is covered in Chapter 31 "Setting Up CIFS/9000".

The CacheFS file system is used to enhance access to a slow file system usually located on a CD or DVD medium by caching its contents in physical memory. A discussion on CacheFS is beyond the scope of this book.

The following sub-sections provide in-depth information on HFS and JFS file systems. A discussion on CDFS follows the two.

15.2.1　The High-Performance File System (HFS)

HFS has been supported on HP-UX for a long period of time. It is designed to work only on hard disk devices.

When an HFS file system is created in a volume, it builds HFS structure in it. The structure is divided into two sets. One set that consists of not too many blocks, holds file system metadata information. The other set that consists of majority of file system blocks, holds actual data.

The metadata contains file system structural information including superblock, cylinder group blocks, and inode table. It also contains pointers that point to specific location in the other set where actual user files are stored. See Figure 15-1.

HFS Superblock

When a file system is built, the first 8KB area is reserved for storing critical file system information. This area is referred to as the *Superblock* and holds the following information about the file system:

- ✓　Type of the file system
- ✓　Size of the file system
- ✓　Number of data blocks in the file system
- ✓　Number of cylinder groups in the file system
- ✓　Data block and fragment sizes used in the file system
- ✓　File system status

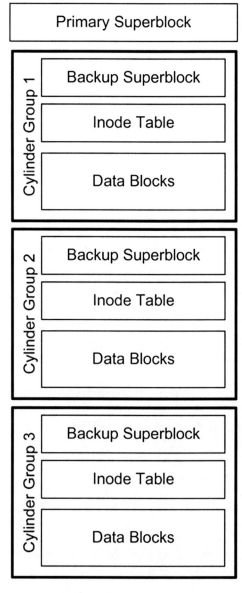

**HFS File System
Structure**

Figure 15-1 HFS File System Structure

Since the superblock holds such vital information, a copy of it is automatically stored in each cylinder group within the file system as well as in the */var/adm/sbtab* file. The superblock at the beginning of the file system is referred to as the *Primary Superblock* and all others as *Backup Superblocks*.

HFS Cylinder Groups

The file system is further divided into *Cylinder Groups* for better performance and manageability. The larger an HFS file system is, the more cylinder groups it will have. Each cylinder group contains a copy of the primary superblock and a portion of both a file system's inodes and data blocks to be used within that cylinder group. Each cylinder group maintains its portion of inodes and data blocks.

HFS Inodes

Each file in HP-UX has an associated *index node* number, which contains information about the file. This information includes the file type, permissions on it, ownership and group membership information, its size, last access/modification time, as well as pointers to data blocks that store the file contents. When a file system is constructed, a fixed number of inodes are generated in each cylinder group and allocated to files as they are created in the file system. This number can be defined to suit your needs at the time of file system construction.

Inodes are maintained in *Inode Table* that contains information about the usage and allocation of each inode in the file system. Within a file system, each inode number is unique. If a file system runs out of inodes, you will not be able to create any more files in it.

HFS Data Blocks

When a file system is formed, several *Data Blocks* are produced in it. These data blocks are used to store file contents. The larger a file is, the more data blocks it requires to store its contents. HFS allows a file to use scattered data blocks in a file system.

The default HFS block size is 8KB, which can be customized to have a value between 4KB and 64KB at the time of file system creation.

HFS Fragments

Each HFS data block is sub-divided into *Fragments*. A fragment is the smallest unit of space allocated to a file. A file system's fragment size is defined at file system creation time and cannot be altered later. The default fragment size is 1KB.

15.2.2   The Journaled File System (JFS)

The *Journaled File System*, popularly known as *Veritas File System* (VxFS), is an extent-based journaling file system, which offers several benefits over conventional HFS file system type. Some of the key advantages are:

✓   Fast file system recovery after a system crash
✓   Online file system resizing
✓   Online backup
✓   Online reorganization and defragmentation

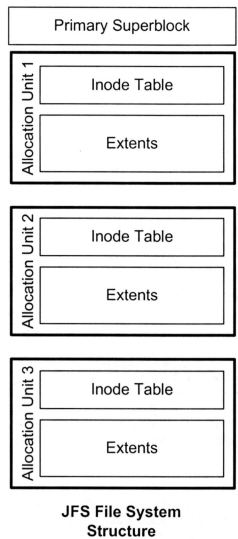

**JFS File System
Structure**

Figure 15-2 JFS File System Structure

JFS Superblock

Like HFS, VxFS has a *Superblock* at the beginning of a file system that describes the file system type, size, number of data blocks and cylinder groups it contains, data block size, fragment size, and file system status information.

Unlike HFS, VxFS does not keep information of its backup superblock locations in a file, rather, it finds them automatically whenever it requires.

JFS Intent Log

The journaled file system keeps track of file system structural updates in *Intent Log*. Each metadata update is written, in its entirety, to the intent log after it is complete. When a system reboots after a crash, it looks in the intent log of each file system and recovers the file system rapidly using the updated structural information stored in its intent log.

JFS Allocation Units

JFS *Allocation Units* are conceptually similar to HFS cylinder groups. A VxFS file system is further divided into allocation units for enhanced performance and manageability. The larger a VxFS file system is, the more allocation units it will have. Each allocation unit contains and maintains a portion of the file system inodes and data blocks.

JFS Inodes

Like HFS, each file has an associated *index node* number, which contains information about the file, such as the file type, permissions, ownership, group membership, size, access time, and pointers to data blocks that store the file contents. When a file system is created, several inodes are generated in each allocation unit. These inodes are allocated to files as they are created. Unlike HFS, when VxFS runs out of inodes, it dynamically creates additional inodes as long as there are free data blocks available in the file system. Each inode number is unique within a file system.

JFS Blocks and Extents

In JFS, a file requires one or more blocks to store its contents. A *Block* is the smallest unit of disk space that can be allocated. The default JFS block size is 1KB, which can be modified at the time the file system is created.

When you make a file, JFS allocates an *Extent* to it. An extent is a contiguous group of blocks in a file system. As the file grows, JFS tries to increase the size of the extent, if contiguous space is available. If contiguous space is not available, JFS uses another extent elsewhere in the file system and moves the file contents there. In order to optimize performance, JFS tries to allocate the next extent in the same allocation unit, if possible. Since file blocks are arranged contiguously in a JFS file system, JFS can read large amounts of data into memory with a single I/O operation.

15.3 Managing HFS and VxFS File Systems

Managing file systems involves creating a file system, mounting it to make it accessible, extending its size, reducing its size, unmounting it to make it inaccessible, and removing it. The following subsections explain how to perform file system management operations.

15.3.1 Creating a File System

In Chapter 13 and 14, you learned about LVM and VxVM and how to create volumes. When a volume is made, only then you can create a file system in it. Without constructing file system structures in a volume, the volume can only be used as a raw partition. In order for a volume to store files and directories, it must be initialized so it can have file system structures created in it.

To make an HFS file system, the *newfs* command is used. This command is the front-end to the *mkfs* command. In other words, when you invoke the *newfs* command, it runs *mkfs* behind the scenes.

In order to understand the behavior of the command, let us assume that you have two LVM logical volumes called *lvol1* and *lvol2* in *vg01* volume group with sizes 1GB and 2GB, respectively. Also assume that you have two VxVM volumes called *vol1* and *vol2* in *dg01* disk group with sizes 3GB and 5GB, respectively. Let us initialize them with the *newfs* command using different options. The general syntax of this command is:

newfs [–F FStype] [–V] [–o specific_options] special

where:

–F FStype denotes the file system type to be created: hfs or vxfs.
–o specific_options specifies any particular options to the type of file system being created.
special is the volume's character special device file.

To create an HFS file system in */dev/vg01/rlvol1* with all default HFS file system characteristics, do the following:

 # newfs –F hfs /dev/vg01/rlvol1
mkfs (hfs): Warning - 608 sector(s) in the last cylinder are not allocated.
mkfs (hfs): /dev/vg01/rlvol1 - 1024000 sectors in 1642 cylinders of 16 tracks, 39 sectors
1048.6Mb in 103 cyl groups (16 c/g, 10.22Mb/g, 1600 i/g)
Super block backups (for fsck -b) at:
    16, 10040, 20064, 30088, 40112, 50136, 60160, 70184, 80208, 90232,
. . . .
. . . .

To create a JFS file system in */dev/vg01/rlvol2* with all default VxFS file system characteristics, run the command as follows:

 # newfs –F vxfs /dev/vg01/rlvol2
    version 4 layout
    2048000 sectors, 2048000 blocks of size 1024, log size 1024 blocks
    unlimited inodes, largefiles not supported
    2048000 data blocks, 2046392 free data blocks
    63 allocation units of 32768 blocks, 32768 data blocks
    last allocation unit has 16384 data blocks

When you create a JFS file system, you do not need to specify "–F vxfs" with *newfs*. The command looks into the */etc/default/fs* file for the variable LOCAL. By default, this variable is set to "vxfs".

The *newfs* command supports various options, some of which are listed in Table 15-1 and used in examples below.

Option	Description
–o largefiles	Enables you to create files of sizes up to 128GB in the file system. Without this option the maximum file size would be 2GB only.
–b	Block size (HFS only).
–m	Minimum amount of free space, as a percent of the total file system size, to be maintained in the file system (HFS only).

Table 15-1 *newfs* Command Options

The following example demonstrates how to create an HFS file system in */dev/vx/rdsk/dg01/vol1* with "largefiles" support and 15% minimum free space to maintain. Run the *newfs* command as follows:

newfs –F hfs –o largefiles –m 15 /dev/vx/rdsk/dg01/vol1
mkfs (hfs): Warning - 592 sector(s) in the last cylinder are not allocated.
mkfs (hfs): /dev/vx/rdsk/dg01/vol1 - 5242880 sectors in 8403 cylinders of 16 tracks, 39 sectors
5368.7Mb in 526 cyl groups (16 c/g, 10.22Mb/g, 1600 i/g)
Super block backups (for fsck -b) at:
   16, 10040, 20064, 30088, 40112, 50136, 60160, 70184, 80208, 90232,
. . . .
. . . .

Let us create a JFS file system in */dev/vx/rdsk/dg01/vol2* with "largefiles" support. Issue the *newfs* command as follows:

newfs –o largefiles /dev/vx/rdsk/dg01/vol2
newfs: /etc/default/fs is used for determining the file system type
/usr/sbin/mkfs -F vxfs -o largefiles /dev/vx/rdsk/dg01/vol2 3145728
   version 4 layout
   3145728 sectors, 3145728 blocks of size 1024, log size 1024 blocks
   unlimited inodes, largefiles supported
   3145728 data blocks, 3143848 free data blocks
   96 allocation units of 32768 blocks, 32768 data blocks

Instead of using *newfs*, you may use its variants to create either the HFS or the VxFS file system. The variants are */sbin/fs/hfs/newfs* for HFS and */sbin/fs/vxfs/newfs* for VxFS. There is no need to use the –F option with them. Here is how you would create the */dev/vg01/rlvol1* and */dev/vx/rdsk/dg01/vol2* file systems using these commands.

/sbin/fs/hfs/newfs /dev/vg01/rlvol1
/sbin/fs/vxfs/newfs –o largefiles /dev/vx/rdsk/dg01/vol2

Notice that the results of these commands and those of the *newfs* command with –F option are identical.

15.3.2   Mounting a File System

Once a file system is created, you want to make it accessible by connecting it to the root of the HP-UX directory hierarchy. There are two steps involved if you are mounting the file system the first time. The first step is to create a directory where you can mount (connect) the file system. This directory is referred to as the *Mount Point*. In the second step, use the *mount* command to mount the file system on the mount point.

Currently, you have four file systems from the previous sub-section with block device files */dev/vg01/lvol1*, */dev/vg01/lvol2*, */dev/vx/dsk/dg01/vol1*, and */dev/vx/dsk/dg01/vol2*. Here is how you would mount them using appropriate options.

To mount */dev/vg01/lvol1* HFS file system on */data1*:

> **# mkdir /data1**
> **# mount –F hfs /dev/vg01/lvol1 /data1**

To mount */dev/vg01/lvol2* JFS file system on */data2*:

> **# mkdir /data2**
> **# mount –F vxfs /dev/vg01/lvol2 /data2**

Note that "–F hfs" and "–F vxfs" are optional. You do not need to specify them when you use the *mount* command. The reason being that the *mount* command senses the file system type. It automatically mounts an HFS file system as HFS and a JFS file system as JFS.

To mount */dev/vx/dsk/dg01/vol1* HFS file system, with "largefiles" support, on */data3*:

> **# mkdir /data3**
> **# mount –F hfs –o largefiles /dev/vx/dsk/dg01/vol1 /data3**

To mount */dev/vx/dsk/dg01/vol2* JFS file system, with "largefiles" support, on */data4*:

> **# mkdir /data4**
> **# mount –o largefiles /dev/vx/dsk/dg01/vol2 /data4**

Instead of using *mount*, you may use its variants to mount either the HFS or the VxFS file system. The variants are */sbin/fs/hfs/mount* for HFS and */sbin/fs/vxfs/mount* for VxFS. There is no need to use the –F option with them. Here is how you would mount the */dev/vg01/lvol1* and */dev/vx/dsk/dg01/vol1* file systems using these commands:

> **# /sbin/fs/hfs/mount /dev/vg01/lvol1 /data1**
> **# /sbin/fs/vxfs/mount –o largefiles /dev/vx/dsk/dg01/vol2 /data4**

When a file system is mounted, an entry is added to the mount table located in the */etc/mnttab* file. Here are the file contents after mounting the four file systems:

```
# cat  /etc/mnttab
/dev/vg00/lvol3         /        vxfs   log                    0   1   1182867277
/dev/vg00/lvol1         /stand   hfs    defaults               0   0   1182867279
/dev/vg00/lvol7         /var     vxfs   delaylog,nodatainlog   0   0   1182867295
/dev/vg00/lvol6         /usr     vxfs   delaylog,nodatainlog   0   0   1182867297
/dev/vg00/lvol5         /tmp     vxfs   delaylog,nodatainlog   0   0   1182867297
/dev/vg00/lvol4         /opt     vxfs   delaylog,nodatainlog   0   0   1182867298
/dev/vg00/lvol8         /home    vxfs   delaylog,nodatainlog   0   0   1182867301
/dev/vg01/lvol1         /data1   hfs    defaults               0   0   1183039596
/dev/vg01/lvol2         /data2   vxfs   log                    0   0   1183039612
/dev/vx/dsk/dg01/vol1   /data3   hfs    largefiles             0   0   1183039778
/dev/vx/dsk/dg01/vol2   /data4   vxfs   log,largefiles         0   0   1183039790
```

15.3.3   Viewing Mounted File Systems

Once file systems are mounted, you have several tools available to list them. Two tools – *bdf* and *mount* – are more common and both read the */etc/mnttab* file to display the information.

Run the *bdf* command to view all mounted file systems. Notice that *lvol1, lvol2, vol1*, and *vol2* file systems are mounted on */data1, /data2, /data3*, and */data4*. Also notice that *vol1* has 15% less space available for use. This is because you defined –m 15% when created the file system.

```
# bdf
File system              kbytes      used       avail      %used   Mounted on
/dev/vg00/lvol3          409600      139752     267784     34%     /
/dev/vg00/lvol1          295024      122112     143408     46%     /stand
/dev/vg00/lvol7          3500000     3274776    223568     94%     /var
/dev/vg00/lvol6          1800000     1500984    296856     83%     /usr
/dev/vg00/lvol5          600000      467448     132096     78%     /tmp
/dev/vg00/lvol4          2000000     1770824    227632     89%     /opt
/dev/vg00/lvol8          600000      389136     209864     65%     /home
/dev/vg01/lvol1          1001729     9          901547     0%      /data1
/dev/vg01/lvol2          2048000     1606       1918502    0%      /data2
/dev/vx/dsk/dg01/vol1    3077449     9          2615822    0%      /data3
/dev/vx/dsk/dg01/vol2    5242880     2385       4912972    0%      /data4
```

Run the *mount* command with and without –v option to view mounted file systems.

```
# mount  –v
/dev/vg00/lvol3   on /      type vxfs log             on  Tue Jun 26 10:14:37 2007
/dev/vg00/lvol1   on /stand type  hfs   defaults      on  Tue Jun 26 10:14:39 2007
/dev/vg00/lvol7   on /var   type  vxfs delaylog       on  Tue Jun 26 10:14:55 2007
/dev/vg00/lvol6   on /usr   type  vxfs delaylog       on  Tue Jun 26 10:14:57 2007
/dev/vg00/lvol5   on /tmp   type  vxfs delaylog       on  Tue Jun 26 10:14:57 2007
/dev/vg00/lvol4   on /opt   type  vxfs delaylog       on  Tue Jun 26 10:14:58 2007
/dev/vg00/lvol8   on /home  type  vxfs delaylog       on  Tue Jun 26 10:15:01 2007
/dev/vg01/lvol1   on /data1 type  hfs   defaults      on  Thu   Jun 28 10:06:36 2007
/dev/vg01/lvol2   on /data2 type  vxfs  log           on  Thu   Jun 28 10:06:52 2007
```

/dev/vx/dsk/dg01/vol1 on /data3 type hfs   largefiles   on Thu Jun 28 10:09:38 2007
/dev/vx/dsk/dg01/vol2 on /data4 type vxfs log,largefiles on Thu Jun 28 10:09:50 2007

15.3.4   Creating, Mounting, and Viewing a File System Using SAM

SAM is available to help you create LVM logical volumes and file systems in them. Follow the steps below:

☞ Go to SAM → Disks and File Systems → Logical Volumes → Actions → Create. Specify a volume group name and then go to Define New Logical Volume(s). Fill in the form with required information. When you hit the OK button, SAM will create a new logical volume with a VxFS file system in it. The file system will be mounted and an entry added to the */etc/fstab* file.

If you already have a logical volume created which does not contain any file system structures in it, follow the steps below to create a file system in it: The same window also displays all mounted file systems.

☞ Go to SAM → Disks and File Systems → File Systems → Actions → Add Local File System → Using the Logical Volume Manager. Highlight the logical volume, provide required information, and hit the OK button. See Figure 15-3.

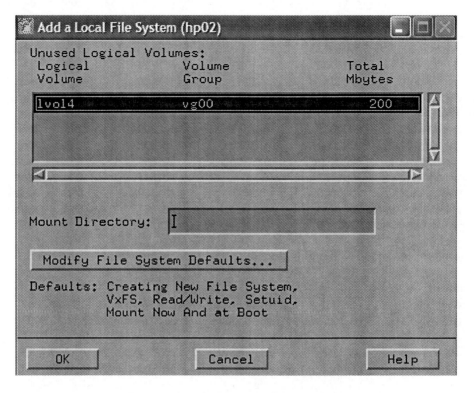

Figure 15-3 SAM – File System Add

15.3.5   Extending a File System

As a system administrator of an HP-UX system, one of your prime responsibilities is to resize file systems as and when required. Most of the time you receive requests to increase the size and occasionally to decrease it.

As you know that there are two types of disk-based file systems: HFS and VxFS. Procedures to extend both types of file system are given below.

Extending an HFS File System Size

To extend an HFS file system that lives in a volume (LVM or VxVM), you need to extend the volume that contains the file system using appropriate procedures outlined in Chapter 13 "Logical Volume Manager" and Chapter 14 "Veritas Volume Manager". Next, unmount the file system and extend it using the *extendfs* command. When done, remount the file system to make it accessible.

Let us extend the HFS file system residing in */dev/vg01/rlvol1* and */dev/vx/rdsk/dg01/vol1* considering that the sizes of the two volumes have already been extended.

> \# **umount /data1**
> \# **extendfs –F hfs /dev/vg01/rlvol1**   (**/dev/vx/rdsk/dg01/vol1** for VxVM volume)
>   max number of sectors extendible is 512000.
>   extend file system /dev/vg01/rlvol1 to have 512000 sectors more.
>   Warning: 288 sector(s) in last cylinder unallocated
>   extended super-block backups (for fsck -b#) at:
>   1028648, 1038672, 1048696, 1058720, 1068744, 1078768, 1088792, 1098816, 1108840, 1118224,
>   . . . .
>   . . . .
> \# **mount –F hfs /dev/vg01/lvol1 /data1**   (**/dev/vx/rdsk/dg01/vol1** for VxVM volume)

Confirm the new sizes using the *bdf* command.

SAM can be used to increase the size of a logical volume as well as the HFS file system that resides in it in one shot. Follow the steps below:

☞ Go to SAM → Disks and File Systems → Logical Volumes (highlight the logical volume) → Actions → Increase Size. Specify a new size and press the OK button.

To extend both a VxVM volume and the HFS file system it contains in one go, use either VEA or the *vxresize* command as explained in Chapter 14 "Veritas Volume Manager". VEA can be run from within SAM GUI as well. You must unmount the HFS file system for the *vxresize* command to act successfully.

Extending a VxFS File System Size

To extend the size of a JFS file system located in an LVM logical volume, follow the procedure outlined above (use –F vxfs instead) or extend the size online if you have the *OnlineJFS* product installed.

The OnlineJFS product is not part of the HP-UX Foundation Operating Environment software but is part of the HP-UX Enterprise OE and Mission-Critical OE.

The following example assumes that you have the OnlineJFS software installed. To extend */dev/vg01/lvol2* mounted on */data2* from 2GB to 2.5GB, first extend the logical volume and then issue the *fsadm* command on the mount point as follows:

> **# fsadm –F vxfs –b 2560000 /data2**
> vxfs fsadm: /dev/vg01/rlvol2 is currently 2048000 sectors - size will be increased

The –b option with *fsadm* specifies the total number of blocks to be allocated to */data2*. The value 2560000 comes by multiplying 2500 MB with 1024.

Confirm the new size using the *bdf* command.

The *fsadm* command works identically on a JFS file system that resides in a VxVM volume.

SAM can be used to increase the size of a logical volume as well as the JFS file system that resides in it in one go. Follow the steps below:

☞ Go to SAM → Disks and File Systems → Logical Volumes (highlight the logical volume) → Actions → Increase Size. Specify a new size and press the OK button.

To extend both a VxVM volume and the JFS file system it contains in one shot, use either VEA or the *vxresize* command as explained in Chapter 14 "Veritas Volume Manager". VEA can be run from within SAM GUI as well. There is no need to unmount the JFS file system for the *vxresize* command.

15.3.6   Reducing a File System

There are times when you need to reduce the size of a file system. It is possible to reduce a JFS file system size online (provided OnlineJFS product is installed) but not possible with HFS type file system. The only way to shrink an HFS file system is to back it up, reduce the volume it resides in, run *newfs* on the volume, mount the file system, and restore the data in it.

To decrease */data2* JFS file system size from 2.5GB to 2GB, reduce the size of the file system using the *fsadm* command and then the volume that the file system resides in using the *lvreduce* command.

> **# fsadm –F vxfs –b 2048000 /data2**
> vxfs fsadm: /dev/vg01/rlvol2 is currently 2560000 sectors - size will be reduced
> vxfs fsadm: allocations found in shrink range, moving data
> **# lvreduce –L 2000 /dev/vg01/lvol2**   (use *vxresize* or *vxassist* to reduce a VxVM volume)
> When a logical volume is reduced useful data might get lost;
> do you really want the command to proceed (y/n) : y
> Logical volume "/dev/vg01/lvol2" has been successfully reduced.
> Volume Group configuration for /dev/vg01 has been saved in /etc/lvmconf/vg01.conf

Observe extreme caution when reducing a file system size. Any data sitting on the blocks being removed from the file system will be lost. It is highly recommended to do a file system backup prior to performing this action.

15.3.7 Tuning a JFS File System

When you mount a JFS file system, you have the choice to supply options for the file system with the *mount* command. There is a command called *vxtunefs* that provides you the ability to display and tune I/O parameters of a mounted JFS file system. The command can be used to display or tune parameters that:

✓ Describe I/O properties of the underlying device
✓ Indicate when to treat an I/O as direct I/O
✓ Control the extent allocation policy

To display existing parameters for the */home* file system, for instance, run the *vxtunefs* command as follows:

```
# vxtunefs  /home
Filesystem i/o parameters for /home
read_pref_io = 65536
read_nstream = 1
. . . . . . . .
. . . . . . . .
```

Any of these parameters can be tuned with the *vxtunefs* command.

15.3.8 Defragmenting a JFS File System

Over the period of time, files are created and removed in a file system. Also, files are edited and their sizes are increased or decreased. Similar functions are performed at the directory level too. These operations result in file system fragmentation causing portions of files to reside in extents and blocks physically away from one another. Fragmentation affects data read and write performance in the file system.

HP-UX allows you to defragment a JFS file system online using the *fsadm* command. In fact, it is not a bad idea to run defragmentation once in a while automatically via cron.

To defragment extents (–e option) and directory entries (–d option) in a JFS file system, */var* for example, do the following:

```
# fsadm  –F  vxfs  –ed  /var
```

Note that it may take several minutes to complete the job.

15.3.9 Unmounting a File System

Unmounting a file system makes the file system inaccessible to users by disconnecting it from the directory structure. The procedure to unmount both HFS and JFS file systems is the same. Use the *umount* command as follows to unmount all the four file systems that you created earlier:

    # umount /data1
    # umount /data2
    # umount /data3
    # umount /data4

The *umount* command scans the */etc/mnttab* file and determine the volume device file associated with the mount point to unmount it.

Occasionally, when you try to unmount a file system, you get the following message:

    # umount /data1
    umount: cannot unmount /data1 : Device busy

This indicates that the specified file system is currently busy. A process or a user may be using it or a file in that file system is open.

To determine who or what processes are using the file system, use the *fuser* command.

    # fuser –cu /data1
    /data1:   26458c(root) 11411c(root)

The –c option tells the process ID and –u gives the user name who owns the process ID.

You can kill all processes that are presently using the file system by running the *fuser* command with the –k option:

    # fuser –ck /data1
    /data1:   26458c 11411c

Now you should be able to unmount */data1* using the *umount* command.

At times, you need to unmount all currently mounted file systems other than */var*, */usr*, and */ that cannot be unmounted. Issue the *umount* command with –a option to do this. Alternatively, you can use the *umountall* command.

    # umount –a
    # umountall
    umountall: umount : has failed.
    umountall: diagnostics from umount
    umount: cannot unmount / : Device busy
    umountall: umount : has failed.
    umountall: diagnostics from umount

umount: cannot unmount /usr : Device busy
umountall: umount : has failed.
umountall: diagnostics from umount
umount: cannot unmount /var : Device busy

15.3.10   Mounting a File System at System Boot

So far, you have mounted file systems from the command line or using SAM. What happens when your system reboots. None of these file systems will be remounted automatically. You will need to mount them manually. To automate mounting of a file system across system reboots, you need to put an entry for it in the */etc/fstab* file.

When your system comes up, the */sbin/init.d/localmount* script is called that executes the *mountall* command, which attempts to mount all file systems listed in the */etc/fstab* file. This file needs to be manually updated to add or remove a file system entry.

Other advantage after adding an entry to this file is that you can mount the file system by only specifying its mount point or the associated device file. You do not have to type in the full command.

The default */etc/fstab* file contains entries only for file systems that make up your root volume group (or disk group). For LVM, this file looks similar to:

cat /etc/fstab
System */etc/fstab* file. Static information about the file systems
See fstab(4) and sam(1M) for further details on configuring devices.

/dev/vg00/lvol3	/	vxfs	delaylog	0	1
/dev/vg00/lvol1	/stand	hfs	defaults	0	1
/dev/vg00/lvol4	/home	vxfs	delaylog	0	2
/dev/vg00/lvol5	/opt	vxfs	delaylog	0	2
/dev/vg00/lvol6	/tmp	vxfs	delaylog	0	2
/dev/vg00/lvol7	/usr	vxfs	delaylog	0	2
/dev/vg00/lvol8	/var	vxfs	delaylog	0	2

For VxVM, it looks like:

cat /etc/fstab
System /etc/fstab file. Static information about the file systems
See fstab(4) and sam(1M) for further details on configuring devices.

/dev/vx/dsk/rootdg/rootvol	/	vxfs	delaylog	0	1
/dev/vx/dsk/rootdg/standvol	/stand	hfs	defaults	0	1
/dev/vx/dsk/rootdg/homevol	/home	vxfs	delaylog	0	2
/dev/vx/dsk/rootdg/optvol	/opt	vxfs	delaylog	0	2
/dev/vx/dsk/rootdg/tmpvol	/tmp	vxfs	delaylog	0	2
/dev/vx/dsk/rootdg/usrvol	/usr	vxfs	delaylog	0	2
/dev/vx/dsk/rootdg/varvol	/var	vxfs	delaylog	0	2

Notice that there are six fields per line entry:

- ✓ The first field defines the volume block device file where your file system resides.
- ✓ The second field defines the mount point.
- ✓ The third field specifies the type of file system. It could be vxfs, hfs, cdfs, swap, swapfs, etc.
- ✓ The fourth field specifies any options to use when mounting the file system. Options available are: defaults, ro, nosuid, quota, delaylog, etc. When you specify the "defaults" option it means rw, suid, and noquota. Some options, such as delaylog, can be used only with JFS file system type.
- ✓ The fifth field is reserved for future use.
- ✓ The last field indicates the sequence number in which to run the file system check and repair utility (*fsck*) on it. It is 1 for both / and /*stand* file systems, and 2 for others, by default.

Add the /*data1*, /*data2*, /*data3*, and /*data4* file system entries to the /*etc/fstab* file using the vi editor. The updated file for LVM would look like:

```
# cat  /etc/fstab
# System /etc/fstab file.  Static information about the file systems
# See fstab(4) and sam(1M) for further details on configuring devices.
/dev/vg00/lvol3         /          vxfs    delaylog        0       1
/dev/vg00/lvol1         /stand     hfs     defaults        0       1
/dev/vg00/lvol4         /home      vxfs    delaylog        0       2
/dev/vg00/lvol5         /opt       vxfs    delaylog        0       2
/dev/vg00/lvol6         /tmp       vxfs    delaylog        0       2
/dev/vg00/lvol7         /usr       vxfs    delaylog        0       2
/dev/vg00/lvol8         /var       vxfs    delaylog        0       2
/dev/vg01/lvol1         /data1     hfs     defaults        0       2
/dev/vg01/lvol2         /data2     vxfs    log             0       2
/dev/vx/dsk/dg01/vol1   /data3     hfs     largefiles      0       2
/dev/vx/dsk/dg01/vol2   /data4     vxfs    log,largefiles  0       2
```

After making these entries, if you wish to mount all file systems listed in the /*etc/fstab* file but are not currently mounted, use one of the following:

```
# mount  −a
# mountall
```

To mount only /*data1*, do one of the following:

```
# mount  /data1
# mount  /dev/vg01/lvol1
```

Remember, the *mount* and *mountall* commands look into the /*etc/fstab* file to mount file systems.

15.3.11 Removing a File System

Removing a file system is a destructive operation, which wipes out all data from the file system. To remove a file system, simply unmount it and remove the volume that holds it. The procedure is same for both HFS and JFS type file systems. Use the *lvremove* command to remove *lvol1* from *vg01*. Type a "y" for confirmation, when prompted. Use the *vxassist* command to remove *vol1* from *dg01*.

> # **lvremove /dev/vg01/lvol1**
> The logical volume "/dev/vg01/lvol1" is not empty;
> do you really want to delete the logical volume (y/n) : y
> Logical volume "/dev/vg01/lvol1" has been successfully removed.
> Volume Group configuration for /dev/vg01 has been saved in /etc/lvmconf/vg01.conf
> # **vxassist –g dg01 remove volume vol1**

To remove a file system using SAM, follow the steps below:

☞ Go to SAM → Disks and File Systems → File Systems (highlight the file system) → Actions → Remove.

To remove a file system that resides in a VxVM volume, use can also use either VEA or the *vxdiskadm* utility.

15.4   Repairing a Damaged File System

The structure of a file system could be damaged when an abnormal system shutdown or crash occurs. To maintain file system integrity, a utility called *fsck* is used. This utility is executed automatically when a reboot occurs following an abnormal system shutdown or crash. It checks file system structures and corrects any inconsistencies found. The utility can also be executed manually on a file system from the command line.

Repairing a Damaged HFS File System

fsck performs multiple checks on an HFS file system and reports any inconsistencies as it finds. It also attempts to fix them. If an inconsistency cannot be resolved, it prompts for your intervention. You run *fsck* manually and try to fix the inconsistencies. The command prompts you for a "yes" or "no" reply. It may take several minutes to check and repair an HFS file system. The following example runs *fsck* on a mounted (use –f option) HFS file system. There is no need to use the –f option, if the command is run on an unmounted file system. Specify appropriate device file for LVM logical volume and VxVM volume.

> # **fsck –F hfs –f /dev/vg01/rlvol1**
> ** /dev/vg01/rlvol1
> ** Last Mounted on /data1
> ** Phase 1 - Check Blocks and Sizes
> ** Phase 2 - Check Pathnames
> ** Phase 3 - Check Connectivity
> ** Phase 4 - Check Reference Counts
> ** Phase 5 - Check Cyl groups
> 2 files, 0 icont, 9 used, 199372 free (12 frags, 24920 blocks)

If the primary superblock is missing or corrupted, check the */var/adm/sbtab* file and use one of the backup superblock locations to repair the primary superblock. Run *fsck* as follows to restore the primary superblock using an alternate location at block number 64. The output will look similar to what is shown below:

```
# fsck –F  hfs  –b  64  /dev/vx/rdsk/dg01/vol1
Alternate super block location: 64
fsck: /dev/vx/rdsk/dg01/vol1: mounted file system

continue (y/n)? y
** /dev/vx/rdsk/dg01/vol1
** Last Mounted on
** Phase 1 - Check Blocks and Sizes
** Phase 2 - Check Pathnames
** Phase 3 - Check Connectivity
** Phase 4 - Check Reference Counts
FREE INODE COUNT WRONG IN SUPERBLK
FIX? y

** Phase 5 - Check Cyl groups
FREE BLK COUNT(S) WRONG IN SUPERBLK
FIX? y

83 files, 0 icont, 3769 used, 33109 free (133 frags, 4122 blocks)

***** FILE SYSTEM WAS MODIFIED *****
```

While checking a file system, *fsck* may encounter a file with a missing name. It moves the file to the *lost+found* directory located in that file system. This file is known as an *Orphan* file and is renamed to correspond to its inode number. You need to figure out the actual name of the file. Use the *file* command to determine the file's type. If this file is a text file, use *cat* or *more* to view contents; otherwise, use the *strings* command to view legible contents in it. You can move the file to its correct directory location, if you determine the whereabouts of it.

Repairing a Damaged JFS File System

Issue the *fsck* command on a VxFS file system the way you ran it on the HFS file system, however, there is no need to specify the file system type. The *fsck* command looks into the */etc/default/fs* file where vxfs is pre-defined as the default file system type. On a VxFS file system, *fsck* simply replays the intent log and completes any pending transactions. It takes only a few seconds to check and fix a VxFS file system. Note that you must unmount a VxFS file system in order to run *fsck* on it. Specify appropriate device file for LVM logical volume and VxVM volume.

```
# fsck  /dev/vg01/rlvol2
file system is clean - log replay is not required
```

You can force *fsck* to do a full check of all file system structures by supplying to the command "–o full" option or simply use "–o nolog" option to prevent an intent log replay.

```
# fsck  –o  full  /dev/vx/rdsk/dg01/vol2
fsck: /etc/default/fs is used for determining the file system type
```

```
log replay in progress
pass0 - checking structural files
pass1 - checking inode sanity and blocks
pass2 - checking directory linkage
pass3 - checking reference counts
pass4 - checking resource maps
OK to clear log? (ynq)y
set state to CLEAN? (ynq)y
```

15.5   Managing CDFS and LOFS File Systems

Other than VxFS and HFS file systems, you may need to manage CDFS and LOFS file systems as well. Managing them usually involves mounting and unmounting them.

15.5.1   Mounting and Unmounting a CDFS File System

Software on CDs and DVDs are available in read-only mode. A CD or DVD contains CDFS file system structure. To mount a CD or DVD, determine its block device file using the *ioscan* command as follows:

 # ioscan –fnkCdisk

Class	I	H/W Path	Driver	S/W State	H/W Type	Description
disk	**0**	**0/0/2/0.0.0.0**	**sdisk**	**CLAIMED**	**DEVICE**	**TEAC DV-28E-N**
		/dev/dsk/c0t0d0 /dev/rdsk/c0t0d0				
disk	1	0/1/1/0.0.0	sdisk	CLAIMED	DEVICE	HP 36.4GST336754LC
		/dev/dsk/c2t0d0 /dev/rdsk/c2t0d0				
disk	2	0/1/1/0.1.0	sdisk	CLAIMED	DEVICE	HP 36.4GST336754LC
		/dev/dsk/c2t1d0 /dev/rdsk/c2t1d0				
disk	3	0/1/1/0.2.0	sdisk	CLAIMED	DEVICE	HP 36.4GST336754LC
		/dev/dsk/c2t2d0 /dev/rdsk/c2t2d0				

The *ioscan* command output indicates that there is a DVD drive at */dev/dsk/c0t0d0*.

Load a CD or DVD in the drive. Create a mount point, such as */cdrom,* to mount the CD/DVD.

 # mkdir   /cdrom

Mount the CD/DVD in read-only mode as follows:

 # mount –F cdfs –o ro /dev/dsk/c0t0d0 /cdrom

–F specifies file system type and –o instructs the command to mount the CD/DVD as read-only.

Now the CD/DVD contents are available for use from the */cdrom* directory.

At times, you need to use the "cdcase" or the "rr" option when mounting a CD/DVD, otherwise, all file names under */cdrom* are displayed in uppercase letters, which is not a desireable condition

---

since HP-UX is case-sensitive and normally works with lowercase letters. Do the following to use the two options:

```
# mount –F cdfs –o cdcase –o ro /dev/dsk/c0t0d0 /cdrom
# mount –F cdfs –o rr –o ro /dev/dsk/c0t0d0 /cdrom
```

To unmount a CD/DVD file system, issue the *umount* command and supply either the mount point or the associated device file as an argument. If mount point is supplied, the command gets the device file name from the */etc/mnttab* file.

```
# umount /cdrom
# umount /dev/dsk/c0t0d0
```

15.5.2 Mounting and Unmounting a LOFS File System

The *LOopback File System* (LOFS) is a virtual file system that provides an alternate path to access an existing directory or file system. The existing directory or file system can be local or remote and of any type (in case of a file system). If there are any local or remote file systems mounted under that directory or file system, they will become available as part of the mount as well. For example, let's mount */usr* as a loopback file system on */lofs* directory.

```
# mkdir /lofs
# mount –F lofs /usr /lofs
```

This makes all files and sub-directories beneath */usr* to become accessible via two paths: */usr* and */lofs*.

15.6 Monitoring File System Space Utilization

File system space monitoring involves checking used and available file system space and inodes. It also includes keeping an eye on space occupied by individual users. Several tools are available to view this information. Some of them are *bdf*, *df*, *du*, and *quot* and discussed in the following sub-sections.

15.6.1 Using *bdf*

bdf is used to view information about file system utilization. Run this command without any options and you would see output similar to the following. It is assumed that all four file systems – *lvol1*, *lvol2*, *vol1*, and *vol2* – still exist and are mounted.

```
# bdf
File system        kbytes      used      avail      %used   Mounted on
/dev/vg00/lvol3    512000      66088     418088     14%     /
/dev/vg00/lvol1    299157      21113     248128     8%      /stand
/dev/vg00/lvol8    2486272     144292    2196087    6%      /var
/dev/vg00/lvol7    1228800     714039    482606     60%     /usr
/dev/vg00/lvol6    512000      1407      478746     0%      /tmp
/dev/vg00/lvol5    1228800     642503    549701     54%     /opt
```

/dev/vg00/lvol4	512000	1252	478827	0%	/home
/dev/vg01/lvol1	1502713	9	1352432	0%	/data1
/dev/vg01/lvol2	2048000	1606	1918502	0%	/data2
/dev/vx/dsk/dg01/vol1	3077449	9	2615822	0%	/data3
/dev/vx/dsk/dg01/vol2	5242880	2385	4912972	0%	/data4

There are six fields in the output. A description of each is given in Table 15-2.

Field	Description
File system	Block device file for the volume that contains the file system.
Kbytes	Total amount of disk space allocated to the file system.
Used	Amount of file system space already used up.
Avail	Amount of file system space available for use.
%Used	Percentage amount of file system space already used up.
Mounted on	Mount point.

Table 15-2 *bdf* Command Output Description

Try running *bdf* with –i option. It adds three columns to the output providing information on inode utilization as well.

```
# bdf  –i
```

Filesystem	kbytes	used	avail	%used	iused	ifree	%iuse	Mounted on
/dev/vg00/lvol3	409600	139752	267784	34%	3707	8421	31%	/
/dev/vg00/lvol1	295024	122112	143408	46%	102	32154	0%	/stand
/dev/vg00/lvol7	3500000	3274792	223552	94%	51091	7021	88%	/var
/dev/vg00/lvol6	1800000	1500984	296856	83%	32098	9342	77%	/usr
/dev/vg00/lvol5	600000	467416	132128	78%	14939	4133	78%	/tmp
/dev/vg00/lvol4	2000000	1770824	227632	89%	29533	7139	81%	/opt
/dev/vg00/lvol8	600000	389160	209840	65%	2581	6571	28%	/home
/dev/vg01/lvol1	1502713	9	1352432	0%	4	246396	0%	/data1
/dev/vg01/lvol2	2048000	1606	1918502	0%	5	511595	0%	/data2
/dev/vx/dsk/dg01/vol1	3077449	9	2615822	0%	4	505596	0%	/data3
/dev/vx/dsk/dg01/vol2	5242880	2385	4912972	0%	4	1310120	0%	/data4

The *bdf* command with –t option displays utilization of only the specified file system type.

```
# bdf  –t  hfs
```

File system	kbytes	used	avail	%used	Mounted on
/dev/vg00/lvol1	299157	21113	248128	8%	/stand
/dev/vg01/lvol1	1502713	9	1352432	0%	/data1
/dev/vx/dsk/dg01/vol1	3077449	9	2615822	0%	/data3

```
# bdf  –t  vxfs
```

File system	kbytes	used	avail	%used	Mounted on
/dev/vg00/lvol3	409600	139752	267784	34%	/
/dev/vg00/lvol7	3500000	3274792	223552	94%	/var
/dev/vg00/lvol6	1800000	1500984	296856	83%	/usr

/dev/vg00/lvol5	600000	467416	132128	78%	/tmp
/dev/vg00/lvol4	2000000	1770824	227632	89%	/opt
/dev/vg00/lvol8	600000	389160	209840	65%	/home
/dev/vg01/lvol2	2048000	1606	1918502	0%	/data2
/dev/vx/dsk/dg01/vol2 5242880		2385	4912972	0%	/data4

15.6.2   Using *df*

df reports on available file system blocks and inodes. It lists each file system with its corresponding volume device file, free blocks (in 512 byte size), and free inodes.

```
# df
/home     (/dev/vg00/lvol8   ):     419712 blocks   6573 i-nodes
/opt      (/dev/vg00/lvol4   ):     455264 blocks   7139 i-nodes
/tmp      (/dev/vg00/lvol5   ):     264176 blocks   4131 i-nodes
/usr      (/dev/vg00/lvol6   ):     593712 blocks   9342 i-nodes
/var      (/dev/vg00/lvol7   ):     447136 blocks   7022 i-nodes
/stand    (/dev/vg00/lvol1   ):     286816 blocks   32154 i-nodes
/         (/dev/vg00/lvol3   ):     535568 blocks   8421 i-nodes
/data1    (/dev/vg01/lvol1   ):     2704864 blocks  246396 i-nodes
/data2    (/dev/vg01/lvol2   ):     3837004 blocks  511595 i-nodes
/data3    (/dev/vx/dsk/dg01/vol1):  5231644 blocks  505596 i-nodes
/data4    (/dev/vx/dsk/dg01/vol2):  9825944 blocks  1310120 i-nodes
```

Try this command with –k option to see results in 1KB block size.

```
# df  –k
/home     (/dev/vg00/lvol8   ) :     599000 total allocated Kb
                                    209848 free allocated Kb
                                    389152 used allocated Kb
                                    64 % allocation used
/opt      (/dev/vg00/lvol4   ) :    1998456 total allocated Kb
                                    227632 free allocated Kb
                                    1770824 used allocated Kb
                                    88 % allocation used
/tmp      (/dev/vg00/lvol5   ) :     599544 total allocated Kb
                                    132120 free allocated Kb
                                    467424 used allocated Kb
                                    77 % allocation used
/usr      (/dev/vg00/lvol6   ) :    1797840 total allocated Kb
                                    296856 free allocated Kb
                                    1500984 used allocated Kb
                                    83 % allocation used
/var      (/dev/vg00/lvol7   ) :    3498344 total allocated Kb
                                    223568 free allocated Kb
                                    3274776 used allocated Kb
                                    93 % allocation used
/stand    (/dev/vg00/lvol1   ) :     265520 total allocated Kb
```

		143408 free allocated Kb
		122112 used allocated Kb
		45 % allocation used
/	(/dev/vg00/lvol3) :	407536 total allocated Kb
		267784 free allocated Kb
		139752 used allocated Kb
		34 % allocation used
/data1	(/dev/vg01/lvol1) :	1352441 total allocated Kb
		1352432 free allocated Kb
		9 used allocated Kb
		0 % allocation used
/data2	(/dev/vg01/lvol2) :	1920108 total allocated Kb
		1918502 free allocated Kb
		1606 used allocated Kb
		0 % allocation used
/data3	(/dev/vx/dsk/dg01/vol1) :	2615831 total allocated Kb
		2615822 free allocated Kb
		9 used allocated Kb
		0 % allocation used
/data4	(/dev/vx/dsk/dg01/vol2) :	4915357 total allocated Kb
		4912972 free allocated Kb
		2385 used allocated Kb
		0 % allocation used

Try running *df* with "–F hfs" and "–F vxfs" options.

15.6.3   Using *du*

du is used to calculate amount of disk space a directory or a file system hierarchy is currently using.

 # du –k /stand

8	/stand/lost+found
65	/stand/krs
2	/stand/system.d
19	/stand/build/mod_wk.d/krm
20	/stand/build/mod_wk.d
1	/stand/build/lib
275	/stand/build
2	/stand/dlkm/system.d
1	/stand/dlkm/node.d
8	/stand/dlkm/mod.d
1	/stand/dlkm/mod_bld.d
905	/stand/dlkm
1	/stand/krs_tmp
65	/stand/krs_lkg
21113	/stand

The –k option displays the output in KBs. The –s option shows only the total count. Try running the command again with –sk options.

15.6.4   Using *quot*

quot gives you information on file system space usage by individual users.

```
# quot  /var
/dev/vg00/rlvol8 (/var):
464971  bin
212162  root
55878  sshd
  296   daemon
  228   lp
   87   adm
   64   uucp
```

The *quot* command picks up the file system type from */etc/default/fs* file. For an HFS file system, you must specify "–F hfs" with the command.

This command, when run with –a option, reports on all file systems; with –f option, reports on number of files owned by individual users; and with –v option, it provides verbose information. Try running *quot* with these options.

Summary

In this chapter, you learned about file systems. You learned concepts and types of file systems supported in HP-UX. You looked in detail at the structure and components of both HFS and JFS file systems.

The chapter then talked about managing file systems, which involved creating, mounting, viewing, extending, reducing, tuning, defragmenting, unmounting, and removing them using both command line and GUI tools. You saw how file systems were defined to get automatically mounted at each system reboot.

You were explained how to check and repair HFS and VxFS file system structures after a system crash and manually. You looked at mounting and unmounting CDFS and LOFS file systems.

Finally, you learned about file system monitoring tools, such as *bdf*, *df*, *du*, and *quot* to monitor file system space utilization.

## 16

Managing Swap Space

This chapter covers the following major topics:

- ✓ Physical memory and how it is used
- ✓ What is swap space and how demand paging works
- ✓ Device and file system swap
- ✓ Primary and secondary swap
- ✓ Create device and file system swap spaces
- ✓ Enable device and file system swap spaces
- ✓ View swap utilization
- ✓ Priority and swap space best practices
- ✓ Swap space kernel parameters

16.1 Understanding Swap

Physical memory installed in your HP-UX machine is a finite temporary storage resource used for loading HP-UX kernel and data structures as well as running user programs. The system automatically reserves a portion of memory, called *Reserved* memory, for the HP-UX kernel and data structures at system startup time. The remaining physical memory, referred to as *Available* memory, is used by the system for two purposes. Some of it is locked by HP-UX subsystems and user processes, and called *Lockable* memory. Data located in the lockable memory cannot be paged out (moved to alternate location). The lockable memory typically holds frequently accessed programs for performance improvement reason. The remaining available memory is used for demand paging purpose. Figure 16-1 shows how physical memory is divided into available and reserved memory areas.

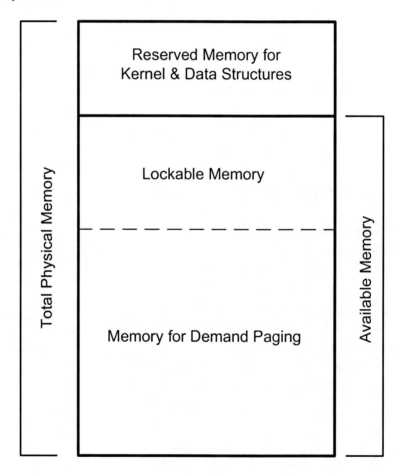

Figure 16-1 Physical Memory Division

The amount of physical, lockable, and available memory is displayed when a system boots up. You can view this information later by running the *dmesg* command or looking into the system log file in */var/adm/syslog/syslog.log*.

The sample *dmesg* command output displays that the total physical memory in the system is 1GB with ~740MB lockable and ~850MB available.

 # dmesg
Memory Information:
    physical page size = 4096 bytes, logical page size = 4096 bytes
    Physical: 1048576 Kbytes, lockable: 759236 Kbytes, available: 877864 Kbytes

To view the information in */var/adm/syslog/syslog.log* file, do a *more* on the file and search for "Memory".

 # more /var/adm/syslog/syslog.log
Dec 19 10:11:36 hp01 vmunix: Memory Information:
Dec 19 10:11:36 hp01 vmunix: physical page size = 4096 bytes, logical page size = 4096 bytes
Dec 19 10:11:36 hp01 vmunix: Physical: 1048576 Kbytes, lockable: 759236 Kbytes, available: 877864 Kbytes

The two example outputs also display the size of physical page, which is, by default, 4KB. When paging occurs, this is the smallest unit of memory content that is paged out or paged in.

16.1.1   Swap Space and Demand Paging

Swap space is a region on a physical disk used for demand paging purposes. When a program or process is started, it requires space in physical memory to run and be processed. Although many programs can run concurrently but the physical memory cannot hold all of them at the same time. The kernel maintains a threshold called *Lotsfree* and it monitors free physical memory. As long as this threshold is not surpassed, no paging occurs. When the amount of free physical memory falls below lotsfree, a daemon called *vhand* comes into action and starts moving selected idle pages of data from physical memory to the swap space to make room to accommodate other programs. This is referred to as *Page Out*. Since system CPU performs process execution in a round-robin fashion, when the time comes for the paged out data to be executed, the CPU looks for that data in the physical memory and *Page Fault* occurs. The pages are then moved back into the physical memory from the swap space. The moving back into the physical memory of paged out data is referred to as *Page In* and the entire process of paging data out and in is known as *Demand Paging*.

HP-UX systems with less physical memory but high memory requirements can become so busy doing paging out and in that they do not have enough time to carry out other useful tasks, causing system performance to degrade. When this occurs you feel as if the system has been frozen. The excessive amount of paging that causes system performance to go down is called *Thrashing*.

When thrashing begins or when free physical memory falls below another threshold, called *Desfree*, the *swapper* process becomes activated, which deactivates idle processes and prevents new processes from initiating. Once the *swapper* process discovers that available physical memory has climbed above the *Minfree* threshold level and thrashing has stopped, it reactivates the deactivated processes and allows new processes to start.

16.1.2   Device and File System Swap

Swap space is of two types: *Device Swap* and *File System Swap*.

The swap space created and enabled in an LVM or a VxVM volume is called the device swap, whereas a file system swap is the portion within an existing, mounted HP-UX file system allocated and enabled for paging purposes.

When file system swap is enabled, a directory called *paging* is created at the root of that file system. Under *paging* directory, files are created for each individual swapchunk used in file system paging. By default, a swapchunk is 2MB in size.

A file system swap can be defined and enabled dynamically. It may be defined to use a fixed amount of file system area or use whatever space it requires. Remember that once a file system has been enabled for swapping, it is not possible to unmount that file system. You must reboot the machine with the swap space line entry commented out, if defined, in the */etc/fstab* file.

16.1.3   Primary and Secondary Swap

The *Primary* swap is the device swap created at the HP-UX system installation time and becomes available each time the system boots up and the HP-UX kernel initializes it. It usually exists in *vg00* volume group (or *rootdg* disk group) with OS file systems and shares the same physical disk.

The primary swap location is defined in LVM structures in the *Boot Disk Reserved Area* (BDRA) or in the private region of the VxVM boot disk. You can change the location of the primary swap using the *lvlnboot* command with –s option. Refer to the *lvlnboot* command man pages.

In addition to the primary swap, one or more *Secondary* swap spaces may be defined based on application demand. It is recommended to always use device swap, whenever required, for improved performance and create it on the physical disk that has no other swap area defined on it.

If you must use a file system swap, always define it as a secondary swap.

Secondary swap spaces can be enabled automatically at boot time if an entry is defined in the */etc/fstab* file. They may also be added manually to a running HP-UX system.

16.2   Managing Swap

Managing swap involves creating device and file system swap areas, enabling them, and viewing their usage. The following sub-sections describe these operations.

16.2.1   Creating and Enabling a Device Swap

To create and enable a device swap called, for instance, *swaplvol*, of size 500MB in *vg01* volume group, perform the following two steps. The first command creates a logical volume and the second enables swapping in it.

---

lvcreate –L 500 –n swaplvol vg01   (use *vxassist* to create a VxVM volume)
Logical volume "/dev/vg01/swaplvol" has been successfully created with
character device "/dev/vg01/rswaplvol".
Logical volume "/dev/vg01/swaplvol" has been successfully extended.
Volume Group configuration for /dev/vg01 has been saved in /etc/lvmconf/vg01.conf
swapon /dev/vg01/swaplvol

The syntax of the *swapon* command for device swap is:

swapon [–p priority] [–e | –f] [–u] device

Run the *swapinfo* command to verify that the new device swap is created and enabled.

swapinfo

TYPE	Kb AVAIL	Kb USED	Kb FREE	PCT USED	START/ LIMIT	Kb RESERVE	PRI	NAME
dev	2097152	0	2097152	0%	0	-	1	/dev/vg00/lvol2
dev	**512000**	**0**	**512000**	**0%**	**0**	**-**	**1**	**/dev/vg01/swaplvol**
reserve	-	189388	-189388					
memory	759864	25484	734380	3%				

Some common options that you can use with the *swapon* command when dealing with device swap are listed in Table 16-1.

Option	Description
–a	Enables all device and file system swap spaces defined in the /etc/fstab file.
–f	Enables force swapping on a volume that contains file system structures. Be careful when using this option; it destroys all file system structures as well as data from the specified volume.
–p	Defines the sequence in which to use a swap space.
Device	Block device file for the volume.

Table 16-1 *swapon* **Options for Device Swap**

SAM can be used to create and enable a device swap in a logical volume. Follow the sequence below:

☞Go to SAM → Disks and File Systems → Swap → Actions → Add Device Swap → Using the Logical Volume Manager. Choose a logical volume and fill out other information as shown in Figure 16-2. Hit the OK button when done.

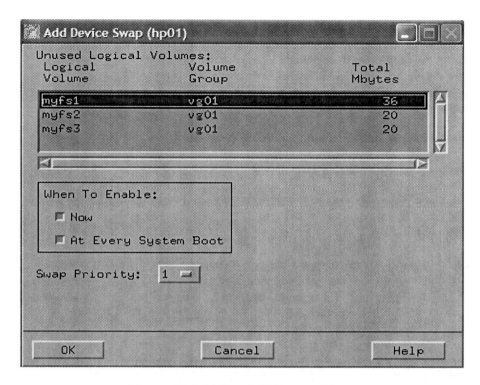

Figure 16-2 SAM – Add Device Swap

16.2.2 Creating and Enabling a File System Swap

To create and enable a file system swap in */data2* file system, for example, and limit it to use not more than 100MB of its space, run *swapon* with –l option as follows:

swapon –l 100m /data2

Run *swapinfo* to verify that the file system swap is enabled.

swapinfo

TYPE	Kb AVAIL	Kb USED	Kb FREE	PCT USED	START/ LIMIT	Kb RESERVE	PRI	NAME
dev	2097152	0	2097152	0%	0	-	1	/dev/vg00/lvol2
dev	512000	0	512000	0%	0	-	1	/dev/vg01/swaplvol
localfs	**102400**	**0**	**102400**	**0%**	**102400**	**0**	**1**	**/data2/paging**
reserve	-	189388	-189388					
memory	759864	25484	734380	3%				

The syntax of the *swapon* command for file system swap is:

swapon [–m min] [–l limit] [–r reserve] [–p priority] directory

Some common options that you can use with *swapon* when dealing with file system swap are listed in Table 16-2.

Option	Description
–a	Enables all device and file system swap spaces defined in the /etc/fstab file.
–m min	Denotes amount of paging space in KBs, MBs, or blocks that the paging system initially reserves.
–l limit	Specifies maximum space in KBs, MBs, or blocks that the swap system can use (default is unlimited).
–r reserve	Specifies total space to be reserved strictly for file system usage. This space will not be used for paging purposes.
–p priority	Defines the order in which to use a swap space.
directory	The file system mount point.

Table 16-2 *swapon* Options for File System Swap

To use SAM to create and enable a file system swap, follow the sequence:

☞ Go to SAM → Disks and File Systems → Swap → Actions → Add File System Swap. Choose a file system to create the swap space and fill out other information as shown in Figure 16-3. Hit the OK button when done.

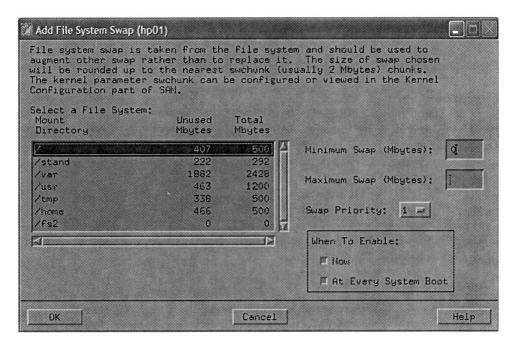

Figure 16-3 SAM – Add File System Swap

16.2.3   Enabling Swap Space at System Boot

In order to make all swap spaces enabled when the system reboots, define them in the /etc/fstab file. During the boot process, the /sbin/init.d/swap_start script is executed, which runs the *swapon*

---

command with –a option. The –a option instructs the command to activate all swap spaces defined in /etc/fstab.

Here is how to add to the /etc/fstab file the device and file system swap entries that you have just created. The updated file will look like:

 # cat /etc/fstab

. . . .

. . . .

/dev/vg01/swaplvol	.	swap	pri=1	0	0
/dev/vg01/lvol2	/data2	swapfs	defaults	0	0

The syntax of /etc/fstab file and description of fields were explained in Chapter 15 "Working with File Systems". Only the third field is different which defines the type of swap. For the device swap, use "swap" and for the file system swap, use "swapfs". If you do not wish to use "defaults", refer to "Creating and Enabling Swap Spaces" earlier in this chapter for options available to set priority, limit, minimum space, etc.

To manually enable all swap spaces listed in the /etc/fstab file, do the following:

 # swapon –a

16.2.4   Viewing Swap Utilization

After activating swap spaces, you can list and view their utilization with the *swapinfo* command.

 # swapinfo

TYPE	Kb AVAIL	Kb USED	Kb FREE	PCT USED	START/ LIMIT	Kb RESERVE	PRI	NAME
dev	2097152	0	2097152	0%	0	-	1	/dev/vg00/lvol2
dev	512000	0	512000	0%	0	-	1	/dev/vg01/swaplvol
localfs	548864	0	548864	0%	none	0	1	/data2/paging
reserve	-	189116	-189116					
memory	759864	21444	738420	3%				

The *swapinfo* output provides a snapshot of swap utilization. There are several columns in the output, which are described in Table 16-3.

Column Title	Description
TYPE	Shows the type of memory/swap. "dev" for device swap, "localfs" for file system swap, "reserve" for reserved paging space, and "memory" for memory-based paging space (a.k.a. pseudo swap).
Kb AVAIL	Amount of swap space in KBs.
Kb USED	Swap space used in KBs.
Kb FREE	Free swap space in KBs.
PCT USED	Swap space used in percentage.

START / LIMIT	For device swap, this value is set to 0 to represent entire volume. For file system swap, START represents the starting block for the swap and LIMIT represents the maximum amount of space that can be used for paging.
Kb RESERVE	For device swap, this value is always –. For file system swap, this value is the amount, in KBs, of swap space that cannot be used as swap.
PRI	Defines the order in which to use a swap space.
NAME	For device swap, this represents block device file. For file system swap, this indicates name of the paging directory.

Table 16-3 *swapinfo* Command Output Explanation

Options available with *swapinfo* are given in Table 16-4. Try each one of these and see results.

Option	Description
–t	Shows total at the bottom.
–m	Displays information in MBs instead of KBs.
–d	Shows information on device swap only.
–f	Shows information on file system swap only.
–q	Shows available KBs only.

Table 16-4 *swapinfo* Command Options

16.3   Priority and Best Practices

Swap spaces are assigned priorities between 0 and 10 with 0 being the highest and 1 being the default. The HP-UX kernel uses a higher priority swap before using a lower priority one. If two swap regions have identical priority, the kernel utilizes them alternately. If multiple devices have the same priority, swap space is allocated from the devices in a round-robin fashion. Thus, to interleave swap requests among a number of device swaps, a common priority should be assigned to them. Similarly, if multiple file system swap areas have identical priority, requests for swap are interleaved among them.

To alter priority of the file system swap you created earlier, use the *swapon* command as follows and verify it with the *swapinfo* command:

```
# swapon –p 2 /data2/paging
# swapinfo
         Kb       Kb     Kb      PCT    START/  Kb
TYPE     AVAIL    USED   FREE    USED   LIMIT   RESERVE    PRI   NAME
dev      2097152  0      2097152 0%     0       -          1     /dev/vg00/lvol2
dev      512000   0      512000  0%     0       -          1     /dev/vg01/swaplvol
localfs  548864   0      548864  0%     none    0          2     /data2/paging
reserve  -        189116 -189116
memory   759864   21444  738420  3%
```

If a device and a file system swap regions carry identical priority, device swap is given preference over file system swap.

When choosing what type of swap space to configure, what priorities to assign, and so on, there are some best practices that you should follow. The following list of best practices is related to swap space management and should be adhered to for better and improved swap performance:

- ✓ Do not configure more than one swap spaces on a single physical disk.
- ✓ Two smaller, same size device swap spaces on two different physical disks are better than one large swap space on one single physical disk.
- ✓ Avoid using file system swap as much as possible. Use it only if there is absolutely no physical disk space left for creating additional device swap.
- ✓ Assign identical priority to all device swap areas. This enables HP-UX to employ them in a round-robin fashion, thus improving performance.
- ✓ Prefer device swap over file system swap.
- ✓ Favor faster devices over slower devices.
- ✓ Choose less utilized file systems over busier file systems.

16.4 Related Kernel Parameters

Tunable kernel parameters, listed in Table 16-5, are available to control swap behavior.

Parameter	Description
maxswapchunks	Defines maximum amount of swap space that can be allocated to both device and file system swap combined. Minimum is 1, maximum is 16384, and the default is 256.
swchunk	Defines swap chunk size. Minimum is 2048, maximum is 16384, and the default is 2048. HP-UX uses chunks from swap space one by one for paging purposes.
nswapdev	Defines maximum number of device swap spaces that can be created. The default is 10 and the maximum is 25.
nswapfs	Defines maximum number of file system swap spaces that can be enabled simultaneously. The default is 10 and the maximum is 25.

Table 16-5 Swap Kernel Parameters

Summary

You learned in this chapter concepts of swapping and paging. You saw how physical memory was divided to be shared and how paging worked on-demand. Device and file system swap and primary and secondary swap regions were discussed along with associated advantages and disadvantages.

You looked at managing swap space areas that covered creating, enabling, and viewing both device and file system swap. You saw how configured swap areas could be enabled manually and at each system reboot.

Finally, swap priority, best practices, and a few key kernel parameters related to swap were covered.

HP Certified Systems Administrator

## 17

Shutting Down and Starting Up an HP-UX System

This chapter covers the following major topics:

- ✓ Explain run control levels and determine current and previous run levels
- ✓ Tools to shutdown and change run control levels
- ✓ Interact with PDC and BCH on an HP 9000 server to view and modify autoboot, autosearch and AUTO file; and view and modify primary, HAA, and alternate boot device paths
- ✓ Interact with BCH and secondary boot loader on an HP 9000 server to boot it normally and into various maintenance states
- ✓ Interact with EFI and Boot Manager on an HP Integrity server to view and modify autoboot, boot delay period, and AUTO file; and view and modify primary, HAA, and alternate boot device paths
- ✓ Interact with EFI and Boot Manager on an HP Integrity server to boot it normally and into various maintenance states
- ✓ Describe HP-UX kernel and initialization phases on HP 9000 and Integrity servers
- ✓ Discuss system startup scripts and associated configuration files

17.1　Shuting Down an HP-UX Server

Servers running HP-UX need to be shutdown periodically for maintenance purposes, such as adding or removing hardware components. Sometimes you install software or apply patches that affect kernel configuration and require a reboot for the configuration to take effect. There may be other situations when a reboot of the server becomes necessary.

HP-UX changes run levels when a system shutdown occurs. Similarly, run levels are changed when a system startup occurs. The following sub-sections discuss system run control levels and how to manipulate them.

 Throughout this chapter, the terms "system", "server", "machine", and "nPar" are used interchangeably.

17.1.1　Run Control Levels

System *Run Control* (rc) levels are pre-defined and determines the current state of the system. HP-UX supports eight such levels of which six are currently implemented. Not all of these are commonly used though. The default rc level is 3. Table 17-1 describes various run levels.

Run Level	Description
0	HP-UX is down and the system is halted.
s	Single user state with critical file systems mounted. The system can be accessed only at the system console.
S	Single user state with critical file systems mounted. The terminal where this run level is invoked from becomes the logical console.
1	Single user state with all file systems mounted and a few critical processes running.
2	Multi-user state. All services running except NFS server processes.
3	Multi-user state. All services including NFS server processes running. This is the default rc level for HP-UX.
4	Other GUI presentation managers are started in addition to some other system processes.
5 and 6	Not implemented. Users may define their own.

Table 17-1 System Run Levels

17.1.2　Checking Current and Previous Run Control Levels

To check the current and previous rc levels of a system, use the *who* command with –r option:

　　# who　–r

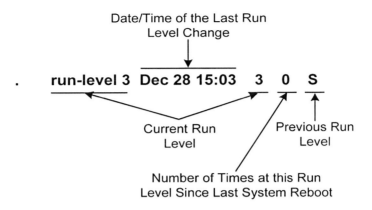

Figure 17-1 Current and Previous System Run Levels

The output of this command, as shown in Figure 17-1, indicates that the system is currently running at run level 3 and its last run level was S. The output also displays date and time of the last system run level change.

17.1.3 Changing Run Control Levels

Run control levels are also referred to as *Init* levels because a system uses the *init* command to alter levels. The *shutdown* and the *reboot* commands are also widely used to change system run levels. Refer to Figure 17-2 that displays various run levels and commands to switch from one run level to another.

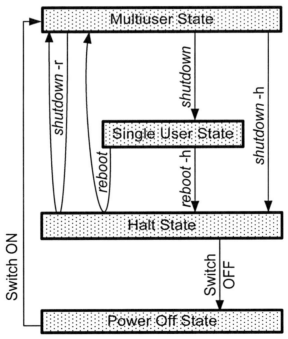

Figure 17-2 System Run Levels

The *init* Command

The *init* command is employed to change run levels. If a system is currently in run level 3 and you want to switch to run level 2, issue the *init* command as follows:

   # **init 2**

This command stops all services and daemons that should not be running in rc level 2 gracefully.

Similarly, by running *init* 1 from run level 2, most system services and daemons can be stopped and the system is transitioned to single user state.

To stop all system services normally and go to system halt state, do the following:

   # **init 0**

The *shutdown* Command

The *shutdown* command is more commonly used than the *init* command or any other system halt commands. It stops all services, processes, and daemons in a sequential and consistent fashion. It broadcasts a message to all logged in users and waits for one minute, by default, for users to log off, after which time it begins stopping services, processes, and daemons. It unmounts non-critical file systems and proceeds according to the options specified with it at the command line.

The following examples show different options and arguments that can be supplied to the *shutdown* command:

# **shutdown**	(broadcasts a message, waits for one minute, prompts the user to confirm the shutdown, and then takes the system to single user mode).
# **shutdown –hy 300**	(broadcasts a message, waits for 5 minutes, and then takes the system to the halt state).
# **shutdown –ry 300**	(broadcasts a message, waits for 5 minutes, stop all services gracefully, shuts down the system and automatically reboots it to the default run control level).
# **shutdown –ry 0**	(broadcasts a message, starts stopping immediately all services gracefully, shuts down the system and automatically reboots it to the default run control level).
# **shutdown –ry now**	(same as "shutdown –ry 0").

When the *shutdown* command is initiated to halt a system, you would see messages similar to the following on system console:

```
SHUTDOWN PROGRAM
12/31/05 07:50:18 EST

Broadcast Message from root (console) Sat Dec 31 07:50:18...
PLEASE LOG OFF NOW ! ! !
     System maintenance about to begin.
```

All processes will be terminated in 0 seconds.
Broadcast Message from root (console) Sat Dec 31 07:50:18...
SYSTEM BEING BROUGHT DOWN NOW ! ! !
/sbin/auto_parms: DHCP access is disabled (see /etc/auto_parms.log)
   System shutdown in progress

   Stopping OpC agent processes (opcagt). .... OK
   Stop CDE login server .... OK
   Stopping the Apache subsystem .... OK
   Stop X print server(s) .... N/A
   Stop NFS server subsystem .... OK
   Shutting down CIFS Client .... N/A
   Stopping Event Monitoring Service .... OK
   Shutting down the SAMBA Server .... N/A
   Stop VMSA Server .... OK

. . . .

. . . .
Closing open logical volumes...
Done

System has halted
OK to turn off power or reset system
UNLESS "WAIT for UPS to turn off power" message was printed above

By default, only *root* can execute the *shutdown* command. If you wish other users of the system to be able to shutdown the machine, you will need to add entries for the users in the /etc/shutdown.allow file. This file controls which users can shutdown the system. For example, the following two entries in the file would enable *user1* and *user2* to bring down *hp01* machine:

   hp01 user1
   hp01 user2

The *shutdown* command actually calls the *init* command behind the scenes to perform run level changes. You may use the *init* command instead. The only two features not available with *init* compared to *shutdown* are that *init* does not broadcast a message and second it does not wait for a specified period of time. It starts the run level change process right away.

When a system is shutdown or rebooted, a timestamp, along with who did the action, is logged to the /etc/shutdownlog file. This log file can also be accessed via /var/adm/shutdownlog file, which has a symbolic link to /etc/shutdownlog. Some sample entries from this file are shown below:

 # cat /etc/shutdownlog
10:28 Sat Feb 25, 2006.   Reboot: (by hp02!root)
10:38 Sat Feb 25, 2006.   Reboot:
10:23 Sun Feb 26, 2006.   Halt: (by hp02!root)
12:23 Mon Mar 6, 2006.   Reboot: (by hp02!root)
12:47 Mon Mar 6, 2006.   Reboot: (by hp02!root)
10:48 Fri May 19, 2006.   Reboot: (by hp02!root)
12:02 Tue May 23, 2006.   Reboot:

```
09:45  Fri May 26, 2006.      Reboot:  (by hp02!root)
09:54  Fri May 26, 2006.      Reboot:
10:08  Fri May 26, 2006.      Reboot:  (by hp02!root)
10:19  Fri May 26, 2006.      Reboot:  (by hp02!root)
```

The *reboot* Command

The *reboot* command calls the *kill* command with signal 9 to terminate all running processes. This makes the system go down very quickly, however, it introduces the risk of damaging application files and file system structure. It is not recommended to use this command from any multi-user run level. The *reboot* command may be used if a system is in single user state or, for some reasons, you wish to bring it down quickly. With no options specified, *reboot* kills all processes, restarts a system, and brings it back to the default run level. With –h option specified, it stops the system and puts it in the halt state.

> **# reboot –h**
> **# reboot**
> Shutdown at 08:05 (in 0 minutes)
>
>   *** FINAL System shutdown message from root@hp01 ***
>
> System going down IMMEDIATELY
>
> System shutdown time has arrived
> Dec 31 08:05:20 /usr/sbin/envd[1169]: terminated by signal 15
> Dec 31 08:05:21 automount[585]: exiting
>
> sync'ing disks (0 buffers to flush):
> 0 buffers not flushed
> 0 buffers still dirty
>
> Closing open logical volumes...
> Done

17.2 Booting an HP 9000 Server

When you power on or reset an HP 9000 system, it goes through the *Boot* process until it displays a login prompt. A step-by-step boot process for a standalone server is highlighted in bulleted form here:

- ✓ Power on external devices.
- ✓ Power on the server.
- ✓ System firmware, called *Processor Dependent Code* (PDC), is initiated, which runs *Power On Self Test* (POST) on the system hardware components, such as processor, memory, and I/O, and initializes them.
- ✓ PDC looks into *Stable Storage* to get hardware addresses for system console display and boot devices. Stable storage is a small non-volatile area in PDC that contains hardware paths of the system console and boot devices. It also stores the values of the Autoboot and

Autosearch flags. The two flags determine if HP-UX kernel is to be booted automatically and from which boot device.
- ✓ PDC initializes the system console display and boot device.
- ✓ PDC locates HP-UX kernel in the boot device.
- ✓ PDC loads *Initial System Loader* (ISL) into memory from the LIF area located on the boot device. The LIF area, also called *Boot Area*, is a small portion on the boot disk reserved to keep boot utilities needed to find and load the HP-UX kernel. The files here are in a special format called *Logical Interchange Format* (LIF). The LIF area contains the ISL, the AUTO file, and the *Secondary Boot Loader* program called *hpux*, among others. The ISL includes utilities to list ISL commands, display AUTO file contents, modify hardware paths for console, primary boot disk, and alternate boot disk, and set Autoboot and Autosearch flags. You can issue the *help* command at the ISL prompt to view available commands.
- ✓ PDC transfers control to ISL.
- ✓ ISL calls the secondary boot loader and loads it into memory.
- ✓ The secondary boot loader uses contents in the AUTO file to locate the kernel file to boot from.
- ✓ The secondary boot loader loads the kernel into memory and initializes it. The default kernel is located in the */stand* file system on the boot disk and is called *vmunix*.
- ✓ The kernel starts the *swapper* daemon.
- ✓ The kernel calls the *init* command and transfers control over to it to initiate the system initialization process.
- ✓ The *init* command looks into the */etc/inittab* file to determine the default run level to boot to.

You can also use the "**lifls –l /dev/dsk/c0t4d0**" at the HP-UX command prompt to view a list of all commands available in the LIF area.

```
# lifls –l /dev/dsk/c0t4d0
volume ISL10 data size 7984 directory size 8 02/05/10 16:25:44
filename  type    start    size    implement    created
=========================================
```

filename	type	start	size	implement	created
ODE		-12960	584	880	0	03/10/15 11:53:05
MAPFILE		-12277	1464	128	0	03/10/15 11:53:05
SYSLIB		-12280	1592	353	0	03/10/15 11:53:05
CONFIGDATA		-12278	1952	250	0	03/10/15 11:53:05
SLMOD2		-12276	2208	141	0	03/10/15 11:53:05
SLDEV2		-12276	2352	157	0	03/10/15 11:53:05
SLDRV2		-12276	2512	689	0	03/10/15 11:53:05
SLSCSI2		-12276	3208	121	0	03/10/15 11:53:05
MAPPER2		-12279	3336	145	0	03/10/15 11:53:05
IOTEST2		-12279	3488	877	0	03/10/15 11:53:05
PERFVER2		-12279	4368	126	0	03/10/15 11:53:05
PVCU		-12801	4496	64	0	03/10/15 11:53:05
SSINFO		-12286	4560	2	0	03/10/15 11:53:05
HPUX		-12928	4568	848	0	02/05/10 16:25:44
ISL		-12800	5416	306	0	00/11/08 20:49:59
AUTO		-12289	5728	1	0	00/11/08 20:49:59
LABEL		BIN	5736	8	0	04/07/07 11:03:03

✓ The *init* command calls */sbin/rc* script which calls all startup scripts needed to bring the system to the specified default run level.
✓ Finally, *init* presents you with a login prompt.

A complete system boot up process from powering up a system to displaying the login prompt on an rp3440 server looks similar to the following:

```
Firmware Version  46.34

Duplex Console IO Dependent Code (IODC) revision 1
-------------------------------------------------------------------------
  (c) Copyright 1995-2004, Hewlett-Packard Company, All rights reserved
-------------------------------------------------------------------------


Processor  Speed         State      CoProcessor State  Cache Size
Number                              State       Inst   Data
--------   -------   --------------------  ----------------  -----------
   0    800  MHz  Active          Functional       67108864 67108    864
   1    800  MHz  Idle            Functional       67108864 67108    864

Central Bus Speed (in MHz) :      200
Available Memory         :  8388608  KB
Good Memory Required     : Not initialized. Defaults to 32 MB.

 Primary boot path:   0/1/1/0.0
 Alternate boot path: 0/1/1/0.1
 Console path:        0/7/1/1.0
 Keyboard path:       0/0/4/0.0


Processor is booting from the first available device.

To discontinue, press any key within 10 seconds.

10 seconds expired.
. . . . . . . .
. . . . . . . .
ISL booting  hpux

Boot
: disk(0/1/1/0.0.0.0.0.0.0;0)/stand/vmunix
11452416 + 2330624 + 38480344 start 0x1fb268

alloc_pdc_pages: Relocating PDC from 0xffffffff0f0c00000 to 0x3f900000.
gate64: sysvec_vaddr = 0xc0002000 for 2 pages
NOTICE: autofs_link(): File system was registered at index 3.
. . . . . . . .
. . . . . . . .
Memory Information:
```

HP Certified Systems Administrator

physical page size = 4096 bytes, logical page size = 4096 bytes
Physical: 8386560 Kbytes, lockable: 6414736 Kbytes, available: 7368540 Kbyte   s

/sbin/ioinitrc:
ioinitrc: /stand mounted on VxVM volume
insf: Installing special files for ipmi instance 0 address 16
/sbin/krs_sysinit:

/sbin/bcheckrc:
Checking for LVM volume groups and Activating (if any exist)
vxfs fsck: /dev/rroot is currently mounted
vxfs fsck: sanity check: /dev/rroot already mounted
Checking hfs file systems
/sbin/fsclean: /dev/vx/dsk/rootdg/standvol (mounted) ok
HFS file systems are OK, not running fsck

. . . .
. . . .
/dev/vx/dsk/rootdg/varvol :
vxfs fsck: sanity check: /dev/vx/dsk/rootdg/varvol OK

Cleaning /etc/ptmp...
. . . .
. . . .
      HP-UX Start-up in progress
      _____

      Configure system crash dumps .... OK
      Removing old vxvm files .... OK
      VxVM device node check .... OK
      VxVM general startup .... OK
      VxVM reconfiguration recovery .... OK
      Mount file systems .... OK
      Update kernel and loadable modules .... N/A
. . . .
. . . .
      Start CDE login server .... OK
      Starting PRNGD (Pseudo Random Number Generator Daemon) .... OK

The system is ready.

The use of this computer is strictly restricted to authorized personnel only.
Console Login:

17.2.1   Processor Dependent Code and Boot Console Handler

The HP-UX system firmware is called the *Processor Dependent Code* (PDC). When a system is
powered on, the PDC runs POST on hardware components and initializes them. It, then, displays a
message on the console prompting to press any key to discontinue the autoboot process. It waits

---

for an input for 10 seconds, by default. If you press any key within that time frame, the PDC loads a menu driven program called the *Boot Console Handler* (BCH). The BCH interface is shown below:

```
Processor is booting from first available device.

To discontinue, press any key within 10 seconds.

Boot terminated.

------- Main Menu -------------------------------------------------------

    Command                              Description
    -------------                        ----------------
    BOot [PRI|ALT|<path>]                Boot from specified path
    PAth [PRI|ALT|CON|KEY] [<path>]      Display or modify a path
    SEArch [DIsplay|IPL] [<path>]        Search for boot devices

    COnfiguration [<command>]            Access Configuration menu/commands
    INformation [<command>]              Access Information menu/commands
    SERvice [<command>]                  Access Service menu/commands

    DIsplay                              Redisplay the current menu
    HElp [<menu>|<command>]              Display help for menu or command
    RESET                                Restart the system
-------
Main Menu: Enter command >
```

You can perform a number of tasks from here. You can search for alternate boot devices, do a manual boot from a non-default boot device or kernel, view or alter configuration, and so on. You do not have to type in an entire command at this level, just type the first two to three letters (displayed in uppercase letters) and hit the *Enter* key.

17.2.2   Viewing and Modifying Autoboot and Autosearch Flags

The settings of the two flags determine the boot behavior of a system. The autoboot flag determines whether or not to boot the system automatically, whereas autosearch determines a boot source.

The following explains the impact of the settings of the two flags on the system boot process:

- ✓ If you wish your system to be able to automatically search for boot sources and boot from a primary, *High-Availability Alternate* (HAA), or an alternate boot source, whichever is available in this sequence, set the autosearch and autoboot flags ON.
- ✓ If you wish your system to be able to automatically search for boot sources and list them but not boot from any of them automatically, set the autosearch flag ON and autoboot flag OFF.
- ✓ If you wish your system to be able to automatically boot from the primary boot source but not attempt to boot or list other boot sources if primary is unavailable, set the autoboot flag ON and autosearch flag OFF.

✓ If you wish to manually supply a bootable device path and interact with BCH each time your system restarts, set both flags OFF.

You can view and set the flag values at the BCH menu, the ISL prompt, or the HP-UX command prompt. The three ways are demonstrated below:

At BCH:

```
Main Menu: Enter Command > co  au              (displays values)
Main Menu: Enter Command > co  au  bo  on      (enables autoboot)
Main Menu: Enter Command > co  au  bo  off     (disables autoboot)
Main Menu: Enter Command > co  au  sea  on     (enables autosearch)
Main Menu: Enter Command > co  au  sea  off    (disables autosearch)
```

Alternatively, you can go to the "Configuration" menu from the main menu and run the above commands without specifying "co". For example, to go to the Configuration menu and set autoboot to ON, do the following:

```
Main Menu: Enter Command > co
Configuration Menu:  au  bo  on              (enables autoboot)
```

At ISL:

```
ISL > display           (displays autoboot/autosearch values)
ISL > autoboot          (enables/disables autoboot)
ISL > autosearch        (enables/disables autosearch)
```

At the command prompt:

```
# setboot               (displays current autoboot/autosearch values)
Primary bootpath : 8/8.4.0
HAA bootpath : 8/8.12.0
Alternate bootpath : 8/16/5.0.0

Autoboot is ON (enabled)
Autosearch is ON (enabled)
# setboot  –b  on       (enables autoboot)
# setboot  –b  off      (disables autoboot)
# setboot  –s  on       (enables autosearch)
# setboot  –s  off      (disables autosearch)
```

17.2.3   Viewing and Setting Primary, HAA, and Alternate Boot Device Paths

You can view and set PRI, HAA, and ALT boot paths as well as path to the system console from the BCH menu, the ISL prompt, or the HP-UX command prompt. Here is how you would do it from the three interfaces:

From BCH:

```
Main Menu: Enter Command > pa               (view paths)
Main Menu: Enter Command > pa pri 8/8.4     (set PRI boot path)
Main Menu: Enter Command > pa haa 8/8.12    (set HAA boot path)
Main Menu: Enter Command > pa alt 8/16/5.2  (set ALT boot path)
```

From ISL prompt:

```
ISL > display       (view paths)
ISL > primpath      (set PRI boot path)
ISL > haapath       (set HAA boot path)
ISL > altpath       (set ALT boot path)
```

From HP-UX Prompt:

```
# setboot            (view paths)
# setboot –p 8/8.4   (set PRI boot path)
# setboot –h 8/8.12  (set HAA boot path)
# setboot –a 8/16/5.2 (set ALT boot path)
```

17.2.4   Booting from Primary, HAA, and Alternate Boot Devices

There are three possible boot sources that you can define on a system to boot from. The *PRImary* (PRI) boot source, the *High-Availability Alternate* (HAA) boot source, and the *ALTernate* (ALT) boot source. The primary boot source is the boot disk that normally boots a system. In case, the primary becomes unavailable for whatever reasons, the system automatically boots via the HAA boot disk. The HAA boot disk is usually a mirror of the primary boot disk. If you wish, you can define an alternate source to boot from, which could be a CD/DVD, a tape drive, or a network boot server. The following few examples show how to boot a system using the three sources:

From the primary boot disk:

```
Main Menu: Enter command or menu > boot
```

From the HAA boot disk:

```
Main Menu: Enter command or menu > boot haa
```

From the alternate boot device:

```
Main Menu: Enter command or menu > boot alt
```

17.2.5   Booting from an Undefined Boot Device

To boot a system from a device other than the three boot sources mentioned, run the *search* command to find all possible boot devices.

Main Menu: Enter command > **sea**

Searching for potential boot device(s)...
This may take several minutes.

To discontinue search, press any key (termination may not be immediate).

Path Number	Device Path (dec)	Device Type
P0	8/8.4	Random access media
P1	8/8.12	Random access media
P2	8/12.1	Random access media
P3	8/12.0	Random access media
P4	8/12.12	Random access media
P5	8/16/5.2	Random access media
P6	8/16/5.0	Sequential access media
P7	8/16/6.0	LAN Module

Main Menu: Enter command >

The output indicates that there are eight possible boot devices. The first five (P0 to P4) are hard drives, the sixth (P5) is the CDROM drive, the seventh (P6) is the tape drive, and the last (P7) is the first network port on the system board. If you know the device path to the boot device you wish to boot from, specify it with the *boot* command. For example, if the boot device path is 8/8.12, do either of the two:

Main Menu: Enter command or menu > **boot 8/8.12**
Main Menu: Enter command or menu > **boot p1**

17.2.6   Booting to Single User State

At times, it is necessary to boot the system to single user mode in order to perform maintenance tasks. After you run the *boot* command at the BCH prompt, you need to answer "yes" to the question "Interact with ISL (Y, N or Cancel ?>". You will be placed at the ISL prompt.

Type *hpux* and supply –is options to go to single user state using the default kernel file */stand/vmunix*. The –i (init) option specifies to boot to (–s) single user state.

ISL> **hpux –is**
Boot
: disc(8/8.4.0;0)/stand/vmunix
8782188 + 1105920 + 666848 start 0x14d968

. . . .

. . . .
INIT: Overriding default level with level 's'
INIT: SINGLE USER MODE
INIT: Running /sbin/sh
#

17.2.7 Booting to LVM and VxVM Maintenance States

Sometimes LVM (or VxVM) structures develop problems due to misconfiguration or abnormal system shutdown. In such a situation, you would want it to boot to LVM (or VxVM) maintenance state so that you can fix issues and bring the system back up normally.

To boot to LVM (or VxVM) maintenance state, you need to answer "yes" to the question "Interact with ISL (Y, N or Cancel?>" after you executed the *boot* command at the BCH menu prompt, as explained above. This will place you at the ISL prompt.

Type *hpux* and supply –lm options (for VxVM, supply –vm options) to boot to LVM (or VxVM) maintenance state using the default kernel file */stand/vmunix*. The –l for LVM and –v for VxVM options force *hpux* secondary boot loader to take the system to maintenance (–m) state.

```
ISL> hpux  –lm              (hpux  –vm for VxVM)
Boot
: disc(8/8.4.0;0)/stand/vmunix
8782188 + 1105920 + 666848 start 0x14d968

. . . . . . . .

. . . . . . . .
INIT: Overriding default level with level 's'
INIT: SINGLE USER MODE
INIT: Running /sbin/sh
#
```

Reboot the system with –n option when you are done with the maintenance work.

```
# reboot  –n
```

17.2.8 Booting without Quorum Checking

With LVM mirrored boot disk configuration, both disks are required to be present for the system to boot up normally. In case one of the disks goes bad, you can still boot the system by ignoring the presence of the other disk. You will need to specify –lq options at the ISL prompt.

```
ISL> hpux  –lq
Boot
: disc(8/8.4.0;0)/stand/vmunix
8782188 + 1105920 + 666848 start 0x14d968

. . . . . . . .

. . . . . . . .
INIT: Overriding default level with level 's'
INIT: SINGLE USER MODE
INIT: Running /sbin/sh
#
```

17.2.9   Viewing and Modifying AUTO File Contents

The AUTO file is located in the LIF area and it contains the command string used to load the secondary boot loader *hpux*. You can view and modify the string at either the ISL prompt or the command prompt. One of the reasons to make this change would be to specify the default kernel file location and ignoring quorum checking after you setup mirroring.

To set the string at the ISL prompt:

ISL > **hpux set autofile "hpux –lq(;0)/stand/vmunix"**

At the command prompt, use the *mkboot* command and specify the boot disk device file.

mkboot –a "hpux –lq(;0)/stand/vmunix" /dev/rdsk/c0t4d0

To view the file's contents from the ISL prompt, do one of the following:

ISL > **lsautofl**
Auto-execute file contains:
hpux –lq(;0)/stand/vmunix

ISL > **hpux show autofile**
Show autofile
: disc(8/8.4.0;0x800000)
AUTO file contains (hpux –lq(;0)/stand/vmunix)

To view the file's contents from the HP-UX command prompt, do the following. Specify raw device file for the boot disk.

lifcp /dev/rdsk/c0t4d0:AUTO –
hpux -lq(;0)/stand/vmunix

17.2.10   Booting from an Alternate Kernel File

Sometimes you need to boot a system from a non-default kernel file. One of the possible reasons would be that you modified the kernel and rebooted the system, and now the system does not want to come up. It is unable to load the new kernel.

To boot from a non-default kernel file, such as */stand/vmunix.prev*, located on the HAA boot disk at 8/8.12.0 hardware address, go to the ISL prompt and type:

ISL> **hpux (8/8.12.0;0)/stand/vmunix.prev**

If the file is located on the primary boot disk, do the following from the ISL prompt:

ISL> **hpux /stand/vmunix.prev**

Run the *hpux* command as follows if you wish to list the contents of the */stand* directory where kernel files are stored:

```
ISL > hpux ll /stand
dr-xr-xr-x      11 2 2 1024      ./
dr-xr-xr-x      11 2 2 1024      ../
drwxr-xr-x       2 0 0 65536     lost+found/
-rw-r--r--       1 0 3 3856      ioconfig
-rw-r--r--       1 0 3 20        bootconf
-r--r--r--       1 0 3 1338      system
drwxr-xr-x       2 0 3 1024      krs/
drwxr-xr-x       2 0 3 1024      system.d/
dr-xr-xr-x       2 2 2 1024      pfil/
dr-xr-xr-x       2 2 2 1024      ipf/
drwxr-xr-x       4 0 3 2048      build/
-rwxr-xr-x       1 0 3 27706244  vmunix*
drwxrwxr-x       6 0 3 1024      dlkm/
-r--r--r--       1 0 3 82        kernrel
-rw-------       1 0 0 12        rootconf
drwxr-xr-x       2 0 0 1024      krs_tmp/
drwxr-xr-x       2 0 0 1024      krs_lkg/
```

Choose the one you want to boot from and specify it with the *hpux* command at the ISL prompt.

17.3   Booting an HP Integrity Server

The HP Integrity servers go through a system boot up process similar to the HP 9000 server boot process with some differences. The differences are discussed in the next sub-section. Here is the step-by-step boot process for an Integrity server.

- ✓ Power on external devices.
- ✓ Power on the server.
- ✓ The system firmware runs **Power On Self Test** (POST) on the system hardware components, such as processor, memory, and I/O, and initializes them.
- ✓ The system locates hardware path to the boot device from the non-volatile area in memory.
- ✓ The boot disk has an EFI partition from where the Boot Manager is automatically launched, which initiates the loading of HP-UX boot loader program called *hpux.efi*.
- ✓ The *hpux.efi* boot loader uses the contents in the AUTO file to locate kernel file to boot from.
- ✓ The *hpux.efi* boot loader loads the kernel into memory and initializes it. The default kernel is located in the */stand* file system on the boot disk and is called *vmunix*.
- ✓ The kernel starts the *swapper* daemon.
- ✓ The kernel calls the *init* command and transfers control over to it to initiate the system initialization process.
- ✓ The *init* command looks into the */etc/inittab* file to determine the default run level to boot to.
- ✓ The *init* command calls */sbin/rc* script which calls all startup scripts needed to bring the system to the specified default run level.
- ✓ Finally, *init* presents you with a login prompt.

17.3.1 Extensible Firmware Interface and Boot Manager

The Integrity systems use *Extensible Firmware Interface* (EFI), which makes the pre-boot level different from the HP 9000 servers. EFI is a hardware and operating system independent interface that contains boot utilities similar to those found on PA-RISC based systems. EFI lives between HP-UX OE and the system firmware, allowing the OE to boot without having to know the details about the underlying hardware and firmware. The two main components of EFI are the *Boot Manager* and the *Shell*. A bootable disk in Integrity systems contains either an EFI operating system loader or an EFI partition. The EFI partition is a small, special area that contains EFI utilities for pre-boot administration tasks. Among such utilities is the Boot Manager. Figure 17-3 shows the EFI Boot Manager interface.

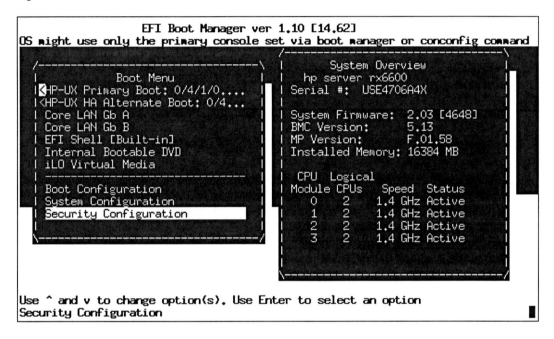

Figure 17-3 EFI Boot Manager

From EFI and the boot manager, you can perform a number of tasks. You can search for alternate boot devices, do a manual boot from a non-default boot device or kernel, view or alter configuration, and so on.

17.3.2 Booting Manually versus Automatically

A system automatically boots up if the autoboot parameter is set to ON and an AUTO file, with a proper string defined in it, is present in the EFI partition on the boot device.

Sometimes you need to boot a system manually to interact with the EFI Boot Manager. To do so, you need to hit any key before autoboot delay period expires. The EFI Boot Manager allows you to specify an alternate boot device to boot from, an alternate kernel file to boot from, view/adjust system's pre-boot settings, and invoke EFI Shell. The following lists steps to use the EFI Shell to boot a system manually:

1. Highlight "EFI Shell [Built-in]" from EFI Boot Manager main menu and hit the *Enter* key to get to the EFI Shell.
2. Use the *map* command to list file systems that are known and mapped. Select a file system to use by entering its mapped name (fs0, fs1, etc.) followed by the colon character and hit the *Enter* key. The prompt changes to reflect the selected file system.

> Shell> **map**
> Device mapping table
> fs0:Acpi(HWP0002,PNP0A03,0)/Pci(2|1)/Usb(0, 0)/CDROM(Entry0)
> fs1:Acpi(HWP0002,PNP0A03,400)/Pci(1|0)/Scsi(Pun5,Lun0)/HD(Part1,Sig03699A00-B066-11DB-8002-D6217B60E588)
> fs2: Acpi(HWP0002,PNP0A03,400)/Pci(1|0)/Scsi(Pun5,Lun0)/HD(Part3,Sig03699A64-B066-11DB-8004-D6217B60E588)
> fs3:Acpi(HWP0002,PNP0A03,400)/Pci(1|0)/Sas(Addr500000E0140986D2,Lun0)/HD(Part1,SigE46 35232-F8B7-11DB-8002-D6217B60E588)
> . . . .
> . . . .
> Shell> **fs1:**

3. Enter *hpux* at the prompt to launch the *hpux.efi* loader. The loader is located in *\EFI\HPUX*.

> fs1:\> **hpux**

4. The *hpux.efi* loader executes the *boot* command using the AUTO file contents located in *\EFI\HPUX* directory on the EFI partition of the selected boot device. The AUTO file typically contains *"boot vmunix"*. If you wish to manually boot the system, interrupt the boot process within the time-out period provided by the loader to get to the HPUX> prompt. You may need to interrupt the boot process at this time to boot from an alternate kernel file, boot to single user mode, boot to LVM or VxVM maintenance mode, and so on.

17.3.3   Configuring Autoboot and Boot Delay Period

You can enable or disable automatic booting of a system and modify the delay time.

The value of autoboot flag can be set from either EFI Shell or HP-UX command prompt. Here is how you would do it:

From the EFI Shell:

> Shell> **autoboot on**   (enables autoboot)
> Shell> **autoboot off**   (disables autoboot)

At the command prompt:

> # **setboot –b on**   (enables autoboot)
> # **setboot –b off**   (disables autoboot)

The default automatic boot delay for is set to 10 seconds. This value can be modified from either EFI Boot Manager or the EFI Shell. The number specified is in seconds.

From the EFI Boot Manager:

Go to "Boot Configuration" → "Auto Boot TimeOut" → "Set TimeOut Value". Specify a number.

From the EFI Shell:

Shell> **autoboot 20**   (Changes to 20 seconds)

17.3.4   Viewing and Setting Primary, HAA, and Alternate Boot Device Paths

You can view and set PRI, HAA, and ALT boot paths from either the EFI Boot Manager or the HP-UX command prompt. Here is how you would do it:

From the EFI Boot Manager:

Go to "Boot Configuration" and use the "Add a Boot Option" to view, add, or modify PRI, HAA, and ALT boot path locations.

At the HP-UX command prompt:

```
# setboot            (displays paths)
# setboot −p 8/8.4   (sets PRI boot path)
# setboot −h 8/8.12  (sets HAA boot path)
# setboot −a 8/16/5.2 (sets ALT boot path)
```

17.3.5   Booting from an Alternate Boot Device

If an alternate boot device is listed in the Boot Menu, select it, and press the *Enter* key, otherwise, go to the EFI Boot Manager and follow the procedure below to choose another boot device:

1. Run the EFI Shell.
2. Enter *map* command to list available bootable devices. Look for entries that begin with *fs#* (where # is 0, 1, 2, and so on).
3. Select the desired entry and hit the *Enter* key.
4. Enter *hpux* to run the boot loader, which then uses the AUTO file to determine which kernel file to use to boot.

17.3.6   Booting to Single User State

From the EFI Shell, boot to single-user state by stopping the boot process at the *hpux.efi* interface and enter the *boot* command with proper switches. Here is the procedure:

1. Run the EFI Shell.
2. Enter *map* command to list available bootable devices. Look for entries that begin with *fs#* (where # is 0, 1, 2, and so on).
3. Select the desired entry and hit the *Enter* key.

4. Run the *hpux* command to invoke the *\EFI\HPUX\HPUX.EFI* loader.
5. Boot to the HP-UX Boot Loader prompt (HPUX>) by hitting any key within 10 seconds.
6. At the *hpux.efi* interface, enter the following to boot the */stand/vmunix* kernel to single-user state:

> HPUX> **boot –is vmunix**
> > System Memory = 4063 MB
> loading section 0
> .... (complete)
> loading section 1
> .... (complete)
> loading symbol table
> loading System Directory(boot.sys) to MFS
> ....
> loading MFSFILES Directory(bootfs) to MFS
> ......
> Launching /stand/vmunix
> SIZE: Text:25953K + Data:3715K + BSS:3637K = Total:33306K
>
> Console is on a Serial Device
> Booting kernel...

17.3.7   Booting to LVM and VxVM Maintenance States

The procedure for booting HP-UX to LVM and VxVM maintenance states is similar to that for booting it to single user state, except that you specify appropriate boot options.

For LVM maintenance mode, use:

> HPUX> **boot –lm vmunix**

For VxVM maintenance mode, use:

> HPUX> **boot –vm vmunix**

17.3.8   Viewing and Modifying AUTO File Contents

The AUTO file is located in *\EFI\HPUX\AUTO* on the boot device. You can modify its contents from the EFI Shell, from *hpux* loader prompt, or from the HP-UX command prompt. Here is the procedure to modify if from the three interfaces.

From the EFI Shell:

1. Use the *map* command to list all available devices.
2. Choose the desired device by selecting its *fs#*.
3. Change to *\EFI\HPUX* directory using the *cd* command.
4. Run the *ls* command to list all boot loader files there.
5. View AUTO file contents with the *cat* command:

```
fs0:\EFI\HPUX> cat AUTO
FILE: fs0:\EFI\HPUX\AUTO, Size 12

boot vmunix
```

6. Use the *edit* command to modify the entry.

```
fs0:\EFI\HPUX> edit AUTO
```

From the HPUX secondary boot loader prompt:

1. Access the *hpux.efi* loader for the boot device that contains the AUTO file to be configured.
2. At the *hpux.efi* boot loader prompt, enter the *showauto* command to display current contents of the AUTO file:

```
HPUX> showauto
```

3. Enter the *setauto* command to delete or modify the AUTO file.

```
HPUX> setauto –d                     (deletes the AUTO file)
HPUX> setauto boot boot_string    (modifies the contents. Specify correct boot string)
```

At the HP-UX command prompt:

1. Copy the AUTO file from the EFI partition to locally on the system:

```
# efi_cp –d /dev/rdsk/c0t4d0s1 –u /EFI/HPUX/AUTO AUTO
```

2. Edit the file and modify contents.
3. Copy the updated AUTO file back to the EFI partition:

```
# efi_cp –d /dev/rdsk/c0t4d0s1 AUTO /EFI/HPUX/AUTO
```

17.3.9   Booting from an Alternate Kernel File

The default kernel file is *vmunix* and is located in the */stand* directory on the boot device. The AUTO file in the EFI partition contains the entry "boot vmunix", which references this kernel file.

If you need to boot using an alternate kernel, such as */stand/vmunix_test*, follow the procedure given below:

1. Go to EFI Boot Manager and then to the EFI shell.
2. Enter the *map* command to list available boot devices.
3. Determine the entry that maps to the device containing the kernel file you want to boot from and enter the *fs#* at the shell prompt.
4. Enter the command *hpux* at the shell prompt and stop the autoboot sequence by hitting any key.

---

5. At the boot loader prompt, enter the command *boot* and specify an alternate kernel file name to boot from.

    HPUX> **boot vmunix_test**

17.4　Initializing HP-UX

HP-UX operating environment initialization phase begins after the *boot* command is executed, with correct boot device and kernel file specified, on either an HP 9000 or Integrity system. The initialization covers everything from loading the kernel to all the way up when you see the login prompt on the screen.

17.4.1　Kernel Initialization

The HP-UX kernel is loaded into the memory and initialized. The kernel starts the *swapper* daemon and runs the */sbin/pre_init_rc* script. This script checks the root file system and executes *fsck* on it, if required.

17.4.2　The init Process

The kernel then calls the */sbin/init* command and transfers the control over to it to initiate the system initialization process. The *init* command looks into the */etc/inittab* file to determine the default run control level for the system to boot to.

A sample */etc/inittab* file is shown below. The first line in the file defines the default run control level, which is 3, for an HP-UX system.

```
# cat /etc/inittab
init:3:initdefault:
ioin::sysinit:/sbin/ioinitrc >/dev/console 2>&1
tape::sysinit:/sbin/mtinit > /dev/console 2>&1
muxi::sysinit:/sbin/dasetup   </dev/console >/dev/console 2>&1 # mux init
stty::sysinit:/sbin/stty 9600 clocal icanon echo opost onlcr ixon icrnl ignpar </dev/systty
vxen::bootwait:/sbin/fs/vxfs/vxenablef -a
vol1::sysinit:/sbin/init.d/vxvm-sysboot </dev/console >/dev/console 2>&1 ##vxvm
vol2::sysinit:/sbin/init.d/vxvm-startup start </dev/console >/dev/console 2>&1 ##vxvm
brc1::bootwait:/sbin/bcheckrc </dev/console >/dev/console 2>&1 # fsck, etc.
link::wait:/sbin/sh -c "/sbin/rm -f /dev/syscon; \
          /sbin/ln /dev/systty /dev/syscon" >/dev/console 2>&1
cprt::bootwait:/sbin/cat /etc/copyright >/dev/syscon        # legal req
sqnc::wait:/sbin/rc </dev/console >/dev/console 2>&1         # system init
#powf::powerwait:/sbin/powerfail >/dev/console 2>&1         # powerfail
cons:123456:respawn:/usr/sbin/getty console console         # system console
#ttp1:234:respawn:/usr/sbin/getty -h tty0p1 9600
#ttp2:234:respawn:/usr/sbin/getty -h tty0p2 9600
#ttp3:234:respawn:/usr/sbin/getty -h tty0p3 9600
#ttp4:234:respawn:/usr/sbin/getty -h tty0p4 9600
#ttp5:234:respawn:/usr/sbin/getty -h tty0p5 9600
```

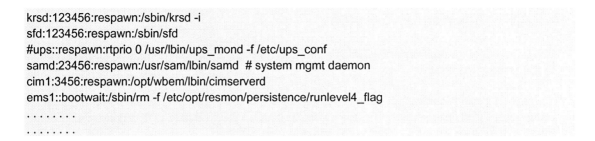

```
krsd:123456:respawn:/sbin/krsd -i
sfd:123456:respawn:/sbin/sfd
#ups::respawn:rtprio 0 /usr/lbin/ups_mond -f /etc/ups_conf
samd:23456:respawn:/usr/sam/lbin/samd  # system mgmt daemon
cim1:3456:respawn:/opt/wbem/lbin/cimserverd
ems1::bootwait:/sbin/rm -f /etc/opt/resmon/persistence/runlevel4_flag
. . . . . . . .
. . . . . . . .
```

As you can see, there are four fields per line separated by the colon character. The fields are explained below:

- ✓ The first field defines a unique identification string containing 1 – 4 characters for each line item.
- ✓ The second field identifies run levels at which the entry is executed. If the field is empty, the entry is valid for all run levels.
- ✓ The third field determines an action. There are many possible actions, some of which are:

  initdefault – this action determines the default run level for the system. The *init* command reads this line and boots the system to the specified run level.
  sysinit – this action executes the specified process before *init* tries to access the system console display.
  bootwait – this action takes place during the system boot process only.
  wait – when an entry with this action is being executed, other entries at the same run level wait for its completion before their turn comes.
  respawn – restarts the specified process as soon as it dies. If the process is running, no action is taken.

- ✓ The fourth field defines the fully qualified pathname to a process or command that is to be executed.

17.4.3   Building Hardware Device Tree

The next command that *init* calls from the */etc/inittab* file is */sbin/ioinitrc*. This command executes the *ioinit* command, which maintains an up to date hardware device information database in the */etc/ioconfig* file. At system boot, *ioinit* tests consistency between hardware available at that time against what is already listed in the */etc/ioconfig* file from the previous reboot. If a new device has been added to the system, the *insf* command is executed, which creates device files for the new device and adds an entry for the device to the file. Similarly, if a device has been removed from the system, the entry pointing to it is removed from the file. A copy of */etc/ioconfig* file is also stored in the */stand* file system.

17.4.4   Checking and Activating Volume Groups

After the hardware information is updated, the */sbin/bcheckrc* command is executed. This command performs several actions including checking and activating LVM volume groups by calling the */sbin/lvmrc* command and checking, cleaning, and mounting all local file systems listed in the */etc/fstab* file.

17.4.5   Starting Up Services

Next, the *init* command calls the */sbin/rc* script, which starts up all HP-UX services configured to run in the default run level.

The */sbin/rc* script locates the services to be started in the sequencer directories */sbin/rc#.d*, gets configuration information from the startup configuration files located in */etc/rc.config.d* directory, and starts up services from the initialization directory */sbin/init.d*.

Here is a list of the sequencer directories:

```
# ll –d /sbin/rc*
dr-xr-xr-x    2    bin    bin    8192    Nov 26 09:07    /sbin/rc0.d
dr-xr-xr-x    2    bin    bin    8192    Nov 29 21:02    /sbin/rc1.d
dr-xr-xr-x    2    bin    bin    8192    Nov 29 21:02    /sbin/rc2.d
dr-xr-xr-x    2    bin    bin    8192    Nov 26 09:32    /sbin/rc3.d
dr-xr-xr-x    2    bin    bin    96      Nov 26 07:57    /sbin/rc4.d
```

The following shows directory contents of the *rc0.d* directory. Notice all scripts here are mere symbolic links to startup scripts located in the */sbin/init.d* directory.

```
# ll /sbin/rc0.d
total 0
lrwxr-xr-x    1    root    root    19    Nov 26 07:57 K480syncer -> /sbin/init.d/syncer
lrwxr-xr-x    1    root    root    15    Nov 26 07:57 K650kl        -> /sbin/init.d/kl
lrwxr-xr-x    1    root    root    20    Nov 26 07:57 K800killall    -> /sbin/init.d/killall
lrwxr-xr-x    1    root    root    19    Nov 26 07:57 K888kminit  -> /sbin/init.d/kminit
lrwxr-xr-x    1    root    root    20    Nov 26 07:57 K890kmbuild -> /sbin/init.d/kmbuild
lrwxr-xr-x    1    root    root    23    Nov 26 07:57 K900localmount  -> /sbin/init.d/localmount
lrwxr-xr-x    1    bin     bin     29    Nov 26 09:07 K930vxvm-daemon-kill ->
/sbin/init.d/vxvm-daemon-kill
```

The following lists directory contents of the *rc3.d* directory. Notice again that all scripts here are symbolic links to startup scripts in the */sbin/init.d* directory.

```
# ll /sbin/rc3.d
total 0
lrwxr-xr-x    1    root    root    23  Nov 26 08:03 S100nfs.server-> /sbin/init.d/nfs.server
lrwxr-xr-x    1    root    sys     21  Nov 26 09:32 S110idsagent-> /sbin/init.d/idsagent
lrwxr-xr-x    1    root    sys     19  Nov 26 08:34 S200tps.rc        -> /sbin/init.d/tps.rc
lrwxr-xr-x    1    bin     bin     24  Nov 26 09:16 S823hpws_apache->/sbin/init.d/hpws_apache
lrwxr-xr-x    1    bin     bin     24  Nov 26 09:17 S823hpws_tomcat-> /sbin/init.d/hpws_tomcat
lrwxr-xr-x    1    bin     bin     24  Nov 26 09:18 S823hpws_webmin->
/sbin/init.d/hpws_webmin
lrwxr-xr-x    1    bin     bin     26  Nov 26 09:18 S823hpws_xmltools->
/sbin/init.d/hpws_xmltools
lrwxr-xr-x    1    root    sys     23  Nov 26 08:26 S990dtlogin.rc-> /sbin/init.d/dtlogin.rc
```

The sequencer directories are *rc0.d, rc1.d, rc2.d, rc3.d,* and *rc4.d*. The *rc4.d* directory is empty. There are two types of scripts located in the sequencer directories: *Start* and *Kill*. The names of the start scripts begin with an uppercase S and that for the kill scripts with an uppercase K. These scripts are symbolically linked to actual startup/shutdown scripts located in the */sbin/init.d* directory. Each startup/shutdown script contains "start" and "stop" functions corresponding to starting and stopping a service. Similarly, each startup/shutdown script contains "start_msg" and "stop_msg" functions. When a service is started, the "start" function of the script is executed and the message defined in the "start_msg" function is displayed. Likewise, when a service is stopped, the "stop" function of the script is executed and the message defined in the "stop_msg" function is displayed. The contents of one of the scripts, */sbin/init.d/lp*, is shown below as an example:

```
# cat  /sbin/init.d/lp
. . . . . . . .
. . . . . . . .
case $1 in
start_msg)
    echo "Start print spooler"
    ;;

stop_msg)
    echo "Stop print spooler"
    ;;

'start')
    if [ -f /etc/rc.config.d/lp ] ; then
        . /etc/rc.config.d/lp
    else
        echo "ERROR: /etc/rc.config.d/lp defaults file MISSING"
    fi

    if [ "$LP" -eq 1 -a -s /var/spool/lp/pstatus ]; then
        ps -ef | grep lpsched | grep -iv grep > /dev/null 2>&1
        if [ $? = 0 ]
        then
           /usr/sbin/lpshut > /dev/null 2>&1
        set_return
        fi
        rm -f /var/spool/lp/SCHEDLOCK
        /usr/sbin/lpsched && echo line printer scheduler started
        set_return
    else
        rval=2
    fi
    ;;

'stop')
    if [ -s /var/spool/lp/pstatus ]; then
        if /usr/sbin/lpshut > /dev/null 2>&1; then
            echo line printer scheduler stopped
```

```
            else
                  set_return
            fi
      fi
      ;;

*)
      echo "usage: $0 {start|stop}"
      ;;
esac

exit $rval
```

All scripts situated in the *rc0.d* directory are kill scripts; *rc1.d* and *rc2.d* contain both start and kill scripts; and *rc3.d* contains only start scripts.

When a system comes up, S scripts are executed one after the other in ascending numbering sequence from *rc1.d*, *rc2.d*, and *rc3.d* directories.

In the same way, when a system goes down, K scripts are executed one after the other in descending numbering sequence from *rc2.d*, *rc1.d*, and *rc0.d* directories.

The following lists configuration files for the startup/shutdown scripts placed in the */etc/rc.config.d* configuration directory:

ll /etc/rc.config.d

```
. . . . . . . .
. . . . . . . .
-r--r--r--      1      bin      bin      1350     Nov 14  2000     crashconf
-r--r--r--      1      bin      bin      122      Nov 14  2000     cron
-r--r--r--      1      bin      bin      2270     Nov 14  2000     dce
-rw-r--r--      1      root     sys      63       Nov 26 09:32     desktop
-r-xr-xr-x      1      bin      bin      921      Feb 13  2003     diagnostic
-r--r--r--      1      bin      bin      122      Nov 26 09:32     egcd
-r--r--r--      1      bin      bin      146      Apr 28  2003     ems
-r--r--r--      1      bin      bin      551      Jul 17  2002     emsagtconf
-r--r--r--      1      bin      bin      264      Mar 28  2000     eus
-r--r--r--      1      bin      bin      475      Jun 18  2002     fc_td_conf
. . . . . . . .
. . . . . . . .
```

Each of these files has a variable value set to either 1 or 0, with 1 means start the service at system boot and 0 means otherwise. A sample startup configuration file for printing services is shown below:

cat /etc/rc.config.d/lp

```
. . . . . . . .
. . . . . . . .
LP=1
```

If you ever required to replace a misconfigured, corrupted, or lost startup configuration file in the */etc/rc.config.d* directory with the original file added at the time of system installation, you can get it from the */usr/newconfig/etc/rc.config.d* directory.

The following directory listing from */sbin/init.d* shows actual startup/shutdown scripts:

```
# ll /sbin/init.d
. . . . . . . .
. . . . . . . .
-r-xr-xr-x   1      bin      bin      1796    Nov 14  2000    crashconf
-r-xr-xr-x   1      bin      bin      1275    Nov 14  2000    cron
-r-xr-xr-x   1      bin      bin      26356   Nov 14  2000    dce
-r-xr-xr-x   1      bin      bin      1894    Nov 14  2000    ddfa
-r-xr-xr-x   1      bin      bin      2140    Feb 13  2003    diagnostic
-r-xr-xr-x   1      bin      bin      3080    Nov 14  2000    dtlogin.rc
-r-xr-xr-x   1      bin      bin      2784    May 23  1995    egcd
-r-xr-xr-x   1      bin      bin      4641    Apr 30  2003    ems
-r-xr-xr-x   1      bin      bin      2373    Jul 17  2002    emsa
-r-xr-xr-x   1      bin      bin      1293    Nov 14  2000    envd
. . . . . . . .
. . . . . . . .
```

17.4.6   Starting and Stopping Services Manually

You can manually start and stop services. For example, to stop the printing service daemon, *lpsched*, do the following:

```
# /sbin/init.d/lp  stop
line printer scheduler stopped
```

To start it, run:

```
# /sbin/init.d/lp  start
scheduler is running
```

17.4.7   System Startup Log File

Log information for each service startup is captured in the */etc/rc.log* file, which has a symbolic link to */var/adm/rc.log* file. Here is a sample from the file.

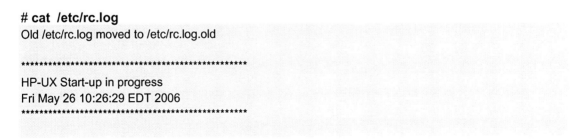

```
# cat  /etc/rc.log
Old /etc/rc.log moved to /etc/rc.log.old

****************************************************
HP-UX Start-up in progress
Fri May 26 10:26:29 EDT 2006
****************************************************
```

Configure system crash dumps
Output from "/sbin/rc1.d/S080crashconf start":

EXIT CODE: 0

VxVM device node check
Output from "/sbin/rc1.d/S091vxvm-nodes-check start":

VxVM general startup
Output from "/sbin/rc1.d/S092vxvm-startup start":

VxVM reconfiguration recovery
Output from "/sbin/rc1.d/S093vxvm-reconfig start":

Mount file systems
Output from "/sbin/rc1.d/S100localmount start":

. . . .
. . . .
Start NFS server subsystem
Output from "/sbin/rc3.d/S100nfs.server start":

NFS_SERVER not set to one in /etc/rc.config.d/nfsconf, exiting.

Starting ids/9000 agent
Output from "/sbin/rc3.d/S110idsagent start":

Skipping idsagent startup as IDS=0 in /etc/rc.config.d/ids
The required IDS/9000 certificates may have not been generated.
Please refer to the configuration chapter of the
HP IDS/9000 Administrator's Guide for further instructions.
"/sbin/rc3.d/S110idsagent start" SKIPPED

Start X print server(s)
Output from "/sbin/rc3.d/S200tps.rc start":

"/sbin/rc3.d/S200tps.rc start" SKIPPED

Start CDE login server
Output from "/sbin/rc3.d/S990dtlogin.rc start":

****

HP-UX run-level transition completed
Fri May 26 10:28:33 EDT 2006
****

Summary

In this chapter, you learned how to shutdown an HP-UX system using various available tools. You saw different run levels that an HP-UX system could run at.

You learned system startup that covered pre-boot administration tasks and kernel and system initialization. Pre-boot administration tasks included interacting with BCH and EFI, setting automatic/manual system boot attributes, setting autosearch attribute for bootable devices, setting and modifying boot device paths, and so on. These tasks were presented for both HP 9000 and Integrity servers.

The following section talked about kernel and system initialization where you studied various commands and scripts that were executed to bring up system services. You were introduced with sequencer directories, startup configuration files, and actual system startup scripts that run to bring an HP-UX system to a fully functional state.

Kernel Reconfiguration Methods

This chapter covers the following major topics:

- ✓ Purpose behind kernel reconfiguration
- ✓ Static and dynamic kernel modules and tunables
- ✓ Reconfigure HP-UX 11iv1 kernel
- ✓ Query, load, and unload DLKMs
- ✓ Query and modify DTKPs
- ✓ Reconfigure HP-UX 11iv2 kernel
- ✓ The kcweb tool
- ✓ Common tunable parameters

18.1   Purpose of Reconfiguring the Kernel

The HP-UX kernel requires a rebuild when a new functionality is added to it. Likewise, when a functionality is removed from the system, kernel needs to be updated to reflect the removal. The new functionality may be introduced by applying a patch, installing a new hardware device, or changing a critical system component. In most cases, the default kernel configuration that comes with HP-UX is sufficient. However, in following situations your kernel needs to be reconfigured.

18.1.1   Installing or Removing an HP-UX Patch

When you install or remove an HP-UX patch that affects kernel configuration, the kernel is rebuilt as part of the installation/removal process.

18.1.2   Adding or Removing a Device Driver

The standard HP-UX kernel includes several software device drivers. Each device driver is used to control a specific type of hardware device. Sometimes, you wish to add a hardware device support for which is not already part of the kernel. In such a situation, you need to add the device's software driver to the kernel so that you can use it. You may, on the other hand, wish to remove a driver from the kernel, if you no longer need it.

18.1.3   Adding or Removing a Subsystem

The kernel includes several subsystems including LVM, CD/DVD-ROM, networking, etc. These subsystems are configured in the kernel so you can use the functionality that they offer. You may add a subsystem to the kernel (or remove from it) depending on whether or not you require the functionality that the subsystem brings. The kernel is rebuilt as part of both processes.

18.1.4   Changing the Primary Swap or the Dump Device

The kernel requires reconfiguration when you modify the location of the primary swap or add or remove a dump device. A dump device is a place on a physical disk that is used by the system to place a dump of the running kernel and memory image in case the system crashes. Some administrators prefer to use the swap space as the dump space; others create a separate volume for it in *vg00* or *rootdg*.

18.1.5   Modifying a Kernel Parameter

Normally, when installing an application or a database software, you are required to modify one or more kernel parameters in order for the application or the database software to function properly. Kernel parameters control the behavior of the HP-UX kernel.

18.2   Static and Dynamic Kernel Components

The HP-UX kernel has two major components: *Modules* and *Tunable Parameters*. Some of the modules and tunable parameters are static while others are dynamic.

18.2.1 Static and Dynamic Kernel Modules

The kernel is composed of a number of modules. Each module contains software that adds a functionality to the system. Modules can be added to or removed from the system using either commands or SAM.

Modules can be either static or dynamic. A static module requires a kernel rebuild and a subsequent system reboot to make it effective. On the contrary, a dynamic module can be added to or removed from the kernel while the system is up and running; there is no need to bounce the server. A dynamic module is automatically loaded into the memory when it is needed by the kernel and gets unloaded by itself when no longer required. Dynamic modules are also referred to as *Dynamically Loadable Kernel Modules* (DLKMs).

18.2.2 Static and Dynamic Kernel Tunable Parameters

There are several tunable parameters defined in the kernel, the values of which affect the overall behavior of the system. The sizes of many kernel tables are determined by these parameters. Parameter values can be altered using either commands or SAM.

Tunable parameters can be either static or dynamic. After modifying the value of a static kernel parameter, the kernel needs to be rebuilt and the server must be rebooted for the new value to take effect. A dynamic tunable parameter, in contrast, does not require a server reboot after its value is altered. The value takes effect as soon as it is changed. Dynamic tunable parameters are also referred to as *Dynamically Tunable Kernel Parameters* (DTKPs).

18.3 Reconfiguring the HP-UX 11iv1 Kernel

The kernel reconfiguration can be done either from the command line or through SAM. The following procedure lists steps to reconfigure an HP-UX 11iv1 kernel from the command line:

1. Change directory to the kernel build environment.

    # cd /stand/build

2. Gather running kernel information using the *system_prep* command and save it to a file called *system* by specifying the –s option with the command.

    # /usr/lbin/sysadm/system_prep –s system

    The *system* file contains drivers, subsystems, and tunable parameter information. The contents of a sample system file are displayed below:

    # cat system
    ```
    *****************************************
    * Source: /ux/core/kern/filesets.info/CORE-KRN/generic
    * @(#)B.11.11_LR
    *
    *****************************************
    * Additional drivers required in every machine-type to create a complete
    ```

```
* system file during cold install.  This list is every driver that the
* master.d/ files do not force on the system or is not identifiable by
* ioscan.
* Other CPU-type specific files can exist for their special cases.
* see create_sysfile (1m).
******************************************
*
* Drivers/Subsystems
c720
sdisk
sctl
Centlf
. . . . . . . .
. . . . . . . .
nfile                  3000
maxfiles               2048
maxfiles_lim           2048
ncallout               6000
maxdsiz                2063835136
maxswapchunks          1024
```

3. Use the *kmsystem* and *kmtune* commands to view and modify this file. *kmsystem* is used to view and modify a driver or subsystem, whereas *kmtune* is used to view and modify the value of a tunable parameter.

    As an example, to view and unconfigure a subsystem called, token2, do the following. Confirm the new status of the subsystem after the change. Use –S option to specify the system file name, –q to state the subsystem name to be queried, and –c to specify whether or not to unconfigure the subsystem.

    ```
    # kmsystem  –S  /stand/build/system  –q  token2
    Module    Configured    Loadable
    ============================
    token2        Y              -
    # kmsystem  –S  /stand/build/system  –c  n  token2
    # kmsystem  –S  /stand/build/system  –q  token2
    Module    Configured    Loadable
    ============================
    token2        N              -
    ```

    Similarly, for instance, to view the value of a tunable parameter called, maxvgs, and modify its value from default 10 to 15, do the following. Confirm the new value after the change. Use –q option to specify the parameter name to be queried and –s to supply a new value.

    ```
    # kmtune  –q  maxvgs  –S  /stand/build/system
    Parameter     Current  Dyn     Planned          Module  Version
    =========================================================
    maxvgs          10       -         10
    # kmtune  –s  maxvgs=15  –S  /stand/build/system
    ```

```
# kmtune -q maxvgs -S /stand/build/system
Parameter      Current Dyn    Planned        Module  Version
===========================================================
maxvgs         10        -     15
```

You can also use the vi editor to modify the *system* file. To remove a driver or subsystem, simply delete the associated line; to add a driver or subsystem, add a line entry for it; and to modify a kernel parameter, change the value listed against the parameter name.

4. Execute the following to generate a new kernel after updating the *system* file with "token2" module information deleted and "maxvgs" tunable parameter value modified. The name of the new kernel file will be *vmunix_test* and it will be located in the */stand/build* directory. The –s option specifies the path and name of the *system* file.

```
# mk_kernel -s ./system
Generating module: krm...
Generating module: pfil...
Generating module: ipf...
Compiling conf.c...
Loading the kernel...
Generating kernel symbol table...
```

5. Move the new kernel, together with associated DLKM directory, to proper location. Issue the *kmupdate* command to rename the existing kernel file */stand/vmunix* and existing DLKM directory */stand/dlkm* as */stand/vmunix.prev* and */stand/dlkm.vmunix.prev,* respectively. The command then moves the newly generated kernel file */stand/build/vmunix_test* and DLKM directory */stand/build/dlkm.vmunix_test* as */stand/vmunix* and */stand/dlkm,* respectively. The new kernel file */stand/vmunix* will be loaded at next system reboot.

```
# kmupdate

Kernel update request is scheduled.

Default kernel /stand/vmunix will be updated by
newly built kernel /stand/build/vmunix_test
at next system shutdown or startup time.
```

6. Reboot the system with the *init* or the *shutdown* command and verify the modifications after the system is back up. For subsystem verification, use the *kmsystem* command. For tunable parameter verification, use either the *sysdef* or the *kmtune* command. These commands look for all module specific information in the */stand/system.d* directory and all master kernel module, parameter, and subsystem specific information in the */usr/conf/master.d* directory.

    To verify that the subsystem "token2" has been unconfigured, do the following:

```
# kmsystem | grep token2
token2          N       -
```

To verify the new value of "maxvgs", use the *kmtune* command:

```
# kmtune –q maxvgs
Parameter      Current Dyn    Planned        Module Version
=========================================================
maxvgs         15      -      10
```

To verify the new value of "maxvgs", run the *sysdef* command:

```
# sysdef | grep maxvgs
maxvgs         15      -      -      -
```

This completes the kernel rebuild process using commands.

If the system has problems booting from the new kernel that you just built, use the old kernel to bring it back up. Refer to Chapter 17 "Shutting Down and Starting Up an HP-UX System" on how to boot a system using alternate kernel file.

The following procedure explains how to tune and rebuild the kernel using SAM. Follow the steps below:

Go to SAM → Kernel Configuration. You will see four options as displayed in Figure 18-1.

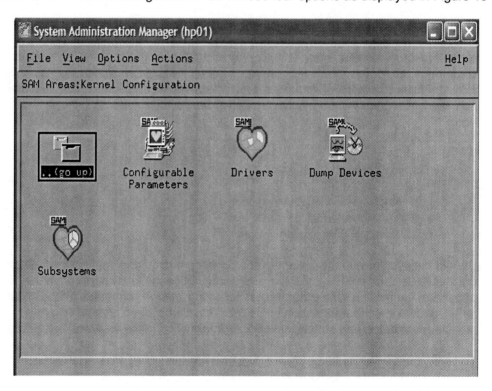

Figure 18-1 SAM – Kernel Administration Main Screen

Here is an explanation for the four options:

✓ Choose "Configurable Parameters" option if you wish to view or modify the value of a tunable parameter. To modify the value, highlight the parameter and go to Actions → Modify Configurable Parameter, as shown in Figure 18-2. Go to Actions → Process New Kernel to regenerate a new kernel.

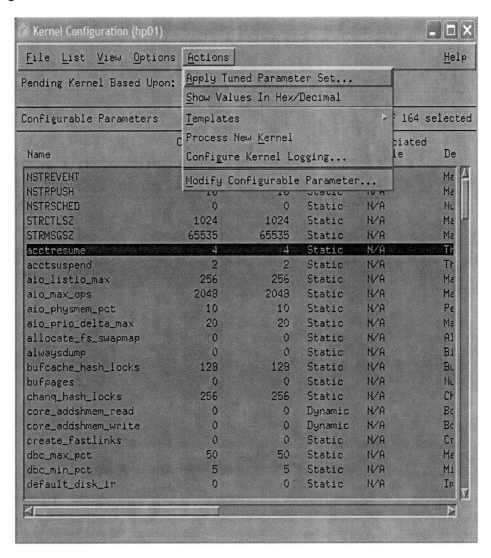

Figure 18-2 SAM – Kernel Configurable Parameter Administration

✓ Select "Drivers" if you want to add or remove a driver support from the kernel. Highlight the driver and go to Actions → Add Driver(s) to Kernel (or Remove Driver(s) from Kernel). When done, go back to Actions → Process New Kernel to regenerate a new kernel. See Figure 18-3.

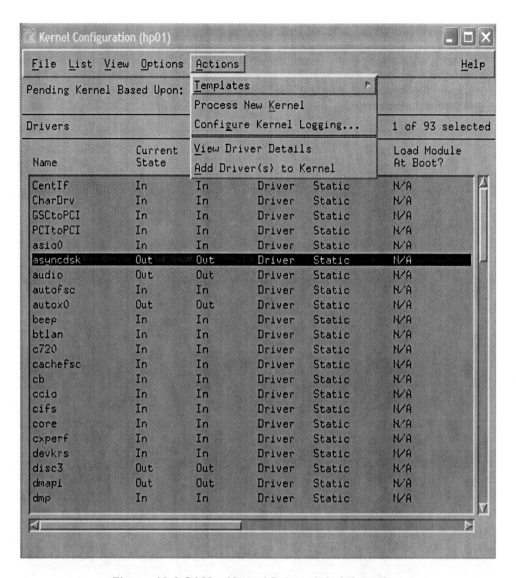

Figure 18-3 SAM – Kernel Driver Administration

✓ Go into "Dump Devices" to add or remove a dump device. Go to Actions → Add Dump Device to add a new dump device. Then again, go to Actions → Process New Kernel to regenerate a new kernel. To remove a dump device, highlight it from the list and go to Actions → Remove. Go back to Actions → Process New Kernel to regenerate a new kernel. Refer to Figure 18-4.

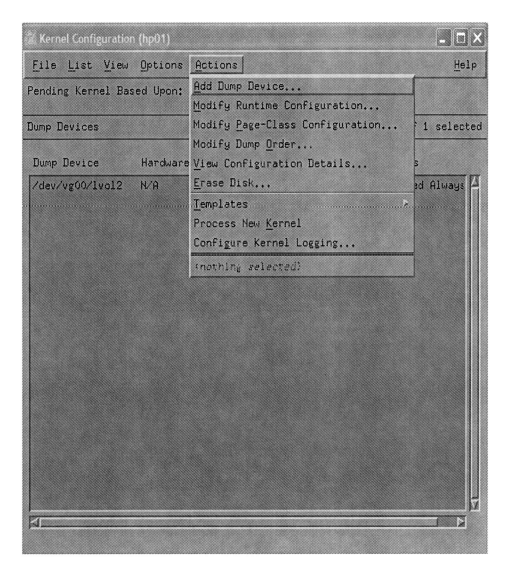

Figure 18-4 SAM – Kernel Dump Device Administration

✓ Opt for "Subsystems" if you wish to add a new subsystem support to the kernel or remove support for an existing subsystem. Go to Actions → Add Subsystem to Kernel (or Remove Subsystem from Kernel) to add or remove a subsystem. Consult Figure 18-5.

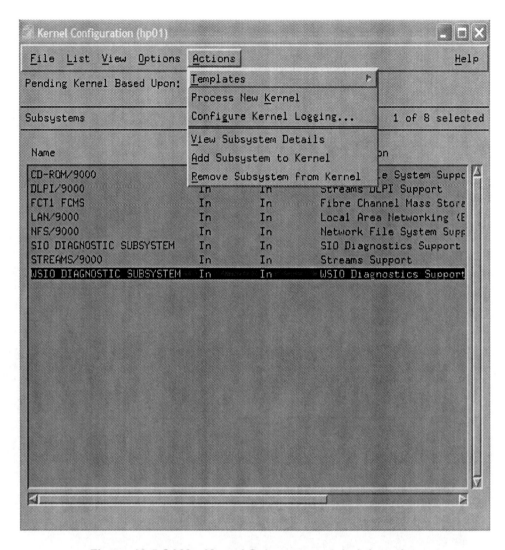

Figure 18-5 SAM – Kernel Subsystems Administration

18.4 Querying, Loading, and Unloading DLKMs

Modules can be loaded or unloaded online and automatically, as well as manually using the *kmadmin* command. This command is also used to query dynamic and static modules. Some examples are given below on the usage of the command.

To query all DLKMs in the running kernel, specify either –s (summary) option or –S (detail) option.

 # kmadmin –s

Name	ID	Status	Type
pfil	1	LOADED	STREAMS
ipf	2	LOADED	WSIO

```
krm         3       UNLOADED    WSIO
```

To query a single DLKM, state either the DLKM name with –Q option or associated DLKM number with –q option:

 # kmadmin –Q ipf

```
Module Name        ipf
Module ID          2
Module Path        /stand/dlkm/mod.d/ipf
Status             LOADED
Size               217088
Base Address       0xf1f000
BSS Size           90112
BSS Base Address   0xf39000
Hold Count         2
Dependent Count    0
Unload Delay       0 seconds
Description        HP IP Filter: v3.5alpha5 (A.03.05.05)
Type               WSIO
Block Major        -1
Character Major    79
Flags              b5
```
 # kmadmin –q 1
```
Module Name        pfil
Module ID          1
Module Path        /stand/dlkm/mod.d/pfil
Status             LOADED
Size               24576
Base Address       0xf19000
BSS Size           4096
BSS Base Address   0xf1e000
Hold Count         6
Dependent Count    1
Unload Delay       0 seconds
Description        pfilm STREAMS module
Type               STREAMS
Switch Number      0
```

To load a DLKM, such as "krm", into the running kernel, do the following:

 # kmadmin –L krm
kmadmin: Module krm loaded, ID = 3

To unload a DLKM, such as "krm", from the running kernel, do one of the following:

 # kmadmin –U krm
Kmadmin: Module 3 unloaded
 # kmadmin –u 3
Kmadmin: Module 3 unloaded

To query all static modules in the running kernel:

```
# kmadmin –k
ufs
kload
nfs_core
nfs_client
nfs_server
cdfs
dlkm
krs
prm
autofsc
inet
ffs
vxfs
lvm
vxdmp
vxvm
. . . . . . . .
. . . . . . . .
```

18.5   Querying and Modifying DTKPs

A few kernel parameters can be modified and loaded dynamically. The *kmtune* command is used for this purpose. Some examples are given below:

To query all tunable parameters, run the *kmtune* command as follows. The third column with a Y tells that the parameter is a DTKP.

```
# kmtune | awk '$3~/Y/{print $0}'
core_addshmem_read       0                Y        0
core_addshmem_write      0                Y        0
maxfiles_lim             1024             Y        1024
maxtsiz                  0x4000000        Y        0x04000000
maxtsiz_64bit            0x40000000       Y        0x0000000040000000
maxuprc                  75               Y        75
msgmax                   8192             Y        8192
msgmnb                   16384            Y        16384
scsi_max_qdepth          8                Y        8
semmsl                   2048             Y        2048
shmmax                   0x4000000        Y        0X4000000
shmseg                   120              Y        120
```

To query a specific DTKP, such as msgmax, do the following:

```
# kmtune –q  msgmax
Parameter    Current        Dyn     Planned        Module  Version
=================================================================
msgmax       8192           Y       8192
```

To modify the value of "msgmax" from 8192 to 16384 and update the running kernel, execute the *kmtune* command as follows:

kmtune –s msgmax=16384

To confirm the change, do one of the following:

kmtune –u
The kernel's value of msgmax has been set to 16384 (0x4000).
kmtune –q msgmax
Parameter   Current   Dyn   Planned   Module Version
===
msgmax   16384   Y   16384

18.6   Reconfiguring the HP-UX 11iv2 Kernel

At HP-UX 11iv2, a new graphical/textual user interface tool called *kcweb* is introduced. Together with *kcweb*, a new set of kernel configuration commands are introduced. With *kcweb* and the set of commands, you can create multiple kernel configurations with only one active at a time. The active kernel configuration is referred to as *current* configuration while others are referred to as *saved* configurations. All configuration information for the current configuration is located under */stand/current* directory while each saved configuration has a directory corresponding to its name under the */stand* directory. You can have as many kernel configurations generated and saved as you need.

The *kcweb* tool automatically saves running kernel configuration before a change is applied to it and maintains a log of all configuration changes.

Table 18-1 provides a list of tasks that this new tool and the set of commands perform:

Command	Description
kclog	It searches the kernel configuration log file */var/adm/kc.log*.
kcmodule	This command is equivalent to *kmsystem* in HP-UX 11iv1. It allows you to: ✓ List and remove modules ✓ Add a module to the configuration in default state ✓ Add a module to the configuration statically bound into the kernel executable ✓ Add a module to the configuration dynamically loaded now and at each system boot ✓ Add a module to the configuration to be auto-loaded at first use ✓ Remove a module from a configuration ✓ Apply changes to a saved configuration
kconfig	Allows you to: ✓ List, load, rename, or delete a saved configuration ✓ Display changes held for next system boot ✓ Force kernel configuration changes to be held for next system boot ✓ Discard kernel configuration changes waiting for next system boot ✓ Create a saved configuration from the running configuration

kcpath	This command is equivalent to *kmpath* in HP-UX 11iv1. It displays the location of the currently running kernel.
kctune	This command is equivalent to *kmtune* in HP-UX 11iv1. It allows you to: ✓ Display and modify tunable parameters ✓ List tunable parameters in a saved configuration ✓ Apply changes to a saved configuration
kcweb	A kernel configuration and management tool that can be invoked from within SAM, from a browser, or from the command prompt. It supports both graphical and textual interfaces.

Table 18-1 HP-UX 11iv2 Kernel Management Commands

18.6.1   The *kcweb* Tool

The *kcweb* tool runs in both graphical and textual modes. It may be invoked from within SAM, from a browser, or from the command prompt in textual user interface (TUI) mode. This tool allows you to configure and manage the kernel. You can query and change the states of kernel modules in the currently running configuration, determine which modules are currently running, view details about a specific module, modify the state of a module, and so on.

With this tool, you can also perform several tasks on kernel tunable parameters including listing and modifying their values.

To access *kcweb* from a browser, type in the following URL. Do not forget to specify your hostname (replace *hp01* with your hostname).

https://hp01:1188/casey/top.cgi

To invoke *kcweb* from the command prompt, do the following:

```
# kcweb
        Kernel Configuration
-------------------------------------------------------------------------
        Tunables       View or modify kernel tunables
        Modules        View or modify kernel modules and drivers
        Log Viewer     View the changes made to kernel tunables or modules
        Usage/Alarms   View kernel usage or set alarms of kernel tunables



-------------------------------------------------------------------------
    ENTER-Select            ESC-Exit Kernel Configuration tool      1-Help
```

This is the main *kcweb* screen. There are four menu items, as you can see from the above output. "Tunables" enables you to view and modify tunable parameter values, "Modules" allows you to view and modify modules and drivers, "Log Viewer" enables you to view modifications made to tunable parameters and modules, and "Usage/Alarms" lets you view kernel usage and set alarms.

Highlight "Tunables" and you would see a screen similar to the following:

```
                Kernel Configuration->Tunables (All)
-----------------------------------------------------------------------------------------
Tunable                   Current        Planned       Dynamic       Auto Tuning
                          Value          Value
=========================================================================================
NSTREVENT                 50             50            no
NSTRPUSH                  16             16            no
NSTRSCHED                 0              0             no
STRCTLSZ                  1024           1024          no
STRMSGSZ                  0              0             no
acctresume                4              4             no
acctsuspend               2              2             no
aio_listio_max            256            256           yes
aio_max_ops               2048           2048          yes
aio_monitor_run_sec       30             30            yes
aio_physmem_pct           10             10            no
aio_prio_delta_max        20             20            yes
aio_proc_thread_pct       70             70            yes
aio_proc_threads          1024           1024          yes
aio_req_per_thread        1              1             yes
allocate_fs_swapmap       0              0             no
-------------------------------------------------------------------------------------\/
ENTER-Details      m-Modify        d-Dynamic       2-kctune Manpage       /-Search
ESC-Go Up          p-Pending       1-Help          3-Tunable Manpage
```

Highlight a tunable to view its details and press the Enter key. To modify any of the kernel tunable parameter value, simply highlight it, and press "m".

From the main menu, if you wish to view or modify modules, highlight "Modules" and you would see a screen similar to the following:

```
                Kernel Configuration->Modules (All)
-----------------------------------------------------------------------------------------
Module                    Current        Planned       Cause
                          State          State
=========================================================================
DeviceFileSystem          static         static        depend
DlkmDrv                   static         static        required
KeyboardMUX               static         static        depend
LCentlf                   static         static        best
LegacyDeviceDriver        static         static        depend
MouseMUX                  static         static        depend
OOCdio                    static         static        depend
PCItoPCI                  static         static        required
UsbBootKeyboard           static         static        depend
UsbBootMouse              static         static        depend
UsbBulkOnlyMS             static         static        best
UsbEhci                   static         static        best
UsbHid                    static         static        best
UsbMiniBus                static         static        best
```

```
UsbOhci                    static        static        best
UsbScsiAdaptor             static        static        best
-------------------------------------------------------------------------------\/
ENTER-Details    p-Pending      m-Modify      2-kcmodule Manpage
ESC-Go Up        r-Required     1-Help        /-Search
```

Highlight a module to view its details and press the Enter key. To modify any of the modules, simply highlight it, and press "m".

18.7   Common Tunable Parameters

A list of some of the commonly used system tunable parameters is given in Table 18-2:

Parameter	Description
dbc_min_pct	Minimum dynamic buffer cache.
dbc_max_pct	Maximum dynamic buffer cache.
maxvgs	Maximum volume groups that can be created.
maxdsiz	Maximum data segment size of a process being executed.
maxssiz	Maximum stack segment size of a process being executed.
maxtsiz	Maximum shared text segment size of a process being executed.
maxuprc	Maximum per user simultaneous processes.
maxfiles	Maximum files a process can open (soft limit).
maxfiles_lim	Maximum files a process can open (hard limit).
msgmax	Maximum message size.
msgmnb	Maximum bytes on the message queue.
mmni	Number of message queues.
mgseg	Number of segments in message queue.
msgssz	Message segment size.
nbuf	Number of buffer headers.
nfile	Maximum open files at any one time.
nflocks	Number of file / record locks.
ninode	Maximum open inodes.
nproc	Maximum simultaneous processes.
npty	Number of pseudo terminal session device files.
semmni	Number of system-wide semaphores.
shmmax	Maximum shared memory segments in bytes.
shmmni	Maximum shared memory identifiers.
shmseg	Maximum simultaneous shared memory segments attached to a process.

Table 18-2 Common Kernel Tunable Parameters

Summary

This chapter talked about HP-UX kernel reconfiguration. You looked at reasons behind reconfiguring a system's kernel. You learned about static and dynamic kernel modules and tunable parameters.

You developed skills to reconfigure HP-UX 11iv1 and HP-UX 11iv2 kernels using command line and SAM. You understood commands and tools available for that purpose. You learned how to query, load into memory, and unload from memory dynamically loadable kernel modules. Similarly, you learned how to query and modify dynamically tunable kernel parameters. You studied *kcweb* tool that enabled you to perform kernel reconfiguration tasks graphically and via menu driven program.

Finally, you were presented with a short description of some of the common kernel tunable parameters that you might want to adjust for your applications.

HP Certified Systems Administrator

## 19

Performing Backup and Restore

This chapter covers the following major topics:

- ✓ Reasons to perform backups
- ✓ Backup, restore, and recovery definitions
- ✓ Backup types – full, incremental, and differential
- ✓ Backup levels
- ✓ Backup schedule
- ✓ Restore from multi-level backups
- ✓ Understand different tools to perform backups
- ✓ Understand different tools to perform restores
- ✓ Introduction to HP's enterprise backup software – Data Protector

19.1 Basics of Backup

Backing up system and data files is a vital function of system administration. To minimize the chance of a complete data loss, you perform backups and store the backup media at an alternate, secure location geographically distant from the system. The alternate location may be another room, another building, another city, or another site.

In order to save your valuable data on external media, you need to come up with a *backup strategy*. The backup strategy is based on several factors. The following sub-sections shed light on backup and restore functions and some critical backup strategy components.

19.1.1   Backup, Restore, and Recovery Functions

Backup is a function that duplicates files and directories from your hard disk to an alternate media for safety purposes. The alternate media could be a tape drive, or another hard drive on a remote system.

Restore is the opposite function of backup. It retrieves one or more files or directories from the alternate media and places them back to where you want them to be on the hard disk.

A similar function called *Recovery* recovers a crashed system to its previous normal state. It may require you to restore lost data files from alternate media.

19.1.2   Types of Backup

There are three common types of backup performed. These are referred to as *Full*, *Incremental*, and *Differential*.

A *Full* backup copies all selected files and directories and, hence, it is self-contained. This type of backup normally takes the most amount of time to complete. A full backup is usually scheduled to occur every week and once every month.

An *Incremental* backup copies only those files that have been modified since their last full, incremental, or differential backup was done. This type of backup usually takes the least amount of time to complete. An incremental backup is usually scheduled to happen on a daily basis.

A *Differential* backup copies only those files that have been modified since they were last backed up as part of a full backup. This type of backup normally takes less amount of time to complete than an incremental backup and more than a full backup. A differential backup may be scheduled to occur on a daily basis in place of an incremental backup or on a weekly basis in place of a full backup. In this situation, you will need to run your full backups once per month.

19.1.3   Levels of Backup

There are certain pre-defined backup levels that you can use for your backups. In fact, employing these backup levels, you make your backups full, incremental, or differential. These levels are relative to one another. There are 10 such levels listed in Table 19-1.

Backup Level	Description
0	Corresponds to a full backup of selected files and directories. This is the default level.
1	Corresponds to an incremental or differential backup since the last level 0 backup occurred.
2	Represents an incremental backup since the last level 1 backup performed and corresponds to a differential backup since the last level 0 backup occurred.
3	Represents an incremental backup since the last level 2 backup performed and corresponds to a differential backup since the last level 0 backup occurred.
4	Represents an incremental backup since the last level 3 backup performed and corresponds to a differential backup since the last level 0 backup occurred.
5 – 9	Follow the same rule as above for all subsequent backup levels.

Table 19-1 Backup Levels

19.1.4   Sample Backup Schedule

Suppose that you want to setup a backup schedule for a file system */opt/oracle* with following scheduling requirements:

- ✓ A monthly full backup on the first Sunday of each month.
- ✓ A weekly differential backup on each Sunday other than the first Sunday of each month.
- ✓ A daily incremental backup, except on Sundays, to backup all files and directories that have changed since the last incremental or differential backup, whichever is more recent, performed.

To setup a backup schedule to meet above requirements, you can use level 0 to represent a full backup, level 1 to correspond to a differential backup, and level 2 to represent an incremental backup. The following displays the schedule for five weeks to accomplish above requirements:

```
Date:  1 2 3 4  5 6 7 8 9 10 11 12 13 14 15 16 17 18 19 20 21 22 23 24 25 26 27 28 29 30 1 2  3 4 5 6
Day:   s m t w t f s s m t  w  t  f  s  s  m  t  w  t  f  s  s  m  t  w  t  f  s  s  m t w t f s s
Level: 0 2 2 2 2 2 1 2 2 2  2  2  2  1  2  2  2  2  2  2  1  2  2  2  2  2  2  1  2  2 2 2 2 2 2 0
```

19.1.5   Restore Procedure for the Sample Backup

From restore perspective, if your data becomes corrupted on Wednesday the 18th before the Wednesday backup is commenced, you will need to perform restores in the following sequence to get your data back to the Tuesday the 17th state:

- ✓ Restore the full backup from Sunday the 1st.
- ✓ Restore the differential backup from Sunday the 15th.
- ✓ Restore the incremental backup from Monday the 16th.
- ✓ Restore the incremental backup from Tuesday the 17th.

This will bring the data in */opt/oracle* file system to the state where it was on Tuesday the 17th.

19.2 Managing Backups and Restores

There are many tools available in HP-UX that you can use to do backups and restores of your files and directories. These tools include *fbackup/frecover*, *dump/restore*, *vxdump/vxrestore*, *tar*, *cpio*, and *dd*. The following sub-sections discuss the tools in detail.

19.2.1 Performing Backups Using *fbackup*

The *fbackup* command is the HP-UX specific native tool for performing full, incremental, and differential backups.

Some essential options *fbackup* takes are listed in Table 19-2.

Option	Description
–f	Specifies the device to be used to do a backup. There is no default tape device for *fbackup*.
[0 – 9]	Defines full, incremental, and differential backups.
–u	Updates */var/adm/fbackupfiles/dates* file at successful completion of a backup. Information written in this file includes start and end backup times, level of backup, and name of the graph file used.
–i	Includes specified files and directories in a backup.
–e	Excludes specified files and directories from a backup.
–g	Specifies name of the file, called *graph* file that contains a list of files and directories to be included in or excluded from a backup. A graph file can be used instead of –i and –e options. Each line in a graph file starts either with an "i" for include or an "e" for exclude followed by a file or directory name.
–I	Specifies name of a file to write index information.
–v	Displays verbose information.

Table 19-2 *fbackup* Command Options

Let us look at a few examples to understand the working of *fbackup*.

To perform a level 0 backup of */home* directory to the tape device at */dev/rmt/0m* and write an index of the files being backed up to */tmp/index.home*, do the following:

 # fbackup –f /dev/rmt/0m –i /home –I /tmp/index.home
fbackup(1004): session begins on Mon May 29 12:44:11 2006
fbackup(3203): volume 1 has been used 2 time(s)
fbackup(3024): writing volume 1 to the output file /dev/rmt/0m
fbackup(3055): total file blocks read for backup: 1239
fbackup(3056): total blocks written to output file /dev/rmt/0m: 1589

To perform a level 0 backup of root (/) directory to the tape device at */dev/rmt/0m* on the first Sunday of a month based on the given graph file contents (include /, exclude */var/adm/crash* and

/tmp), write an entry to */var/adm/fbackupfiles/dates* file and generate an index of the files in */tmp/index.full*, do the following:

i /
e /var/adm/crash
e /tmp

fbackup –f /dev/rmt/0m –u0g graph –I /tmp/index.full

To perform an incremental backup of the files and directories the next six days (Monday to Saturday) based on the contents in the graph file mentioned above, update the */var/adm/fbackupfiles/dates* file, and create an index file */tmp/index.incremental*, do the following:

fbackup –f /dev/rmt/0m –u2g graph –I /tmp/index.incremental

To perform a differential backup of the files and directories on the following Sunday based on the contents in the graph file mentioned above, update the */var/adm/fbackupfiles/dates* file, use tape drive at */dev/rmt/1m,* and create an index file */tmp/index.differential*, do the following:

fbackup –f /dev/rmt/1m –u1g graph –I /tmp/index.differential

To do the same level 0 backup (from above) over the network on another machine's tape device at */dev/rmt/2m*. Suppose the remote machine is *hp02* and you are on *hp01*. The index file */tmp/index.full* will be created on *hp01*.

fbackup –f hp02:/dev/rmt/2m –u0g graph –I /tmp/index.full

19.2.2   Performing Restores Using *frecover*

The *frecover* command is the HP-UX specific native tool for performing restores done using *fbackup*.

Some important options *frecover* takes are listed in Table 19-3.

Option	Description
–f	Specifies the device to be used to do a restore. The default is */dev/rmt/0m*.
–g	Specifies name of a file that contains a list of files and directories to be included in or excluded from a restore.
–r	Restores an entire backup. This is default.
–x	Restores selected files and directories only.
–v	Displays verbose information.
–F	Ignores leading directories from the path names of files being restored, hence, if you restore */usr/bin/cat* in */root* directory, the result would be */root/cat*.
–I	Specifies name of a file to write index information.

Table 19-3 *frecover* Command Options

Let us look at a few examples to understand the working of *frecover*.

To restore all files from the default tape device */dev/rmt/0m* and display details, do the following:

> **# frecover –rv**

To extract only */home* from a full backup using tape device at */dev/rmt/1m*, do the following:

> **# frecover –f /dev/rmt/1m –i /home –xv**

To do the same restore (from above) over the network from another machine's tape device at */dev/rmt/2m*. Suppose the remote machine is *hp02* and you are on *hp01*.

> **# frecover –f hp02:/dev/rmt/2m –rv**

19.2.3   *fbackup* and *frecover* via SAM

SAM provides backup and restore functionalities by calling *fbackup* and *frecover* commands in the background. Follow the steps below:

☞ Go to SAM → Backup and Recovery → Automated Backups if you wish to schedule backups to be run at specified date and time for selected files, directories, and file systems on local or remote tape devices. See Figure 19-1.

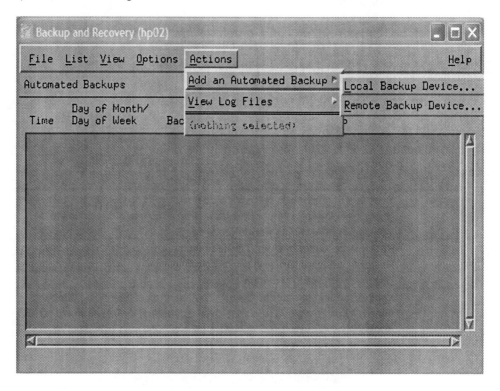

Figure 19-1 SAM – Automated Backups

☞Go to SAM → Backup and Recovery → Interactive Backup and Recovery to perform backups and restores interactively from local or remote tape devices. See Figure 19-2.

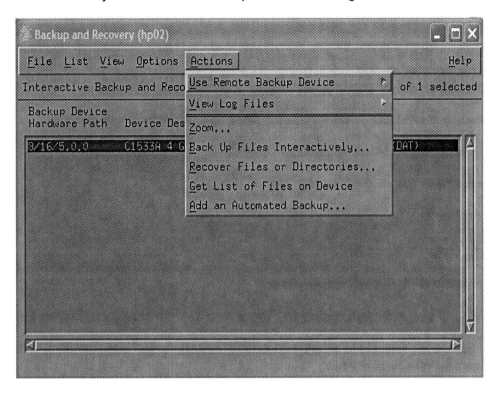

Figure 19-2 SAM – Interactive Backup and Restore

19.2.4 Performing Backups/Restores Using *dump/restore*

These tools work similar to the way *fbackup* and *frecover* work with two major differences. One, these tools work at the file system level and not on individual files and directories, and two, they can backup and restore only an HFS file system. Both tools support multi-level backups, store time stamp information in */var/adm/dumpdates* file, and use various levels of backups described earlier in the chapter.

Let us look at a couple of examples.

To do a level 0 backup of the */stand* file system to the default tape device at */dev/rmt/0m* and update the */var/adm/dumpdates* file, issue the following:

dump 0u /stand
    DUMP: Date of this level 0 dump: Mon May 29 14:38:46 2006
    DUMP: Date of last level 0 dump: the epoch
    DUMP: Dumping /dev/vg00/rlvol1 (/stand) to /dev/rmt/0m
    DUMP: This is an HP long file name filesystem
    DUMP: mapping (Pass I) [regular files]
    DUMP: mapping (Pass II) [directories]

DUMP: estimated 58029 tape blocks on 1.49 tape(s).
DUMP: dumping (Pass III) [directories]
DUMP: dumping (Pass IV) [regular files]
DUMP: DUMP: 58612 tape blocks on 1 tape(s)

DUMP: DUMP: /dev/vg00/rlvol1 has 0 inodes with unsaved optional acl entries
DUMP: DUMP IS DONE
DUMP: Date of completion of this level 0 dump: Mon May 29 14:40:30 2006

The */var/adm/dumpdates* file will contain the following after the backup is complete:

/dev/vg00/rlvol1 0 Mon May 29 14:38:46 2006

To restore the above, do the following:

restore r

> You can use the same syntax to backup to or restore from a tape device connected to a remote system as was demonstrated with *fbackup* and *frecover* previously.

19.2.5   Performing Backups/Restores Using *vxdump/vxrestore*

These tools work identically as *dump* and *restore* but backs up and restores only JFS file systems. Here are a couple of examples.

To do a level 0 backup of the */opt* file system to a non-default tape device at */dev/rmt/1m* and update the */var/adm/dumpdates* file, run the following:

vxdump 0uf /dev/rmt/1m /home
vxfs vxdump: Date of this level 0 dump: Mon May 29 14:44:59 2006
vxfs vxdump: Date of last level 0 dump: the epoch
vxfs vxdump: Dumping /dev/vg00/rlvol5 (/home) to /dev/rmt/1m
vxfs vxdump: mapping (Pass I) [regular files]
vxfs vxdump: mapping (Pass II) [directories]
vxfs vxdump: estimated 1456 blocks (728KB).
vxfs vxdump: dumping (Pass III) [directories]
vxfs vxdump: dumping (Pass IV) [regular files]
vxfs vxdump: vxdump: 970 tape blocks on 1 volumes(s)
vxfs vxdump: level 0 dump on Mon May 29 14:44:59 2006
vxfs vxdump: Closing /dev/rmt/1m
vxfs vxdump: vxdump is done

To restore the above from the same tape device, do the following:

vxrestore r /dev/rmt/1m

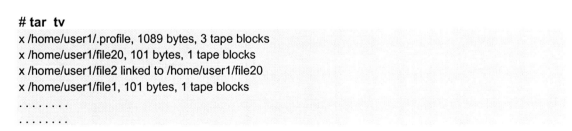You can use the same syntax to backup to and restore from a tape device connected to a remote system as was demonstrated with *fbackup* and *frecover* previously.

19.2.6   Using *tar*

The *tar (tape archive)* command archives, lists, and extracts files to and from a single file called a *tar* file. A tar file can be created as a regular file on disk or tape.

Certain switches used with *tar* are summarized in Table 19-4.

Switch	Definition
c	Creates a backup.
t	Lists backup contents.
x	Extracts from a backup.
f	Specifies backup destination.
v	Verbose mode.

Table 19-4 *tar* Command Options

A few examples follow to explain how *tar* works.

To create an archive on default tape device at */dev/rmt/0m* of the */home* directory, execute the following:

```
# tar  cv  /home
a /home/user1/.profile 3 blocks
a /home/user1/file20 1 blocks
a /home/user1/file2 link to /home/user1/file20
a /home/user1/file1 1 blocks
. . . . . . . .
. . . . . . . .
```

To create a single archive file called */tmp/files.tar* containing files – *file1*, *file2*, *file3*, and *file4* – use the following:

```
# tar  cvf  /tmp/files.tar  file1  file2  file3  file4
```

To view contents of files in the default tape device, execute the following. Note that *tar* automatically uses the default tape device.

```
# tar  tv
x /home/user1/.profile, 1089 bytes, 3 tape blocks
x /home/user1/file20, 101 bytes, 1 tape blocks
x /home/user1/file2 linked to /home/user1/file20
x /home/user1/file1, 101 bytes, 1 tape blocks
. . . . . . . .
. . . . . . . .
```

To view contents of the archive file, *files.tar*, execute the following:

 # tar tvf /tmp/files.tar

To restore */home* directory from the default tape device, do the following:

 # tar xv

To extract files from */tmp/files.tar*, execute the following:

 # tar xvf /tmp/files.tar

19.2.7   Using *cpio*

The *cpio* (**c**opy **i**n/**o**ut) command archives, lists, and extracts files to and from a tape or single file. The *cpio* command packs data more efficiently than *tar* does.

Certain options available with *cpio* are summarized in Table 19-5. The *cpio* command requires that o, i, or p option be specified.

Option	Description
o	Creates a backup.
i	Extracts from a backup.
c	Reads or writes header information in ASCII format.
t	Lists backup contents.
v	Verbose mode.
p	Reads from backup to get pathnames.
a	Resets access times of files after they are copied.

Table 19-5 *cpio* Command Options

Here are a few examples to explain the usage.

To archive current directory contents and copy them to the */dev/rmt/0m* tape device:

 # find . | cpio –ocv > /dev/rmt/0m
(Using tape drive with immediate report mode enabled (reel #1).)

.
lost+found
ids
user1
user1/.profile
user1/file20
user1/file2
user1/file1
user1/file4
. . . .
. . . .

To archive only those files in the current directory that have changed within the last week and copy them to a file called */tmp/mod.cpio*:

```
# find  .  –mtime –7  |  cpio  –ocv  >  /tmp/mod.cpio
```

To list the two archive files created:

```
# cpio  –itvc  <  /dev/rmt/0m
# cpio  –itvc  <  /tmp/mod.cpio
```

To restore files from */tmp/mod.cpio:*

```
# cpio  –ivc  <  /tmp/mod.cpio
```

19.2.8   Using *dd*

The *dd* command performs a bit for bit duplication. This command is useful in some limited situations and is technically not a backup command. Here is how it works:

To duplicate everything that resides under *lvol1* in *vg00* to *lvol1* in *vg01*, do the following:

```
# dd  if=/dev/vg00/lvol1  of=/dev/vg01/lvol1
112373+0 records in
112372+0 records out
```

where:

   "if" stands for input file and "of" for output file.

 The destination *lvol1* in *vg01* must be either of the same size as *lvol1* in *vg00* or larger.

19.3   Introduction to HP Data Protector Software

HP Data Protector software is an enterprise client/server backup and restore management software product that offers advantages unavailable to any of the tools discussed thus far. Some of the key benefits the Data Protector software offers are listed below:

   ✓ High-performance automated backup on tape or disk.
   ✓ High-performance automated restore from tape or disk.
   ✓ Centralize backup and restore management for hundreds of client systems from a single server.
   ✓ Supports backing up multi-vendor hardware and heterogeneous operating system platforms including UNIX, Linux, Windows, NetWare, and other operating systems.
   ✓ Supports online backup of Oracle, Informix, Sybase, MS Exchange, MS SQL, SAP, and so on.
   ✓ Supports backing up open files.
   ✓ Supports local and remote replication of data with zero downtime.

A detailed coverage on Data Protector software is beyond the scope of this book.

Summary

In this chapter, you learned reasons to perform backups of your system and data files. You learned definitions of backup, restore, and recovery functions. You saw types of backup, such as full, incremental, and differential that were based on backup levels you defined when setting up or running a backup.

You looked at various tools, such as *fbackup/frestore*, *dump/restore*, *vxdump/vxrestore*, *tar*, *cpio*, and *dd*. You used these tools to perform data backups and restores.

At the end of the chapter, you were presented with introduction to HP's enterprise data backup and restore software called Data Protector. You looked at the benefits that this software offered.

## 20

Print Services Management

This chapter covers the following major topics:

✓ Print spooler concepts and directory tree
✓ Local and remote printing daemons
✓ Types of printer setups – local, remote, and network
✓ Why define printer classes
✓ Setup local, remote, and network printers
✓ Administer printers – configure default print destination, enable and disable a printer, allow and disallow users to submit print requests, check printer status, modify a printer priority, modify a printer's fence level, and remove a printer.
✓ Administer print requests – submit, list, modify, move, and cancel a print request

20.1 Understanding Print Spooler

The HP-UX *Line Printer* (LP) spooler sub-system is a set of utilities to:

- ✓ Setup, modify, and remove printers.
- ✓ Manage user print requests.

The print spooler sub-system is based on client/server architecture where a print client sends a file to a print server for printing. The print client is typically the *lp* or the *lpr* command that submits a file to the print server. The print server is the print scheduler daemon called *lpsched*.

When a print request comes in from a local system user, *lpsched* takes care of it until it is printed on the specified printer. This daemon is automatically started at boot time by */sbin/rc2.d/S720lp* script or when a system enters the run level 2.

When a print request comes in over the network from a remote system user, a master internet services daemon called *inetd* intercepts it. This daemon consults its configuration file */etc/inetd.conf* and starts the remote print daemon called *rlpdaemon* and hooks the client request up with it. This daemon then accepts or rejects the incoming remote print request. If the print request is accepted, it is passed to the *lpsched* daemon, which gets the print request printed; otherwise, the request is rejected.

20.1.1 Print Spooler Directory Hierarchy

The print spooler directory hierarchy comprises of two types of files: *static* and *dynamic*. Static files reside in */etc* and */usr* directories and include configuration files, commands, interface scripts, model scripts, etc. Dynamic files reside in */var* directory and include printer status files, log files, and so on. The dynamic directory structure also holds print requests temporarily in a printer spool directory before they are sent to a printer for printing.

Table 20-1 lists and explains some important directories pertaining to the printing sub-system.

Directory	Purpose
Static Files	
/etc/lp	Parent directory for all printer-related configuration.
/etc/lp/class	Contains information that tells which printers belong to which printer classes.
/etc/lp/interface	Contains one file per configured printer that includes interface program to be used for the printer.
/etc/lp/member	Contains one file per configured printer that includes printer port/device file information.
/usr/lib/lp/model	Contains scripts for various printer models. Copied to */etc/lp/interface* and renamed to match the printer name at the time of printer setup.
/usr/lib/lp/fonts	Contains printer fonts.
/usr/bin	Contains user-specific print commands, such as *lp*, *lpalt*, *lpstat*, *cancel*, *enable*, and *disable*.

/usr/sbin	Contains superuser-specific print administration commands, such as *lpadmin*, *lpsched*, *lpshut*, *lpana*, *lpmove*, *lpfence*, *accept*, and *reject*.
Dynamic Files	
/var/spool/lp	Parent directory for LP spooler. Information about printer status, print requests, etc. is located here.
/var/spool/lp/request	Print requests are temporarily held here before being sent to a printer for printing.
/var/adm/lp	Contains print spooler log files.

Table 20-1 Print Spooler Directory Hierarchy

20.1.2   Starting and Stopping Print Spooler Daemon

The *lpsched* daemon is started by the *lpsched* command and stopped by the *lpshut* command. The daemon is started automatically at system boot up or when a system changes to run level 2.

If you wish to manually start the daemon, do one of the following:

> **# /sbin/init.d/lp start**
> scheduler is running
> line printer scheduler started
> **# lpsched**
> scheduler is running

Similarly, to stop the daemon manually, you can do either of the following:

> **# /sbin/init.d/lp stop**
> line printer scheduler stopped
> **# lpshut**
> scheduler stopped

To do the above using SAM, follow the steps below:

☞ Go to SAM → Printers and Plotters → LP spooler → Printers and Plotters → Actions → Stop (or Start) Print Spooler.

Sometimes you try to start or stop the scheduler daemon and it does not come up or go down. For the startup problem, check if */var/spool/lp/SCHEDLOCK* file exists. If it does, remove it, and then retry starting the scheduler. For the stop problem, terminate the *lpsched* process by specifying its PID with the *kill* command, and then retry stopping it.

20.2 Types of Printer Setups

Printers are normally setup in three ways, referred to as *local*, *remote*, and *network* printer setups. Figure 20-1 demonstrates four systems (*hp01*, *hp02*, *hp03*, and *hp04*) and one printer (*prn2*)

---

connected on the network. There is another printer (*prn1*) shown, which is connected directly to *hp01* machine.

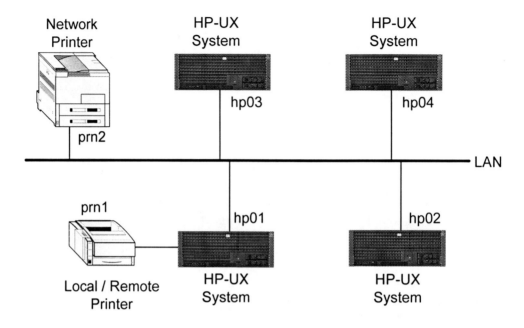

Figure 20-1 Types of Printer Setups

20.2.1 Local Printer

A printer attached physically to a system's parallel or serial port and accessed by users of that system only is called a *local* printer. In Figure 20-1, *prn1* is shown physically connected to *hp01* and acts as a local printer to users on *hp01* system.

When a print request is submitted by a user on *hp01* using the *lp* or *lpr* command to print to *prn1*, the request goes to the print scheduler daemon, *lpsched*, and a unique print request ID is generated and assigned to it. The *lpsched* daemon uses the interface program defined for the printer, spools the request in */var/spool/lp/request* directory, and, finally, forwards the request to *prn1* to get it printed.

20.2.2 Remote Printer

A local printer acts as a *remote* printer to users on remote systems. In Figure 20-1, *prn1* acts as a remote printer to *hp02*, *hp03*, and *hp04* users. The system that has the local printer connected, must have a daemon called, *rlpdaemon,* enabled through *inetd* in order for it to receive and process remote print requests. In Figure 20-1, *hp01* must have this daemon enabled.

When a print request is submitted by a user on *hp03*, for example, using *lp* or *lpr* command to print to the remote printer *prn1*, the request goes directly to the *inetd* daemon running on *hp01*, which looks into its configuration file */etc/inetd.conf* to figure out if the remote printing daemon service, *rlpdaemon*, is enabled. If it is, *inetd* starts it up and establishes a connection between the client print request and this daemon. The *rlpdaemon* daemon then forwards the request to the local *lpsched* daemon and a unique print request ID is generated and assigned to it. The *lpsched* daemon on *hp01* uses the interface program defined for the printer, spools the request in */var/spool/lp/request* directory, and, finally, forwards the print request to *prn1* to get it printed.

20.2.3   Network Printer

A *network* printer has a network card installed and is physically connected to a network port. It has its own hostname and IP address. It is configured on an HP-UX system after which it becomes accessible by users. A software program called *JetDirect **HP Printer Installer*** (hppi) or the *addqueue* command is typically used on HP-UX to configure a network printer.

In Figure 20-1, *prn2* is a network printer and is accessible by users of all four systems.

20.3   Setting Up Printers

To setup local, remote, and network printers on HP-UX systems, some printer attributes are needed. Table 20-2 lists various attributes required by local, remote, and/or network printer setups. Note that not all attributes are required by all types of setups.

Attribute	Description	Which Setup Needs It
Printer name	A unique name with up to 14 alphanumeric characters.	Local, remote, network
Printer model/interface	Each printer has an interface model script defined that enables the print spooler to access special features of the printer. These scripts are located in */usr/lib/lp/model*.	Local, network
Printer class	A group of similar printers combined to form a single print destination for increased availability and utilization. When a print request is sent to a class of printers, the first available printer in the class prints it. A class name can include up to 14 alphanumeric characters.	Local, network
IP Address	A unique IP address of the printer.	Network
Default request priority	Default priority level. Any print request submitted to a printer uses this priority level, unless it is explicitly set to a different value using –p option with the *lp* command. Priorities range between 0 and 7 with 0 being the lowest.	Local, remote, network
Default destination	All print requests sent by the *lp* command without –d option are sent to default printer, unless LPDEST variable is set in user's shell environment.	Local, remote, network
Remote system name	Remote system name where a printer is physically connected.	Remote
Remote printer name	Printer name on the remote machine.	Remote

BSD system	Check mark if both print client and print server are HP-UX machines.	Remote
Remote cancel model	Interface program to cancel print requests on a remote system. Use "rcmodel" for remote printers.	Remote
Remote status model	Interface program to obtain status of print requests on a remote system. Use "rsmodel" for remote printers.	Remote
Allow anyone to cancel	Say "yes" if you wish users to cancel other users' print requests. Say "no" if you wish otherwise.	Remote

Table 20-2 Printer Setup Attributes

20.3.1 Setting Up a Local Printer

Let us setup a local printer, *prn1*, on *hp01*, with "laserjet" printer model, default priority, default fence level, and */dev/c3t0d0_lp* as the parallel port device file. Use the *lpadmin* command as follows:

 # lpadmin –pprn1 –v/dev/c3t0d0_lp –mlaserjet

Create a printer class "prn_class" on *hp01* and define and add to it another local printer, *prn3*, with "laserjet" printer model, default priority, default fence level, and */dev/c4t0d0_lp* as the parallel port device file. Use the *lpadmin* command as follows:

 # lpadmin –pprn3 –v/dev/c4t0d0_lp –cprn_class –mlaserjet

Now add *prn1* to *prn_class*:

 # lpadmin –pprn1 –cprn_class

To do the above using SAM, follow the steps below:

☞Go to SAM → Printers and Plotters → LP spooler → Printers and Plotters → Actions → Add Local Printer/Plotter. See Figure 20-2.

SAM presents a list of types of local printers to choose from including parallel and serial. SAM scans for appropriate available devices. You need to highlight the device file you wish to use and press OK. SAM then displays a form to setup a printer. Fill out the form using attributes listed in Table 20-2. Press OK when done. SAM shuts the *lpsched* daemon down and restarts it to complete the printer setup process.

Anytime a printer is configured, SAM stops and restarts the *lpsched* daemon. This causes all print jobs currently being scheduled for printing to restart from the beginning.

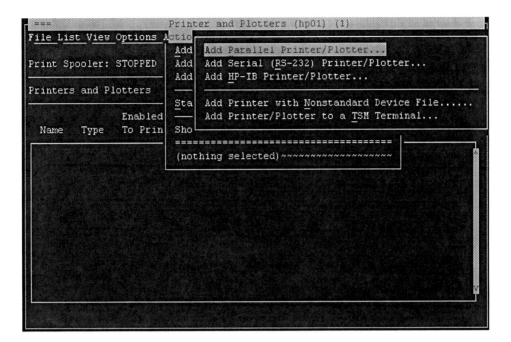

Figure 20-2 SAM – Add Local Printer

20.3.2 Setting Up a Remote Printer

A remote printer is a printer that has already been configured on another system as a local printer. A remote printer is only defined on remote machines that wish to access that printer.

To add access to *prn1* on *hp01* from another HP-UX system, run the following on that system. Assign the printer a name, *prn1* (for example), same as on *hp01*, and specify remote model, remote cancel model, and remote printer status access model.

    # lpadmin –pprn1 –v/dev/null –mrmodel –ocmrcmodel –osmrsmodel –ormhp01 \
    –orpprn1 –v/dev/null

To do the above using SAM, follow the steps below:

☞ Go to SAM → Printers and Plotters → LP spooler → Printers and Plotters → Actions → Add Remote Printer/Plotter. SAM presents you with a form as shown in Figure 20-3. Fill out the form with attributes outline in Table 20-2 and hit the OK button.

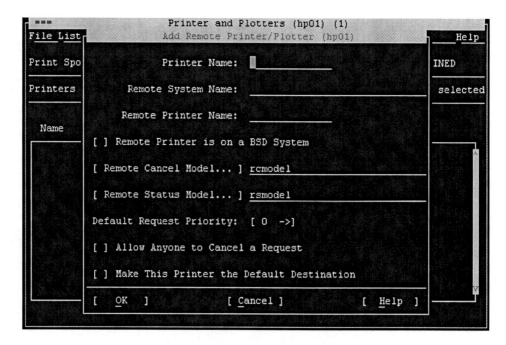

Figure 20-3 SAM – Add Remote Printer

20.3.3   Setting Up a Network Printer

To setup a network printer on HP-UX, you need to have JetDirect HP Printer Installer (hppi) software loaded on the system. You require a hostname and an IP address in addition to other attributes listed in Table 20-2. Use the *hppi* command to setup *prn2* network printer.

 # /opt/hpnpl/bin/hppi

```
********************************************************************
*****]        ****
**** ]        ****    JetDirect Printer Installer for UNIX
**** ]]]]] ]]]]] ****    Version E.10.34
**** ]  ]]  ] ****
**** ]  ] ]]]] ****    M A I N    M E N U
*****      ]      ****
******    ]    ****    User: (root)    OS: (HP-UX B.11.11)
   I N V E N T
********************************************************************


1) Spooler Administration (super-user only)
2) JetDirect Configuration (super-user only)
   - TCP/IP configurable parameters
3) Diagnostics:
   - diagnose printing problems


        ?) Help        q) Quit
```

Select option #1 to go to Spooler Administration.

```
Please enter a selection (q - quit): 1
        ******************************************************************

        *****]        ****
        **** ]        ****     JetDirect Printer Installer for UNIX
        **** ]]]]] ]]]]] ****  Version E.10.34
        **** ] ]] ] ****
        **** ] ] ]]]] ****     Spooler Administration
        *****    ]    ****
        ******   ]   ****      User: (root)   OS: (HP-UX B.11.11)
           I N V E N T
        ******************************************************************


        Spooler:
           1) Add printer to local spooler
           2) Delete printer from local spooler
           3) Modify existing spooler queue(s)
           4) Install New Model Script
           5) Remove Model Script

              ?) Help          q) Quit
```

Select option #1 to add printer to local spooler. You will be prompted to enter hostname or IP address of the printer. Note that if you specify a hostname, it should have already been defined in the /etc/hosts file. Next, a list of various printer models appear. Choose the one that fits your needs.

Finally, you will be presented with a list of suggested parameter values. If you are satisfied, press "0" to complete the procedure.

```
    The following is a list of suggested parameter values for this queue. You
    may change any settings by selecting the corresponding non-zero numbers.
    The values will be used to configure this queue when '0' is selected.
    To abort the operation, press 'q'.

    Configurable Parameters:            Current Settings
    -------------------------------     --------------------
    1) Lp destination (queue) name:     [prn2_1]
    2) Status Log                       [(No Log)]
    3) Queue Class                      [(Not assigned)]
    4) Default Queue                    [NO]
    5) Additional printer configuration...

Select an item for change, or '0' to configure (q - quit): 0

Ready to shut down the spooler and configure the new print queue.
The spooler will be running again after the configuration is done.
```

WARNING: If there are jobs currently being printed, and the page count is enabled (i.e. when True End-of-Job is turned on), this shutdown and rerun of the spooler may result in incorrect page count.

OK to continue? (y/n/q, default=y) **y**

......

Finished adding "prn2" to the spooler.

 The *lpsched* daemon is stopped and restarted to complete the network printer add process.

You can use the *addqueue* command as well to define a network printer. Suppose you wish to define a network printer called *prn4* with IP address *192.168.1.250.* Here is how you would do it with the *addqueue* command:

> **# addqueue –h 192.168.1.250 –q prn4**

To do a network printer setup using SAM, follow the steps below:

☞ Go to SAM → Printers and Plotters → LP spooler → Printers and Plotters → Actions → Add Network-Based Printer/Plotter → Add Printer/Plotter Connected to HP JetDirect. SAM will now execute the */opt/hpnpl/bin/hppi* command. Supply the required information.

20.4   Administering Printers

Administering printers include performing tasks, such as setting default print destination, enabling and disabling a printer, making a printer accept or reject print requests, checking printer status, setting printer priority, modifying printer fence level, and removing a printer. The following sub-sections elaborate these tasks.

20.4.1   Setting Default Print Destination

A printer, or a printer class, can be defined as the default print destination for all user print requests. Here is how to do it.

To make *prn1* the default printer, use the –d option with the *lpadmin* command.

> **# lpadmin –dprn1**

To make *prn_class* the default print destination, use the –d option with the *lpadmin* command.

> **# lpadmin –dprn_class**

To view current default print destination setting.

> **# lpadmin –d**

To do this using SAM, follow the steps below:

☞ Go to SAM → Printers and Plotters → LP spooler → Printers and Plotters. A list of existing printers is displayed. Highlight a printer and go to Actions → Set as System Default Destination. Press the OK button to complete the task.

20.4.2 Enabling and Disabling a Printer

A printer must be activated before it can print. The *enable* command activates the specified printer and enables it to print requests. The *disable* command deactivates the specified printer and disables it from printing requests.

To enable *prn1*, do the following:

> # **enable prn1**
> printer "prn1" now enabled

To disable *prn1*, do the following:

> # **disable prn1**
> printer "prn1" now disabled

To disable *prn1* and specify a reason for disabling it, use the –r option with the *disable* command. The specified reason will be displayed on the user terminal, when he or she tries to submit a print request to it.

> # **disable –r "prn1 is disabled for maintenance for 1 hour" prn1**

To do the above using SAM, follow the steps below:

☞ Go to SAM → Printers and Plotters → LP spooler → Printers and Plotters. A list of existing printers is displayed. Highlight a printer and go to Actions → Enable (or Disable).

20.4.3 Accepting and Rejecting Print Requests

A printer must be accepting requests in its queue before it can actually print them. The *accept* command allows user print requests to be queued for printing. The *reject* command denies queuing user print requests.

To accept user print requests in *prn1* or *prn_class* queue:

> # **accept prn1**
> destination "prn1" now accepting requests
> # **accept prn_class**
> destination "prn_class" now accepting requests

To reject user print requests from being queued in *prn1* and *prn_class*:

> # **reject –r "prn1 is down for 15 minutes for toner replacement" prn1**
> destination "prn1" will no longer accept requests

 # reject prn_class
destination "prn_class" will no longer accept requests

The –r option allows you to specify some text to explain a reason for rejecting user requests. This text is displayed on the user terminal, when he or she attempts to send a print request to *prn1*.

To do the above using SAM, follow the steps below:

☞ Go to SAM → Printers and Plotters → LP spooler → Printers and Plotters. A list of existing printers and printer classes is displayed. Highlight a printer or printer class and go to Actions → Accept (or Reject) Requests.

20.4.4   Checking Printer Status

To check the status of printers and user print requests, use the *lpstat* command. Several options are available to it. Some of the more commonly used options are listed in Table 20-3.

Option	Description
–a	Displays accept/reject status.
–d	Displays default destination printer or printer class.
–o	Displays queued print requests only.
–p	Displays enable/disable status.
–r	Displays scheduler status.
–s	Displays summary information.
–t	Displays detailed information about all configured printers and all queued requests.
–v	Displays printer device file.

Table 20-3 *lpstat* Command Options

 # lpstat –t
scheduler is running
system default destination: prn1
device for prn1: /dev/c3t0d0_lp
prn1 accepting requests since Feb 3 13:10
printer prn1 enabled since Feb 3 16:16 -
fence priority : 0

20.4.5   Setting Printer Priority

Priorities are set for both printers and user print requests. A printer priority is set when a printer is setup and can be altered later. If a priority is not specified when issuing the *lp* or *lpr* command, the request is sent with the printer's default priority, which is 0.

To change a printer's priority to 5, for instance, you must first stop the *lpsched* daemon and then make the modification using the *lpadmin* command. Do as follows:

```
# lpadmin  –pprn1  –g5
```

20.4.6   Setting Printer Fence Level

A printer's fence level defines the minimum required priority for a submitted print request to be printed. The fence level is configured with the *lpfence* command or SAM. A print request with a priority lower than the printer's fence level will sit in the printer's queue forever until either the print request's priority is raised or the fence level is lowered.

To increase a printer's fence level to 4, run the *lpfence* command as follows:

```
# lpfence  prn1  5
```

To reset it to default:

```
# lpfence  prn1  0
```

The *lpalt* command can be issued by ordinary users as well, while the *lpfence* command requires root privileges.

To modify fence level using SAM, follow the steps below:

☞Go to SAM → Printers and Plotters → LP spooler → Printers and Plotters. A list of existing printers is displayed. Highlight the printer and then go to Actions → Modify Fence Priority. Specify the fence priority and hit the OK key.

20.4.7   Removing a Printer

To remove a printer, *prn1*, use the *lpadmin* command with –x option. Make sure to execute the *reject* and *disable* commands on the printer before removing it. Follow the steps below:

```
# reject  prn1
# disable  prn1
# lpadmin  –xprn1
```

To do the above using SAM, follow the steps below:

☞Go to SAM → Printers and Plotters → LP spooler → Printers and Plotters. A list of existing printers is displayed. Highlight a printer and go to Actions → Remove.

20.5 Administering Print Requests

Administering print requests involve submitting, listing, modifying, moving, and canceling a print request. The following sub-sections describe these tasks.

20.5.1   Submitting a Print Request

To submit a print request to a printer or printer class, use the *lp* command. The *lp* command supports several options. Some of the options are captured in Table 20-4.

Option	Description
–c	Copies the specified file to the spool directory and then sends it to a printer or printer class for printing.
–d	Sends a print request to the specified destination printer.
–m	Notifies the user by sending a mail, when a print request submitted by that user is finished printing.
–n	Defines number of copies to print.
–p	Denotes a priority for the print request.
–t	Specifies a title to be printed on the first page. By default, username is printed.
–w	Writes a message to the user's terminal, when the print request is finished. If the user is logged off, a mail is sent to him/her.

Table 20-4 *lp* Command Options

Let us take a look at some examples.

To print */etc/group* file on the default printer, *prn1*, do the following:

> # **lp /etc/group**
> request id is prn1-0

The output indicates that this (prn1-0) is the first print request submitted to this printer.

To print */etc/passwd* file on a non-default printer, *prn2*, do the following:

> # **lp –dprn2 /etc/passwd**
> request id is prn2-0

To submit */etc/passwd* file to *prn_class*, do the following:

> # **lp –dprn_class /etc/passwd**
> request id is prn_class-0

All print requests are queued in their destination printer's spool directory in priority order. A print request with a higher priority gets printed before a lower priority print request is printed. If two requests have an identical priority, both are printed in the order in which they are submitted. For example:

To send */etc/group* to *prn2* and *prn_class* at priority 5:

> # **lp –p5 –dprn2 /etc/group**
> # **lp –p5 –dprn_class /etc/group**

To raise the priority of a submitted print request, such as prn2–2 or prn_class–2, to 5, use the *lpalt* command as follows:

```
# lpalt  prn2–2  –p5
# lpalt  prn_class–2  –p5
```

20.5.2   Listing a Print Request

To list all print requests submitted to all defined printer queues on the system, use the *lpstat* command with –o option:

```
# lpstat  –o
```

To do the above using SAM, follow the steps below:

☞Go to SAM → Printers and Plotters → LP spooler → Print Requests. A list of existing print requests will be displayed.

20.5.3   Modifying a Print Request

A print request can be modified after it is submitted for printing and before it actually gets on to the printer. The *lpalt* command is used for this purpose. The following raises the priority of the queued print requests prn2-0 and prn_class-0 to 6:

```
# lpalt  prn2–0  –p6
# lpalt  prn_class–0  –p6
```

20.5.4   Moving a Print Request

You can move one or all print requests from one printer queue to another using either *lpmove* or *lpalt* command. You must stop the *lpsched* daemon before successfully running the two commands.

For example, to move all print requests from *prn1* to *prn2*, stop the scheduler, move all requests, and restart the scheduler:

```
# lpshut
# lpmove  prn1  prn2
# lpsched
```

To move only prn1-0 print request from *prn1* to *prn2*, use either of the following:

```
# lpalt  prn1–0  prn2
# lpmove  prn1–0  prn2
```

20.5.5   Canceling a Print Request

To cancel a single print request, use the *cancel* command as follows:

```
# cancel  prn2-0
# cancel  prn_class-0
```

To cancel all print requests queued on *prn2* and *prn_class*, use the *cancel* command as follows:

```
# cancel  -e  prn2
# cancel  -e  prn_class
```

To do the above using SAM, follow the steps below:

☞ Go to SAM → Printers and Plotters → LP spooler → Print Requests. A list of existing print requests is displayed. Highlight the one you wish to cancel and go to Actions → Cancel Request.

Summary

You learned inside-out of printing in HP-UX in this chapter. You developed a good understanding of print spooler, the directory structure where files related to print spooling were stored, and daemons that enabled you to print to printers. You looked at local, remote, and network printer definitions, and reasons behind combining printers into classes. You setup local, remote, and network printers and defined default printer and printer class. You looked at starting and stopping the print scheduler daemon automatically and manually.

You studied print spooler administration that involved activating and deactivating a printer, allowing and disallowing users to submit print requests, verifying if a printer is working, modifying a printer priority and fence level, and removing a printer from the system.

Finally, you learned how to submit print requests to a printer or printer class; list, cancel, and modify submitted print requests; and move submitted print requests to another printer or printer class.

## 21

Job Scheduling and System Logging

This chapter covers the following major topics:

- ✓ What is job scheduling?
- ✓ Start and stop the cron daemon
- ✓ Allow and disallow users to schedule jobs
- ✓ Log cron activities
- ✓ Schedule, list, and remove at jobs
- ✓ Schedule, list, and remove jobs using crontab command
- ✓ What is system logging?
- ✓ Types of messages and level of criticality
- ✓ Where to send messages
- ✓ Syslog and syslog configuration files

21.1   What is Job Scheduling?

Job scheduling is a feature that allows a user to schedule a command to be executed at the specified time in future. The execution of the command could be one time in future or at regular intervals based on a pre-defined time schedule.

Usually, one-time command execution is scheduled for an activity that is to be performed at a time when there is low system usage. One example of such an activity is running a lengthy shell program.

In contrast, recurring activities could include performing backups, creating system recovery archives, trimming log files, and removing unwanted files from the system.

21.1.1   Starting and Stopping the *cron* Daemon

A system daemon called *cron* controls all scheduled jobs. This daemon is started when the system boots up and enters run level 2. At run level 2, a script called */sbin/rc2.d/S730cron,* which is symbolically linked to the actual startup script */sbin/init.d/cron,* executes the "start" function (defined in the script) based on the setting of a variable CRON in the */etc/rc.config.d/cron* file. If the variable is set to 1, the daemon is started.

To start or stop the *cron* daemon manually, do the following:

> **# /sbin/init.d/cron start**
> cron started
> **# /sbin/init.d/cron stop**
> cront stopped

When a system changes its run level to 1 or when it shuts down, a script called */sbin/rc1.d/K270,* which is symbolically linked to */sbin/init.d/cron*, executes the "stop" function (defined in the script) to terminate the daemon.

21.1.2   Controlling User Access

Which users can or cannot submit an *at* or *cron* job is controlled through files located in the */var/adm/cron* directory. For *at* job control, the *at.allow* and *at.deny* files are used. For *cron* job control, the *cron.allow* and *cron.deny* files are used.

The syntax of all four files is identical. You only need to list user names who you want to permit or deny access to these tools. Each file takes one user name per line.

Table 21-1 shows various combinations and the impact on user access.

at.allow / cron.allow	at.deny / cron.deny	Impact
Exists and contains user entries	Does not matter if exists or not	All users listed in *.allow* files are permitted.

Exists but empty	Does not matter if exists or not	No user is permitted.
Does not exist	Exists and contains user entries	All users, other than those listed in *.deny files, are permitted.
Does not exist	Exists but empty	All users are permitted.
Does not exist	Does not exist	No user, other than root, is permitted.

Table 21-1 Controlling User Access

By default, the *.allow files exist and *.deny files do not.

If you attempt to execute the at command and you are not authorized, you get the following message:

    you are not authorized to use at. Sorry.

If you attempt to execute the crontab command and you are not authorized, you get the following message:

    crontab: you are not authorized to use cron. Sorry.

21.1.3   cron Log File

All activities, wherein the cron daemon is involved, are logged in the /var/adm/cron/log file. Information about each activity's start time, end time, and owner is captured. The file also keeps track of when the cron daemon is started, PID associated with it, spooled at and cron jobs, etc. Sample entries from the log file are shown below:

```
# cat  /var/adm/cron/log
! *** cron started ***   pid = 1253 Sat Feb  4 08:27:51 EST 2006
> CMD: 1139284800.a
> root 8832 a Mon Feb  6 23:00:00 EST 2006
< root 8832 a Mon Feb  6 23:00:19 EST 2006
```

21.2 Job Scheduling Using *at*

The at command is used to schedule a one-time execution of a program in future. All submitted jobs are spooled in the /var/spool/cron/atjobs directory.

21.2.1   Setting Up an *at* Job

In order to schedule an at job to run the find command to look for all core files in the system and remove them at 11pm tonight, do the following:

```
# at  11pm  find  /  –name  core  –exec  rm  {}  \;
ctrl+d
```

Warning: commands will be executed using /usr/bin/sh
job 1139284800.a at Mon Feb 6 23:00:00 2006

You have to press *ctrl+d* to submit an *at* job. When you submit it, an ID is assigned to it along with a time stamp. The job ID is a long integer value followed by a dot and an a. The integer value is a number, in seconds, calculated from the epoch time, January 01, 1970, all the way up to the job execution time. A file is created in the */var/spool/cron/atjobs* directory by the same name as the job ID. This file includes all variable settings that are to be used when the job is actually executed. These variables establish the user's shell environment so that the job is properly carried out. This file also includes the command or the script name that is to be executed.

There are multiple ways of mentioning an execution time with the *at* command. Some examples are:

at 11am	(executes the task at next 11am)
at 23:00	(another way of specifying 11pm tonight)
at 17:30 tomorrow	(executes the task at 5:30 pm next day)
at now + 5 days	(executes the task at this time after 5 days)

 When year is not mentioned, the current year is assumed; when no date is mentioned, today's date is assumed.

If you wish to run a series of commands or scripts that reside in a file, you can supply the file's name as input to the *at* command using the –f option. Here is how you would do it:

   # at –f file1 now + 5 days

In the above example, the contents of *file1* will be executed at the current time after 5 days.

21.2.2   Listing and Removing *at* Jobs

Use the *at* command to list and remove *at* jobs.

To list the current spooled *at* jobs, use the –l option. This option lists all job IDs along with their execution time.

   # at –l
   user = root   1139284800.a   Mon Feb 6 23:00:00 2006

Alternatively, you can do an *ll* on the spool directory to view a list of all spooled jobs.

   # ll /var/spool/cron/atjobs
   total 16
   -r-Sr-Sr-- 1 root   sys   1752 Feb 6 13:01 1139284800.a

To remove a spooled *at* job, use the –r option and specify a job ID you want to remove.

   # at –r 1139284800.a

21.3   Job Scheduling Using *crontab*

Using the *crontab* command is the other method for setting up tasks to be executed in future. Unlike *at*, *crontab* executes jobs on a regular basis and at specified time defined in the *crontab* file. Crontab files for users are located in the */var/spool/cron/crontabs* directory. Each user, who is allowed and has scheduled a cron job, has a file by his or her login name created in this directory. The *cron* daemon scans entries in these files to determine job execution times. The daemon then runs the commands or scripts at the specified time and puts a log entry into the */var/adm/cron/log* file.

The *crontab* command is used to edit, list, and remove *crontab* files.

21.3.1   Syntax of the *crontab* File

In a crontab file, each line that contains an entry for a scheduled job comprises of 6 fields. These fields must be in the correct sequence in order for the *cron* daemon to interpret them correctly. See Figure 21-1 for syntax of the *crontab* file.

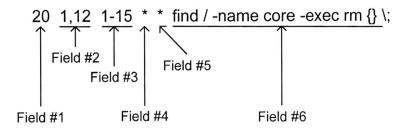

Figure 21-1 Syntax of the crontab File

A description of each field is given in Table 21-2.

Field #	Field Content	Description
1	Minute of the hour.	Valid values are from 0 (represents exact hour) to 59. You can define this field to have one specific value (see Field #1 for usage), multiple comma-separated values (see Field #2 for usage), a range of values (see Field #3 for usage), or the * character to represent every minute of the hour (see Field #4 and #5).
2	Hour of the day.	Valid values are from 0 (represents midnight) to 23. Values in this field are defined exactly the way they are defined for Field #1, except that the * character represents every hour of the day.
3	Date of the month.	Valid values are from 1 to 31. Values in this field are defined exactly the way they are defined for Field #1, except that the * character represents every day of the month.

4	Month of the year.	Valid values are from 1 to 12 with 1 represents January, 2 represents February, and so on. Values in this field are defined exactly the way they are defined for Field #1, except that the * character represents every month of the year.
5	Day of the week.	Valid values are from 0 to 6 with 0 represents Sunday, 1 represents Monday, and so on. Values in this field are defined exactly the way they are defined for Field #1, except that the * character represents every day of the week.
6	Command to execute.	Specifies the full path name of the command or script to be executed.

Table 21-2 *crontab* File Description

21.3.2 Setting Up a *cron* Job

To set up a cron job, execute the *crontab* command with –e option:

$ crontab –e

This opens up for editing the crontab file for the user who has executed this command based on permissions defined for that user in the *cron.allow* or the *cron.deny* file. Note that *root* can modify the contents of any other user's crontab file. For example, to open up the crontab file for *user1* as *root*, do the following:

 # crontab –e user1

The name of the crontab file for a user matches the user's login name. For example, crontab file for *root* is called *root*, crontab file for *user1* is called *user1*, and so on.

You do not have to be in the */var/spool/cron/crontabs* directory to open your crontab file. In fact, you can be anywhere in the directory structure.

Let us put the following entry in the *root* user's crontab file:

 # crontab –e
20 1,12 1-15 * * find / -name core –exec rm {} \;

This entry tells the *cron* daemon to execute the *find* command at 1:20 am and 12:20 pm every day from the 1st of the month to the 15th.

21.3.3 Listing and Removing *cron* Jobs

Use the *crontab* command to list and remove cron jobs. See following examples to understand the usage.

To list contents of the crontab file for *user1*, use –l option and run it as *user1*:

   $ **crontab –l**

To list contents of the crontab file for *user1* as *root*:

   # **crontab –l user1**

To remove an entry from a user crontab file, use –e option to open the file and remove the desired entry.

To remove a crontab file completely, use –r option. This will remove the crontab file for the user who has executed the command.

   # **crontab –r**

To remove *user1*'s crontab file as *root*:

   # **crontab –r user1**

21.4   System Logging

System logging is performed to keep track of messages generated by various sources, such as kernel, daemons, and commands. A daemon called, *syslogd*, is responsible for all logging activities. It is started at system boot time by the */sbin/rc2.d/S220syslogd* script, which is symbolically linked to the actual startup script */sbin/init.d/syslogd*, when the system enters run level 2. The daemon reads its configuration file, */etc/syslog.conf*, when coming up.

You can manually start or stop this daemon. Here is how:

   # **/sbin/init.d/syslogd start**
   System message logger started
   # **/sbin/init.d/syslogd stop**
   syslogd stopped

When the *syslogd* daemon is started, the process ID assigned to it is stored in the */var/run/syslogd.pid* file.

21.4.1   The System Log Configuration File

The system log configuration file resides in the */etc* directory and is called *syslog.conf*. The contents of the default *syslog.conf* file are shown below:

   # **cat /etc/syslog.conf**
   . . . .
   . . . .
   mail.debug   /var/adm/syslog/mail.log
   *.info;mail.none   /var/adm/syslog/syslog.log

```
*.alert              /dev/console
*.alert              root
*.emerg              *
```

Notice that each line entry consists of two fields. The left field is called *Selector* and the right field is called *Action*. The selector field is further divided into two sub-fields, which are separated by the period character. The left sub-field, called *Facility*, represents various system process categories that can generate messages. You can define multiple facilities, with each facility separated from the other by the semicolon (;) character. The right sub-field, called *Level*, represents severity associated with the message. The *Action* field determines where to send the message.

Some of the facilities are kern, user, mail, daemon, and cron. The * character represents all of them.

In the same way, there are multiple severity levels, such as emergency (emerg), critical (crit), error (err), warning (warn), and none. The * character represents all of them.

In the sample */etc/syslog.conf* file above, the following entries are defined. The last two entries are added for explanation purposes.

```
mail.debug           /var/adm/syslog/mail.log
*.info;mail.none     /var/adm/syslog/syslog.log
*.alert              /dev/console
*.alert              root
*.emerg              *
cron.err             user1,user2,user3
kern.err             @hp02
```

In the first line entry, facility is "mail", level is "debug", and the action field is */var/adm/syslog/mail.log*. This tells the *syslogd* daemon to log all debug messages generated by the mail subsystem to the */var/adm/syslog/mail.log* file.

In the second line entry, two facilities are defined. The first facility tells the *syslogd* daemon to capture all informational messages generated by any service on the system and log them to *syslog.log* file. The second facility tells the daemon not to capture any messages generated by the mail subsystem.

The third and the fourth lines tell the daemon to capture all alerts and display them on the system console as well as on the terminals where the *root* user is logged in.

The fifth line indicates that the *syslogd* daemon will display all emergency messages on the terminals of all logged in users.

The sixth line tells the *syslogd* daemon to display error messages generated by *cron* daemon on the terminals of *user1*, *user2*, and *user3*.

The last line entry forwards all kernel error messages to another system, *hp02*, to let the *syslogd* daemon running on that machine to handle them.

21.4.2   The System Log File

The default system log file is located in the */var/adm/syslog* directory and is called *syslog.log*. This is a plain text file and can be viewed with *cat*, *more*, *pg*, *head*, *tail*, or other such file display utility. This file may be viewed in real time using the *tail* command with –f option. The file captures time stamp, hostname, daemon or command executed, PID of the process, and other related information.

The following shows sample entries from the *syslog.log* file:

```
# cat /var/adm/syslog/syslog.log
Feb  4 08:27:48 hp02  pwgrd: Started at Sat Feb  4 08:27:48 2006, pid = 1220
Feb  4 08:27:53 hp02  LVM [1261]: lvlnboot -v
Feb  4 08:27:55 hp02  diagmond[1274]: started
Feb  4 08:27:55 hp02  /usr/sbin/envd[1277]: restart, and read the configuration file
Feb  4 08:28:20 hp02  krsd[1504]: Delay time is 300 seconds
Feb  4 17:28:41 hp02  rlogind[4414]: Login failure (exit (1) from login(1))
Feb  4 22:54:45 hp02  su: + 0 root-user1
Feb  6 13:42:04 hp02  rlogind[8104]: Login failure (exit (2) from login(1))
Feb  6 13:42:13 hp02  su: + 0 root-user1
```

Summary

You learned two system administration areas in this chapter. First, you learned how to schedule commands and scripts to run automatically at pre-determined time in future. This included two tools: *at* and *crontab*. Both used a common daemon called *cron*. Normal users could automate their own tasks, if they were permitted. You looked at how to permit and prohibit users to use the tools. Furthermore, you were presented with examples that listed and removed spooled jobs.

Second, you looked at system activity logging functionality of HP-UX. You understood contents of the */etc/syslog.conf* configuration file. You looked at the */var/adm/syslog/syslog.log* file, where all system activities were logged based on the configuration defined in */etc/syslog.conf*.

Performance Monitoring

This chapter covers the following major topics:

- ✓ Performance bottleneck areas
- ✓ Performance monitoring tools, such as uptime, w, sar, top, glance, swapinfo, vmstat, iostat, ps, ipcs, time, timex, and Performance Manager
- ✓ Monitor CPU, memory, swap, disk, process, and network adapter performance
- ✓ Fix performance issues

22.1   Performance Monitoring

As a system administrator, it is one of your responsibilities to ensure the systems you manage are operating at optimum performance levels and there are no bottlenecks affecting performance. If there are any bottlenecks, you need to address them appropriately.

Performance monitoring is the process of acquiring performance data from different system components, such as CPU, memory, swap, disk, processes, and network adapters. This data is analyzed and results generated are utilized to understand trends as they develop, prevent unsatisfactory performance, and optimize system resources. It helps locate bottlenecks and identify under- and over-utilized resources. You can then make arrangements to carry out necessary changes to component(s) affecting performance.

A system may perform slowly or sluggishly for numerous reasons. You need to be sure what exactly causing the problem. There are several tools available to obtain performance data to identify potential cause. The topics to follow cover these tools in detail.

You need to focus on three performance-related areas in order to effectively monitor a system. These areas are *throughput*, *response time*, and *resource utilization*. Throughput is the amount of work done within certain time limits. It is normally measured in *Transactions Per Second* (TPS) or *Million Instructions Per Second* (MIPS). Response time is the wait time for the completion of a task. Resource utilization tells how much resources of a system are being used to conduct a task.

22.1.1   Performance Monitoring Tools

There are numerous tools available for performance monitoring of system components including CPU, memory, swap, disk, process, and network adapter. Most tools are built-in to HP-UX. Table 22-1 lists and describes them.

Tool	Description
uptime / w	Shows CPU load averages.
sar	Reports on CPU, virtual memory, disk, and network activities.
top	Displays CPU, memory, swap, disk, processes, and network activities.
glance or gpm	Reports on CPU, memory, swap, disk, processes, and network utilization in both text and graphics modes. This tool comes standard with HP-UX EOE and MCOE.
swapinfo	Shows memory and swap usage.
vmstat	Reports on virtual memory statistics.
iostat	Monitors disk I/O activities.
ps	Displays detailed process activities.
ipcs	Displays information about active IPC (*Inter Process Communication*) facilities, such as semaphores, message queues, and shared memory segments.
time / timex	Measures elapsed time, in seconds, for the specified command and displays actual time spent, time spent in user space, and time spent in the system.

netstat / lanadmin	Displays network adapter activities.
Performance Manager / Performance Agent	A client/server software tool primarily used for performance monitoring and trending. The server portion is called *Performance Manager* (PM) and the client portion is known as *Performance Agent* (PA). PA comes standard with HP-UX EOE and MCOE. The server portion is separately purchasable.

Table 22-1 Performance Monitoring Tools

22.1.2   Monitoring CPU Performance

To monitor CPU performance, use the *uptime, sar*, *top*, and *glance* commands.

The *uptime* command gives you a rough, quick estimate of system load, in addition to showing you how long the system has been up for.

> **# uptime**
> 3:41pm up 4 days, 7:16, 1 user, load average: 0.51, 0.53, 0.53

The load average displays a rough estimate of CPU utilization over the past 1, 5, and 15 minutes. The higher the load average numbers are, the heavier the system utilization is. Normally, a load average of 3 or less is considered good. The *w* command also shows the same estimates in the first line of output.

The *sar* command automates gathering of system activity data. It collects performance data from all major system components. Some essential options to the *sar* command are listed in Table 22-2.

Option	Action
A	Reports on overall system performance.
b	Monitors buffer activities.
d	Monitors disk activities.
k	Checks kernel memory allocation.
o	Specifies the output file.
q	Monitors queue length.
r	Checks unused memory.
u	Reports on CPU utilization.
w	Checks swapping activities.

Table 22-2 *sar* Command Options

Use the –u option with the *sar* command to display CPU activities. The following runs the command every 5 seconds for 5 times:

> **# sar –u 5 5**
> HP-UX hp02 B.11.11 U 9000/871   02/09/06
> 09:47:34   %usr   %sys   %wio   %idle
> 09:47:39   0   0   0   100
> 09:47:44   0   0   0   100

```
09:47:49    0       0       0       100
09:47:54    0       0       0       100
09:47:59    0       0       0       100
Average     0       0       0       100
```

The output is displayed in five columns. The first column shows the five second sampling time. The second and the third columns demonstrate percentages of time the CPU spends to execute the user and system processes, respectively. The fourth column lists the wait time for an I/O operation to complete. If this value is too high, check disk, network adapter, and NFS I/O operations. The last column shows CPU time spent on nothing. If this value is too low, it indicates that the CPU is heavily used.

The *top* command exhibits quantity of CPUs installed in a system and their utilization. The following *top* command output shows the main window:

```
# top
System: hp02                        Sun Feb 12 12:30:28 2006
Load averages: 0.53, 0.51, 0.51
103 processes: 87 sleeping, 16 running
Cpu states:
CPU        LOAD   USER  NICE   SYS  IDLE   BLOCK  SWAIT INTR  SSYS
0          0.06   0.0%  0.0%   0.0% 100.0% 0.0%   0.0%  0.0%  0.0%
1          1.00   0.0%  0.0%   0.4% 99.6%  0.0%   0.0%  0.0%  0.0%

---  ----  -----  -----  -----  -----   -----   -----  -----
avg        0.53   0.0%  0.0%   0.2% 99.8%  0.0%   0.0%  0.0%  0.0%

Memory: 95012K (67748K) real, 365780K (307692K) virtual, 623844K free  Page# 1/10

CPU TTY   PID USERNAME PRI  NI SIZE    RES    STATE TIME  %WCPU %CPU COMMAND
0   ?     1620 root    154  10 324K    544K   sleep 1:27  1.42  1.41 memlogd
1   ?     1384 root    152  20 7968K   10140K run   61:34 0.54  0.54 prm3d
1   pts/1 17745 root   178  20 2644K   464K   run   0:00  0.69  0.39 top
0   ?     35   root    152  20 0K      2912K  run   8:10  0.37  0.37 vxfsd
1   ?     1136 root    152  20 1964K   2288K  run   0:24  0.23  0.23 dmisp
0   pts/1 17730 root   158  20 316K    252K   sleep 0:00  0.29  0.22 sh
. . . . . . . .
. . . . . . . .
```

The *glance* command starts the HP *GlancePlus* software in text mode. To run it in graphical mode, use the *gpm* command. This tool displays quantity of CPUs installed in a system and their utilization. When *glance* is executed, the output looks similar to the following:

```
# glance
B3692A GlancePlus C.03.70.00   15:57:30   hp02 9000/871  Current Avg High
--------------------------------------------------------------------------------
CPU  Util  A                                         |  1%   3%   11%
Disk Util  F F                                       |  6%   3%    6%
Mem  Util  S     SU   UB   B                          | 41%  41%   41%
Swap Util  U  UR R                                    | 13%  13%   13%
```

Process Name	PID	PPID	Pri	User Name	CPU Util (200% max)	Cum CPU	Disk IO Rate	Thd RSS	Cnt
					PROCESS LIST Users= 2				
glance	17959	17730	154	root	2.0 / 5.5	0.5	0.0 / 0.0	3.7mb	1
vxfsd	35	0	138	root	0.0 / 0.1	494.8	9.3 / 0.9	2.8mb	16

The main Glance window in GUI, when you issue the *gpm* command, is shown in Figure 22-1. It takes you directly to the window that displays graphical utilization of CPU, memory, network, and disk, when it is started.

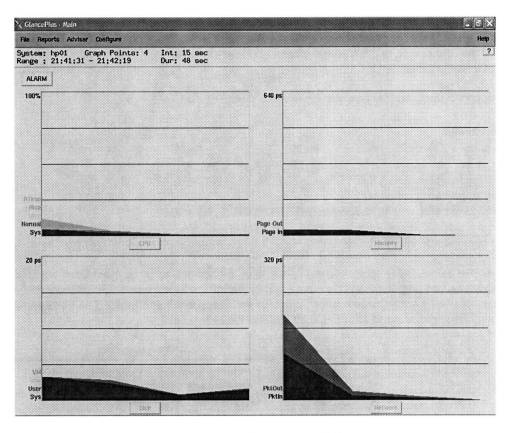

Figure 22-1 GlancePlus GUI

22.1.3   Monitoring Physical Memory and Swap Performance

To monitor physical memory and swap consumption, use the *swapinfo*, *top*, and *glance* commands. The *vmstat* and *sar* commands may also be used to monitor swap.

Use the *swapinfo* command as follows to display physical memory and swap information:

```
# swapinfo  –at
              Kb              Kb     Kb     PCT    START/    Kb
  TYPE        AVAIL           USED   FREE   USED   LIMIT  RESERVE  PRI   NAME
  dev         2097152         0      2097152  0%    0       -       1    /dev/vg00/lvol2
  reserve     -               163424  -163424
  memory      753984          206924  547060   27%
  total       2851136         370348  2480788  13%   -       0       -
```

The above output depicts information about the device swap and its utilization. It also shows physical memory usage. The last column displays the sum of the two. The first three columns show the total of swap and memory, and how much they are used and free. A very high value (80% plus) would most likely mean that you need to add more physical memory to your system.

The *top* and *glance* (or *gpm*) commands show amount and utilization of physical memory and swap space. See the output of the *top* and *glance* commands in section "Monitoring CPU Performance" earlier in this chapter.

The *vmstat* command displays virtual memory statistics.

```
# vmstat
  procs      memory           page                   faults       cpu
  r  b  w   avm   free    re   at  pi po fr de sr   in  sy   cs   us sy id
  1  0  0  13660  1721   233  103  3  0  0  0  6   108 1443 1191   6  4 90
```

The following tells *vmstat* to run every 15 seconds for 10 times:

```
# vmstat  15  10
```

The *vmstat* command outputs several columns of information with the main header across the top and sub-heading underneath. The output is divided into two sections: a VM section and a CPU section. The VM section covers information on memory, page, and faults. The CPU section covers information on procs and CPU. Table 22-3 describes each field.

Main Heading	Sub-Heading	Description
procs	r	Processes waiting to be processed by CPU.
procs	b	Kernel threads blocked while waiting for I/O.
procs	w	Swapped out idle processes.
memory	avm	Free, unreserved, active virtual memory space.
memory	free	Free memory.
page	re	Pages reclaimed. The higher this number is, the more the shortage of physical memory is.
page	at	Address translation.
page	pi	Paged in from swap.
page	po	Paged out to swap.
page	fr	Freed pages.
page	de	Anticipated short-term memory shortfall.
page	sr	Scan rate. This number is reported as a total number of pages scanned.
faults	in	Interrupts per second.

faults	sy	System calls per second.
faults	cs	Context switches per second.
cpu	us	CPU time taken by users.
cpu	sy	CPU time taken by system (kernel).
cpu	id	CPU idle time.

Table 22-3 *vmstat* Command Output Description

The *sar* command also displays virtual memory statistics. The following runs the command every 5 seconds for 5 times:

```
# sar –w 5 5
HP-UX hp02 B.11.11 U 9000/871    02/09/06
09:51:11    swpin/s  bswin/s  swpot/s  bswot/s  pswch/s
09:51:16    0.00     0.0      0.00     0.0      103
09:51:21    0.00     0.0      0.00     0.0      100
09:51:26    0.00     0.0      0.00     0.0      94
09:51:31    0.00     0.0      0.00     0.0      92
09:51:36    0.00     0.0      0.00     0.0      100
Average     0.00     0.0      0.00     0.0      98
```

22.1.4   Monitoring Disk Performance

Use the *iostat, sar*, and *glance* commands to check disk load I/O activities.

The *iostat* command is used to monitor and gather disk performance data. Use the command during peak hours and observe I/O requests being directed at disk devices.

```
# iostat
device      bps      sps      msps
c0t10d0     0        0.0      1.0
c0t11d0     0        0.0      1.0
```

The *iostat* command generated several columns of information and are described in Table 22-4.

Column	Description
bps	Kilobytes transferred per second.
sps	Number of disk seeks per second.
msps	Milliseconds per average disk seek.
device	Disk device name.

Table 22-4 *iostat* Command Output Description

If you see high values for a device in the output, it indicates that the particular disk device is being used heavily. That device may have an extensively-used swap on it. You need to determine the root cause.

The following tells *iostat* to run every 5 seconds for 5 times:

iostat 5 5

Use the *sar* command with –d option for 5 times at every 5th second to display disk device activities.

sar –d 5 5

09:54:41	device	%busy	avque	r+w/s	blks/s	avwait	avserv
09:54:46	c0t10d0	0.80	0.50	1	4	4.30	13.67
	c0t11d0	0.80	0.50	1	4	4.35	13.78
09:54:51	c0t10d0	1.80	0.50	2	6	4.75	22.41
	c0t11d0	1.20	0.50	1	4	5.44	17.28
09:54:56	c0t10d0	2.40	0.50	3	10	3.19	24.30
	c0t11d0	2.60	0.50	3	10	3.23	25.86
09:55:01	c0t10d0	5.40	0.50	6	14	5.48	9.63
	c0t11d0	2.80	0.50	6	14	5.15	5.89
09:55:06	c0t10d0	0.20	0.50	0	3	0.83	14.83
	c0t11d0	0.20	0.50	0	3	0.87	16.96
Average	c0t10d0	2.12	0.50	2	8	4.65	15.48
Average	c0t11d0	1.52	0.50	2	7	4.56	13.00

The *glance* (or *gpm*) command displays overall disk utilization. See the output of the *glance* command in section "Monitoring CPU Performance" earlier in this chapter.

22.1.5   Monitoring System Processes

You can view process statistics using the *ps*, *top*, and the *glance* commands and active IPC facilities' status using the *ipcs* command. In addition, *time* and *timex* commands are available that measure time spent on a given process or command.

The *ps* command displays detailed information about processes running on a system. There are several options available to it but normally –e, –f, and –l are used. These options provide a complete picture of all running processes.

ps –elf

F S	UID	PID	PPID	C PRI NI	ADDR	SZ	WCHAN	STIME	TTY	TIME	COMD
3 S	root	0	0	0 128 20	c7df10	0	-	Feb 4	?	007	swapper
3 S	root	8	0	0 100 20	5397040	0	cc1ff8	Feb 4	?	0:00	supsched
3 S	root	9	0	0 100 20	5397100	0	c7d87c	Feb 4	?	0:00	strmem
3 S	root	10	0	0 100 20	53971c0	0	cc1038	Feb 4	?	0:00	strweld
3 S	root	11	0	0 100 20	5397280	0	cc0a14	Feb 4	?	0:00	strfreebd

. . . .
. . . .

The *top* and the *glance* (or *gpm*) commands show a list of all processes currently running on the system along with relevant details. See the output of *top* in section "Monitoring CPU Performance" earlier. The thread list is shown by *gpm* as demonstrated in Figure 22-2.

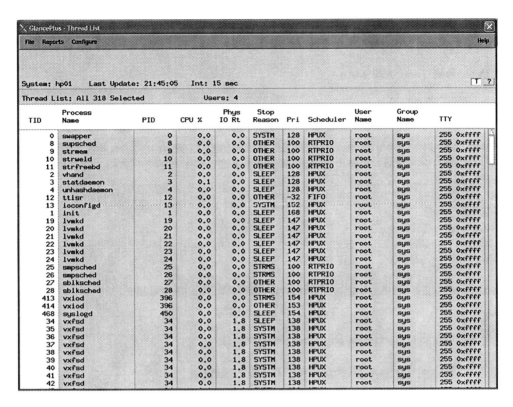

Figure 22-2 *gpm* Process List

The *ipcs* command displays status information about active IPC facilities. With no options specified, information about active message queues, shared memory segments, and semaphores is shown.

ipcs
IPC status from /dev/kmem as of Mon Apr 9 14:12:05 2007

T	ID	KEY	MODE	OWNER	GROUP
Message Queues:					
q	0	0x3c240734	-rrw--w--w-	root	root
q	1	0x3e240734	--rw-r--r--	root	root
Shared Memory:					
m	0	0x41240846	--rw-rw-rw-	root	root
m	1	0x4e000002	--rw-rw-rw-	root	root
m	2	0x41281314	--rw-rw-rw-	root	root
m	204	0x0c6629c9	--rw-r-----	root	root
m	405	0x491c8a91	--rw-r--r--	root	root
Semaphores:					
s	0	0x41240846	--ra-ra-ra-	root	root
s	1	0x4e000002	--ra-ra-ra-	root	root
s	2	0x41281314	--ra-ra-ra-	root	root
s	3	0x00446f6e	--ra-r--r--	root	root
s	4	0x00446f6d	--ra-r--r--	root	root
s	5	0x01090522	--ra-r--r--	root	root

. . . .
. . . .

The *time* command reports, in seconds, on the elapsed time during the execution of a command, time in the system, and execution time of itself.

```
# time  find  /  –name  core
real        2.4
user        0.4
sys         1.9
```

The *timex* command reports, in seconds, on the elapsed time, user time, and system execution time. For example, run SAM and determine the time measurements on it. Exit out of SAM to see the numbers.

```
# timex  sam
real        26.09
user        4.73
sys         1.63
```

The above output indicates that SAM was run for total 26.09 seconds.

 Both *time* and *timex* commands produce similar outputs.

22.1.6   Monitoring Network Performance

To monitor network adapter activities, use the *lanadmin* and *netstat* commands. See Chapter 26 "Network Connectivity Troubleshooting and Overview of Network Management" for a detailed understanding of these tools.

22.2   Fixing a Performance Problem

When you have identified the root cause of a bottleneck in a system, arrange to perform necessary modifications to the area or areas affecting performance. In case multiple areas are required to be modified, implement your fixes one at a time.

It is highly recommended that you monitor systems proactively on a regular basis and capture any bottlenecks before it starts affecting system performance.

Summary

In this chapter, you learned about performance bottlenecks and tools to monitor performance. You looked at common performance bottleneck areas including CPU, memory, swap, disk, process, and LAN adapters. You used performance monitoring tools, such as *uptime, w, sar, top, glance, swapinfo, vmstat, iostat, ps, ipcs, time,* and *timex,* and how to use them to measure performance.

## 23

POSIX Shell Scripting

This chapter covers the following major topics:

- ✓ What is shell scripting?
- ✓ Write scripts to display basic system information, set local and environment variables, use values of pre-defined environment variables, parse command outputs to variables, understand usage of command line arguments, and understand the role the shift command plays
- ✓ Execute and debug scripts
- ✓ Write interactive scripts
- ✓ Write scripts to create logical constructs using if-then-fi, if-then-else-fi, if-then-elif-fi, and case structures
- ✓ Write scripts to create looping constructs using for-do-done, while-do-done, and until-do-done structures
- ✓ Understand exit codes and test conditions
- ✓ Control loops using break, continue, and sleep
- ✓ Ignore signals using the trap command

23.1   Shell Scripting

Shell Scripts (a.k.a. *Shell Programs*, or simply *Scripts*) are text files that contain UNIX commands and control structures to automate long, repetitive tasks. Commands are interpreted and run by the shell one at a time in the order they are listed in a script. Control structures are utilized for creating and managing logical and looping constructs. Comments are also usually included in shell scripts to add general information about the script, such as author name, creation date, last modification date, and purpose of the script.

Although shell scripting is typically part of UNIX fundamentals, which were covered in the first few chapters of this book, it is purposely included here after discussing all system administration topics. The reason is to provide better and useful example scripts that employ the system administration knowledge you have gained.

Throughout this chapter, the approach will be to write scripts and examine them line-by-line. You will start with simple scripts and move forward to more complicated ones. As with any other programming languages, your shell scripting skill will develop overtime as you write, read, and understand more and more scripts.

Scripts, you will be looking at in this chapter, are written for the POSIX shell */usr/bin/sh*. These scripts can be used in Korn shell without any modifications, but not all of them can be run in Bourne and C shells.

Shell scripting enables you to create programs for various purposes including automation of system and network administration tasks, such as manipulating several volume groups, disk groups, volumes, and file systems, monitoring file system utilization, trimming log files, performing tape and network recovery archives, doing system backups, removing core and other temporary files, automating software and patch management tasks, generating reports, creating users, and other lengthy tasks.

When a script is executed, the shell reads its contents line by line. Each line is executed as if it is typed and executed at the command prompt. If the script encounters an error, the error message is displayed on the screen. There is nothing that you can place in a script but cannot run at the command prompt.

Scripts do not need to be compiled as many other programming languages do.

23.2   Creating Shell Scripts

Use the *vi* editor to create example shell scripts given in this chapter. This gives you an opportunity to practice the *vi* editor. The *cat* command is used to display the contents of the scripts. It is recommended to store these scripts under */usr/local/bin* directory and add the directory to your PATH. Following example scripts are created in */usr/local/bin* directory with an assumption that */usr/local/bin* is in defined in the PATH variable.

23.2.1   Displaying Basic System Information

Let us create the first script called *sys_info.sh* and then examine it. When you are ready to go, *cd* into */usr/local/bin* directory and use the *vi* editor to open a new file. Type in what you see in the box.

```
# cat sys_info.sh
#!/usr/bin/sh
# The name of this script is sys_info.sh.
# The author of this script is Asghar Ghori.
# The script is created on February 24, 2006.
# This script is last modified by Asghar Ghori on March 1, 2006.
# This script should be located in /usr/local/bin directory.
# The purpose of this script is to explain construct of a simple shell program.
echo "Display Basic System Information"
echo "-------------------------------------------"
echo
echo "The hardware model of this machine is:"
/usr/bin/model
echo "This machine is running the following version of HP-UX Operating Environment:"
/usr/bin/uname –r
```

 To view line numbers associated with each line entry while you are in vi, type (:set nu)

In this script, comments and commands are used.

The first line indicates which HP-UX shell the script is to be run in. This line must start with the "#!" character combination followed by the full pathname to the shell file.

The next six lines contain comments, which include script name, author name, creation time, modification time, where it should be located, and what the script do. The # sign indicates that anything written to the right of this character is for informational purposes only and will not be executed when the script is run. Note that line 1 uses this character too followed by the "!" mark; this combination has a special meaning to the shell, which specifies the location of the shell file. Do not get confused between the two usages.

Line number 8 has the first command of the script. The *echo* command prints on the screen whatever follows it. In this case, you will see "Display Basic System Information" printed.

Line number 9 underlines the "Display Basic System Information" heading.

Line number 10 has the *echo* command followed by nothing. This means an empty line will be inserted in the output.

Line number 11 prints on the screen "The hardware model of this machine is:".

Line number 12 executes the HP-UX *model* command. This command displays the hardware model of the machine you are currently working on.

Line number 13 prints on the screen "This machine is running the following version of HP-UX Operating Environment:".

Line number 14 executes the *uname* command with –r option. This command returns the HP-UX Operating Environment version that you are currently running.

23.2.2   Executing a Script

When you have a script created, it is usually not executable, since the *umask* value is typically set to 022, which allows only rw- permissions to the owner and r-- permission to group members and public on new files. You need to run the script as follows while you are in */usr/local/bin* directory:

> # **sh   ./sys_info.sh**

The alternate way to run the script is to give the owner of the file execute permission:

> # **chmod +x sys_info.sh**

Now you can run it using either its relative path or fully qualified path:

> # **./sys_info.sh**   or   # **/usr/local/bin/sys_info.sh**

Add the absolute path to your PATH variable for the */usr/local/bin* directory where this script resides, so you do not have to retype the relative or absolute pathname to run it. You may wish to define the path in either */etc/profile* or */etc/PATH* file so whoever logs in to the system has this path set. The following shows how to set the path at the command prompt:

> # **PATH=$PATH:/usr/local/bin**
> # **export PATH**

Now let us run *sys_info.sh* and see what the output will look like:

> # **sys_info.sh**
> Display Basic System Information
> --
>
> The hardware model of this machine is:
> 9000/800/S16K-A
> This machine is running the following version of HP-UX Operating Environment:
> B.11.11

23.2.3   Debugging a Shell Script

If you would like to use a basic debugging technique, when you see that your script is not functioning the way it should be, you may want to append –x to #!/usr/bin/sh in the first line of the script to look like "#!/usr/bin/sh –x". Alternatively, you can execute the script as follows:

```
# sh –x /usr/local/bin/sys_info.sh
+ echo Display Basic System Information
Display Basic System Information
+ echo ---------------------------------------------
---------------------------------------------
+ echo

+ echo The hardware model of this machine is:
The hardware model of this machine is:
+ model
9000/800/S16K-A
+ echo This machine is running the following version of HP-UX Operating Environment:
This machine is running the following version of HP-UX Operating Environment:
+ uname -r
B.11.11
```

With a + sign the actual line from the script is echoed to the screen followed in the next line by what it would produce in the output.

23.2.4   Using Local Variables

You have dealt with variables previously and seen how to use them. To recap, you know there are two types of variables: *Local* (or *Private*) and *Global* (or *Environment*). The way you define and use local and global variables in scripts is exactly the same as you would at the command line. A local variable defined in a script disappears once the script execution is finished, whereas a global variable persists even after the script execution is finished. This is because when the script is executed, it opens up a sub-shell, runs the script in it, and then comes back to the current shell.

In the second script called *loc_var.sh,* a local variable is defined and its value displayed. After the script execution is complete, check the value of the variable again.

cat loc_var.sh

```
#!/usr/bin/sh
# The name of this script is loc_var.sh.
# The author of this script is Asghar Ghori.
# The script is created on February 24, 2006.
# This script is last modified by Asghar Ghori on March 1, 2006.
# This script should be located in /usr/local/bin directory.
# The purpose of this script is to explain how a local variable is defined and used in a shell
# program.
echo  "Setting a Local Variable".
echo  "--------------------------------"
echo
SYS_NAME=hp01
echo  "The hostname of this system is $SYS_NAME".
```

When you execute this script, the result will be:

 # loc_var.sh
Setting a Local Variable.

The hostname of this system is hp01.

Now since it was a local variable and the script was run in a sub-shell, the variable disappeared after the script execution was complete. Here is what you will see, if you try to sthe variable value:

 # echo $SYS_NAME
sh: SYS_NAME: Parameter not set

23.2.5 Using Pre-Defined Environment Variables

In the next script called *pre_env.sh,* values of two pre-defined environment variables, SHELL and LOGNAME, are displayed.

 # cat pre_env.sh

```
#!/usr/bin/sh
# The name of this script is pre_env.sh.
# The author of this script is Asghar Ghori.
# The script is created on February 24, 2006.
# This script is last modified by Asghar Ghori on March 1, 2006.
# This script should be located in /usr/local/bin directory.
# The purpose of this script is to explain how a pre-defined environment variable is used in a
# shell program.
echo "The location of my shell command is:"
echo $SHELL
echo "You are logged in as $LOGNAME".
```

The output will be:

 # pre_env.sh
The location of my shell command is:
/sbin/sh
You are logged in as root.

23.2.6 Setting New Environment Variables

In the next script, *new_env.sh,* two environment variables, SYS_NAME and OP_ENV, are set during script execution. Once the script execution is finished, you will see that the two variables still exist.

 # cat new_env.sh

```
#!/usr/bin/sh
# The name of this script is new_env.sh.
# The author of this script is Asghar Ghori.
# The script is created on February 24, 2006.
```

```
# This script is last modified by Asghar Ghori on March 1, 2006.
# This script should be located in /usr/local/bin directory.
# The purpose of this script is to explain how environment variables are defined and used in
a
# shell program.
echo  "Setting New Environment Variables".
echo  "---------------------------------------------"
echo
SYS_NAME=hp01
OP_ENV="HP-UX 11i"
export  SYS_NAME  OP_ENV
echo  "The hostname of this system is $SYS_NAME".
echo  "This system is running $OP_ENV Operating Environment software".
```

The output will be:

 # new_env.sh
Setting New Environment Variables.

The hostname of this system is hp01.
This system is running HP-UX 11i Operating Environment software.

The *export* command makes the specified variables, environment variables. Now even though the script was run in a sub-shell, both environment variables retained their values. Do an *echo* to check the values:

$ echo $SYS_NAME
hp01
$ echo $OP_ENV
HP-UX 11i

23.2.7   Parsing Command Output

Shell scripts allow you to run an HP-UX command and capture its output into a variable. For example, the following script called *cmdout.sh* is a modified form of *new_env.sh* script. You must enclose the commands *hostname* and *uname* in forward quotes.

 # cat cmdout.sh
```
#!/usr/bin/sh
# The name of this script is cmdout.sh.
# The author of this script is Asghar Ghori.
# The script is created on February 24, 2006.
# This script is last modified by Asghar Ghori on March 1, 2006.
# This script should be located in /usr/local/bin directory.
# The purpose of this script is to display how a command output is captured and stored in a
# variable.
echo  "Parsing Command Output".
```

```
echo "-----------------------------------"
echo
SYS_NAME=`hostname`
OP_ENV_VER=`uname -r`
export  SYS_NAME OP_ENV_VER
echo  "The hostname of this system is $SYS_NAME".
echo  "This system is running $OP_ENV_VER of HP-UX Operating Environment software".
```

The output will be:

 # new_env.sh
Parsing Command Output.

The hostname of this system is hp01.
This system is running B.11.11 of HP-UX Operating Environment software.

23.2.8   Using Command Line Arguments

Command Line Arguments (also called *Positional Parameters*) are the arguments specified at the command line with a command or script when you execute it. The locations at the command line of the arguments as well as the command or script itself, are stored in corresponding variables. These variables are special shell variables. Figure 23-1 and Table 23-1 help you understand them.

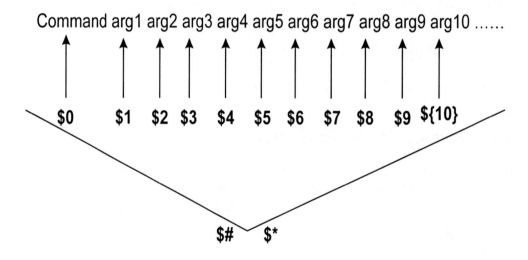

Figure 23-1 Command Line Arguments

Variable	Description
$0	Represents the command or script.
$1 to $9	Represents arguments 1 through 9.
${10} and so on	Represents arguments 10 and further.
$#	Represents total number of arguments.
$*	Represents all arguments.
$$	Represents the PID of a running script.

Table 23-1 Command Line Arguments Description

The script *com_line_arg.sh* shows what command line arguments are provided, a count of them, value of the first argument, and the process ID of the script itself.

 # cat com_line_arg.sh

```
#!/usr/bin/sh
# The name of this script is com_line_arg.sh.
# The author of this script is Asghar Ghori.
# The script is created on February 24, 2006.
# This script is last modified by Asghar Ghori on March 1, 2006.
# This script should be located in /usr/local/bin directory.
# The purpose of this script is to explain the usage of command line arguments.
echo  "There are $# arguments specified at the command line".
echo  "The arguments supplied are: $*"
echo  "The first argument is: $1"
echo  "The Process ID of the script is: $$"
```

When you execute this script with four arguments toronto, chicago, london, and washington specified, the result will be as shown below:

 # com_line_arg.sh toronto chicago london washington
```
There are 4 arguments specified at the command line.
The arguments supplied are: toronto chicago london washington
The first argument is: toronto
The Process ID of the script is: 15420
```

23.2.9   Shifting Command Line Arguments

The *shift* command is used to move command line arguments one position to the left. The first argument gets lost. *com_line_arg_shift.sh* script below uses the *shift* command.

 # cat com_line_arg_shift.sh

```
#! /usr/bin/sh
# The name of this script is com_line_arg_shift.sh.
# The author of this script is Asghar Ghori.
# The script is created on February 24, 2006.
# This script is last modified by Asghar Ghori on March 1, 2006.
```

```
# This script should be located in /usr/local/bin directory.
# The purpose of this script is to show you impact of the shift command on command line
# arguments.
echo  "There are $# arguments specified at the command line".
echo  "The arguments supplied are: $*"
echo  "The first argument is: $1"
echo  "The Process ID of the script is: $$"
shift
echo  "The new first argument after the first shift is: $1"
shift
echo  "The new first argument after the second shift is: $1"
```

Let us execute *com_line_arg_shift.sh* with four arguments toronto, chicago, london, and washington. You can see that after each *shift*, a new value is assigned to $1.

 # com_line_arg_shift.sh toronto chicago london washington
There are 4 arguments specified at the command line.
The arguments supplied are: toronto chicago london washington
The first argument is: toronto
The Process ID of the script is: 15423
The new first argument after the first shift is: chicago
The new first argument after the second shift is: london

You can perform multiple shifts in one go by supplying a digit as an argument to it. For example, "shift 2" will shift two arguments to the left, "shift 3" will shift three arguments to the left, and so on.

23.2.10   Writing an Interactive Script

Interactive shell scripts are written where you want the script to prompt to type in something as input. This input gets stored into a variable. The *read* command is used for this purpose. Usually, the *echo* command is used, prior to *read* command prompts you for input, to display an informational message.

inter_read.sh lists files and prompts you to enter a name of the file you want to remove. The script acts based on the input provided. Note that a \c is used at the end of the eleventh line. This is one of the *Escape Sequences*. It tells the *echo* command not to send a carriage return and line feed after displaying "Enter name of file you want to remove:". When you enter a file name, you will be typing it on the same line and right after the colon (:) character. Try running this script with and without \c. Also, a pre-defined environment variable called PWD is used in the script. This will display your location in the directory tree.

 # cat inter_read.sh
```
#! /usr/bin/sh
# The name of this script is inter_read.sh.
# The author of this script is Asghar Ghori.
# The script is created on February 24, 2006.
# This script is last modified by Asghar Ghori on March 1, 2006.
# This script should be located in /usr/local/bin directory.
```

```
# The purpose of this script is to show you an example of how an interactive script works.
echo  "Here is a list of all files in $PWD directory:"
/usr/bin/ls  −l
echo
echo  "Enter name of file you want to remove: \c".
/usr/bin/read  FILE
echo  "Type 'y' to remove it, 'n' if you do not want to:"
/usr/bin/rm  −i  $FILE
echo  "The file is removed".
```

Let us assume that you are in */var/adm/syslog* directory when you execute this script. Here is what the *inter_read.sh* script will do:

 # inter_read.sh
Here is a list of all files in /var/adm/syslog directory:
total 128

-rw-r--r--	1	root	root	8706	Jan 9 11:37	OLDsyslog.log
-r--r--r--	1	root	root	74095	Feb 4 17:48	mail.log
-rw-r--r--	1	root	root	15921	Feb 4 10:28	syslog.log

Enter name of file you want to remove:
Type 'y' to remove it, 'n' if you do not want to:
<filename>: ? (y/n)
The file is removed.

There are some other escape sequences, such as \t for tab, \n for new line, \a for beep, \f for form feed, \r for carriage return, and \b for backspace that you can use in shell scripts to increase readability. Try using a few of them in *inter_read.sh* script.

Another example of an interactive script is given below. Script *userc.sh* prompts you to input required user information. Each value entered is stored in a variable and finally the *useradd* command is executed to create an account based on the input provided, followed by the *passwd* command to set an initial password.

 # cat userc.sh
```
#! /usr/bin/sh
# The name of this script is userc.sh.
# The author of this script is Asghar Ghori.
# The script is created on February 24, 2006.
# This script is last modified by Asghar Ghori on March 1, 2006.
# This script should be located in /usr/local/bin directory.
# The purpose of this script is to show you how a user can be created using an interactive
# script.
echo  "This simple program creates user accounts based on input provided."
echo  "Enter required information."
echo  "---------------------------------"
echo
```

```
echo  "Enter username:\c"
read  USER
echo  "Enter user ID:\c"
read  UID
echo  "Enter primary group name or group ID:\c"
read  GID
echo  "Enter shell:\c"
read  SH
echo  "Enter home directory for the user:\c"
read  HD
echo  "Enter comments:\c"
read  COMMENT
/usr/sbin/useradd –u $UID –g $GID –s $SH –m –d $HD –c $COMMENT $USER
passwd  $USER
```

When running this script, make sure that username and UID you supply are unique, otherwise the script will fail.

Once this script is finished running, do a *tail* on the */etc/passwd* file and check if an entry is appended at the very bottom of the file. Try logging in as this user.

23.3   Logical Constructs

In shell scripting, there are times when you need to make a decision whether or not to do something. For example, you are provided with two options and you want to make a decision based on a logic (or test condition) defined in the program. In other words, you define a test condition in a script and based on the true or false status of the condition, the script decides what to do next.

The shell provides you with two logical constructs: the "if-then-fi" construct and the "case" construct. The "if-then-fi" construct has a few variations that you will see later in this chapter.

Before looking at example scripts that use logical constructs, let us discuss *Exit Codes* and *Test* conditions. These will be used in logical construct example scripts.

23.3.1   Exit Codes

Exit Codes refer to the value returned when a program or script is finished running. This value is based on the outcome of the program. If the program ran successfully, you will get a zero exit code. If the program ran unsuccessfully, you will get a non-zero exit code.

Note that you may use terms "zero status code", "zero exit code", "successful script completion", or "true value", interchangeably. Similarly, you may use terms "non-zero status code", "failed script completion", or "false value", interchangeably. These values or codes are also referred to as *Return Codes* and are stored in a special shell variable called ?. Let us look at the following two examples to understand them:

ls
file1 file2 file3 file4 file5 file6

```
# echo $?
0

# man
Usage: man [-M path] [-T macro-package] [ section ] name ...
or: man -k keyword ...
or: man -f file ...
# echo $?
1
```

In the first example, the *ls* command ran successfully and it produced desired results, hence a zero return code. In the second example, the *man* command did not run successfully since it required an argument, hence a non-zero return code. To display the value stored in the special variable ?, the *echo* command was used as shown in both examples above.

Within your script, you may wish to define exit codes at different locations. This would help debug by letting you know where exactly the script quit.

23.3.2   What You Can Test

Test conditions can be set on numeric values, string values, or on files using the *test* command. You may, instead, enclose a test condition inside the square brackets [ ] without using the *test* command explicitly. This is exhibited in logical construct examples later.

Table 23-2 shows various testing condition operations that you can perform.

Operation on Numeric Value	Meaning
integer1 –eq integer2	Integer1 is equal to integer2.
integer1 –ne integer2	Integer1 is not equal to integer2.
integer1 –lt integer2	Integer1 is less than integer2.
integer1 –gt integer2	Integer1 is greater than integer2.
integer1 –le integer2	Integer1 is less than or equal to integer2.
integer1 –ge integer2	Integer1 is greater than or equal to integer2.
Operation on String Value	**Meaning**
string1–string2	Checks if the two strings are identical.
string1! –string2	Checks if the two strings are not identical.
–l string or –z string	Checks if string length is zero.
–n string	Checks if string length is non-zero.
string	Same as "–n string".
Operation on File	**Meaning**
–b file	Checks if file exists and is a block device file.
–c file	Checks if file exists and is a character device file.
–d file	Checks if file is a directory.
–e file	Checks if file exists.
–f file	Checks if file exists and is a normal file.
–g file	Checks if file exists and has setgid bit on it.

−L file	Checks if file exists and is a symbolic link.
−r file	Checks if file exists and is readable.
−s file	Checks if file exists and is non-zero in length.
−u file	Checks if file exists and has setuid bit set on it.
−w file	Checks if file exists and is writable.
−x file	Checks if file exists and is executable.
file1 −nt file2	Checks if file1 is newer than file2.
file1 −ot file2	Checks if file1 is older than file2.
Logic Operator	**Meaning**
!	Opposite result of expression.
−a	AND operator.
−o	OR operator.

Table 23-2 Testing Conditions

Having described exit codes and various test condition operations, let us take a look at a few scripts and see how some of these can be utilized in them.

23.3.3   The if-then-fi Construct

The if-then-fi construct checks a condition for either true or false using the *test* command. If the condition is true, an action is performed, otherwise, it gets you out of the "if" statement. The "if" statement ends with a "fi". The syntax of this construct is:

```
if
        condition
then
        action
fi
```

You have seen earlier how to check number of arguments specified at the command line. You can write a shell script to determine that number and print an error message if there is none specified at the command line. The *if_then_fi.sh* does that.

 # cat if_then_fi.sh

```
#!/usr/bin/sh
# The name of this script is if_then_fi.sh.
# The author of this script is Asghar Ghori.
# The script is created on February 24, 2006.
# This script is last modified by Asghar Ghori on March 1, 2006.
# This script should be located in /usr/local/bin directory.
# The purpose of this script is to explain the usage of if-then-fi logical construct.
if
        [ $# −ne 2 ]        # You can also use it as "test $# −ne 2" in explicit mode.
then
    echo  "Error: Invalid number of arguments supplied."
        echo  "Usage: $0 source_file destination_file
        exit  2
```

```
fi
echo  "Script terminated."
```

This script will display the following message on the screen, if executed without specifying exactly two arguments at the command line:

```
Error: Invalid number of arguments supplied.
Usage: if_then_fi.sh source_file destination_file
```

Now, if you check the return code, a value of 2 will appear. This value reflects the exit code defined in the action.

```
# echo  $?
2
```

On the other hand, if you supply two arguments, the return code will be 0 and the message on your screen will be:

```
Script terminated.
```

```
# echo  $?
0
```

23.3.4   The if-then-else-fi Construct

This construct is used when you want to execute one or the other action, depending on the result of a test. The general syntax of the structure is:

```
if
          condition
then
          action1
else
          action2
fi
```

If the result of the condition is true, action1 is executed, otherwise action2.

The following script called *if_then_else_fi.sh* accepts an integer value as an argument and tells if it is positive or negative. If no argument is provided, it displays script usage.

```
# cat  if_then_else_fi.sh
```
```
#!/usr/bin/sh
# The name of this script is if_then_else_fi.sh.
# The author of this script is Asghar Ghori.
# The script is created on February 24, 2006.
# This script is last modified by Asghar Ghori on March 1, 2006.
# This script should be located in /usr/local/bin directory.
```

```
# The purpose of this script is to explain the usage of if-then-else-fi logical construct.
if
        [ $1 –gt 0 ]              # You can also use it as "test  $1  –ge  0" in explicit mode.
then
        echo  "$1 is a positive integer value".
else
        echo  "$1 is a negative integer value".
fi
```

Run this script one time with a positive integer value and the next time with a negative value.

 # if_then_else_fi.sh 10
10 is a positive integer value.

 # if_then_else_fi.sh –10
-10 is a negative integer value.

23.3.5   The if-then-elif-fi Construct

This construct defines multiple conditions; whichever is met, an action associated with it, is executed. The general syntax of the structure is:

```
if
              condition1
then
              action1
elif
              condition2
then
              action2
elif
              condition3
then
              action3
.............
.............
else
              action(n)
fi
```

The following script called *if_then_elif_fi.sh* is an upgraded form of *if_then_else_fi.sh* script. It accepts an integer value as an argument and tells if it is positive, negative, or zero. If a non-integer value or no command line argument is supplied, the script complains about it.

 # cat if_then_elif_fi.sh
```
#!/usr/bin/sh
# The name of this script is if_then_elif_fi.sh.
# The author of this script is Asghar Ghori.
```

```
# The script is created on February 24, 2006.
# This script is last modified by Asghar Ghori on March 1, 2006.
# This script should be located in /usr/local/bin directory.
# The purpose of this script is to explain you the usage of if-then-elif-fi logical construct.
if
        [ $1 –gt 0 ]
then
        echo "$1 is a positive integer value".
        exit 1
elif
    [ $1 –eq 0 ]
then
    echo "$1 is zero integer value".
    exit 2
elif
    [ $1 –lt 0 ]
then
    echo "$1 is a negative integer value".
    exit 3
else
    echo "$1 is not an integer value. Please supply an integer".
    exit 4
fi
```

Run this script one time with a positive value, second time with zero, third time with a negative value, and fourth time with a non-integer value. Each time you run it, check the value of exit code to see where the script actually exits out.

```
# if_then_elif_fi.sh  10
10 is a positive integer value.
# echo  $?
1

# if_then_elif_fi.sh  0
0 is zero integer value.
# echo  $?
2

# if_then_elif_fi.sh  –10
-10 is a negative integer value.
# echo  $?
3

# if_then_elif_fi.sh  abcd
abcd is not an integer value. Please supply an integer.
# echo  $?
4
```

23.3.6   The case Construct

The case construct compares a value against listed patterns. If a match is made, the commands associated with that pattern are executed and $? is assigned a 0 value. If a match is not made, $? is assigned a value other than 0.

Wildcard characters, such as *, ?, and [ ], can be used in patterns. The pipe | character can be used for logical OR operation. If you make an invalid choice, the last part of the case construct (followed by *)) is executed.

The general syntax of the case construct is given below:

```
case VAR in
        pattern1)
        command(s)
        ;;
        pattern2)
        command(s)
        ;;
......
......
        patternx)
        command(s)
        ;;
        *)
        command(s)
        ;;
esac
```

VAR is a variable whose value is checked against each pattern listed in the case statement. Note the two semicolon ;; characters. When the value of VAR matches a pattern, commands corresponding to that pattern are executed up to the next occurrence of the ;; characters. The) character marks the end of a pattern. If VAR matches none of the patterns, commands after *) are executed. The "case" statement ends with "esac".

The following example script called *case_menu.sh* is a menu-driven program and uses case construct:

 # cat case_menu.sh

```
#!/usr/bin/sh
# The name of this script is case_menu.sh.
# The author of this script is Asghar Ghori.
# The script is created on February 24, 2006.
# This script is last modified by Asghar Ghori on March 1, 2006.
# This script should be located in /usr/local/bin directory.
# The purpose of this script is to explain you the usage of the logical case construct.
clear
echo
echo "                        Menu "
```

```
echo "      --------------------------------------------------------"
echo "     [1] Display System's Current Date and Time".
echo "     [2] Display Boot Paths and Autoboot/Autosearch Settings".
echo "     [3] Run ioscan with –fnk options to list all disks".
echo "     [4] Run SAM".
echo "     ==================================="
echo
echo "Enter Your Choice [1-4] \c: "
/usr/bin/read  VAR
case  $VAR  in
    1) echo  "Current System Data and Time is `date`"
       echo
       echo  "Press any key to go back to the Menu......"
       /usr/bin/read
       ;;
    2) /usr/sbin/setboot
       echo
       echo  "Press any key to go back to the Menu......"
       /usr/bin/read
       ;;
    3) /usr/sbin/ioscan  –fnkCdisk
       echo  "Press any key to go back to the Menu......"
       /usr/bin/read
       ;;
    4) /usr/sbin/sam
       ;;
    *) echo  "You have selected an invalid choice".
       ;;
esac
```

When you execute *case_menu.sh* script, it will clear the screen and display a menu and four choices on the screen. If you choose option 1, the *date* command will be executed; if you opt for option 2, the *setboot* command will be executed; if you enter a 3, the *ioscan* command will be executed with –fnkCdisk; if you go with option 4, the *sam* command will be executed; and if you enter any other characters, the message "You have selected an invalid choice" will appear on the screen and the script terminate.

After finishing execution of a command associated with the first four options, a message "Press any key to go back to the Menu......" will appear on the screen. Notice, in the script that two commands *date* and *pwd* are executed and their outputs are used. When you enclose a command within forward quotes, the command gets executed and its result displayed.

23.4 Looping Constructs

In shell scripting, there are times when you need to perform a task on a number of given values or until a specified condition becomes true or false. For example, you are provided with a list of several physical disk device files and asked to issue the *pvcreate* command on each one of them. Instead of typing the command repetitively specifying one physical device file at a time, you can use a loop to perform the action on all the physical devices in one go. Likewise, based on a defined condition, you may want your program to continue to run until the condition becomes either true of false.

There are three constructs that implement looping: the "for-do-done" construct, the "while-do-done" construct, and the "until-do-done" construct.

The for-do-done construct performs an operation on a list of given elements until the list is exhausted. The while-do-done construct performs an operation repeatedly based on a specified condition until the condition becomes false. The until-do-done construct does the opposite of what the while-do-done construct does. It performs an operation repeatedly based on a specified condition until the condition becomes true.

23.4.1   What You can Test

The *let* command is used in looping constructs to check a condition every time a repetition is made. It compares the value stored in a variable against a defined value. Every time a loop does an iteration, the value in the variable is altered. You can enclose the test condition within (( )) or double quotes " ", instead of using the *let* command explicitly. This is exhibited in looping construct examples that follow shortly.

Table 23-3 lists operators that can be used with the *let* command.

Operator	Description
–	Unary minus.
!	Unary negation (same value but with a negative sign).
+	Addition.
–	Subtraction.
*	Multiplication.
/	Integer division.
%	Remainder.
<	Less than.
<=	Less than or equal to.
>	Greater than.
>=	Greater than or equal to.
=	Assignment.
==	Comparison for equality.
!=	Comparison for non-equality.

Table 23-3 *let* Operators

Having described various test condition operators, let us take a look at a few scripts and see how some of these can be utilized.

HP Certified Systems Administrator

23.4.2   The for-do-done Loop

The for-do-done loop is executed on a list of given elements until all the elements on the list are used up by the loop. Each element on the list is assigned to a variable one after the other and processed inside the loop. The syntax of this loop is:

```
for  VAR  in  list
do
            command block
done
```

The *for_do_done.sh* script below initializes a variable COUNT to 0. An array of items are supplied to a variable ALPHABET. The for-do-done loop reads the ALPHABET value one after the other, assigns it to another variable LETTER, and displays it on the screen. The *expr* command is an arithmetic processor and it simply increments the COUNT by 1 at each iteration of the loop.

 # cat for_do_done.sh

```
#!/usr/bin/sh
# The name of this script is for_do_done.sh.
# The author of this script is Asghar Ghori.
# The script is created on February 24, 2006.
# This script is last modified by Asghar Ghori on March 1, 2006.
# This script should be located in /usr/local/bin directory.
# The purpose of this script is to explain you the usage of the for-do-done looping construct.
COUNT=0
ALPHABET=A B C D E F G H I J K L M N O P Q R S T U V W X Y Z
for  LETTER  in  $ALPHABET
do
        COUNT=`/usr/bin/expr  $COUNT + 1`
        echo  "Letter $COUNT is [$LETTER]"
done
```

The output of the script will be:

 # for_do_done.sh
```
Letter 1 is [A]
Letter 2 is [B]
Letter 3 is [C]
Letter 4 is [D]
. . . . . . . .
. . . . . . . .
Letter 24 is [X]
Letter 25 is [Y]
Letter 26 is [Z]
```

The following for-do-done loop example script called *pvcreate_many.sh* defines a variable called *j* and contains a list of disk drives you want to *pvcreate*. When this script is executed, it takes the device name specified on the list one by one and executes the *pvcreate* command on it.

```
#!/usr/bin/sh
# The name of this script is pvcreate_many.sh.
# The author of this script is Asghar Ghori.
# The script is created on February 24, 2006.
# This script is last modified by Asghar Ghori on March 1, 2006.
# This script should be located in /usr/local/bin directory.
# The purpose of this script is to perform LVM pvcreate operation on a number of physical
# disk devices.
for  j  in  c2t2d0  c2t3d0  c2t4d0 c2t5d0  c2t6d0
do
     echo  "Creating LVM Structures on $j".
     /usr/sbin/pvcreate  /dev/rdsk/$j
done
```

The execution of the script will produce the following output:

 # pvcreate_many.sh
Creating LVM Structures on c2t2d0.
Physical volume "/dev/rdsk/c2t2d0" has been successfully created.
Creating LVM Structures on c2t3d0.
Physical volume "/dev/rdsk/c2t3d0" has been successfully created.
Creating LVM Structures on c2t4d0.
Physical volume "/dev/rdsk/c2t4d0" has been successfully created.
Creating LVM Structures on c2t5d0.
Physical volume "/dev/rdsk/c2t5d0" has been successfully created.
Creating LVM Structures on c2t6d0.
Physical volume "/dev/rdsk/c2t6d0" has been successfully created.

Another example is given below. This script called *create_user.sh* creates specified user accounts. As each account is created, the value of $? is checked. If the value is 0, a message saying that the account is created successfully, is displayed on the screen. If not, the script is terminated. In case of a successful user account creation, the *passwd* command is invoked on the user account to assign password to it.

 # cat create_user.sh

```
#!/usr/bin/sh
# The name of this script is create_user.sh.
# The author of this script is Asghar Ghori.
# The script is created on February 24, 2006.
# This script is last modified by Asghar Ghori on March 1, 2006.
# This script should be located in /usr/local/bin directory.
# The purpose of this script is to create multiple user accounts in one go.
for  USER  in  user10  user11  user12  user13  user14
do
     echo  "Creating account for user $USER".
     /usr/sbin/useradd  –m  –d  /home/$USER  –s  /usr/bin/sh  $USER
     if  [  $?  =  0  ]
             then
```

```
                    echo "$USER is created successfully."
        else
                    echo "Failed to create user account $USER".
                    exit
    fi
passwd  $USER
done
```

23.4.3   The while-do-done Loop

The while-do-done loop checks for a condition and goes on executing a block of commands until the specified condition becomes false. The general syntax of the loop is:

```
while
        condition
do
        command block
done
```

The condition is usually an expression containing a *test* or *let* command in either implicit or explicit mode, but they are normally used in implicit mode.

Let us look at the *while_do_done.sh* script below. This is an upgraded form of *case_menu.sh* that you created earlier in this chapter. The entire case statement is defined as a block of commands within the while-do-done loop here. When you choose one of the options listed, the command associated with that option is executed. Once the command is finished executing, you are prompted to press a key to go back to the menu. The loop continues until you choose option 5.

cat while_do_done.sh

```
#!/usr/bin/sh
# The name of this script is while_do_done.sh.
# The author of this script is Asghar Ghori.
# The script is created on February 24, 2006.
# This script is last modified by Asghar Ghori on March 1, 2006.
# This script should be located in /usr/local/bin directory.
# The purpose of this script is to show you an example of how a menu driven program can
# be included in a while loop so it continues to run until a specific option from the menu is
# chosen to exit out.
while  true
do
        clear
        echo "                    Menu "
        echo "    ----------------------------------------------------------"
        echo "    [1] Display System's Current Date and Time".
        echo "    [2] Display Boot Paths and Autoboot/Autosearch Settings".
        echo "    [3] Run ioscan with –fnk options to list all disks".
        echo "    [4] Run SAM".
        echo "    [5] Exit".
```

```
            echo "  ===================================="
            echo
            echo "Enter Your Choice [1-5] \c: "
            read VAR
            case $VAR in
                1) echo "Current System Data and Time is `date`"
                   echo
                   echo "Press any key to go back to the Menu......"
                   /usr/bin/read
                   ;;
                2) /usr/sbin/setboot
                   echo
                   echo "Press any key to go back to the Menu......"
                   /usr/bin/read
                   ;;
                3) /usr/sbin/ioscan –fnkCdisk
                   echo "Press any key to go back to the Menu......"
                   /usr/bin/read
                   ;;
                4) /usr/sbin/sam
                   echo "Press any key to go back to the Menu......"
                   /usr/bin/read
                   ;;
                5) echo "Exiting ........."
                   exit 0
                   ;;
                *) echo "You have selected an invalid choice".
                   echo "Please make a valid choice".
                   echo "Press any key to go back to the Menu......"
                   /usr/bin/read
                   ;;
            esac
done
```

23.4.4 The until-do-done Loop

The until-do-done loop repeats execution of a block of commands, until the specified condition becomes true. The only difference between this and the while-do-done loop is that it tests condition for false. The general syntax is:

```
until
        condition
do
        command block
done
```

The next script called *until_do_done.sh* does exactly what the *while_do_done.sh* script does. The only difference between the two is that you define "until false" instead of "while true".

---

cat until_do_done.sh

```
#!/usr/bin/sh
# The name of this script is until_do_done.sh.
# The author of this script is Asghar Ghori.
# The script is created on February 24, 2006.
# This script is last modified by Asghar Ghori on March 1, 2006.
# This script should be located in /usr/local/bin directory.
# The purpose of this script is to explain the usage of the until-do-done loop construct.
until false
do
        clear
        echo "                    Menu "
        echo "    ---------------------------------------------------------"
        echo "    [1] Display System's Current Date and Time".
        echo "    [2] Display Boot Paths and Autoboot/Autosearch Settings".
        echo "    [3] Run ioscan with –fnk options to list all disks".
        echo "    [4] Run SAM".
        echo "    [5] Exit".
        echo "    ===================================="
        echo
        echo "Enter Your Choice [1-5] \c: "
        read VAR
        case $VAR in
            1) echo "Current System Data and Time is `date`"
               echo
               echo "Press any key to go back to the Menu......"
               /usr/bin/read
               ;;
            2) /usr/sbin/setboot
               echo
               echo "Press any key to go back to the Menu......"
               /usr/bin/read
               ;;
            3) /usr/sbin/ioscan –fnkCdisk
               echo "Press any key to go back to the Menu......"
               /usr/bin/read
               ;;
            4) /usr/sbin/sam
               echo "Press any key to go back to the Menu......"
               /usr/bin/read
               ;;
            5) echo "Exiting ........."
               exit 0
               ;;
            *) echo "You have selected an invalid choice".
               echo "Please make a valid choice".
               echo "Press any key to go back to the Menu......"
               read
```

```
          ;;
    esac
done
```

23.4.5   Controlling Loop Behavior

There are three commands that may be used to control the behavior of a loop. These commands are *break*, *continue,* and *sleep.*

The *break* command discontinues the execution of a loop immediately and transfers control to the command following the done keyword.

The *continue* command skips execution of the remaining part of the loop and transfers control back to the start of the loop for next iteration.

The *sleep* command suspends the execution of a loop for a specified time period. It takes the value in seconds. The default is one second.

Your next script *file_remove.sh* is a simple text file removal program. It displays a list of files in the current directory and prompts you to enter a text file name. If the name you enter is a directory, a block special file, a character special file, or a symbolic link, the execution of the while-do-done loop will be broken (the *break* command) and the control transferred to the command that immediately follows the done keyword (which is *echo* in *file_remove.sh* script).

If the name you supply is a text file, the script executes the *rm* command with –i option, asking whether or not you wish to remove the file. If you reply "y", the file will be deleted and the control of the loop will be given back to the start of the loop. This is done only if you entered a text file name. In all other cases, the *break* command terminates loop execution.

The *sleep* command is supplied with an argument 5. This forces the loop to wait for 5 seconds before running *ls* –F.

The \t escape sequence is used to insert a tab before the text "Here are $PWD Contents:". This is done for better readability.

The last line of the script contains the *exit* command with 0 as an argument. Right after the program is finished, execute "*echo $?*" to verify whether or not the script ran successfully. A 0 status code would mean a success and a non-zero otherwise.

Notice that the colon ":" character is used with the *while* command in the script. This is another way of specifying "true" with *while*.

cat file_remove.sh

```
#!/usr/bin/sh
# The name of this script is file_remove.sh.
# The author of this script is Asghar Ghori.
# The script is created on February 24, 2006.
# This script is last modified by Asghar Ghori on March 1, 2006.
```

```
# This script should be located in /usr/local/bin directory.
# The purpose of this script is to explain the usage of the break, continue, and sleep
# commands in looping constructs.
PWD=`/usr/bin/pwd`
while  :
do
      echo
      echo  "\t Here are $PWD Contents:"
      echo  "\t ----------------------------------------"
      echo
      sleep  5
      /usr/bin/ls  −F
      echo
      echo  "Enter name of text file you want to remove: \c"
      read  FILE
      if  [  −d  $FILE  ]
         then
            echo  "This is a directory, not a text file. Please enter a text file name."
            break
      elif  [  −L  $FILE  ]
         then
            echo  "This is a symbolic link, not a text file. Please enter a text file name."
            break
      elif  [  −c  $FILE  ]
         then
            echo  "This is a character special file, not a text file. Please enter a text file
name."
            break
      elif  [  −b  $FILE  ]
         then
            echo  "This is a block special file, not a text file. Please enter a text file name."
            break
      elif  [  −p  $FILE  ]
      then
            echo  "This is a named pipe, not a text file. Please enter a text file name."
            break
      elif  [  −f  $FILE  ]
         then
            echo  "Type y to remove $FILE, n if you do not want to:\c"
            /usr/bin/rm  −i  $FILE
            echo  "The file is removed."
            continue
      fi
done
echo
echo  "Good Bye. See you later."
exit  0
```

Try running this script and supply a directory name, a block/character special file name, a symbolic file name, and a regular text file name, and see the results.

23.4.6   Ignoring Signals

A shell script is terminated when a user interrupts it by pressing the *ctrl+c* sequence or by executing the *kill* command with −1, −2, −3, −9, or −15 signal on the script's PID. If you want these signals to be ignored while your script is running, you can make use of the *trap* command. The *trap* command catches a specified signal and ignores it. For example, in *ignore_signals.sh* script, signals 1, 2, 3, and 15 are ignored when the script runs. These signals represent hangup, interrupt, quit, and terminate, respectively.

 # cat ignore_signals.sh

```
#!/usr/bin/sh
# The name of this script is ignore_signals.sh.
# The author of this script is Asghar Ghori.
# The script is created on February 24, 2006.
# This script is last modified by Asghar Ghori on March 1, 2006.
# This script should be located in /usr/local/bin directory.
# The purpose of this script is to see how the trap command can be used in scripts to ignore
# signals.
trap " 1 2 3 15
until  false
do
        clear
        echo "                    Menu "
        echo "    ---------------------------------------------------------"
        echo "    [1] Display System's Current Date and Time".
        echo "    [2] Display Boot Paths and Autoboot/Autosearch Settings".
        echo "    [3] Run ioscan with −fnk options to list all disks".
        echo "    [4] Run SAM".
        echo "    [5] Exit".
        echo "    ====================================="
        echo
        echo "Enter Your Choice [1-5] \c: "
        read  VAR
        case $VAR  in
            1) echo  "Current System Data and Time is `date`"
               echo
               echo  "Press any key to go back to the Menu......"
               /usr/bin/read
               ;;
            2) /usr/sbin/setboot
               echo
               echo  "Press any key to go back to the Menu......"
               /usr/bin/read
               ;;
            3) /usr/sbin/ioscan  −fnkCdisk
```

```
            echo
            echo  "Press any key to go back to the Menu......"
            /usr/bin/read
            ;;
        4) /usr/sbin/sam
            echo  "Press any key to go back to the Menu......"
            /usr/bin/read
            ;;
        5) echo  "Exiting ........."
           exit  0
           ;;
        *) echo  "You have selected an invalid choice".
           echo  "Please make a valid choice".
           echo  "Press any key to go back to the Menu......"
           /usr/bin/read
           ;;
       esac
done
```

Run this script and try to stop it by sending signals 1, 2, 3, and 15 using the *kill* command. You will notice that the script will continue to run, until you choose option 5 from the menu or send signal –9 with the *kill* command to the script's PID from another terminal window.

The *trap* command is normally used in scripts to perform some sort of cleanup or rollback function prior to ending a program after the program encounters a hangup, quit, kill, or terminate signal.

Summary

Shell scripting allows you to enclose one or more long and repetitive set of tasks into files, called scripts, and run them when needed to accomplish desired results. This saves you a lot of typing. In this chapter, you started off with an introduction to shell scripting. You were introduced to the components of a shell script. You wrote simple scripts to gather basic system information, define and manipulate local and environment variables, use and move command line arguments, and prompt for user input. You looked at requirements to run scripts and how to debug them.

You then moved on to more sophisticated and complicated scripts. You wrote and analyzed logical constructs based on the if-then-fi, if-then-else-fi, if-then-elif-fi, and case structures. You understood the purpose of exit codes and test conditions.

Finally, you learned how to create scripts that used for-do-done, while-do-done, and until-do-done looping constructs. You understood the use of the *break*, *continue*, and *sleep* commands within these loops. At the end you looked at an example that explained the usage of the *trap* command to ignore signals.

## 24

Introduction to Networking

This chapter covers the following major topics:

- ✓ What is a Network?
- ✓ Network topologies – bus, star, ring, and hybrid
- ✓ Network access methods – CSMA/CD, token passing, FDDI, ATM, and HPPI
- ✓ LAN cables
- ✓ Introduction to OSI Reference Networking Model
- ✓ The seven layers of the OSI Model
- ✓ Basic network terminology – gateway, protocol, port, socket, router, switch, bridge, repeater, and hub
- ✓ Understand packet encapsulation and de-encapsulation
- ✓ What is peer to peer networking?
- ✓ Introduction to the TCP/IP protocol stack and the TCP/IP layers
- ✓ Understand and use MAC addresses, ARP, and RARP
- ✓ Understand and define a system's hostname
- ✓ Understand IP addresses, network classes, and IP multiplexing
- ✓ Divide a network into multiple, smaller sub-networks and the role of subnet mask
- ✓ Introduction to Virtual Private Network (VPN)

24.1 What is a Network?

A network is formed when two or more nodes are interconnected to share resources and information. A node is any device connected directly to a network by wired or wireless means. A node can be a computer, such as a PC, a server, or a workstation; a printer, a hub or switch, a router, a data storage device, such as disk or tape, and so on.

To connect two nodes together, you need a cable, connectors, network ports, and the software that support the connectivity. To connect a number of nodes together so they can talk to one another, you need devices, such as hubs, switches, routers, gateways, etc. in addition to cables and connectors.

A network can be composed of several nodes located at a single physical location, such as a building or a campus. This type of network is called a *Local Area Network* (LAN) . Devices, such as hubs and switches, are used to provide inter-node connectivity. Figure 24-1 illustrates a typical LAN.

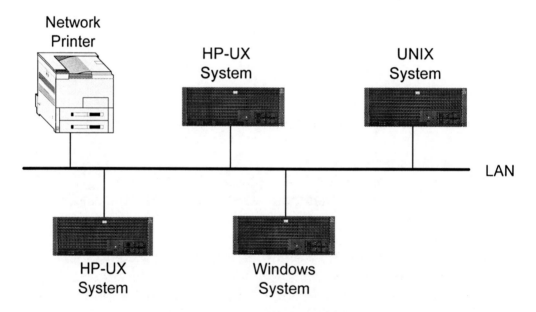

Figure 24-1 Local Area Network

LANs typically use Ethernet protocol to transfer data from one to the other node. Ethernet was developed in the late 1970's and has now become the global standard of data transmission in today's computer networks. Some of the reasons for its popularity include support for a variety of cable types, topologies, affordability, scalability, and native support within almost all network operating systems out there. The data transmission speed on an Ethernet LAN ranges from 10Mbps (*Mega Bits Per Second*) to 1Gbps (*Giga Bits Per Second*).

The other type of network can be composed of individual nodes or entire LANs that may be located geographically apart in different cities, countries, or continents. This type of network is called a

---

Wide Area Network (WAN). Devices, such as routers and gateways, are used to form a WAN using telephone lines, satellites, wireless, or other means. Figure 24-2 shows a typical WAN.

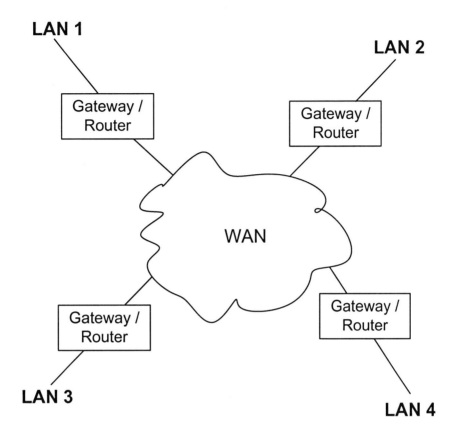

Figure 24-2 Wide Area Network

24.2   Network Topologies

A network topology refers to how computers, peripherals, interconnect devices, and physical media are coupled with one another. There are three common types of physical topologies: *Bus*, *Star*, and *Ring*. The fourth type is a combination of bus and star, and is known as *Hybrid*.

The following sub-sections discuss these topologies.

24.2.1   Bus Topology

The bus topology consists of a main backbone cable with a terminator connector at either end. All nodes are attached to the backbone. This type of topology is relatively inexpensive and easy to install for small networks. Figure 24-3 shows a bus topology network diagram with a thick line across representing the backbone cable.

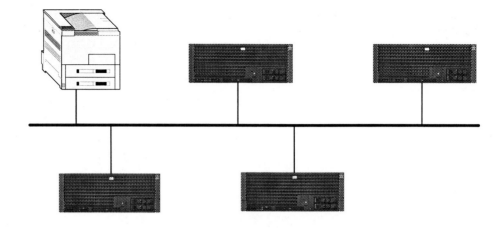

Figure 24-3 Bus Topology

The primary disadvantage with the bus topology is that a break in the backbone cable or fault in one of the terminators, shuts the entire network down.

24.2.2 Star Topology

The star topology uses a device called switch (or hub), with each node connected directly to it. Data packets must pass through this device to reach their destination. Ethernet networks typically use this topology. Figure 24-4 illustrates a star topology based network diagram.

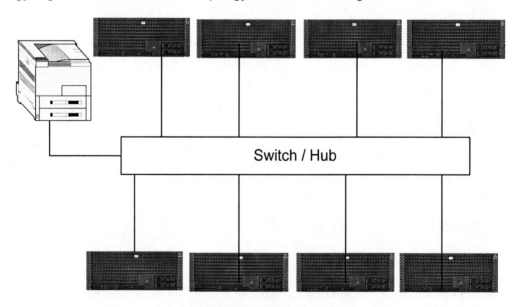

Figure 24-4 Star Topology

Star topology networks are easier to deploy and manage, and are highly scalable. Nodes can be connected or disconnected without any disruption to the function of the network. If there is a broken cable, only one node is affected; but if the switch or hub is down, all nodes connected to it, become inaccessible.

24.2.3　Ring Topology

The ring topology is a wiring scheme that allows information to pass from one node to another in a circle or ring. Nodes are joined in the shape of a closed loop, so that each node is connected directly to two other nodes, one on either side of it. Figure 24-5 shows a ring topology network diagram.

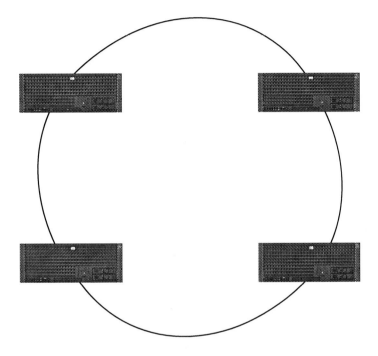

Figure 24-5 Ring Topology

The disadvantage with the ring topology is that if one of the cables in the ring breaks, all nodes in the ring become unreachable. This type of topology is more difficult to configure and wire than other topologies. The Token Ring protocol uses this topology on Token Ring networks.

24.2.4　Hybrid Topology

Corporate networks are generally formed using a combination of bus and star topologies. Switches (or hubs) installed on different floors of a building or in different buildings and campuses, are inter-connected using the bus topology scheme, whereas the start topology is employed to connect individual nodes to switches (or hubs). Figure 24-6 shows a hybrid topology network diagram.

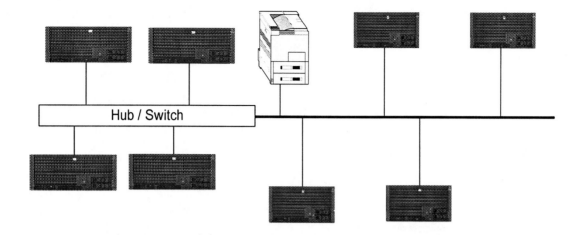

Figure 24-6 Hybrid Topology

24.3 Network Access Methods

Network access refers to the technique to send data over a physical medium. When a node wants to send a data packet to another node, it first needs to know if another node on the network is currently using the medium. There are two methods commonly employed for network access: *Carrier Sense Multiple Access with Collision Detection* (CSMA/CD) and *Token Passing*. CSMA/CD is used on Ethernet networks and Token Passing on IBM's Token Ring networks.

24.3.1 CSMA/CD

When data transfer occurs from one node to another on a network, the Ethernet protocol tries to determine whether or not the network medium is presently being used by another node. In case the medium is in use, the Ethernet protocol waits until the medium gets freed up. If, by chance, two nodes detect that the medium is free, both try to transmit their data packets simultaneously. This results in a collision situation. With Ethernet, each node that sends data over the medium also, at the same time, continuously checks if there is a collision occurred. If it detects a collision, it forces other nodes on the network to wait and retry later at random time instances.

24.3.2 Token Passing

Token Passing is a technique in which a node that wants to send data over the medium must capture a data frame called *Token*. The token travels on the ring constantly from node to node in a defined sequence. If a node wants to transmit data, it has to await and get the token. As soon as it gets the token, it attaches its data to the token and passes the token to the next node in the series. Each node along the way determines if the attached data is intended for it. If the destination address does not match the node address, the token is passed to the next node until it reaches the correct destination node. The receiving node detaches the data, frees up the token, and passes it on to the next node.

One of the nodes on the token ring network monitors the token activity so that if the token is lost, it generates a new one. If the destination node dies and no node is able to receive data attached to the token, this node detaches the data and mark the token free.

24.3.3   Other Network Access Methods

HP-UX natively support other physical medium technologies including *Fiber Distributed Data Interface* (FDDI), *Asynchronous Transfer Mode* (ATM), *High Performance Parallel Interface* (HIPPI), and *Hyperfabric*.

FDDI uses fiber cables in a dual ring topology that provides redundancy. ATM uses switching techniques. HIPPI and Hyperfabric allow high-speed point-to-point and node-to-node data communication links, respectively.

24.4   LAN Cables

Cables are run to connect LAN nodes together so that data can be transported among them. There are two types of physical medium protocols commonly employed in computer networks: Ethernet and Token Ring.

Ethernet LANs primarily use three types of cables: *Coaxial*, *Twisted Pair* (*Shielded Twisted Pair* – STP and *Unshielded Twisted Pair* – UTP), and *Fiber*. The Ethernet naming convention is based on the type of cable, supported maximum speed, and allowable maximum distance. For example, 10Base-2 Ethernet supports a maximum speed of 10Mbps and up to 185 meters per single segment. 10Base-5 Ethernet supports a maximum speed of 10Mbps and up to 500 meters per single segment. Both are coaxial cables and commonly used in bus topology networks. They are also referred to as *Thin Net* and *Thick Net*, respectively. Ethernet standards 10Base-T, 100Base-T, and 1000Base-T normally use UTP cables and are employed in star topology networks. They support maximum 10Mbps, 100Mbps, and 1Gbps speeds at distances of up to 100 meters. All five cable types mentioned use copper wires.

Ethernet is also supported on fiber cables at 1Gbps and on much longer distances. Ethernet standard for fibre is called 1000Base-FX and is used with 1000BaseSX card types.

Token ring networks usually use STP cables and support up to 1000Mbps data transfer rate.

Cables are categorized based on their electrical characteristics. Category 5 (or Cat 5) and Category 5e (or Cat 5 enhanced) copper cables are widely used today. These cables are good to support data transmission at up to 100Mbps speed. For 1000Mbps LANs, Cat 6 cables are available.

24.5   Introduction to OSI Reference Model

The *Open Systems Interconnection* (OSI) is a reference networking model developed in the early 1980's by the *International Organization for Standardization* (universally abbreviated as ISO) to provide guidelines to networking product manufacturers. These guidelines enabled them to develop products that can communicate with each other's software and hardware network products in a heterogeneous computing environment. The OSI reference model is defined and divided for ease in seven layers, with each layer performing a unique function independently from the other layer. Refer to Figure 24-7.

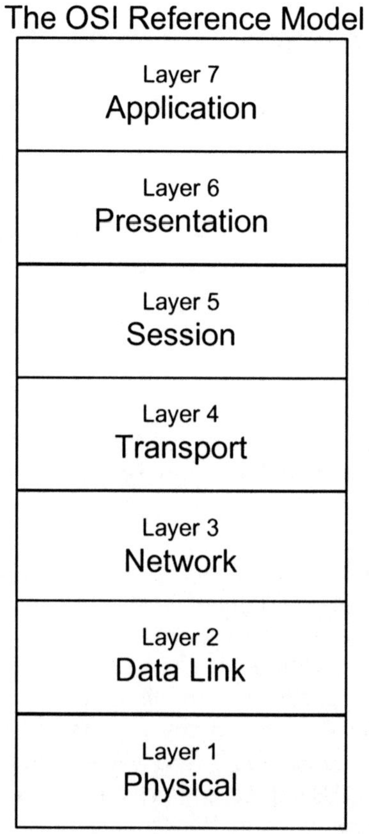

The OSI Reference Model

| Layer 7 |
| Application |
| |
| Layer 6 |
| Presentation |
| |
| Layer 5 |
| Session |
| |
| Layer 4 |
| Transport |
| |
| Layer 3 |
| Network |
| |
| Layer 2 |
| Data Link |
| |
| Layer 1 |
| Physical |

Figure 24-7 The OSI Reference Model

Each layer in the model interacts directly with two layers, one above it and one below it, except the top and the bottom layers. Functionality provided by the seven layers, can be divided into three categories: an application (such as FTP or telnet), a set of transport/network protocols (such as TCP and IP), and related software and hardware.

The function of the seven layers can be segregated into two groups. One group, containing the upper three layers (layers 5 to 7), relates to user applications, such as formatting of data. The other group, containing the lower four layers (layers 1 to 4), add transport information, such as address of the destination system.

Each of the seven layers of the OSI reference model are explained in the following sub-sections.

24.5.1   Layer 7: The Application Layer

The *Application* layer is where a user or program requests initiation of some kind of service on a remote system. Utilities and programs that work at this layer include *File Transfer Protocol* (FTP), *telnet, rlogin, remsh, rcp, Simple Network Management Protocol* (SNMP), *Simple Mail Transfer Protocol* (SMTP), *Hyper Text Transfer Protocol* (HTTP), *Trivial File Transfer Protocol* (TFTP), *Network File System* (NFS), *Dynamic Host Configuration Protocol* (DHCP), *Secure Shell (SSH), X Windows*, etc. On the remote system, server daemons for these services (*ftpd, telnetd, rlogind*, and so on) respond by providing requested services.

In other words, client and server programs for *ftp, telnet, http*, etc. work at this layer.

Gateway

A device called *Gateway* works at this layer. Actually, it works in such a way that it covers all seven layers. A gateway links two networks that run completely different protocols, viz., TCP/IP and NetBEUI, or TCP/IP and IPX/SPX, and enables them to talk to each other.

Protocol

A protocol is a set of rules governing the exchange of data between two nodes. These rules include how data is formatted, coded, and controlled. The rules also provide error handling, speed matching, and data packet sequencing. In other words, a protocol is a common language that all nodes on a network speak and understand. Some of the more common protocols are TCP, IP, ICMP, Ethernet, NetBEUI, and AppleTalk. Protocols are defined in the */etc/protocols* file. A sample */etc/protocols* file is shown below:

```
# cat /etc/protocols
. . . . . . . .
. . . . . . . .
ip       0     IP       # internet protocol, pseudo protocol number
icmp     1     ICMP     # internet control message protocol
igmp     2     IGMP     # internet group management protocol
ggp      3     GGP      # gateway-gateway protocol
tcp      6     TCP      # transmission control protocol
egp      8     EGP      # exterior gateway protocol
pup      12    PUP      # PARC universal packet protocol
udp      17    UDP      # user datagram protocol
. . . . . . . .
. . . . . . . .
```

The first column lists a protocol's official name, the second column shows the protocol number, and the third column identifies any associated aliases.

24.5.2   Layer 6: The Presentation Layer

This layer converts incoming data from the application layer into a format understandable by the remote machine where this message is to be sent. The layer manages the presentation of the data to be independent of the computer hardware architecture.

24.5.3　Layer 5: The Session Layer

This layer sets up, synchronizes, sequences, and terminates communication session established between a client program at source node and corresponding server program at the destination node. It deals with session and connection coordination between source and destination nodes.

24.5.4　Layer 4: The Transport Layer

This layer manages end-to-end data transfer reliability. It makes sure that data from the source to destination arrives error-free. It retransmits the data, if it does not reach the destination error-free. The protocols that work at this layer are *Transmission Control Protocol* (TCP) and *User Datagram Protocol* (UDP).

TCP

TCP is reliable, connection-oriented, point-to-point, and slow. When a stream of packets is sent to the destination node using TCP, the destination node checks for errors and packet sequencing upon its arrival. Each packet contains information, such as IP addresses for both source and destination nodes, data, a sequence number, source and destination port numbers, and checksum fields. The TCP protocol, at the source node, establishes a point-to-point connection with the peer TCP protocol at the destination. When the packet is received by the receiving TCP, an acknowledgement is sent back. If the packet contains an error or is lost while in transit, the destination node requests the source node to resend the packet. This ensures guaranteed data delivery and makes TCP reliable. Due to acknowledgment and handshaking, some overhead signals are added to TCP, making it slow. TCP is analogous to a telephone communication session between two parties.

TCP Window

It is important to mention the concept of *TCP Window* here that affects data packet transmission performance and, therefore, contribute to overall network performance. As you know, TCP, at the destination node, acknowledges all data packets as it receives them. The source node does not send more data packets than what the TCP window on the destination node can hold, until the source node gets an acknowledgment back from the destination node. Upon receiving an acknowledgment, the source node sends another stream of packets that the TCP window on the destination node can hold. The default TCP window size is 64KB. If you increase this value, the source node is able to transmit more data packets to the destination. This results in less number of acknowledgment signals going back, which contributes to improve overall network performance.

UDP

UDP, on the other hand, is unreliable, connectionless, multi-point, and faster than TCP. If a packet is lost or contains errors upon arrival at the destination node, the source node remains unaware of it. The destination node does not send an acknowledgement back to the source node. UDP is normally used for broadcast purposes. There are no overhead signals involved, which makes UDP faster than TCP. UDP is analogous to a radio broadcast, where there is no connection between parties.

TCP vs. UDP

Differences between TCP and UDP are summarized in Table 24-1.

TCP	UDP
Reliable	Unreliable
Connection-oriented	Connectionless
Point-to-point	Multipoint
Slow	Fast
Sequenced	Unsequenced
Acknowledgement	No acknowledgement
Uses TCP window for flow control	No such thing

Table 24-1 TCP vs. UDP

Ports and Sockets

Both TCP and UDP use ports and sockets for data transmission between a client and its associated server program. A port is either well-known or private. A well-known port is pre-defined and is used by a specific application. It is standardized across all network operating systems including all flavors of UNIX. Well-known ports are defined in the /etc/services file, an excerpt of which is shown below:

```
# cat  /etc/services
. . . . . . . .
. . . . . . . .
# The form for each entry is:
# <official service name>  <port number/protocol name>  <aliases>
#
ftp          21/tcp                          # File Transfer Protocol (Control)
telnet       23/tcp                          # Virtual Terminal Protocol
smtp         25/tcp                          # Simple Mail Transfer Protocol
time         37/tcp     timeserver           # Time
time         37/udp     timeserver           #
rlp          39/udp     resource             # Resource Location Protocol
whois        43/tcp     nicname              # Who Is
domain       53/tcp     nameserver           # Domain Name Service
domain       53/udp     nameserver           #
bootps       67/udp                          # Bootstrap Protocol Server
. . . . . . . .
. . . . . . . .
```

The first column lists a network service's official name, the second column contains the well-known port number and the transport layer protocol the service uses, and the third column identifies any associated aliases.

Some of the more commonly used services and the ports they listen on are: telnet on port 23, ftp on 21, sendmail on 25, http on 80, ntp on 123, and so on. Well-known ports range between 0 to 1023, inclusive.

A private port, on the other hand, is a random number generated when a client application attempts to establish a communication session with a server process. Private port numbers usually range between 1024 and 65535.

When a telnet request is initiated on *hp01* (source node with IP address 192.168.1.201) to get into *hp02* (destination node with IP address 192.168.1.202), a private port number (4352, for example) is generated and appended to the IP address of *hp01* to form a source-side socket. This socket information is included in data packets carrying the telnet request to *hp02*. Similarly, the IP address of *hp02* is appended by the well-known telnet port number from the */etc/services* file to form a destination-side socket. This socket information, too, is added to data packets. Here is what the two sockets will look like:

Source node (hp01):	192.168.1.201.4352	(IP address + private port number)
Destination node (hp02):	192.168.1.202.23	(IP address + well-known port number)

A combination of the two sockets distinctively identifies this telnet communication session from among several other possible telnet sessions established at that time.

24.5.5   Layer 3: The Network Layer

This layer routes and forwards data packets to the right destination using the right network path. It manages data addressing and delivery functions. Protocols that work at this level are *Internet Protocol* (IP), *Address Resolution Protocol* (ARP), *Reverse Address Resolution Protocol* (RARP), *Internet Control Message Protocol* (ICMP), *Serial Line Internet Protocol* (SLIP), *Point to Point Protocol* (PPP), *BootP*, etc.

Router

A router works at the network layer. It is a device that routes data packets from one network to another. The source and destination networks may be located thousands of miles apart. A router is widely used on corporate networks and the internet.

24.5.6   Layer 2: The Data Link Layer

This layer manages the delivery of data packets beyond the physical network. It does packet framing and provides error detection functionality. Protocols available at this layer are *Ethernet*, *IEEE 802.3*, *Fast Ethernet*, *Gigabit Ethernet*, *Token Ring*, *IEEE 802.5*, *Fibre Distributed Data Interchange* (FDDI), and so on.

Switch and Bridge

Network devices, switches and bridges, work at the data link layer. A switch determines, by looking at the MAC address contained within each incoming packet, which output port to forward the packet to. Once it determines that, it switches the packet to the port, which ultimately reaches the destination node. A switch offers dedicated bandwidth to data flow.

A bridge connects two LANs together, provided both use a common protocol (for example, Ethernet-Ethernet or Token Ring-Token Ring). A bridge examines MAC address contained within each data packet. If it matches one of the MAC addresses on the local network, the packet is passed to it. If it does not, the packet is forwarded to the destination on the other LAN.

24.5.7 Layer 1: The Physical Layer

This layer transmits data packets through the network. It describes network hardware characteristics including electrical, mechanical, optical, and functional specifications to ensure compatibility between communicating nodes. Protocols available at this layer are 10Base-T, 100Base-T, 1000Base-T, and so on.

Repeater and Hub

Network devices, repeaters and hubs, work at this layer. Also fall under this layer are cables, connectors, and LAN cards.

A repeater is a network device that takes data signals as input, filters out unwanted noise, amplifies the signals, and regenerates them to cover extended distances.

A hub is a network device that receives data from one or more directions and forwards it to one or more directions. The bandwidth of a hub is shared among connected, active nodes. For example, the speed per port on a 100Mbps, 12-port hub is 100/12, which is approximately equal to 8Mbps. This means each node is able to communicate at 8Mbps. This calculation is based on the assumption that all ports on the hub have nodes hooked up and being used.

24.5.8 Summary of OSI Layers

Table 24-2 summarizes OSI layer functions.

OSI Layer	Description
Application (7)	Users and programs request initiation of some kind of service on a remote system. Protocols/applications used at this layer are telnet, ftp, rlogin, rcp, remsh, SMTP, SNMP, NFS, HTTP, DNS, TFTP, DHCP, X Windows, and so on.
Presentation (6)	Manages presentation of data to be independent of computer hardware architecture.
Session (5)	Establishes, synchronizes, sequences, and terminates communication session setup between source and destination nodes.
Transport (4)	Manages end-to-end data transfer reliability. Protocols used at this level are TCP and UDP.
Network (3)	Manages data addressing and delivery functions. Protocols used at this level are IP, ARP, RARP, ICMP, SLIP, PPP, BootP, and so on.
Data Link (2)	Performs packet framing and provides error detection functionality. Protocols used at this layer are Ethernet, IEEE 802.3, Fast Ethernet, Gigabit Ethernet, Token Ring, IEEE 802.5, FDDI, and so on.
Physical (1)	Describes network hardware characteristics including electrical, mechanical, optical, and functional specifications.

Table 24-2 OSI Layer Functions

24.5.9 Encapsulation and De-encapsulation

Data transmission from source node to destination node takes place in the form of packets. When a message is created at the application layer, subsequent layers add header information to the message as it passes down towards the physical layer. Headers contain layer-specific information. When the message, along with header information, reaches the physical layer, it is referred to as a *Packet*. The process of forming a packet through the seven layers is called *Encapsulation*.

The packet is, then, transmitted as a stream of 1s and 0s through the medium to the destination node, where the physical layer receives the data stream and a reverse process is started. Headers are detached at each subsequent layer as the message passes up towards the application layer. This reverse process is referred to as *De-encapsulation*. Figure 24-8 illustrates encapsulation and de-encapsulation.

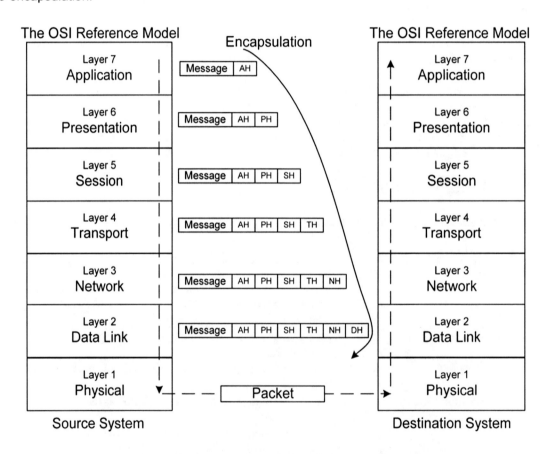

Figure 24-8 Encapsulation and De-encapsulation

24.5.10 Peer-to-Peer Model

Each layer on the source node acts as a peer layer to its corresponding layer on the destination node, making the OSI model peer-to-peer. Header information attached at the application layer can only be read, understood, and removed by the application layer on the receiving side. Similarly, header attached at the session layer can only be read, understood, and removed by the session layer on the receiving node, and so on for the other layers.

24.6 Introduction to TCP/IP

The *Transmission Control Protocol / Internet Protocol* (TCP/IP) is a suite of protocols developed by the US Department of Defense in 1969. Today, it is the global standard of information exchange. Although, there are scores of protocols within the TCP/IP protocol suite, the name is derived from the two key protocols: *Transmission Control Protocol* (TCP) and *Internet Protocol* (IP).

TCP/IP uses the client/server model of communication in which a client program on a source machine requests a service and the server program on the destination system responds. TCP/IP communication is primarily point-to-point, meaning each communication is between two nodes.

24.6.1 TCP/IP Layers

TCP/IP is layered similar to the OSI model. It is, in fact, based on the OSI reference model. Some vendors have defined TCP/IP suite in four layers, while others in five. In this sub-section, you will be presented with the model defined in four layers. Figure 24-9 shows the TCP/IP suite and compares it with the OSI reference model.

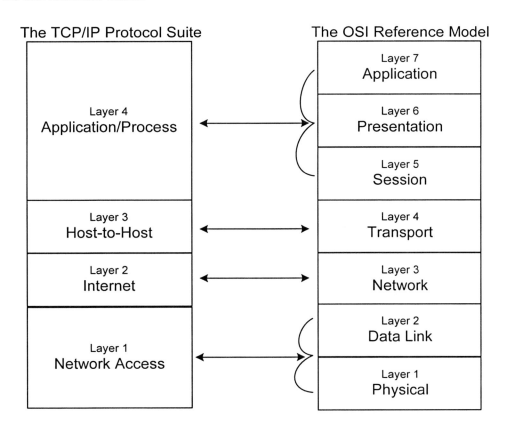

Figure 24-9 TCP/IP Protocol Suite

Figure 24-9 illustrates the TCP/IP protocol stack on the left hand side. It is compared with the OSI reference model. Notice that the bottom four layers are the same. The difference lies at the top three layers, where TCP/IP merges the application, presentation, and session layer functionalities into one layer, collectively called the *Application* Layer. For a detailed understanding of each layer and how they interact, refer to the previous sub-section on Introduction to OSI Reference Model.

24.6.2   MAC Address

Medium Access Control (MAC) is a unique 48-bit address used to identify the correct destination node for data packets transmitted from a source node. The data packets include MAC addresses for both the source and the destination nodes. A network protocol called *Address Resolution Protocol* (ARP), maps the MAC address to the destination node's IP address.

MAC address is also referred to as *Station* address, *Physical* address, *Link Level* address, *Ethernet* address, and *Hardware* address.

Use the *lanscan* command to list all LAN cards installed in your HP-UX system, along with their associated MAC (station) addresses.

```
# lanscan
Hardware    Station            Crd    Hdw     Net-Interface    NM MAC  HP-DLPI  DLPI
Path        Address            In#    State   Name PPA         ID Type  Support  Mjr#
8/16/6      0x0060B0B6CAE3     0      UP      lan0  snap0      1  ETHER  Yes      119
8/20/5/1    0x0060B058A2FA     1      UP      lan1  snap1      2  ETHER  Yes      119
```

The station addresses shown in the output are in hexadecimal notation preceded by 0x.

You can also use the *lanadmin* command to determine the hardware address of a LAN card. Run the command as follows to find the MAC address for *lan0* adapter. Specify only the card instance number.

```
# lanadmin –a  0
Station Address          = 0x001083362050
```

To view MAC addresses using SAM, follow the links:

☞ Go to SAM → Networking & Communications → Network Interface Cards.

24.6.3   Address Resolution Protocol (ARP)

As you know that IP and MAC addresses work hand in hand with each other and a combination of both is critical to identifying the correct destination node. A protocol called *Address Resolution Protocol* (ARP), is used to enable IP and MAC addresses to work with each other. Basically, the protocol is used to determine the MAC address of the destination node, when you already know its IP address.

ARP sends out a broadcast message across the network requesting each node alive to reply with its MAC and IP addresses. The MAC and IP addresses, thus received, are then cached locally by

---

the node in a special memory area called *ARP Cache*. If you wish to view all cached IP and MAC addresses, you can run the *arp* command with –a option as follows:

```
# arp  –a
192.168.1.1  (192.168.1.1)  at 0:40:f4:e3:ce:64  ether
sun05  (192.168.1.80)  at 8:0:20:a4:76:ab  ether
hp02  (192.168.1.202) at 0:60:b0:b6:ca:e3  ether
```

Entries in the ARP cache are normally kept for 10 minutes and then removed. These entries can be added to or removed/modified using the *arp* command.

To remove an entry from the ARP cache for the host *hp02*, do the following:

```
# arp  –d  hp02
```

Issue the *arp* command on *hp03* to determine MAC address for *hp02* as follows:

```
# arp  hp02
hp02 (192.168.1.202) at 0:60:b0:b6:ca:e3 ether
```

The *arp* command proves useful when you suspect duplicate IP addresses on the network. Check its output for any duplicate entries.

24.6.4   Reverse Address Resolution Protocol (RARP)

The reverse of ARP is possible with the *Reverse Address Resolution Protocol* (RARP). This protocol gets you the IP address of a remote node, if you already know the remote node's MAC address. It is typically used by DHCP and old diskless HP-UX workstations, X terminals, and network printers that only know their MAC addresses and not IP addresses. Refer to Chapter 35 "Introduction to BootP and TFTP Services" for detailed information.

24.6.5   Hostname

A hostname is a unique alphanumeric name assigned to a node. It is normally allotted based on the purpose and primary use of the node. You can choose any naming standard in accordance with your corporate IT naming convention policy. For example, the hostname "*hpdbp001*" in a multi-vendor environment can be assigned to the first HP-UX production database server and *sndbd003* can be given to the third SUN Solaris development database server.

The hostname is defined in the startup configuration file */etc/rc.config.d/netconf* via a variable. It can be set or modified using the *set_parms* command or SAM.

```
# set_parms  hostname
```

For the system to operate correctly, you must assign it a unique
system name or "hostname". The hostname can be a simple name
(example: widget) or an Internet fully-qualified domain name
(example: widget.redrock-cvl.hp.com).

A simple name, or each dot (.) separated component of a domain name, must:

 * Start and end with a letter or number.

 * Contain no more than 63 characters.

 * Contain only letters, numbers, underscore (_), or dash (-).
    The underscore (_) is not recommended.

The current hostname is hp03.

_____

Enter the system name, then press [Enter] or simply press [Enter]
to retain the current host name (hp03):
You have chosen hp03 as the name for this system.
Is this correct?
Press [y] for yes or [n] for no, then press [Enter]

 The hostname should contain eight characters or less for compatibility with some HP-UX utilities, such as *uname*, and applications.

To set hostname using SAM, follow the links:

☞ Go to SAM → Networking & Communications → Network Interface Cards. Highlight the network card and then Actions → Modify System Name.

24.6.6   IP Address

IP stands for *Internet Protocol* and represents a unique 32-bit software address that every single node on the network must have in order to communicate with other nodes. Every data packet sent out from a source node contains the destination node's IP address to determine the correct recipient of the packet and the route to be taken to reach that destination. MAC and IP addresses work hand in hand with each other to identify the correct LAN card or the correct port on a multi-port LAN card.

A multi-port LAN card is a LAN card that contains more than one LAN ports each with a unique MAC address.

An IP address consists of four 8-bit octets separated by the period (.) character. Each octet can have values between 0 and 255 (00000000 to 11111111), inclusive, based on 2^8 (2x2x2x2x2x2x2x2=256) formula. An IP address can be determined in both binary and decimal notations. Given an IP address in a binary notation, you can convert it into decimal notation, and vice versa. For instance, an IP address 192.168.1.202 is shown below in both binary and decimal notations:

```
11000000.10101000.00000001.11001010        (binary notation)
128+64   128+32+8      1      128+64+8+2
  192  .   168  .      1  .     202          (decimal notation)
```

Each bit in an octet has a weight based on its position in the octet. Figure 24-10 depicts that information as either "0" or "1".

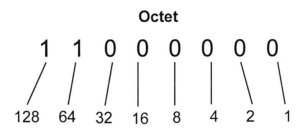

Figure 24-10 Binary to Decimal Conversion

Based on this formula, the first octet of the IP address given above, the two left-most bits are 1. When you sum them up, it comes to 192. The second octet has the 1st, 3rd, and the 5th left-most bits set to 1. When you sum them up, you get 168; and so on for the last two octets.

To view IP addresses assigned to LAN cards on a system, use the *netstat* or *ifconfig* commands:

```
# netstat –in
```

Name	Mtu	Network	Address	Ipkts	Opkts
lan1*	1500	1.0.0.0	1.1.1.2	14	16
lan0	1500	192.168.1.0	192.168.1.202	168284	158707
lo0	4136	127.0.0.0	127.0.0.1	2644	2644

```
# ifconfig lan0
lan0: flags=843<UP,BROADCAST,RUNNING,MULTICAST>
       inet 192.168.1.202 netmask ffffff00 broadcast 192.168.1.255
```

You can also use SAM to view IP addresses. Follow the links below:

☞ Go to SAM → Networking & Communications → Network Interface Cards.

The explosive growth of the internet and the presence of an extremely large number of nodes, with each requiring a unique IP address, the conventional IP address space, which is 2^{32} (four octets) and provides approximately 4.3 billion addresses, is almost used up. To overcome the shortage of IP addresses in the near future, a new version of IP address space is now available, and is referred to as IPv6 (IP version 6). IPv6 addresses are 128-bit, which means 2^{128} (16 octets) additional IP addresses. Also, IPv6 provides simplified packet header format, better routing capabilities, enhanced security controls, and many other new and enhanced features as compared to the conventional IP address space.

24.6.7   Network Classes

Each IP address is divided into two portions: a *Network* portion and a *Node* portion. The network portion identifies the correct destination network and the node portion identifies the correct destination node on that network.

Based on how many bits are allocated to the network portion, there are five useable IP address classes: A, B, C, D, and E. Classes A, B, and C are widely used, while classes D and E are dedicated, respectively, for multicast networks and scientific purposes. The following provides an explanation of classes A, B, and C.

Class A

Class A IP addresses are used for networks with an extremely large number of nodes. The first octet of a 32-bit IP address defines the network address; the remaining three octets are allocated to nodes. Figure 24-11 displays the division of bits in a class A IP address.

Figure 24-11 Class A Address

The total number of useable networks in class A can be up to $2^{8-1} - 2$ (126) and the total number of nodes can be up to $2^{24} - 2$ (16,777,214). Two is subtracted from both calculations above because IP addresses with all 0's in the first octet and all 1's in the last octet are reserved. Also, one network bit is subtracted from 8 to get 2^7 network numbers since 0 is always reserved. The network address range for class A networks is between 0 and 127 (**0**0000000 to **0**1111111), inclusive. See the example below that also shows reserved addresses:

    00001010.01111001.00110011.11010001 (binary notation)
       10   .   121 .   51   .   209   (decimal notation)

    10.121.51.**0**   (network address)
    10.121.51.**255** (broadcast address)

Notice "0" and "255" in the decimal notation of the IP address. Network and broadcast addresses are always reserved. Class A IP addresses always start with a "0" as shown in the binary notation.

Class B

Class B IP addresses are used for mid-sized networks. The first two octets of a 32-bit IP address define the network address; the remaining two octets are allocated to nodes. See Figure 24-12.

Figure 24-12 Class B Address

The total number of networks in class B can be up to 2^{16-2}, which is 16,384 (the first two bits in class B network addresses are reserved and, hence, not used in calculation). The total number of nodes can be up to $2^{16} - 2$, which comes to 65,534. The network address range for class B networks is between 128 and 191 (**10**000000 to **10**111111), inclusive. See the example below for a class B address that also shows reserved addresses.

    10100001.01111001.00110011.11010001 (binary notation)
       161 .   121 .   51   .   209   (decimal notation)

```
161.121.51.0          (network address)
161.121.51.255        (broadcast address)
```

Notice "10" in the binary notation of the IP address. Class B IP addresses always start with "10".

Class C

Class C IP addresses are used for networks with not more than 254 nodes. The first three octets of a 32-bit IP address define the network address; the remaining octet is allocated to nodes. Refer to Figure 24-13.

| Network Bits | . | Network Bits | . | Network Bits | . | Host Bits |

Figure 24-13 Class C Address

The total number of networks in class C can be up to 2^{24-3}, which is 2,097,152 (the first three bits in the network address are reserved and, hence, not used in calculation). The total number of nodes can be up to $2^8 - 2$, which is 254. The network address range for class C networks is between 192 and 223 (**110**00000 to **110**11111), inclusive. See the example below for a class C network address that also shows reserved addresses.

```
11010111.01111001.00110011.11010001  (binary notation)
  215  .  121  .  51  .  209      (decimal notation)

215.121.51.0          (network address)
215.121.51.255        (broadcast address)
```

Notice "110" in the binary notation of the IP address. Class C IP addresses always start with "110".

 Class D ranges from 224 to 239 and class E from 240 to 255.

24.6.8   Subnetting

Subnetting is a method by which a large network IP address space is divided into several smaller and more manageable logical sub-networks, commonly referred to as *Subnets*. Subnetting usually results in reduced network traffic, improved network performance, and de-centralized and easier administration, among other benefits.

As you are aware that an IP address contains a network portion and a node portion. Subnetting does not touch the network bits, rather, it makes use of the node bits only.
The following should be kept in mind when working with subnetting:

✓   Subnetting does not increase the number of IP addresses in a network. In fact, it reduces the number of useable IP addresses.
✓   All nodes in a given subnet must have the same subnet mask. Subnet mask is explained in the next section.
✓   Each subnet acts as a separate network and requires a router to talk to other subnets.

✓ The first and last IP addresses in a subnet (similar to a network) are reserved. The first address points to the subnet itself and the last is the broadcast address.

Subnetting employs using required number of node bits. For example, if you wish to divide a class C network address of 192.168.12.0 with default netmask of 255.255.255.0 into 6 useable subnets each with 30 useable node IP addresses, you need 3 left-most node bits (highlighted) from the right-most octet (node octet), as shown below:

$$192 \quad . \quad 168 \quad . \quad 12 \quad . \quad 0$$
$$11000000.10101000.00001100.\mathbf{000}00000$$

Here is the formula to calculate useable subnets. 2 subnet bits give you $2^2 - 2 = 2$ subnets, 3 subnet bits give you $2^3 - 2 = 6$ subnets, 4 subnet bits give you $2^4 - 2 = 14$ subnets, 5 subnet bits give you $2^5 - 2 = 30$ subnets, 6 subnet bits give you $2^6 - 2 = 62$ subnets, 7 subnet bits give you $2^7 - 2 = 126$ subnets, and so on. This formula is applicable to determine number of useable subnets created out of a class A, B, or C network address.

Similarly, use the same formula to determine number of useable node addresses. 2 node bits give you $2^2 - 2 = 2$ IP addresses, 3 node bits give you $2^3 - 2 = 6$ IP addresses, 4 node bits give you $2^4 - 2 = 14$ IP addresses, 5 node bits give you $2^5 - 2 = 30$ IP addresses, 6 node bits give you $2^6 - 2 = 62$ IP addresses, 7 node bits give you $2^7 - 2 = 126$ IP addresses, and so on. This formula is applicable to determine number of useable node addresses created out of a class A, B, or C network address.

As an example, suppose you have 3 subnet bits available to work with. The 3 bits would generate eight combinations – 000, 001, 010, 011, 100, 101, 110, and 111. The first and the last set of values (000 and 111), as you know, are reserved for network and broadcast addresses. This leaves the remaining 6 combinations useable. Table 24-3 lists the combinations along with subnet IP, range of useable IP addresses available within the subnet that you can assign to nodes, and broadcast subnet addresses.

Subnet Bits	Subnet IP	First Useable IP	Last Useable IP	Broadcast Subnet IP
000	Reserved for subnet address			
001	192.168.12.32	192.168.12.33	192.168.12.62	192.168.12.63
010	192.168.12.64	192.168.12.65	192.168.12.94	192.168.12.95
011	192.168.12.96	192.168.12.97	192.168.12.126	192.168.12.127
100	192.168.12.128	192.168.12.129	192.168.12.158	192.168.12.159
101	192.168.12.160	192.168.12.161	192.168.12.190	192.168.12.191
110	192.168.12.192	192.168.12.193	192.168.12.222	192.168.12.223
111	Reserved for subnet broadcast address			

Table 24-3 Subnetting

24.6.9   Subnet Mask

Once you have your network IP address subnetted, you need to determine something called *Subnet Mask* or *Netmask*. The subnet mask is the network portion plus the subnet bits. In other words, the subnet mask segregates the network bits from the node bits. It is used by routers and

HP Certified Systems Administrator

other network devices to determine the start and end of the network/subnet portion and the start and end of the node portion of a given IP address.

The subnet mask, like an IP address, can be represented in either decimal or binary notation. The 1s in the subnet mask identify subnet bits and 0s identify node bits. The default subnet masks for class A, B, and C networks are 255.0.0.0, 255.255.0.0, and 255.255.255.0, respectively.

To determine the subnet mask of the class C address 192.168.12.0 in the example earlier, set all network and subnet bits to 1 and all node bits to 0. This means the first 3 octets in the network portion plus the first 3 left-most bits in the node portion are set to 1 and the remaining 5 right-most node bits to 0.

11111111.11111111.11111111.**111**00000
255 . 255 . 255 . 224

This gives the netmask of 255.255.255.224. In class A networks, there are 22 valid netmasks. Consult Table 24-4.

Subnet Mask	# of Subnet Bits	Useable Subnets	Nodes per Subnet
255.128.0.0	1	1	8,388,606
255.192.0.0	2	2	4,194,302
255.224.0.0	3	6	2,097,150
255.240.0.0	4	14	1,048,574
255.248.0.0	5	30	524,286
255.252.0.0	6	62	262,142
255.254.0.0	7	126	131,070
255.255.0.0	8	254	65,534
255.255.128.0	9	510	32,766
255.255.192.0	10	1,022	16,382
255.255.224.0	11	2,046	8,190
255.255.240.0	12	4,094	4,094
255.255.248.0	13	8,190	2,046
255.255.252.0	14	16,382	1,022
255.255.254.0	15	32,766	510
255.255.255.0	16	65,534	254
255.255.255.128	17	131,070	126
255.255.255.192	18	262,142	62
255.255.255.224	19	524,286	30
255.255.255.240	20	1,048,574	14
255.255.255.248	21	2,097,150	6
255.255.255.252	22	4,194,302	2

Table 24-4 Subnet Masks for Class C

In class B networks, there are 14 valid netmasks. Consult Table 24-5.

Subnet Mask	# of Subnet Bits	Useable Subnets	Nodes per Subnet
255.255.128.0	1	1	32,766
255.255.192.0	2	2	16,382
255.255.224.0	3	6	8,190
255.255.240.0	4	14	4,094
255.255.248.0	5	30	2,046
255.255.252.0	6	62	1,022
255.255.254.0	7	126	510
255.255.255.0	8	254	254
255.255.255.128	9	510	126
255.255.255.192	10	1,022	62
255.255.255.224	11	2,046	30
255.255.255.240	12	4,094	14
255.255.255.248	13	8,190	6
255.255.255.252	14	16,382	2

Table 24-5 Subnet Masks for Class B

In class C networks, there are 6 valid netmasks. Consult Table 24-6.

Subnet Mask	# of Subnet Bits	Useable Subnets	Nodes per Subnet
255.255.255.128	1	1	126
255.255.255.192	2	2	62
255.255.255.224	3	6	30
255.255.255.240	4	14	14
255.255.255.248	5	30	6
255.255.255.252	6	62	2

Table 24-6 Subnet Masks for Class C

To determine the subnet IP for a given IP address, such as 192.168.12.72 with netmask 255.255.255.224, write the IP address in binary format. Then write the subnet mask in binary format with all network and subnet bits set to 1 and all node bits set to 0. Now perform the logical AND operation. For each matching 1, you get 1, otherwise 0. The following highlights ANDed bits:

```
11000000.10101000.00001100.01001000       (IP address)
11111111.11111111.11111111.11100000       (subnet mask)
==================================
11000000.10101000.00001100.01000000       (subnet IP)
   192  .  168  .  12  .   64             (subnet IP in decimal format)
```

This calculation enables you to determine subnet IP from a given IP address and subnet mask.

24.6.10   IP Multiplexing

A single physical LAN card can have multiple IP addresses assigned to it to create multiple logical interfaces. Each IP address then points to a unique hostname. Assigning multiple IP addresses to a single physical LAN card/port is called *IP Multiplexing*.

IP multiplexing enables a single system with single LAN card to be seen as multiple systems, with each system having its own IP address and unique hostname. This functionality allows several applications that need to be run on separate systems to appear to users as if the applications reside on separate, physical systems.

Each logical interface uses a unique logical instance number. For example, the first logical interface on lan2 would be lan2:1, the second would be lan2:2, and so on. In this naming convention, "lan" refers to the network interface card, digit "2" represents the *Physical Point of Attachment* (PPA), which is a numerical index for the physical card within its class, and ":1" and ":2" represent logical instances corresponding to logical interfaces for the specified card. The default is 0. The interface name lan2 is same as lan2:0.

The first logical instance 0 in lan0:0, lan1:0, and so on, is known as the *Initial* interface. The initial interface for a LAN card must be configured before any subsequent logical interfaces, such as lan2:1, lan2:2, lan3:3 can be configured on it. Note that the logical interfaces do not have to be assigned in this sequence; in fact, lan3:3 can be configured even if lan2:1 and lan2:2 are not configured.

24.7   Virtual Private Network

A *Virtual Private Network* (VPN) is a network that uses the public network infrastructure, such as the internet, to transfer information confidentially and securely in the form of data packet streams. Corporations and organizations throughout the world allow their employees and other privileged users, regardless of their physical location, to connect to the corporate network remotely over the internet using VPN. The connection into the corporate network via VPN provides them with exact same access to corporate computing resources that they get when they are physically on the company premises with their computers connected to the network.

Since a VPN makes use of the public network, tools and techniques are widely available and employed by companies and organizations to secure information transfer. VPNs typically cost a lot lower than having dedicated leased lines.

Summary

In this chapter, you were introduced to basics of networking. The chapter started off with providing an understanding of network, types of network, and various common network topologies and access methods being employed in the industry.

The next section covered the OSI reference networking model in detail. You learned about the layers of the model, how packets were encapsulated and de-encapsulated, and the peer-to-peer nature of the model. You looked at a few other sub-topics including key transport protocols, concepts of ports and sockets, and definitions of devices, such as gateways, routers, switches, repeaters, hubs, and so on.

The TCP/IP protocol stack and concepts related to it were discussed in detail. Topics, such as TCP/IP layers, MAC address, ARP, RARP, hostname, IP address, network classes, and IP multiplexing provided you good understanding of the basics of TCP/IP. Finally, you were explained what the concepts of subnetting and subnet mask were, how to divide a network address into multiple sub-networks, and the role subnet mask played. At the end, you looked at some basic information on virtual private network that allowed secure transmission of confidential data over public network infrastructure.

## 25

LAN Card Administration and Routing

This chapter covers the following major topics:

- ✓ Configure a LAN card/port and assign a single IP address
- ✓ Configure a LAN card/port and assign multiple IP addresses
- ✓ Enable a LAN card/port to activate at each system reboot
- ✓ The role of the /etc/hosts file
- ✓ What is routing?
- ✓ Add, delete, and display routes
- ✓ Establish default routes and flush routing table
- ✓ Activate DHCP client functionality

25.1 LAN Card Administration

In order for an HP-UX system to communicate with other nodes on the network, one of its LAN cards (or a LAN port on a multi-port LAN card) must be configured with a unique IP address, hostname, and other associated network parameters. The following sub-sections provide procedure on how to configure LAN cards/ports.

25.1.1 Configuring a LAN Card/Port

To successfully configure a LAN card/port, follow the steps below:

1. Ensure HP-UX networking software, which includes TCP/IP, is installed. Execute the *swlist* command to verify the presence of the software.

    # swlist –l product | grep –i networking
    Networking   B.11.11   HP-UX_Lanlink_Product

    If the software is not loaded, use the *swinstall* command to install it from the HP-UX CD/DVD.

2. Verify if proper software drivers are loaded in the HP-UX kernel for the LAN cards to operate properly. The drivers for most LAN cards get automatically installed and configured, when HP-UX is initially installed. Use the *ioscan* command as follows:

    # ioscan –fnkClan

Class	I	H/W Path	Driver	S/W State	H/W Type	Description
lan	0	8/16/6	lan2	**CLAIMED**	INTERFACE	Built-in LAN
		/dev/diag/lan0 /dev/ether0				
lan	1	8/20/5/1	btlan0	**CLAIMED**	INTERFACE	EISA card INP0500

    The output shows the S/W State of the two LAN cards as "CLAIMED", which indicates that their driver is installed and the LAN cards are bound to it. If it has "UNCLAIMED" state, then you would have to install a proper driver, regenerate the kernel, and reboot the machine.

    You can also use the *lsdev* command to list driver:

    # lsdev –C lan

Character	Block	Driver	Class
5	-1	btlan	lan
23	-1	fcT1_cntl	lan
31	-1	fddi4	lan
37	-1	btlan0	lan
44	-1	fddi0	lan
45	-1	fddi3	lan
48	-1	btlan1	lan

    · · · · · · · ·
    · · · · · · · ·

3. Identify what LAN card/port you want to use. The *ioscan* (as displayed in the previous step) and *lanscan* commands (shown below) list all LAN cards/ports.

 # lanscan

Hardware Path	Station Address	Crd In#	Hdw State	Net-Interface NamePPA	NM ID	MAC Type	HP-DLPI Support	DLPI Mjr#
8/16/6	0x0060B0B6CAE3	0	UP	lan0 snap0	1	ETHER	Yes	119
8/20/5/1	0x0060B058A2FA	1	UP	lan1 snap1	2	ETHER	Yes	119

On this HP-UX machine, *hp02*, from the output of the two commands above, it is obvious that there are two LAN cards installed. The default naming convention is lan0 (*/dev/lan0*) for the first LAN card, lan1 (*/dev/lan1*) for the second card, lan2 (*/dev/lan2*) for the third card, and so on. The numbers 0, 1, 2, etc. refer to the **P**hysical **P**oint of **A**ttachment (PPA) of the card in the system and are preceded by "lan". This is the standard naming convention for LAN cards in HP-UX.

4. Assign IP address and other network parameters to the LAN card/port using the *ifconfig* command. For this example, you are going to use lan1 to have class C IP address of 193.11.211.2, default netmask of 255.255.255.0, and broadcast address of 193.11.211.255.

**# ifconfig lan1 inet 193.11.211.2 netmask 255.255.255.0 broadcast \
193.11.211.255 up**

You can also achieve the above by running the *ifconfig* command as follows:

 # ifconfig lan1 193.11.211.2 255.255.255.0

The *ifconfig* command is used to assign an IP address to a LAN card/port, setup local loopback interface, activate or deactivate a LAN card/port, and assign a subnet mask. It is executed automatically at boot time through the */sbin/init.d/net* startup script. The keywords "inet", "netmask", "broadcast", and "up" are defaults.

5. Run the *ifconfig* and *netstat* commands to verify the new IP assignment:

 # ifconfig lan1
lan1: flags=843<**UP**,BROADCAST,**RUNNING**,MULTICAST>
        inet **193.11.211.2** netmask **ffffff00** broadcast **193.11.211.255**

The output demonstrates that the IP address 193.11.211.2 is assigned to lan1 with netmask 255.255.255.0 and broadcast address 193.11.211.255. It also shows that the LAN card is up and running.

 # netstat –in

Name	Mtu	Network	Address	Ipkts	Opkts
lan1*	1500	193.11.211.0	193.11.211.2	0	0
lan0	1500	192.168.1.0	192.168.1.202	90173	68601
lo0	4136	127.0.0.0	127.0.0.1	2337	2337

25.1.2   Configuring IP Multiplexing

If you plan to run multiple applications on a single system, you can have multiple IP addresses and hostnames assigned to a single physical LAN card/port. Users of each application will be given a different hostname/IP address to access the same system. The *ifconfig* command below assigns three additional logical IP addresses to lan1 with default netmask.

```
# ifconfig  lan1:1  193.12.211.2
# ifconfig  lan1:2  193.13.211.2
# ifconfig  lan1:3  193.14.211.2
```

Note that when you execute *ifconfig* to set multiplexing, you specified lan1:1, lan1:2, lan1:3, and so on. You did not use lan1:0. This is based on the fact that 0 always point to the first IP address assigned to a LAN card. In the example above, the first IP address is 193.11.211.2 that you assigned earlier. Run the *netstat* command to check the results.

```
# netstat  –in
```

Name	Mtu	Network	Address	Ipkts	Opkts
lan1:1*	1500	193.12.211.0	193.12.211.2	0	0
lan1*	1500	193.11.211.0	193.11.211.2	0	0
lan0	1500	192.168.1.0	192.168.1.202	90496	68791
lo0	4136	127.0.0.0	127.0.0.1	2337	2337
lan1:3*	1500	193.14.211.0	193.14.211.2	0	0
lan1:2*	1500	193.13.211.0	193.13.211.2	0	0

25.1.3   Setting a LAN Card/Port to Activate at System Boot

The LAN card/port configuration you did in previous sub-sections, is not going to survive across system reboots. If you want the settings to be preserved and automatically assigned to the LAN card/port at each system reboot, you need to define them in the */etc/rc.config.d/netconf* startup configuration file. This is the source file for */sbin/init.d/net* startup script, which is executed at boot time, when the system reaches run level 2. This script reads the configuration file and executes *ifconfig* on all LAN card/port entries that it finds in the file.

Edit the */etc/rc.config.d/netconf* file and add entries as follows for the four IP addresses that you assigned above:

```
INTERFACE_NAME[1]=lan1
IP_ADDRESS[1]=193.11.211.2
SUBNET_MASK[1]=255.255.255.0
BROADCAST_ADDRESS[1]=""
INTERFACE_STATE[1]=up

INTERFACE_NAME[2]=lan1:1
IP_ADDRESS[2]=193.12.211.2
SUBNET_MASK[2]=255.255.255.0
BROADCAST_ADDRESS[2]=""
INTERFACE_STATE[2]=up
```

INTERFACE_NAME[3]=lan1:2
IP_ADDRESS[3]=193.13.211.2
SUBNET_MASK[3]=255.255.255.0
BROADCAST_ADDRESS[3]=""
INTERFACE_STATE[3]=up

INTERFACE_NAME[4]=lan1:3
IP_ADDRESS[4]=193.14.211.2
SUBNET_MASK[4]=255.255.255.0
BROADCAST_ADDRESS[4]=""
INTERFACE_STATE[4]=up

The */sbin/init.d/net* script can be run manually to activate the entries.

 # /sbin/init.d/net start

Use the *netstat* command with –in switches to verify the settings.

 # netstat –in

With SAM too, you can perform the above tasks. Follow the links below:

☞Go to SAM → Networking & Communications → Network Interface Cards. Highlight a LAN card/port from the list and go to Actions → Configure. Answer questions in the dialog box that follows. See Figure 25-1.

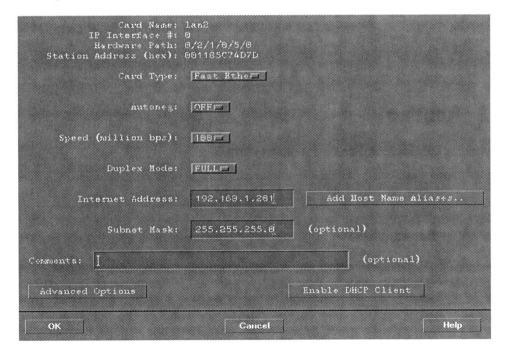

Figure 25-1 SAM – LAN Card Configuration

25.1.4   Defining an IP Address and Hostname in the */etc/hosts* File

You need to choose hostnames to be assigned to each individual IP address. For example, the system you configured four IP addresses on, requires four hostnames, such as server1, server2, server3, and server4. The entries in the */etc/hosts* file will look like:

```
193.11.211.2        server1        db01     # first logical server
193.12.211.2        server2        db02     # second logical server
193.13.211.2        server3        db03     # third logical server
193.14.211.2        server4        db04     # fourth logical server
```

The */etc/hosts* file is typically used, if you need to access systems on a local network only. This file must be maintained locally on each system.

Each line in the */etc/hosts* file contains an IP address in the first column followed by the official (or *Canonical*) hostname associated with it in the second column. You may also define one or more aliases per entry (*db01*, *db02*, *db03*, and *db04* in the above example). The official hostname and one or more aliases, allow you to have multiple hostnames assigned to a single IP address. This way, you can access the same system using any of the names.

Since */etc/hosts* is maintained locally, you must update it manually on each system to maintain consistency, whenever an update is required.

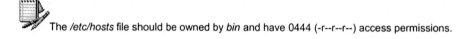 The */etc/hosts* file should be owned by *bin* and have 0444 (-r--r--r--) access permissions.

You can use SAM to add or remove entries to and from the */etc/hosts* file. Follow the steps below:

☞ Go to SAM → Networking and Communications → Internet Addresses → Select Actions and Add.

25.2   Routing

The following sub-sections discuss the basics of routing.

25.2.1   Routing Concepts

Routing refers to the process of choosing a path over which to send a data packet, and router is the device that performs this function.

When nodes on two different networks (or subnets) want to communicate with each other, proper route(s) must be setup in order for them to talk to each other. For instance, if a node on network A, sends a data packet to a node on network B, one or more routing devices come in between to route the packet to the correct destination network. The two networks can be located in the same data center or thousands of miles apart. Once the data packet reaches a router, the router selects the next router along the path toward the destination node. The packet passes from router to router, until it reaches the router that can deliver the packet directly to the destination node.

When a node sends out a packet, one of the following happens:

✓ If both the source and the destination nodes are on the same network (or subnet), the packet is sent directly to the destination node. A router extracts the network portion of the destination node's address and compares it to the network portion of its own IP address to see if the destination node lies on its own network. A match indicates that the packet can be sent directly to the destination node.

✓ If the source and the destination nodes are on two different networks, all defined routes are tried one after the other. If a proper route is found, the packet is forwarded to that specific router, which then forwards the packet to the destination node.

✓ If the source and the destination nodes are on two different networks but no routes are defined, the packet is forwarded to the *Default Router* (or *Default Gateway*), which tries to find a route to the destination. If found, it delivers the packet to the destination node.

An HP-UX system passes all data destined to other networks through the default router. By default, HP-UX is able to deliver data to any system on its network once its IP address and subnet mask have been set. An HP-UX system can be configured to perform the function of a router.

Routes are either *Static* or *Dynamic*. A static route is fixed and does not get changed across system reboots. It is defined in the */etc/rc.config.d/netconf* file.

A dynamic route, on the other hand, changes constantly. Some of the more common dynamic routing protocols used in the industry are *Routing Information Protocol* (RIP), *Open Shortest Path First* (OSPF), *Exterior Gateway Protocol* (EGP), and *Border Gateway Protocol* (BGP). All these protocols are supported by HP-UX.

Routing protocols are classified in two major groups based on the mechanism they use to determine the best route between the source and destination nodes. These are referred to as *Distance Vector* protocols and *Link State* protocols. Distance vector protocols choose a routing path that has the least number of routers (or hops). RIP uses this routing mechanism.

Link state protocols use additional factors, such as link bandwidth and reliability, to determine the best route. OSPF uses this routing mechanism.

25.2.2   Routing Table

A *Routing Table* maintains information about available routes and their status. It is maintained by the HP-UX kernel in memory. You can view the routing table with the *netstat* command as follows:

```
# netstat –r
Routing tables
Destination          Gateway          Flags    Refs    Interface      Pmtu
localhost            localhost        UH       0       lo0            4136
hp02                 hp02             UH       0       lan0           4136
192.168.1.0          hp02             U        2       lan0           1500
127.0.0.0            localhost        U        0       lo0            0
default              hp02             U        0       lan0           1500
```

You may want to specify the –n option to see the output in numerical format:

```
# netstat –rn
Routing tables
Destination        Gateway          Flags   Refs   Interface      Pmtu
127.0.0.1          127.0.0.1        UH      0      lo0            4136
192.168.1.202      192.168.1.202    UH      0      lan0           4136
192.168.1.0        192.168.1.202    U       2      lan0           1500
127.0.0.0          127.0.0.1        U       0      lo0            0
default            192.168.1.202    U       0      lan0           1500
```

As you notice, there are six columns in the output of the *netstat* command. These are explained in Table 25-1:

Column	Description
Destination	Destination route to a host or network.
Gateway	Packets are routed to the destination through this address.
Flags	Displays route type. Following are various flags: U – route is up and it is a network route. H – route is a host route. UH – route is up and it is a host route. G – route is through a gateway. D – route is created dynamically. M – gateway route has been modified. ? – gateway route is unknown.
Refs	Displays current route usage.
Interface	LAN interface used by the route.
Pmtu	*Path Maximum Transfer Unit*. Default for Ethernet is 1500 and that for loopback is 4136.

Table 25-1 *netstat* Command Output Description

25.3   Managing Routes

Managing routes involves adding a route, deleting a route, flushing the routing table, and modifying the default route. You can use either the *route* command or SAM to perform these tasks. Alternatively, you can manually edit the */etc/rc.config.d/netconf* file to add, delete, flush, or modify route entries.

25.3.1   Adding a Route

A route can be set to a network or host. Following provides procedures for both:

Adding a Route to a Network

To add a route to a network, such as 192.168.2 with default class C netmask and gateway 192.168.1.1, do the following:

 # route add net 192.168.2.0 netmask 255.255.255.0 192.168.1.1 1

If you want this route setting to be available across system reboots, edit the */etc/rc.config.d/netconf* file and add the following entry to it. The */sbin/init.d/net* script executes the *route* command at each system reboot and sources these entries from the */etc/rc.config.d/netconf* file.

ROUTE_DESTINATION[0]="net 192.168.2.0"
ROUTE_MASK[0]="255.255.255.0"
ROUTE_GATEWAY[0]=192.168.1.1
ROUTE_COUNT[0]=1
ROUTE_ARGS[0]=""

After placing the entry, you may wish to manually set it by running the following. Note that this will also execute other entries defined in the */etc/rc.config.d/netconf* file.

 # /sbin/init.d/net start

Use the *netstat* command with –rn switches to verify the settings.

 # netstat –rn

Adding a Route to a Host

To add a route to a host , such as192.168.3.31 with default class C netmask and gateway 192.168.1.1, do the following:

 # route add host 192.168.3.31 netmask 255.255.255.0 192.168.1.1 1

If you want this route setting to be available across system reboots, edit the */etc/rc.config.d/netconf* file and add the following entry to it. The */sbin/init.d/net* script executes the *route* command at each system reboot and sources these entries from the */etc/rc.config.d/netconf* file.

ROUTE_DESTINATION[0]="192.168.3.31"
ROUTE_MASK[0]="255.255.255.0"
ROUTE_GATEWAY[0]=192.168.1.1
ROUTE_COUNT[0]=1
ROUTE_ARGS[0]=""

After placing the entry, you may wish to manually set it by running the following. Note that this will also execute other entries defined in the */etc/rc.config.d/netconf* file.

 # /sbin/init.d/net start

Use the *netstat* command with –rn switches to verify the settings.

> # netstat –rn

25.3.2 Deleting a Route

To delete the two routes you just added, do the following:

> # route delete net 192.168.2.0 192.168.1.1
> delete net 192.168.2.0: gateway 192.168.1.1
>
> # route delete host 192.168.3.31 192.168.1.1
> delete host 192.168.3.31: gateway 192.168.1.1

Verify the deletion with the *netstat* command.

25.3.3 Flushing Routing Table

To flush the entire routing table, run the *route* command with –f option as follows:

> # route –f

This will remove all routing entries from the routing table. At this point, you may wish to re-execute the */sbin/init.d/net* script or define routes manually.

25.3.4 Setting the Default Route

To reach other networks, most nodes define the nearest dedicated router as the *Default* route in their routing table. The default route is used if there is no other route exists in the routing table to a destination. Only one default route may be defined on a host. Issue the *route* command as follows to define the default route through 192.168.1.1:

> # route add default 192.168.1.1 1

You can also use the *set_parms* command to configure the default route. Use the command with caution. It prompts to keep or modify several other network parameters too.

> # set_parms initial

To configure the default route using SAM, follow the steps below:

☞ Go to SAM → Networking & Communications → Routes → Actions. You will see options to add, modify, or remove default route, as shown in Figure 25-2.

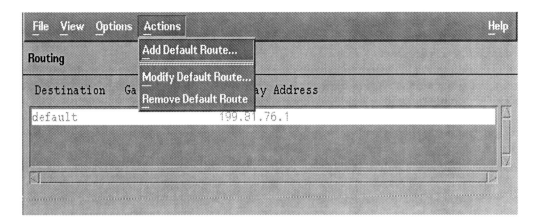

Figure 25-2 SAM – Default Gateway

The default route can be permanently defined in the */etc/rc.config.d/netconf* file too. For instance, see the following sample entries:

```
HOSTNAME=hp01
IP_ADDRESS[0]=192.168.1.201
SUBNET_MASK[0]=255.255.255.0
INTERFACE_NAME[0]=lan0
ROUTE_DESTINATION[0]=default
ROUTE_GATEWAY[0]=192.168.1.1
ROUTE_COUNT[0]=1
```

25.4   Enabling DHCP Client Service

Dynamic Host Configuration Protocol (DHCP) enables a system that acts as a *DHCP Server,* to provide IP address and other network parameters including subnet mask, default route, DNS/NIS/NTP server IP, to other systems automatically. These other systems are called *DHCP Client*s.

When an HP-UX system, with DHCP client functionality enabled, boots up, it broadcasts a message on the network requesting an available DHCP server to provide an IP address and network parameter information. An available DHCP server responds and sends the requested information back to the client. When the client gets the required information, it sets it up accordingly. The IP address is leased to the DHCP client for a specific amount of time.

DHCP client functionality can be enabled by inserting an entry for it in the */etc/rc.config.d/netconf* file, running the *set_parms* command, or using SAM.

The following two step procedure shows how to enable DHCP client functionality for lan0. The first step edits the *netconf* file and adds entry for the specified LAN card or port. The second step executes the */sbin/init.d/net* startup script manually to re-execute entries in the file.

```
# vi /etc/rc.config.d/netconf
DHCP_ENABLE[0]=1
# /sbin/init.d/net start
```

To enable the functionality using the *set_parms* command, do the following. Use this tool with caution. It prompts to keep or modify several other network parameters.

```
# set_parms initial
```

To enable DHCP client functionality using SAM, follow the links:

☞ Go to SAM → Communication and Networking → Network Interface Cards. Highlight the LAN card for which you want to enable DHCP client functionality. Go to Actions → Modify. Highlight the "Enable DHCP Client" and hit the *Enter* key. Refer to Figure 25-3.

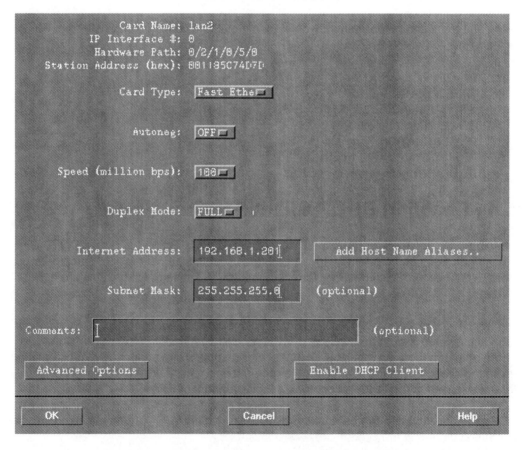

Figure 25-3 SAM – DHCP Client Enable/Disable

Summary

In this chapter, you learned how to assign network parameters to a LAN card including assigning it a single IP address and multiple IP addresses. You looked at how to edit the network startup

---

configuration file, so the entries become activated, whenever a system reboot occurs. You then defined IP addresses and hostnames in *letc/hosts* database.

The next major topic in the chapter was on routing. You studied routing concepts and how it worked. You understood the concept of default route. You used examples to add, delete, and display routes. You saw how to zero out routing table entries by using the *route* command.

The last topic explained briefly Dynamic Host Configuration Protocol and how it worked. You used ways of activating DHCP client functionality.

HP Certified Systems Administrator

Network Connectivity Troubleshooting and Overview of Network Management

This chapter covers the following major topics:

✓ Understand network connectivity troubleshooting
✓ Perform network connectivity troubleshooting using tools, such as ioscan, lanscan, linkloop, lanadmin, ping, netstat, traceroute, ndd, and nettl
✓ Overview of network management via SNMP

26.1   Network Connectivity Troubleshooting

Network problems usually surround physical connectivity or incorrect setup. Physical connectivity issues may involve LAN card not seated properly in the slot, cable plugged into wrong LAN card or port, a broken cable, a bad or loose connector at cable ends, cable length too long, router, switch, or hub not functioning or malfunctioning, and so on.

Setup issues may include LAN card software driver not installed, duplicate IP addresses on the network, wrong IP address assignment, incorrect subnet mask, incorrect routing table entries, IP address and other network parameters lost at system reboot, LAN card or port not in UP state, and so on.

In the following sub-sections, you will look at various network troubleshooting tools that help troubleshoot physical connectivity issues. These tools come standard with HP-UX. For incorrect setup related problems, check network assignments in key configuration files, such as */etc/hosts* and */etc/rc.config.d/netconf*. Refer to Chapter 24 "Introduction to Networking" and Chapter 25 "LAN Card Administration and Routing" for in-depth coverage on network parameter configuration.

To troubleshoot connectivity problems, HP-UX offers tools, such as *ioscan, lanscan, linkloop, lanadmin, ping, netstat, traceroute, ndd*, and *nettl*. Let us take a look at each one of these and see how they can help identify issues.

26.1.1   Using *ioscan*

The *ioscan* command is a powerful tool. It looks into the running kernel or scans the entire system and displays useful output pertaining to peripheral devices and their status. From network connectivity troubleshooting perspective, you may want to run this command to determine if a LAN card has the proper software driver installed, configured, and bound to it.

```
# ioscan –fnkC lan
Class   I  H/W Path  Driver   S/W State    H/W Type      Description
=================================================================
lan     0  8/0/1/0   btlan    CLAIMED      INTERFACE     HP J3515A HSC 10/100
Base-TX D-Class 1 port
                 /dev/diag/lan0 /dev/ether0    /dev/lan0
lan     1  8/4/1/0   fddi3    UNCLAIMED    UNKNOWN       PCI FDDI (107e0003)
lan     2  8/16/6    lan2     CLAIMED      INTERFACE     Built-in LAN
                 /dev/diag/lan2 /dev/ether2
lan     3  8/20/5/1  btlan0   UNCLAIMED    UNKNOWN       EISA card INP0500
```

Check under the column "S/W State" for the "CLAIMED" or "UNCLAIMED" state. A "CLAIMED" state indicates that a software driver is properly loaded, configured, and the LAN card is bound to it. An "UNCLAIMED" state means that you need to install a software driver for the associated LAN card. In the above *ioscan* output, lan0 and lan2 are CLAIMED, and lan1 and lan3 are not.

Run this command and analyze results on both machines between which you want to test physical connectivity.

There are several options available with the *ioscan* command. Some of them are described in Table 26-1.

Option	Description
–f	Displays full information including module's class, instance number, hardware path, driver, software state, hardware type, and a brief description.
–n	Displays device files.
–k	Reads information from the running kernel data structures.
–C	Displays information about devices belonging to the specified class.
–d	Displays information about devices controlled by the specified software driver.
–H	Displays information about devices attached at the specified hardware path.
–I	Displays information about devices at the specified instance number.
–u	Displays information about devices that have CLAIMED state and an assigned instance number.

Table 26-1 *ioscan* Command Options

Try running the command with options listed in Table 26-1 and compare results.

Refer to Chapter 07 "System Administration and HP-UX Server Hardware" for detailed information on output produced by running the *ioscan* command.

26.1.2   Using *lanscan*

Once you have determined that a proper software driver is installed and configured for your LAN card on both systems, you need to determine MAC address of the LAN cards or ports on both machines between which you want to check physical connectivity. Run the *lanscan* command on both systems to obtain this information.

```
# lanscan
Hardware    Station          Crd    Hdw     Net-Interface  NM   MAC    HP-DLPI   DLPI
Path        Address          In#    State   NamePPA        ID   Type   Support   Mjr#
8/0/1/0     0x001083F546F5   0      UP      lan0 snap0     1    ETHER  Yes       119
8/16/6      0x0060B0D286AB   2      UP      lan2 snap2     2    ETHER  Yes       119
```

A short description of each column is given in Table 26-2.

Column	Description
Hardware Path	Displays each LAN card/port's physical path.
Station Address	Displays each LAN card/port's MAC address.
Card Instance #	Displays each LAN card/port's instance number, also called *Physical Point of Attachment* (PPA).
Hardware State	Displays UP or DOWN status.
Net Interface Name PPA	Displays LAN card/port's name. By default, the name is "lan" followed by the card's PPA.
NM ID	Displays a unique *Network Management ID* used by *lanadmin* command and other network management tools.

MAC Type	Displays LAN card/port's access method. Default is ETHER for Ethernet.
HP-DLPI Support	Tells if the LAN card/port supports *Data Link Provider Interface* (DLPI). Required by *linkloop* and *lanadmin* commands.
Major Number	Displays associated major number for DLPI.

Table 26-2 *lanscan* Command Output Description

There are several options available to the *lanscan* command. Some of them are described in Table 26-3. Try running the command with these options and compare results.

Option	Description
–a	Displays MAC address.
–v	Displays detailed information.
–i	Displays interface name.
–m	Displays MAC types.
–n	Displays network management ID.
–p	Displays PPA.

Table 26-3 *lanscan* Command Options

26.1.3   Using *linkloop*

This command tests physical connectivity between LAN cards/ports installed in two different systems and are physically connected via a cable. For example, when you run this command on *hp02* and specify with it *hp03's* MAC address (use *lanscan* to get MAC address), it reports whether or not physical connectivity is OK. This command works at the physical layer level and does not require TCP/IP parameters configured. Specify the MAC address in hexadecimal notation.

 # linkloop 0x0060B0B6CAE3
Link connectivity to LAN station: 0x0060B0B6CAE3
   -- OK

There are several options available with the *linkloop* command. Some of them are described in Table 26-4. Try running the command with these options and compare results.

Option	Description
–i	Specifies the PPA number. Default is the first available.
–n	Denotes the number of data frames to be sent to destination.
–s	Defines the size of data frame.
–t	Specifies time, in seconds, to wait for a reply before aborting.
–v	Displays detailed information.

Table 26-4 *linkloop* Command Options

26.1.4   Using *lanadmin*

The *lanadmin* command is a menu-driven utility for displaying a LAN card/port's statistics and changing its characteristics. This command can be useful in troubleshooting LAN card/port related issues. It does the following:

- ✓ Displays or changes MAC address.
- ✓ Displays or changes *Maximum Transmission Unit* (MTU) size.
- ✓ Displays or changes speed.
- ✓ Displays statistics including inbound/outbound traffic, errors, etc.
- ✓ Resets a LAN card/port and execute self-test on it.

When you invoke *lanadmin*, the following pops up:

```
# lanadmin
      LOCAL AREA NETWORK ONLINE ADMINISTRATION, Version 1.0
            Thu, Mar 9,2006  14:04:08


      Copyright 1994 Hewlett Packard Company.
            All rights are reserved.

Test Selection mode.


      lan     = LAN Interface Administration
      menu    = Display this menu
      quit    = Terminate the Administration
      terse   = Do not display command menu
      verbose = Display command menu
```

The only option to work with here is "lan". Others are self-explanatory. Type "lan" and you will see the following:

```
LAN Interface test mode. LAN Interface PPA Number = 0


      clear    = Clear statistics registers
      display  = Display LAN Interface status and statistics registers
      end      = End LAN Interface Administration, return to Test Selection
      menu     = Display this menu
      ppa      = PPA Number of the LAN Interface
      quit     = Terminate the Administration, return to shell
      reset    = Reset LAN Interface to execute its selftest
      specific = Go to Driver specific menu
```

At this stage, various choices are available for the LAN card/port. For example, "clear" clears statistics registers, "display" displays status and statistics, "end" takes you back to the main menu, "menu" redisplays the menu options, "ppa" allows you to choose a LAN card/port's instance number to test, "quit" takes you back to the command prompt, "reset" resets and runs self-test, and "specific" takes you to the driver-specific sub-menu.

To view statistics, for example, choose the "display" option.

```
                    LAN INTERFACE STATUS DISPLAY
                   Thu, Mar 9,2006  14:13:50
PPA Number                      = 0
Description                     = HP J3515A HSC 10/100Base-TX D-Class 1 port [10
BASE-T,HD,AUTO,TT
Type (value)                    = Ethernet-csmacd(6)
MTU Size                        = 1500
Speed                           = 10000000
Station Address                 = 0x1083f546f5
Administration Status (value)   = up(1)
Operation Status (value)        = up(1)
Last Change                     = 73919604
Inbound Octets                  = 137904088
Inbound Unicast Packets         = 47055
Inbound Non-Unicast Packets     = 207200
Inbound Discards                = 0
Inbound Errors                  = 0
Inbound Unknown Protocols       = 0
Outbound Octets                 = 5360913
Outbound Unicast Packets        = 98811
Outbound Non-Unicast Packets= 238
Outbound Discards               = 1
Outbound Errors                 = 0
Outbound Queue Length           = 0
Specific                        = 655367

Ethernet-like Statistics Group

Index                           = 1
Alignment Errors                = 0
FCS Errors                      = 0
Single Collision Frames         = 31
Multiple Collision Frames       = 5
Deferred Transmissions          = 446
Late Collisions                 = 0
Excessive Collisions            = 0
Internal MAC Transmit Errors    = 0
Carrier Sense Errors            = 0
Frames Too Long                 = 0
Internal MAC Receive Errors     = 0
```

The *lanadmin* command has several options available to do things without having to enter the menu. Some of the more common options are listed in Table 26-5.

Option	Description
–a / –A	Displays / Changes MAC address.
–m / –M	Displays / Changes MTU size.
–s / –S	Displays / Changes speed.
–x / –X	Displays / Changes current configuration.

Table 26-5 *lanadmin* **Command Options**

Let us see in the following examples how these options can be used.

To display MAC address of LAN card/port at PPA 1, do the following:

```
# lanadmin –a  1
Station Address        = 0x001083f546f5
```

To display MTU size of LAN card/port at PPA 1, do the following:

```
# lanadmin –m  1
MTU Size               = 1500
```

To display LAN card/port speed at PPA 1, do the following:

```
# lanadmin –s  1
Speed                  = 10000000
```

To display current configuration for LAN card/port at PPA 1, do the following:

```
# lanadmin –x  1
Current Config         = 10 Half-Duplex AUTONEG
```

To change the current configuration for LAN card/port at PPA 1 to full-duplex:

```
# lanadmin –X  fd  1
WARNING: an incorrect setting could cause serious network problems!!!

Driver is attempting to set the new speed
Reset will take approximately 11 seconds
```

With –X option, the following choices are available:

"hd" to change to half duplex
"fd" to change to full duplex
"10hd" to change to half duplex at 10 Mbps
"10fd" to change to full duplex at 10 Mbps
"100hd" to change to half duplex at 100 Mbps
"100fd" to change to full duplex at 100 Mbps
"auto_on" to enable automatic detection of speed and duplex mode

26.1.5 Using *ping*

ping tests connectivity at the TCP/IP level, when physical connectivity is ok and proper IP address and network assignments are in place. It sends out a series of 64-byte *Internet Control Message Protocol* (ICMP) test packets to a destination IP address and waits for a response.

```
# ping  192.168.1.202
PING hp02: 64 byte packets
64 bytes from 192.168.1.202: icmp_seq=0. time=2. ms
64 bytes from 192.168.1.202: icmp_seq=1. time=0. ms
64 bytes from 192.168.1.202: icmp_seq=2. time=0. ms
64 bytes from 192.168.1.202: icmp_seq=3. time=0. ms
64 bytes from 192.168.1.202: icmp_seq=4. time=0. ms
64 bytes from 192.168.1.202: icmp_seq=5. time=0. ms
64 bytes from 192.168.1.202: icmp_seq=6. time=0. ms
64 bytes from 192.168.1.202: icmp_seq=7. time=0. ms
ctrl+c

----hp02 PING Statistics----
8 packets transmitted, 8 packets received, 0% packet loss
round-trip (ms)  min/avg/max = 0/0/2
```

You have to press *ctrl+c* to terminate the command execution. Notice under "hp02 PING Statistics" at the bottom, the number of packets transmitted, received, and lost are shown. The packet loss should be 0% and the round trip time should not be high. You may want to ping your system's own IP, the loopback address (127.0.0.1), the default route, a node on the local network, and a node through a router to check if your system is properly set to communicate to itself, nodes on local network, and nodes beyond the local network.

Another item to notice in the output is that the first ICMP reply took longer than subsequent replies to come back. This is based on the fact that the command broadcasts the card/port's MAC address over the network using *arp,* and a node with that MAC address replies. This process takes additional time and results in a longer reply time for the first packet. It might not be the case always.

If *ping* fails in any of the situations, check if the LAN card seated in the slot properly, its driver installed and configured (use *ioscan*), LAN cable secured appropriately, IP and subnet mask set correctly (use *ifconfig* and *netstat*), and the default route configured right (use *netstat*). Verify entries in the */etc/hosts* and */etc/rc.config.d/netconf* files as well.

26.1.6 Using *netstat*

netstat reports the status of LAN cards/ports. For example, when this command is executed with –i option, it displays the hostname and IP addresses and incoming and outgoing packet information. Examine its output when you suspect an issue with one of the LAN cards/ports. By default, this command resolves hostnames to IP addresses, but if you like to see results in numerical format, add –n option.

```
# netstat  –i
```

Name	Mtu	Network	Address	Ipkts	Opkts
lan1:1*	1500	193.12.211.0	193.12.211.2	0	0
lan1*	1500	193.11.211.0	193.11.211.2	0	0
lan0	1500	192.168.1.0	hp02	4592	3823
lo0	4136	127.0.0.0	localhost	1267	1267
lan1:3*	1500	193.14.211.0	193.14.211.2	0	0
lan1:2*	1500	193.13.211.0	193.13.211.2	0	0

The *netstat* command with –r option generates routing information.

```
# netstat  –r
```
Routing tables

Destination	Gateway	Flags	Refs	Interface	Pmtu
localhost	localhost	UH	0	lo0	4136
hp02	hp02	UH	0	lan0	4136
192.168.1.0	hp02	U	2	lan0	1500
default	hp02	U	0	lan0	1500

Above output in numerical format.

```
# netstat  –rn
```
Routing tables

Destination	Gateway	Flags	Refs	Interface	Pmtu
127.0.0.1	127.0.0.1	UH	0	lo0	4136
192.168.1.202	192.168.1.202	UH	0	lan0	4136
192.168.1.0	192.168.1.202	U	2	lan0	1500
default	192.168.1.202	U	0	lan0	1500

With –a option, this command displays status of socket connections.

```
# netstat  –a
```
Active Internet connections (including servers)

Proto	Recv-Q	Send-Q	Local Address	Foreign Address	(state)
tcp	0	0	*.discard	*.*	LISTEN
tcp	0	0	*.chargen	*.*	LISTEN
tcp	0	0	*.echo	*.*	LISTEN

. . . .
. . . .

With –s option, it displays network activity statistics.

```
# netstat  –s
```
tcp:
         58907 packets sent
             45019 data packets (3013575 bytes)
             88 data packets (387 bytes) retransmitted
             13881 ack-only packets (7779 delayed)
             5 keepalive probes sent

```
        1 connection dropped by keepalive
        0 connect requests dropped due to full queue
        1 connect request dropped due to no listener
udp:
        0 incomplete headers
        0 bad checksums
ip:
        205656 total packets received
        0 bad IP headers
        0 fragments received
        0 packets not forwardable
icmp:
        30176 calls to generate an ICMP error message
        0 ICMP messages dropped
        address mask reply: 0
        15 responses sent

. . . . . . . .
. . . . . . . .
```

From network connectivity troubleshooting perspective, use this command to check if proper routes and IP addresses are set and if packets are going out and coming in.

26.1.7   Using *traceroute*

traceroute tests connectivity at the TCP/IP level between hosts. It sends out packets to the destination host and displays the route the packets take to reach it. As an example, issue the following on *hp01*:

```
# traceroute  hp02
traceroute to hp02 (192.168.1.202), 30 hops max, 40 byte packets
 1  192.168.1.1 (192.168.1.1)  0.264 ms  0.197 ms  0.201 ms
 2  hp02 (192.168.1.202)  0.197 ms  0.163 ms  0.165 ms
```

The output indicates that the packets got out of the system via the default gateway (192.168.1.1) to reach *hp02*.

If *traceroute* fails, check if the IP and subnet mask are set correctly (use *ifconfig* and *netstat*) and the default route configured right (use *netstat*). Verify entries in the */etc/hosts* file.

26.1.8   Using *ndd*

ndd displays TCP/IP tunable parameter information and allows you to fine tune them. Its output can be used to troubleshoot a network problem. A list of supported ndd tunable parameters on HP-UX is displayed using the –h option.

ndd –h supported

SUPPORTED ndd tunable parameters on HP-UX:
IP:

ip_def_ttl	- Controls the default TTL in the IP header
ip_forward_directed_broadcasts	- Controls subnet broadcasts packets
ip_forward_src_routed	- Controls forwarding of source routed packets
ip_forwarding	- Controls how IP hosts forward packets
ip_fragment_timeout	- Controls how long IP fragments are kept
ip_icmp_return_data_bytes	- Maximum number of data bytes in ICMP

. . . .
. . . .

TCP:

tcp_conn_request_max	- Max number of outstanding connection request
tcp_ignore_path_mtu	- Disable setting MSS from ICMP 'Frag Needed'
tcp_ip_abort_cinterval	- R2 during connection establishment
tcp_ip_abort_interval	- R2 for established connection
tcp_ip_notify_cinterval	- R1 during connection establishment
tcp_ip_notify_interval	- R1 for established connection

. . . .
. . . .

A list of unsupported ndd parameters on HP-UX is displayed using the –h option.

ndd –h unsupported

UNSUPPORTED ndd tunable parameters on HP-UX:

This set of parameters are not supported by HP and modification of
these tunable parameters are not suggested nor recommended.

IP:

ip_bogus_sap	- Allow IP bind to a nonstandard/unused SAP
ip_check_subnet_addr	- Controls the subnet portion of a host address
ip_debug	- Controls the level of IP module debugging
ip_dl_snap_sap	- The SAP to use for SNAP encapsulation
ip_dl_sap	- Set the SAP when IP binds to a DLPI device
ip_encap_ttl	- Set the TTL for the encapsulated IP header

. . . .
. . . .

TCP:

tcp_conn_grace_period	- Additional time for sending a SYN packet
tcp_debug	- Internal TCP debug option
tcp_deferred_ack_interval	-Timeout interval for deferred ACK
tcp_discon	- Terminate a TCP connection
tcp_discon_by_addr	- Terminate a TCP connection
tcp_dupack_fast_retransmit	- No. of ACKs needed to trigger a retransmit

. . . .
. . . .

The *ndd* command allows you to display or set any of these parameter values. For example, to display the value of a parameter "ip_def_ttl", do the following:

> # **ndd –h ip_def_ttl**
> ip_def_ttl:
>
> Sets the default time to live (TTL) in the IP header.
> [1,225] Default: 255

To change its value to 100, do the following:

> # **ndd –set /dev/ip ip_def_ttl 100**

Parameters for *ndd* can be set in the */etc/rc.config.d/nddconf* file so that they automatically get set at each system reboot. The default *nddconf* file is shown below:

> # **cat /etc/rc.config.d/nddconf**
> . . . .
> . . . .
> # Example 4: Change the UDP default ttl parameter to 128
> # TRANSPORT_NAME[3]=udp
> # NDD_NAME[3]=udp_def_ttl
> # NDD_VALUE[3]=128
> #
> # Example 5: Change the amount of time that ARP entries can stay in
> #   ARP cache to 10 minutes.
> #
> # TRANSPORT_NAME[4]=arp
> # NDD_NAME[4]=arp_cleanup_interval
> # NDD_VALUE[4]=600000

26.1.9   Using *nettl*

nettl controls network tracing and logging activities. Tracing captures inbound and outbound packets going through the network, as well as loopback or header information. Logging captures network activities, such as connection establishment, errors, and state changes.

To start *nettl* service, first make sure that the variable NETTL is set to 1 in */etc/rc.config.d/nettl* file and then execute one of the following:

> # **/sbin/init.d/nettl start**   or # **nettl –st**
> Initializing Network Tracing and Logging...
> Done.

To stop *nettl*, do the following:

> # **/sbin/init.d/nettl stop**   or # **nettl –sp**
> nettl stopped

To check the status of logging and tracing, execute *nettl* as follows:

```
# nettl -status
Logging Information:
Log Filename:                /var/adm/nettl.LOG*
Max Log file size(Kbytes):   1000        Console Logging:        On
User's ID:                   0           Buffer Size:            8192
Messages Dropped:            0           Messages Queued:        0

Subsystem Name:         Log Class:
NS_LS_LOGGING                           ERROR DISASTER
NS_LS_NFT                               ERROR DISASTER
NS_LS_LOOPBACK                          ERROR DISASTER
NS_LS_NI                                ERROR DISASTER
NS_LS_IPC                               ERROR DISASTER
NS_LS_SOCKREGD                          ERROR DISASTER
........
........
Tracing Information:
Trace Filename:
Max Trace file size(Kbytes): 0
No Subsystems Active
```

26.2 Overview of Network Management

A computer network is formed, as you know, when two or more nodes are inter-connected to share resources. A network may include any number of devices, such as computers, storage devices, printers, routers, switches, bridges, hubs, and so on. Network management refers to monitoring, supporting, and administering these devices.

Network management covers tasks, such as fault isolation and fix, performance monitoring and optimization, configuration and security management, bandwidth and accounting management, and so forth. It supports notifying administrators via pager and email in case of critical events.

There are several protocols available to monitor and manage network devices, of which the most common is the *Simple Network Management Protocol* (SNMP), which uses TCP/IP protocol stack to function.

An SNMP-managed network consists of three key components:

Managed Device

A *Managed Device* is a node that runs SNMP agent software and resides on a managed network.

Agent

An *Agent* is a piece of software that runs on a managed device. Its responsibility is to collect management information and present it to management station. The management information describes the system configuration information, which is defined in the form of variables, such as "free memory", "system name", "number of running processes", and "default route". These variables are organized in hierarchies and are described by *Management Information Bases* (MIBs). Some capabilities of the agent are to:

- ✓ Gather information from managed devices.
- ✓ Configure parameters of the managed devices.
- ✓ Respond to management station's requests.
- ✓ Generate alarms or traps.

Management Station

A *Management Station* is responsible for monitoring and controlling managed devices. It communicates with managed devices via agents for management operations.

Summary

In this chapter, you studied the basic network connectivity troubleshooting techniques and looked at network management concepts in brief.

You were presented with various native HP-UX tools that helped you with troubleshooting. The tools included *ioscan, lanscan, linkloop, lanadmin, ping, netstat, traceroute, ndd*, and *nettl.*

## 27

Setting Up and Administering Internet Services and Sendmail

This chapter covers the following major topics:

- ✓ Introduction to Berkeley and ARPA internet services
- ✓ The role of internet services daemon
- ✓ The role of internet service daemon configuration and security files
- ✓ Enable internet services logging
- ✓ Establish user and host equivalency
- ✓ Use Berkeley services
- ✓ Enable and Disable ARPA services
- ✓ Use ARPA services
- ✓ Enable and use anonymous ftp
- ✓ Setup sendmail and verify functionality
- ✓ Update sendmail aliases database

27.1 The Internet Services

HP-UX internet services enable a system to be used as a provider of one or more services to remote client systems over the network. These services include allowing users on the remote machines to log in, transfer files, send and receive emails, execute commands without logging in, getting list of logged in users, synchronize time, and so on.

When services are used over the network, two pieces of software program get involved. One is the client program and the other is the server program. The client program requests for a service running on a remote system. The server program (or daemon), on the remote system, serves or responds to the client request. This way a client/server communication channel establishes. At any given time, an HP-UX machine can act as both a server and a client. It may provide services to other machines and may use their services as a client.

Server programs are started in one of two ways: via startup scripts located in sequencer directories or via the master server program daemon called *inetd*. A detailed discussion on the startup scripts and sequencer directories is covered in Chapter 17 "Shutting Down and Starting Up an HP-UX System".

The *inetd* daemon itself is started by one of the startup scripts when a system boots up to run level 2. When this daemon is started, it reads its configuration file */etc/inetd.conf* and sits in the memory. It listens on ports listed in the */etc/services* and */etc/rpc* files for services defined in its configuration file. It waits for a client request to come in requesting for one of the *inetd*-controlled services. When one such request arrives on a particular port, this daemon starts the server program corresponding to that port. It hooks the client and server pieces up, gets itself out of that communication, and starts listening on that port again on behalf of that server program. Remember, every service uses a unique port number defined in either the */etc/services* or the */etc/rpc* file.

27.1.1 Berkeley and ARPA Services

There are two major categories of the internet services: one developed at the University of California at Berkeley and referred to as *UCB* (or *Berkeley*) services; second developed for the US *Department of Defense's Advanced Research Project Agency* (ARPA) and referred to as *ARPA* services.

The Berkeley services include BIND (DNS), *sendmail, finger, rexec, rcp, rlogin, remsh, ruptime, rup, rwho*, etc. Berkeley Services were primarily developed to run on UNIX platform, however, most of them today run on non-UNIX platforms too. The names of most Berkeley services begin with an "r" and hence referred to as "r" commands.

The ARPA services, on the other hand, include *ftp* and *telnet*, which can be used on both UNIX and non-UNIX platforms.

Table 27-1 lists and describes some commonly used internet services.

Service	Description
rlogind	Enables a user to log in to a remote system using the *rlogin* command. This daemon is started by *inetd* and uses port 513. The *rlogind* entry in the */etc/inetd.conf* file looks like: login stream tcp nowait root /usr/lbin/rlogind rlogind
remshd	Enables two services: file transfer via *rcp,* and command execution and remote login using *remsh* on to a remote system. This daemon is started by *inetd*. The *remshd* entry in the */etc/inetd.conf* file looks like: shell stream tcp nowait root /usr/lbin/remshd remshd
rexecd	Enables executing a command on a remote system. The daemon is started by *inetd*. The *rexecd* entry in the */etc/inetd.conf* file looks like: exec stream tcp nowait root /usr/lbin/rexecd rexecd
rwhod	Enables *rup, ruptime*, and *rwho* commands to display remote system information. This daemon is started by the */sbin/init.d/rwhod* script at system boot up if the RWHOD variable is set to 1 in the */etc/rc.config.d/netdaemons* file.
fingerd	Enables the *finger* command to display information about users on local and remote systems. The *fingerd* daemon is started by *inetd* and uses port 79. The *fingerd* entry in the */etc/inetd.conf* file looks like: finger stream tcp nowait bin /usr/lbin/fingerd fingerd
telnetd	Enables a user to log in to a remote machine. The client program is *telnet*. *telnetd* is started by *inetd* and uses port 23. The *telnetd* entry in the */etc/inetd.conf* file looks like: telnet stream tcp nowait root /usr/lbin/telnetd telnetd
ftpd	Enables file transfer between UNIX to UNIX and UNIX to non-UNIX systems. The client program is *ftp*. *ftpd* is started by *inetd* and uses port 21. The *ftpd* entry in the */etc/inetd.conf* file looks like: ftp stream tcp nowait root /usr/lbin/ftpd ftpd -l
sendmail	Sendmail is the most widely used mail transport and delivery program on large networks and the internet. It works with a client mail program. It is started by the */sbin/init.d/sendmail* script at boot time, if the SENDMAIL_SERVER variable is set to 1 in the */etc/rc.config.d/mailservs* file. It uses port 25.
rlpdaemon	Enables a print request to print to a remote printer. This daemon is started by *inetd*. A detailed discussion on printers is covered in Chapter 20 "Print Services Management".
xntpd	Keeps an HP-UX system clock in sync with a more reliable and accurate source of time. A detailed discussion is covered in Chapter 28 "Setting Up and Administering NTP".

named	Enables hostname-to-IP and IP-to-hostname resolution. The *named* daemon responds to many commands, such as *nslookup* and *nsquery*. It is started via a startup script. A detailed discussion is covered in Chapter 33 "Setting Up and Administering DNS".
bootpd	Enables diskless systems, X stations, Ignite-UX clients, and old network printers to boot from a remote boot server. The daemon provides network configuration information to them. A detailed discussion is captured in Chapter 35 "Introduction to BootP and TFTP Services".
tftpd	Works with *bootpd* to enable diskless systems, X stations, Ignite-UX clients, and old network printers to transfer files containing boot and other configuration data. The client program is *tftp*. A detailed discussion is covered in Chapter 35 "Introduction to BootP and TFTP Services".
gated	Dynamically determines which of the several available routes to use to transport data from one machine to another on large networks and the internet. Updates routing table dynamically and automatically based on the updated routing information it discovers over time. Its configuration file is */etc/gated.conf* and is started by the */sbin/init.d/gated* script at system boot up if the GATED variable is set to 1 in the */etc/rc.config.d/netconf* file. A detailed discussion on *gated* is beyond the scope of this book. Refer to its manual pages.

Table 27-1 Internet Services

27.1.2   The *inetd* Daemon and the */etc/inetd.conf* File

The *inetd* daemon is the master server daemon for many internet services. This daemon is started automatically at system boot, when the */sbin/init.d/inetd* script is executed. It listens for connection requests for the services listed in its configuration file */etc/inetd.conf* over the ports defined in the */etc/services* and */etc/rpc* files and starts up the appropriate server process, when a request arrives.

The contents of */etc/inetd.conf* look similar to the following:

```
# cat /etc/inetd.conf
. . . . . . . .
. . . . . . . .
##
#       ARPA/Berkeley services
#
ftp           stream   tcp    nowait   root /usr/lbin/ftpd  ftpd  -l
telnet        stream   tcp    nowait   root /usr/lbin/telnetd      telnetd
tftp          dgram    udp    wait     root /usr/lbin/tftpd        tftpd   /opt/ignite  /var/opt/ignite
#bootps       dgram    udp    wait     root /usr/lbin/bootpd       bootpd
#finger       stream   tcp    nowait   bin  /usr/lbin/fingerd      fingerd
login         stream   tcp    nowait   root /usr/lbin/rlogind      rlogind
shell         stream   tcp    nowait   root /usr/lbin/remshd       remshd
exec          stream   tcp    nowait   root /usr/lbin/rexecd       rexecd
. . . . . . . .
. . . . . . . .
```

There are at least seven columns per line entry for each non-RPC and nine columns per line entry for each RPC service defined in the file. Table 27-2 lists and explains each column. Line entries commenced with the # character, represents disabled services.

Column	Description
1	Service name as listed in the */etc/services* file. Lines, defining RPC services, begin with "rpc".
2	Socket type. "Stream" for TCP and "dgram" (datagram) for UDP.
3	Protocol to use (TCP or UDP). Defined in the */etc/protocols* file.
4	"wait" is used with UDP and tells *inetd* not to start another instance (or thread) of the same process, until this one finishes. "nowait" is used with TCP and tells *inetd* to go ahead and start another instance (or thread) of the same process, if additional requests come in. For example, you can have multiple *telnetd* daemons running simultaneously serving multiple *telnet* requests.
5	Run the server program as this user.
6	Full pathname to the server process.
7	Name of the server process in case of a non-RPC service; RPC program number in case of an RPC service.
8	Any options or arguments.
9	Name of the server process in case of an RPC service.

Table 27-2 Explanation of the */etc/inetd.conf* File Contents

Line entries for some internet services are extracted from the */etc/services* file and displayed below. The output shows service name in the first column, port number and protocol it uses in the second column, associated alias in the third column, and comments in the last column.

 # cat /etc/services
```
. . . . . . . .
. . . . . . . .
# The form for each entry is:
# <official service name>  <port number/protocol name>  <aliases>
#
ftp          21/tcp                          # File Transfer Protocol (Control)
telnet       23/tcp                          # Virtual Terminal Protocol
smtp         25/tcp                          # Simple Mail Transfer Protocol
time         37/tcp          timeserver      # Time
time         37/udp          timeserver      #
rlp          39/udp          resource        # Resource Location Protocol
whois        43/tcp          nicname         # Who Is
domain       53/tcp          nameserver      # Domain Name Service
domain       53/udp          nameserver      #
bootps       67/udp                          # Bootstrap Protocol Server
. . . . . . . .
. . . . . . . .
```

Line entries for some RPC-based services are extracted from the */etc/rpc* file and displayed below. It shows service name in the first column, followed by port number and any associated aliases.

```
# cat /etc/rpc

........
........
rpcbind       100000  portmap sunrpc rpcbind
rstatd        100001  rstat rup perfmeter
rusersd       100002  rusers
nfs           100003  nfsprog
ypserv        100004  ypprog
mountd        100005  mount showmount
ypbind        100007
walld         100008  rwall shutdown
yppasswdd     100009  yppasswd
rquotad       100011  rquotaprog quota rquota
sprayd        100012  spray
pcnfsd        150001  pcnfs
rexd100017    rex
llockmgr      100020
nlockmgr      100021
status        100024
keyserv       100029  keyserver
ypxfrd        100069
automountd    100099

........
........
```

Whenever a modification is made to the */etc/inetd.conf* file, the *inetd* daemon must be restarted with the –c option for the modifications to take effect.

The */etc/inetd.conf* file should have "root" ownership and "other" group membership with 444 permissions.

27.1.3 Securing *inetd*

By default, when a user on a client machine requests for a service managed by *inetd* on a remote system, he or she is served, if the service is enabled in */etc/inetd.conf* file. This access can be controlled at the user, system, or network level by inserting proper entries in *inetd* daemon's security file */var/adm/inetd.sec*.

The following shows typical */var/adm/inetd.sec* file contents, appended by three example entries:

```
# cat /var/adm/inetd.sec

........
........
# For example:
#
# login     allow  10.3-5 192.34.56.5 ahost anetwork
#
```

```
# The above entry allows the following hosts to attempt to access your system
# using rlogin:
#             hosts in subnets 3 through 5 in network 10,
#             the host with Internet Address of 192.34.56.5,
#             the host by the name of "ahost",
#             all the hosts in the network "anetwork"
#
# mountd    deny    192.23.4.3
#
# The mountd entry  denies host  192.23.4.3  access to the NFS  rpc.mountd
# server.
#
# Hosts and network names must be official names, not aliases.
# See the inetd.sec(4) manual page for more information.
telnet         allow    193.11.211.*
finger         deny     hp05  hp06
ftp            deny     *
```

The first line allows *telnet* access from only those machines that are on the 193.11.211 network. The second line denies *finger* access from *hp05* and *hp06* systems. The third line denies everyone access to using *ftp* service.

This file should have "root" ownership and "other" group membership with 444 permissions. Use of this security control is optional.

 Only the services configured in */etc/inetd.conf* can be controlled via */var/adm/inetd.sec*.

The */var/adm/inetd.sec* file can be managed using SAM as well. Follow the links below:

Go to SAM → Networking and Communications → System Access → Internet Services. Highlight a service, then go to Actions → Modify and choose "Selected-Allowed" or "Selected-Denied" and specify what systems and networks to be allowed or denied access. See Figure 27-1.

27.1.4   Enabling *inetd* Connection Logging

The *inetd* daemon starts logging connection requests for all services listed in the */etc/inetd.conf* file through *syslogd* in */var/adm/syslog/syslog.log* file immediately, if the –l option is used with it at the command line. By default, *inetd* connection logging is disabled.

 # inetd –l

To make this change permanent, so every time a system reboots, *inetd* connection logging gets enabled, edit the */etc/rc.config.d/netdaemons* file and set the INETD_ARGS variable as follows:

INETD_ARGS="–l"

From now on, whenever *inetd* is called either at system startup or manually through */sbin/init.d/inetd* script, it will use this variable setting and start itself accordingly.

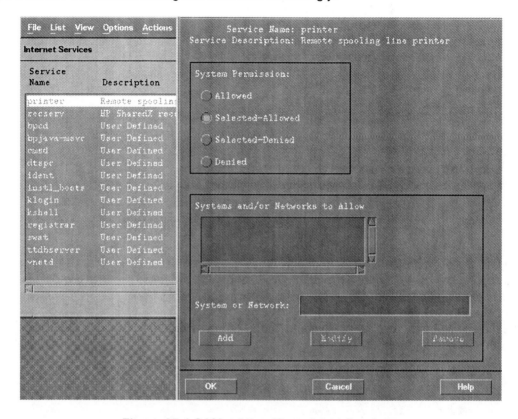

Figure 27-1 SAM – Allow/Deny inetd Services

27.2 Using the Internet Services

The following sub-sections talk about how to use the Berkeley internet services. Note that only selective services are covered.

Before looking at how Berkeley internet services are used, let us understand the concept of trust relationship.

27.2.1 Establishing Trust Relationship

Making a system trusted on a remote machine means that any user from that system can run the *rlogin*, *rcp*, or *remsh* command, without being prompted for a password, on the remote machine. This is called *Host Equivalency*. The equivalency information is stored in the */etc/hosts.equiv* file on the remote machine. This includes hostnames of those systems whose users are to be allowed passwordless entry into the remote machine for the three commands. Note that the same user must exist on both systems. This file does not support trusting *root* user account.

By default, */etc/hosts.equiv* file does not exist. You must create it, if you wish to use host equivalency.

To understand the concept, assume that you are on *hp03* and following entries exist in the */etc/hosts.equiv* file:

```
hp01
hp02      user1
+

-
```

Here is the explanation for the four entries:

✓ The first line entry allows all users from *hp01*, passwordless access into *hp03*.
✓ The second line entry allows only *user1* from *hp02*, passwordless access into *hp03*.
✓ The third line entry allows all users from all hosts, passwordless access into *hp03*.
✓ The fourth line entry allows no users from any hosts, passwordless access into *hp03*.

The */etc/hosts.equiv* file is created and maintained by *root*.

Unlike the */etc/hosts.equiv* file, a user on a system can create a *.rhosts* file in his or her home directory and allow a remote user, by the same username, to execute the three commands without furnishing a password. This is known as *User Equivalency*. This file may be created for any user including *root*.

By default, *.rhosts* file does not exist in any user home directories. The syntax of this file is identical to that of the */etc/hosts.equiv* file.

To understand the concept, assume that you are on *hp04* and following entries exist in *.rhosts* file located in *user2*'s home directory:

```
hp02
+
```

Here is the explanation for the two entries:

✓ The first line entry allows *user2* from only *hp02* system, passwordless access into *hp04*.
✓ The second line entry allows *user2* from any system on the network, passwordless access into *hp04*.

You can setup both host equivalency and user equivalency via SAM too. Follow the links below:

☞ Go to SAM → Networking and Communications → System Access → Remote Logins → Actions → Add. Fill out the form based on your requirements and press the OK button. See Figure 27-2.

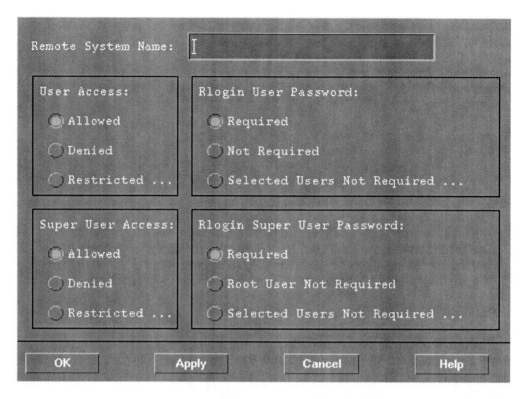

Figure 27-2 SAM – Remote Access

27.2.2   Using Berkeley Services

After understanding the concept of host and user equivalencies, let us now look at the usage of some client programs, such as *rlogin*, *rcp*, *remsh*, *rexec*, *rup*, *ruptime*, *rwho*, and *finger*, included in the Berkeley internet services. The usage is explained using examples. Make sure that none of these services are restricted in */var/adm/inetd.sec* file.

The following examples assume that you have *hp02* trusted on *hp03,* and vice versa, for *root.*

To use *rlogin* to enter from *hp02* into *hp03*, run the following on *hp02*:

> **# rlogin hp03**
> Please wait...checking for disk quotas
> (c)Copyright 1983-2000 Hewlett-Packard Co., All Rights Reserved.
> (c)Copyright 1979, 1980, 1983, 1985-1993 The Regents of the Univ. of California
> . . . .
> . . . .
> Value of TERM has been set to "ansi".
> WARNING: YOU ARE SUPERUSER !!
> #

HP Certified Systems Administrator

You must have the "login" line entry in the */etc/inetd.conf* file uncommented to enable the *rlogind* service to serve a client *rlogin* request.

To use *rcp* to copy *.dtprofile* from *root's* home directory on *hp02* to its home directory on *hp03*, run the following on *hp02*:

rcp $HOME/.dtprofile hp03:$HOME

You must have the "shell" line entry in the */etc/inetd.conf* file uncommented to enable the *remshd* service to serve a client *rcp* request.

To use *rcp* to copy *.dtprofile* from *root's* home directory on *hp02* to its home directory on *hp03*, run the following on *hp03*:

rcp hp02:$HOME/.dtprofile $HOME

The *remsh* command can be used to perform two functions: it can do the *rlogin* function and can execute a command on a remote machine without logging on to it. The first example below lets *root* log in to *hp02* from *hp03*. The second example runs the *ls* command on the */etc* directory on *hp02* from *hp03*.

remsh hp02
remsh hp02 ls /etc

You must have the "shell" line entry in the */etc/inetd.conf* file uncommented to enable the *remshd* service to serve a client *remsh* request.

The following examples use neither */etc/hosts.equiv* nor *.rhosts* file. You must enter the correct password in order to get in.

The example below runs the *ls* command on the */etc* directory on *hp02* from *hp03*.

rexec hp02 ls /etc
Password (hp03:root):

You must have the "exec" line entry in the */etc/inetd.conf* file uncommented to enable the *rexecd* service to serve a client *rexec* request.

The *rup* command broadcasts over the network and all machines running the *rpc.rstatd* daemon responds with a brief status of them.

rup
hp02   up 13 days, 13:50,   load average: 0.50, 0.50, 0.50
hp03   up 3 days, 10 mins, load average: 2.32, 2.46, 2.50

You must have the "rpc.rstatd" line entry in the */etc/inetd.conf* file uncommented to enable the *rpc.rstatd* service to serve a the client *rup* request.

The *ruptime* command broadcasts over the network and all machines running the *rwhod* daemon responds with a brief status of them.

ruptime
```
hp02      up  13+13:45,   2 users,  load 0.50, 0.50, 0.50
hp03      up   3+00:02,   1 user,   load 2.53, 2.59, 2.51
```

You must have the "rwhod" line entry in the */etc/inetd.conf* file uncommented to enable the *rwhod* service to serve a client *ruptime* request.

The *rwho* command broadcasts over the network and all machines running the *rwhod* daemon responds with a list of logged on users.

rwho
```
root      hp02:0     Feb  8 15:18
user1     hp02:1     Feb 17 21:32
root      hp03:0     Feb 17 21:35
```

You must have the "rwhod" line entry in the */etc/inetd.conf* file uncommented to enable the *rwhod* service to serve a client *rwho* request.

The *finger* command broadcasts over the network and all machines running the *fingerd* daemon responds with a list of logged on users.

finger @hp03
```
[hp02]
Login     Name      TTY  Idle         When     Bldg.     Phone
root      ???       *0   9d Wed 15:18
root      ???       *1   Fri 21:32
```

You must have the "finger" line entry in the */etc/inetd.conf* file uncommented to enable the *fingerd* service to serve a client *finger* request..

These client programs cannot be used from SAM, but you can enable or disable them. Follow the links below:

Go to SAM → Networking and Communications → System Access → Internet Services. Highlight a service and go to Actions → Modify. Select either "Allowed" or "Denied". This will update the */etc/inetd.conf* file and execute the *inetd* command with –c switch. Consult Figure 27-3.

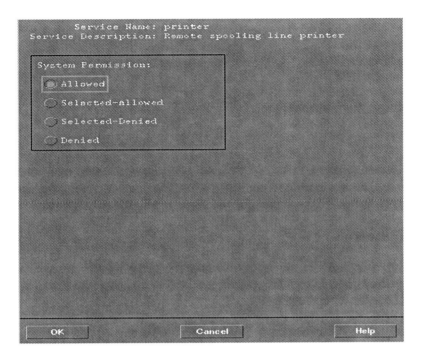

Figure 27-3 SAM – Internet Services Allow/Deny

27.2.3   Using ARPA Services

In this sub-section, you are going to look at two renowned ARPA services: *telnet* and *ftp*.

Enabling *telnet* Access

To enable a *telnet* client request coming in from over the network into a system, you must enable the *telnetd* daemon in the */etc/inetd.conf* file and make sure that *telnet* is not disallowed in the */var/adm/inetd.sec* file for that system.

To enable or disable telnet access using SAM, follow the links:

 Go to SAM → Networking and Communications → System Access → Internet Services. Highlight *telnet* and go to Actions → Modify. Choose either "Allowed" or "Denied" to enable or disable it. This will update the */etc/inetd.conf* file and execute the *inetd* command with –c switch.

By default, *telnet* is enabled and all users from all systems have access to using it.

Using *telnet*

The procedure to use *telnet* is such that you specify the hostname or IP address of the remote machine you want to log in to. You can execute *telnet* from a Windows prompt or from another UNIX machine. For example, the following invokes a *telnet* session from a Windows prompt to enter *hp02* with IP address 192.168.1.202:

```
C:\> telnet  192.168.1.202
Trying 192.168.1.202...
Connected to hp02.
Escape character is '^]'.

HP-UX hp02 B.11.11 U 9000/871 (ta)

login:
```

As soon as *telnet* contacts *hp02* on port 23, *inetd* starts the *telnetd* daemon, which then takes over and establishes a communication session with *telnet*. You must enter correct username and password to get into *hp02*. To exit out of *telnet* session, use the *exit* command or press *ctrl+d*.

Enabling *ftp* Access

To enable an *ftp* client request coming in from over the network into a system, you must enable the *ftpd* daemon in the */etc/inetd.conf* file and make sure that *ftp* is not disallowed in the */var/adm/inetd.sec* file for that system.

To enable or disable FTP access using SAM, follow the links:

 Go to SAM → Networking and Communications → System Access → Internet Services. Highlight *ftp* and go to Actions → Modify. Choose either "Allowed" or "Denied" to enable or disable it. This will update the */etc/inetd.conf* file and execute the *inetd* command with –c switch.

By default, *ftp* is enabled and all users from all systems have access to using it.

Using *ftp*

The procedure to use *ftp* is such that you specify the hostname or IP address of the remote machine you want to log in to. You can execute this command from a Windows prompt or from another UNIX machine. For example, the following runs *ftp* from a Windows prompt to enter *hp02* with IP address 192.168.1.202:

```
C:\> ftp  192.168.1.202
220 hp02 FTP server (Version 1.1.214.4 Wed Aug 23 03:38:25 GMT 2000) ready.
Name (192.168.1.202:root):
331 Password required for root.
Password:
230 User root logged in.
Remote system type is UNIX.
Using binary mode to transfer files.
ftp>
```

As soon as *ftp* contacts *hp02* on port 21, *inetd* starts the *ftpd* daemon, which then takes over and establishes a communication session with *ftp*. You must supply correct username and password to get into *hp02*.

Available commands at the *ftp* prompt can be listed by typing a *?* at the ftp> prompt:

```
ftp> ?
!            debug        mget      put       size
$            dir          mkdir     pwd       status
account      disconnect   mls       quit      struct
append       form         mode      quote     system
ascii        get          modtime   recv      sunique
. . . . . . . .
. . . . . . . .
```

To quit *ftp* session, use the *quit* or *bye* command at the ftp> prompt.

Controlling Access to *ftp*

You can specify the names of users who you do not want to allow entering a system via *ftp*. These username entries can be put into a file called */etc/ftpd/ftpusers*, one line per user name.

By default, this file does not exist, which means any user from any remote machine can *ftp* into a system, provided he or she knows a username and associated password on the system.

Enabling Anonymous *ftp* Access

Anonymous *ftp* access into a system allows a user, without knowing a username/password on the system, to upload or download files to and from a public directory. The user types the *ftp* command to connect to the system, then enters "anonymous" as the login name, and any string of characters (preferably his or her email address) as the password. Here is the procedure on how to enable it.

1. Add the following entry to the system's */etc/passwd* file:

    ftp:*:500:1:Anonymous FTP user:/home/ftp:/usr/bin/false

2. Create a home directory for *ftp* account in */home* with following permissions and ownership/membership:

    dr-xr-xr-x   6 root   other   96 Feb 17 10:55 ftp

3. Create *dist, etc, pub*, and *usr* sub-directories under */home/ftp* and modify permissions and ownership as per below:

dr-xr-xr-x	2 root	other	96 Feb 17 10:55 dist
dr-xr-xr-x	2 root	other	96 Feb 17 10:55 etc
drwxrwxrwx	2 ftp	other	96 Feb 17 10:55 pub
dr-xr-xr-x	4 root	other	96 Feb 17 10:55 usr

4. Copy */etc/passwd* and */etc/group* files to */home/ftp/etc* and modify permissions as per below:

-r--r--r--	2 root	other	223 Feb 17 10:55 group
-r--r--r--	1 root	other	641 Feb 17 10:55 passwd

---

5. Under */home/ftp/usr*, create *bin* sub-directory:

    dr-xr-xr-x   2 root   other   96 Feb 17 10:55 bin

6. Copy the *ls* command to */home/ftp/usr/bin* and modify permissions as per below:

    ---x--x—x   1 root   other   286720 Nov 14 2000 ls

The anonymous *ftp* is all set. You can start using it now.

You can use SAM, too, to enable anonymous *ftp* access. Follow the links below to enable file uploads:

☞Go to SAM → Networking and Communications → Network Services. Highlight "Anon FTP Deposit" and go to Actions → Enable. See Figure 27-4.

Follow the links below to enable file downloads:

☞Go to SAM → Networking and Communications → Network Services. Highlight "Anon FTP Retrieval" and go to Actions → Enable. See Figure 27-4.

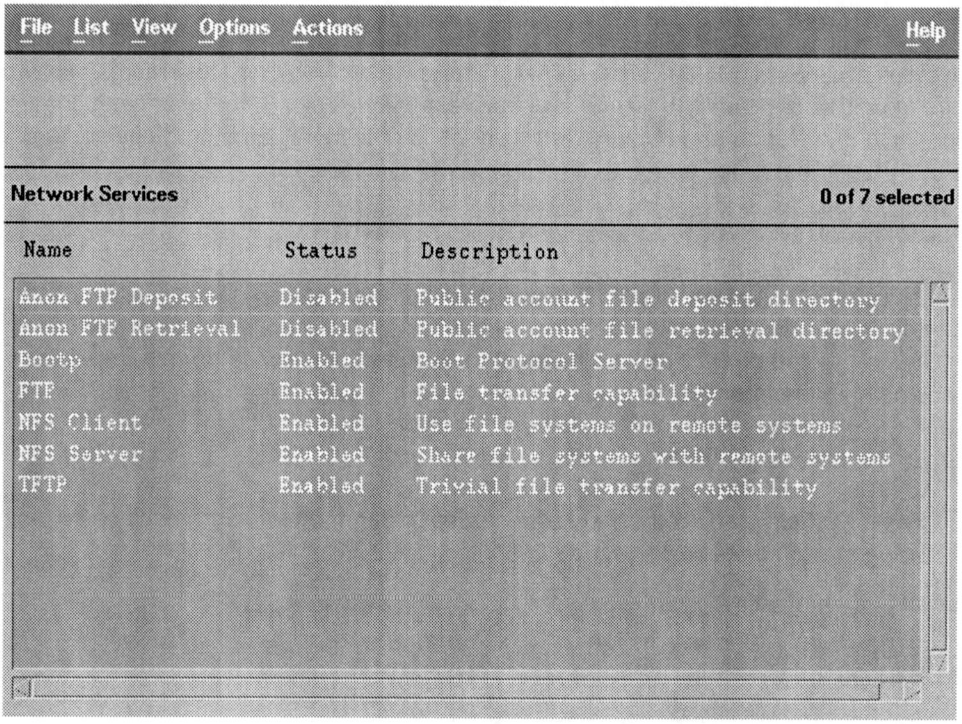

Figure 27-4 SAM – Anonymous FTP

Using Anonymous *ftp*

The following runs *ftp* from a Windows prompt to enter *hp02* with IP address 192.168.1.202 to log in as user "anonymous":

```
C:\> ftp  192.168.1.202
Connected to hp02.
220 hp02 FTP server (Version 1.1.214.4 Wed Aug 23 03:38:25 GMT 2000) ready.
Name (hp02:root): anonymous
331 Guest login ok, send your complete e-mail address as password.
Password:
230 Guest login ok, access restrictions apply.
Remote system type is UNIX.
Using binary mode to transfer files.
ftp>
```

Enabling *ftp* Logging

You can log *ftp* session and file transfer activities for auditing purposes in the */var/adm/syslog/xferlog* file. Session activities include commands used, successful and unsuccessful login attempts, etc. File transfer activities include file transfer time, remote system name, name of the file transferred, its size, and transfer mode (ASCII or binary) used. To enable *ftp* session logging, specify the –L option. To enable incoming and outgoing file transfer activities, specify the –i and –o options, respectively, with the *ftp* entry in the */etc/inetd.conf* file as follows:

```
ftp  stream  tcp  nowait  root  /usr/lbin/ftpd  ftpd  –L  –i  –o
```

Force *inetd* to reload updated configuration from */etc/inetd.conf*. Run the following command:

```
# inetd  –c
```

27.3   Setting Up Basic Sendmail Functionality

Sendmail is the most widely used email routing and delivery application on the internet. In other words, it is the most widely used *Mail Transport Agent* (MTA) and *Mail Delivery Agent* (MDA). Since sendmail is used on the internet, it requires that your system is setup to use *Domain Name System* (DNS) for hostname resolution. The */etc/hosts* file may be employed, if sendmail is to be used on the internal network.

Sendmail works with a client mail program, such as *mailx*, and routes mail messages using *Simple Mail Transfer Protocol* (SMTP). It is started by the */sbin/init.d/sendmail* script at boot time, if the SENDMAIL_SERVER variable is set to 1 in the */etc/rc.config.d/mailservs* file. Sendmail uses port 25.

The following sub-sections explain how to setup and verify sendmail, and update its aliases file.

27.3.1   Setting Up Sendmail to be Used by Single System Users

When HP-UX is installed, sendmail is ready to go by default. The *sendmail* daemon is started automatically and users can send and receive mail. The default setup is restricted to users of that system only. The following is done as part of HP-UX installation for sendmail configuration and automatic startup:

✓   The SENDMAIL_SERVER variable in */etc/rc.config.d/mailservs* is set to 1.
✓   The system's hostname is appended to the */etc/mail/sendmail.cw* file.
✓   Default */etc/mail/sendmail.cf* and */etc/mail/aliases* files are created.
✓   The sendmail startup script */sbin/init.d/sendmail* is executed that generates the aliases database file */etc/mail/aliases.db* from */etc/mail/aliases*, and starts the *sendmail* daemon.

If, for some reasons, sendmail setup is removed, follow the above steps to redo the configuration.

27.3.2   Setting Up Sendmail in Client/Server Environment

You can setup one of the HP-UX systems as a sendmail server so that it receives and sends out mail messages for users on that system as well as on other systems on the network. The user mail is stored in the */var/mail* directory. This directory can be NFS exported to client machines for user mail retrieval on those systems. Similarly, for sending mail out, the sendmail client forwards to the sendmail server any mail destined for local or over the internet delivery.

To setup an HP-UX system, *hp02* for example, as both NFS and sendmail servers, do the following:

1.   Make sure all mail users have accounts on the mail server and that their UIDs and GIDs on the mail server are consistent with the ones on the client machines.
2.   Edit */etc/rc.config.d/nfsconf* and set the NFS_SERVER variable to 1.
3.   Add the following line to */etc/exports* (create the file, if unavailable):

    /var/mail

4.   Edit */etc/rc.config.d/mailservs* and set the SENDMAIL_SERVER variable to 1.
5.   Edit */etc/mail/sendmail.cw* file and list names of all client machines at the bottom.
6.   Edit the sendmail configuration file */etc/mail/sendmail.cf* and append the following to the "Fw" keyword to look like:

    Fw/etc/mail/sendmail.cw

7.   Execute the NFS server and sendmail startup scripts:

    # /sbin/init.d/nfs.server start
    # /sbin/init.d/sendmail start
    /etc/mail/aliases: 7 aliases, longest 9 bytes, 88 bytes total

The next step would be to setup all client machines to forward and receive mail to and from *hp02* sendmail server defined above. Here is what you will need to perform on the client systems:

1. Edit */etc/rc.config.d/mailservs* and set the SENDMAIL_SERVER variable to 0 and SENDMAIL_SERVER_NAME variable to the hostname or IP address of the sendmail server:

    SENDMAIL_SERVER=0
    SENDMAIL_SERVER_NAME=hp02

2. Edit */etc/rc.config.d/nfsconf* and set the NFS_CLIENT variable to 1.
3. Add the following line to */etc/fstab*:

    hp02:/var/mail /var/mail nfs defaults 0 0

4. Start *sendmail* and NFS client functionalities:

    # **/sbin/init.d/sendmail start**
    # **/sbin/init.d/nfs.client start**

The client/server setup is complete and your client machines are ready to forward local mail to the sendmail server.

27.3.3   Verifying Sendmail Functionality

You can verify that sendmail has been setup properly by sending out a test mail.

To test local mail functionality, mail a message to a local user (for example, *user1*) on your system. The result follows the command.

    # **date | mailx –s "Local sendmail Test" user1**
    From user1 Thu Feb 16 09:18 EDT 2006
    Received: by hp02; Thu, 16 Feb 06 09:18:53 edt
    Date: Thu, 16 Feb 06 09:18:53 edt
    From: user1 User <user1>
    Return-Path: <user1>
    To: **user1**
    Subject: Local sendmail Test
    Thu Feb 16 09:18:49 EDT 2006

To test network mail functionality, mail a message to a remote user (for example, to *user1* on *hp01*):

    # **date | mailx –s "Remote sendmail Test" user1%hp02@hp01**

When a mail is sent out, it is stored temporarily in the mail queue located in the */var/spool/mqueue* directory. You can display it with the *mailq* command. Use –v for detailed output.

    # **mailq –v**

The user, *user1*, can view his/her mail by running the *mailx* command on *hp01* as follows:

```
$ mailx
From user1@hp02 Wed Aug  6 14:22 MDT 1986
Received: from hp01 by hp02; Wed, 6 Aug 86 14:22:56  mdt
Return-Path: <user1@hp02>
Received: from hp02 by hp01; Wed, 6 Aug 86 14:25:04  mdt
Received: by hp02; Wed, 6 Aug 86 14:22:31 mdt
Date: Wed, 6 Aug 86 14:22:31 mdt
From: user1 User <user1@hp02>
To: user1%hp02@hp01
Subject: Round Robin SMTP

Wed Aug  6 14:22:28 MDT 1986
```

An entry for both mail messages above will be logged in the */var/adm/syslog/mail.log* file.

27.3.4   Updating Aliases File

When you need to add a new alias to the */etc/mail/aliases* database file, you are required to execute the *newaliases* command to update the *sendmail* daemon about the change. Here is what this command produces when executed.

```
# newaliases
/etc/mail/aliases: 8 aliases, longest 9 bytes, 107 bytes total
```

Summary

This chapter introduced you to the internet services and sendmail functionality.

You learned Berkeley and ARPA internet services and looked at how to activate/deactivate and use them. You understood the concept of trust relationship and how to setup user and host equivalency. You looked at how the internet services daemon worked and understood the contents of its configuration and security files.

Finally, you studied a little bit about sendmail. You were presented with step-by-step procedure on how to configure basic sendmail server and client functionality. You sent mail messages to local and network users and displayed the messages to verify client/server component functionality.

Setting Up and Administering NTP

This chapter covers the following major topics:

- ✓ NTP concepts and components
- ✓ Setup an NTP server
- ✓ Setup an NTP peer
- ✓ Setup an NTP client
- ✓ Configure authentication
- ✓ Use ntpdate to update system clock
- ✓ Query NTP servers
- ✓ Trace NTP server roots
- ✓ Basic troubleshooting

28.1 NTP Concepts and Components

The *Network Time Protocol* (NTP) service maintains the system clock on an HP-UX system synchronized with a more accurate and reliable time source. Providing accurate and uniform time for systems on the network allows time-sensitive applications, such as backup software, job scheduling tools, and billing systems to perform correctly and precisely. NTP uses port 123 on the HP-UX system.

In order to understand NTP, a grasp of NTP components and roles is necessary. The following subsections explain them.

28.1.1 Time Source

A time source is a server that synchronizes its time with *Universal Coordinated Time* (UTC). Care should be taken when choosing a time source for a network. Preference should be given to a time server that is physically close to the system location and takes the least amount of time to send and receive NTP packets.

The most common time sources available are:

- ✓ A local system clock from one of the HP-UX systems on the network.
- ✓ An internet-based public time server.
- ✓ A radio clock.

Local System Clock

You can arrange for one of the HP-UX systems on the network to function as a provider of time for other machines. This requires the maintenance of correct time on this local server either manually or automatically via cron. However, keep in mind that since this server is using its own system clock, it has no way of synchronizing itself with a more reliable and accurate external time source. Therefore, using a local system that relies on its own clock as a time server is the least recommended option.

Internet-Based Public Time Server

Several public time servers that can be employed for the provision of correct time are available via the internet. One of the systems on the network must be connected to one or more such time servers. To make use of such a time source, a port in the firewall may need to be opened to allow for the flow of NTP traffic. Internet-based public time servers are typically operated by government organizations and universities. This option is more popular than using a local time server.

Several public time servers are available for access on the internet. Visit *www.ntp.org* to obtain a list.

Radio Clock

A radio clock is considered the most accurate source of time. Some popular radio clock methods include *Global Positioning System* (GPS), *National Institute of Science and Technology* (NIST) radio broadcasts in Americas, and DCF77 radio broadcasts in Europe. Of theses methods, GPS-based sources are the most accurate. In order to use them, some hardware must be added to one of the local systems on the network.

28.1.2   Stratum Levels

As you are aware that there are numerous time sources available to synchronize the system time with. These time sources are categorized into levels, called *Stratum Levels*, based on their reliability and accuracy. There are 15 stratum levels ranging from 1 to 15, with 1 being the most accurate. The radio clocks are at stratum 1 as they are the most accurate. However, stratum 1 time sources cannot be used on a network directly. Therefore, one of the machines on the network at stratum 2, for instance, needs to be configured to get time updates from a stratum 1 server. The stratum 2 server then acts as the primary source of time for secondary servers and/or clients on the network. It can also be configured to provide time to stratum 3 or lower-reliability time servers.

If a secondary server is also configured to get time from a stratum 1 server directly, it will act as a peer to the primary server.

28.1.3   NTP Roles

A role is a function that an HP-UX system performs from the NTP standpoint. A system can be configured to assume one or more of the following roles:

Primary NTP Server

A *Primary NTP Server* gets time from one of the time sources mentioned above and provides time to one or more secondary servers or clients, or both. It can also be configured to broadcast time to secondary servers and clients.

Secondary NTP Server

A *Secondary NTP Server* receives time from a primary server or from one of the time sources mentioned above. It can be used to provide time to a set of clients to offload the primary server or, as a redundant time server when the primary becomes unavailable. Having a secondary server is optional, but highly recommended. It can be configured to broadcast time to clients and peers.

NTP Peer

An *NTP Peer* provides time to an NTP server and receives time from that server. They usually work at the same stratum level. Both primary and secondary servers can be peers of each other.

NTP Client

An *NTP Client* receives time from either a primary or a secondary time server. A client can be configured in one of the following two ways:

✓ As a *Polling* client that contacts a primary or a secondary NTP server directly to get time updates to synchronize its system clock.
✓ As a *Broadcast* client that listens to time broadcasts by a primary or a secondary NTP server. A broadcast client binds itself with the NTP server that responds to its requests and synchronizes its clock with it. The NTP server must be configured in broadcast mode in order for the broadcast client to bind to it.

28.2   Setting Up NTP

The following sub-sections provide step-by-step procedures on how to setup an NTP server, peer, and client.

28.2.1   Setting Up NTP Server and Peer

To setup an NTP server or peer (primary or secondary), follow the steps below:

1. Select an appropriate time source.
2. Add the time source information to the */etc/ntp.conf* configuration file:

For local system clock, add the following two lines. The 127.127.1.1 is a reserved IP address, which is always used in this case. The "fudge" keyword defines the stratum level.

```
server      127.127.1.1
fudge       127.127.1.1      stratum  9
```

For an internet-based time server, specify either fully qualified hostname or IP address of the server. For example, if the IP address is 11.59.99.3, then an entry will look like:

```
server      11.59.99.3
```

For a radio clock-based source of time, connect special hardware device to the system's serial port and add the following line to the file. The first three octets of the IP address (127.127.4) indicates that an external source of time is used. The last octet of the IP address (2, in this example) means that the radio clock hardware is connected to the second serial port of the system.

```
server      127.127.4.2
```

To setup a peer, specify the hostname or IP address of the NTP server with the keyword "peer". For example, to define that this machine is a peer of *hp03*, enter the following:

```
peer        hp03
```

It is recommended to choose a minimum of two time servers located apart physically and accessed via different network routes for redundancy purposes. NTP automatically starts using the secondary server, should the primary becomes unavailable. The servers can act as peers of each other, if they are at the same stratum level.

---

3. Edit the */etc/rc.config.d/netdaemons* file:

Set the variable NTPDATE_SERVER to the hostname of an NTP time server that is reachable (say 11.59.99.3). This will run the *ntpdate* command just before the NTP daemon is started at boot time and will bring the system clock very close to the NTP server clock. Setting this variable is not required, but recommended.

NTPDATE_SERVER=11.59.99.3

Set the XNTPD variable to 1, so the *xntpd* daemon starts automatically at each system reboot.

XNTPD=1

4. Start the daemon manually:

 # /sbin/init.d/xntpd start

An NTP server can be setup via SAM as well. Follow the links below:

Go to SAM → Time → NTP Network Time Sources → Actions. Select an appropriate choice from:

✓ Add Remote Server or Peer
✓ Configure NTP Local Clock
✓ Stop or Start NTP

Refer to Figure 28-1.

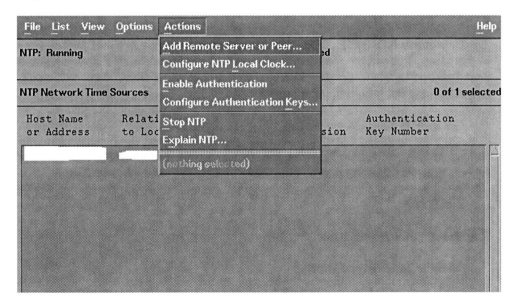

Figure 28-1 SAM – NTP Server Administration

28.2.2   Setting Up an NTP Client

To setup an NTP client, follow the steps below:

1.   Add the following lines to the */etc/ntp.conf* file:

To setup the client as a polling client to synchronize time with NTP server *hp01*:

```
server       hp01
driftfile    /etc/ntp.drift
```

The *xntpd* daemon computes the clock frequency error in the local system every 64 seconds, by default. It may take *xntpd* hours after it is started to compute a good estimate of the error. The current error value is stored in the */etc/ntp.drift* file (or any other file or directory location specified with the "driftfile" keyword). This allows *xntpd* to reinitialize itself to the estimate stored in the driftfile, saving time in recomputing a good frequency estimate. In short, the usage of driftfile helps *xntpd* track local system clock accuracy. A driftfile is not required, but recommended.

To setup the client as a broadcast client:

```
broadcastclient      yes
driftfile            /etc/ntp.drift
```

To setup a broadcast client, define the broadcast network address in */etc/ntp.conf* on the NTP server and restart *xntpd* on it. An example entry would be: broadcast 11.69.99.255

2.   Edit the */etc/rc.config.d/netdaemons* file:

Set the variable NTPDATE_SERVER to the hostname of one of the NTP time servers (*hp01* in this case). This will run the *ntpdate* command just before the NTP daemon is started at boot time and force the system clock to come very close to the NTP server's clock. Setting this variable is not required, but recommended.

```
NTPDATE_SERVER=hp01
```

Set the XNTPD variable to 1, so the *xntpd* daemon starts automatically at each system reboot. You may start the daemon manually by calling the script (step 3).

```
XNTPD=1
```

3.   Start the daemon manually:

 # /sbin/init.d/xntpd start

SAM can be used to setup an NTP client. Follow the links:

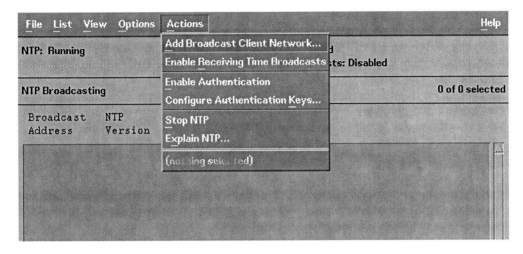Go to SAM → Time → NTP Broadcasting → Actions. You will see the following choices:

- ✓ Add Broadcast Client Network
- ✓ Enable Receiving Time Broadcasts
- ✓ Stop or Start NTP

See Figure 28-2.

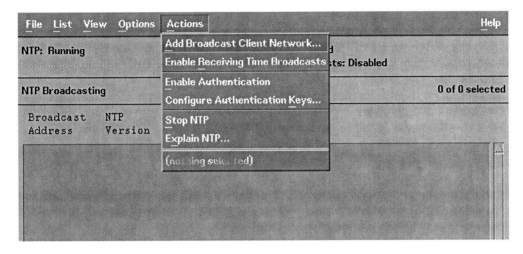

Figure 28-2 SAM – NTP Client Administration

28.2.3 Enabling Authentication

Enabling authentication on an NTP client helps protect against unauthorized access. It allows only those NTP servers that send messages encrypted with a configured key, to be candidates to which your system is synchronized.

An authentication key file */etc/ntp.key* is configured on the NTP client. This file contains a list of keys and corresponding key numbers. Each key-key number combination is further defined by a key format, which determines the encryption method to be used.

To enable NTP authentication, include the following statement in the */etc/ntp.conf* file on an NTP client, and restart the daemon:

    authenticate yes

You can enable NTP authentication using SAM as follows:

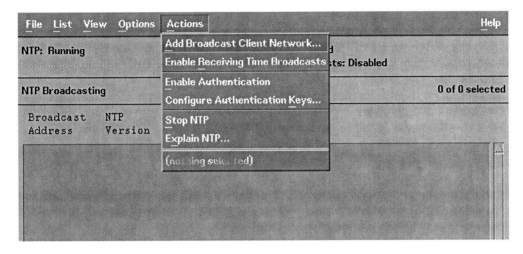Go to SAM → Time → NTP Network Time Sources → Actions → Enable Authentication. See Figures 28-1 and 28-2.

28.3 Managing NTP

Managing NTP involves updating system clock manually, querying NTP servers, and tracing roots of an NTP server.

28.3.1 Updating System Clock Manually

You can run the *ntpdate* command anytime to bring the system clock close to the time on an NTP server. You can also schedule a cron job to execute this command periodically as an alternative to setting up the system as an NTP client. The *xntpd* daemon must not be running, when *ntpdate* is executed. Run *ntpdate* manually and specify either the hostname, *hp01.ntp.org* as an example, or IP address of the time server:

> # ntpdate hp01.ntp.org
> 9 Feb 14:00:29 ntpdate[6704]: adjust time server 19.33.42.222 offset 0.000023 sec

28.3.2 Querying NTP Servers

You can run the *ntpq* command to query NTP servers about time synchronization and server association status. This command sends out requests to and receives responses from NTP servers. The command may be run in interactive mode as well.

Run *ntpq* with –p option to print a list of NTP servers known to your system, along with a summary of their states.

```
# ntpq  –p
     remote         refid        st  t  when  poll  reach  delay   offset  disp
==============================================================
*19.33.42.222  hp01.ntp.org   2   u   180   1024   377    28.95   -0.437  0.61
```

Each column from the above output is explained in Table 28-1.

Column	Description
remote	Shows IP addresses or hostnames of all NTP servers and peers. Each IP/hostname may be preceded by one of the following characters: * → Indicates current synchronization source. # → Indicates the server selected for synchronization, but distance exceeds maximum. o → Displays server selected for synchronization. + → Indicates the system considered for synchronization. x → Designated false ticker by the intersection algorithm. . → Indicates the systems picked from the end of the candidate list. - → Indicates the system not considered for synchronization. Blank → Indicates the server rejected because of high stratum level or failed sanity checks.
refid	Shows current source of synchronization.

st	Shows stratum level of the server.
t	Shows available types, which include l=local (such as a GPS clock), u=unicast, m = multicast, b= broadcast, - = netaddr (usually 0).
when	Shows time, in seconds, since a response was received from the server.
poll	Shows polling interval. Default is 64 seconds.
reach	Shows number of successful attempts to reach the server. The value 001 indicates that the most recent probe was answered, 357 indicates that one probe was not answered, and the value 377 indicates that all recent probes were answered.
delay	Shows how long, in milliseconds, it took for the reply packet to come back in response to the query sent to the server.
offset	Shows time difference, in milliseconds, between the server and the client clocks.
disp	Dispersion. Shows how much the "offset" measurement varies between samples. This is an error-bound estimate.

Table 28-1 *ntpq* Command Output Description

28.3.3   Tracing Roots of an NTP Server

You can trace the roots of an NTP server starting from the specified server, using the *ntptrace* command. For example, if a time server, such as *hp01.ntp.org*, is configured at stratum 2, the following will locate the stratum 1 server where *hp01.ntp.org* is getting time from:

 # ntptrace hp01.ntp.org
hp01.ntp.org: stratum 1, offset 0.000247, synch distance 0.00607, refid 'GPS'

The output shows that *hp01.ntp.org* is at stratum 1 and using GPS. Try running *ntptrace* with –d and –v options to display debug and detailed information, respectively.

28.4 Troubleshooting Basic Issues

This section lists a few common NTP-related error messages with an explanation and how to resolve them.

No Suitable Server for Synchronization Found

This message means that the NTP server is not responding for some reasons. Try stopping *xntpd* and running the *ntpdate* command with –d (debug) option to print information about the requests sent to the time server and the replies from it.

Startup Delay

This message indicates that there is a delay in the response from the server. What happens is that when *xntpd* first starts, it takes five poll cycles to bind itself with a server or peer. During this time, *xntpd* does not respond to client requests. A server must be bound to a time server before it gives time to clients or peers.

Synchronization Lost

When this message appears, it indicates that NTP has lost synchronization with the time server it was bound to and now it is in the process of choosing one and making time adjustments with it. If a system makes these adjustments frequently, you might have network congestions. Use the *ntpq* command with –p option and examine dispersion statistics.

Time Difference Over 1000 Seconds

When this message appears, it means that the difference in time is over 1000 seconds between a server and its peer or client and hence they have started to reject time updates coming from the NTP server. Try stopping *xntpd* and running *ntpdate* to get time from some other server or peer. Restart *xntpd*.

Summary

This chapter provided an introduction to Network Time Protocol and how to set it up. You learned concepts and components of it. You looked at configuring an NTP server, peer, and client. You understood the rationale behind enabling authentication on NTP clients. You saw how to update the system clock manually, query NTP servers, and trace roots of an NTP server.

Finally, you were presented with a few common error messages while working with NTP, along with an explanation and basic techniques to fix problems that potentially caused them.

## 29

Setting Up and Administering NFS

This chapter covers the following major topics:

- ✓   Understand NFS concepts and benefits
- ✓   Understand NFS versions, daemons, commands, related files, and startup scripts
- ✓   How NFS client and server interact with each other
- ✓   Setup an NFS server and client
- ✓   Display exported and mounted NFS resources
- ✓   Unmount and unexport a resource
- ✓   Monitor NFS activities
- ✓   Basic troubleshooting

29.1   Understanding Network File System (NFS)

The *Network File System* (NFS) service is based on the client/server architecture whereby users on one system access files, directories, and file systems (called *Resources*) residing on a remote system as if they exist locally on their system. The remote machine that makes its resources available to be accessed over the network is called an *NFS Server* and the process of making them accessible over the network is referred to as *Export*. The resources exported by an NFS server can be accessed by one or more systems. These systems are called *NFS Clients* and the process of making the resources accessible is referred to as *Mount*.

A system can function as both an NFS server and NFS client at the same time. When a directory or file system resource is exported, the entire directory structure beneath it becomes available to be mounted on an NFS client. A sub-directory or the parent directory of an exported resource cannot be exported, if it exists in the same file system. Similarly, a resource mounted by an NFS client cannot be re-exported.

NFS uses *Remote Procedure Call* (RPC) to allow an NFS server and client to talk to each other. RPC provides a common "language" that both the server and client understand. This is standardized based on the fact that the NFS server and client may be running two totally different operating systems. RPC uses program numbers defined in the */etc/rpc* file.

The following data is extracted from */etc/rpc* file. It shows official service names in the first column, followed by program numbers and associated alias names in subsequent columns.

```
# cat  /etc/rpc
. . . . . . . .
. . . . . . . .
rpcbind    100000    portmap    sunrpc      rpcbind
rstatd     100001    rstat      rup         perfmeter
mountd     100005    mount      showmount
pcnfsd     150001    pcnfs
. . . . . . . .
. . . . . . . .
```

29.1.1   Benefits

Some benefits associated with using NFS are listed below:

- ✓ Supports heterogeneous operating system platformss including all flavors of the UNIX operating system as well as Linux and Windows.
- ✓ Several client systems can access a single resource simultaneously.
- ✓ Enables sharing common application binaries and read-only information, such as the *man* pages, instead of loading them on each single machine. This results in reduced overall disk storage cost and administration overhead.
- ✓ Gives users access to uniform data.
- ✓ Useful when many users exist on many systems with each user's home directory located on every single machine. NFS enables you to create all user home directories on a single machine under */home*, for example, and export */home*. Now, whichever machine a user logs

on to, his/her home directory becomes available there. The user will need to maintain only one home directory and not a lot.

29.1.2   NFS Versions

When working with a mix of HP-UX versions newer and older than 11.0, ensure that proper NFS versions are specified in the configuration. The older versions supported NFS v2 and the newer versions are at NFS v3. The benefits you get with NFS v3 are:

✓ Files of sizes up to 128GB (64-bit) are supported as compared to 2GB (32-bit) limitation in v2.
✓ Uses TCP compared with UDP in v2.
✓ Enhanced performance.
✓ AutoFS is supported versus Automounter in v2. AutoFS has better features than Automounter. See Chapter 30 "Setting Up and Administering AutoFS" for details.

29.1.3   NFS Daemons, Commands, Configuration Files, and Scripts

When working with NFS, several daemons, commands, configuration files, and scripts are involved. The tables given below list and explain them.

Table 29-1 describes NFS daemons.

Daemon	Description
rpc.mountd	Server side daemon that responds to client requests to: ✓ mount a resource. ✓ provide status of exported or mounted resources.
rpc.pcnfsd	Server side daemon for PC-based operating systems.
Nfsd	Server side daemon that responds to client requests to access files.
rpcbind	Server and client side daemon that is responsible for forwarding incoming RPC requests to the appropriate RPC daemons.
portmap	Same as rpcbind but used in versions of HP-UX prior to 11.0.
biod	Server and client side daemon. Stands for *Block I/O Daemon*. Clients use it to handle buffer cache read-ahead and write-behind.
rpc.statd	Server and client side daemon. A client application may request this daemon to place a lock on the file it is accessing to prevent other programs from modifying the file while in use.
rpc.lockd	Server and client side daemon that keeps an eye on the NFS client that has requested a lock on a file to make sure the client is up and running. If the client reboots unexpectedly, this daemon removes all locks placed on any files by applications from that client, so other NFS client applications may use them.

Table 29-1 NFS Daemons

Table 29-2 describes NFS commands.

Command	Description
exportfs	Server side command that can be used to: ✓ export resources listed in the */etc/exports* file. ✓ display exported resources listed in the */etc/xtab* file.
showmount	Server and client side command that can be used to: ✓ display which resources are exported to which clients (consults */etc/xtab* file on NFS server). ✓ display which clients have those resources mounted (consults */etc/rmtab* file on NFS server).
mount	Client side command that can be used to: ✓ mount a resource specified at the command line or listed in the */etc/fstab* file, followed by adding an entry to client's */etc/mnttab* file, and server's */etc/rmtab* file via the *rpc.mountd* daemon. ✓ display mounted resources listed in the */etc/mnttab* file.
mountall	Client side command that mounts all resources listed in the */etc/fstab* file, followed by adding entries to client's */etc/mnttab* file, and server's */etc/rmtab* file via the *rpc.mountd* daemon.
umount	Client side command that unmounts a single resource specified at the command line or listed in the */etc/mnttab* file, followed by removing corresponding entry from this file, and server's */etc/rmtab* file via the *rpc.mountd* daemon.
umountall	Client side command that unmounts all resources listed in the */etc/mnttab* file, followed by removing corresponding entries from this file, and server's */etc/rmtab* file via the *rpc.mountd* daemon.
rpcinfo	Server side command that checks whether or not NFS server daemons are registered with RPC.
nfsstat	Server and client side command that displays NFS and RPC statistics.

Table 29-2 NFS Commands

Table 29-3 describes NFS configuration and functional files.

File	Description
/etc/exports	Server side file that contains a list of resources to be exported.
/etc/xtab	Server side file that contains a list of exported resources. When a resource is exported, an entry is added to this file. When a resource is unexported, the entry is removed. This file is maintained by the *rpc.mountd* daemon.
/etc/rmtab	Server side file that contains a list of exported resources that have been mounted by clients. When a resource is mounted, an entry is added to this file. When a resource is unmounted, the entry is removed. This file is maintained by the *rpc.mountd* daemon.
/etc/fstab	Client side file that contains a list of resources to be mounted at each system reboot, or manually using the *mount* or *mountall* commands.

HP Certified Systems Administrator

/etc/mnttab	Client side file that contains a list of mounted resources. The *mount*, *umount*, *mountall*, and *umountall* commands update this file.
/etc/rc.config.d/nfsconf	Server and client side configuration file used by NFS startup scripts.

Table 29-3 NFS Configuration and Functional Files

Table 29-4 describes NFS startup and shutdown scripts.

Startup Scripts	Description
/sbin/init.d/nfs.core	Runs at run level 2 on both NFS server and client. Starts the *rpcbind* daemon. Looks into the */etc/rc.config.d/nfsconf* file for startup configuration information.
/sbin/init.d/nfs.server	Runs at run level 3 on the NFS server. Looks into the */etc/rc.config.d/nfsconf* file for startup configuration information.
/sbin/init.d/nfs.client	Runs at run level 2 on the NFS client. Looks into the */etc/rc.config.d/nfsconf* file for startup configuration information.

Table 29-4 NFS Startup and Shutdown Scripts

29.1.4   How NFS Works?

When an NFS server exports a resource and an NFS client mounts the resource, the following happens. It is assumed that the startup configuration file */etc/rc.config.d/nfsconf* is properly configured.

✓ The */etc/exports* file contents are evaluated for any syntax problems and access issues.
✓ Each resource listed in this file is exported and an entry is put in the */etc/xtab* file on the server. The *showmount* command looks into this file to display exported resource information.
✓ The client issues the *mount* command to request the NFS server to provide file handle for the requested resource.
✓ The request goes to the *rpc.mountd* daemon on the NFS server through the *rpcbind* daemon that runs on both the server and the client.
✓ The *rpc.mountd* daemon performs an access check to validate if the client is authorized to mount the resource.
✓ The *rpc.mountd* daemon sends the file handle for the requested resource to the client.
✓ The client mounts the resource, if the correct *mount* command syntax is used. To automate the mount process, an entry for the resource can be added to the */etc/fstab* file, which ensures that the resource will get automatically mounted when the client reboots.
✓ The *mount* command tells the *rpc.mountd* daemon on the NFS server that the resource has been mounted successfully. Upon receiving that confirmation, the daemon puts an entry in the */etc/rmtab* file. The *showmount* command uses this file to display remotely mounted NFS resources. When the resource is unmounted on the client, the *umount* command sends a request to the *rpc.mountd* daemon to remove corresponding entry from this file.
✓ The *mount* command also puts an entry in the */etc/mnttab* file for the mounted resource. The *mount*, *bdf*, and *df* commands reference this file to display information about mounted

resources. The *mount, umount, mountall,* and *umountall* commands update this file whenever they execute successfully.

✓ Any file access request by the client on the mounted resource is now going to be handled by the server's *nfsd* daemon.

✓ The *rpc.lockd* and *rpc.statd* daemons are involved, when the client requests the server to place a lock on a file.

29.2 Setting Up NFS

This section discusses procedures on configuring an NFS server and client.

29.2.1 Setting Up an NFS Server

Let us look at the step-by-step procedure to setup a machine (*hp02*, for example) to act as an NFS server and export several resources. Prior to setting up an NFS environment, ensure that UIDs and GIDs are consistent across all systems that will be configured and used as NFS servers and clients. Here is the procedure.

1. Edit */etc/exports* file and insert following entries one per line. Create this file if it does not already exist. Make sure the file has 644 permissions and *root* ownership.

   ```
   /usr/share/man        -ro
   /home                 -access=hp03:hp04
   /var/mail             -root=hp03:hp04
   /opt/samba            -anon=104
   /opt/perl             -async
   /var/opt/samba        -anon=65535
   ```

   Refer to Table 29-5 for option details.

2. Edit */etc/rc.config.d/nfsconf* file and set the NFS_SERVER and START_MOUNTD variables to 1. This ensures that NFS server functionality is started at each system reboot.

   ```
   NFS_SERVER=1
   START_MOUNTD=1
   ```

3. Execute the following command to start NFS server processes and export entries you inserted in */etc/exports* file:

   # /sbin/init.d/nfs.server start
   ```
   starting NFS SERVER networking

   starting up the rpcbind daemon
       rpcbind already started, using pid: 685
   Reading in /etc/exports
   starting up the mount daemon
       /usr/sbin/rpc.mountd
   starting up the NFS daemons
   ```

```
            /usr/sbin/nfsd 16
         starting up the Status Monitor daemon
            /usr/sbin/rpc.statd
         starting up the Lock Manager daemon
            /usr/sbin/rpc.lockd
```

If the processes are already running, simply execute the following:

exportfs −a

Note that you can run the *exportfs* command with −i option and specify a resource name to export it temporarily without making an entry in */etc/exports*. This resource will stay exported until you manually unexport it or reboot the server.

Some common options that you can use when exporting or mounting a resource are described in Table 29-5. Notice that server side options are used when exporting resources and client side options are used when mounting them on NFS clients.

Option	Description
rw (read/write) / ro (read-only) (default: rw)	Server and client side options. Used on NFS server when exporting a resource and on NFS client when mounting a resource. "rw" enables users to modify files. "ro" prevents users from modifying files.
−access=client1:client2	Server side option. Gives access to specified clients only.
−root=client1:client2	Server side option. Gives *root* access to specified clients only.
−anon=UID	Server side option. Anonymous users are assigned the specified UID. If UID 65535 is supplied, users without a valid UID are denied access. If this option is not used, the default UID of −2 is allocated, which belongs to user "nobody" and provides limited access to anonymous users.
−async	Server side option. NFS writes are made asynchronously (in parallel).
hard / soft (default: hard)	Client side option. Use "hard" if users will be either writing to the mounted resource or running programs located in it. When an NFS client attempts to mount a resource with this option, it keeps trying until it succeeds or is interrupted. If the NFS server goes down, any processes using the mounted resource hang until the server comes back up. "hard" mounts with "intr" option set, may be interrupted with *ctrl+c* or *kill* command. Use "soft" to prevent NFS clients from being hung, if the NFS server goes down. When an NFS client attempts to mount a resource with this option unsuccessfully for "retrans" times, it displays an error message.
vers=*n* (default=3)	Client side option. NFS version to be used.

suid / nosuid (default: suid)	Client side option. "suid" enables users on an NFS client to execute a setuid-enabled program, located on the NFS mounted resource, with the same privileges as the owner of the program has on it. If such a program has *root* ownership on it, it is executed with *root* privileges, regardless of who runs it. "nosuid" prevents users from running setuid programs.
intr (interruptible) / nointr (Non-interruptible) (default: intr)	Client side option. Use "intr" if users do not wish to manually interrupt an NFS request. Use "nointr" for the opposite.
fg (foreground) / bg (background) (default: fg)	Client side option. Use "fg" for resources that must be available to the NFS client to boot or operate correctly. If a foreground mount fails, it is retried in the foreground until it succeeds or is interrupted. With "bg" option set, mount attempts are tried and retried in the background enabling an NFS client to continue to boot.
timeo=n (default=7)	Client side option. The timeout, in tenths of a second, for NFS read and write requests. If an NFS request times out, this value is doubled and the request is attempted again for "retrans" times. When number of "retrans" attempts are made, a "soft" mount displays an error message, while a "hard" mount continues to retry.
retrans=n (default=5)	Client side option. This many times an NFS client retransmits a read or write request after the first transmission times out. If the request does not succeed after n retransmissions, a "soft" mount displays an error message, while a "hard" mount continues to retry.
retry=n (default=1)	Client side option. This many times an NFS client tries to mount a resource after the first try fails. If you specify "intr", you can interrupt the mount before n retries. However, if you specify "nointr", you must wait until n retries have been made, mount succeeds, or you reboot the client.
rsize=n (default=8k)	Client side option. Size of each read request from NFS client to NFS server.
wsize=n (default=8k)	Client side option. Size of each write request from NFS client to NFS server.

Table 29-5 *export* and *mount* Command Options

You can setup an NFS server using SAM as well. Follow the links below:

☞Go to SAM → Networking and Communications → Networked File Systems → Exported Local File Systems → Actions → Add Exported File System. Fill out the form based on requirements and hit the OK button. See Figure 29-1.

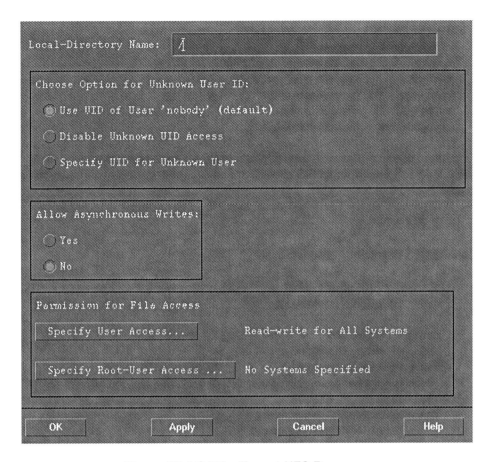

Figure 29-1 SAM – Export NFS Resource

29.2.2 Setting Up an NFS Client

Here is the procedure to setup an NFS client successfully.

1. Execute the following command on the NFS server to determine available exported resources:

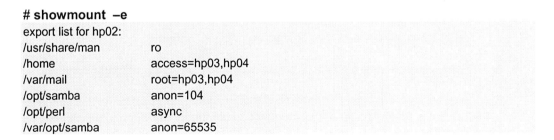

You can also use the *exportfs* command without any options, or do a *cat* on the */etc/xtab* file, to display the above information.

---

exportfs
```
/usr/share/man    -access=ro
/home             -access=access=hp03:hp04
/var/mail         -access=root=hp03:hp04
/opt/samba        -access=anon=104
/opt/perl         -access=async
/var/opt/samba    -access=anon=65535
```

2. Edit */etc/rc.config.d/nfsconf* file on NFS client (*hp03*, for example) and set NFS_CLIENT variable to 1 to ensure that NFS client functionality gets started each time you reboot the machine.

    NFS_CLIENT=1

3. Run the NFS client startup script:

    # **/sbin/init.d/nfs.client start**
    starting NFS CLIENT networking

    starting up the rpcbind
       rpcbind already started, using pid: 542
    starting up the BIO daemons
       biod(s) already started, using pid(s): 587 585 584 586 588 589 590 591 592 593 594 595 596
    597 598 599
    starting up the Status Monitor daemon
       rpc.statd already started, using pid: 607
    starting up the Lock Manager daemon
       rpc.lockd already started, using pid: 613
    mounting remote NFS file systems ...

4. Edit */etc/fstab* and add the following lines for each of the seven resources. This is done to ensure that each time this client reboots, the defined resources get automatically mounted.

    ```
    hp02:/usr/share/man    /usr/share/man    nfs    ro          0  0
    hp02:/home             /home             nfs    defaults    0  0
    hp02:/var/mail         /var/mail         nfs    defaults    0  0
    hp02:/opt/samba        /opt/samba        nfs    defaults    0  0
    hp02:/opt/perl         /opt/perl         nfs    defaults    0  0
    hp02:/var/opt/samba    /var/opt/samba    nfs    defaults    0  0
    ```

5. Create required mount points, if not already exist, using the *mkdir* command.

6. Execute either the *mountall* command that attempts to mount all local and remote resources listed in the */etc/fstab* file or the *mount* command with –aF nfs options to mount only remote resources.

    # **mountall**
    # **mount –aF nfs**

___

Alternatively, you can manually mount resources in one of two ways as well. Repeat the first command below for each resource to be mounted and specify correct options with –o switch. The second command gets additional required information from the */etc/fstab* file.

> # **mount –F nfs –o ro hp02:/usr/share/man /usr/share/man**
> # **mount /usr/share/man**

A mount point should be empty and not in use, when an attempt is made to mount a resource on it, otherwise, the contents of the mount point will be hidden.

You can setup an NFS client using SAM, too. Follow the links below:

Go to SAM → Networking and Communications → Networked File Systems → Mounted Remote File Systems → Actions → Add Remote File System → Using NFS. Fill out the form and hit the OK button. See Figure 29-2.

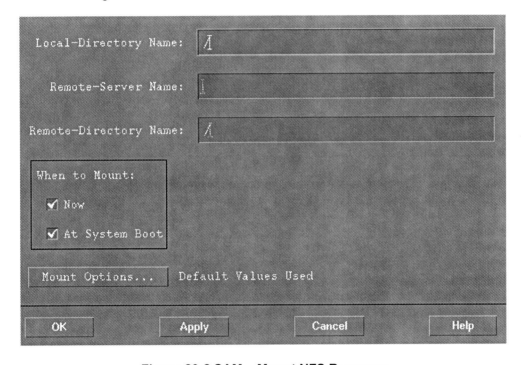

Figure 29-2 SAM – Mount NFS Resource

29.3   Managing NFS

Managing NFS involves displaying exported and mounted resources, and, unmounting and unexporting resources. Following sub-sections explain the management operations.

29.3.1   Viewing Exported and Mounted Resources

To verify the functionality of) both the server and the client, *cd* into resource mount points and run the *ll* command. If both commands run successfully, it means that the resource is exported and mounted. There are several commands, such as *showmount*, *exportfs*, *bdf*, and *mount* that allow you to view what resources are exported by the server, what resources are available to a particular client to be mounted, what resources are mounted on a client, and so on. Let us look at some examples here.

To view what resources are currently exported, execute any of the following on the NFS server:

> # **exportfs**
> # **showmount –e**
> # **cat /etc/xtab**

To view what resources are currently mounted by which NFS client, execute any of the following on the NFS server:

> # **showmount –a**
> hp03:/home
> hp03:/usr/share/man
> hp03:/opt/perl
> hp03:/opt/samba
> hp03:/var/mail
> hp03:/var/opt/samba
> # **cat /etc/rmtab**

To view what remote resources are currently mounted, execute any of the following on the NFS client:

> # **mount –v**
> # **bdf –t nfs**

File system	kbytes	used	avail	%used	Mounted on
hp02:/var/opt/samba	3006464	1665784	1330360	56%	/var/opt/samba
hp02:/var/mail	3006464	1665784	1330360	56%	/var/mail
hp02:/opt/samba	1785856	1241872	539752	70%	/opt/samba
hp02:/opt/perl	1785856	1241872	539752	70%	/opt/perl
hp02:/usr/share/man	1257472	905600	349352	72%	/export/man
hp02:/home	20480	3112	17296	15%	/export/home

> # **df –k**
> # **cat /etc/mnttab | grep –i nfs**

You can also view exported and mounted resources using SAM. Follow the links in sections 29.2.1 and 29.2.2.

29.3.2   Unmounting a Resource

Follow the steps below to unmount a remote resource on an NFS client.

HP Certified Systems Administrator

1. Make sure no users are) accessing the resource (*/usr/share/man*, for example). If a non-critical process is using the resource, or simply, a user is sitting in it, list PIDs and user names of all that are using it:

   # **fuser –cu /usr/share/man**
   /usr/share/man: 2805c(root)   26159c(root)

2. Kill any processes using the resource or wait until the processes terminate. To kill all processes using the resource, do the following:

   # **fuser –ck /usr/share/man**
   /usr/share/man: 2805c   26159c

3. Run the following to unmount the resource:

   # **umount /usr/share/man**

4. If you wish to remove this resource permanently, edit */etc/fstab* and remove the associated entry.

29.3.3   Unexporting a Resource

After making sure, with the *showmount* command) that the resource to be unexported, is not mounted by any clients, do the following on the NFS server to unexport it:

exportfs –u /usr/share/man

If you unexport a mounted resource, the next time a user on that client requests access to the resource, NFS will return "NFS stale file handle" error message.

To unexport all resources listed in */etc/exports* file, use the *exportfs* command as follows:

exportfs –au

29.4 Monitoring NFS Activities

There is a tool called *nfsstat* that you can use to monitor NFS activities, such as read and write. You can specify the –c, –s, and –r options to capture client, server, and RPC activities, respectively. With –m all mounted resource activities are displayed.

Here is the output of this command. Without any options, it displays all information.

nfsstat
Server rpc:
Connection oriented:
calls   badcalls nullrecv badlen   xdrcall   dupchecks dupreqs
49646 0   0   0   0   210   0

Setting Up and Administering NFS

Connectionless oriented:

calls	badcalls	nullrecv	badlen	xdrcall	dupchecks	dupreqs
0	0	0	0	0	0	0

Server nfs:

calls	badcalls
49646	0

Version 2: (0 calls)

null	getattr	setattr	root	lookup	readlink	read
0 0%	0 0%	0 0%	0 0%	0 0%	0 0%	0 0%

wrcache	write	create	remove	rename	link	symlink
0 0%	0 0%	0 0%	0 0%	0 0%	0 0%	0 0%

mkdir	rmdir	readdir	statfs
0 0%	0 0%	0 0%	0 0%

Version 3: (49646 calls)

null	getattr	setattr	lookup	access	readlink	read
21 0%	31596 63%	19 0%	93 0%	15330 30%	0 0%	411 0%

. . . .
. . . .

29.5   Basic NFS Troubleshooting

When you encounter an issue in the functionality of NFS, you need to revisit NFS server and client configurations. A good understanding of how NFS works, along with proper knowledge of individual files involved, daemons, commands, startup scripts, and options used, help resolve most NFS-related problems quickly and with less pain. Since NFS uses the network, a stable and robust network infrastructure is necessary for its proper operation.

Some common error messages, generated on NFS clients, are explained below:

NFS Server Not Responding

Use *ping* on the NFS client to ensure the NFS server is up and reachable. If this command fails, the server might be down, is too busy, or something wrong with the network.

Run the *rpcinfo* command as follows on the client to ensure the server is running all required processes:

```
# rpcinfo –p  hp02
  program vers proto  port service
  100000   4   tcp   111  rpcbind
  100000   3   tcp   111  rpcbind
  100000   2   tcp   111  rpcbind
  100000   4   udp   111  rpcbind
  100000   3   udp   111  rpcbind
  100000   2   udp   111  rpcbind
  100068   2   udp  49153 cmsd
  100068   3   udp  49153 cmsd
```

```
100068  4  udp  49153  cmsd
100068  5  udp  49153  cmsd
100083  1  tcp  49152  ttdbserver
100002  1  udp  49154  rusersd
100002  2  udp  49154  rusersd
100001  2  udp  49155  rstatd
100001  3  udp  49155  rstatd
100001  4  udp  49155  rstatd
. . . . . . . .
. . . . . . . .
```

The following specifically checks if the *mountd* daemon is running:

 # rpcinfo –u hp02 mountd
program 100005 version 1 ready and waiting
rpcinfo: RPC: Program/version mismatch; low version = 1, high version = 3
program 100005 version 2 is not available
program 100005 version 3 ready and waiting

The *rpcinfo* command has –s and –m options available too for display purposes. Try running the command with these options and see the results.

Run the *nslookup* or *nsquery* command on both the server and the client to check that they "see" each other correctly. Refer to Chapter 33 "Setting Up and Administering DNS" on how to use *nslookup* and *nsquery*.

Stale File Handle

This message occurs when the server unexports a resource which the client still has mounted. To quickly resolve the issue, re-export the resource, unmount it on the client, and then unexport it.

Too Many Levels of Remote in Path

This message occurs on the client when it attempts to mount a resource from a server that has that resource NFS-mounted from another server.

Access Denied

This error message is displayed on the client when it tries to mount a resource. Use the *showmount* command to check if the resource is really exported. Also check if the resource is exported with proper access options and the client's name is on it.

Permission Denied

When this message is generated, do the following:

- ✓   Check if the resource does not use read-only option in client's */etc/fstab* file.
- ✓   Check if the resource does not use read-only option in server's */etc/exports* file.

- ✓ Check */etc/passwd* file on both server and client to ensure you have a valid login on both machines and the UID is consistent.
- ✓ Check for the setuid bit in */etc/fstab* file.

Device Busy

If you get this message while attempting to mount a resource, check to see if the resource is not already mounted.

If you get this message while attempting to unmount a resource, check to see if no user or process is currently accessing it.

Summary

This chapter introduced you to one of the most commonly managed system administration task. You learned and understood concepts, benefits, different versions, daemons, commands, related files, and startup scripts pertaining to Network File System. You comprehended how NFS server and client interact with each other. You looked at procedures for setting up NFS server and client. You used commands that displayed exported and mounted NFS resources, unmounted and unexported resources, and captured and displayed NFS activity data.

Finally, common NFS error messages were presented along with a brief explanation on how to resolve them.

30

Setting Up and Administering AutoFS

This chapter covers the following major topics:

- ✓ Understand AutoFS
- ✓ Features and benefits
- ✓ How AutoFS works
- ✓ AutoFS startup script and configuration file
- ✓ Configure AutoFS maps – the master, special, direct, and indirect maps
- ✓ Access an AutoFS resource from multiple NFS servers
- ✓ Mount user home directories
- ✓ Compare AutoFS with Automounter

30.1   Understanding AutoFS

In Chapter 29, you learned about NFS and how to mount an NFS exported resource on the client. This is the standard mount method. In this chapter, you are going to look at the AutoFS (*Auto File System*) facility of HP-UX that offers another method of mounting a resource.

AutoFS is the NFS client-side service that automatically mounts an NFS resource on an as-needed basis. When an activity occurs in the mount point by using a command, such as *ls* or *cd*, the configured NFS resource gets mounted. When the resource is no longer accessed for a pre-defined period of time, it automatically gets unmounted.

30.1.1   Features and Benefits

There are several features and benefits associated with AutoFS mount method compared with standard NFS mount method. These are described below:

- ✓ AutoFS requires that you define NFS resources in text configuration files called *AutoFS Maps,* which are typically located in the */etc* directory. These maps may be managed centrally via NIS, NIS+, or LDAP. In contrast, standard NFS mount information is defined in */etc/fstab* file for each NFS resource that you want to get automatically mounted when the system reboots. Additionally, you must maintain */etc/fstab* file separately on each NFS client.
- ✓ AutoFS does not require *root* privileges to mount available NFS resources, whereas with standard NFS mount method, only *root* can mount them.
- ✓ With AutoFS, the NFS client boot process never hangs if the NFS server is down or inaccessible. With standard NFS mount, when a client system boots up and an NFS server listed in */etc/fstab* file is unavailable, the client hangs until either the mount request times out or the NFS server becomes available.
- ✓ With AutoFS, a resource is unmounted automatically if it is not accessed for five minutes, by default. With standard NFS mount method, a resource stays mounted until you unmount it manually or the client system shuts down.
- ✓ AutoFS provides load balancing and high availability capabilities by automatically accessing a resource available from multiple, replicated NFS servers. In this case, whichever NFS server responds first, AutoFS mounts the resource from that server. This feature is not available with standard NFS mount method.
- ✓ AutoFS supports wildcard characters and environment variables whereas standard NFS mount method does not.
- ✓ A special map is available with AutoFS that mounts all available NFS resources from a reachable NFS server, when a user requests access to a resource on that server without explicitly defining each one of them. The standard mount method does not have any such features available.

30.1.2   How AutoFS Works?

AutoFS consists of the following components:

1. The *automount* command that loads AutoFS maps into memory.
2. The *automountd* daemon that mounts a resource automatically, when it is accessed.
3. An AutoFS resource.

The *automount* command is invoked at system boot up. It reads the AutoFS master map and creates initial mount point entries in the */etc/mnttab* file, however, the resources are not actually mounted at this time. When a user activity occurs later under one of the initial mount points, the *automountd* daemon contacts the *rpc.mountd* daemon on the NFS server and actually mounts the requested resource. The *autofs_proc* daemon monitors all AutoFS-mounted resources. If an Auto-mounted resource is idle for a certain time period, *autofs_proc* notifies *automountd*, which unmounts the idle resource.

The *automountd* daemon and the *automount* command are completely independent of each other, enabling you to modify AutoFS map contents without having to restart the daemon.

30.1.3   Starting and Stopping AutoFS

In order to start AutoFS functionality automatically on a client at every system reboot, set the following variables in the */etc/rc.config.d/nfsconf* startup configuration file. These settings are also required, if you start AutoFS manually.

```
NFS_CLIENT=1
AUTOMOUNT=1
AUTOFS=1
AUTOMOUNT_OPTIONS=""
AUTOMOUNTD_OPTIONS=" "
```

The last two variables can be used to define additional options for the AutoFS daemons. Some common options are given in Table 30-1.

Option	Description
AUTOMOUNT_OPTIONS="–t 600"	Specifies, in seconds, the maximum idle time after which AutoFS automatically unmounts the resource.
AUTOMOUNT_OPTIONS="–v"	Displays a message on the screen, when AutoFS configuration is altered.
AUTOMOUNTD_OPTIONS="–v –T"	Logs all AutoFS mount and unmount requests in */var/adm/automount.log* file.

Table 30-1 AutoFS Options

Execute the NFS client startup script to bring both NFS client as well as AutoFS functionalities up. This script also mounts all NFS resources listed in the */etc/fstab* file.

```
# /sbin/init.d/nfs.client  start
   starting NFS CLIENT networking
   starting up the rpcbind
      rpcbind already started, using pid: 673
   starting up the BIO daemons
      /usr/sbin/biod 16
   starting up the Status Monitor daemon
      /usr/sbin/rpc.statd
```

```
        starting up the Lock Manager daemon
            /usr/sbin/rpc.lockd
        starting up the AutoFS daemon
            /usr/lib/netsvc/fs/autofs/automountd
            Running the AutoFS command interface
            /usr/sbin/automount
    automount: /net: already mounted
        mounting remote NFS file systems ...
```

Alternatively, you can manually start AutoFS functionality by executing the following two commands. The first command starts the *automountd* daemon and the second command copies the AutoFS map contents into */etc/mnttab,* so *automountd* knows which resources it is responsible for mounting.

 # /usr/lib/netsvc/fs/autofs/automountd
 # /usr/lib/netsvc/fs/autofs/automount –v

To bring both AutoFS and NFS client functionalities down, execute the same startup script again but with "stop" argument:

 # /sbin/init.d/nfs.client stop
killing rpc.lockd
killing rpc.statd
killing biod
killing automountd

30.2   The AutoFS Maps

As you know, AutoFS mounts NFS resources on-demand only. In order to perform this, it needs to know which resources to mount, which NFS servers export them, and what mount options to use when mounting them. This information is defined in AutoFS map files.

There are four types of AutoFS maps, viz. *master, special, direct,* and *indirect.* Let us look at each one of these and see how these are setup.

30.2.1   Setting Up the Master Map

The */etc/auto_master* file is the master map, which contains special, direct, and indirect map information. A sample */etc/auto_master* file is shown below that displays how the three map entries look like:

 # cat /etc/auto_master
/net –hosts –nosuid,soft
/– auto_direct
/home auto_indirect

The first entry is for a special map telling AutoFS to use –hosts special map, whenever a user attempts to access anything under */net.*

The second entry is for a direct map telling AutoFS to look for information in the */etc/auto_direct* file.

The last entry is for an indirect map telling AutoFS to refer to the */etc/auto_indirect* file for further information. The umbrella mount point, */home*, precedes all relative mount point entries in the */etc/auto_indirect* file.

The */etc/auto_master* file does not exist by default. When AutoFS is first started, a minimal */etc/auto_master* file is created automatically containing the following entry:

    /net   –hosts   –nosuid,soft

 Execute the *automount* command every time you modify */etc/auto_master*.

30.2.2   Setting Up the Special Map

The –hosts special map allows all resources exported by all accessible NFS servers to get mounted under the */net* directory without explicitly mounting each one of them. Accessing */net/<NFS_Server>* causes AutoFS to automatically mount all resources available to the client from the specified NFS server. Here is the two step procedure to set it up.

1.   Edit */etc/auto_master* and enter the following line, if it does not already exist:

        /net   –hosts   –soft,nosuid

2.   Execute the *automount* command to force AutoFS to re-read the maps:

    # /usr/lib/netsvc/fs/autofs/automount –v

At this point, if you run the *mount* command, you will see nothing mounted from NFS servers:

    # mount –v
    –hosts on /net type autofs ignore, indirect,soft,nosuid

Even if you do an *ll* on the */net* directory, nothing appears. However, if you try to access a specific NFS server (*hp02*, for example, with */usr/share/man*, */home*, */var/mail*, */opt/samba*, */opt/perl*, and */var/opt/samba* exported) under */net*, the *automountd* daemon mounts all resources available from that server.

    # ll /net/hp02

drwxr-xr-x	7	root	root	96	Feb 17 11:06	home
dr-xr-xr-x	2	root	root	4	Feb 22 10:42	opt
dr-xr-xr-x	2	root	root	4	Feb 22 10:42	usr
dr-xr-xr-x	2	root	root	4	Feb 22 10:42	var

The output does not indicate how many resources are mounted under */net/hp02*. Use the *mount* command to display all automounted resources.

 # mount −v

-hosts on /net type autofs ignore,indirect,nosuid,soft on Wed Feb 22 10:38:29 2006

hp02:/home on /net/hp02/home type nfs nosuid,soft,rsize=32768,wsize=32768,NFSv3 on Wed Feb 22 10:41:26 2006

hp02:/var/mail on /net/hp02/var/mail type nfs nosuid,soft,rsize=32768,wsize=32768,NFSv3 on Wed Feb 22 10:41:26 2006

hp02:/opt/perl on /net/hp02/opt/perl type nfs nosuid,soft,rsize=32768,wsize=32768,NFSv3 on Wed Feb 22 10:41:26 2006

hp02:/opt/samba on /net/hp02/opt/samba type nfs nosuid,soft,rsize=32768,wsize=32768,NFSv3 on Wed Feb 22 10:41:26 2006

hp02:/usr/share/man on /net/hp02/usr/share/man type nfs nosuid,soft,rsize=32768,wsize=32768,NFSv3 on Wed Feb 22 10:41:26 2006

hp02:/var/opt/samba on /net/hp02/var/opt/samba type nfs nosuid,soft,rsize=32768,wsize=32768,NFSv3 on Wed Feb 22 10:41:26 2006

The −hosts map is not recommended in an environment where there are many NFS servers exporting many resources, because AutoFS mounts all available resources whether you need them or not.

30.2.3   Setting Up a Direct Map

A direct map is used to mount resources automatically on any number of unrelated mount points. Some key points to note, when working with direct maps, are:

✓   Direct mounted resources are always visible to users.
✓   Local and direct mounted resources can co-exist under one parent directory.
✓   Each direct map entry adds an entry to the */etc/mnttab* file.
✓   When a user or program accesses a directory containing many direct mount points, all resources get mounted.

Let us use a direct map to mount the six resources from NFS server *hp02*. Perform the following three steps:

1.   Edit */etc/auto_master* and add a direct map entry, if it does not already exist. For this example, let us use */etc/auto_direct* file.

   /−   /etc/auto_direct

Each direct map entry consists of three fields: the first field always contains /−, which identifies the entry as a direct map entry, the second field (which is optional) specifies any mount options (not shown), and the third field points to the direct map file where actual NFS server resource and mount point information are located.

2.   Create */etc/auto_direct* file and input the following entries:

   /usr/share/man   −ro   hp02:/usr/share/man
   /home   hp02:/home
   /var/mail   hp02:/var/mail

```
/opt/samba          –ro     hp02:/opt/samba
/opt/perl           –ro     hp02:/opt/perl
/var/opt/samba              hp02:/var/opt/samba
```

3. Execute the *automount* command to make the changes take effect:

 # automount –v

Run the *automount* command each time you add a new entry to a direct map or remove an existing entry from it. There is not need to run it, if the contents of an existing entry are modified.

Now, execute the *mount* command to check mount status of the automounted resources. Note that resource information is visible, but none of them has actually been mounted yet.

```
# mount –v
auto_direct on /usr/share/man type autofs ignore,direct, on Wed Feb 22 11:25:36 2006
auto_direct on /home type autofs ignore,direct, on Wed Feb 22 11:25:36 2006
auto_direct on /var/mail type autofs ignore,direct, on Wed Feb 22 11:25:36 2006
auto_direct on /opt/samba type autofs ignore,direct, on Wed Feb 22 11:25:36 2006
auto_direct on /opt/perl type autofs ignore,direct, on Wed Feb 22 11:25:36 2006
auto_direct on /var/opt/samba type autofs ignore,direct, on Wed Feb 22 11:25:36 2006
```

The first time a user accesses one of these mount points, AutoFS automatically mounts the resource associated with that mount point. Do an *ll* on all six resources and then run the *mount* command again.

```
# ll /usr/share/man /home /var/mail /opt/samba /opt/perl /var/opt/samba
# mount –v
auto_direct on /usr/share/man type autofs ignore,direct, on Wed Feb 22 11:25:36 2006
auto_direct on /home type autofs ignore,direct, on Wed Feb 22 11:25:36 2006
auto_direct on /var/mail type autofs ignore,direct, on Wed Feb 22 11:25:36 2006
auto_direct on /opt/samba type autofs ignore,direct, on Wed Feb 22 11:25:36 2006
auto_direct on /opt/perl type autofs ignore,direct, on Wed Feb 22 11:25:36 2006
auto_direct on /var/opt/samba type autofs ignore,direct, on Wed Feb 22 11:25:36 2006
hp02:/home on /home type nfs ro,rsize=32768,wsize=32768,NFSv3 on Wed Feb 22 11:25:47 2006
hp02:/var/mail on /var/mail type nfs rsize=32768,wsize=32768,NFSv3 on Wed Feb 22 11:26:59 2006
hp02:/opt/perl on /opt/perl type nfs ro,rsize=32768,wsize=32768,NFSv3 on Wed Feb 22 11:28:13 2006
hp02:/opt/samba on /opt/samba type nfs ro,rsize=32768,wsize=32768,NFSv3 on Wed Feb 22 11:28:13 2006
hp02:/var/opt/samba on /var/opt/samba type nfs rsize=32768,wsize=32768,NFSv3 on Wed Feb 22 11:28:13 2006
hp02:/usr/share/man on /usr/share/man type nfs ro,rsize=32768,wsize=32768,NFSv3 on Wed Feb 22 11:29:28 2006
```

30.2.4   Setting Up an Indirect Map

An indirect map is used to automatically mount resources under one common parent directory. Some key points to note, when working with indirect maps, are:

- ✓ Indirect mounted resources only become visible after being accessed.
- ✓ Local and indirect mounted resources cannot co-exist under same parent directory.
- ✓ Each indirect map puts only one entry in the */etc/mnttab* file.
- ✓ There is no need to execute the *automount* command after adding, removing, or modifying an indirect map entry.
- ✓ When a user or program accesses a directory containing many indirect mount points, only the directories that are already mounted, appear.

Let us use an indirect map to mount the */opt/samba* and */opt/perl* resources from NFS server *hp02*. Perform the following:

1. Edit */etc/auto_master* and add the following indirect map entry to it. There is no default map file for defining indirect map entries, however, you can use any name you want.

        /opt1   auto_indirect

2. Execute the *automount* command to make the changes take effect:

     # automount −v

3. Create */etc/auto_indirect* file. Each entry in this map has three fields: the first field identifies the relative pathname of a mount point directory, the second field (which is optional) specifies any mount options, and the third field identifies the resource to be mounted on the mount point identified in the first field.

        samba   −ro   hp02:/opt/samba
        perl   −ro   hp02:/opt/perl

Now, execute the *mount* command to see mount status of the resources:

     # mount −v
     /etc/auto_indirect on /opt1 type autofs ignore,indirect

At this point */opt1* looks empty. The first time when a user accesses these resources, AutoFS creates necessary mount points and mounts associated resources. Do an *ll* on the two resources and then run the *mount* command:

     # ll /opt1/samba /opt1/perl
     # mount −v
     /etc/auto_indirect on /opt1 type autofs ignore,indirect
     auto_indirect on /opt1/samba type autofs ignore,direct, on Wed Feb 22 12:15:19 2006
     auto_indirect on /opt1/perl type autofs ignore,direct, on Wed Feb 22 12:15:19 2006

30.2.5   Setting Up AutoFS Maps via SAM

You can setup AutoFS maps using SAM also. Follow the links below:

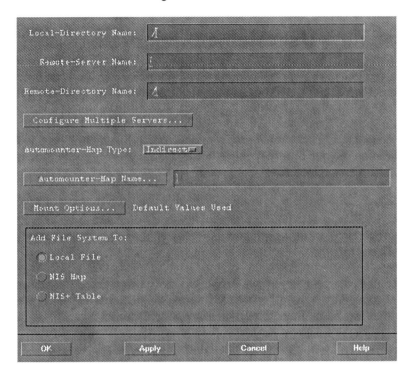Go to SAM → Networking and Communications → Networked File Systems → Mounted Remote File Systems → Actions → Add Remote File System → Using the NFS Automounter. Fill out the form and hit the OK button. See Figure 30-1.

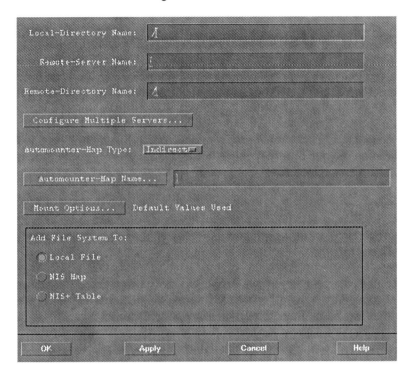

Figure 30-1 SAM – AutoFS Mount

30.3   Accessing Replicated Servers

AutoFS allows you to mount a resource exported simultaneously by more than one NFS servers. This means if one of the NFS servers becomes unavailable, the resource gets automatically mounted from the second NFS server, and so on. The resource must be exported and mounted read-only to ensure data integrity. Either direct or indirect map may be used for this purpose.

Suppose, you have four NFS servers: *hp01*, *hp02*, *hp03*, and *hp04* with all four having an identical copy of */usr/share/man* directory and are exporting it. When a user tries to access the resource on an NFS client, the *automountd* daemon contacts all four servers at the same time and mounts the resource from the server that responds first. This functionality provides several advantages including quicker response time, minimized network traffic, load balancing, and better availability.

The following shows how an entry for such a setup will look like in a direct map:

```
/usr/share/man        -ro        hp01,hp02,hp03,hp04:/usr/share/man
```

The following shows what it will look like in the */etc/auto_master* and */etc/auto_indirect* maps:

```
/usr/share          auto_indirect                          # in auto_master
man-ro              hp01,hp02,hp03,hp04:/usr/share/man      # in auto_indirect
```

30.4   Mounting User Home Directories

AutoFS allows you to use two special characters when defining maps in an indirect map. These special characters are & and *, and are used to replace references to NFS servers and mount points.

When user accounts exist under the */home* directory located on more than one NFS servers, the *automountd* daemon mounts only that user's home directory who logs in. The indirect map entry for this type of substitution will look like:

```
*      &:/home/&
```

Now if, for example, only *user1*, *user2*, and *user3* log in, then only */home/user1*, */home/user2*, and */home/user3* will get mounted.

This simple, single-line map entry allows AutoFS to mount user home directories from any accessible NFS server. Moreover, if more NFS servers with */home* exported are added to the environment, there will be no need to update client AutoFS maps.

30.5   Comparing AutoFS and Automounter

AutoFS has been a part of HP-UX beginning v10.20. Prior to that, Automounter used to provide AutoFS-like functionality. Although Automounter is still included in HP-UX 11i and is still the default, it will be removed from future HP-UX Operating Environment software releases based on the following disadvantages it has, compared with AutoFS:

- ✓ Automounter does not support NFS v3, which enables support for files of sizes up to 128GB, offers better performance, uses TCP protocol, and so on. Automounter uses NFS v2.
- ✓ Automounter always mounts NFS resources under */tmp_mnt* directory and then creates symbolic links to actual mount points.
- ✓ The *automountd* daemon must be stopped and restarted, if there is any modification made to either the master or a direct map. To stop the daemon, you have to kill it.

Summary

This chapter provided coverage on Auto File System. You learned concepts, features, and benefits associated with it. You were presented with information that helped you understand how it worked. You looked at associated daemons, command, and startup configuration file.

You studied the four types of AutoFS maps, their relationship, and how to set them up. You looked at related advantages and disadvantages.

You were explained how AutoFS could be setup to mount NFS resources from multiple, replicated NFS servers to increase availability. Similarly, you looked at how only needed home directories could be mounted from whichever NFS server it resided on.

Finally, a summarized comparison between AutoFS and old Automounter was given.

Setting Up CIFS/9000

This chapter covers the following major topics:

✓ Describe CIFS/9000 product suite and its use
✓ Features of CIFS/9000
✓ What is Samba and how to access it?
✓ Configure a CIFS server on HP-UX
✓ Access an HP-UX CIFS share on a Windows system
✓ Access a Windows CIFS share on an HP-UX system

31.1 Understanding CIFS/9000

Common Internet File System (CIFS), originally called *Server Message Block* (SMB), is a networking protocol, developed by Microsoft in late 1980's to enable Windows-based PCs to share file and print resources. This protocol has been used in Windows operating systems as the native and primary protocol for sharing file and print resources. As time passed, the need to share the two types of resources with non-Windows systems arose. Operating system vendors started to develop and implement products based on the CIFS protocol to fulfill the sharing requirements in their operating system software. One such vendor was HP. HP introduced CIFS/9000 software product in HP-UX. CIFS/9000 is a client/server implementation of CIFS protocol on HP-UX. The product enabled heterogeneous operating systems, including Windows and Linux, to share the two resource types with HP-UX. In the CIFS/9000 terminology, the system that offers its file and print resources for sharing purposes is referred to as the *CIFS Server* and the system that accesses the resources is called the *CIFS Client*.

31.1.1   Features of CIFS/9000

Some common features of CIFS/9000 are:

- ✓ CIFS exported resources from an HP-UX server can be accessed on Windows-based CIFS clients as standard drive letters and can be navigated via "Windows Explorer" or "Network Neighborhood".
- ✓ Windows-based shares can be mounted as CIFS resources on HP-UX.
- ✓ An HP-UX CIFS server can be configured as the *Primary Domain Controller* (PDC) in Windows environment.
- ✓ An HP-UX CIFS server can act as a print server for Windows-based CIFS clients.
- ✓ HP-UX and Windows domain usernames and passwords can be used on either platform for authentication.

31.1.2   Introduction to Samba

The server component of CIFS/9000 is based on the freeware file and print software called *Samba*. Samba is an open source software, which may be freely acquired, modified, and used. HP added enhancements to the Samba source code and implemented the product in HP-UX as part of CIFS/9000 product. Throughout this chapter, the terms CIFS server and Samba will be used interchangeably.

Samba can be configured and administered using the browser-based GUI called *Samba Web Administration Tool* (SWAT), the X Windows-based GUI by running */opt/samba/bin/swat*, or the command line. In order to bring up the graphical interface using a web browser, you need to ensure that the following line is uncommented in the */etc/inetd.conf* file. If not, uncomment the line, and execute "inetd −c" to make the change take effect.

```
swat        stream  tcp     nowait.400      root    /opt/samba/bin/swat     swat
```

Type in the following URL in a browser window (replace *hp01* with your system's hostname). The default port used is 901. Enter a UNIX username and password when prompted to log in to Samba GUI.

---

http://hp01:901

The main Samba screen comes up as shown in Figure 31-1. You can make local resources available to remote systems, access remote resources, and view status of resources, in addition to several other tasks that you can perform from this GUI.

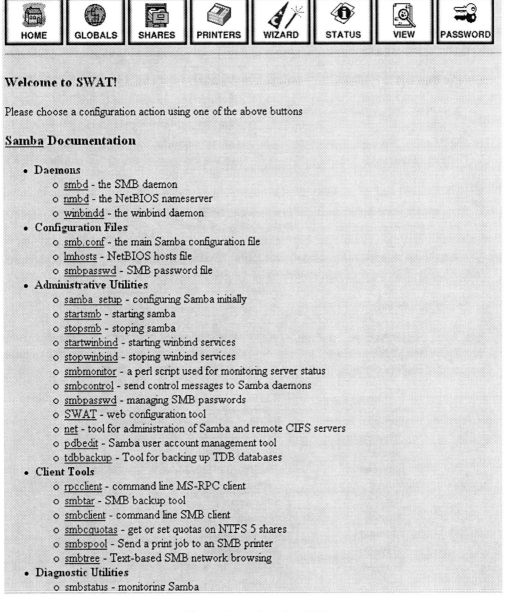

Welcome to SWAT!

Please choose a configuration action using one of the above buttons

Samba Documentation

- **Daemons**
    - smbd - the SMB daemon
    - nmbd - the NetBIOS nameserver
    - winbindd - the winbind daemon
- **Configuration Files**
    - smb.conf - the main Samba configuration file
    - lmhosts - NetBIOS hosts file
    - smbpasswd - SMB password file
- **Administrative Utilities**
    - samba_setup - configuring Samba initially
    - startsmb - starting samba
    - stopsmb - stoping samba
    - startwinbind - starting winbind services
    - stopwinbind - stoping winbind services
    - smbmonitor - a perl script used for monitoring server status
    - smbcontrol - send control messages to Samba daemons
    - smbpasswd - managing SMB passwords
    - SWAT - web configuration tool
    - net - tool for administration of Samba and remote CIFS servers
    - pdbedit - Samba user account management tool
    - tdbbackup - Tool for backing up TDB databases
- **Client Tools**
    - rpcclient - command line MS-RPC client
    - smbtar - SMB backup tool
    - smbclient - command line SMB client
    - smbcquotas - get or set quotas on NTFS 5 shares
    - smbspool - Send a print job to an SMB printer
    - smbtree - Text-based SMB network browsing
- **Diagnostic Utilities**
    - smbstatus - monitoring Samba

Figure 31-1 Samba GUI

31.2 Setting Up CIFS

This section covers setting up a CIFS server on HP-UX to export a resource and accessing the resource on a Windows CIFS client. It also describes how to mount a Windows share on HP-UX.

31.2.1 Setting Up a CIFS Server on HP-UX

Here are the steps to setup a CIFS server on HP-UX to share */usr/share/man*, */home*, and */var/mail* directories using the commands.

1. Ensure that the CIFS/9000 software is loaded on the system. To verify, do the following:

    # swlist –l product | grep CIFS
CIFS-Client	A.02.01	CIFS Client
CIFS-Development	A.01.10	HP CIFS Server Source Code Files
CIFS-Server	A.01.10	HP CIFS Server (Samba) File and Print Services

    If the software is not loaded, go to *software.hp.com* and then "Internet ready and networking". Download both HP CIFS Client and Server components, and install them using *swinstall*.

2. Edit */etc/rc.config.d/samba* file and set RUN_SAMBA variable to 1. This is to ensure that the functionality gets started automatically at each system reboot.

    RUN_SAMBA=1

3. Edit */etc/opt/samba/smb.conf* and specify names of resources that you want to share. There are a number of parameters that can be set in this file, but you are going to use only a few selected. Description of some common parameters is given in Table 31-1.

Parameter	Description
NetBIOS name	Name of the HP-UX CIFS server.
Workgroup	Name of Windows workgroup or domain.
Server string	Any description.
Hosts allow	IP address of the network or individual hosts to access the shares.
Security	Security level.
Encrypt passwords	Password to be encrypted or not.
Comment	Any description.
Writeable	Write enabled.
Browseable	Users can browse files/folders.
Path	Absolute path to the share.
Default case	Upper or lowercase letters.

    Table 31-1 CIFS Configuration Parameters

4. Perform modifications to the *smb.conf* file to look like the following:

```
[global]
        netbios name            = hp02
        workgroup               = localwg
        server string           = CIFS Server
        hosts allow             = 192.168.1
        security                = user
        encrypt passwords       = yes
        default case            = lower
[man]
        comment                 = UNIX manual pages
        writeable               = no
        browseable              = no
        path                    = /usr/share/man
[home]
        comment                 = User home directories
        writeable               = yes
        browseable              = yes
[mail]
        comment                 = Mail directory
        path                    = /var/mail
        writeable               = yes
        browseable              = no
```

5. Execute the *testparm* command to check for any syntax errors in the file.

 # /opt/samba/bin/testparm
Load smb config files from /etc/opt/samba/smb.conf
Processing section "[man]"
Processing section "[home]"
Processing section "[mail]"
Loaded services file OK.
Press enter to see a dump of your service definitions

Global parameters
[global]
     workgroup = LOCALWG
     netbios name = HP02
     server string = CIFS Server
     bind interfaces only = No
     security = USER
     encrypt passwords = Yes
     update encrypted = No
     allow trusted domains = Yes
     hosts equiv =
     min passwd length = 5
     null passwords = No
     smb passwd file = /var/opt/samba/private/smbpasswd
     root directory = /
     passwd program = /bin/passwd

```
        username map = /etc/opt/samba/username.map
. . . . . . . .
. . . . . . . .
        hosts allow = 192.168.1
        hosts deny =
        print command = lp -c -d%p %s; rm %s
        lpq command = lpstat -o%p
        lprm command = cancel %p-%j
        printer driver file = /etc/opt/samba/printers.def
        default case = lower
        case sensitive = No
        browseable = Yes
        fstype = NTFS

[man]
        comment = UNIX manual pages
        path = /usr/share/man
        browseable = No

[home]
        comment = User home directories
        read only = No

[mail]
        comment = Mail directory
        path = /var/mail
        read only = No
        browseable = No
```

6. Create the CIFS password file */var/opt/samba/private/smbpasswd* to be used for authentication purposes to determine which users on the CIFS clients are allowed to access these resources. Note that user accounts must already be present in the */etc/passwd* file. Use the following procedure to add *user1*:

```
# touch  /var/opt/samba/private/smbpasswd
# chmod  600  /var/opt/samba/private/smbpasswd
# chmod  500  /var/opt/samba/private
# /opt/samba/bin/smbpasswd  –a  user1
New SMB password:
Retype new SMB password:
Added user user1.
```

7. Start CIFS server daemons using one of the following:

```
# /sbin/init.d/samba  start                    (or  # startsmb)
Samba started successfully; process ids: smbd: 8481, nmbd: 8479
```

8. Check the status of CIFS server:

```
# smbstatus
Samba version 2.2.8a based HP CIFS Server A.01.10
Service        uid     gid    pid    machine
-----------------------------------------------------------------
user1          user1   users  1802   hp02 (192.168.1.202) Tue May 15 11:22:53 2007

No locked files
```

Instead of using the manual method or one of the GUI methods for setting up a CIFS server, you can use a command line utility called *samba_setup*. This command prompts you to supply configuration information for setup.

31.2.2   Accessing Exported CIFS Share on a Windows System

Verify that the Windows machine is a member of the same workgroup or domain as the CIFS server. Go to Start → Settings → Control Panel → Network and Internet Connections → Network Connections. Click on Advanced menu option and select Network Identification. You should be able to see the domain or workgroup information here.

To access the share, use one of the following methods:

- ✓ Go to "Network Neighborhood" and you should be able to see an icon "hp02" (the CIFS server name). Double click on it. You will be prompted to enter a username and password to connect. Enter *user1* and associated SMB password. All CIFS shares will become visible to you.
- ✓ Start the Windows Explorer. Go to Tools and choose Map Network Drive. Enter the following in the little window right next to "Folder" and click on OK:

    \\hp02\user1

This will connect to the CIFS share and display the contents.

31.2.3   Accessing a Windows Share on HP-UX

Here are the steps to setup CIFS client functionality on an HP-UX system called *hp01*. This procedure assumes that a share called *data* is available from a Windows server called *win-serv01*, with IP address 192.168.1.220. It is also assumed that a user account *testuser* with password *test!123* exists on both *win-serv01* and *hp01*.

1. Download the latest version of CIFS client software from *software.hp.com*. Use the *swinstall* command to install it on *hp01*. The system will reboot after the software installation is finished.

2. Edit the */etc/rc.config.d/cifsclient* file and set the variable RUN_CIFSCLIENT to 1.

    RUN_CIFSCLIENT=1

3. Define the Windows domain or workgroup in the */etc/opt/cifsclient/cifsclient.cfg* file.

       domain = "LOCALWG"

4. Start the CIFS client daemon. This script executes */opt/cifsclient/bin/cifsclient* command.

   # /sbin/init.d/cifsclient start
   CIFS Client daemon cifsclientd is up; process id 24778, started 10:56:13

5. Create a mount point on *hp01* as required. Let us call it */mntdata*.

   # mkdir /mntdata

6. Edit */etc/fstab* file and add an entry for the share, so that it automatically gets mounted at each system reboot.

       win-serv01:/data   /mntdata cifs   defaults   0   0

7. Edit the */etc/hosts* file and insert an entry for *win-serv01* and its IP address.

       192.168.1.220 win-serv01

8. Mount the share using the *mount* command.

   # mount –aF cifs

9. Logon to the CIFS share using the *cifslogin* command. Do the following as user *testuser*:

   # su – testuser
   $ cifslogin win-serv01 testuser –P test!123 –s

   This command creates a password database file */var/opt/cifsclient/cifsclient.udb* for CIFS and add to it an entry for the user *testuser*.

10. Run the following command to verify the share:

    # cifslist

Mounted Object	Mountpoint	State
\\win-serv01\data	/data	MS

Server	Local User	Remote User	Domain	State
win-serv01	root	testuser		LS
win-serv01	testuser	testuser		LS

If you do not wish to automatically mount the CIFS share at each system reboot, you do not need to add an entry to the */etc/fstab* file. You can use the following command as *testuser* to mount and logon to the share:

```
# su  -  testuser
$ cifsmount  //win-serv01/data  /data  -U  testuser
```

This command will prompt you to enter the password defined for *testuser* on *win-serv01*. After entering the correct password, the share becomes available to you.

Summary

This chapter discussed CIFS/9000. It provided an understanding of the CIFS protocol, the CIFS/9000 product suite, and Samba. It explained how to configure a CIFS server on HP-UX, access an HP-UX exported CIFS share on a Windows system, and access a Windows exported share on HP-UX.

HP Certified Systems Administrator

## 32

Setting Up and
Administering NIS

This chapter covers the following major topics:

✓ NIS concepts and components – domain, maps, master server, slave server, client, and daemons
✓ Setup master and slave NIS servers
✓ Setup an NIS client
✓ Configure /etc/nsswitch.conf file
✓ Verify NIS master, slave, and client functionality
✓ Display and search NIS maps
✓ Modify NIS user password
✓ Update NIS maps on master and slave NIS servers
✓ Manually bind a client to alternate NIS server
✓ Use alternate passwd file
✓ Secure access to NIS servers

32.1 NIS Concepts and Components

Every networked HP-UX system requires some administrative work to be performed on it in order to stay current, and up and running. For example, when a user requires access to all networked HP-UX systems, a user account is created on each individual machine for him/her. Likewise, when a new system is brought on the network, the */etc/hosts* file is updated on every existing HP-UX system to include the hostname and IP address of the new system. As long as the number of users and systems, and other system management requirements are low, administrative work can be done without much difficulty. However, when this number grows or requirements increase, system administration and updates to administrative files become tedious and time consuming.

Rather than managing user accounts, hostnames, etc. on each individual system, an HP-UX facility called **Network Information Service** (NIS) may be used to maintain administrative files for these and other services centrally on a single system. Other systems are then configured to reference the central system to obtain user information, hostnames, and so on. In an NIS environment, a new user account is setup on the central system (and not on individual systems). This allows the user to log in to any system on the network with his/her credentials authenticated by the central system.

Another key advantage with central management of administrative files is that the data stay consistent and uniform across all systems.

 NIS was derived from Yellow Pages. The Yellow Pages were developed by the British Telecom in the UK. Most NIS commands and daemon names precede yp (for yellow pages).

When working with NIS, certain components and roles are used. These are explained in the following sub-sections.

32.1.1 NIS Domain

An *NIS domain* is a set of NIS-managed systems sharing common NIS-converted administrative data files called *NIS Maps*.

NIS maps are stored under a sub-directory beneath */var/yp* on an NIS server. The sub-directory is created, when an NIS server is setup. The name of the sub-directory matches the name of the NIS domain.

 There is no relationship between NIS domain and DNS domain.

32.1.2 NIS Maps

There are several administrative files that exist on an HP-UX system and most of them are located in the */etc* directory. These files are text files and can be managed with a text editor or through system commands.

When a Master NIS Server is created on a machine, the information in these files is converted into a special NIS format and saved into new files under the domain directory beneath /var/yp. These special files are called *NIS Maps*.

By default, NIS manages twelve administrative files: /etc/passwd, /etc/group, /etc/hosts, /etc/networks, /etc/rpc, /etc/services, /etc/protocols, /etc/netgroup, /etc/mail/aliases, /etc/publickey, /etc/netid, and /etc/auto.master. The names of these files are defined in the NIS configuration file called /var/yp/Makefile. Do a *more* on the file and search for "all" and you should be able to verify this information.

When an NIS server is setup, three types of map files are created under the /var/yp/<domainname> directory. Run the *ll* command on the domain directory as follows to view the map file types:

 # ll /var/yp/<domainname>

```
. . . . . . . .
. . . . . . . .
-r--r--r--    1    root    sys    0       Feb 12 16:58    hosts.byaddr.dir
-r--r--r--    1    root    sys    1024    Feb 12 16:58    hosts.byaddr.pag
-r--r--r--    1    root    sys    0       Feb 12 16:58    hosts.byname.dir
-r--r--r--    1    root    sys    1024    Feb 12 16:58    hosts.byname.pag
-rw-r--r--    1    root    sys    0       Feb 12 16:58    hosts.time
. . . . . . . .
. . . . . . . .
-r--r--r--    1    root    sys    0       Feb 12 16:58    passwd.byname.dir
-r--r--r--    1    root    sys    1024    Feb 12 16:58    passwd.byname.pag
-r--r--r--    1    root    sys    0       Feb 12 16:58    passwd.byuid.dir
-r--r--r--    1    root    sys    1024    Feb 12 16:58    passwd.byuid.pag
-rw-r--r--    1    root    sys    0       Feb 12 16:58    passwd.time
. . . . . . . .
. . . . . . . .
```

Files with *.dir* extension contain indexing information for the *.pag* files provided *.pag* files are too big, files with *.pag* extension hold actual data, and files with *.time* extension display map creation or modification time stamp. Maps are indexed based on names and numbers. For example, "passwd" maps are indexed by user name and by user ID, "group" maps are indexed by group name and group ID, and so on for others.

32.1.3   NIS Server

There are two types of NIS server setups. These are referred to as *Master NIS Server* and *Slave NIS Server*.

A master NIS server is the system on which the original (or master) administrative files are kept and maintained. These files are translated into NIS maps, which are stored under NIS domain directory beneath /var/yp. Any modifications to NIS maps must be made in the master administrative files on the master server.

A slave NIS server is, although, not required for NIS functionality, but to have at least one is highly recommended for redundancy and load balancing purposes. Each slave server has an identical directory structure under */var/yp* containing a copy of NIS maps that it pulls from the master server.

32.1.4   NIS Client

An NIS client does not store a copy of master server's administrative files or NIS maps locally. It does have its own administrative files but may not be referenced, when NIS client functionality is invoked. When an NIS client is started, it sends out a broadcast message on the network. Any server on the client's network that holds NIS maps for the client's domain, responds. The NIS client forms binding with the first NIS server that responds. Subsequently, all client queries are replied to by that server.

32.1.5   NIS Daemons

When NIS functionality on master and slave servers, and on clients, is initiated, NIS daemons begin to run. Table 32-1 lists and explains the daemons.

Daemon	Runs On			Purpose
	Master	Slave	Client	
ypserv	Yes	Yes	–	Responds to client requests.
ypbind	Yes	Yes	Yes	Binds with a *ypserv* daemon to send and obtain requested information. Binding information is stored in the */var/yp/binding/<domainname>* file. This daemon dynamically binds itself to another NIS server should the one, it was bound to, fail.
rpcbind	Yes	Yes	–	Must be up and running prior to starting any RPC-based services including NIS and NFS.
rpc.yppasswdd	Yes	–	–	When a user changes his/her password on a client using the *yppasswd* or *passwd* command, *ypbind* sends the password change request to this daemon, which updates the */etc/passwd* file on the master server, regenerates "passwd" maps, and pushes them out to slave servers.
rpc.ypupdated	Yes	–	–	Provides a secure mechanism to update NIS maps on the master server using configuration information located in the */var/yp/updaters* file.
ypxfrd	Yes	–	–	Responds to slave server's *ypxfr* command to pull maps.
keyserv	Yes	–	–	Stores private encryption keys of each logged in user.

Table 32-1 NIS Daemons

32.2   Setting Up NIS

This section provides detailed information on how to setup master and slave NIS servers, and NIS clients.

32.2.1   Set Up Considerations

When setting up an NIS environment, keep the following design considerations in mind:

- ✓ A system cannot be the master server for more than one NIS domains.
- ✓ The master server for one domain may be used as a slave server for another domain.
- ✓ A system can be a slave server for multiple domains.
- ✓ Each system in an NIS environment, including the master and any slave servers, is an NIS client as well.
- ✓ A client belongs to only one NIS domain.
- ✓ Each subnet in an NIS domain must have an NIS server on it. When the NIS client functionality is started, it broadcasts a message on the network to search for a server to bind itself with. These broadcasts cannot pass through gateways and routers, so each subnet must have at least one slave NIS server. The master NIS server can exist on any subnet.

32.2.2   Setting Up a Master NIS Server

To setup an HP-UX machine, *hp02* for instance, to act as a master NIS server, perform the following steps:

1. Update administrative files on *hp02* that you want to bring under NIS control. For example, if you want */etc/passwd* file to be managed by NIS, consolidate all user entries from all systems that are going to be part of the NIS domain and append them to the */etc/passwd* file on *hp02*. Remove all duplicate entries and fix any inconsistencies.

2. Define a unique NIS domain name, for example, "nis_domain". Run the following command to set it:

   # domainname nis_domain

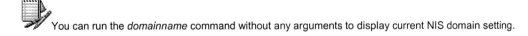 You can run the *domainname* command without any arguments to display current NIS domain setting.

3. Edit */etc/rc.config.d/namesvrs* file and make the following modifications:

   Set the NIS_DOMAIN variable to the domain name:

   NIS_DOMAIN=nis_domain

   Set the NIS_MASTER_SERVER and NIS_CLIENT variables to 1, so the master server and client functionalities start automatically at each system reboot when

---

/sbin/rc2.d/S410nis.server script, which is symbolically linked to */sbin/init.d/nis.server*
script, is executed.

```
NIS_MASTER_SERVER=1
NIS_CLIENT=1
```

4. Execute the *ypinit* command on *hp02* to create the master NIS server. This command calls
    the *makedbm* command in the background to generate NIS maps from the administrative
    files. Specify system names (*hp03*, for example) that you wish to setup as slave NIS servers,
    followed by *ctrl+d*.

    # ypinit –m
    You will be required to answer a few questions to install the Network Information Service.
    All questions will be asked at the beginning of this procedure.

    Do you want this procedure to quit on non-fatal errors? [y/n: n] **n**
    OK, but please remember to correct anything which fails.
    If you do not, some part of the system (perhaps the NIS itself) won't work.

    At this point, you must construct a list of the hosts which will be
    NIS servers for the "nis_domain" domain.
    This machine, hp02, is in the list of Network Information Service servers.
    Please provide the hostnames of the slave servers, one per line.
    When you have no more names to add, enter a <ctrl+d> or a blank line.

        next host to add: **hp02**
        next host to add: **hp03**
        next host to add:
    The current list of NIS servers looks like this:

    hp02
    hp03

    Is this correct? [y/n: y] **y**

    There will be no further questions. The remainder of the procedure should take
    5 to 10 minutes.

    Building the ypservers database... ypservers build complete.

    Running make in /var/yp:
    updated passwd
    updated group
    updated hosts
    . . . .
    . . . .
    hp02 has been set up as a master Network Information Service server without any errors.

    If there are running slave NIS servers, run yppush(1M) now for any databases

---

which have been changed. If there are no running slaves, run ypinit on
those hosts which are to be slave servers.

This command creates */var/yp/nis_domain* directory and runs *ypmake*. The *ypmake*
command looks into its configuration file */var/yp/Makefile* to get a list of administrative files to
be translated into NIS maps. As the maps are created, they are saved in the
/var/yp/nis_domain directory.

5. Start NIS functionality by running the following two scripts. The first script starts *ypserv,*
   rpc.yppasswdd, and *rpc.ypupdated* daemons from the */usr/lib/netsvc/yp* directory and *ypxfrd*
   daemon from the */usr/sbin* directory. The second script starts *ypbind* and *keyserv* daemons
   from the */usr/lib/netsvc/yp* and */usr/sbin* directories, respectively.

```
# /sbin/init.d/nis.server  start
    starting NIS SERVER networking
    starting up the rpcbind
        rpcbind already started, using pid: 669
        domainname nis_domain
    starting up the Network Information Service
        starting up the ypserv daemon
        /usr/lib/netsvc/yp/ypserv
        starting up the ypxfrd daemon
        /usr/sbin/ypxfrd
        starting up the rpc.yppasswdd daemon
        /usr/lib/netsvc/yp/rpc.yppasswdd /etc/passwd -m passwd PWFILE=/etc/passwd
        starting up the rpc.ypupdated daemon
        /usr/lib/netsvc/yp/rpc.ypupdated
        starting up the keyserv daemon
        /usr/sbin/keyserv
# /sbin/init.d/nis.client  start
    starting NIS CLIENT networking
    starting up the rpcbind
        rpcbind already started, using pid: 669
        domainname nis_domain
    starting up the Network Information Service
        starting up the ypbind daemon
        /usr/lib/netsvc/yp/ypbind
        Checking NIS binding.
        Bound to NIS server using domain nis_domain.
        starting up the keyserv daemon
        keyserv already started, using pid: 18410
```

The master NIS server is set and ready to go.

You can also setup the master NIS server using SAM. Follow the links below:

☞ Go to SAM → Networking and Communications → NIS → Actions → Set Domain Name. Set
the NIS domain name here. Refer to Figure 32-1.

Figure 32-1 SAM – NIS Domain Setup

Go back to Actions after setting the domain. You will see following choices:

- ✓ Set Domain Name
- ✓ Configure Master Server
- ✓ Configure Slave Server
- ✓ Enable Client
- ✓ Modify
- ✓ Remove

See Figure 32-2.

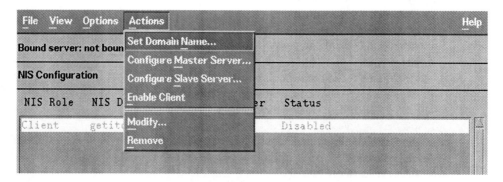

Figure 32-2 SAM – NIS Administration

From here, you can setup, modify, or remove the master server, a slave server, or a client.

32.2.3   Setting Up a Slave NIS Server

To setup an HP-UX machine, *hp03* for instance, to act as a slave NIS server, perform the following steps:

1. Set the NIS domain name "nis_domain". Run the following command:

   # **domainname nis_domain**

2. Edit */etc/rc.config.d/namesvrs* file and make the following modifications:

   Set the NIS_DOMAIN variable to the domain name:

   NIS_DOMAIN=nis_domain

Set the NIS_SLAVE_SERVER and NIS_CLIENT variables to 1:

```
NIS_SLAVE_SERVER=1
NIS_CLIENT=1
```

3. Execute the following command to transfer all NIS maps from the master server and save them into */var/yp/nis_domain* directory on the slave server, *hp03*:

   # **ypinit –s hp02**
   You will be required to answer a few questions to install the Network Information Service.
   All questions will be asked at the beginning of this procedure.

   Do you want this procedure to quit on non-fatal errors? [y/n:] **n**
   OK, but please remember to correct anything which fails.
   If you do not, some part of the system (perhaps the NIS itself) won't work.

   There will be no further questions asked. The remainder of the procedure will copy NIS map files over from *hp02* and will take some time. If you see "no such map" messages produced during file transfer, ignore them.

   ```
   Transferring group.bygid for domain nis_domain from hp02...
   Transferring group.byname for domain nis_domain from hp02...
   Transferring hosts.byaddr for domain nis_domain from hp02...
   Transferring hosts.byname for domain nis_domain from hp02...
   Transferring netgroup for domain nis_domain from hp02...
   Transferring netgroup.byhost for domain nis_domain from hp02...
   Transferring netgroup.byuser for domain nis_domain from hp02...
   Transferring networks.byaddr for domain nis_domain from hp02...
   Transferring networks.byname for domain nis_domain from hp02...
   Transferring passwd.byname for domain nis_domain from hp02...
   Transferring passwd.byuid for domain nis_domain from hp02...
   . . . . . . . .
   . . . . . . . .
   hp03 has been set up as a slave Network Information Service server without errors.
   ```

4. Start NIS functionality by running the following two scripts:

   # **/sbin/init.d/nis.server start**
   # **/sbin/init.d/nis.client start**

A slave NIS server is set and ready to go.

You can also setup a slave NIS server using SAM. Refer to the previous sub-section "Setting Up the Master NIS Server" for details.

32.2.4   Setting Up an NIS Client

To setup an HP-UX machine to act as an NIS client, perform the following steps on that machine:

1. Set the NIS domain name "nis_domain" as follows:

   # **domainname nis_domain**

2. Modify the */etc/rc.config.d/namesvrs* startup file and make the following modifications:

   Set the NIS_DOMAIN variable to the domain name:

   NIS_DOMAIN=nis_domain

   Set the NIS_CLIENT variable to 1 so NIS client functionality gets started at each system reboot when */sbin/rc2.d/S420nis.client* script, which is symbolically linked to */sbin/init.d/nis.client* script, is executed.

   NIS_CLIENT=1

3. Start NIS functionality by running the following script:

   # **/sbin/init.d/nis.client start**

An NIS client is set and ready to go.

You can also setup NIS client using SAM. Refer to sub-section "Setting Up the Master NIS Server" for details.

32.2.5 Configuring */etc/nsswitch.conf* File

In HP-UX, more than one sources can be employed to get information from. For example, user authentication information can be obtained from */etc/passwd* file, NIS, NIS+, or LDAP. Which of these sources to obtain information from and in what order, is determined by entries defined in the **Name Service Switch** configuration file called *nsswitch.conf*. This file is located in the */etc* directory. An example entry from the file below consults local */etc/passwd* file first and then an NIS server for user authentication:

    passwd: files   nis

By default, this file does not exist, however, there are several template files available in the */etc* directory. These templates include *nsswitch.files, nsswitch.compat, nsswitch.nis, nsswitch.nisplus*, and *nsswitch.hp_defaults*. Copy one of these files as *nsswitch.conf* and modify entries according to requirements. The following is an excerpt from */etc/nsswitch.nis*:

    # **cat /etc/nsswitch.nis**
    passwd: files   nis
    group: files   nis
    hosts: nis   [NOTFOUND=return] files
    networks: nis   [NOTFOUND=return] files
    protocols: nis   [NOTFOUND=return] files
    rpc: nis   [NOTFOUND=return] files

```
publickey:   nis    [NOTFOUND=return]  files
netgroup:    nis    [NOTFOUND=return]  files
automount:   files  nis
aliases:     files  nis
services:    files  nis
```

There are four keywords used, when more than one potential sources are referenced in the
/etc/nsswitch.conf file. These keywords are listed in Table 32-2 with their meanings.

Keyword	Meaning
SUCCESS	Information found.
UNAVAIL	Source down or not responding.
NOTFOUND	Information not found.
TRYAGAIN	Source busy. Try again later.

Table 32-2 Name Service Source Status

Based on the status code for a source, one of two actions, given in Table 32-3, take place.

Action	Meaning
continue	Try the next source listed.
Return	Do not try the next source.

Table 32-3 Name Service Source Actions

As an example, if the "passwd" entry looks like:

```
passwd:     nis [NOTFOUND=return] files
```

This would mean that if the required user information is not found in NIS, terminate the search and
do not look into the /etc/passwd file.

Each keyword defined in Table 32-2 has a default action associated. If no keyword/action
combination is specified, actions listed in Table 32-4 will be assumed.

Keyword	Default Action
SUCCESS	return
UNAVAIL	continue
NOTFOUND	continue
TRYAGAIN	continue

Table 32-4 Name Service Source Default Actions

32.2.6　Testing NIS Master, Slave, and Client Functionality

To test which NIS server a client is bound to, run the *ypwhich* command without any options. Note that every system in an NIS domain, including master and slave servers, is a client. With –m option, this command also displays what maps are available from that NIS server.

```
# ypwhich
hp02
# ypwhich –m
. . . . . . . .
. . . . . . . .
hosts.byaddr hp02
hosts.byname hp02
group.bygid hp02
group.byname hp02
passwd.byuid hp02
passwd.byname hp02
ypservers hp02
```

Since NIS is based on RPC, you can use the *rpcinfo* command to list what NIS daemons are currently running.

```
# rpcinfo
```

program	version	netid	address	service	owner
100000	3	ticots	hp02.rpc	rpcbind	superuser
100000	3	ticotsord	hp02.rpc	rpcbind	superuser
100000	3	ticlts	hp02.rpc	rpcbind	superuser
100000	3	tcp	0.0.0.0.0.111	rpcbind	superuser
100000	3	udp	0.0.0.0.0.111	rpcbind	superuser
100004	1	udp	0.0.0.0.3.105	ypserv	superuser
100004	1	tcp	0.0.0.0.3.106	ypserv	superuser
100069	1	udp	0.0.0.0.3.111	ypxfrd	superuser
100069	1	tcp	0.0.0.0.3.112	ypxfrd	superuser
100009	1	udp	0.0.0.0.3.254	yppasswdd	superuser
100028	1	tcp	0.0.0.0.3.121	ypupdated	superuser
100028	1	udp	0.0.0.0.3.122	ypupdated	superuser
100029	1	ticlts	hp02.keyserv	keyserv	superuser
100029	1	ticotsord	hp02.keyserv	keyserv	superuser
100029	1	ticots	hp02.keyserv	keyserv	superuser
100007	1	tcp	0.0.0.0.253.255	ypbind	sys
100007	1	udp	0.0.0.0.254.127	ypbind	sys

The output indicates that all NIS daemons: *rpcbind, ypserv, ypxfrd, yppasswdd, ypupdated, keyserv*, and *ypbind* are registered and running.

To obtain user information, on *user5* for instance, use the *nsquery* command and specify the type of source you want to search into. You have two choices: passwd and group. This command consults the */etc/nsswitch.conf* file to determine potential sources for lookup. The last line of the output tells that the search is terminated, since the information is found.

```
# nsquery  passwd  user5
Using "files nis" for the passwd policy.
Searching /etc/passwd for user5
User name: user5
User Id: 107
Group Id: 20
Gecos:
Home Directory: /home/user5
Shell: /sbin/sh
Switch configuration: Terminates Search
```

32.3 Managing NIS

Managing NIS involves tasks, such as displaying and searching NIS maps, changing a user password, updating maps on master and slave servers, changing client binding, and using alternate passwd file.

32.3.1 Displaying and Searching NIS Maps

The administrative data files are in plain ascii text. When they are translated into NIS, the resulting map files contain data in non-text format. These map files require different set of commands to be viewed and searched.

To display, for example, the "passwd" NIS map contents, use the *ypcat* command, which performs equivalent function to the *cat* command. Note that there is no need to specify the location of the map. The *ypcat* command, by default, looks into the domain directory.

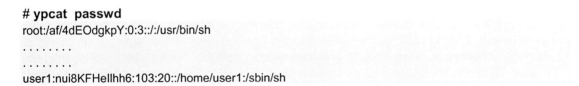

```
# ypcat  passwd
root:/af/4dEOdgkpY:0:3::/:/usr/bin/sh
. . . . . . . .
. . . . . . . .
user1:nui8KFHellhh6:103:20::/home/user1:/sbin/sh
```

To search for a string "users" in the "group" NIS map, use the *ypmatch* command, which performs equivalent function to the *grep* command. Again, there is no need to specify the domain directory.

```
# ypmatch  users  group
users::20:root
```

The *yppoll* command is another NIS command, which is used to display the time stamp of the creation of an NIS map. The time displayed is calculated in seconds from the epoch time.

yppoll passwd.byuid
Domain nis_domain is supported.
Map passwd.byuid has order number 1139927840.
The master server is hp02.

32.3.2   Changing a User Password

Once an NIS environment is established, use either the *yppasswd* or *passwd* command to change user passwords. For example, to change *user1*'s password, do either of the following from any NIS client:

$ **yppasswd user1**
Changing password for user1 on NIS server
Old NIS password:
New password:
Re-enter new password:
NIS(YP) passwd/attributes changed on hp02, the master NIS server.

$ **passwd –r nis**
Changing password for user1 on NIS server
Old NIS password:
New password:
Re-enter new password:
NIS(YP) passwd/attributes changed on hp02, the master NIS server.

Both commands contact the *rpc.yppasswdd* daemon on the master NIS server, replace existing encrypted passwd entry in the local */etc/passwd* file on that server, regenerate NIS "passwd" maps from the updated */etc/passwd* file, and then push the "passwd" maps out to slave servers.

32.3.3   Updating NIS Maps on the Master Server

The administrative files change over time when they are updated. In an NIS environment, you need to make sure that the updates are performed on the master server and then pushed out to slave servers. For example, if you want to add a new group, add it to the */etc/group* file on the master server. Then execute the *yppush* command from the */var/yp* directory to regenerate the "group" maps and push them out to slave servers. When *yppush* is executed on the master server, it initiates the *ypxfr* command on the slave server, which then pulls maps from it.

./ypmake group
For NIS domain nis_domain:

Building the group map(s)... group build complete.
  Pushing the group map(s): group.bygid.
 group.byname.

ypmake complete: no errors encountered.

HP Certified Systems Administrator

If you execute the *ypmake* command without any arguments, it will update all maps and calls the *yppush* command to transfer maps to slave servers.

> **# ./ypmake**
> For NIS domain nis_domain:
>
> The passwd map(s) are up-to-date.
> Building the group map(s)... group build complete.
>   Pushing the group map(s): group.bygid.
>   group.byname.
> . . . .
> . . . .
> The publickey map(s) are up-to-date.
> Building the netid map(s)... netid build complete.
>   Pushing the netid map(s): netid.byname.
> The auto_master map(s) are up-to-date.
> ypmake complete: no errors encountered.

You can also use the *make* command instead of *ypmake*.

32.3.4   Updating NIS Maps on a Slave Server

There are three scripts in the */var/yp* directory on slave servers, which are *ypxfr_1perday*, *ypxfr_2perday*, and *ypxfr_1perhour*. These scripts can be scheduled to run via *cron* to pull maps over from the master server. This ensures that no updates performed on the master server are missed.

Do the following as root on slave servers:

> **# crontab –e**
>
> | 0 | 0 | * | * | * | /var/yp/ypxfr_1perday |
> |---|------|---|---|---|------------------------|
> | 0 | 0,12 | * | * | * | /var/yp/ypxfr_2perday |
> | 0 | * | * | * | * | /var/yp/ypxfr_1perhour |

The *ypxfr_1perday* script will be executed at midnight each night, the *ypxfr_2perday* script at midnight and midday each day, and the *ypxfr_1perhour* script will be executed each hour.

The *ypxfr_1perday* script pulls, by default, *group.bygid*, *group.byname*, *networks.byaddr*, *networks.byname*, *protocols.byname*, *protocols.bynumber*, *rpc.bynumber*, *services.byname*, and *ypservers* maps.

The *ypxfr_2perday* script pulls, by default, *ethers.byaddr*, *ethers.byname*, *hosts.byaddr*, *hosts.byname*, *mail.aliases*, *netgroup*, *netgroup.byhost*, and *netgroup.byuser* maps.

The *ypxfr_1perhour* script pulls, by default, *passwd.byname* and *passwd.byuid* maps.

You may consolidate them into a single script and then schedule the consolidated script to run via *cron*. Also, you can include or exclude any maps that you do or do not wish to be pulled.

32.3.5 Manually Binding a Client to Another NIS Server

In order for a client system to be able to reference NIS information, it must be bound to an NIS server. This binding is set automatically when either the client system reboots or you manually start the NIS functionality on it.

If you wish to manually change the binding to another NIS server, such as *hp04*, use the *ypset* command as follows:

 # ypset hp03

Verify the change with the *ypwhich* command.

32.3.6 Using Alternate passwd File

The */etc/passwd* file stores information about the system and regular user accounts. This includes the *root* user. When *root* or any other user is authenticated via NIS, associated password travels over the network, which introduces security concerns especially for the *root* account. Therefore, for security purposes, you do not want to have *root* and other system user accounts under NIS control.

To manage this situation, you can use an alternate passwd file when setting up NIS and later too, when rebuilding NIS maps. Follow the steps below on the master server:

1. Copy */etc/passwd* as */etc/passwd.nis*.
2. Edit */etc/passwd.nis* and remove users who should not be authenticated via NIS, including *root*, *bin*, *uucp*, and *listen*. The system user accounts typically have UIDs less than 100.
3. Edit */var/yp/Makefile* file and replace the value of the variable PWFILE from PWFILE=$(DIR)/passwd with PWFILE=$(DIR)/passwd.nis.
4. Edit */etc/rc.config.d/namesvrs* and do the following:

    Replace YPPASSWDD_OPTIONS="/etc/passwd –m passwd PWFILE=/etc/passwd" with YPPASSWDD_OPTIONS="/etc/passwd.nis –m passwd PWFILE=/etc/passwd.nis".

5. Execute the *ypmake* command from the */var/yp* directory to regenerate the "passwd" maps and push them out to slave servers. You can use the *make* command instead too.

    # ./ypmake passwd
    For NIS domain nis_domain:

    Building the passwd map(s)... passwd build complete.
      Pushing the passwd map(s): passwd.byname.
    passwd.byuid.

    ypmake complete: no errors encountered.

Now, whenever a new user account is created, which you want to be part of NIS, append that user's entry to the */etc/passwd.nis* file and run either *ypmake* or *make* command.

32.4 Securing Access to NIS Servers

By default, with *root* privileges, a user on any machine outside of NIS domain and located on any subnet, can make a system part of an existing NIS domain. To control this to happen, you can limit NIS domain access by specific systems and specific networks only. Perform the following on both the master and slave servers to implement the control:

1. Create */var/yp/securenets* file.
2. Specify netmask and IP address of the system or network to be allowed access. The example entries below restrict all machines other than the ones residing on the 192.168.1 network and a particular machine with IP address 192.168.2.201.

255.255.255.0	192.168.1.0
255.255.255.255	192.168.2.201

3. Bounce NIS server daemons on both master and slave servers:

   # /sbin/init.d/nis.server stop
   # /sbin/init.d/nis.server start

This procedure can also be used to prevent one or more existing NIS client systems from requesting information from NIS servers. Similarly, the procedure is valid to restrict one or more slave servers from transferring maps over.

Summary

In this chapter, you learned about NIS. You looked at its concepts and components – domain, maps, master server, slave server, client, and daemons. You performed configuration of master and slave NIS servers. You setup an NIS client including configuring the name service switch file.

You were presented with procedures on how to test the functionality of NIS master and slave servers, and client. You displayed NIS map contents and searched them for text using special commands. You saw how a user password was modified in an NIS environment. You looked at procedures to update NIS maps on both master and slave servers, manually bind a client to an alternate NIS server, and use alternate passwd file.

The last section explained to you reasons behind securing NIS servers and how to implement that security feature.

## 33

Setting Up and Administering DNS

This chapter covers the following major topics:

- ✓ What is name resolution?
- ✓ Various name resolution approaches
- ✓ DNS concepts and components – name space, domain, zone, zone files, master DNS server, slave DNS server, caching-only DNS server, DNS client, and BIND versions
- ✓ How DNS works
- ✓ Setup master DNS server
- ✓ Understand DNS boot and zone files
- ✓ Setup slave and caching-only DNS servers
- ✓ Setup DNS client – the name service switch and resolver files
- ✓ Verify DNS functionality
- ✓ Update master, slave, and caching-only DNS servers

33.1 Understanding Name Resolution

Name resolution is a technique for determining the IP address of a system by providing its hostname. In other words, name resolution is a way of mapping a hostname with its associated IP address. Name resolution is used on the internet and corporate internal networks. When you type the address of a website in a browser window, you actually specify the hostname of a remote machine that exists somewhere in the world. You do not know its exact location, but you do know its hostname. There is a complex web of hundreds of thousands of routers configured on the internet at various service provider locations. These routers maintain information about routers closer to them. When you hit the *Enter* key after typing in a website name, the hostname (the website name) is passed to a DNS server, which tries to get the IP address associated with the website's hostname. Once it gets the IP address, your request to access the website is forwarded to the web server from one router to another, until the request reaches the destination system. Determining IP address by providing a hostname is referred to as *Name Resolution* (a.k.a. *Name Lookup* or *DNS Lookup*), determining hostname by providing an IP address is referred to as *Reverse Name Resolution* (a.k.a. *Reverse Name Lookup* or *Reverse DNS Lookup*), and the service employed to perform name resolution is called *Domain Name System* (DNS) service. DNS is commonly recognized by the name *Berkeley Internet Name Domain* (BIND) in the UNIX world. BIND is an implementation of DNS on UNIX platforms, developed at the University of California, Berkeley. You will see the two terms used interchangeably throughout this chapter.

33.1.1 Name Resolution Approaches

There are four methods available in HP-UX for hostname resolution. These are:

- ✓ The */etc/hosts* file
- ✓ Network Information Service (NIS)
- ✓ Network Information Service Plus (NIS+)
- ✓ Domain Name System (DNS)

Let us look at them one by one.

The */etc/hosts* File

The */etc/hosts* file is typically used when you need to access systems on the local network only. This file is maintained locally on each system.

Each line in the */etc/hosts* file contains an IP address in the first column, followed by an official (or *Canonical*) hostname associated with it. You may also define one or more aliases per entry. Aliases are nicknames. The official hostname, and one or more aliases, allow you to assign multiple hostnames to a single IP address. This way you can access the same system using any of these names. A few sample entries below from */etc/hosts* file display *hp01, hp02, hp03, hp04, and hp05* systems with IP addresses 192.168.1.201, 192.168.1.202, 192.168.1.203, 192.168.1.204, and 192.168.1.205, and aliases *h1, h2, h3, h4,* and *h5*, respectively. Notice that comments follow the # character.

```
192.168.1.201    hp01    h1      # Production database server
192.168.1.202    hp02    h2      # Development web server
192.168.1.203    hp03    h3      # Production application server
192.168.1.204    hp04    h4      # Production application server
192.168.1.205    hp05    h5      # Production backup server
```

Since the */etc/hosts* file is maintained locally, you must update it manually on each system to maintain consistency, whenever an update is required.

NIS and NIS+

An NIS server can serve only the systems on its local network. NIS clients send out broadcasts to locate and bind to NIS servers. Each NIS server is able to respond to hostname queries on its local network.

NIS and NIS+ are not used for hostname resolution because of limitations and security issues.

DNS

DNS is the de facto standard for name resolution used on the internet and on corporate networks.

Systems using DNS send name resolution requests to a DNS server, instead of the */etc/hosts* file, NIS, or NIS+.

The remainder of this chapter furnishes detailed information on DNS and how to set it up.

33.2   DNS Concepts and Components

This sections covers DNS concepts and components at length. It explains the concepts, identifies the components, describes the roles, and explains how DNS works.

33.2.1   DNS Name Space and Domains

The DNS *Name Space* is a hierarchical organization of all the domains on the internet. The root of the name space is represented by the (.) dot character. The hierarchy, right below the root, is divided into top-level (first-level) domains, such as *com*, *gov*, *edu*, *mil*, *net*, *org*, *biz*, *tv*, *info*, and two-character country-specific domains, such as *ca*, *uk*, and *au*. A *DNS Domain* is a collection of one or more systems. Sub-domains fall under domains. For example, the *com* domain consists of second-level sub-domains, such as *hp*, *ibm*, and *sun*. Sub-domains can then be further divided into multiple, smaller third-level sub-domains, each of which may contain one or several systems. For example, *hp.com* may contain a sub-domain represented as *ca.hp.com*. Within a domain, you can setup as many sub-domains as you wish.

Figure 33-1 shows the hierarchical structure of the DNS name space. It also shows domain levels.

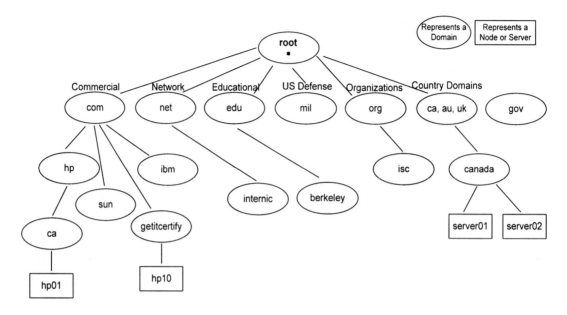

Figure 33-1 DNS Hierarchy

At the deepest level of the hierarchy, are the *Leaves* (systems) of the name space. For example, a system, *hp01*, in *ca.hp.com* will be represented as *hp01.ca.hp.com*. If the dot character is appended to this name to look like *hp01.ca.hp.com.*, it will be referred to as the *Fully Qualified Domain Name* (FQDN) for *hp01*.

A system in the DNS name space may be a computer, a router, a switch, a network printer, etc. that has an IP address associated with it.

The DNS name space is structurally similar to the UNIX directory hierarchy. Here are a few similarities that both share:

✓ DNS uses the dot character to represent the root of the name space; UNIX uses the forward slash character to represent the root of the directory tree.
✓ DNS uses domains to contain systems; UNIX uses directories to store files.
✓ DNS uses the dot character to separate domain levels; UNIX uses the forward slash character to separate directory levels.

The hierarchical structure of DNS enables you to sub-divide a domain into multiple sub-domains and delegate management responsibility of each sub-domain to different groups of administrators. In this type of setup, each sub-domain will have its own DNS server, which will have "authority" on the information it contains. This distributed management approach simplifies overall DNS administration.

In order to run a server directly facing the internet, you must get a domain name registered for it. Contact one of the accredited domain registrars licensed by the *Internet Corporation for Assigned Names and Numbers* (ICANN). Visit *www.icann.com* to obtain a list of licensed registrars or simply contact an ISP to get you a domain registered.

33.2.2　DNS Zones and Zone Files

Every DNS server maintains complete information about the portion of the DNS name space for which it is responsible. This information includes a complete set of authoritative data files. The portion of the name space for which a DNS server has a complete set of authoritative data files is known as the server's *Zone* and the set of authoritative data files is known as *Zone Files, Zone Databases*, or simply *Databases*.

33.2.3　DNS Roles

A role is a function that an HP-UX system performs from DNS standpoint. A system is typically configured to function as a DNS server or client.

Master DNS Server

A *Master DNS Server* (called *Primary DNS Server* in older versions) has the authority for its domain and contains that domain's data. Each domain must have one master server. When a system is added to or removed from a domain, master server's zone files must be updated. A master server may delegate responsibility of one or more sub-domains to other DNS servers, referred to as *Slave* and *Caching-Only DNS Servers*.

Slave DNS Server

A *Slave DNS Server* (called *Secondary DNS Server* in older versions) also has the authority for its domain and stores that domain's zone files, however, the zone files are copied from the master server. When updates are made to zone files on the master server, the slave server may get the updated zone files automatically. This type of DNS server is normally setup for redundancy purposes in case the master server fails and for sharing master server's load. It is highly recommended to have at least one slave server per domain to work with the master.

Caching-Only DNS Server

A *Caching-Only DNS Server* has no authority for any domains. It gets data from the master or slave server and caches it locally in its memory. Like a slave server, a caching-only server is normally used for redundancy and load-sharing purposes. The replies to queries from a caching-only server are normally quicker than replies from either a master or a slave server. This is because a caching-only server keeps data in memory rather than on disk. This type of DNS server is typically used by ISPs where hundreds of thousands of queries for name resolution arrive every minute.

DNS Client

A *DNS Client* normailly has two files configured that are used to resolve hostname queries by referencing information defined in them.

33.2.4   BIND Versions

The latest version of BIND software is 9.3.2 at the time of writing this chapter. Note that BIND is an implementation of DNS on UNIX systems. You can download the latest version available for HP-UX from *software.hp.com* → Internet Ready and Networking, as exhibited in Figure 33-2.

Figure 33-2 *software.hp.com* Main Page

The HP-UX 11iv1 comes standard with BIND version 8.1.2.

 Starting BIND 8.1.2, the boot file is called */etc/named.conf*. In previous versions, it was called */etc/named.boot*.

To check the version of BIND on a system, use the *what* command as follows:

```
# what  /usr/sbin/named
/usr/sbin/named:
     $Revision: vw: -RW   selectors:  'ic27d' -proj integ -- ph_ic27d_i80 '
cupi80_ic27dbase_pb(08-Nov-00.16:48:14)' 'BE11.11_IC27A'
     Wed Nov  8 18:20:04 PST 2000 $
     Copyright (c) 1986, 1989, 1990 The Regents of the University of California.
     ns_sort.c     4.10 (Berkeley) 3/3/91
     named 8.1.2 Tue Feb 15 06:58:53 GMT 2000
```

The last line indicates that the BIND version is 8.1.2.

33.2.5   How DNS Works

The following illustrates what occus when a user on *server01.canada.ca* initiates access to *hp10.getitcertify.com* using the *telnet* command:

- ✓ The *telnet* command calls the *gethostbyname* routine to get the IP address of *hp10.getitcertify.com*.
- ✓ The *gethostbyname* routine looks into the */etc/nsswitch.conf* file to check what name resolution methods are available.
- ✓ If DNS is selected, the *gethostbyname* routine invokes the DNS resolver to query DNS servers.
- ✓ If *server01.canada.ca* is a DNS server itself, the query is forwarded to it. If not, the resolver looks into the */etc/resolv.conf* file to get the IP address of the DNS server that serves the *canada.ca* domain.
- ✓ The DNS server receives the query, but it is unable to answer it since it has information about systems in its local domain *canada.ca* only.
- ✓ The DNS server queries a root DNS server, which typically stores information about DNS servers one or two levels below it.
- ✓ The root DNS server forwards the query to *.com* domain, which passes the query to the DNS server for *getitcertify.com* domain.
- ✓ The DNS server for *getitcertify.com* returns the authoritative address of *hp10.getitcertify.com* to the DNS server of *canada.ca* domain.
- ✓ The DNS server for *canada.ca* passes the requested IP address to the resolver, which passes it to *gethostbyname* routine, which finally returns it to the *telnet* command.

33.3   Setting Up DNS

Let us look at step-by-step procedures on how to setup a master, a slave, and a caching-only DNS server. You will also look at DNS maps generated and procedure on how to setup a DNS client.

33.3.1   Setting Up a Master DNS Server

To setup an HP-UX machine, *hp01* for instance, to act as a master DNS server for domain *getitcertify.com*, perform the following steps:

1. Get the domain *getitcertify.com* registered.
2. Update the */etc/hosts* file on the master server with canonical hostnames of all systems on the network. Enter aliases as required. For example, *hp01*, *hp02*, *hp03*, *hp04*, and *hp05* are five systems with official hostnames (after appending the domain name) *hp01.getitcertify.com*, *hp02.getitcertify.com*, *hp03.getitcertify.com*, *hp04.getitcertify.com*, and *hp05.getitcertify.com*. The */etc/hosts* file will look like:

192.168.1.201	hp01.getitcertify.com	hp01	# Production database server
192.168.1.202	hp02.getitcertify.com	hp02	# Development web server
192.168.1.203	hp03.getitcertify.com	hp03	# Production application server
192.168.1.204	hp04.getitcertify.com	hp04	# Production application server
192.168.1.205	hp05.getitcertify.com	hp05	# Production backup server

Note that aliases *h1*, *h2*, *h3*, *h4*, and *h5* defined previously are removed.

3. Create */etc/dns* directory to store DNS zone files:

   # mkdir /etc/dns

4. Change directory to */etc/dns* and run the *hosts_to_named* command. This command scans the */etc/hosts* file and generates several files, such as *named.conf*, *db.127.0.0*, *db.domain*, and *db.net*. The zone files *db.domain* and *db.net* are created one per each domain and network, specified with –d and –n options, respectively. The –z option creates zone files for the slave DNS server that you will be setting up in the next sub-section. The –b option specifies the location of the BIND boot configuration file.

   # cd /etc/dns
   **# hosts_to_named –d getitcertify.com –n 192.168.1 –z 192.168.1.202 **
   –b /etc/named.conf
   Translating */etc/hosts* to lowercase ...
   Collecting network data ...
       192.168.1
   Creating list of multi-homed hosts ...
   Creating "A" data (name to address mapping) for net 192.168.1 ...
   Creating "PTR" data (address to name mapping) for net 192.168.1 ...
   Creating "MX" (mail exchanger) data ...
   Building default named.boot file ...
   Building default db.cache file ...

   WARNING: db.cache must be filled in with
            the name(s) and address(es) of the rootserver(s)

   Building default boot.sec.save for secondary servers ...
   Building default boot.sec for secondary servers ...
   Building default boot.cacheonly for caching only servers ...
   done

   Alternatively, you can create a param file, *param.dns* for example, using the vi editor and pass the file name as an argument to the *hosts_to_named* command. Include all options and parameters in the file that you supplied at the command line above. This saves you from some typing.

   # vi param.dns
   –d getitcertify.com   # Name of the domain.
   –n 192.168.1   # IP address of the network.
   –z 192.168.1.202   # IP address of the slave DNS server.
   –b /etc/named.conf   # location of the DNS boot file.
   # hosts_to_named –f param.dns

5. Download the *db.cache* file from *ftp://ftp.internic.net/domain* and copy it to the */etc/dns* directory. Overwrite existing *db.cache* in that directory. This file contains an updated list of root name servers.

HP Certified Systems Administrator

6. Edit */etc/rc.config.d/namesvrs* file and set the variable NAMED to 1:

    NAMED=1

7. Start the BIND service:

    # /sbin/init.d/named start

Here is a list of the boot and zone database files created by running the *hosts_to_named*
command:

 # ll /etc/dns
total 14
-rw-rw-rw-	1	root	sys	146	Feb 28 18:31	boot.cacheonly
-rw-rw-rw-	1	root	sys	644	Feb 28 18:32	conf.cacheonly
-rw-rw-rw-	1	root	sys	439	Feb 28 18:32	conf.sec
-rw-rw-rw-	1	root	sys	439	Feb 28 18:32	conf.sec.save
-rw-rw-rw-	1	root	sys	251	Feb 28 18:31	db.127.0.0
-rw-rw-rw-	1	root	sys	399	Feb 28 18:31	db.192.168.1
-rw-rw-rw-	1	root	sys	972	Feb 28 18:32	db.getitcertify

SAM can also do the job of setting up a master DNS server. Follow the links below:

☞ Go to SAM → Networking and Communications → DNS (BIND) → DNS Local Name Server
→ Actions → Add Master/Slave Information. Fill out the form and click on "Start the DNS Name
Server" from the Actions menu to run the *named* daemon.

33.3.2   Understanding DNS Boot and Zone Files

The *hosts_to_named* command generates DNS boot files and several zone files. The syntax of all
these files is almost identical. Table 33-1 describes them.

File	Description
Boot Files for BIND Versions 8 and Up	
/etc/named.conf	Boot configuration file used on the master server.
/etc/dns/conf.sec	Boot configuration file used as */etc/named.conf* on a slave DNS server that does not save zone files locally. A slave server with this configuration only works if the master DNS server is up and running.
/etc/dns/conf.sec.save	Boot configuration file used as */etc/named.conf* on a slave server that saves zone files locally. A slave server with this configuration does not require that the master server be up and running.
/etc/dns/conf.cacheonly	Boot configuration file used as */etc/named.conf* on a caching-only server.
Zone Files for BIND Versions 8 and Up	
db.getitcertify	Contains hostname to IP address mappings.
db.192.168.1	Contains IP address to hostname mappings.

db.127.0.0	Contains mapping for loopback addresses.
db.cache	Contains root name server database.
Boot and Zone Files for Older BIND Versions	
boot.sec	Boot configuration file used as *etc/named.boot* on a slave server that does not save zone files locally. A slave server only works with this configuration, if the master DNS server is up and running.
boot.sec.save	Boot configuration file used as *etc/named.boot* on a slave server that saves zone files locally. A slave server with this configuration does not require that the master server be up and running.
boot.cacheonly	Boot configuration file used as *etc/named.boot* on a caching-only server.

Table 33-1 DNS Zone Files

Let us look at the boot and zone files used in BIND versions 8 and up and see what kind of information they store.

The */etc/named.conf* Boot File

This file is read each time the DNS server daemon, *named*, is started or restarted either at boot time or manually after the system is up. It tells the master server the location of all the zone databases for all domains that this DNS server serves. In your case the contents of this file will look like:

 # cat /etc/named.conf
```
. . . . . . . .
. . . . . . . .
zone "0.0.127.IN-ADDR.ARPA" {
        type master;
        file "db.127.0.0";
};

zone "getitcertify.com" {
        type master;
        file "db.getitcertify";
};

zone "1.168.192.IN-ADDR.ARPA" {
        type master;
        file "db.192.168.1";
};

zone "." {
        type hint;
        file "db.cache";
};
```

HP Certified Systems Administrator

Comments begin with // or can be contained within /* and */. Options can be defined at both the global and individual levels. The keyword "Options" defines global options. Individual options are defined with each zone statement, which includes the characteristics of a zone, such as the location of its database files, and so on. This statement can be used to override the global options statements.

The "type" zone statement option defines zone type and has the following valid choices:

- ✓ "master" designates the master DNS server as authoritative for the specified zone.
- ✓ "slave" designates the specified server as a slave DNS server for the specified zone. Also defines the master server's IP address.
- ✓ "hint" points to root DNS servers for resolving queries.

The /etc/dns/conf.sec and /etc/dns/conf.sec.save Boot Files

One of these files (see Table 33-1 on difference between the two) is copied over to a slave DNS server and renamed to /etc/named.conf. The contents of the two files are almost identical to that of the /etc/named.conf file for the master server with some exceptions.

```
# cat  /etc/dns/conf.sec
. . . . . . . .
. . . . . . . .
//
// type       domain            source file
//
zone "0.0.127.IN-ADDR.ARPA" {
     type master;
     file "db.127.0.0";
};

zone "getitcertify.com" {
     type slave;
     masters {
          192.168.1.202;
     };
};

zone "1.168.192.IN-ADDR.ARPA" {
     type slave;
     masters {
          192.168.1.202;
     };
};

zone "." {
     type hint;
     file "db.cache";
};
```

```
# cat  /etc/dns/conf.sec.save
. . . . . . . .
. . . . . . . .
//
// type        domain              source file
//
zone "0.0.127.IN-ADDR.ARPA" {
      type master;
      file "db.127.0.0";
};

zone "getitcertify.com" {
      type slave;
      file "db.getitcertify";
      masters {
            192.168.1.202;
      };
};

zone "1.168.192.IN-ADDR.ARPA" {
      type slave;
      file "db.192.168.1";
      masters {
            192.168.1.202;
      };
};

zone "." {
      type hint;
      file "db.cache";
};
```

The */etc/dns/conf.cacheonly* Boot File

This file is copied over to a caching-only DNS server and renamed to */etc/named.conf*. The contents of this file includes information about *db.127.0.0* and *db.cache* databases only.

```
# cat  /etc/dns/conf.cacheonly
. . . . . . . .
. . . . . . . .
//
// type        domain              source file
//
zone "0.0.127.IN-ADDR.ARPA" {
      type master;
      file "db.127.0.0";
};

zone "." {
```

```
    type hint;
    file "db.cache";
};
```

The *db.getitcertify* Zone File

This is the domain database file that resides on the master server. This file contains address record for each system in the zone.

 # cat /etc/dns/db.getitcertify

```
@       IN    SOA    hp01.getitcertify.com.  root.hp01.getitcertify.com. (
                         1              ; Serial
                         10800          ; Refresh every 3 hours
                         3600           ; Retry every hour
                         604800         ; Expire after a week
                         86400 )        ; Minimum ttl of 1 day
        IN    NS     hp01.getitcertify.com.

localhost   IN    A                  127.0.0.1
hp01        IN    A                  192.168.1.201
hp01        IN    CNAME              hp01.getitcertify.com.
hp02        IN    A                  192.168.1.202
hp02        IN    CNAME              hp02.getitcertify.com.
hp03        IN    A                  192.168.1.203
hp03        IN    CNAME              hp03.getitcertify.com.
hp04        IN    A                  192.168.1.204
hp04        IN    CNAME              hp04.getitcertify.com.
hp05        IN    A                  192.168.1.205
hp05        IN    CNAME              hp05.getitcertify.com.
hp01        IN    MX        10       hp01.getitcertify.com.
hp02        IN    MX        10       hp02.getitcertify.com.
hp03        IN    MX        10       hp03.getitcertify.com.
hp04        IN    MX        10       hp04.getitcertify.com.
hp05        IN    MX        10       hp05.getitcertify.com.
```

Table 33-2 explains various entries from this zone file. These entries are called *Resource Records*.

Record	Description
SOA	*Start Of Authority*. Designates start of a domain. Indicates the DNS server (*hp01.getitcertify.com*) authoritative for the domain, the address (*root.hp01.getitcertify.com*) of the user responsible for the DNS server, and the following values: Serial → Denotes zone file version and is incremented each time the files are refreshed. Slave servers look at this number and compare it with the one they have. If the number is higher on the master server, a transfer of the updated files takes place. Refresh → Indicates how often a slave server refreshes itself with the master.

	This number is in seconds. Retry → Indicates how often a slave server retries to get updates from the master after the previous refresh attempt fails. This number is in seconds. Expire → Indicates how long a slave server can use the zone data before the data is considered expired. This number is in seconds. Minimum ttl → Indicates the minimum amount of time (*Time To Live*) to keep an entry. This number is in seconds.
NS	*Name Server*. Lists DNS servers along with domains for which they have authority.
A	*Address*. Assigns IP address to the corresponding system.
CNAME	*Canonical **Name***. Official hostname of a system.
MX	*Mail eXchanger*. Specifies a weighted list of systems to try when sendmail'ing to a destination on the internet. MX data points to one or more alternate systems that accept emails for the target system, if the target system is down or unreachable.

Table 33-2 Resource Records Description

The *db.192.168.1* Zone File

This database contains a *Pointer* (PTR) for every host in the zone. It enables DNS to map IP addresses to their corresponding hostnames for reverse lookup.

```
# cat  /etc/dns/db.192.168.1
@     IN   SOA  hp01.getitcertify.com.  root.hp01.getitcertify.com. (
                     1                ; Serial
                     10800            ; Refresh every 3 hours
                     3600             ; Retry every hour
                     604800           ; Expire after a week
                     86400 )          ; Minimum ttl of 1 day
      IN   NS   hp01.getitcertify.com.
201   IN   PTR  hp01.getitcertify.com.
202   IN   PTR  hp02.getitcertify.com.
203   IN   PTR  hp03.getitcertify.com.
204   IN   PTR  hp04.getitcertify.com.
205   IN   PTR  hp05.getitcertify.com.
```

The *db.127.0.0* Zone File

Each DNS server is authoritative of the network 127.0.0 and has the zone file *db.127.0.0*. This file includes the resource record that maps 127.0.0.1 to the name of the loopback (localhost) address. In other words, this file contains a pointer to the localhost.

```
# cat  /etc/dns/db.127.0.0
@     IN   SOA  hp01.getitcertify.com.  root.hp01.getitcertify.com. (
                     1                ; Serial
                     10800            ; Refresh every 3 hours
                     3600             ; Retry every hour
```

```
                    604800          ; Expire after a week
                    86400 )         ; Minimum ttl of 1 day
      IN    NS    hp01.getitcertify.com.
1     IN    PTR   localhost.
```

The *db.cache* Zone File

The *db.cache* file lists servers for the root domain. Every DNS server must have a cache file. When a DNS server cannot resolve a hostname query from its local maps or local cache, it queries a root server.

Although the *hosts_to_named* command creates this file, but it is recommended that you download it from *ftp://ftp.internic.net/domain*. Following is an excerpt from this file:

```
.                 3600000 IN  NS   A.ROOT-SERVERS.NET.
A.ROOT-SERVERS.NET.    3600000    A    198.41.0.4
;
; formerly NS1.ISI.EDU
;
.                 3600000    NS   B.ROOT-SERVERS.NET.
B.ROOT-SERVERS.NET.    3600000    A    192.228.79.201
;
; formerly C.PSI.NET
;
.                 3600000    NS   C.ROOT-SERVERS.NET.
C.ROOT-SERVERS.NET.    3600000    A    192.33.4.12
. . . . . . . .
. . . . . . . .
```

33.3.3   Setting Up a Slave DNS Server

To setup an HP-UX machine, *hp02* for instance, to act as a slave DNS server, do the following:

1. Copy *boot.sec.save* file from the master server over into the */etc* directory and rename the file to */etc/named.conf*.
2. Create */etc/dns* directory to store DNS zone files and *cd* into it:

    # mkdir /etc/dns
    # cd   /etc/dns

3. Copy the */etc/dns/db.cache* and */etc/dns/db.127.0.0* files over from the master server.
4. Edit */etc/rc.config.d/namesvrs* file and set the variable NAMED to 1:

    NAMED=1

5. Start the BIND service:

    # /sbin/init.d/named start

To setup a slave DNS server using SAM, follow the links below:

☞ Go to SAM → Networking and Communications → DNS (BIND) → DNS Local Name Server → Actions → Add Master/Slave Information. Fill out the form and click on "Start the DNS Name Server" from the Actions menu to run the *named* daemon.

33.3.4   Setting Up a Caching-Only DNS Server

To setup an HP-UX machine, *hp03* for instance, to act as a caching-only DNS server, perform the following steps:

1. Copy */etc/dns/boot.cacheonly* file from the master server over into the */etc* directory and rename the file to */etc/named.conf*.
2. Create the */etc/dns* directory to store DNS zone files and *cd* into it:

    # **mkdir /etc/dns**
    # **cd /etc/dns**

3. Copy the */etc/dns/db.cache* and */etc/dns/db.127.0.0* files over from the master server.
4. Edit */etc/rc.config.d/namesvrs* file and set the variable NAMED to 1:

    NAMED=1

5. Start the BIND service:

    # **/sbin/init.d/named start**

To setup a caching-only DNS server using SAM, follow the links below:

☞ Go to SAM → Networking and Communications → DNS (BIND) → DNS Local Name Server → Actions → Configure Caching-Only Server. Fill out the form and click on "Start the DNS Name Server" from the Actions menu to run the *named* daemon.

33.3.5   Setting Up a DNS Client

To setup an HP-UX machine to act as a DNS client, you need to configure */etc/nsswitch.conf* and */etc/resolv.conf* files.

The */etc/nsswitch.conf* File

In HP-UX, more than one sources can be employed to get information from. For example, host information can be obtained from */etc/hosts* file, NIS, NIS+, or DNS. Entries defined in the **Name Service Switch** configuration file called *nsswitch.conf* determines which of these sources to obtain information from and in what order. This file is located in the */etc* directory. An example entry from the file below consults local */etc/hosts* file first and then a DNS server for hostname resolution:

    hosts: files   dns

By default, this file does not exist, however, there are several template files available in the */etc* directory. These templates include *nsswitch.files*, *nsswitch.compat*, *nsswitch.nis*, *nsswitch.nisplus*, and *nsswitch.hp_defaults*. Copy one of these files as *nsswitch.conf* and modify entries according to requirements. The following is an excerpt from */etc/nsswitch.files*:

```
# cat  /etc/nsswitch.files
passwd:      files
group:       files
hosts:       files
networks:    files
protocols:   files
. . . . . . . .
. . . . . . . .
```

There are four keywords used when more than one potential sources are referenced in the */etc/nsswitch.conf* file. These keywords are listed in Table 33-3 with their meanings.

Keyword	Meaning
SUCCESS	Information found.
UNAVAIL	Source down or not responding.
NOTFOUND	Information not found.
TRYAGAIN	Source busy. Try again later.

Table 33-3 Name Service Source Status

Based on the status code for a source, one of two actions take place. Refer to Table 33-4.

Action	Meaning
continue	Try the next source listed.
Return	Do not try the next source.

Table 33-4 Name Service Source Actions

As an example, if the "hosts" entry looks like:

```
hosts:       dns [NOTFOUND=return]  files
```

This would mean that if the required host information is not found in DNS, terminate the search and do not look into the */etc/hosts* file.

Each keyword defined in Table 33-3 has a default action associated with it. If no keyword/action combination is specified, actions listed in Table 33-5 are assumed.

Keyword	Default Action
SUCCESS	return
UNAVAIL	continue
NOTFOUND	continue
TRYAGAIN	continue

Table 33-5 Name Service Source Default Actions

The */etc/resolv.conf* File

The next file to configure is the resolver file, which is called */etc/resolv.conf*. You can define three keywords in this file, as described in Table 33-6.

Keyword	Description
domain	Followed by the default domain name. This keyword tells the *gethostbyname* and *gethostbyaddr* routines to search the specified default domain for incoming name resolution queries. This keyword is defined when you have multiple domains. For a single domain environment, this keyword need not be defined.
search	Followed by up to six domain names. The first domain listed must be the local domain. The resolver appends these domain names one at a time in the order they are listed to the hostname you specify when it constructs queries to send to a DNS server.
nameserver	Followed by up to three DNS server IP addresses. These DNS servers are used for name resolution queries one at a time in the order they are listed. If none specified, the local DNS server is used.

Table 33-6 The */etc/resolv.conf* File Description

In your case, the DNS client will have the following entries in the */etc/nsswitch.conf* and */etc/resolv.conf* files:

/etc/nsswitch.conf file:

    hosts: dns   files

/etc/resolv.conf file:

    search   getitcertify.com
    nameserver   192.168.1.201   # IP address of the master DNS server
    nameserver   192.168.1.202   # IP address of the slave DNS server

To setup a DNS client using SAM, follow the links below:

☞Go to SAM → Networking and Communications → DNS (BIND) → DNS Resolver → Actions. You will see two choices here: Specify Name Servers and Set Default Domain. Fill out the form for each and you are done.

33.4 Managing DNS

Managing DNS involves verifying DNS functionality and updating master, slave, and caching-only DNS srevers.

33.4.1 Verifying DNS Functionality

HP-UX provides a few utilities to test DNS functionality. These utilities are *nsquery, nslookup,* and *dig*.

To obtain IP address of a system, *hp05*, use the *nsquery* command and specify the type of source to be searched. This command consults the */etc/nsswitch.conf* file to determine sources for lookup. The last line of the output tells that the search is terminated since the information is found.

```
# nsquery  hosts  hp05
Using "dns" for the hosts policy.

Searching dns for hp05
Hostname: hp05.getitcertify.com
Aliases:
Address: 192.168.1.205
Switch configuration: Terminates Search
```

To obtain IP address of a system, *hp05*, use the *nslookup* command as follows:

```
# nslookup  hp05
Name Server:  hp01.getitcertify.com
Address:  192.168.1.201

Trying DNS
Name:   hp05.getitcertify.com
Address:  192.168.1.205
```

The *nslookup* command can be run in interactive mode as well:

```
# nslookup
>
```

At the > prompt, you may run the *server* command to force *nslookup* to use an alternate DNS server. For example, to resolve hostnames using the slave DNS server, *hp02*, instead of the master, do the following:

```
> server  hp02
```

Type a system name to lookup its IP address:

> hp05
Name Server: getitcertify.com
Addresses: 192.168.1.202

Name: hp05.getitcertify.com
Address: 192.168.1.205

Type exit to quit *nslookup*.

Domain Information Groper (dig) is a DNS lookup utility and also used for troubleshooting DNS issues. This command looks into the */etc/resolv.conf* to determine DNS server information.

To obtain IP address of a system, *hp05*, use the *dig* command as follows:

 # dig hp05
; <<>> DiG 9.1.1 <<>> hp05
;; global options: printcmd
;; Got answer:
;; ->>HEADER<<- opcode: QUERY, status: NOERROR, id: 39720
;; flags: qr aa rd ra; QUERY: 1, ANSWER: 1, AUTHORITY: 1, ADDITIONAL: 1

;; QUESTION SECTION:
;hp05.getitcertify.com.   IN   A

;; ANSWER SECTION:
hp05.getitcertify.com.   16000   IN   A   192.168.1.205

;; AUTHORITY SECTION:
getitcertify.com.   16000   IN   NS   hp01.getitcertify.com.

;; ADDITIONAL SECTION:
hp01.getitcertify.com.   16000   IN   A   192.168.1.201

;; Query time: 1 msec
;; SERVER: 192.168.1.201#53(192.168.1.201)
;; WHEN: Sat Mar 31 22:27:39 2007
;; MSG SIZE rcvd: 83

33.4.2   Updating Master, Slave, and Caching-Only DNS Servers

To update zone files on the master server, make required modifications to the */etc/hosts* file, run the *hosts_to_named* command as discussed earlier, and restart the *named* daemon with the *sig_named* command as follows:

 # sig_named restart
Name server is running and its process id is 5007.
Name server restarted

The slave and caching-only servers update their zone files automatically from the master server based on the SOA records in their database files. Refer to Table 33-2 for detailed information.

```
@    IN    SOA    hp01.getitcertify.com.  root.hp01.getitcertify.com. (
                         1            ; Serial
                         10800        ; Refresh every 3 hours
                         3600         ; Retry every hour
                         604800       ; Expire after a week
                         86400 )      ; Minimum ttl of 1 day
```

Summary

This chapter introduced you to name resolution and DNS. You learned name resolution concepts, how name resolution and reverse of it worked, and what name resolution methods were available.

You studied DNS components including name space, domain, zone, zone files, master server, slave server, caching-only server, and client. You looked at various versions of BIND available in HP-UX.

On the implementation side, you were presented with step-by-step procedure on how to setup master, slave, and caching-only DNS servers. You looked at the contents of the boot and zone files. You looked at files involved in DNS client setup.

The last couple of sections explained to you how to verify the functionality of DNS and how to update maps on master, slave, and caching-only DNS servers.

LDAP Basics

This chapter covers the following major topics:

- ✓ LDAP introduction
- ✓ Features and benefits
- ✓ LDAP terminology – directory, entry, attribute, matching rule, object class, schema, LDIF, DN, and RDN
- ✓ LDAP roles – server, replica, client, and referral
- ✓ Basic install of Netscape Directory Server software
- ✓ Basic install of LDAP-UX client software

34.1   What is LDAP?

Lightweight Directory Access Protocol (LDAP) is a trivial, simplified networking protocol for obtaining directory information, such as email messaging, user authentication, and calendar services over a TCP/IP network. LDAP was derived from *Directory Access Protocol* (DAP), which is one of the protocols within X.500 specification developed jointly by the *International Telecommunication Union* (ITU) and the *International Organization for Standardization* (ISO). One of the major disadvantages with DAP was that it required too much computing resources to work efficiently. LDAP (also referred to as *X.500 Lite*), on the other hand, is thinner and requires less client-side computing resources. This protocol is platform-independent which makes it available on a variety of vendor hardware platforms running heterogeneous operating system software.

LDAP is hierarchical and similar to the structure of UNIX directory tree and DNS. It can be based on logical boundaries defined by geography or organizational arrangement. A typical LDAP directory structure for a company, ABC, with domain *ABC.com* and offices in Canada, USA, UK, and Australia, is shown in Figure 34-1.

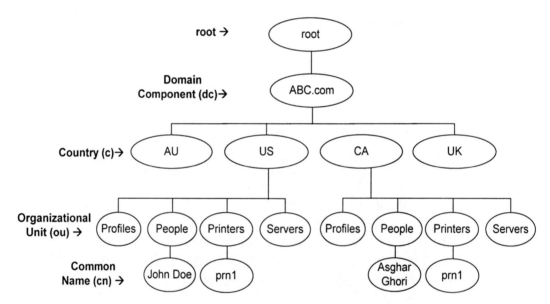

Figure 34-1 LDAP Directory Hierarchy

The top of the company is referred to as the *root* of the LDAP directory hierarchy. Underneath it, is located *Domain Component* (dc), which is usually the name of the company. *Country* (c) falls under domain component. *Organizational Units* (OU) separate various categories of directory information and may be country-specific. The actual information is at the lowest level of the hierarchy, which may include resources, such as users, profiles, people, printers, servers, photos, text, URLs, pointers to information, binary data, public key certificates, and so on.

34.1.1   Features and Benefits of Using LDAP

Some of the features and key benefits of using LDAP are listed below:

- ✓ It has a hierarchical directory structure that allows organization of information and resources in a logical fashion.
- ✓ It allows consolidating common information, such as user information within an OU.
- ✓ It has lower overhead than X.500 DAP.
- ✓ It provides users and applications with a unified, standard interface to a single, extensible directory service making it easier to rapidly develop and deploy directory-enabled applications.
- ✓ It reduces the need to enter and coordinate redundant information in multiple services scattered across an enterprise.
- ✓ It enables fast searches, cost-effective management of users and security, and a central integration point for multiple applications and services.
- ✓ It maintains directory-wide consistent information.

34.2 LDAP Terminology

In order to comprehend LDAP thoroughly, an understanding of the following key terms is essential.

34.2.1 Directory

An LDAP *Directory* is like a specialized database that stores information about objects, such as people, profiles, printers, and servers. It organizes information in such a way that it becomes easier to find and retrieve needed information. It lists objects and gives details about them. An LDAP directory is similar in concept to the UNIX directory hierarchy. The LDAP directory is also referred to as *Directory Information Tree* (DIT).

34.2.2 Entry

An *Entry* is a building block of a directory and represents a specific record in it. In other words, an entry is a collection of information consisting of one or more attributes for an object. An LDAP directory, for instance, might include entries for employees, printers, servers, and so on.

34.2.3 Attribute

An *Attribute* contains two pieces of information: *Attribute Type* and *Attribute Values* and is associated with one or more entries. The attribute type tells the type of information the attribute contains, for example "jobTitle". The attribute value is the specific information contained in that entry. For instance, the value for the "jobTitle" attribute type could be "director". Table 34-1 lists some common attribute types.

Attribute Type	Description
CommonName (cn)	Common name of an entry – for example cn=John Doe
DomainComponent (dc)	The distinguished name (DN) of the component in DNS – for example dc=ca, dc=ABC, dc=com.
Country (c)	Country – for example c=CA.
Mail (mail)	Email address.
Organization (o)	Name of an organization – for example o=ABC.

OrganizationalUnit (ou)	Name of a unit within an organization – for example ou=Printers.
Owner (owner)	Owner of an entry – for example cn=John Doe, ou=Printers, dc=ABC, c=ca.
Surname (sn)	A person's last name – for example Doe.
TelephoneNumber (telephoneNumber)	Telephone number – for example (123) 456-7890 or 1234567890.

Table 34-1 Common LDAP Attribute Types

 Long names and corresponding abbreviations can be used interchangeably.

34.2.4   Matching Rule

A *Matching Rule* matches the attribute value sought against the attribute value stored in the directory in a search and compare task.

For example, matching rules associated with the telephoneNumber attribute could cause "(123) 456-7890" to be matched with either "(123) 456-7890" or "1234567890", or both. When an attribute is defined, a matching rule is associated with it.

34.2.5   Object Class

Each entry belongs to one or more *Object Classes*. An object class is a group of required and optional attributes that defines the structure of an entry.

For example, an organizationalUser object class may include commonName and Surname as required attributes and telephoneNumber, UID, streetAddress, and userPassword as optional attributes. Minimum required attributes must be defined when an entry is defined.

34.2.6   Schema

Schema is a collection of attributes and object classes along with matching rules and syntax, and other related information.

34.2.7   LDAP Data Interchange Format (LDIF)

LDAP Data Interchange Format (LDIF) is a special format for importing and exporting LDAP records from one LDAP server to another. The data is in text format and consists of entries or alterations to entries, or both.

Each record is represented as a group of attributes, with each individual attribute listed on a separate line comprising "name:value" pair. The following is a sample directory entry with attributes representing a record in LDIF:

```
dn: cn=John Doe,ou=People, c=CA,dc=ABC
objectClass: inetLocalMailRecipient
sn: Doe
mail: john.doe@ABC.com
cn: John Doe
givenName: John
uid: jdoe
telephoneNumber: (416) 123-4567
```

34.2.8   Distinguished Name and Relative Distinguished Name

A *Distinguished Name* (DN) uniquely identifies an entry in the entire directory tree. You can relate a distinguished name of an entry to a fully qualified pathname of a file in the UNIX directory hierarchy.

A *Relative Distinguished Name* (RDN), in contrast, represents individual components of a DN. You can relate a relative distinguished name to a relative pathname of a file in the UNIX directory hierarchy.

As an example, the DN for the printer *prn1* under Printers located in Canada (See Figure 34-1) is:

```
cn=prn1,ou=Printers,c=CA,dc=ABC
```

In this example, the RDN for *prn1* is cn=prn1. Similarly, the RDN for Printers is ou=Printers, the RDN for CA is c=CA, and that for ABC is dc=ABC. A DN is thus a sequence of RDNs separated by commas.

34.2.9   LDAP Roles

There are four roles that systems within an LDAP environment may perform. These are:

- ✓ An LDAP Server
- ✓ An LDAP Replica
- ✓ An LDAP Client
- ✓ An LDAP Referral

One system may be configured to perform more than one roles. The roles are defined below:

An *LDAP Server* is a system that houses LDAP directory information. It may be referred to as the *Master* LDAP srever. There must be one such server configured to offer directory services.

An *LDAP Replica* is a system that contains a copy of the information that the LDAP server maintains. A replica may be referred to as a *Slave* LDAP server. It is recommended that at least one replica be configured together with an LDAP server to achieve enhanced availability and load balancing.

An *LDAP Client* is a system that binds itself with a server or replica to establish a communication session. Once a session is established, it can perform queries on directory entries and carry out necessary modifications.

An *LDAP Referral* is an entity on a server that redirects an LDAP client's request to some other LDAP server or replica if it does not contain the requested information. A referral contains names and locations of other LDAP servers where requested information may be found.

34.3   Installing Netscape Directory Server Software

The LDAP directory information is stored on an LDAP server. On HP-UX, *Netscape Directory Server* and *Novell eDirectory* software are available that enable an HP-UX system to be configured and used as an LDAP directory server. Both software may also be downloaded from *software.hp.com,* if needed. The following procedure demonstrates how to install the Netscape Directory Server software and perform a basic setup of it:

1.   If not already installed, go to *software.hp.com* → Security and Manageability, as shown in Figure 34-2.

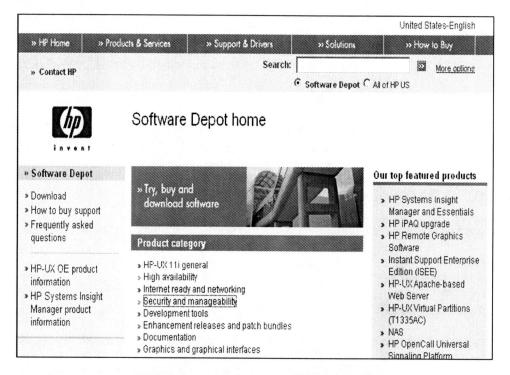

Figure 34-2 *software.hp.com* Main Page

Currently, version 6 of the software is available. Download it into */tmp* directory. The file name would be *Netscape_Directory_Server.depot*.

2.   Install the software using the *swinstall* command as follows:

swinstall –s /tmp/Netscape_Directory_Server.depot

3. Make sure that the SHLIB_PATH environment variable is set for *root* user:

   # export SHLIB_PATH=$(cat /etc/SHLIB_PATH)

4. Run the *setup* command as *root* to configure the software. Choose all defaults. A detailed explanation of LDAP implementation and configuration is out of scope.

   # cd /var/opt/netscape/servers/setup
   # ./setup

Some of the vital data needed during the execution of the *setup* program, is given below:

- ✓ License terms = yes
- ✓ Choose typical install (option 2)
- ✓ Machine's name = specify full hostname of the system (for example, hp01.getitcertify.com)
- ✓ System user = www
- ✓ System group = other
- ✓ Register with existing Netscape ….. = no
- ✓ Another directory to store data = no
- ✓ Directory server network port = 389
- ✓ Directory server identifier = you may want to put just the directory server hostname
- ✓ Netscape administrator ID = admin (supply a password of your choice)
- ✓ Suffix = specify a domain name (for example, getitcertify.com)
- ✓ Directory manager DN = cn=Directory Manager (supply a password of your choice)
- ✓ Administration domain = specify a domain name (for example, getitcertify.com)
- ✓ Administration port = 7764
- ✓ Run administration server as = root

5. After the *setup* program is finished, the Netscape Directory Server will be started. Verify the software functionality using the *ldapsearch* command. An example construct of the command would be:

   **# ldapsearch –D 'uid=user1,ou=class,o=getitcertify.com' –w <password> **
   –b 'o=getitcertify.com' uid=user1

34.4   Installing an LDAP-UX Client

In order to use the Netscape Directory Server software, install and configure the client software called *LDAP-UX Integration* on HP-UX client systems. This software may be downloaded from *software.hp.com,* if needed. The following procedure demonstrates how to install it and perform a basic setup of it. Choose defaults for most questions. Follow the steps below:

1. Run the *setup* command to setup the LDAP-UX client software. Respond to setup questions. This command updates the */etc/opt/ldapux/ldapux_client.conf* file.

   # cd /opt/ldapux/config
   # ./setup

2. Edit */etc/nsswitch.conf* file and make proper modifications to have the client system look for information in the LDAP sources. There is a */etc/nsswitch.ldap* template file that you can copy as */etc/nsswitch.conf*, if one does not already exist.
3. Edit the */etc/pam.conf* file and make proper modifications to ensure that user logins reference Netscape Directory Server for authentication. You may want to copy the */etc/pam.ldap* template file as */etc/pam.conf*, if one does not already exist.

4. Start the LDAP-UX client functionality:

    # **/sbin/init.d/ldapclientd.rc start**

5. Execute the *nsquery* command to verify that the LDAP client is configured and referencing the Netscape Directory Server:

    # **nsquery passwd user1 ldap**

Summary

In this chapter, you were provided with an introduction to LDAP. You looked at features, benefits, and definitions of LDAP components, such as directory, entry, attribute, matching rule, object class, schema, LDIF, DN, RDN, server, replica, client, and referral.

You were presented with high-level information on how to obtain, install, and configure Netscape Directory Server and LDAP-UX client software.

Introduction to BootP and TFTP Services

This chapter covers the following major topics:

- ✓ What are BootP and TFTP services?
- ✓ How BootP and TFTP client and server work?
- ✓ Activate BootP and TFTP
- ✓ Configure /etc/bootptab file
- ✓ Add and verify a BootP client
- ✓ Add and verify BootP relay information

35.1   BootP / TFTP Services

The *Bootstrap Protocol* (BootP) and the *Trivial File Transfer Protocol* (TFTP) services enable client systems to obtain boot and network information from a server on the network that provides boot services. Such systems include Ignite-UX clients, X terminals, diskless HP-UX workstations, network printers, and so on. Ignite-UX clients require access to a boot server to install HP-UX OE on them. See Chapter 36 "Using Ignite-UX" for details. On the contrary, the other clients mentioned, always require the presence of a boot server in order to function and be up and running. The boot server is referred to as the *BootP* server.

The boot information provided by a BootP server include IP address of the BootP server and name of a bootfile to use. The network information include client's IP address and subnet mask, and optionally, gateway and nameserver addresses.

35.1.1   How It Works?

The way it works is that a client broadcasts over the network a *bootrequest* containing its MAC address. Any server on the network running the *bootpd* daemon intercepts the bootrequest and compares the MAC address contained in the bootrequest against a list of configured MAC addresses in its configuration file. If a match is found, the bootp server sends back a *bootreply* consisting of client's boot and network information. The client transfers the bootfile specified in the bootreply over using the *tftp* protocol, loads and executes the bootfile, and configures itself using the network parameters.

If a match is not found, the bootp server checks to see whether or not any relay information is defined. Relay information defines the IP address of some other BootP server that might have the requested information. If available, the client bootrequest is forwarded to it, otherwise, it is denied.

35.2   Configuring BootP and TFTP

Configuring BootP and TFTP services involves configuring a few files. The following sub-sections explain and show how to define appropriate entries to make BootP/TFTP work.

35.2.1   Configuration Files

Three configuration files are typically involved when working with BootP and TFTP services. These files are */etc/services*, */etc/inetd.conf*, and */etc/bootptab*.

The */etc/services* File

Entries for the two protocols in the */etc/services* file should look similar to the following:

```
bootps    67/udp    # Bootstrap Protocol Server
tftp      69/udp    # Trivial File Transfer Protocol
```

The */etc/inetd.conf* File

Entries for the two protocols in the */etc/inetd.conf* file should look similar to the following:

```
bootps   dgram  udp  wait  root  /usr/lbin/bootpd  bootpd
tftpd    dgram  udp  wait  root  /usr/lbin/tftpd  tftpd  /home/tftp/incoming  /home/tftp/outgoing
```

If any modifications are performed in this file, restart the *inetd* daemon to ensure updated entries are read and loaded:

 # inetd –c

Make sure that *tftpd* daemon has *root* user access on all files and sub-directories under */home/tftp/incoming* and */home/tftp/outgoing*.

The */etc/bootptab* File

This is the main BootP configuration file where entries for client and relay are defined. This file is referenced by the *bootpd* daemon.

A sample */etc/bootptab* file looks similar to the following:

 # cat /etc/bootptab
```
. . . . . . . .
. . . . . . . .
#
# Fourth example: bootp relay entries:
#
# Common relay entry.
#
# relay-default:\
#    ht=Ethernet:\
#    bp=15.4.3.136 15.13.6.192:\
#    th=2:\
#    hp=1
#
# Relay entry for node2
#
# node2:\
#    tc=relay-default:\
#    ha=08000902CA00
. . . . . . . .
. . . . . . . .
```

This file contains global and per-client parameters. Global parameters affect all clients, whereas per-client parameters are specific to individual clients. Each line entry for per-client parameter definition has the following syntax:

```
hostname:tag=value:tag=value: ……...
```

The syntax contains a hostname and associated tag values. "hostname" is the client system name and tag=value is a combination of two-character case-sensitive tag with a value. The *bootpd* daemon compares client bootrequest information with these values to decide if it should send a bootreply back to the client, forward to an alternate BootP server, or simply reject the bootrequest.

Some significant tags are listed in Table 35-1.

Tag	Description
hn	Bootreply to include the client hostname.
ht	Hardware type of the client NIC card.
ha	Hardware address (MAC address) of the client NIC card.
ip	Client's IP address.
sm	Subnet mask.
gw	Gateway IP address.
ds	DNS server IP address.
bf	Client's bootfile name.
bp	BootP relay server.
ba	Broadcast address.

Table 35-1 */etc/bootptab* Tags

35.2.2   Adding and Verifying a BootP Client

To add a BootP client, information, such as hostname, LAN interface type, MAC address, IP address, subnet mask, gateway address, nameserver address, and name of the bootfile to be transferred is needed. This information is added to the */etc/bootptab* file.

The example below defines client information on a BootP server, such as *hp01*, for an HP X terminal, *hpxt01*:

1. Edit */etc/bootptab* on *hp01* and input client information:

    hpxt01: hn: ht=ether: ha=080009032354: ip=192.168.1.200: sm=255.255.255.0: \
    gw=192.168.1.1: ds=192.168.1.251: bf=/hpxterm01 ba:

2. Run the following on *hpxt01* to send a *bootpquery* to *hp01* to see how *bootpd* responds to the bootrequest:

    ```
    # bootpquery  080009032354  –s  hp01
    Received BOOTREPLY from hp01 (192.168.1.201)
        Hardware Address:          08:00:09:03:23:54
        Hardware Type:             Ethernet
        IP Address:                192.168.1.200
        Boot file:                 /hpxterm01
        Subnet Mask:               255.255.255.0
        Gateway:                   192.168.1.1
        Domain Name Server:        192.168.1.251
        Host Name:                 hpxt01
    ```

This confirms that the BootP server, *hp01*, is setup correctly.

35.2.3 Adding and Verifying BootP Relay Information

To make a relay entry for the client to boot from another BootP server, such as *hp02*, perform the following modifications:

1. Edit */etc/bootptab* on both *hp01* and *hp02* and input client information:

    hpxt01: hn: ht=ether: ha=080009032354: ip=192.168.1.200: sm=255.255.255.0: \
    gw=192.168.1.1: ds=192.168.1.251: bf=/hpxterm01 ba:

2. Edit */etc/bootptab* on *hp01* and specify the IP address of *hp02* as the BootP "bp" relay server. The "ha" entry specifies the MAC address of the client X terminal. Requests from this client will be forwarded to *hp02* automatically.

    ha=080009032354: bp:192.168.1.202:

3. Run the following on *hpxt01* to see how BootP server responds to the bootrequest:

    ```
    # bootpquery  080009032354  –s  hp02
    Received BOOTREPLY from hp02 (192.168.1.202)
        Hardware Address:        08:00:09:03:23:54
        Hardware Type:           Ethernet
        IP Address:              192.168.1.200
        Boot file:               /hpxterm01
        Subnet Mask:             255.255.255.0
        Gateway:                 192.168.1.1
        Domain Name Server:      192.168.1.251
        Host Name:               hpxt01
    ```

This confirms the relay functionality.

Summary

This chapter provided introductory information on BootP and TFTP services. It explained to you how communication between a BootP client and server took place. You looked at enabling the two services in */etc/services* and */etc/inetd.conf* files. You understood the contents and syntax of the BootP configuration file. You learned how to define a BootP client and relay information in the */etc/bootptab* file and verify functionality.

HP Certified Systems Administrator

## 36

Using Ignite-UX

This chapter covers the following major topics:

- ✓ Introduction of Ignite-UX and benefits of it
- ✓ Install Ignite-UX product
- ✓ Registered and anonymous clients
- ✓ Configure an Ignite-UX server via GUI and command line
- ✓ Boot clients and perform HP-UX OE installation from Ignite-UX server
- ✓ Create golden image and use it to clone another machine
- ✓ Create system recovery archive and use it to recover a non-bootable system

36.1   Introduction to Ignite-UX

HP Ignite-UX software product is a set of tools that allows the installation of HP-UX OE using different methods. The toolset provides the ability to perform local and over-the-network installations. In addition, it offers the capability to clone other systems and create system recovery archives of individual machines. Chapter 09 "HP-UX Operating Environment Installation" described how to perform a local installation of HP-UX. In this chapter, you are going to learn over-the-network installation methods using an Ignite-UX server, how cloning is performed and recovery archives are created locally as well as across the network, and how recovery archives are used to recover a corrupted or unbootable HP-UX system.

36.1.1   Benefits of Using Ignite-UX

Ignite-UX supports both PA-RISC and Itanium2 client systems and offers several benefits. With this product you can:

   ✓ Install HP-UX on a number of systems concurrently.
   ✓ Have different versions of HP-UX (11iv1, 11iv2, or 11iv3) loaded on different client machines from a single Ignite-UX server.
   ✓ Perform a fully customized and automated installation with no questions for configuration asked.
   ✓ Carry out a fresh installation or re-installation.
   ✓ Perform either a push install or a pull install. Push install runs the user interface on the Ignite-UX server, whereas pull install runs the user interface on the client system.
   ✓ Copy the entire image of a running HP-UX system (called *Golden Image*) and use it to clone other systems.
   ✓ Create a recovery archive of a running HP-UX system and use it in case of emergency when the system becomes unbootable or corrupted.

36.2   Setting Up an Ignite-UX Server

To setup a server to provide installation services, an HP-UX system needs to be configured as an Ignite-UX server. The configuration can be done using GUI (or TUI) and command line. The GUI and TUI interfaces provide identical functionality. The GUI is automatically invoked if the DISPLAY environment variable is set properly, otherwise, the text interface is initiated.

36.2.1   Installing the Ignite-UX Product

If Ignite-UX is not already installed on the server, either install it from the HP-UX OE media or download it from *software.hp.com* and install it using *swinstall*. There are five bundles available to choose from. Table 36-1 lists and briefly describes them.

Bundle	Description
IGNITE	Complete Ignite-UX product that supports HP-UX 11.00, 11iv1, 11iv2, and 11iv3.
Ignite-UX-11-00	Supports only HP-UX 11.00.
Ignite-UX-11-11	Supports only HP-UX 11iv1.

Ignite-UX-11-23	Supports only HP-UX 11iv2.
Ignite-UX-11-31	Supports only HP-UX 11iv3.

Table 36-1 Ignite-UX Bundles

36.2.2   Registered and Anonymous Clients

When a client boots up via an Ignite-UX server, the server supplies an available IP address to the client from a pool of addresses defined on it. A client that gets any available IP address is referred to as an *Anonymous Client*. The same IP address can be reserved for that client as well, so that it cannot be assigned to any other booting client. This is accomplished by associating the MAC address of the client with the IP address. Now this client will be referred to as a *Registered Client*.

For PA-RISC clients, the IP and MAC information is stored in the */etc/opt/ignite/instl_boottab* file, which is referenced by the Ignite-UX daemon called *instl_bootd*.

For Itanium2 systems, the */etc/bootptab* file is referenced by another Ignite-UX server daemon called *bootpd*. This file is manually edited to insert entries for booting clients. The same rules that apply to PA-RISC anonymous and registered client setups, are applicable with Itanium2 client setups too. A sample entry from the */etc/bootptab* file is shown below. The definition starts with the keyword IADEF and the sample name of the client used here is *hp10*.

```
IADEF:\
ht=ethernet:\
hn:\
bf=/opt/ignite/boot/npd.efi\
bs=48:\
sm=255.255.255.0:\
gw=192.168.1.1:\
ds=192.168.1.254:
hp10:tc=IADEF:ip=192.168.1.210:ha=00306A6A4396
```

For explanation of tags, refer to Chapter 35 "Introduction to BootP and TFTP Services".

In case an Ignite-UX server is not setup, a DHCP server may be configured instead to respond to boot requests coming from PA-RISC and Itanium2 clients. A DHCP server is able to respond and send back an IP address from its pool of available IP addresses. This is the recommended method for assigning IP addresses to booting Itanium2 clients.

36.2.3   Setting Up an Ignite-UX Server from the GUI

To setup an Ignite-UX server from the GUI on *hp01* to boot PA-RISC clients, follow the steps below:

1.   Edit */etc/inetd.conf* file and uncomment, if commented, the *tftp* entry. This protocol is used by the server to transfer files to a booting client. Do not forget to run the *inetd* command with –c option.

```
tftp  dgram  udp  wait  root  /usr/lbin/tftpd  tftpd  /opt/ignite  /var/opt/ignite
```

2. Make sure *tftp* user entry exists in the */etc/passwd* file. If not, create it.

   tftp:*:510:1:Trivial FTP user:/home/tftpdir:/usr/bin/false

3. Execute the *ignite* command to bring up the GUI:

   # **/opt/ignite/bin/ignite**

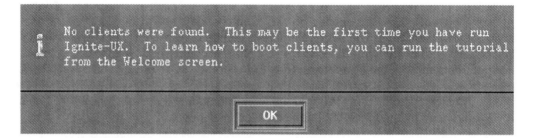

Figure 36-1 Ignite-UX – Message When no Clients are Configured

Click on OK when you see this message.

4. A "Welcome To Ignite UX" screen pops up as displayed in Figure 36-2.

Figure 36-2 Ignite-UX – Welcome Screen

Click on "Server Setup". This executes the Ignite-UX command called *setup_server* located in the */opt/ignite/lbin* directory. The next two screens display "Server Setup: Overview". Click on Next on both.

5. The window shown in Figure 36-3 is where one or more IP addresses and/or MAC addresses for PA-RISC clients are defined. It accepts a range of IP addresses as well. Click on Add when done and then on OK. It saves the supplied information in the */etc/opt/ignite/instl_boottab* file. For Itanium2 clients, edit the */etc/bootptab* file manually and insert information as explained earlier.

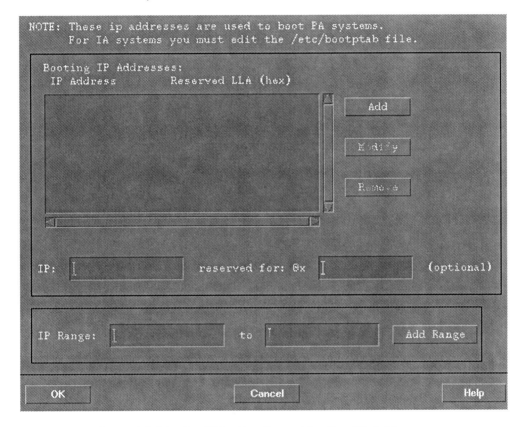

Figure 36-3 Ignite-UX – Configure Booting IP Addresses

6. The next window brings up the "Server Setup: DHCP (optional)" window. Choose "Skip DHCP Setup" and then click on Next to go to the "Server Setup: Software Depot Setup" screen shown in Figure 36-4.

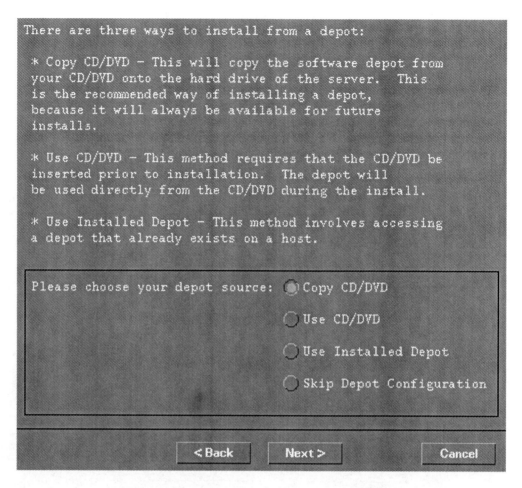

Figure 36-4 Ignite-UX – Software Depot Setup

7. Four choices are available to specify the depot source. The booting client uses the source defined here to pull and *swinstall* the OE software. The four choices are:

✓ Copy CD/DVD – This option swcopies the HP-UX OE software image to the specified directory on the Ignite-UX server. The CD/DVD containing the depot must be loaded in the drive. When the Next button is pressed, the following message appears asking to insert the CD/DVD:

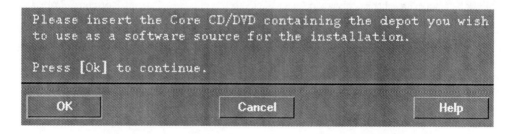

Figure 36-5 Ignite-UX – Prompt to Insert the CD/DVD

Press OK. Confirm the CD/DVD device path as shown in Figure 36-6:

Figure 36-6 Ignite-UX – Prompt for Source Depot Location

Click on OK. The CD/DVD is automatically mounted and the default target location to swcopy the software is displayed. See Figure 36-7. You have the option to specify an alternate location.

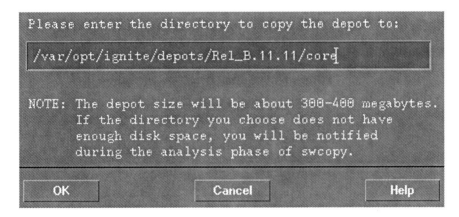

Figure 36-7 Ignite-UX – Target Depot Location

✓ Use CD/DVD – This option installs the HP-UX OE software directly from the specified CD or DVD drive. The installation CD/DVD must be loaded in the drive.
✓ Use Installed Depot – This option is selected when a depot containing the HP-UX OE installation software is configured and available. You need to supply the hostname of the depot server and the directory location for the depot.
✓ Skip Depot Configuration – This option skips the depot setup.

8. At this point, if you wish to setup more depots or exit out of Ignite-UX GUI, simply follow the screens.

This completes the procedure for setting up an Ignite-UX server using GUI.

The GUI also presents two tabs to set "Server Options" and "Session Options". See Figures 36-8 and 36-9.

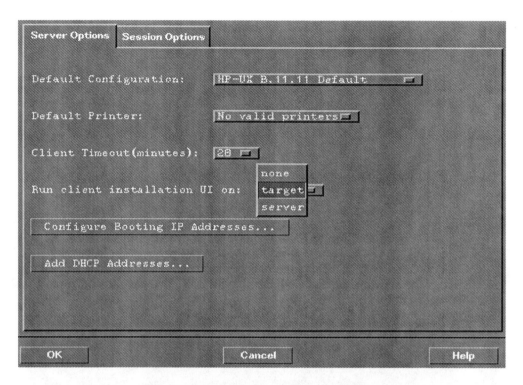

Figure 36-8 Ignite-UX – Server Options

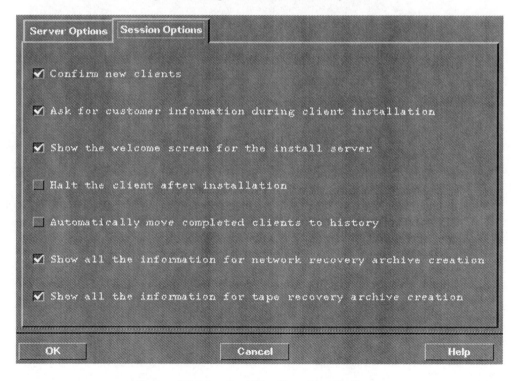

Figure 36-9 Ignite-UX – Session Options

Server options are explained in Table 36-2. Leave the Session options to the defaults.

Server Options	Description
Default configuration	Choose a default configuration for future client installs. This may be overridden for individual clients.
Default printer	Choose a printer (if configured), if you wish to print a history of the install session.
Client timeout (minutes)	Define a timeout value. If turned off, no notification is generated for the *install.log* file on the client for not being updated. Default is usually good in most cases.
Run client installation UI on	Run user interface on the client in TUI mode or on the Ignite-UX server in either GUI or TUI mode. If disabled, non-interactive installs are performed.

Table 36-2 Ignite-UX Server Options

36.2.4   Setting Up an Ignite-UX Server from the Command Line

To setup an Ignite-UX server from the command line on *hp01* to boot PA-RISC clients, follow the steps below:

1. Edit */etc/inetd.conf* file and uncomment, if commented, the *instl_boots* and *tftp* entries. These protocols are used for booting and transferring files. Do not forget to run the *inetd* command with –c option after the changes are put in place:

    tftp   dgram udp wait root /usr/lbin/tftpd tftpd /opt/ignite /var/opt/ignite
    instl_boots dgram udp wait root /opt/ignite/lbin/instl_bootd instl_bootd

    # inetd –c

2. Make sure *tftp* user entry exists in the */etc/passwd* file. If not, create it. Create */home/tftpdir* as well with proper ownership and group membership:

    tftp:*:510:1:Trivial FTP user:/home/tftpdir:/usr/bin/false

3. Edit */etc/opt/ignite/inst_boottab* file and add either IP addresses only (for anonymous clients) or both IP and corresponding MAC addresses (for registered clients). This file is sourced by the *instl_bootd* daemon. Sample entries are:

    192.168.1.251   # Entry for an anonymous client
    192.168.1.252:070001234567::reserve   # Entry for a registered client

4. Edit */etc/exports* file and add the following entry for */var/opt/ignite/clients* directory, which contains the HP-UX mini kernel used by the client when it boots up:

    /var/opt/ignite/clients –anon=2

5. Execute the following command to export the directory. Make sure NFS server daemons are already running:

    # exportfs –a

---

6. Edit the PATH variable to include */opt/ignite/bin* directory:

   # PATH=$PATH:/opt/ignite/bin
   # export PATH

7. Create a depot for HP-UX 11i OE software at, for example, */var/softdepot/HP-UX11i/core*. Make sure that the CD/DVD drive contains the 11i OE software media and is mounted on */SD_CDROM* directory:

   # make_depots –d /var/softdepot/HP-UX11i/core –s /SD_CDROM

8. Execute the *make_config* command to examine the contents of the depot created in the previous step. Specify the name and location of the configuration file with –c option where you want the output of this command to be saved. Speficy the location of the depot with –s option.

   **# make_config –c /var/opt/ignite/data/Rel_B.11.11/core.conf –s **
   /var/softdepot/HP-UX11i/core
   NOTE: make_config can sometimes take a long time to complete. Please be patient!

   Here is some key data extracted from the *core.conf* file:

```
####################
##  Software Sources
####################

sw_source "core" {
   description = "HP-UX Core Software"
   source_format = SD
   sd_server = "192.168.1.201"
   sd_depot_dir = "/var/softdepot/HP-UX11i/core"
   source_type = "NET"
   load_order = 0
}


###################
##  HPUX Base OS
###################

sw_sel "HPUXBase64" {
   description = "HP-UX 64-bit Base OS"
   sw_source = "core"
   sw_category = "HPUXBaseOS"
   sd_software_list = "HPUXBase64,r=B.11.11,a=HP-UX_B.11.11_64,v=HP"
   impacts = "/opt" 61011Kb
   impacts = "/usr" 666578Kb
   impacts = "/etc" 22Kb
   impacts = "/var" 98Kb
   impacts = "/sbin" 24636Kb
   impacts = "/" 861Kb
   exrequisite = sw_category
}
(sw_sel "HPUXBase64") {
   _hp_os_bitness = "64"
```

```
}

init sw_sel "OE90BaseOS64" {
   description = "HP-UX 11i Base OS-64bit"
   sw_source = "core"
   sw_category = "HPUXEnvironments"
   corequisite = "HPUXBase64"
   visible_if = can_run_64bit
} = (can_run_64bit)

########################
##  Operating Environments
########################

sw_sel "HPUX11i-OE-Ent" {
   description = "HP-UX Enterprise Operating Environment Component"
   sw_source = "core"
   sw_category = "OpEnvironments"
   sd_software_list = "HPUX11i-OE-Ent,r=B.11.11.0612,a=HP-UX_B.11.11_32/64,v=HP"
   (_hp_os_bitness == "32") {
      impacts = "/usr" 3149Kb
      impacts = "/etc" 9419Kb
      impacts = "/var" 58Kb
      impacts = "/sbin" 40Kb
      impacts = "/opt" 157522Kb
      impacts = "/" 12Kb
   }
   (_hp_os_bitness == "64") {
      impacts = "/usr" 3149Kb
      impacts = "/etc" 9419Kb
      impacts = "/var" 58Kb
      impacts = "/sbin" 40Kb
      impacts = "/opt" 157546Kb
      impacts = "/" 12Kb
   }
}

sw_sel "HPUX11i-OE" {
   description = "HP-UX 11i Operating Environment Component"
   sw_source = "core"
   sw_category = "OpEnvironments"
   sd_software_list = "HPUX11i-OE,r=B.11.11.0612,a=HP-UX_B.11.11_32/64,v=HP"
   (_hp_os_bitness == "32") {
      impacts = "/var" 4Kb
      impacts = "/etc" 2738Kb
      impacts = "/sbin" 16Kb
      impacts = "/opt" 73739Kb
      impacts = "/usr" 1689Kb
      impacts = "/" 1Kb
   }
   (_hp_os_bitness == "64") {
      impacts = "/var" 4Kb
      impacts = "/etc" 2738Kb
      impacts = "/sbin" 16Kb
      impacts = "/opt" 73763Kb
      impacts = "/usr" 1689Kb
```

```
        impacts = "/" 1Kb
    }
}
```

9. The */var/opt/ignite/INDEX* file maintains a list of available configurations that are presented in the user interface after a client successfully boots up. You choose from one of them (See Figure 36-8 above). Execute the *manage_index* command with –l option to display the current selected configuration.

> # manage_index –l
> HP-UX B.11.11 Default

The default entries for HP-UX B.11.11 in the *INDEX* file look like:

> # more /var/opt/ignite/INDEX
> cfg "HP-UX B.11.11 Default" {
>   description "This selection supplies the default system configuration that HP supplies for the B.11.11 release."
>   "/opt/ignite/data/Rel_B.11.11/config"
>   "/var/opt/ignite/data/Rel_B.11.11/hw_patches_cfg"
>   "/var/opt/ignite/config.local"

Execute the *manage_index* command to update the B.11.11 configuration in the *INDEX* file to reflect the settings created in the previous step:

> # manage_index –a –f /var/opt/ignite/data/Rel_B.11.11/core.conf –r "B.11.11"

10. Execute the *instl_adm* command to setup parameters to be used by the client during installation. To check the default entries, use –d option with the *instl_adm* command:

> # instl_adm –d
> # instl_adm defaults:
>
> # NOTE: Manual additions between the lines containing "instl_adm defaults"
> # and "end instl_adm defaults" will not be preserved.
> server="192.168.1.201"
> netmask[]="0xfffffff0"
> # end instl_adm defaults.

Modify the parameters by saving the defaults into a file and editing the file. Comments follow parameter definitions:

> # instl_adm –d > /var/tmp/instl_adm.conf
> # vi /var/tmp/instl_adm.conf
> # instl_adm defaults:
> # NOTE: Manual additions between the lines containing "instl_adm defaults"
> # and "end instl_adm defaults" will not be preserved.
> server="192.168.1.201"   # Ignite-UX server IP address.
> netmask[]="0xfffffff0"   # Subnet mask.
> # end instl_adm defaults.
> sd_server="192.168.1.201"   # IP address of the Ignite-UX server.
> route_gateway[0]=""   # Route gateway.
> route_destination[0]="default"   # Route destination.

```
timezone="EST5EDT"                      # Time zone to be set.
control_from_server=true                # installation process is controlled from Ignite-UX server.
root_password="fn3,d7a.1Bp,."           # copy and paste password from /etc/passwd file for
root.
is_net_info_temporary=false             # The TCP/IP parameters supplied are permanent.
disable_dhcp=true                       # Disable DHCP.
_hp_keyboard="PS2_DIN_US_English"       # Keyboard type to be set.
```

Execute the *instl_adm* command again to update the */opt/ignite/data/INSTALLFS* file with the new values:

instl_adm –f /var/tmp/instl_adm.conf

Configuration information stored in */var/opt/ignite/INDEX*, */opt/ignite/data/INSTALLFS*, and */var/opt/ignite/clients/<client_MAC_address>/config* is used for a client when it is ignited.

This completes the procedure for setting up an Ignite-UX server from the command line.

36.3   Booting Clients and Installing HP-UX OE

Once an Ignite-UX server is setup, it is ready to be used to install HP-UX OE on client systems. The client systems may or may not already have HP-UX running. You can initiate a push install from the server or a pull install from a client. There are multiple ways of installing HP-UX. Table 36-3 categorizes them in three classes for clarity.

Installation Class	Available Methods
Booting and installing with UI running on client console.	Local boot and local install.
	Local boot with HP-UX OE software located in a network depot.
	Local boot and pull install.
	Remote boot and pull install.
Booting and installing with UI running on Ignite-UX server.	Remote boot and push install.

Table 36-3 Installation Methods

The following sub-sections cover them one by one.

36.3.1   Booting and Installing with UI Running on Client Console

This sub-section outlines installing HP-UX with user interface running on client console.

Local Boot and Local Install

This method employs booting the system locally with the CD/DVD media, performing customization, and installing the OE software from the CD/DVD. Refer to Chapter 09 "HP-UX Operating Environment Installation" for details on how to perform installation using local media.

Local Boot with HP-UX OE Software Located in a Network Depot

In Chapter 09 "HP-UX Operating Environment Installation", when the *User Interface and Media Options* screen appeared after the system was booted locally with the HP-UX 11i OE CD/DVD, a few choices were presented to choose source location. See Figure 36-10.

The first choice was selected in Chapter 09 to demonstrate local install of the OE. The second choice enables the system to contact a network depot server that has the HP-UX 11i OE image sitting in a depot directory. Supply the hostname or IP address of the depot server as well as the depot directory. Choosing this option does not install the OE software locally from the CD/DVD media, rather it pulls the software over the network from the depot server.

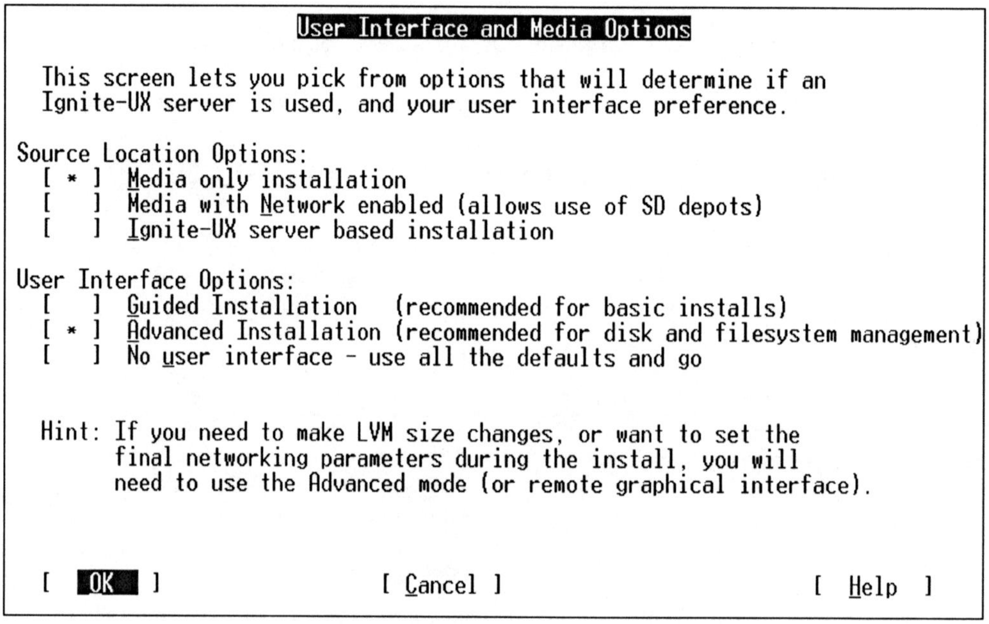

```
┌──────────────────────────────────────────────────────────────────────────────┐
│                      User Interface and Media Options                          │
│     This screen lets you pick from options that will determine if an           │
│     Ignite-UX server is used, and your user interface preference.              │
│                                                                                │
│   Source Location Options:                                                     │
│     [ * ]  Media only installation                                             │
│     [   ]  Media with Network enabled (allows use of SD depots)                │
│     [   ]  Ignite-UX server based installation                                 │
│                                                                                │
│   User Interface Options:                                                      │
│     [   ]  Guided Installation   (recommended for basic installs)              │
│     [ * ]  Advanced Installation (recommended for disk and filesystem management)│
│     [   ]  No user interface - use all the defaults and go                     │
│                                                                                │
│                                                                                │
│   Hint: If you need to make LVM size changes, or want to set the               │
│            final networking parameters during the install, you will            │
│            need to use the Advanced mode (or remote graphical interface).       │
│                                                                                │
│                                                                                │
│   [   OK   ]                  [ Cancel ]                    [  Help  ]          │
└──────────────────────────────────────────────────────────────────────────────┘
```

Figure 36-10 HP-UX Installation – User Interface and Media Options

Local Boot and Pull Install

The third option in Figure 36-10 utilizes a configured Ignite-UX server to pull the software image from. The system prompts to input the IP address of the Ignite-UX server and the directory location where the HP-UX OE image resides. The next window, Figure 36-11, brings up the *itool* interface that allows you to perform any customization. This is the same interface that was used to customize the OE installation in Chapter 09.

HP Certified Systems Administrator

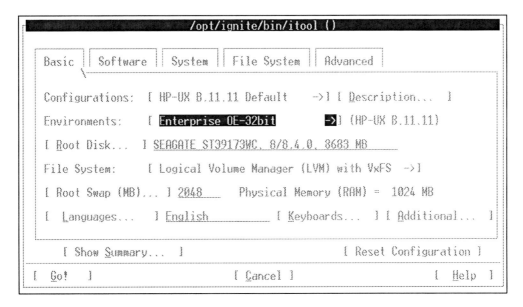

Figure 36-11 HP-UX Installation – Configuration Screen

When done, press the Go! button to continue the OE installation process. The client performs the customization and pulls the OE image from the Ignite-UX server.

Remote Boot and Pull Install

Similar to the "Local boot and pull install" method, the user interface with this method runs on the client console. The only difference being that instead of booting the client locally using the CD/DVD media, it is booted remotely from the Ignite-UX server. Make sure that both the Ignite-UX server and the client are on the same subnet since the *instl_bootd* daemon can only listen and respond to boot requests coming from systems that reside on the same subnet. There are two ways to boot a client remotely:

✓ If the client already has HP-UX 11.0 or later version running, run the following on it with –c option to specify the Ignite-UX server name:

    # bootsys –c hp01

✓ If the client does not have any OS running on it, go to the BCH prompt on it and run the following:

    Main Menu: Enter command > **boot lan.192.168.1.201 install**

Both examples above use the Ignite-UX server *hp01* with IP address 192.168.1.201.

36.3.2 Booting and Installing with UI Running on Ignite-UX Server

With this method, the client is booted from the Ignite-UX server. A few screens appear on the client console that require your input. Any further information needs to be supplied on the Ignite-UX

---

server. This method requires that the client already has HP-UX 11.0 or later running. From the Ignite-UX server, boot the client by either issuing the *bootsys* command or highlighting the client icon in Ignite-UX GUI and choosing the "client boot" option.

Here is an example to boot a client, *hp05*, using the *bootsys* command issued on the Ignite-UX server:

bootsys –a hp05:192.168.1.205
Rebooting hp05 now.

This example assigns the client *hp05* as the hostname and 192.168.1.205 as the IP address. Here is what you would see on the console of *hp05*:

Processor is booting from the first available device.

To discontinue, press any key within 10 seconds.

10 seconds expired.
Proceeding...

Trying Primary Boot Path

Booting...
Boot IO Dependent Code (IODC) revision 1

HARD Booted.

ISL Revision A.00.43 Apr 12, 2000

. . . .

. . . .

The "Welcome to Ignite-UX!" screen appears on the client console, as shown in Figure 36-12. Highlight "Install HP-UX" and hit the Enter key.

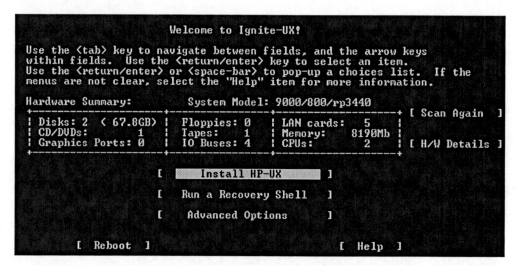

Figure 36-12 HP-UX Installation – Welcome Screen

On the "User Interface and Media Options" window, Figure 36-13, select "Ignite-UX server based installation" and "Remote graphical interface running on the Ignite-UX server" options.

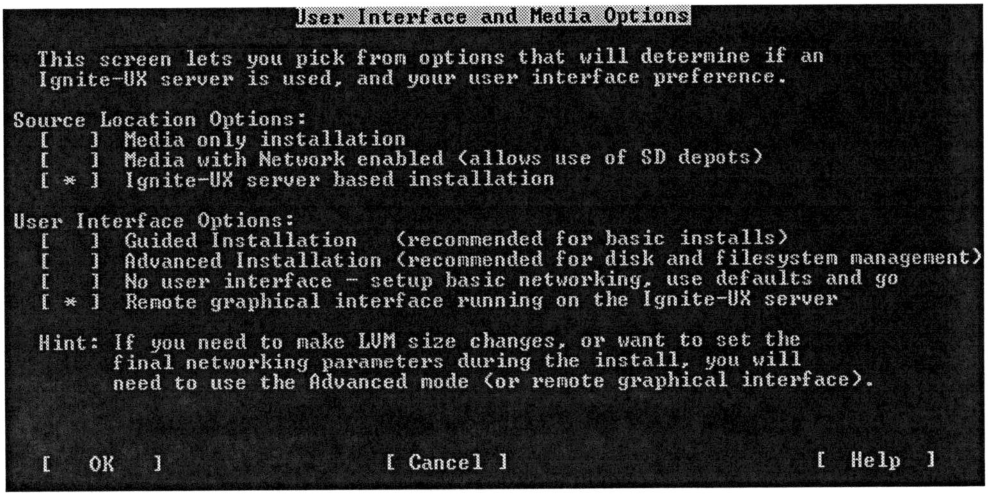

```
                    User Interface and Media Options

    This screen lets you pick from options that will determine if an
    Ignite-UX server is used, and your user interface preference.

  Source Location Options:
      [   ]  Media only installation
      [   ]  Media with Network enabled (allows use of SD depots)
      [ * ]  Ignite-UX server based installation

  User Interface Options:
      [   ]  Guided Installation   (recommended for basic installs)
      [   ]  Advanced Installation (recommended for disk and filesystem management)
      [   ]  No user interface - setup basic networking, use defaults and go
      [ * ]  Remote graphical interface running on the Ignite-UX server

  Hint: If you need to make LVM size changes, or want to set the
        final networking parameters during the install, you will
        need to use the Advanced mode (or remote graphical interface).


    [  OK   ]                   [ Cancel ]                   [ Help  ]
```

Figure 36-13 HP-UX Installation – User Interface and Media Options

Press the OK button. A list of all LAN cards installed in the system is displayed. Choose the one that has network connectivity and hit the Enter key. A summary of the network information is displayed for review:

NETWORK CONFIGURATION

This system's hostname: hp05
Internet protocol address (eg. 15.2.56.1) of this host: 192.168.1.205
Default gateway routing internet protocol address: 192.168.1.1
The subnet mask (eg. 255.255.248.0 or 0xfffff800): 0xffffff00
IP address of the Ignite-UX server system: 192.168.1.201
Is this networking information only temporary? [No]

Press the OK button to see the following on the console screen:

Ignite-UX

Waiting for installation instructions from server: 192.168.1.201   [-]

Icon Name Shown in GUI: hp05
Active System Name/IP: hp05/192.168.1.205
You may now complete the installation using the "ignite" graphical
interface on the Ignite-UX server (See ignite(1M)). If you are not
already running "/opt/ignite/bin/ignite" on the server, do so now.

No further action is required at this console.
[Perform Installation from this Console]
[View Active Network Parameters]
[Change Icon Name Shown in GUI]

At this point, an icon for *hp05* on the Ignite-UX server becomes visible in the GUI. Select "New Install" by right-clicking on *hp05* icon. See Figure 36-14.

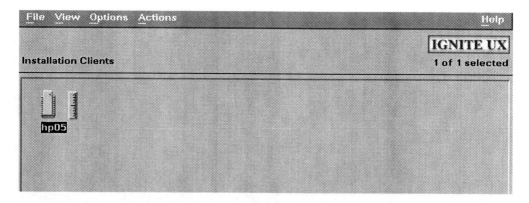

Figure 36-14 HP-UX Installation – Installation Clients

The *itool* interface appears, as shown in Figure 36-15. Consult Chapter 09 to modify any of the installation parameters. Press "Go!" when done.

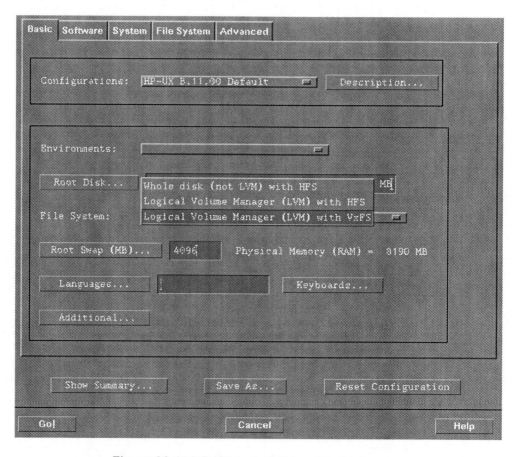

Figure 36-15 HP-UX Installation – itool Interface

36.4 Cloning (Golden Image)

This feature of Ignite-UX is used to clone multiple systems with identical configuration. It requires that you install HP-UX 11i OE on one system, install common applications on it, and configure and patch the system according to requirements. When installation and customization is complete, take a snapshot, called *Golden Image*, of the entire system either on tape or network directory. The following sub-sections demonstrate procedures on creating and using golden images.

36.4.1 Creating a Golden Image on Tape

To create a golden image of *hp05* on a tape device at */dev/rmt/1m* (default is */dev/rmt/0m*), run the *make_tape_recovery* command as follows. The –v option displays output in detail, the –x inc_entire option specifies to include the entire volume group (replace *vg00* with *rootdg* if using Veritas Volume Manager), and –a option tells which tape device to be used.

```
# make_tape_recovery –v –x inc_entire=vg00 –a /dev/rmt/1m
      * Creating local directories for configuration files and archive.

====== 02/01/06 09:28:02 EST  Started make_tape_recovery. (Wed Feb 01 09:28:02 EST 2006)
         @(#) Ignite-UX Revision B.4.2.110
         @(#) net_recovery (opt) $Revision: 10.601 $


      * Testing pax for needed patch
You have 10 seconds to cancel archive creation...
Do you want to cancel? (y or n)
      * Recovery Archive Description = Recovery Archive
      * Recovery Archive Location   = /dev/rmt/0mn
      * Number of Archives to Save  = 2
      * Pax type  = tar
   In?   dsk/vg name          minor# Associated disks/mountpoints
   2     v    /dev/vg00        0x00   /dev/dsk/c0t10d0  /dev/dsk/c0t11d0
                     /dev/vg00/lvol1 /stand  2
                     /dev/vg00/lvol2
                     /dev/vg00/lvol3 /      2
                     /dev/vg00/lvol4 /tmp    2
                     /dev/vg00/lvol5 /home   2
                     /dev/vg00/lvol6 /opt    2
                     /dev/vg00/lvol7 /usr    2
                     /dev/vg00/lvol8 /var    2
. . . . . . . .
. . . . . . . .
      * Creating The Tape Archive
      * Checking configuration file for Syntax
      * Writing boot LIF to tape
74439+1 records in
74439+1 records out
      * Complete writing boot LIF onto tape.
      * /opt/ignite/data/scripts/make_sys_image -c n -d /dev/rmt/0mn -t n -s
```

```
local -n 2006-02-01,09:28 -m t -w
/var/opt/ignite/recovery/2006-02-01,09:28/recovery.log -u -R -g
/var/opt/ignite/recovery/2006-02-01,09:28/flist -a 3344790

    * Preparing to create a system archive
    * Archiving contents of hp05 via tar image to local device /dev/rmt/0mn.
. . . . . . . .
. . . . . . . .
```

Notice from the output that a utility called *make_sys_image* is called during the execution of the *make_tape_recovery* command. This utility is responsible for creating a compressed archive of a running system. It may also be invoked directly from the command line. See its man pages for details on its usage.

36.4.2   Creating a Golden Image on a Network Directory

To create a golden image of *hp05* on *hp01* under the */var/opt/ignite/recovery/archives/hp05* directory, first create the directory to store the image, assign proper ownership and group membership to the directory, and then export the directory via NFS. Perform the following on *hp01*:

 # mkdir –p /var/opt/ignite/recovery/archives/hp05
 # chown bin:bin /var/opt/ignite/recovery/archives/hp05
 # vi /etc/exports
/var/opt/ignite/recovery/archives/hp05 anon=2,access=hp01
 # exportfs –av

Run the *make_net_recovery* command on *hp05* to create its image on *hp01* at */var/opt/ignite/recovery/archives/hp05*. The command automatically NFS mounts the directory from *hp01*. With –s option, specify the Ignite-UX server name and with –a, the directory location to store the archive.

 # make_net_recovery –v –s hp01 –a hp01:/var/opt/ignite/recovery/archives/hp05
    * Creating NFS mount directories for configuration files.
    * Recovery Archive Name = 2006-05-01,15:44

    * Lanic Id = 0x0060B0B6CAE3

    * Ignite-UX Server = hp01

======= 05/01/06 15:44:38 EDT Started make_net_recovery. (Mon May 01 15:44:38
    EDT 2006)
    @(#) Ignite-UX Revision C.6.1.44
    @(#) net_recovery (opt) $Revision: 10.672 $

    * Testing for necessary pax patch.
    * Passed pax tests.
    * Recovery Archive Description = Recovery Archive
    * Recovery Archive Location   = hp01:/var/opt/ignite/recovery/archives/hp05

```
        * Number of Archives to Save  = 2
          pax type  = tar
. . . . . . . .
. . . . . . . .
```

36.4.3   Cloning a System Using Golden Image on Tape

To clone a PA-RISC system with identical configuration (except hostname and IP address) using the golden image residing on tape, do the following:

1. Power on the system.
2. Insert the golden image tape into the tape drive.
3. Interrupt the boot sequence by pressing *Esc* to go to BCH.
4. Execute *sea ipl* to get a list of devices containing bootable media.
5. Execute the *boot* command with proper tape device path specified.
6. Do not interact with ISL.
7. Interrupt the boot process within 10 seconds when prompted. Follow the screens and set the hostname, IP address, and other TCP/IP parameters to be assigned to the client. Continue the boot process, when finished.

Here is the procedure for an Integrity machine:

1. Power on the system.
2. Insert the golden image tape into the tape drive.
3. Interrupt the boot sequence by pressing *Esc* and go to EFI Boot Manager.
4. Go to Boot Option Maintenance menu and select Add a Boot Option.
5. Select appropriate tape device.
6. Enter an appropriate boot option name at the message prompt.
7. Go back to the main menu. The new boot option appears in the EFI Boot Manager main menu.
8. Select the new boot option and boot the system.
9. Interrupt the boot process within 10 seconds when prompted. Follow the screens and set the hostname, IP address, and other TCP/IP parameters to be assigned to the client. Continue the boot process, when finished.

36.4.4   Cloning a System Using Golden Image on a Network Directory

To clone a PA-RISC system with identical configuration using the golden image residing on a remote server, do the following. You must have the Ignite-UX server, where the network-based image resides, properly configured.

1. Power on the system.
2. Interrupt the boot sequence by pressing *Esc* to go to BCH.
3. Execute the following at the BCH prompt:

    Main Menu: Enter command > **boot lan install**

4. Do not interact with IPL.

---

5. Interrupt the boot process within 10 seconds when prompted. Follow the screens and set the hostname, IP address, and other TCP/IP parameters to be assigned to the client. Continue the boot process, when finished.

Here is the procedure for an Integrity machine:

1. Power on the system.
2. Interrupt the boot sequence by pressing *Esc* and go to EFI Boot Manager.
3. Go to Boot Option Maintenance menu and select Add a Boot Option.
4. Select an appropriate network interface.
5. Enter an appropriate boot option name, such as LAN1 at the message prompt.
6. Go back to the main menu. The new boot option appears in the EFI Boot Manager main menu.
7. Select the new boot option and boot the system.
8. Interrupt the boot process within 10 seconds when prompted. Follow the screens and set the hostname, IP address, and other TCP/IP parameters to be assigned to the client. Continue the boot process, when finished.

36.5 System Recovery

System recovery needs to be performed in the event of a catastrophic failure of the system disk, root volume/disk group, or when the root disk becomes corrupt. In each of these situations, the system is rendered unbootable and cannot continue to function. An Ignite-UX functionality, called *System Recovery*, that utilizes the same commands and procedures described earlier in this chapter to create and use golden image, may be employed to recover the system. Note that the purpose and usage of system recovery is slightly different from that of golden image's. The key differences are:

✓   Golden image is typically created for the purpose of cloning a number of new servers, whereas system recovery is host-specific and used primarily to recover an unbootable system or, corrupt or failed root disk.
✓   Golden image is normally produced one time and used many times, whereas system recovery archive is made once every week or month via cron to capture the OS image. It is used only when needed.

For system recovery standpoint, *make_tape_recovery* creates a bootable system recovery tape archive of either selected, essential files and directories of *vg00* (or *rootdg*) or the entire *vg00* (or *rootdg*). This archive is system-specific and includes hostname, IP address, copy of boot area, LVM (or VxVM) structures, and data that reside within *vg00* (or *rootdg*), among other information.

make_tape_recovery is an advanced form of another system recovery tool called *make_recovery,* which has been discontinued in HP-UX 11i, however, an example is included here on how to use it.

make_net_recovery does exactly what *make_tape_recovery* does with the exception that the archive is stored in a directory on another system on the network rather than on tape.

In the event a system recovery is required, either of these archives can be used to recover the system. The tape archive boots a system directly from the BCH prompt and requires no further interaction by default. On the other hand, the network recovery archive requires that you boot the system locally via the HP-UX OE CD/DVD and specify the server and directory location where the archive is located. Booting from either archive, rebuilds the boot area on the root disk, regenerates LVM structures for *vg00* (or VxVM structures for *rootdg*), creates and mounts all file systems, and restores data along with all configuration information. Within an hour or so, the system is back up and running.

36.5.1 Creating and Using Recovery Archives

To create tape and network images for system recovery purposes, follow the procedures outlined in the previous section. A recovery archive should be made on a weekly or monthly basis via cron. It should also be made manually if any updates are made to the operating system.

To use tape and network images for system recovery purposes, follow the procedures outlined in the previous section. The only difference is that you do not need to interrupt the boot process to set any TCP/IP parameters.

36.5.2 Creating and Checking Tape Recovery Archive

To create a system recovery tape archive using the old *make_recovery* command at an alternate tape device, such as */dev/rmt/1m* (–d option) that includes (with –A option) the entire *vg00* volume group (or *rootdg* disk group) and creates a system status file */var/opt/ignite/recovery/makrec.last* (–C option) to contain names, modification times, checksums, etc. for all core OS files being copied to the recovery tape, run the following:

> # **make_recovery –ACv –d /dev/rmt/1m**

The contents of the */var/opt/ignite/recovery/makrec.last* file is compared to the current system file states when *check_recovery* utility is executed to determine whether or not a new *make_recovery* archive needs to be created. If *check_recovery* reports any additions, deletions, or modifications, then re-run *make_recovery* to capture the updated image.

> # **check_recovery**

This command may be executed on a weekly or monthly basis via cron. It should also be run manually, if any updates are made to the operating system.

Summary

In this chapter, you learned about benefits and usage of the Ignite-UX product. You developed an understanding of what registered and anonymous clients were. You saw procedures on how to configure an Ignite-UX server via GUI and command line.

You looked at how to install and re-install HP-UX on client systems. You saw how the user interface could be brought up on either client or server.

Finally, you studied how to create golden image and recovery archives on tape and network directory. You used *make_tape_recovery* and *make_net_recovery* tools for these purposes. You saw procedures to clone other machines using golden image. You looked at procedures on how to recover an unbootable system to its previous running state using the tape and network archives.

37

Introduction to High Availability and Clustering

This chapter covers the following major topics:

✓ Describe HP-UX high-availability and clustering features
✓ Traditional and high-availability network computing models
✓ Risks with single points of failure
✓ Explain key HA terms – downtime, uptime, reliability, fault tolerance, availability, high-availability, ultra high-availability, cluster, floating IP address, failover, failback, primary node, and adoptive node

37.1 Introduction to High Availability

High Availabililty is a design technique whereby a computer system is architected and built in such a way that it recovers quickly from a hardware or software failure and restores to normal the service it is designed to run. A hardware failure could be a fault in a computer system component that makes the computer unable to deliver the required service. Likewise, a software failure could be a fault in HP-UX kernel or the application running on it. In either case, users are unable to access and use the system.

The following sub-sections provide an overview of different design techniques used in computing environments.

37.1.1 Traditional Network Computing Model

In the traditional network computing environment, a single computer runs user applications. Users access these applications over the network. The application data may reside on local drives inside the computer or disk drives in an external disk storage subsystem. In this model, the key hardware components used are:

- ✓ A hard disk that has the operating system loaded on it.
- ✓ One or more disks where user data and applications reside.
- ✓ A SCSI (or fibre) controller card that connects the system to external disks.
- ✓ A network card that connects the computer to the network via a switch or hub for user access.
- ✓ A power supply connected to a UPS.

And the key software components involved are:

- ✓ The operating system software.
- ✓ User data and applications.

Figure 37-1 shows a traditional computer environment.

In the traditional network computing environment configuration, there are many *Single Points Of Failure* (SPOF). For example, if the OS disk goes bad, the entire system will crash. Similarly, if the SCSI/FC adapter fails, access to data and application will be lost. The power supply or the UPS failure will result in no power to the system. A bug in the OS kernel will crash the entire system. In other words, a single hardware or software component failure would cause interruption to the business that depends on it. The interruption may last for minutes or it could extend to several hours or even days until the cause of the failure is identified and fixed. Some of the SPOFs are listed below including the ones just described:

- ✓ SCSI or Fibre Channel adapter
- ✓ OS disk
- ✓ Data disk
- ✓ Network connectivity
- ✓ Power supplies
- ✓ UPS

- ✓ Computer system
- ✓ Racking
- ✓ Data

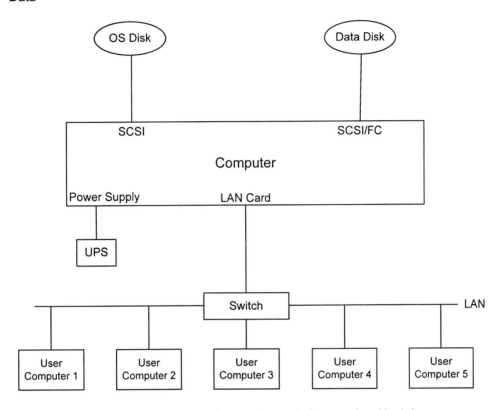

Figure 37-1 Traditional Network Computing Model

37.1.2 Redundant-Component Network Computing Model

As businesses started to rely more and more on computing infrastructure, the need arose to reduce the amount of time it took to overcome the interruption and bring the system back to normal operation. This need resulted in designs that led to deploying duplicate hardware components in the computer system to minimize the SPOFs. The duplicate hardware components introduced *Redundancy* and increased the *Availability* of the system. Redundancy allowed systems to continue to function should one of the two redundant components fail. The resultant increased availability decreased considerably the amount of system recovery time. Figure 37-2 shows the traditional computer model with redundancy added.

It is obvious from Figure 37-2 that some of the hardware components are made redundant. The disk that houses the HP-UX operating environment software, now has a redundant disk connected to the system via a separate SCSI card and cable. Both disks are mirrored using a mirroring software, such as HP-UX MirrorDisk/UX or Veritas Volume Manager.

Similarly, data and application now sit in an external disk storage subsystem that has protection added via RAID 1, RAID 5, RAID 1+0, or RAID 0+1. The external disk storage is connected to the system via two separate controller cards and cables.

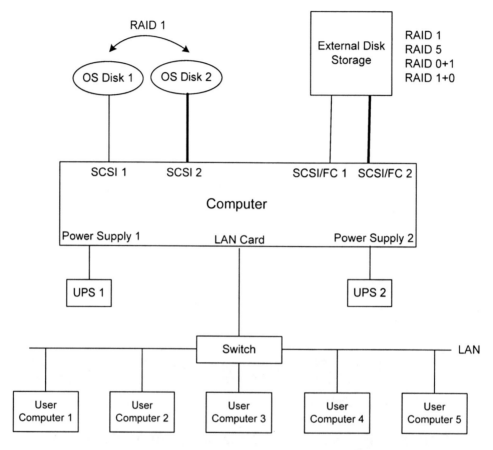

Figure 37-2 Redundant-Component Network Computing Model

There is a pair of UPS providing power to the computer system. One backs up the other. Both should be connected to separate power sources.

37.1.3 High-Availability Network Computing Model

There still are SPOFs in the design. The connectivity to the network is still non-redundant. Similarly, the application that resides in the disk storage is non-redundant. Although the data itself is protected against disk breakdown, but what if the application crashes due to a CPU failure or failure in memory or some other non-redundant component. Generally, when a CPU fails, memory malfunctions, or other system component faults, the system panics and reboots. This results in the business service that relies on it to become unavailable, until the system is recovered from the hardware failure and application is restored to normal operation. When this type of outage, referred to as *Unplanned Downtime,* occurs, the business suffers.

HP Certified Systems Administrator

Figure 37-3 shows more redundancy added to the system environment to remove the remaining SPOFs. Now you have two systems, each with redundant OS disks, connectivity to separate networks via separate physical switches, and redundant connectivity to shared external disk storage. You need to configure the two systems in such a manner that both work as a single entity. This type of setup would create a *Cluster* of systems, whereby failure of one system or a pair of any redundant components would cause the business service to be unavailable for a short period of time only. A cluster of systems (or simply, a cluster) is formed using a cluster management software, such as HP ServiceGuard or Veritas Cluster Server (VCS).

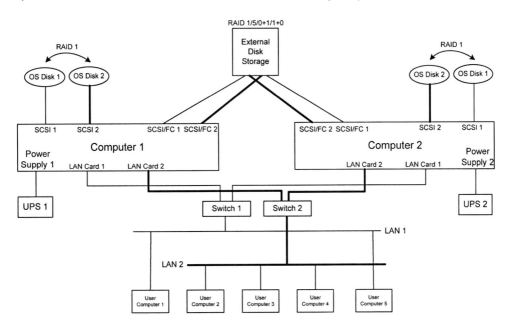

Figure 37-3 High-Availability Network Computing Model

You also need to ensure that both systems are deployed in separate physical racks to remove the SPOF from server racking perspective.

37.1.4   Ultra High-Availability Network Computing Model

Although the computer system design is now fully redundant, however, there still is a SPOF – the data center where this setup is deployed. What if the data center becomes inaccessible or destroyed for reasons, such as fire, flood, or other natural or human-caused disasters? You may want to have one of the nodes of the cluster to be placed at an alternate data center physically apart from the primary data center. The alternate data center could be hundreds or thousands of miles away in another city, country, or continent. For this type of setup, the standard HP ServiceGuard and Veritas Cluster Server software would not work. You will need to obtain an appropriate version of the software that supports such a setup. By implementing this configuration, any mission-critical business applications that run on these systems, become even more available. This type of setup may be referred to as *Ultra High-Availability* or *Continuously Available* setup.

Note that such a setup would require plenty of design consideration from the network as well as disk storage perspective and be very expensive to implement and maintain. You would have to implement *Storage Area Network* (SAN) solution and connect nodes in the cluster to disk storage subsystems that reside locally in each of the two data centers. The system located in the primary data center would store data locally on the local disk storage subsystem. This data is synchronously or asynchronously replicated in real time to the disk storage subsystem that reside in the alternate data center. The second node of the cluster is attached to the second disk storage subsystem. In case a disaster strikes causing the primary data center to become inaccessible, the cluster management software would *Failover* the applications running on the primary node to the *Adoptive* (second) node in the alternate data center. Since all the data was being replicated to the disk storage subsystem in the alternate data center location, the cluster node will have access to the latest data and hence the applications and services may become available within minutes. The remote users will automatically connect to the adoptive node and re-gain access to the applications.

37.2 Key HA Terms

This section defines a few terms that are commonly used in an HA environment. Some of them have already been covered earlier in this chapter.

37.2.1 Downtime

Downtime refers to a length of time during which a business application is unavailable or non-functional due to a failure. Downtime is of two types – *Planned* and *Unplanned*. A *Planned Downtime* is a pre-scheduled maintenance window for performing any hardware, OS, or application repair task. An *Unplanned Downtime,* on the other hand, refers to a sudden interruption in business application accessibility. An unplanned downtime may also be referred to as an *Outage*.

37.2.2 Uptime

Uptime is the opposite of downtime. It refers to a length of time during which a business application remains up and available for user access.

37.2.3 Reliability

Reliability is the ability of a computer system to carry out and keep up its function in normal as well as abnormal circumstances. Ususally, branded computers are manufactured using high quality hardware components. These components are tested and certified before being used to produce better quality and more reliable computer systems.

37.2.4 Fault Tolerance

Fault Tolerance refers to the ability of a computer system to survive and continue to function in the event a sudden hardware or software failure occurs. Fault tolerance is built by adding redundant hardware components to a computer system.

37.2.5 Availability

Availability is a measure of overall system uptime minus any unplanned downtime.

37.2.6   High-Availability

High-Availability (HA) refers to a system design in which failure of a single hardware or software component interrupts only briefly the service offered by the system. The purpose of designing an HA system is to minimize the duration of a possible interruption to the service offered by the system.

37.2.7   Ultra High-Availability

Ultra High-Availability is one level higher than normal HA. It generally includes two or more cluster nodes that reside in distant data centers with data mirrored in real time and is continuously available to both or all nodes in the cluster. In the event one of the nodes faults, the other takes over the control and starts applications on it.

37.2.8   Cluster

A *Cluster* is a group of two or more independent systems that work in conjunction with each other under the control of a management software to provide higher availability to business applications. The clustered systems are configured to work coherently as a single entity and share the same data. Certain key benefits achieved by implementing a cluster are:

Load Balancing

When several applications require varying amount of compute capacity to run in a multi-node cluster, the cluster is configured in such a way that application load is evenly distributed across the nodes in the cluster. This is called *Load Balancing* and is done to avoid any single node from being swamped.

Rolling Upgrades

Without requiring a large amount of time to perform an OS or application upgrade, a cluster allows to manually failover applications running on the node to be upgraded to another node in the cluster. This leaves the node free for any upgrade work. Move the application back to this node after the upgrade is complete.

37.2.9   Floating (Virtual) IP Address

When clusters are formed, applications are packaged to run on cluster nodes. Each application package is assigned an IP address, which is associated with a defined LAN port on the system where the package is to be run. This IP address is referred to as the *Floating* (or *Virtual)* IP address. When the package fails over to another node in the cluster, the floating IP address goes with the package to that node and is assigned to a LAN port there. A floating IP address is not tied to a specific node in a cluster.

37.2.10 Failover

The responsibility of a cluster management software is to keep an eye on the availability of the hardware and software components of nodes within a cluster it is configured to manage. If an event occurs that renders a cluster node inoperative, the cluster management software transfers the control of the software package to another configured node in the cluster and starts the package on that node. This stop-transfer-start operation is referred to as *Failover*. Clustered nodes in production services are almost always configured to perform failover function automatically without human intervention. The cluster management software does not fix any problems, rather it monitors hardware and software components and transfers the control to another configured node should a critical fault occurs on the primary node that makes it unable to perform the desired role.

37.2.11 Failback

Failback is opposite of failover. It refers to the tasks to be performed to transfer the control of the failed over package back to its primary node and bring it up there. Failback is not configured to happen automatically in production services, rather it is done manually during a customer-approved scheduled maintenance or specially-arranged window.

37.2.12 Primary (Active) Node

From a package standpoint, a *Primary* (or *Active)* node is that where the package is configured to automatically start when cluster services are brought up.

37.2.13 Adoptive (Standby or Passive) Node

When a primary node faults, the package running on it fails over to an *Adoptive* node and starts there. The adoptive node may or may not already be running a different package on it. The adoptive node is also referred to as the *Standby* or *Passive* node.

HP ServiceGuard and Veritas Cluster Server software can be configured in active/active and active/standby modes. In active/active configuration, each node in the cluster runs at least one package. Iin active/standby configuration, in contrast, one of the nodes remains idle (standby) until some other node in the cluster dies and the package running there fails over to this standby node.

Summary

In this chapter, you learned concepts around high-availability and clustering. You looked at various network computing models that helped you understand risks associated with having single points of failure. You saw how those risks could be minimized by adding redundant components.

Finally, several key HA terms, such as downtime, uptime, reliability, fault tolerance, availability, high-availability, ultra high-availability, cluster, floating IP address, failover, failback, primary node, and adoptive node were presented to enhance your understanding of HA and clustering.

## 38

Administering HP-UX Security

This chapter covers the following major topics:

✓ Ways to secure HP-UX systems
✓ Password aging and how to use it
✓ Benefits of shadow password and how to implement it
✓ Trusted mode security level and how to convert an HP-UX system to and unconvert it from trusted mode
✓ Standard mode security extensions and its benefits and use
✓ Secure shell benefits and how ssh encryption takes place
✓ Access HP-UX systems via ssh
✓ Pluggable Authentication Module (PAM) and its use
✓ Describe chroot jail
✓ Security monitoring, hardening, and reporting tools
✓ Common HP-UX system hardening tasks

38.1 Securing an HP-UX System

When HP-UX is newly installed, standard security mechanism is put in place to control user access to the system. The user security controls normally cover authentication, authorization, and network access into the system.

Authentication identifies a user to the system. When a user enters credentials by entering his/her username and password, the system checks whether or not the credentials are valid and based on the outcome the user is either allowed or denied access.

Authorization determines what privileges a user has on using programs and managing resources. The default authorization is put in place for normal users when HP-UX OE is installed. The root user is authorized to use any programs and can manage any system resources. Additional privileges may be granted to normal users by root, if required. For instance, SAM is only allowed to be run by root. However, root can delegate management of a subset of resources via SAM to other users.

Many incoming client requests over the network from remote systems must pass through the *inetd* daemon on the system in order to be serviced. Security at this level can be controlled in two ways:

✓ Disable the service no longer required in the *inetd* daemon's configuration file */etc/inetd.conf*.
✓ Limit access into the system by specific systems, networks, and domains in the *inetd* daemon's security file */var/adm/inetd.sec*.

The following sub-sections describe methods available to secure an HP-UX system from user authentication perspective. The later sections explain additional topics surrounding further securing an HP-UX system.

38.1.1 Setting Password Aging Attributes

In Chapter 12 "User and Group Account Administration", user creation and password settings were discussed. Rules that must be adhered to when setting a user password were outlined. *Password Aging* provides enhanced control on user passwords. It allows to set certain limits on user passwords in terms of expiration, warning period, etc. The *passwd* command is used to alter these parameters for a user account. The general syntax of the command with password aging options is:

passwd –r files [–d | –l] [–f] [–n min] [–w warn] [–x max] username

where:

✓ "–r files" specifies that this change is made in the */etc/passwd* file.
✓ "–d" unlocks a locked user account by deleting its password.
✓ "–l" locks a user account.
✓ "–f" forces a user to change password upon next login by expiring existing password.
✓ "–n" specifies that the password cannot be changed before this many days are elapsed.
✓ "–w" defines number of days a user gets warning messages to change password. If the password is not changed during this period, the user account gets locked. This option is only available when a system is converted to trusted mode security.
✓ "–x" denotes maximum days of validity of the password before a user starts getting warning messages to change password.

The following example sets password aging on user *bghori*. The "min" value is set to 7, the "max" is set to 28, and the user is forced to modify password at next login.

```
# passwd –f –n 7 –x 28 bghori
<min> argument rounded up to nearest week
<max> argument rounded up to nearest week
```

When done, verify the attributes:

```
# passwd –s bghori
bghori PS   00/00/00   7  28
```

38.1.2   Implementing Shadow Password Mechanism

The default location to store user passwords on a standard HP-UX system is the */etc/passwd* file. By implementing *Shadow Password*, all passwords from the */etc/passwd* file as well as any associated password aging attributes are moved to the */etc/shadow* file. Now both these files will be used for user authentication.

The process of implementing shadow password is very simple. First, install the software if it is not already loaded. Download it from *software.hp.com* and install it using *swinstall* command.

```
# swlist | grep –i shadow
ShadowPW    B.11.11.03   HP-UX 11.11 Shadow Password Enablement Product
```

The next step is to execute the *pwconv* command. This command creates */etc/shadow* file and moves over all password entries and aging attributes.

```
# pwconv
# ll /etc/shadow
-r-------- 1 root     sys        428 Apr  9 12:46 /etc/shadow
# cat /etc/shadow
root:xPk1ieoqpwl7E:13612::::::
daemon:x:13612::::::
bin:x:13612::::::
sys:x:13612::::::
adm:x:13612::::::
. . . . . . . .
. . . . . . . .
```

If, at any stage, you wish to revert to the original non-shadow password environment, execute the *pwunconv* command. This command removes the */etc/shadow* file also.

38.1.3   Converting a System to Trusted Mode Security

Trusted Mode Security implements additional system access protection from user authentication perspective. It complies with C2 level of security and based on *Trusted Computing Base* (TCB). Note that applications may malfunction if this security level is implemented. Check with application administrators before implementing it.

Any or all of the following capabilities can be achieved by converting a system to trusted mode security:

- ✓ If a user account remains dormant for a set period of time, his/her account gets locked. The default time period is 30 days.
- ✓ If a user attempts to log in unsuccessfully, his/her account is locked. The default number of unsuccessful attempts after which a user account is locked is 3.
- ✓ *root* user password must be entered in order to get into the single user state.
- ✓ Enhanced password aging attributes, such as minimum time before which a user cannot change his/her password, warning time before a user account is locked, expiration time for a user account, and account lifetime are enabled.
- ✓ When a user wants to change his/her password, he/she has three options to choose a password from: *select a randomly generated password string*, *select a pronounceable password*, or *enter own password*.
- ✓ A user can be restricted to log in to a system within a specified time period and/or from specified terminals only.
- ✓ Auditing for user activities and system calls is enabled.

To convert an HP-UX system to trusted mode security, either command line or SAM may be used. The following example demonstrates how to do it from the command line using the *tsconvert* command:

> # **/etc/tsconvert**
> Creating secure password database...
> Directories created.
> Making default files.
> . . . .
> . . . .
> Moving passwords...
> secure password database installed.
> Converting at and crontab jobs...
> At and crontab files converted.

This command creates a new directory structure */tcb/files/auth* that contains sub-directories "a" through "z". Each sub-directory contains files for user accounts that begin with the sub-directory's name. For instance, user accounts beginning with an "a" have their files under */tcb/files/auth/a* sub-directory, user accounts beginning with a "b" have their files under */tcb/files/auth/b* sub-directory, and so on for other users. All password fields in the */etc/passwd* file are replaced with an " * " character and the password and password aging information is moved to this new directory structure. To view user *bghori's* security file, go to */tcb/files/auth/b*. You will find a file that matches the user name. Do a *cat* on this file to view what it contains.

> # **cat bghori**
> bghori:u_name=bghori:u_id#101:\
>   :u_pwd=:\
>   :u_auditid#12:\
>   :u_auditflag#1:\
>   :u_minchg#604800:u_exp#2419200:u_succhg#1132185600:u_pswduser=bghori:\
>   :u_suclog#1135355071:u_lock@:chkent:

This file holds all standard and extended password aging attributes for user *bghori*. The numbers in the file are in seconds.

If a user is activated, the @ sign followed by u_lock, is displayed, otherwise it is not. For example, the line below means that user *bghori* is locked:

    :u_suclog#1135355071:u_lock:chkent:

If *bghori* tries to log in to the system now, the following message will be displayed:

    Account is disabled - see Account Administrator

To unlock a user account, there is a command called *modprpw* that must be used to unlock the user. This command only works in trusted mode security. For example, the following will unlock user *bghori*:

    # /usr/lbin/modprpw –k –l bghori

The –w option with the *passwd* command can now be used to set warning period. This option was unavailable when the system was not converted to trusted mode security. Here is an example:

    # passwd –f –w 5 –n 7 –x 28 bghori
    <warn> argument rounded up to nearest week
    <min> argument rounded up to nearest week
    <max> argument rounded up to nearest week

To restore the system back to standard security level, run the *tsconvert* command with –r option as follows:

    # /etc/tsconvert –r
    Restoring /etc/passwd...
    /etc/passwd restored.
    Deleting at and crontab audit ID files...
    At and crontab audit ID files deleted.

To convert an HP-UX system to trusted mode security via SAM, perform the following:

☞ Go to SAM → Auditing and Security → System Security Policies. Follow screen prompts to run the conversion process.

38.1.4   Implementing Standard Mode Security Extensions

Standard Mode Security Extensions (SMSE) is a set of advanced security features that are made available in HP-UX 11iv2 as a bundled product called *StdModSecExt*. This product can be downloaded from *software.hp.com* as well. The purpose of the product is to provide features that are otherwise only available on a system that is converted into trusted mode.

The product targets two major areas from security perspective and supports these features:

1. *Enhanced Authentication Controls*: Enhanced user authentication controls via password and login policies to:

   ✓ Lock a user account after a certain number of failed login attempts made.
   ✓ Display last successful and unsuccessful login attempts.
   ✓ Prevent using previously-used passwords.
   ✓ Disallow zero-length passwords.
   ✓ Limit user logins to specific time durations.
   ✓ Expire inactive user accounts.

2. *Auditing*: System and user activity auditing for analysis purposes.

Most of these features can be configured on a per-user basis as well, as compared to system-wide basis in trusted mode.

To check whether or not the software is loaded on the machine, run the following:

   # **swlist | grep –i stdmodsecext**

To download it, go to *software.hp.com* and click on "Security and manageability". You should be able to see "HP-UX Standard Mode Security Extensions" product on this page. Click on "Receive for Free" and follow the procedure to download it.

Copy the software to a temporary location, such as */tmp* or */var/tmp* or a software depot directory location. Execute the *swinstall* command. The following assumes that the product is located in the */var/tmp* directory. Notice that the install of this product requires a system reboot.

   # **swinstall –x autoreboot=true –s **
   /var/tmp/StdModSecExt_B.11.23.02_HP-UX_B.11.23_IA+PA.depot

Enhanced Authentication Controls

There are three files where user security attributes are defined. These are:

   /var/adm/userdb – This per-user security file is checked for login and password attributes at the time a user logs in, in addition to */etc/passwd* and */etc/shadow* (if available) files.

   /etc/default/security – This system-wide security file is checked for login and password attributes if a per-user attribute is not defined in */var/adm/userdb*. Attributes defined in this file are applicable to all users logging in.

   /etc/security.dsc – This system-wide security file contains pre-defined default security attributes. If the authentication process does not find a defined attribute for the user in */var/adm/userdb* and */etc/default/security* files, it uses default security attributes listed in this file.

Table 38-1 lists and describes configurable per-user security attributes.

Attribute	Function
ALLOW_NULL_PASSWORD	Allow or deny null passwords.
AUDIT_FLAG	Enable or disable user auditing.
AUTH_MAXTRIES	Maximum unsuccessful login tries before a user is locked.
DISPLAY_LAST_LOGIN	Whether or not to display information about user's last login.
LOGIN_TIMES	Limit user login time periods.
MIN_PASSWORD_LENGTH	Minimum number of characters a user password must have.
NUMBER_OF_LOGINS_ALLOWED	Number of concurrent logins per user.
PASSWORD_HISTORY_DEPTH	Depth of password history.
PASSWORD_MIN_LOWER_CASE_CHARS	Minimum number of lowercase alphabets a user password must have.
PASSWORD_MIN_UPPER_CASE_CHARS	Minimum number of uppercase alphabets a user password must have.
PASSWORD_MIN_DIGIT_ CHARS	Minimum number of digits a user password must have.
PASSWORD_MIN_SPECIAL_CHARS	Minimum number of special characters a user password must have.
UMASK	Default user umask value.

Table 38-1 Per-User Security Attributes

SMSE offers a set of commands to set, view, and verify security attributes. These commands are:

✓ *userdbset* – sets user attributes.
✓ *userdbget* – displays user attributes
✓ *userdbck* – verifies the integrity of per-user security file contents.

The following examples demonstrate how these commands are used.

To force user *bghori* to have at least 2 uppercase letters in his/her password, execute the following:

 # userdbset –u bghori PASSWORD_MIN_UPPER_CASE_CHARS=2

To view defined security attributes for user *bghori*, enter the following:

 # userdbget –u bghori

If you suspect inconsistencies in the user security file */var/adm/userdb*, run the following command to check the integrity of the contents:

 # userdbck

Auditing

The auditing feature of SMSE enables you to record user and system activities in log files. These log files may be reviewed later to spot potential security breaches. Some configuration files and commands are added to the system when SMSE product is installed. The configuration files are used to define how auditing should be done and recorded. The commands are used to modify audit settings in the configuration files.

The configuration files are */etc/rc.config.d/auditing* and */etc/default/security*. The former is used to define audit parameters for system events and the latter for user activities.

Commands available for system event auditing are *audevent, audisp, audomon,* and *audsys*. Here is a short description of these commands:

- ✓ audevent – displays and sets system events.
- ✓ audisp – displays audit records.
- ✓ audomon – sets audit file monitoring and size parameters.
- ✓ audsys – used for two purposes: 1) stop and start auditing 2) display and set audit file/directory information.

In order to use and enable auditing, the AUDIT_FLAG and AUDIT variables must be set to 1 in the */etc/default/security* and */etc/rc.config.d/auditing* files, respectively.

The following three points should be considered when implementing auditing:

- ✓ Auditing to be performed for individual user accounts or for all system users.
- ✓ What system events to audit?
- ✓ Where to record audit information?

38.2 The Secure Shell

You have seen a number of ways so far to make an HP-UX system more secure. This includes using ACLs; setting setuid, setgid, and sticky bits; disabling unnecessary services in the */etc/inetd.conf* file, controlling access to the network services via */var/adm/inetd.sec* file, enabling logging for network services by specifying the –l option to the *inetd* daemon in the */etc/rc.config.d/netdaemons* file; setting password aging attributes; implementing shadow password mechanism; converting a system to trusted mode security; implementing standard mode security extensions; configuring user and host equivalency; and so on.

Secure SHell (ssh) provides users with secure login access to an HP-UX system over the network using hidden encryption. Due to better security features, ssh utilities are preferred over conventional, unsecured *telnet, rlogin, remsh, rcp,* and *ftp*. Once ssh is successfully implemented for each individual user of the system including the *root* user, the *rlogind, rexecd, remshd, ftpd,* and *telnetd* services can be disabled in the */etc/inetd.conf* file provided no user or application functionality is impacted. The secure command that replaces *rlogin, remsh,* and *telnet* is called *ssh*. The secure commands that replace *rcp* and *ftp* are called *scp* and *sftp*, respectively.

38.2.1   How SSH Encryption Takes Place

ssh is based on the client/server model. The client piece (*ssh*, *scp*, and *sftp*) makes a connection request and the server process (*sshd*) responds to it. Here is how a secure communication channel is established when using an ssh utility:

- ✓ The client program sends a connection request to the specified server.
- ✓ The *sshd* daemon on the server receives the incoming request on the pre-defined port. The configuration file for *sshd* is */opt/ssh/etc/sshd_config*. The *sshd* daemon may be controlled via *inetd* daemon.
- ✓ Both client and server processes share ssh protocol versions and switch to a packet-based protocol for communication.
- ✓ The server supplies session information to the client.
- ✓ The client acknowledges the server's session information and responds with a session key.
- ✓ Both client and server enable encryption at their ends.
- ✓ This completes authentication process and a communication channel is established between the two.

38.2.2   Accessing HP-UX Server via SSH

telnet and *ftp* client and server software are installed as part of all UNIX and most non-UNIX operating systems, whereas ssh utilities (client and server programs) may need to be installed. By default, HP-UX 11i comes standard with ssh utilities and the *sshd* server daemon is enabled and running. If not, install the utilities and perform the following two steps to enable and run it:

1. Edit the */etc/rc.config.d/sshd* file and set the variable SSHD_START to 1:

   SSHD_START=1

2. Start the daemon:

   # **/sbin/init.d/secsh start**
   HP-UX Secure Shell started

On Windows side, several ssh client programs, such as PuTTY are available. PuTTY can be downloaded free of charge from the internet. Figure 38-1 shows the PuTTY interface.

Supply a hostname or an IP address of the system where you want to log on and check "SSH" under "Protocol". The ssh protocol uses port 22 by default. Save this session by assigning a name to it so that you do not have to type in this information repeatedly.

The first time you try to ssh into an HP-UX server, *hp02* for instance, information similar to the following will be displayed:

The authenticity of host 'hp02 (192.168.1.202)' can't be established.
RSA key fingerprint is d3:a4:4e:c1:9f:de:00:e7:4a:55:ac:a9:e6:5e:ff:a9.
Are you sure you want to continue connecting (yes/no)? yes
Warning: Permanently added 'hp02,192.168.1.202' (RSA) to the list of known hosts.

This sets up encryption keys for the user and the client system. This message is not displayed on subsequent login attempts.

Figure 38-1 PuTTY Interface

38.2.3   Setting Up Passwordless User Access via ssh

Similar to the way user-level trust relationship works for the "r" commands, ssh access can be setup as well for passwordless user access. The following outlines step-by-step procedure on how to setup passwordless ssh authentication for a user. For the purpose of understanding this procedure, assume that the user is *user1* and the system is *hp01*.

1. Log on to *hp01* as *user1*.
2. Run the following command. This command creates a *.ssh* sub-directory under *user1*'s home directory along with three files: *id_dsa*, *id_dsa.pub*, and *prng_seed* underneath *.ssh*. Press *Enter* for the three questions it asks.

> **$ ssh–keygen –t dsa**
> Generating public/private dsa key pair.
> Enter file in which to save the key (/home/user1/.ssh/id_dsa):
> . . . .
> . . . .
> Your public key has been saved in /home/user1/.ssh/id_dsa.pub.
> The key fingerprint is:
> 7f:21:56:85:70:a8:f6:b9:37:8c:d2:05:cf:10:27:9b user1@hp01

DSA is an encryption method and stands for *Digital Security Algorithm*. There are a couple of other methods, but DSA is preferred.

3. Change to the *.ssh* sub-directory.
4. Save the key located in the *id_dsa.pub* file into a new file called *authorized_keys*.

   $ cat id_dsa.pub >> authorized_keys

5. Repeat steps 2 through 4 on each system on the network where *user1* requires passwordless access using the *ssh* command. On each system where you run *ssh-keygen*, copy the contents of *id_dsa.pub* file and append to the *authorized_keys* file on *hp01*. The *authorized_keys* file on *hp01* will eventually contain public authentication keys for all the systems where *ssh-keygen* is run.

   $ cat /home/user1/.ssh/authorized_keys
   ssh-dss
   AAAB3NzaC1kc3MAAACBAPbRCVE820BIPMUNV2VdIKoq/s0tD3hqvIR5z+sarhbbjO218M7i
   9AUA6mmvVizC0fxRxIpiNIIdB42H58dK5hvHgeJR/fQTmPkAgvVirXIsJNTfe2x7H7YoV4FqynEm9a
   G9BuWqxPbVZPty/jawb7mJ9TR+E++k8Xnfnm/lvq5pAAAAFQCuqafHQAz23bQzPJi8HFYS3SbTb
   QAAAIB1d3Go+MVEKMs/CbFPItDRowITHICO/sK6zHnhZhpjY90i5L0EhgbATu2Y2wlmOtZ6BMkea
   m6sBrdjxj1UtS1vwE9xXjJ3afJBUheVzLjrV4dyaZP6D1P9vjSiBfty/PEQh8gKcql7rEg+vYBYUao7qR
   vAL9dSVhEzwNsxApZyiQAAAIEAmiWdn3u7FThSWzbpbd0svu74waYvdqFl1Hepj/t23DdLqEBeKs
   TzsIqpx5MSEdgxEII159zkPdj5PaiD8GCJvJ1+xHBv37ZUVYtY1s0KDILSYY277T/p0MAEpla73fY8Z
   gm2ZuadzxuKt5Cx2GGGv2jJH+ZMXtZsNdKxAcRZ2xl= user1@hp01
   ssh-dss
   AAAAB3NzaC1kc3MAAACBAJ2vUeZCBV1nTNJSg8/4vMo+kcrowRDAJzOFM4aokUI5YleFOBGQr
   cUwTA+t76j+HNRMkR0375fzf2OjXNcK3jRxJLDUID3aWIp7Ifzh95dHQEvaCV890clp0IC+6twapejN
   LR7gg9dmZgIB+3kIbNR6qgel4ddIDFfIGHDWA9arAAAAFQD2g7oI+M8XCqqMa0QQqrj/seLnVQAA
   AIB92R3QVPKgv5T7ERWfIhrW1rVmYJ6X7/davPjoL0PU1ecAmC0zaG5EAwS1ybZQv4sB0JOcJnI
   oKaDWaahb2dYYA2TW6EzDYTXoD8tF8CjhTUwo7CA7GMitJZJ7SQi3gQTKY3GK6c48o14GoWv
   2oAMKxVpneS192kcbvdjmGgmO5gAAAIAL3+TEYAhSRdd9LuMHrYTEF3FIZVDqBIMa0nYO5siC
   LFWRoiLqXqtkz5aJmZSDw9hdOEBLd01zDqHEylfVGSXbL2IIFrrmGUm8dSj48utefuPz8jS/eknAAB
   WQQxg5b52qSksWGW6HsicG2sf5a4866Lk8kII+YbnPH9Sq+LIvyg== user1@hp02

6. Ensure that the *authorized_keys* file has 644 permissions. If not, modify them.

   $ chmod 644 authorized_keys

7. Modify permissions on *user1*'s home directory to 755.

   $ chmod 755 $HOME

8. Copy the *authorized_keys* file from *hp01* to *$HOME/.ssh* sub-directory of *user1* on other systems. This way *user1* will have identical file contents for *authorized_keys* across the board.
9. Login as *user1* from *hp01* to *hp02* using the *ssh* command. Answer "yes" to the question it asks and then supply *user1*'s password.

```
$ ssh  hp02
```
The authenticity of host 'hp02 (192.168.1.202)' can't be established.
RSA key fingerprint is 25:24:a0:e7:e8:25:96:7d:70:bd:72:db:9b:ff:1c:1b.
Are you sure you want to continue connecting (yes/no)? **yes**
Warning: Permanently added 'hp02,192.168.1.202' (RSA) to the list of known hosts.
Password:
. . . .

. . . .
Rights for non-DOD U.S. Government Departments and Agencies are as set
forth in FAR 52.227-19(c)(1,2).

This creates a file called *known_hosts* under *$HOME/.ssh* directory on *hp01*. The
known_hosts file contains something similar to the following:

```
$ cat  /home/user1/.ssh/known_hosts
```
hp02,192.168.1.202 ssh-rsa
AAAAB3NzaC1yc2EAAAABlwAAAIEAxFjYK353o1fgXMBfySxgPLnhg5oWS+f8nAJx3SO40pfB3Dc
A1HLIEV0w2NKmEfgFQYOeoeMfp0IRqYxnyqNo33v3qbRjAxm6emgB2Q0xcUvL55bem0q6IMEfV
n+ycrHsEMu1B1c1pa4b3G1HX1hjcHwp3PA4MmIsyLArRbybWEU=

On each subsequent login from *hp01* to *hp02*, this file is referenced and *user1* will be allowed
a passwordless entry into *hp02*.

This completes the procedure for setting up passwordless entry into *hp02* from *hp01* for *user1* for
ssh, scp, and *sftp* commands.

38.3   Pluggable Authentication Module (PAM)

The *Pluggable Authentication Module* (PAM) is a standard set of library routines that allows using
any authentication service available on a system for user authentication, password modification,
and user account validation purposes. For example, when a user authentication is required, the
request first goes to PAM which determines the correct verification method to be used and returns
an appropriate response. The user authentication methods supported include the */etc/passwd* file,
NIS, NIS+, and trusted system. Users and programs that require authentication do not know what
method is being used. The PAM framework provides easy integration of additional security
technologies into HP-UX system entry commands.

There are two PAM configuration files: */etc/pam.conf* and */etc/pam_user.conf*. The former controls
system-wide user authentication and the latter controls per-user authentication.

The default */etc/pam.conf* file is shown below:

```
# cat  /etc/pam.conf
# PAM configuration
#
# Authentication management
login          auth      required      /usr/lib/security/libpam_unix.1
su             auth      required      /usr/lib/security/libpam_unix.1
```

```
. . . . . . . .
. . . . . . . .
# Account management
login          account        required        /usr/lib/security/libpam_unix.1
su             account        required        /usr/lib/security/libpam_unix.1
. . . . . . . .
. . . . . . . .
# Session management
login          session        required        /usr/lib/security/libpam_unix.1
dtlogin        session        required        /usr/lib/security/libpam_unix.1
. . . . . . . .
. . . . . . . .
# Password management
login          password       required        /usr/lib/security/libpam_unix.1
passwd         password       required        /usr/lib/security/libpam_unix.1
. . . . . . . .
. . . . . . . .
```

In this file, four security mechanisms are defined for authenticating users: *Authentication Management*, *Account Management*, *Session Management*, and *Password Management*.

Authentication management authenticates a user. Account management determines if a user's account is valid by checking for password and password aging attributes. Session management establishes and terminates user login sessions. Password management changes a user's password.

Each line under the four authentication management headings contain five columns. The first column depicts the name of the service, such as *login*, *ftp*, etc. The second column categorizes the module in one of the four authentication mechanisms. The third column tells how to control more than one definitions for the same service: "required", "optional", or "sufficient" keywords can be used. The fourth column lists pathname to the library file to be used to implement the service. The last column is optional and may contain any options, such as debug and nowarn.

This file must be owned by *root* with 444 permissions.

The default */etc/pam_user.conf* file is shown below:

```
# cat  /etc/pam_user.conf
. . . . . . . .
. . . . . . . .
# user_name  module_type  module_path options
#
# For example:
#
# user_a     auth           /usr/lib/security/libpam_unix.1    debug
# user_a     auth           /usr/lib/security/libpam_dce.1     try_first_pass
# user_a     password       /usr/lib/security/libpam_unix.1    debug
. . . . . . . .
. . . . . . . .
```

This file consists of four columns. The first column contains name of the user, the second column categorizes the service, the third column lists pathname to the library file to be used to implement the service, and the last column specifies any options to be used. The second, third, and fourth columns correspond to second, third, and fourth columns, respectively, in the */etc/pam.conf* file.

SAM can be used to control system-wide PAM configuration. Follow the links below:

☞Go to SAM → Auditing and Security → Authenticated Commands. Add, remove, or modify a service as desired.

38.4 The *chroot* Jail

The *chroot* (**change root**) utility changes the directory specified at the command line to become the root directory for the specified command. The new path will be seen by the command as root (/) and it will not be able to see any other directory paths outside of this new path. This creates a *chroot* jail for the command. If the command being executed requires any additional files in the *chroot* directory path, those files are required to be copied there, otherwise you will get an error message.

For example, to change root directory for the *ioscan* command so */etc* becomes the root directory for it and files outside of */etc* become invisible, execute the following:

> **# chroot /etc ioscan**
> ioscan: not found

The *ioscan* command is located in */usr/sbin* directory. When you specified */etc* with the *chroot* command, you restricted *chroot* not to look for *ioscan* outside the boundaries of */etc*. An error message "ioscan: not found" was displayed as it was unable to find the command under */etc*.

38.5 Security Monitoring, Hardening, and Reporting Tools

Several built-in HP-UX and third-party security tools are available that can be employed to perform security vulnerability tests on an HP-UX system. Some of these tools include *Crack, COPS, ISS, SATAN, Bastille,* and *HIDS* and are described briefly in the following paragraphs.

Crack identifies dictionary-based easily crackable passwords in the */etc/passwd* file. This tool allows to configure different types of password guesses.

Computer Oracle and Password System (COPS) is a collection of tools that gathers operating system security weaknesses and generates reports for review. In some cases it automatically fixes one or more weaknesses. It can be configured to send alerts. COPS can be downloaded from the internet.

Internet Security Scan (ISS) checks for a number of known security holes, such as problems with sendmail and improperly configured NFS. ISS can be downloaded from the internet.

Security Administrators Tool for Analyzing Networks (SATAN) gathers network security weaknesses and generates reports for review. SATAN can be downloaded from the internet.

Bastille is a security hardening and lockdown tool that enhances the security of an HP-UX system by implementing various levels of hardening. It allows you to configure various services and settings to make them more secure and turn unneeded services off. This tool can be run in either interactive or non-interactive mode. Bastille is part of HP-UX 11i.

Host Intrusion Detection System (HIDS) is a client/server tool that monitors one or more systems for unauthorized access and suspicious activities that might cause damage. It detects possible attacks on HP-UX systems. HIDS gathers security information from all configured systems and displays results in GUI form. The activities that HIDS monitor include system and application programs with associated configuration and log files, file additions and deletions, public writable files, newly created setuid programs, and files modified by non-owners.

38.6   Common HP-UX System Hardening Tasks

Some HP-UX system hardening recommendations are listed below. Implementing all (or part that suits your requirements) in an HP-UX environment helps ensure systems are safer and more protected against unknown and outside threats.

1. Convert a system to trusted mode security, if applications allow.
2. Implement standard mode security extensions, if you have HP-UX 11iv2 or 11iv3.
3. Implement password aging on HP-UX 11iv1. Disable accounts that are no longer accessed over a certain period of time. Force users to change their passwords periodically.
4. Implement shadow password with 400 permissions to *root* user.
5. Disable use of the *write* command by defining "mesg –n" in the system-wide user profiles.
6. Create hidden home directory, such as */home/.root,* for *root* user account at an alternate directory location. Set 700 permissions on the directory.
7. Set the umask value to 077 in *root* user's .profile.
8. Set TMOUT variable in *root* user's .profile to, for example 900 (seconds). This would force *root* to log off if it has been idle for 900 seconds.
9. Check the contents of */etc/passwd* and */etc/group* files periodically using the *pwck* and *grpck* commands, respectively, for any discrepancies, including non-*root* users with UID 0, no passwords, and no home directories.
10. Check log files, including */var/adm/sulog, /var/adm/wtmp, /etc/utmp, /var/adm/btmp* on a regular basis for user login activities.
11. Set 644 permissions on */var/adm/btmp, /var/adm/wtmp*, and */etc/utmp* files.
12. Control the usage of setuid and setgid programs. Use the *find* command to list all files owned by *root* that have setuid and setgid bits set. Analyze the file usage and unset the bits, if not needed.
13. Execute security vulnerability tests on a regular basis. You may want to schedule such tests to run automatically via *cron*.
14. Disable network services, such as *rlogin, remsh, rexec, ident, rusers, finger, tftp, bootps, instl_bootd, uucp, ntalk*, and *rpc.ttdbserver* in */etc/inetd.conf* file. Ensure they are not being used before disabling them.
15. Disable network services, such as *rbootd, routed, mrouted, gated*, and *rdpd* in */etc/rc.config.d/netdaemons* file. Ensure they are not being used before disabling them.

16. Disable *telnet* and *ftp* and use *ssh, scp*, and *sftp* instead. Perform enough due diligence prior to disabling these services. Many applications rely on them.
17. Disallow system users – *uucp, nuucp, sys, lp, hpdb, www, webadmin, smbnull, nobody, adm, bin*, and *daemon* – from using FTP. Update */etc/ftpd/ftpusers* file accordingly.
18. Enable *inetd* logging.
19. Set 777 permissions and sticky bit on all world-writeable directories, such as */tmp* and */var/tmp*.
20. Disable NFS client, NFS server, PC NFS, and AutoFS functionalities in */etc/rc.config.d/nfsconf* file. Before disabling, ensure they are not in use. If you must use the NFS server functionality, make sure that the exported resources are only available to the specific systems that need access to them.
21. Configure */var/adm/inetd.sec* file to control access to network services.
22. Control the use of *cron* and *at* via user entries in *cron.allow, cron.deny, at.allow*, and *at.deny* files in the */var/adm/cron* directory. It is better to remove both *at.allow* and *at.deny*, if this service is not used. Remove *cron.deny* and update *cron.allow* file with entries for only those users that must require *cron* scheduling.
23. Maintain and monitor user (*$HOME/.rhosts*) and system (*/etc/hosts.equiv*) equivalency files. These files are referenced by *remsh, rlogin, rcp*, and *rexec* utilities for passwordless entry into a system. Discourage the use of this trust mechanism especially for the *root* user. Use *ssh* instead. See section on Secure Shell earlier in this chapter.
24. Disable direct *root* login. The *root* user should only be allowed to login at the system console. Create */etc/securetty* file and define "console" in it to disable *root* access via *telnet*. This file should have 400 permissions on it. Update */etc/opt/sshd/sshd_config* file and define "PermitRootLogin no" in it to disable *root* access via *ssh*.
25. Change the password for the *Admin* MP user.
26. Implement the use of *sudo*. Force administrators to log in with their user IDs and then use *sudo* if needed. Allow limited access to privileged commands, if needed, to non-system administrators via *sudo*. Update the */etc/sudoers* file accordingly.
27. Implement *IPSec* and *IPFilter* to secure IP packets transmitted over the network to control their flow.
28. Implement *TCP Wrapper* for *telnet* and *ftp*, if you must keep the two services enabled. Update */etc/inetd.conf* file accordingly.

Summary

This chapter discussed various ways of securing an HP-UX system. You looked at password aging and how to define aging parameters for user accounts. You learned benefits associated with shadow password and how to implement and reverse its implementation. You studied trusted mode security and how to convert and unconvert an HP-UX system to and from this level of user security mechanism. You learned standard mode security extensions that has recently been made available in HP-UX. This product provides features that are otherwise available only after converting a system to trusted security mode.

You looked at benefits associated with using secure shell. How ssh encrypts information. You saw how to access a remote HP-UX machine via ssh and setup a passwordless user entry onto a system. You looked at Pluggable Authentication Module, associated benefits, and how to configure its files for authentication purposes. You learned the concept of *chroot* and how to create it.

At the end of the chapter, a few security hardening and scanning tools were discussed. Finally, you were supplied with a list of common system security recommendations that you should look at implementing in an HP-UX system environment to elevate system security level.

Appendix A

Sample CSA Exam Questions

This appendix covers sample questions for HP Certified Systems Administrator exam. Answers to these questions are given in Appendix B. I recommend that you first read and understand the material in this book thoroughly and then take this quiz.

1. What benefit you get by adding a journal to a file system?
   - A. Automatic defragmentation   B. Better buffer cache utilization C. Faster recovery time
   - D. Guaranteed data integrity   E. Provides an audit trail

2. Which LVM structure holds a file system?
   - A. Volume group   B. VGRA area   C. Physical volume   D. Logical volume

3. Choose TWO significant features of VxVM on HP-UX.
   - A. Online administration and backup   B. Only choice for swap partition
   - C. Runs independently from the HP-UX kernel   D. Supports RAID 0, 1, 5, 1+0, and 0+1

4. Why do you use the su command?
   - A. To log out of the system   B. To shutdown the system
   - C. To switch your user id   D. To display a list of logged in users

5. What command is used to display your current group?
   - A. newgroup   B. who   C. id   D. whoami

6. Which key combination is used for command line completion in the POSIX shell?
   - A. <tab> <tab>   B. <esc> <k>   C. <esc> <esc>   D. <up arrow> <up arrow>

7. Which command determines how many disks are attached to a SCSI controller?
   - A. diskinfo   B. lsdev   C. cat /etc/scsiconf   D. pvdisplay   E. ioscan

8. What does the PATH variable contain?
   - A. Directories you can cd into
   - B. Access paths to a disk
   - C. Directory search order when using the find command
   - D. Directory search order used when locating a command for execution

9. What is the purpose of a MAC address?
   - A. Controls the processor   B. Points to a location in physical system memory
   - C. Identifies a LAN card port   D. Locates a block of data on a disk

10. Which of the following THREE ways can you boot to install HP-UX?
   - A. An NFS mounted file system   B. LAN   C. CD-ROM/DVD-ROM

D. Tape   E. IDE drive F. Mirrored disk

11. Why do you use CIFS/9000 software product?
  A. To share directories between Windows and Mainframe computers
  B. To share directories between UNIX and Mainframe computers
  C. To share directories between UNIX and Windows systems
  D. None of the above

12. What Online JFS command is used to increase the size of a file system without unmounting it.
  A. fsadm   B. lvextend   C. extendfs   D. fsextend

13. Which of the following TWO file transfer protocols are used by Ignite-UX server?
  A. FTP   B. TFTP   C. NFS   D. CIFS

14. List THREE advantages of Online JFS product.
  A. It can extend the size of a file system online. B. It defragments a file system automatically.
  C. It can reduce a file system size online.   D. It can increase a logical volume size online.
  E. None of the above.

15. What is the main difference between PCI and PCI-X cards?
  A. PCI-X cards are smaller than PCI cards.
  B. PCI cards are smaller than PCI-X cards.
  C. PCI cards are faster than PCI-X cards (almost double speed).
  D. PCI-X cards are faster than PCI cards (almost double speed).

16. What additional benefit do scp and sftp commands have over cp and ftp commands, respectively?
  A. Enhanced security   B. Enhanced speed
  C. Enhanced command line options   D. All of the above

17. Why quoting is used in shell scripts?
  A. To treat special characters as regular characters B. To ensure uppercase letters are displayed
  C. To set command substitution   D. To highlight special characters

18. Which of the following extracts all lines from a file that do not contain the specified pattern?
  A. egrep –v pattern filename   B. grep -v pattern filename
  C. grep –n pattern filename   D. fgrep -v pattern filename

19. How do you rename a directory called "scripts1" to a directory called "scripts2" in the present working directory?
  A. ln scripts1 scripts2   B. ren scripts1 scripts2
  C. mv scripts1 scripts2   D. mv scripts2 scripts1

20. What does the command chown used for?
  A. To change your user id
  B. To make you the owner of all files in your directory
  C. To change the time stamp of a file or directory
  D. To change the ownership of a file or directory

21. What signifies the end of an "if" statement in the POSIX Shell?

A. endif   B. fi   C. }   D. elseif

22. Access control list (ACL) allow(s):
    A. Controlling file access based on time-of-day restrictions
    B. Extending file mode on top of standard UNIX file permissions
    C. Listing all resources from which a user is currently granted access
    D. Controlling who has permission to use the chown and chmod commands

23. The "break" command in the POSIX shell is used to break out of a:
    A. Shell script   B. Function   C. Loop   D. Sleep routine

24. How would you capture the result of the "who" and the "date" commands into a variable called VAR in the POSIX Shell?
    A. VAR=$(who|date)   B. VAR=$(who;date)
    C. VAR=$(who,date)   D. Who>VAR;date>VAR

25. What key in the POSIX shell, when repeated twice, completes file names?
    A. [space]   B. *   C. [ESC]   D. [TAB]

26. What command counts the number of lines in a file?
    A. fcount   B. wc   C. wordc   D. grep

27. As a root user, what command would you use to influence the priority that a command runs at?
    A. pri   B. priority   C. nice   D. chpri

28. HP-UX _____ swap space for each new process spawned.
    A. Frees   B. Builds   C. Locks   D. Reserves

29. On an HP-UX system the command to view disk space utilization is:
    A. freedisk   B. scandisk   C. bdf   D. diskinfo

30. Which command lists full details of a device file?
    A. listf   B. lsdev   C. lssf   D. ls

31. The Software Distributor tools will only run if the following daemon is running:
    A. swinstalld   B. swdistd   C. swlogd   D. swagentd

32. Can a user define a default printer for himself (separate from the system's default printer)?
    A. Yes, using SAM   B. Yes, using the lpadmin command
    C. Yes, using the LPDEST environmental variable   D. No, users are not allowed to define a default
    printer for themselves

33. The command to submit a cron job is?
    A. cronfile   B. crontab   C. cron.allow   D. /usr/sbin/cron

34. If you create a sub-directory by the name "custom" under the /etc/skel/ directory and it
contains a file by the name "config", then new user accounts created via Sam will:
    A. Contain a symbolic link to this file structure
    B. Have a local file, ~/config, which is read-only for the account owner

C. Not have any access to the file custom

D. Have a local file, ~/custom/config, belonging to the new user

35. The which command is used to determine:
    A. The current version and release of an executable
    B. Pseudo terminal your session is running from.
    C. The absolute path where an executable is run from.
    D. Which compiler options were used to create an executable.

36. The main function of the hpux utility is to:
    A. Load the kernel into memory
    B. List the /stand directory contents
    C. Execute ISL
    D. Rebuild the kernel

37. What command is used to create the whatis database to facilitate keyword search in man pages?
    A. catman   B. man –k   C. echo $MANPATH   D. All of the above.

38. Which of the THREE are the main components of an HP-UX system?
    A. Kernel   B. Directory Structure   C. Shell   D. User

39. Which of the following are features of HP-UX? Choose THREE.
    A. Multi-tasking   B. Multi-user   C. Time sharing   D. Single-user

40. Which of the following can be used to log in to an HP-UX system?
    A. At the CDE console
    B. Using the telnet command
    C. At the system console
    D. Using the ssh command
    E. All of the above.

41. What component of the HP-UX structure the user interacts with?
    A. The directory structure   B. The kernel   C. The shell   D. All of the above.

42. True or False. A user password is case-insensitive.
    A. True   B. False

43. What is the default user password length in HP-UX?
    A. 10 characters   B. 6-8 characters   C. 6-10 characters   D. 7 characters

44. Can a normal user change other users' passwords?
    A. Yes   B. No

45. Which command is used to change a user password?
    A. passwd   B. password   C. pass   D. None of the above.

46. How many arguments are in "cal 12 2006" command?
    A. 3   B. 2   C. 1   D. 0

47. The pwd command:
    A. Changes directory path
    B. Displays current absolute directory path
    C. Displays current relative directory path
    D. Both A and B

48. Where does "cd ~users" takes you if run as user1?

A. To user1's home directory   B. To user2's home directory
C. To user2 sub-directory under user1's home directory   D. To root user's home directory

49. What information do logname and whoami commands return?
     A. Your home directory path   B. Your login information
     C. Your UID   D. Your user name

50. Which command only displays a user's group memberships?
     A. id   B. id –a   C. groups   D. usermod

51. Which commands display hardware model of a system? Choose TWO.
     A. model   B. system   C. getconf   D. id

52. Which of the following shows current system run level?
     A. rwho   B. who   C. uptime   D. who –r

53. Which command compares two text files and displays the differences?
     A. comp   B. diff   C. differ   D. All of the above.

54. Which command enables you to view syntax of the */etc/passwd* file?
     A. man 4 passwd   B. man passwd   C. man –k passwd   D. help passwd

55. If lost+found directory is removed, what is the recommended method of recreating it.
     A. mkdir lost+found   B. touch lost+found   C. mklost+found   D. mkdir l+f

56. Which directory is typically used to hold additional software products installed on a system?
     A. /opt   B. /var   C. /etc   D. /usr

57. What is the default location where user home directories are created?
     A. /export/home   B. /home   C. /usr   D. /usr/home

58. The path, /home/user1/dir1/scripts1, is absolute or relative.
     A. Absolute   B. Relative

59. Which command gives you the type of file?
     A. filetype   B. filename   C. file   D. type

60. What information does the inode of a symbolic link file contains?
     A. Nothing   B. The creation time of the linked file
     C. The name of the linked file   D. The path to the linked file

61. What type of file contains major and minor numbers in its inode?
     A. Regular files   B. Named pipes   C. Directory files   D. Device Files

62. What is the maximum number of alphanumeric characters that a file or directory name can contain?
     A. 128   B. 8   C. 256   D. 255

63. What option with the ls command is used to list hidden files?
     A. –d   B. –l   C. –a   D. –h

64. To create a file of size zero, which command would you use.
     A. touch   B. vi   C. cat   D. edit

65. To view all lines in a file starting from line number 100 onwards, which command would you run.
     A. tail filename   B. tail +100 filename   C. tail –100 filename   D. tail 100 filename

66. Which command displays the legible contents of a non-text file?
     A. strings   B. cat   C. view   D. vi

67. The grep command is used to display lines in a file that match a certain pattern. What modifications does the grep command make in the file?
     A. None   B. Removes the matched lines from the file
     C. Removes the file contents   D. Modifies the file

68. What is not a criteria for finding a file using the find command?
     A. Modification time   B. hostname   C. Directory name   D. File name

69. Can you link files or directories across file systems using symbolic link?
     A. Yes   B. No

70. Can you link two directories using hard link?
     A. Yes   B. No

71. In vi, to copy 5 lines and paste them above cursor position, which one of the following would you use.
     A. 5yyP   B. 5yyp   C. 5pyy   D. yy5P

72. What two modes are available to modify file permissions? Choose TWO.
     A. chmod   B. Symbolic   C. chown   D. Octal

73. To modify a file permissions to get 751, which of the following would you run? Choose TWO.
     A. chmod +751 filename   B. chmod rwxr-x--x filename
     C. chmod u+rwxrxx filename   D. chmod 751 filename

74. What is the default umask value in HP-UX?
     A. 022   B. 027   C. 000   D. 777

75. What option would you use with the umask command to display umask value in symbolic notation?
     A. –A   B. –B   C. –S   D. –s

76. The following are default permissions on files and directories.
     A. 777 on files and 666 on directories   B. 666 on files and 777 on directories
     C. 777 on both files and directories.   D. 666 on both files and directories.

77. What command is used to change a user's primary group temporarily?
     A. chgrp   B. newgrp   C. chsh   D. newgroup

78. What two commands are used to change file ownership and group membership? Choose TWO.
     A. chown   B. chgrp   C. chowner   D. chgroup

79. To prevent users from removing other users' files in a public directory, what would you do?
- A. Set setuid bit on the directory
- B. Set setgid bit on the directory
- C. Set setpid bit on the directory
- D. Set sticky bit on the directory

80. Which option with the chmod command enables you to set permissions recursively?
- A. –R
- B. –A
- C. –r
- D. –a

81. To search for all files in the /usr file system that have setgid bit set on them, which of the following would you run?
- A. find /usr –perm 1000
- B. find /usr –perm 2000
- C. fine /usr –perm 4000
- D. find /usr –perm 4000 –exec rm {} \;

82. Which command prints ACL on a file?
- A. getacl
- B. getfacl
- C. All of the above
- D. None of the above

83. What does the following do?

    setacl –m u:user2:7 file10

- A. Allocates read, write, and execute permissions to user2 on file10.
- B. Removes read, write, and execute permissions for user2 on file10.
- C. Allocates read, write, and execute permissions to user1 on file10.
- D. Removes read, write, and execute permissions for user1 on file10

84. What does the following command do?

    setacl –s u::rwx,g::rw,o:r,u:user3:rwx file9

- A. Recalculates existing permissions on file9 based on the new ACL mask
- B. Substitutes existing permissions on file9 based on the new ACL mask
- C. Substitutes existing permissions on file9 with the ones specified with the command
- D. All of the above.

85. What does]] do in vi?
- A. Takes you to the last line of the file
- B. Takes you to the first line of the file
- C. Takes you to the end of the line
- D. Takes you to the start of the line

86. What commands are available in vi to get you to edit mode?
- A. A, a, I, i, o, and O
- B. A, I, and O
- C. a, i, and o
- D. Append, Insert, and Open

87. Which command in vi removes a character preceding the current cursor position?
- A. R
- B. x
- C. X
- D. r

88. What does the following do in vi?
    :%s/old_text/new_text/g

- A. Replaces all occurrences of old_text with new_text
- B. Replaces the next occurrence of old_text with new_text
- C. Replaces all occurrences of new_text with old_text
- D. Replaces the previous occurrence of old_text with new_text

89. What does $0 represent with the awk command?
    A. The command name   B. The first command line argument
    C. All command line arguments   D. The last command line argument

90. What does the following sed command do?
    sed –n '/root/p' /etc/group

    A. Displays lines from the /etc/group file containing the pattern root
    B. Displays lines from the /etc/group file not containing the pattern root
    C. Hides lines from the /etc/group file containing the pattern root
    D. Displays lines in duplicate from the /etc/group file containing the pattern root

91. Which option is used with the sed command to perform multiple edits in a file?
    A. –e   B. –l   C. –s   D. –E

92. Which is the default shell in HP-UX?
    A. Bourne   B. POSIX   C. BASH   D. Korn

93. Which of the following is used to display the value contained in the variable EDITOR?
    A. display $EDITOR   B. display EDITOR   C. echo EDITOR   D. echo $EDITOR

94. Which of the following is not a pre-defined environment variable?
    A. HOME   B. LOGNAME   C. NAME   D.TZ

95. Which of the following alters your primary command prompt to look like the following. Choose TWO.
    < user2@hp01:/usr/bin >

    A. PS2="< `logname`@`hostname`:\$PWD >"   B. PS1="< $LOGNAME@`hostname`:\$PWD
    >"
    C. PS2="< $LOGNAME@`hostname`:\$PWD >"   D. PS1="< `logname`@`hostname`:\$PWD >"

96. Which symbol redirects error messages to alternate location?
    A. #   B. | C. <   D. >

97. Which command is used to unset an alias?
    A. unsetalias   B. unalias   C. alias rm   D. unset alias

98. What does a pipe do?
    A. Takes the output of one command and pass it as input to the next command
    B. Takes the input from one command and pass it as input to the next command
    C. Takes the output from two files and pass it as input to the next command
    D. None of the above

99. Which command is used to change the priority of a running process?
    A. renicing   B. nice   C. renice   D. niceagain

100. Which of the following are immune to hangup signals? Choose TWO.
    A. nohup cp –rp /dir1 /dir2   B. nohup cp /dir1 /dir2
    C. cp –rp /dir1 /dir2   D. nohup rcp –rp /dir1 server2:/dir2

101. Which character when specified at the end of a command runs the command in background?
    A. @   B. %   C. $ D. &

102. Which of the following is not a system administrator resource?
    A. docs.hp.com   B. help.com   C. Online man pages   D. itrc.hp.com

103. How would you run SAM in restricted mode?
    A. sam   B. sam &   C. sam –restricted   D. sam –r

104. Which directory the samlog file is located?
    A. /var/adm/sam   B. /var/adm/sam/log   C. /var/sam/log   D. /var/adm/log

105. Which command is used to view sam log?
    A. sam_view   B. samlog_view   C. samlog_viewer   D. samview

106. What major categories of HP-UX systems are available? Choose TWO.
    A. HP Proliant   B. HP Netfinity   C. HP 9000   D. HP Integrity

107. Which feature of HP-UX Operating Environment software allows you to replace a PCI card online?
    A. PCI/R   B. Card/R   C. OLA/R   D. A/R

108. What is the number of slots in a Superdome PCI I/O chassis?
    A. 8   B. 4   C. 12   D. 16

109. What is the maximum number of processors that can be installed on a single cell board?
    A. 8   B. 4   C. 16   D. 12

110. What is the minimum and maximum number of node partitions that an HP-UX server can have?
    A. 2 and 16   B. 2 and 8   C. 1 and 8   D. 1 and 16

111. What is the maximum number of virtual partitions that you can have in an HP-UX server?
    A. 32   B. 64   C. 128   D. 1

112. What does the CLAIMED status under 'S/W State' of the ioscan command mean? Choose TWO.
    A. The software driver for the device is properly bound to it
    B. The software driver for the device is not properly bound to it
    C. The device is available for use
    D. Both A and B

113. Which option with the ioscan command reads and displays device information from running kernel?
    A. –H   B. –f   C. –r   D. –k

114. Which option with ioscan command displays logical device file associated with a device in the output?
    A. –m   B. –n   C. –k   D. –l

115. Which directory under /dev holds device files for tape devices?
    A. rmt   B. mt   C. dev/mt   D. dev/rmt

116. Major number points to the device driver in the kernel. True or False?

A. True   B. False

117. What kind of information the minor number points to?
    A. It points to a specific device within a category of devices
    B. It lists a specific device within a category of devices
    C. It points to the type of device
    D. None of the above

118. Which command displays you major numbers for device drivers configured into the kernel?
    A. lsview   B. lsdev   C. ioscan   D. lanscan

119. Which of the three commands can be used to create device files? Choose THREE.
    A. mksf   B. insf   C. mkfs   D. mknod

120. Which command displays diagnostic messages?
    A. dmesg   B. ioscan   C. lsdev   D. lssf

121. HP-UX 11iv2 runs on both HP 9000 and HP Integrity architecture systems. True or False?
    A. True   B. False

122. HP-UX 11iv1 runs on HP Integrity systems. True or False?
    A. True   B. False

123. HP Online JFS and MirrorDisk/UX software are included in which operating environment bundles. Choose TWO.
    A. Foundation OE   B. Enterprise OE   C. Mission Critical OE   D. Both A and C

124. HP ServiceGuard software is part of which operating environment software bundle?
    A. Mission Critical OE   B. Enterprise OE
    C. Foundation OE   D. You always have to purchase separately

125. Management Processor is also called?
    A. Guardain System Performance   B. Guardian System Processing
    C. General Service Processor   D. Guardian Service Processor

126. Which command at the BCH level on an HP 9000 PA-RISC machine is used to find and display all possible bootable devices on the system?
    A. fi   B. find   C. se   D. search

127. What two methods are available to you to setup network parameters? Choose TWO.
    A. At the installation time
    B. Using set_parms initial after the installation
    C. You must set them up at the installation time
    D. You cannot set them up at the installation time

128. What is the default primary swap partition size?
    A. Same as the size of system's physical memory   B. Twice the size of system's physical memory
    C. Half the size of system's physical memory   D. Four times the size of system's physical memory

129. By default, HP-UX installation program creates eight logical volumes in vg00 viz., /, /usr, /var, swap, /tmp, /home, /opt, and /stand. True or False?
    A. True   B. False

130. Which is the only file system in HP-UX that must be HFS?
    A. /stand   B. /   C. /var   D. Any application-specific file systems

131. HP Software Distributor is a client/server software. True or False?
    A. True   B. False

132. What system run levels the HP software distributor runs?
    A. Power off mode   B. Multiuser mode   C. Single user mode   D. Both B and C

133. What is the smallest unit of software management with SD-UX?
    A. Sub-product   B. Product   C. Bundle   D. Fileset

134. What is the location in the directory hierarchy of the Installed Product Database?
    A. /var/sw/products   B. /var/adm/products
    C. /var/adm/sw/products   D. /var/adm/sw/software

135. Which SD-UX command uses IPD to search and display installed software information?
    A. swlist   B. swverify   C. swinstall   D. swconfig

136. Protected software require customer ID and codeword to be installed. True or False.
    A. True   B. False

137. What are the two SD-UX agents that make SD-UX utilities to work? Choose TWO.
    A. swagent   B. swd   C. swagentd   D. swagentdaemon

138. Which is not an SD-UX command?
    A. swpackage   B. swinstall   C. swunreg   D. swreg

139. Where is the HP-UX daemon log file located in the directory hierarchy?
    A. /var/adm/sw   B. /var/adm/sw/products   C. /var/adm/products   D. /var/sw/products

140. Which of the two methods can be used to stop the swagentd daemon? Choose TWO.
    A. swagentd –k   B. swagentd –s   C. /sbin/init.d/swagentd shut   D. /sbin/init.d/swagentd stop

141. By default, the swlist command displays the following software component?
    A. Bundle   B. Product   C. Sub-product   D. Fileset

142. Which is the correct method of using the swinstall command to load software called soft1 located in the depot /opt/depots?
    A. swinstall –s soft1   B. swinstall soft1 –s
    C. swinstall /opt/depots/soft1 –s   D. swinstall –s /opt/depots

143. Which commands are used to package, unconfigure, and verify software? Choose THREE.
    A. swpackage   B. swunconfig   C. swconfig   D. swverify

144. What is the equivalent of IPD in depot?
    A. Software files   B. Software installation files   C. Log files   D. Catalog files

145. Which command copies the perl software from CD to /opt/depot depot?
    A. swcopy –s /SD_CDROM perl @ /opt/depot   B. swcopy –s /SD_CDROM/perl @ /opt/depot
    C. swcopy –s /SD_CDROM perl –d /opt/depot   D. swcopy –s /SD_CDROM/perl –d /opt/depot

146. Which SD-UX command is used to unregister a software depot?
    A. No need to unregister.   B. swunreg   C. swreg   D. Either B or C can be used.

147. Which command displays all software depots located on a remote system hp02?
    A. swlist –l depot @ hp02   B. swlist depot @ hp02
    C. swlist –l depots @ hp02   D. swlist –l depot@hp02

148. Which command removes all software from a depot /var/opt/mx/depot11 and unregisters it?
    A. swremove –d* @/var/opt/mx/depot11   B. swremove –d * @ /var/opt/mx/depot11
    C. swremove –r * @ /var/opt/mx/depot11   D. swremove * -r @ /var/opt/mx/depot11

149. What three commands are typically used for user account management? Choose THREE.
    A. useradd   B. usermod   C. userrem   D. userdel

150. The /etc/passwd file contains how many fields?
    A. Six   B. Seven   C. Eight   D. Nine

151. A user password is saved in encrypted form. How many characters does it contain?
    A. 8   B. 11   C. 13   D. 15

152. What permissions should the /etc/passwd file have?
    A. 444   B. 555   C. 440   D. 400

153. How many fields does the /etc/group file line entries contain?
    A. 3   B. 4   C. 5   D. 6

154. Which commands are used to fine syntax errors and verify the consistency of the /etc/passwd and /etc/group files? Choose TWO.
    A. passwdck   B. groupck   C. grpck   D. pwck

155. To lock the /etc/passwd file while editing, which command do you use to open it?
    A. vi /etc/passwd –l   B. pwvi   C. vi –l /etc/passwd   D. vipw

156. What is the impact of using the –o option with the useradd command have?
    A. Prevents from assigning duplicate GIDs   B. Allows to assign duplicate GIDs
    C. Prevents from assigning duplicate UIDs   D. Allows to assign duplicate UIDs

157. Which of the following command creates a user account called user5 with UID 105, belonging to primary group dba and secondary groups dba1 and unixadm. The user should have /usr/bin/sh with a new home directory created in /home?
    A. useradd –u 105 –g dba –G dba1,unixadm –m –d /home/user5 –s /usr/bin/sh user5
    B. useradd –u 105 –g dba,dba1,unixadm –m –d /home/user5 –s /usr/bin/sh user5

HP Certified Systems Administrator

C. useradd –u 105 –g dba –G dba1,unixadm –m /home/*user5* –s /usr/bin/sh *user5*
D. useradd –u 105 –G dba,dba1,unixadm –m –d /home/*user5* –s /usr/bin/sh *user5*

158. What does the following command do?
    useradd –D –b /u01/home

    A. Changes the default home directory to /u01/home for new user accounts created onwards
    B. Changes the default home directory to /u01/home for all existing users' home directories
    C. Changes the default home directory to /u01/home for all existing and new users
    D. None of the above

159. Which command locks *user5* and prevents him from logging in?
    A. passwd *user5* –lock   B. passwd –lock *user5*   C. passwd –l *user5*   D. passwd *user5* –l

160. To remove a user account along with its home directory, which command would you use?
    A. userdel *user5*   B. userdel –r *user5*   C. userdel *user5* –r   D. userrem –r *user5*

161. To force a user to change his/her password at next login, which command would you run?
    A. passwd –m *user5*   B. passwd –n *user5*   C. passwd –f *user5*   D. passwd –c *user5*

162. Which command converts a system to trusted mode and unconverts it back to normal? Choose TWO.
    A. convertts –r   B. tsconvert –r   C. converts   D. tsconvert

163. What three commands are typically used for group account management? Choose THREE.
    A. groupadd   B. groupmod   C. grouprem   D. groupdel

164. What is the name of the system-wide user initialization file for Bourne, Korn, and POSIX shell users?
    A. /etc/profile   B. $HOME/profile   C. /etc/.profile   D. /etc/swprofile

165. Which command is used to broadcast a message to all logged in users?
    A. write   B. talk   C. wall   D. broadcast

166. Which file does the last command look into?
    A. /var/adm/wtmp   B. /var/adm/btmp   C. /var/adm/utmp   D. /var/adm/ltmp

167. Which file does the lastb command look into?
    A. /var/adm/wtmp   B. /var/adm/btmp   C. /var/adm/utmp   D. /var/adm/ltmp

168. Which file does the who command look into?
    A. /var/adm/wtmp   B. /var/adm/btmp   C. /var/adm/utmp   D. /var/adm/ltmp

169. Which three solutions are available in HP-UX for disk management? Choose THREE.
    A. Logical Volume Manager   B. DiskSuite
    C. Whole disk solution   D. Veritas Volume Manager

170. You can span a file system on two disks using the whole disk solution. True or False.
    A. True   B. False

171. With LVM and VxVM, you can span a file system on multiple disks. True or False.

A. True   B. False

172. Which of the following are VxVM objects? Choose FOUR.
     A. Disk   B. Volume   C. DVD   D. Subdisk   E. Volume group F. Plex

173. Which RAID level is not supported by VxVM?
     A. 0+1   B. 1+0   C. 1   D. 5   E. 9

174. Which statement about RAID 0+1 is correct?
     A. Mirroring a concatenated volume   B. Striping a mirrored volume
     C. Mirroring a striped volume   D. Concatenating a striped volume

175. Which of the following are components of LVM? Choose THREE.
     A. Physical volume   B. Disk group   C. Volume group   D. Logical volume

176. Which command below brings a disk under LVM control and creates BDRA on it too?
     A. pvcreate –fB /dev/dsk/c1t4d0   B. pvcreate /dev/rdsk/c1t4d0
     C. pvcreate –fB /dev/rdsk/c1t4d0   D. pvcreate –f /dev/rdsk/c1t4d0

177. The group file for a volume group in LVM is a block device file. True or False.
     A. True   B. False

178. Which LVM structure is used to hold one or more physical volumes?
     A. Logical volume   B. Volume group   C. Physical volume   D. Plex

179. What is the default first minor number assigned to a logical volume device file?
     A. 0   B. 1   C. 2   D. 3

180. Which of the following is part of the LVM data structure?
     A. VGSA   B. PVRA   C. VGRA   D. BDRA   E. All of the above

181. Which command displays all devices visible to your HP-UX system?
     A. lsdev   B. lssf   C. ioscan   D. diskinfo

182. Which command displays the boot devices only?
     A. lssf   B. diskinfo   C. ioscan   D. setboot

183. Which command at the OS level displays the settings for autoboot and autosearch flags?
     A. lssf   B. setboot   C. ioscan   D. diskinfo

184. Which command displays the size and manufacturer information of a disk?
     A. diskinfo   B. ioscan   C. lsdev   D. setboot

185. Which one of the following will work?
     A. diskinfo /dev/rdsk/c1t0d0   B. diskinfo /dev/dsk/c1t0d0
     C. diskinfo c1t0d0   D. diskinfo /dev/vx/rdsk/c1t0d0

186. What is the correct syntax of the mknod command to create a device file?
     A. mknod c 64 group 0x010000   B. mknod group 64 c 0x010000

C. mknod group c 64 0x010000   D. mknod group c 0x010000 64

187. Which command displays a volume group information in detail?
    A. display   B. vgdisplay –v   C. lvdisplay   D. vgdisplay

188. Which three commands (in order) are typically used to display physical volume, logical volume, and volume group information?
    A. pvdisplay, lvdisplay, vgdisplay   B. vgdisplay, lvdisplay, pvdisplay
    C. lvdisplay, vgdisplay, pvdisplay   D. pvdisplay, vgdisplay, lvdisplay

189. Which of the following create a logical volume, lvol1, of size 500MB in vg01? Choose TWO.
    A. lvcreate –L 500 –n lvol1 /dev/vg01   B. lvcreate /dev/vg01/lvol1
    C. lvcreate –l 500 vg01 lvol1   D. lvcreate –L 500 –n lvol1 vg01

190. Which of the following extends the size of a logical volume, lvol1, located in vg01, to 800MB?
    A. lvextend –l 800 /dev/vg01/lvol1   B. lvextend –L 800 /dev/vg01/lvol1
    C. lvextend –L 800 /dev/vg01 lvol1   D. lvextend /dev/vg01/lvol1 –L 800

191. How do you view the contents of the /etc/lvmtab file?
    A. Using the strings command   B. Using the tail command
    C. Using the more command   D. Using the cat command

192. What do you mean by increasing the size of a volume group?
    A. Adding a logical volume to it   B. Adding a physical volume to it
    C. Merging with another volume group to increase the size   D. None of the above

193. Which command is used to reduce a logical volume and a volume group? Choose TWO.
    A. vgshrink   B. vgreduce   C. lvreduce   D. lvshrink

194. A disk group of VxVM is equivalent to a _____ of LVM.
    A. Logical extent   B. Physical volume   C. Logical volume   D. Volume group

195. What is the default number of file systems created at HP-UX installation time?
    A. 6   B. 7   C. 8   D. 9

196. How do you view a list of supported file systems type on HP-UX?
    A. fstyp –l   B. showfstyp –l   C. fstype –l   D. cat /etc/vfstab

197. What is the purpose of JFS intent log? Choose TWO.
    A. Keeps file system structural updates log   B. Quick system recovery after a crash
    C. Backs up file system data   D. Maintains file system data

198. Which command is correct to create a JFS file system?
    A. newfs –F vxfs vg01   B. newfs –F vxfs rlvol1
    C. newfs /dev/vg01/rlvol1 vxfs   D. newfs –F vxfs /dev/vg01/rlvol1

199. Which file contains the location information of backup superblocks for a HFS file system?
    A. /etc/sbtab.conf   B. /etc/superblock.conf   C. /etc/sbtab   D. /etc/sb.tab

200. Which of the following is correct to mount a file system?
   A. mount –F vxfs lvol1 fs1
   B. mount –F vxfs /fs1 /dev/vg01/lvol1
   C. mount –F vxfs /dev/vg01/lvol1 /fs1
   D. mount –F vxfs /dev/vg01/lvol1 fs1

201. Which file contains a list of all file systems to be mounted at system boot?
   A. /etc/vfstab   B. /etc/fstab   C. /etc/sbtab   D. /etc/fs.conf

202. What does the mount command with –a option do?
   A. Mounts all CIFS file systems listed in the /etc/fstab file
   B. Mounts all file systems that are currently not mounted and are listed in the /etc/fstab file
   C. Mounts all NFS file systems listed in the /etc/fstab file
   D. Mounts all CDFS file systems listed in the /etc/fstab file

203. Which file does the umountall command look into to unmount file systems?
   A. /etc/mnttab   B. /etc/fstab   C. /etc/vfstab   D. /etc/mnttab.conf

204. What does the mount command do when run without any options?
   A. Mounts all file systems in /etc/fstab file   B. Mounts all NFS file systems in /etc/fstab file
   C. Displays currently mounted file systems   D. Mounts all CIFS file systems in /etc/fstab file

205. An entry is made into which file when a file system is mounted?
   A. /etc/fstab   B. /etc/mnttab   C. /etc/vfstab   D. /etc/mnttab.conf

206. Which command is used to increase the size of an HFS file system online?
   A. extendfs   B. fsadm   C. extendhfs   D. None of the above

207. To increase an HFS file system size listed in /etc/fstab file, what command sequence will you run?
   A. lvextend –L 300 /dev/vg01/lvol1, fsadm –F hfs /dev/vg01/rlvol1
   B. umount /fs1, extendfs –F hfs /dev/vg01/rlvol1, lvextend –L 300 /dev/vg01/lvol1, mount /fs1
   C. umount /fs1, lvextend –L 300 /dev/vg01/lvol1, extendfs –F hfs /dev/vg01/rlvol1, mount /fs1
   D. Both B and C

208. Which of the following is correct to reduce the size of a JFS file system to 200MB? You have OnlineJFS product installed.
   A. lvreduce –L 200 /dev/vg01/lvol2
   B. umount /fs2, lvreduce –L 200 /dev/vg01/lvol2, reducefs –F hfs /dev/vg01/rlvol2, mount /fs2
   C. lvreduce –l 200 /dev/vg01/lvol2
   D. lvreduce –L 200 /fs2

209. Which command is used to see what processes are using a file system?
   A. fuser –cU /fs2   B. fuser –Cu /fs2   C. fuser –ck /fs2   D. fuser –cu /fs2

210. Which command would you use to mount a DVD?
   A. mount /dev/dsk/c1t4d0 /SD_CDROM   B. mount –F cdfs /dev/dsk/c1t4d0
   /SD_CDROM
   C. mount –F dvdfs /dev/dsk/c1t4d0 /SD_CDROM   D. mount –F cdfs /dev/rdsk/c1t4d0
   /SD_CDROM

211. Which command is used to check and repair a damaged CD file system?

A. fsck   B. fsdvd   C. fscd   D. None of the above.

212. Which of the following works to check and repair an entire JFS file system?
      A. fsck –F vxfs –o log /dev/vg01/rlvol2   B. fsck –F vxfs /dev/vg01/rlvol2
      C. fsck –F vxfs –o full /dev/vg01/rlvol2   D. fsck –F vxfs full /dev/vg01/rlvol3

213. What command would you use to find HFS superblock locations?
      A. newfs –N /dev/vg01/rlvol1   B. find / -name sb –print
      C. newfs –F hfs /dev/vg01/rlvol1   D. None of the above

214. How would you check the amount of physical memory in your system? Choose TWO.
      A. grep physical /var/adm/syslog/syslog.log B. grep –i physical /etc/rc.log
      C. dmesg   D. grep –i physical /var/adm/syslog/syslog.log

215. Which type of file system swap area is fastest?
      A. Device swap   B. File system swap   C. Both A and B   D. None of the
above

216. Which command enables device swap space in a logical volume?
      A. lvchange –a y /dev/vg01/swaplvol   B. swapon /dev/vg01/swaplvol
      C. swap /dev/vg01/swaplvol   D. swapon –enable /dev/vg01/swaplvol

217. Which command displays utilization of all swap spaces configured on your system?
      A. swapinfo   B. swapon   C. swap –a   D. swapon –a

218. What directory is created underneath the file system where you enable file system swap space?
      A. fsswap   B. swaping   C. paging   D. None of the above

219. Which of the following TWO entries enable a device swap and a file system swap at system boot?
      A. /dev/vg02/lvol2 /fs2 swapfs defaults 0 0   B. /dev/vg02/rlvol2 /fs2 swapfs defaults 0 0
      C. /dev/vg01/swaplvol … swap defaults 0 0   D. /dev/vg01/rswaplvol … swap defaults 0 0

220. How would you enable all swap areas defined in the /etc/fstab file manually?
      A. swapon –e   B. swapon –a   C. swapon –s   D. swapon –r

221. What is the default number of each of the file system and device swap space areas that you can define in your system?
      A. 5   B. 10   C. 15   D. 25

222. How many run control levels are currently implemented?
      A. 4   B. 5   C. 6   D. 8

223. Which of the following would you run to view the current and previous system run levels?
      A. uptime   B. w   C. who –s   D. who –r

224. What is the default HP-UX run level?
      A. 1   B. 2   C. 3   D. 4

225. To shutdown the system gracefully, which two commands are used? Choose TWO.

A. shutdown   B. init   C. reboot   D. halt

226. What does the shutdown command, by default, do which the init command does not? Choose TWO.
     A. Starts the shutdown process right away
     B. Waits for one minute before actual system shutdown commences
     C. Broadcasts a message to all logged in users
     D. Both A and C

227. When you run the shutdown command without any options, where does it take you to?
     A. Displays syntax error   B. Default run level   C. Reboots the system   D. Single user
     mode

228. To allow a normal user to be able to shutdown a system, which file you need to update?
     A. /etc/shutdown.allow   B. /etc/shutdown.enable
     C. /etc/shutdown.conf   D. /etc/shutdownallow

229. How would you boot your system to single user state from ISL prompt?
     A. hpux –i   B. hpux –s   C. hpux –is   D. hpux s

230. What script is executed at boot time that checks the root file system and repairs it, if necessary?
     A. /sbin/pre_boot   B. /sbin/pre_initial   C. /sbin/init   D. /sbin/pre_init_rc

231. What would you type at the ISL prompt to boot your system to LVM maintenance state?
     A. hpux –is   B. hpux –lm   C. hpux –ls   D. hpux –im

232. Which of the following would you type at the command to view the AUTO file contents?
     A. lifcp /dev/dsk/c0t4d0:AUTO   B. lifcp –d /dev/rdsk/c0t4d0 AUTO
     C. lifcp /dev/rdsk/c0t4d0:AUTO -   D. lifcp AUTO /dev/rdsk/c0t4d0

233. How would you set the alternate boot path to 8/8.12 disk?
     A. setboot –h 8/8.12   B. setboot –haa 8/8.12   C. setboot –alt 8/8.12   D. setboot –a 8/8.12

234. Which file determines the default boot level at the system startup time?
     A. /etc/inittab   B. /etc/init.conf   C. /etc/inittab.conf   D. /sbin/init

235. Which file maintains I/O configuration across reboots?
     A. /etc/ioconfig   B. /sbin/ioconfig   C. /var/adm/ioconfig   D. /etc/ioconfig.conf

236. Which script at system startup checks file systems listed in /etc/fstab file?
     A. /sbin/lvmrc   B. /sbin/bcheckrc   C. /etc/fstab   D. /sbin/inittab

237. Which is system startup log file?
     A. /etc/rc.log   B. /var/adm/startup.log   C. /etc/rc.log.log D. /var/adm/rc.log.log

238. Which directory contains configuration files for all startup and shutdown scripts?
     A. /etc/init.d   B. /sbin/init.d   C. /etc/rc#.d   D. /etc/rc.config.d

239. Which directory contains startup and shutdown scripts?
     A. /sbin/init.d   B. /etc/init.d   C. /etc/rc.config.d   D. /sbin/inittab

240. Which is not a reason to reconfigure the kernel?
   A. Install patches
   B. Add/remove device drivers
   C. Add/remove subsystems
   D. Add swap space

241. Which command is used in HP-UX 11.0 version to gather running kernel information?
   A. /usr/lbin/system/system_prep
   B. /usr/lbin/admin/system_prep
   C. /usr/lbin/sysadm/system_prep
   D. /usr/sbin/system_prep

242. Which command displays the value of maxvgs kernel parameter defined in the system file?
   A. kmsystem –q maxvgs –S /stand/build/system
   B. kmupdate –q maxvgs –S /stand/build/system
   C. kmtune –q maxvgs
   D. kmtune –q maxvgs –S /stand/build/system

243. Which TWO commands can you use to change the value of a kernel parameter in the system file?
   A. vi
   B. system_prep
   C. kmsystem
   D. kmtune

244. Which command is used to regenerate the kernel?
   A. kmsystem
   B. kmupdate
   C. mk_kernel
   D. kmtune

245. Which command is used to make a newly generated kernel the default kernel at next system reboot?
   A. kmtune
   B. kmsystem
   C. mk_kernel
   D. kmupdate

246. Which of the following can you use to determine the value of a kernel parameter? Choose TWO.
   A. kmtune
   B. kmsystem
   C. sysdef
   D. ioscan

247. Which command is used to query all static and DLKM modules in the running kernel?
   A. kmsystem
   B. sysdef
   C. kmadmin
   D. kmtune

248. Which version of HP-UX supports kcweb command?
   A. HP-UX 11iv1   B. HP-UX 11iv2   C. HP-UX 11.00   D. HP-UX 10.20

249. Which command is equivalent to kmsystem in HP-UX 11iv2?
   A. kconfig
   B. kctune
   C. kcsystem
   D. kcmodule

250. kcweb provides GUI interface to modify kernel tunable parameters?
   A. True
   B. False

251. What is system recovery?
   A. It is a function that crashes your system
   B. It is a function that performs a backup
   C. It is a function that recovers a crashed system to its previous normal state
   D. It is a function that only restores data from backup

252. How many levels of backups are supported by fbackup command?
   A. 9   B. 10   C. 8   D. 11

253. Which digit represents an entire file system backup with fbackup?
   A. 9   B. 2   C. 1   D. 0

254. What is a graph file?
- A. It is a file that contains a list of files/directories to be included in and /excluded from the backup
- B. It is a log file that is updated for each file/directory that is being backed up
- C. This file maintains backup history
- D. This file maintains backup logs

255. Which one of the following is correct?
- A. fbackup –f /dev/rmt/0m –g /home
- B. fbackup /home /tmp/index.home
- C. fbackup –f /home –i index.home
- D. fbackup –f /dev/rmt/0m –i /home –I index.home

256. Where does the fbackup command puts a time stamp if the –u option is used with it?
- A. /usr/dumpdates
- B. /var/adm/dumpdates
- C. /var/adm/fbackupfiles/dates
- D. /etc/dates

257. Where does the dump and vxdump commands put a time stamp if the –u option is used with them?
- A. /usr/dumpdates
- B. /etc/dates
- C. /var/adm/fbackupfiles/dates
- D. /var/adm/dumpdates

258. Which command restores only /home file system from a full system backup?
- A. frecover –xv
- B. frecover –f /dev/rmt/1m –i /home –xv
- C. frecover –f /dev/rmt/1m –xv
- D. Any of the above

259. Which TWO commands can be used to archive /etc directory to a non-default tape device?
- A. tar cvf /dev/rmt/1m /etc
- B. tar –cvf /dev/rmt/1m /etc
- C. tar cv /etc
- D. tar c /etc

260. Which of the following would work to backup /etc directory using the cpio command?
- A. find /etc –mtime –7 | cpio –icv mod.lst
- B. find /etc –mtime –7 | cpio –Ocv mod.lst
- C. find /etc –mtime –7 | cpio –ocv –O mod.lst
- D. find /etc –mtime –7 | cpio -itv

261. Which two tools are included in HP-UX 11i to perform recovery archives? Choose TWO.
- A. make_net_recovery
- B. create_net_recovery
- C. create_tape_recovery
- D. make_tape_recovery

262. How would you create a network system recovery archive of hp01 on hp02 at /var/recovery directory and include the entire vg00?
- A. create_net_recovery –v –s hp02 –a hp02:/var/recovery/hp01.archive –x inc_entire=vg00
- B. make_net_recovery –v –s hp02 –a hp02:/var/recovery/hp01.archive –x inc_entire=vg00
- C. make_tape_recovery –v –s hp02 –a hp02:/var/recovery/hp01.archive –x inc_entire=vg00
- D. create_tape_recovery –v –s hp02 –a hp02:/var/recovery/hp01.archive –x inc_entire=vg00

263. Which directory in the print spooling system holds temporarily print requests before they are forwarded to a printer?
- A. /var/spool/request
- B. /var/adm/lp/request
- C. /var/spool/lp/request
- D. /var/adm/request

264. The lpsched is a local print daemon. Which script starts it at boot time?
- A. /sbin/rc3.d/S720lp
- B. /sbin/rc2.d/S720lp
- C. /sbin/rc2.d/lp
- D. /sbin/rc3.d/lp

265. What is the configuration file for the master internet daemon, inetd?

A. /etc/inetd.conf   B. /etc/inet.conf   C. /etc/internet.conf   D. /etc/net.conf

266. What is the range of print request priorities?
        A. 1 – 9   B. 0 – 9   C. 1 – 7   D. 0 – 7

267. Which syntax for the lpadmin command is correct to create a local printer named prn3 of type "laserjet", and a printer class prn_class, and add prn3 to the class?
        A. lpadmin –pprn3 –v/dev/c3t0d0_lp –cprn_class –mlaserjet
        B. lpadmin –c prn3 –v /dev/c3t0d0_lp –p prn_class –m laserjet
        C. lpadmin –p prn3 –c prn_class –m laserjet
        D. lpadmin –pprn3 –v/dev/c3t0d0_lp –cprn_class

268. Which of the following tools is not used to setup printers?
        A. lpadmin   B. prnadmin   C. SAM   D. None of the above

269. Which of the following sets prn1 as the default print destination?
        A. SAM –d prn1   B. lpadmin –d prn1   C. lp –d prn1   D. lpadmin –p prn1

270. What command sequence would you run to take a printer off for maintenance and then back online?
        A. reject, disable, accept, enable   B. enable, accept, disable, reject
        C. disable, reject, enable, accept   D. reject, accept, disable, enable

271. Which command displays the status of all printers configured on your system?
        A. lpadmin –d   B. lp –t   C. lpadmin –t   D. lpstat –t

272. Which command is used to set printer fence level?
        A. lpalt   B. lpadmin   C. lpfence   D. lp

273. Which command is used to change print priority of a submitted print request?
        A. lpadmin   B. lpalt   C. lpfence   D. lp

274. Which command is used to cancel a print request?
        A. lpalt   B. lpcancel   C. cancel   D. lpadmin

275. What script is executed at system boot time that calls the /sbin/init.d/cron script to start cron daemon?
        A. /sbin/rc2.d/S730cron   B. /sbin/rc3.d/S730cron   C. /sbin/rc2.d/cron   D. /sbin/cron

276. What happens if both cron.allow and cron.deny files do not exist?
        A. All users excluding root can schedule a cron job
        B. All users including root can schedule a cron job
        C. No user excluding root can schedule a cron job
        D. No users including root can schedule a cron job

277. Which is the log file for cron daemon?
        A. cron has no log files   B. /var/adm/logs   C. /var/logs/cron   D. /var/adm/cron/log

278. What does the following do?
        # at 11pm find / -name core –exec rm {} \;

A. Executes find command at 11pm next week   B. Executes find command at 11pm tonight
C. Executes find command every night at 11pm   D. None of the above

279. Where does the at jobs spool?
    A. /var/spool/at/atjobs   B. /var/spool/cron/atjobs
    C. /var/spool/atjobs   D. /var/spool/cron/jobs

280. What does the following crontab entry do?
    20 1,12 1-15 * * find / -name core –exec rm {} \;

    A. Runs the find command at 20:01 and 20:12 the first fifteen days of the month
    B. Runs the find command at 1:20 and 12:20 the first fifteen days of the month
    C. Both of the above
    D. None of the above

281. Which option with the crontab command allows you to modify your crontab file?
    A. –e   B. –a   C. –m   D. -l

282. What are the names of the logging daemon and configuration file?
    A. syslog and /etc/syslog.conf   B. syslogd and /etc/syslog.conf
    C. syslog and /etc/syslog.log   D. sysloagd and /etc/syslog.log

283. What is the default system logging file?
    A. /var/spool/syslog.log   B. /var/adm/syslog.log
    C. /var/adm/syslog/syslog.log   D. /var/adm/syslog/log

284. Which of the following cannot be used as a performance monitoring tool?
    A. ioscan   B. top   C. iostat   D. uptime   E. glance

285. Which looping constructs are supported in shell scripts? Choose THREE.
    A. for-do-done   B. while-do-done C. until-do-done   D. if-then-else-fi

286. What is the command that is used in shell scripts to make it interactive?
    A. input   B. get   C. write   D. read

287. What logical constructs are supported in shell scripts ? Choose TWO.
    A. while-done   B. case-esac   C. for-done   D. if-fi

288. Which command quits a running shell script?
    A. break   B. exit   C. sleep   D. out

289. Which command suspends a loop execution?
    A. break   B. exit   C. sleep   D. wait

290. Which command takes the loop control back to the start of the loop?
    A. break   B. continue   C. exit   D. back

291. How would you check the status code of the last running command?
    A. echo $*   B. echo $#   C. echo $0   D. echo $?

292. What is the minimum number of nodes that you require to form a network?
    A. 1   B. 2   C. 3   D. Many

293. Which is the most commonly used network topologies today?
    A. Star   B. Bus   C. Token-ring   D. Ethernet

294. What is the most common network access method in use today?
    A. Token passing   B. Ethernet   C. Fibre   D. All of the above

295. How many layers are in the OSI model?
    A. 8   B. 9   C. 7   D. 5

296. What is the term used for adding a header message when creating a packet with respect to the OSI reference model?
    A. De-encapsulation   B. Encapsulation   C. Packet-forming   D. Message-forming

297. Which layers TCP and IP protocols are defined? Choose TWO.
    A. Data link layer   B. Application layer   C. Transport layer   D. Network layer

298. What layers do the routers work?
    A. Physical   B. Data link   C. Network   D. Transport

299. Which command displays MAC addresses of all LAN cards installed in your system?
    A. lanscan   B. ioscan   C. lanshow   D. lsdev

300. Which command can be used to change hostname, timezone, etc.
    A. ifconfig   B. set_parms   C. hostname   D. timezone

301. Which command is used to configure LAN cards?
    A. ifconfig   B. set_parms   C. hostname   D. lanadmin

302. Which command displays routing information?
    A. netstat   B. ifconfig   C. networkstat   D. iostat

303. What is the default netmask for a class B IP address?
    A. 255.255.255.255   B. 255.255.255.0   C. 255.255.0.0   D. 255.0.0.0

304. What is IP multiplexing?
    A. Having a single IP address assigned to multiple LAN cards
    B. Having multiple IP addresses assigned to a single LAN card
    C. Not supported in HP-Ux
    D. Both A and B

305. How many useable subnets can you create with 3 host bits in a class C network?
    A. 2   B. 4   C. 8   D. 6

306. What is the netmask for a class C network divided into 6 useable subnets?
    A. 255.255.255.252   B. 255.255.255.248   C. 255.255.255.244   D. 255.255.255.224

---

307. How many nodes can you have in a subnet with netmask of 255.255.255.128?
     A. 30   B. 126   C. 62   D. 14

308. Which file defines well-known ports?
     A. /etc/inetd.conf   B. /etc/protocols C. /etc/services   D. Both B and C

309. Which of the following THREE can you use to display installed LAN cards in your system?
     A. ioscan   B. lanscan   C. iostat   D. netstat

310. What does the following command do?
     # ifconfig lan1:1 150.11.211.100

     A. Assigns a logical IP address to lan1
     B. Deassigns a logical IP address from lan1
     C. Changes the network address to class B for lan1:1
     D. Changes the primary IP address of the LAN card

311. Which file is consulted at boot time to assign IP addresses to LAN cards?
     A. /etc/rc.config.d/namesvrs   B. /etc/rc.config.d/netconf
     C. /etc/rc.config.d/net.conf   D. /etc/rc.config.d/route

312. Which file contains the IP address to hostname mapping?
     A. /etc/hosts   B. /etc/rc.config.d/route   C. /etc/hostnames   D. /etc/ipnodes

313. Which file contains routing information that takes affect at system boot?
     A. /etc/route.conf   B. /etc/rc.config.d/route
     C. /etc/rc.config.d/netconf   D. /etc/rc.config.d/route.conf

314. To add a route to network 192.168.5 with gateway 182.0.1.1, which command would you run?
     A. route add net 192.168.5.0 182.0.1.1 1   B. route add 192.168.5.0 182.0.1.1 0
     C. route add default 192.168.5.0   D. route add 192.168.5.0 net 182.0.0.1

315. Which command is used to test physical network connectivity between two nodes?
     A. ping   B. linkloop   C. ioscan   D. linkcheck

316. Which command would you use to display and modify LAN card configuration?
     A. lanscan   B. lanadmin   C. lanadm   D. lanmod

317. Which command would you use to check connectivity between two nodes at the TCP/IP level?
     A. linkloop   B. netstat   C. ping   D. linkstat

318. Which command displays TCP/IP parameter information?
     A. netstat   B. ioscan   C. ndd   D. lanadmin

319. What would you run after modifying the /etc/inetd.conf file to make the changes effective?
     A. inetd –f   B. inetd –s   C. inetd –c   D. inetd –r

320. Which file defines the port numbers for RPC-based services?
     A. /etc/services B. /etc/rpc   C. /etc/protocols   D. /etc/inetd.conf

321. Which is the security file for the inetd daemon?
    A. /var/adm/inetdsec   B. /etc/inetd.sec C. /var/inetd.sec D. /var/adm/inetd.sec

322. Which of the following commands use trust relationship defined in $HOME/.rhosts or */etc/hosts*.equiv and without which you cannot get desired results? Choose THREE.
    A. rlogin   B. rexec   C. rcp   D. remsh

323. The root user uses the */etc/hosts*.equiv file?
    A. True   B. False

324. What is the correct syntax for transferring files between two systems? Choose TWO.
    A. rcp $HOME/.dtprofile hp02:$HOME   B. rcp hp02:$HOME/.dtprofile .
    C. rcp $HOME/.dtprofile $HOME   D. rcp $HOME/.dtprofile .

325. Which line entry in /etc/inetd.conf enables logging for all FTP activities including incoming/outgoing file transfer?
    A. ftp stream tcp nowait root /usr/lbin/ftpd ftpd -L
    B. ftp stream tcp nowait root /usr/lbin/ftpd ftpd -i -o
    C. ftp stream tcp nowait root /usr/lbin/ftpd ftpd –l –i -o
    D. ftp stream tcp nowait root /usr/lbin/ftpd ftpd

326. What two functions does sendmail provide? Choose TWO.
    A. Mail reading   B. Mail transport agent   C. Mail delivery agent   D. Mail display

327. What is the default configuration file for sendmail?
    A. /etc/sendmail.conf   B. /etc/mail/sendmail.conf
    C. /etc/mail/sendmail.cf   D. */etc/hosts*

328. What is the alternate secure tools to access an HP-UX system? Choose THREE.
    A. ssh   B. telnet   C. sftp   D. scp

329. To setup ssh, which command do you use to generate keys?
    A. ssh   B. ssh-keygen   C. ssh.key.gen   D. ssh.keygen

330. What port ssh uses by default?
    A. 21   B. 22   C. 23   D. 24

331. Can PAM be used with DNS?
    A. Yes   B. No

332. Which is the system-wide configuration file for PAM?
    A. /etc/pam.conf   B. /etc/pamconf
    C. /etc/rc.config.d/pam.conf   D. /etc/rc.config.d/pamconf

333. Which command is used to create a chroot jail?
    A. su   B. suroot   C. changeroot   D. chroot

334. What are the common sources of obtaining time for your network? Choose THREE.
    A. An internet-based time server   B. A radio clock

C. A time clock   D. Local system clock

335. Clocks working at what stratum level are considered the most accurate?
      A. 0   B. 1   C. 10   D. 15

336. When two time servers work at the same stratum level, they are called Peers?
      A. True   B. False

337. What files are typically involved with NTP configuration? Choose THREE.
      A. /etc/ntp.drift   B. /etc/ntp.conf   C. /etc/rc.config.d/netdaemons   D. /etc/ntp/ntp.conf

338. Which command can be used at the command line or run via cron to update system time manually?
      A. xntp   B. ntpdate   C. chdatentp   D. ntpchdate

339. Which command is used to check the status of NTP and its associated bindings?
      A. ntpd   B. xntpd   C. ntptrace   D. ntpq

340. Which is the widely used naming service on the internet?
      A. DNS   B. NIS   C. NIS+   D. LDAP

341. Which command displays NFS activities?
      A. nfs –t   B. nfs –s   C. nfsact   D. nfsstat

342. What two daemons are not required on a slave NIS server? Choose TWO.
      A. ypserv   B. ypxfrd   C. ypbind   D. rpc.yppasswdd

343. What script is executed at system bootup to bring up the NIS client functionality and what startup configuration file it uses? Choose TWO.
      A. /etc/rc.config.d/netconf   B. /etc/rc.config.d/namesvrs
      C. /sbin/init.d/nis.client   D. /sbin/init.d/ypclient

344. Which command does the ypxfrd daemon respond to?
      A. ypserv   B. ypxfr.server   C. nisxfr   D. ypxfr

345. Which command would you use to determine the NIS server your machine is bound to?
      A. ypwhich   B. ypwho   C. ypmatch   D. ypcat

346. Which command would you use to list all RPC-based services currently running on your system?
      A. rpc –d   B. rpclist   C. rpcinfo   D. rpc –l

347. Which command would you use to display an NIS map contents?
      A. cat   B. ypcat   C. strings   D. ypmatch

348. What commands can you use to change your NIS password? Choose TWO.
      A. yppasswd   B. yppasswd   C. passwd   D. nispasswd

349. What does the following command do?
      # ypset hp03

A. Does nothing
B. Binds your system to NIS server hp03 in addition to the one your machine is already bound to
C. Unbinds your system from hp03
D. Binds your system to NIS server hp03

350. Which commands can you use to update NIS maps? Choose TWO.
    A. niscreate   B. ypcreate   C. make   D. ypmake

351. Which file contains network security settings for NIS?
    A. /var/yp/securenets   B. /var/yp/security   C. /etc/securetty D. /etc/nis/securenets

352. An NFS server _____ a file system and an NFS client _____ it.
    A. exports, accesses   B. shares, mounts   C. exports, mounts   D. shares, accesses

353. NFS is an RPC-based service. True or False.
    A. True   B. False

354. Which is not a benefit of using NFS?
    A. Sharing common application binaries
    B. Multiple NFS client machines can access an NFS file system simultaneously
    C. Sharing user authentication information
    D. Sharing user home directories

355. Which NFS server daemon responds to the mount command request?
    A. rpc.mountd   B. mountd   C. nfsd   D. rpc.nfsd

356. Which NFS server daemon responds to NFS client file access requests?
    A. rpc.mountd   B. mountd   C. nfsd   D. biod

357. Which NFS daemon has replaced the portmap daemon used in earlier HP-UX versions?
    A. rpc.mountd   B. rpcbind   C. rpc.bind   D. rpc.portmapd

358. Which file is looked into by the exportfs command to export listed resrouces?
    A. /etc/exportfs   B. /etc/exports   C. /etc/dfs/dfstab   D. /etc/rc.config.d/namesvrs

359. What two NFS daemons provide crash recovery? Choose TWO.
    A. nfsd   B. rpc.mountd   C. rpc.statd   D. rpc.lockd

360. When an NFS file system is mounted by a client, which file on NFS server stores an entry for it?
    A. /etc/mnttab   B. /etc/xtab   C. /etc/rmtab   D. /etc/exports

361. When an NFS file system is mounted by a client, which file is updated on the NFS client?
    A. /etc/mnttab   B. /etc/fstab   C. /etc/rmtab   D. /etc/exports

362. When you execute the mount command with –v option, which file it reads to display the output?
    A. /etc/mnttab   B. /etc/fstab   C. /etc/rmtab   D. /etc/exports

363. When a file system is exported by an NFS server, which file on NFS server stores an entry for it?
    A. /etc/mnttab   B. /etc/rmtab   C. /etc/xtab   D. /etc/exports

364. Which is the startup configuration file for NFS service?
    A. /etc/rc.config.d/namesvrs
    C. /etc/rc.config.d/netdaemons
    B. /etc/rc.config.d/netconf
    D. /etc/rc.config.d/nfsconf

365. When you execute mountall command, which file the command looks into to mount unmounted file systems?
    A. /etc/exports
    B. /etc/fstab
    C. /etc/mnttab
    D. /etc/rmtab

366. Which of the following scripts starts the rpcbind daemon?
    A. /sbin/init.d/rpcbind
    C. /sbin/init.d/nfs.client
    B. /sbin/init.d/nfs.server
    D. /sbin/init.d/nfs.core

367. Which version of NFS is supported in HP-UX 11i?
    A. v1
    B. v2
    C. v3
    D. v4

368. What does the following entry in /etc/exports file mean?
    /usr/bin –access=hp03:hp04

    A. Only hp03 and hp04 will be able to mount /usr/bin
    B. All systems other than hp03 and hp04 will be able to mount /usr/bin
    C. All systems including hp03 and hp04 will be able to mount /usr/bin
    D. All of the above

369. What does the following entry in /etc/exports file mean?
    /var/opt/samba –anon=65535

    A. 65535 systems will be able to mount /var/opt/samba
    B. 655535 users can access /var/opt/samba at a time
    C. Anonymous users will be assigned 65535 UID
    D. Both A and B are correct

370. What variables in the /etc/rc.config.d/nfsconf file need to be set to 1 in order to have NFS server functionality startup at system boot? Choose TWO.
    A. NFS_MASTER
    B. NFS_SERVER
    C. NFS_SLAVE
    D. START_MOUNTD

371. Which command exports all resources listed in the /etc/exports file?
    A. exports –a
    B. exportfs
    C. exportfs –a
    D. exports

372. Which is not a default option when exporting a file system?
    A. suid
    B. ro
    C. rw
    D. intr

373. Which THREE would tell you what resources are exported from hp02? You use them on hp02.
    A. showmount –e
    B. cat /etc/xtab
    C. exportfs
    D. showmount –a

374. Which one of the following is correct?
    A. mount –o ro,nfs hp02:/usr/share/man /usr/share/man
    B. mount –o nfs,ro hp02:/usr/share/man /usr/share/man
    C. mount –F nfs –o ro hp02:/usr/share/man /usr/share/man
    D. mount –F ro –o nfs hp02:/usr/share/man /usr/share/man

375. Which TWO would tell you what resources are mounted by NFS client? You use them on NFS server.
   A. showmount –a   B. cat /etc/xtab   C. exportfs   D. showmount –e

376. Which commands would you use to kill all processes using a file system? Choose TWO.
   A. umount –f /home   B. fuser –k /home   C. fuser –cu /home   D. fuser –ck /home

377. What is the other name for CIFS Server product?
   A. Samba   B. CIFS/NFS   C. NFS   D. There is no other name for it.

378. Which ones are true for sharing directories using CIFS? Choose THREE.
   A. Windows and Windows can share directories   B. UNIX and Windows can share directories
   C. UNIX and UNIX can share directories   D. UNIX and UNIX cannot share directories

379. Which is the CIFS server configuration file?
   A. /etc/opt/cifs/smb.conf   B. /etc/opt/samba/smb.conf
   C. /etc/samba/smb.conf   D. /etc/cifs/smb.conf

380. What variable would you set in /etc/rc.config.d/samba file to have CIFS server start at system boot?
   A. CIFS=1   B. RUN_CIFS=1   C. RUN_SAMBA=1   D. SAMBA=1

381. Which of the following would you run to start CIFS server in GUI mode?
   A. /opt/cifs/bin/swat   B. /opt/samba/bin/swat   C. /usr/samba/bin/swat   D. /usr/bin/swat

382. Which command would you run to check the syntax errors in the CIFS server configuration file?
   A. testcifsserv   B. testparm   C. cifstest   D. sertestcifs

383. Which is the startup configuration file for CIFS client on HP-UX?
   A. /etc/rc.config.d/cifsclient   B. /etc/rc.config.d/samba
   C. /etc/rc.config.d/cifsserver   D. /etc/rc.config.d/sambaclient

384. Which two commands can you use on HP-UX to mount a CIFS share? Choose TWO.
   A. sharemount   B. sambamount   C. cifsmount   D. mount

385. AutoFS requires entries in the /etc/fstab file to work properly? True or False.
   A. True   B. False

386. For how long, by default, an AutoFS file system is kept idle before it is automatically unmounted?
   A. 5 sec   B. 5 min   C. 1 min   D. 10 min

387. What are AutoFS command and daemon?
   A. automount, autofsd   B. autofs, autofsd
   C. automount, automountd   D. autofs, automountd

388. What two variables in the /etc/rc.config.d/nfsconf file must you set to have AutoFS client funcationality started on your system at each system reboot?
   A. AUTOFS   B. NFS_CLIENT   C. AUTOMOUNT   D. AUTOMOUNTD

389. What change is required on the NFS server in order to mount them on a client system using AutoFS?
   A. You restart the NFS server daemons

B. You must reboot the NFS server

C. You must re-export the file system to be mounted by AutoFS on client.

D. No change is required

390. What is the directory location for the automount and automountd for AutoFS?

    A. /usr/sbin/autofs   B. /usr/lib/netsvc/fs/autofs

    C. /usr/lib/netsvc/fs/automount   D. /opt/autofs/bin

391. What four are AutoFS maps? Choose FOUR.

    A. indirect   B. direct   C. hosts   D. special   E. master

392. Which of the following are true about a direct AutoFS mount? Choose TWO.

    A. Always visible to users

    B. Always invisible to users unless there is an activity inside the mount point

    C. Both local and direct-mounted maps can co-exist under the same parent directory

    D. Both local and direct-mounted maps cannot co-exist under the same parent directory

393. You must run the automount command manually to make the modifications in a direct map take effect? True or False.

    A. True   B. False

394. What does the following mean on an NFS client?

    *   &:/home/&

    A. Mount from an available NFS server only the home directory of the user who logs in

    B. Mount from all configured NFS servers only the home directory of the user who logs in

    C. Mount home directories of all users from all NFS servers

    D. Mount home directories of all users from only one NFS server

395. Which is not true about AutoFS?

    A. It supports files larger than 2GB in size

    B. It supports NFS v3 protocol

    C. It always mounts AutoFS file systems under /tmp_mnt directory

    D. You do not have to restart the automountd daemon everytime you modify any of the map files to take effect.

396. Which of the naming services are supported for host name resolution? Choose THREE.

    A. CIFS   B. DNS   C. NIS   D. NIS+

397. In a small environment of a few HP-UX servers what host name resolution method is preferred?

    A. LDAP   B. DNS   C. NIS   D. /etc/hosts

398. Which of the following do not have hierarchical structure? Choose TWO.

    A. LDAP   B. DNS   C. NIS   D. NIS+   E. /etc/hosts

399. What is the DNS boot file in BIND version 8.1.2 and later?

    A. /etc/named.dns   B. /etc/named.boot   C. /etc/named.data   D. /etc/named.bind

400. What three DNS server configurations are supported? Choose THREE.

A. Master   B. Slave   C. Peer   D. Caching-Only

401. Which command is used to create DNS zone files?
     A. createdns   B. converthosts   C. hosts_to_named   D. host_to_named

402. What is the name of the DNS daemon?
     A. named   B. name   C. dnsd   D. inetd

403. On what DNS server would you update your host entries to be included in DNS?
     A. Caching-Only   B. Slave   C. Master   D. Client

404. What daemon must be running on all DNS servers as well as clients?
     A. named   B. name   C. dnsd   D. inetd

405. Which file is referenced to determine sources to look up information?
     A. /etc/inetd.conf   B. /etc/nsswitch.conf   C. /etc/resolv.conf   D. /etc/named.boot

406. What is the DNS resolver file name?
     A. /etc/resolve.conf   B. /etc/nsswitch.conf   C. /etc/named.boot   D. /etc/resolv.conf

407. How many nameserver entries can you defined in DNS resolver file?
     A. 1   B. 2   C. 3   D. 4

408. What three entries can be defined in the DNS resolver file? Choose THREE.
     A. defaultdomain   B. search   C. domain   D. nameserver

409. What commands can you use to verify DNS funcationality? Choose TWO.
     A. nsfind   B. nslookup   C. nsquery   D. nstrace

410. What does the db.cache file contain?
     A. Mapping for loopback address   B. Used on slave servers as /etc/named.conf
     C. Root name server database   D. Used on caching-only server as /etc/named.conf

411. What does the db.127.0.0 file contain?
     A. Root name server database   B. Mapping for loopback address
     C. Used on slave servers as /etc/named.conf   D. Used on clients as /etc/named.conf

412. What is the purpose of conf.sec.save file?
     A. Used on slave servers as /etc/named.conf   B. Root name server database
     C. Mapping for loopback address   D. Used on master server as /etc/named.conf

413. What is the purpose of conf.sec.cacheonly file?
     A. Used on slave servers as /etc/named.conf   B. Root name server database
     C. Used on caching-only servers as /etc/named.conf   D. Mapping for loopback address

414. What does the keyword "hint" represents in the /etc/named.conf file?
     A. Points to root DNS servers   B. Points to master DNS server
     C. Points to slave DNS server   D. Points to caching-only DNS server

415. What command is used to restart the DNS daemon?
　　　A. named restart　　　B. sig_named restart　　　C. sig_named start　　　D. named start

416. What is the configuration file for bootpd daemon?
　　　A. /etc/bootp.conf　　　B. /etc/bootpdtab　　　C. /etc/boottab　　D. /etc/bootptab

417. Which command would you use to manually send a message to BootP server to verify if it is setup properly?
　　　A. nslookup　　　B. bootpquery　　　C. bootquery　　　D. bootqueryp

418. In which file would you define the BootP relay information?
　　　A. /etc/bootp.conf　　　B. /etc/bootpdtab　　　C. /etc/bootptab　　　D. /etc/boottab

419. Which of the following is true about LDAP?
　　　A. Provides user authentication　　　B. Provides calendar service
　　　C. Provides email messaging service　　　D. All of the above

420. Which protocol is LDAP derived from?
　　　A. X.500 DAP　　　B. X.25 DAP　　　C. TCP/IP　　　D. NFS

421. What is a directory in LDAP terminology?
　　　A. An inode that points to where the directory information is located in LDAP
　　　B. A file that stores information you type in using the vi editor
　　　C. A UNIX-like conventional directory that holds file information
　　　D. A database that stores information about objects

422. What information does an LDAP attribute contain? Choose TWO.
　　　A. Attribute class　　　B. One or more attribute values
　　　C. One or more attribute classes　　　D. Attribute type

423. Which of the following is a collection of LDAP attributes, object classes, matching rules and syntax, and other related information?
　　　A. Schematics　　　B. Object Class　　　C. Object　　　D. Schema

424. What is the special format for importing and exporting LDAP data among LDAP servers?
　　　A. LDAPIF　　　B. DIF　　　C. LDIF　　　D. LIF

425. What identifies an entry starting from the root of the LDAP directory?
　　　A. Relative distinguished name (RDN)　　　B. Distinguished name (DN)
　　　C. Common name (CN)　　　D. Domain component (DN)

426. What is the purpose of a referral in LDAP?
　　　A. Redirects an LDAP request to some other LDAP server
　　　B. Gets unfound information from another LDAP server and sends back to the client
　　　C. It is a dedicated machine that performs a referral action in a large environment
　　　D. None of the above

427. What is the purpose of replica in LDAP? Choose TWO.
　　　A. It can be used to provide redundancy

B. It can be called a referral

C. It can be referred to as a caching-only LDAP server

D. It can be referred to as a slave LDAP server

428. What command would you use to configure Netscape Directory server software on HP-UX?

    A. run   B. setup   C. swinstall   D. sh

429. What script is used at system startup to bring the LDAP client services up?

    A. /sbin/init.d/ldapclientd.rc   B. /sbin/init.d/ldapclient

    C. /sbin/init.d/ldap   D. /sbin/init.d/ldapclientd

430. What is the UID of the root user?

    A. 1   B. 0   C. 3   D. 2

431. What is the name and location of the history file for the POSIX shell?

    A. ~/.history.sh   B. ~/.history_sh   C. ~/.posix_history   D. ~/.sh_history

432. What option would you use with the ls command to display hidden (or dot) files?

    A. –d   B. –l   C. –h   D. –a

433. Which of the following are vi editor modes? Choose THREE.

    A. Edit mode   B. Last line mode   C. Command mode   D. Save mode

434. Which is the default directory location for storing NIS maps?

    A. /var/yp   B. /var/adm/yp   C. /etc/yp   D. /usr/yp

435. What is the default subnet mask for a class A IP address?

    A. 255.255.255.0   B. 255.255.0.0   C. 255.0.0.0   D. 0.0.0.255

436. What is the default subnet mask for a class B IP address?

    A. 255.255.255.0   B. 255.255.0.0   C. 255.0.0.0   D. 0.0.0.255

437. What is the default gateway IP address for an HP-UX system with IP address 192.168.1.202?

    A. 192.168.1.1   B. 192.168.1.202   C. 192.168.1.255   D. 192.168.1.0

438. What is a system's loopback IP address?

    A. 0.0.0.127   B. 127.0.0.0   C. 127.0.0.1   D. 1.0.0.127

439. Which option with the netstat command displays the routing information for your system?

    A. –a   B. –i   C. –r   D. –n

440. Which is not another name for the MAC address?

    A. Station address   B. Hardware address   C. IP address   D. Ethernet address

441. What is the lowest priority target ID in a SCSI chain?

    A. 0   B. 7   C. 8   D. 15

442. What does the following command do?

    echo $?

A. Echoes the character ?
B. Display the message "command not found"
C. Displays total number of command line arguments specified at the last executed command
D. Displays status code for the last executed command

443. What is the default shell in HP-UX and what is the default shell for the root user?
    A. Bourne, POSIX   B. Bourne for both   C. POSIX for both   D. POSIX, Bourne

444. What is the purpose of output redirection?
    A. Send the output to an alternate destination   B. Take the input from an alternate source
    C. Send the output to /dev/null   D. Always send the output to a file

445. What is the major number for LVM subsystem in HP-UX?
    A. 32   B. 64   C. 96   D. 128

446. What would be the sequence of commands to create a file system on a brand new disk online?
    A. ioscan, insf, pvcreate, vgextend, lvcreate, newfs   B. ioscan, insf, pvcreate, lvcreate, newfs
    C. pvcreate, lvcreate, newfs, vgextend   D. ioscan, pvcreate, vgextend, lvcreate, newfs

447. What is the root volume group in HP-UX?
    A. vgroot   B. vg01   C. vgboot   D. vg00

448. Which command puts boot utilities on a disk?
    A. mkdisk   B. mkutil   C. mkboot   D. pvcreate

449. Which command would you use to display a volume group configuration in detail?
    A. vgdisplay –a   B. vgdisplay –v   C. vgdisplay –t   D. vgdisplay –o

450. Which command would you use to display a logical volume details?
    A. lvdisplay –a   B. lvdisplay –v   C. lvdisplay –t   D. lvdisplay –o

451. Which command would you use to increase the size of an HFS file system?
    A. fsadm   B. lvextend   C. extendfs   D. fsextend

452. Which command would you run to restore a backup made with fbackup tool?
    A. vxrestore   B. cpio   C. tar   D. frecover

453. Which three layers of the OSI reference model corresponds with the application layer of TCP/IP?
    A. Application, presentation, session   B. Application, session, network
    C. Physical, data link, network   D. Network, transport, application

454. At which layer of the OSI model does the TCP and UDP protocols are used?
    A. Transport   B. Network   C. Data link   D. Session

455. Which protocol is used by a BootP client to get its IP address?
    A. RARP   B. ARP   C. TFTP   D. FTP

456. Which command displays information as to which user is using how much space?
    A. du   B. bdf   C. quot   D. ff

457. What is the purpose of the cron daemon?
    A. Run scheduled jobs every hour   B. Run scheduled jobs at their specified times
    C. Run all scheduled jobs simultaneously   D. Run all scheduled jobs every hour

458. Which OSI layer does the switch work?
    A. Transport   B. Network   C. Data link   D. Physical

459. Which OSI layer does the fibre channel cable work?
    A. Transport   B. Network   C. Data link   D. Physical

460. What is the maximum speed on a fast ethernet network adapter?
    A. 1000 Mbps   B. 100 Mbps   C. 10 Mbps   D. 1 Mbps

461. Which command displays IP addresses and MAC addresses of all systems on the network ?
    A. arp   B. bootp –a   C. arp –a   D. None of the above

462. Which command would you use to setup a master NIS server?
    A. setup   B. ypsetup   C. init   D. ypinit

463. At what run level does the NFS client functionality becomes available?
    A. 4   B. 3   C. 2   D. s

464. What is the well-known port number for ftp?
    A. 21   B. 22   C. 23   D. 25

465. What command can be used to set or modify system hostname, IP address, date/time, and root password?
    A. set_parms –m   B. set_parms initial   C. set_parms ip   D. ifconfig

466. In which file is the primary group for a user defined?
    A. /etc/passwd   B. /etc/default/useradd   C. /etc/group   D. /etc/profile

467. In which file are the secondary group memberships for a user defined?
    A. /etc/passwd   B. /etc/default/useradd   C. /etc/group   D. /etc/profile

468. What command would you run to set your terminal settings to default?
    A. setterm   B. termset   C. stty   D. stty sane

469. What initializes and loads the HP-UX kernel into memory?
    A. Primary boot loader   B. Secondary boot loader   C. The init program   D. The /etc/inittab file

470. What two commands can you use to display values contained in variables? Choose TWO.
    A. display   B. print   C. show   D. echo

471. Which is the default kernel parameter file?
    A. /etc/system   B. /stand/system   C. /stand/build/system   D. /stand/system.conf

472. What is the meaning of the character "t" if it appears in the ll command output right after the permissions column?

A. setuid bit is set   B. setgid bit is set   C. sticky bit is set   D. nothing special

473. What would the following command do:
    chmod a=666 file1

A. Grants rw permissions to the owner, group members, and public
B. Revokes rw permissions from the owner, group members, and public
C. Grants 666-022=644 permissions to the owner, group members, and public
D. Revokes 666-022=644 permissions from the owner, group members, and public

474. Which of the following commands would display all available tape devices on your system? Choose THREE.

A. ioscan –fnkC tape   B. ioscan –fnkCtape   C. ioscan –fnC tape   D. ioscan –tape

475. Where does your HP UNIX system store autoboot information?

A. PDC   B. Stable storage   C. AUTO file   D. Both AUTO file and stable storage

476. Which of the following are metacharacters? Choose THREE.

A. *   B. \   C. $ D. A tab

477. To bring a disk to LVM control with BDRA created on it, which command would you use?

A. mkboot –a   B. pvcreate –fB /dev/dsk/c0t2d0
C. pvcreate –fB /dev/rdsk/c0t2d0   D. pvcreate –f /dev/rdsk/c0t2d0

478. Where is the default file system type defined?

A. /etc/fs   B. /etc/default/fs   C. /etc/fs.conf   D. /etc/vfstab

479. What is the default file system type for the /var file system?

A. UFS   B. VxFS   C. LOFS   D. HFS

480. What is the source file for the make utility?

A. /etc/Makefile   B. /var/yp/make   C. /var/yp/Makefile   D. /var/yp/makefile

481. What five objects are used in Veritas Volume Manager? Choose FIVE.

A. Volume group   B. Disk group   C. Plex
D. Disk   E. Volume   F. Subdisk

482. To boot a system to ignore quorum, what would you type at the ISL prompt?

A. hpux –iq   B. hpux –lq   C. hpux –is   D. hpux –lm

483. Which command would you use to display the contents of the AUTO file at the ISL prompt?

A. hpux display autofile   B. hpux autofile
C. hpux show autofile   D. lifcp /dev/dsk/c0t0d0:AUTO -

484. Which shell would you assign to a Bourne shell user who you do not want to change directories?

A. rsh   B. rksh   C. rcsh   D. sh

485. What is stored in the AUTO file by default?
    A. hpux   B. hpux –lq   C. hpux –is   D. isl

486. Which commands are used to query and set kernel parameters and modules respectively?
    A. kmadmin, kmtune   B. kmsystem, kmtune
    C. kmtune, kmsystem   D. kmadmin, kmsystem

487. Which of the following would display the correct information?
    A. pg /etc/lvmtab   B. more /etc/lvmtab   C. cat /etc/lvmtab   D. strings
/etc/lvmtab

488. Which command lists running processes?
    A. prstat   B. ps   C. psstat   D. proc

489. If /etc/lvmtab file is lost, which command would you use to recreate it?
    A. vgrecreate   B. vgsync   C. vgscan   D. mklvm

490. Which one of the following is not a network monitoring tool?
    A. nfsstat   B. netstat   C. nettl   D. top

491. What directory structure is created under root when your system is converted to trusted mode security?
    A. /tcb/files/auth   B. /tcb/auth/files/a   C. /tcb/files/auth/ts   D. /ts/auth/tcb

492. How many host bits are there in class A network?
    A. 8   B. 16   C. 24   D. 32

493. Which signal is sent by default with the kill command?
    A. 15   B. 9   C. 2   D. 1

494. How many network bits are there in class B network?
    A. 8   B. 16   C. 24   D. 32

495. Which file is created in /var/spool/lp directory to prevent multiple lpsched daemons from running?
    A. .lck   B. LOCK   C. SCHED   D. SCHEDLOCK

496. Which command would display all available signals?
    A. kill –s   B. kill –l   C. kill –list   D. kill

497. What would the following command do?
    lp –d prn1 */etc/hosts*

    A. Prints the */etc/hosts* file on prn1 printer
    B. Sets prn1 as the default printer
    C. Sets prn1 as the default printer and prints the */etc/hosts* file
    D. Prints the */etc/hosts* file on the default printer and deletes it

498. Where would you start entering the text in vi when you press the A key while in command mode?
    A. Beginning of the current line   B. End of the current line
    C. Middle of the current line   D. Opens up a new line and you insert text there

499. What would the following do in vi?
    :%s/old/new

    A. Replaces the first occurrence of the pattern "new" with "old"
    B. Replaces the first occurrence of the pattern "old" with "new"
    C. Replaces all occurrences of the pattern "old" with "new"
    D. Replaces all occurrences of the pattern "new" with "old"

500. What would be the result of the following grep command?
    grep ^$ /etc/group

    A. Displays from the /etc/group file all lines that contain at least one character
    B. Displays from the /etc/group file no lines
    C. Displays from the /etc/group file all lines that begin with the character ^ and end with the character $
    D. Displays from the /etc/group file all lines that are empty

501. What command is used in HP-UX to find help on a command?
    A. The catman command   B. The help command   C. The man command   D. Any of the above

502. Which command shows you your user ID?
    A. The id command   B. The groups command
    C. The usermod command   D. The uid command

503. Which command would you use to navigate within HP-UX directory tree?
    A. The pwd command   B. The cd command   C. The nav command   D. The id command

504. How would you create a symbolic link?
    A. ln –s existing_file link_file   B. ln existing_file link_file
    C. ln –c existing_file link_file   D. link –s link_file existing_file

505. What does the execute permission on a directory mean?
    A. You can create files in the directory   B. You can execute a command located in the directory
    C. You can execute the directory   D. You can cd into the directory

506. Which one is correct to view the value contained in a variable?
    A. echo $VAR   B. display $VAR   C. show $VAR   D. echo VAR

507. Which file transfer protocol is used by Ignite-UX?
    A. FTP   B. TFTP   C. BootP   D. rcp

508. Which special character would you use at the end of a command to run it in the background?
    A. ~   B. ^   C. $ D. &

509. What kind of files are typically stored in the /opt directory?
    A. Configuration files   B. Variable files   C. Application files   D. Kernel files

510. What is the recommended way of bringing your HP-UX system down?
    A. init 6   B. shutdown –h   C. shutdown -6   D. reboot

511. Which script calls and runs startup scripts at boot time?
    A. /etc/rc   B. /sbin/init   C. /sbin/rc   D. /etc/init

512. When does your .profile file is executed?
    A. When a user logs in   B. When a user logs off
    C. When an administrator runs a command   D. At system boot up

513. Which utility allows you to create a bootable system tape?
    A. make_net_recovery   B. make_tape_recovery   C. make_tape   D. tape_create

514. What is the most common backup command found on UNIX systems?
    A. cpio   B. dump   C. tar   D. fbackup

515. Which of the following gives you number of lines in file15?
    A. wc –w file15   B. wc –a file15   C. wc –c file15   D. wc –l file15

516. Which two commands show you the device file associated with a device? Choose TWO.
    A. lssf   B. lsdev   C. insf   D. ioscan

517. What happens if you do not specify the size of a logical volume when you run the lvcreate command to create a new logical volume?
    A. It will use entire disk space of the volume group it is created in
    B. It will be created with zero size
    C. It will result in syntax error
    D. It will destroy existing logical volumes in that volume group

518. Which directory holds most log files?
    A. /var/logs   B. /var/adm/logs   C. /var/adm   D. /var/adm/syslog

519. Which directory contains default user startup template files?
    A. /etc/skeleton   B. /etc/default/user   C. /etc/default   D. /etc/skel

520. What is the purpose of using NTP?
    A. Administration files synchronization   B. Time synchronization
    C. Sending packets to check remote system connectivity   D. All of the above with proper options
    and arguments

521. Which of the following is not a correct class C netmask?
    A. 255.255.0.0   B. 255.255.255.128   C. 255.255.255.192   D. 255.255.255.0

522. What permissions does the chmod command set with 755 on file10?
    A. r-wr-wr-w   B. rwxr-wr-x   C. rwxr-xr-x   D. rwxrwxrwx

523. If you assign UID 0 to a normal user, what will happen? Choose THREE.
    A. The user will get root privileges
    B. The user will still be able to do his normal work and will not be able to do anything additional
    C. The user will be able to run SAM
    D. The user will be able to run all system administration tasks

524. What kind of file systems can newfs command create? Choose TWO.
    A. vxfs   B. cdfs   C. hfs   D. swapfs

525. What is the default location for the software depot?
    A. /var/spool/products   B. /var/spool/sw   C. /var/spool/software   D. /var/spool/depot

526. What class does the IP address 199.81.51.231 belong to?
    A. Class A   B. Class B   C. Class C   D. Class D

527. What two portions each IP address contains? Choose TWO.
    A. A protocol portion   B. A network portion   C. A host portion D. All three portions

528. Which file is consulted at boot time to configure LAN cards?
    A. /sbin/init.d/netconf   B. /etc/rc.config.d/netconf
    C. /etc/netconf   D. /etc/rc.config.d/netdaemons

529. Which directories should not be shared via NFS with other systems? Choose THREE.
    A. /opt   B. /stand   C. /etc   D. /dev

530. What does a direct map contain?
    A. Any number of related mount points   B. Any number of unrelated mount points
    C. No related mount points   D. No unrelated mount points

531. What does the alias command used for?
    A. To create nick names for users   B. To create nick names for groups
    C. To create shortcuts to commands   D. To setup cron jobs

532. What does ACL do? Choose THREE.
    A. Allows you to set extended permissions on top oF standard UNIX permissions
    B. Provides same functionality as the chmod command does
    C. Allocates permissions to specific users or groups
    D. Revokes permissions from specific user and groups

533. Which command enables you to make a local variable an environment variable?
    A. echo   B. set   C. env   D. export

534. What does the pipe character do in a command?
    A. Takes input from an alternate location
    B. Sends output of an command as input to another command
    C. Sends output to the system log file only
    D. Takes input from user

535. Where does the cpio command sends its output by default?
    A. stderr   B. stdout   C. stdin   D. stddis

536. Which command would display only the third column from the output of the ls –l command?
    A. ls –l | cut –f2 –d " "   B. ls –l | cut –f3 –d " "
    C. ls –l | cut –d "" –f3   D. ls –l | cut –d " " –f2

537. Which of the following prints the contents of the /etc/profile file on printer prn3? Choose TWO.
  A. lp –p prn3 /etc/profile
  B. lp –dprn3 /etc/profile
  C. lp –d prn3 /etc/profile
  D. lp –pprn3 /etc/profile

538. Which sequence of commands would you run to force unmount a file system?
  A. fuser –cu, umount
  B. fuser –ck, umount
  C. umount –f
  D. fuser, umount

539. What is the purpose of subnetting?
  A. To create multiple smaller networks out of an IP address
  B. To divide a network portion of an IP address into multiple addresses to create subnets
  C. To create larger networks
  D. To concatenate multiple IP addresses to form a very large network

540. OSI layers provide a set of rules for data transmission. True or False.
  A. True
  B. False

541. The lpadmin command is used to create a new printer when the scheduler is running. True or False.
  A. True
  B. False

542. Who can change a user password?
  A. Only the user himself
  B. Only the root user
  C. Both the user and the root
  D. Any users on the system

543. Which file would you modify to prevent users from only one remote host from printing to a printer on your system?
  A. /etc/inetd.sec
  B. /etc/securenets
  C. /etc/inetd.conf
  D. /var/adm/inetd.sec

544. Which kernel parameter defines maximum number of swap spaces that you can configure?
  A. maxswapchunks
  B. maxswap
  C. maxswapspace
  D. maxswapslice

545. What is the meaning of initiator in the output of ioscan?
  A. SCSI disk array
  B. SCSI bus controller
  C. SCSI hard disk
  D. SCSI DVD-ROM

546. Ethernet and IEEE 802.3 use what kind of network access method?
  A. Fibre
  B. Token passing
  C. CSMA/CD
  D. SCSI protocol

547. What is the maximum cable length for a 10BaseT segment?
  A. 10 meters
  B. 100 meters
  C. 1000 meters
  D. 10 kilometers

548. At what system run level, NFS server functionality becomes available?
  A. 2
  B. 3
  C. 4
  D. 5

549. Which one of the following would never be used by your system to deliver a packet to a local system?
  A. /etc/hosts
  B. DNS
  C. NFS
  D. CIFS

550. Which of the following is a correct $HOME/.rhosts and /etc/hosts.equiv file format?
  A. user1 ~
  B. ~ user1
  C. user1 +
  D. + user1

551. What are the default primary command prompts for root user, POSIX shell users, and C shell users?

A. $, $, %   B. #, $, %   C. $, #, %   D. #, %, $

552. What is the default secondary command prompt displayed if a command misses information?
A. >   B. <   C. $ D. #

553. VAR=`hostname` and VAR=(hostname) are examples of:
A. Filename completion   B. Command completion
C. Tilde substitution   D. Command substitution

554. Where does, by default, the error messages are sent?
A. /var/adm/syslog/syslog.log   B. /var/adm/console
C. Other user's screen   D. Root's screen

555. What is the default UID for 'nobody' user?
A. 1   B. -1   C. 2   D. -2

556. Which of the following is the correct /etc/passwd file entry?
A. username:actual password:UID:GID:Comments:Home directory:Shell
B. username:encrypted password:UID:GID:Comments:Home directory:Shell
C. username:encrypted password:UID:GID:Home directory:Comments:Shell
D. username:encrypted password:GID:UID:Comments:Home directory:Shell

557. What does the following do?
    mailx user1 < $HOME/.profile

A. Mail the contents of the sending user's .profile file
B. Mail the sending user's .profile file as an attachment
C. Mail user1's .profile file from his home directory
D. Saves a receiving mail to user1's home directory as .profile

558. What is a socket address?
A. PID appended by an IP address   B. IP address appended by a PID
C. IP address appended by a port number D. Port number appended by an IP address

559. What would be the device name for a tape device connected to controller 1 and target 2 with best performance and no rewind?
A. /dev/rmt/c1t2d0BEST   B. /dev/dsk/c1t2d0BESTn
C. /dev/rdsk/c1t2d0BESTn   D. /dev/rmt/c1t2d0BESTn

560. Which command can you use to recreate lost device files?
A. lsdev   B. ioscan   C. insf   D. lssf

561. Which directory does the .rhosts file reside in?
A. $HOME   B. /etc   C. /var   D. /usr

562. What are three ways of saving and exiting vi? Choose THREE.
A. :x!   B. ZZ   C. :wq!   D. :q!   E. :w!

563. Which combination of NFS mount options would reduce the chances of an NFS client hang up when NFS server is unavailable?

    A. retry=3,soft,nointr   B. retry=2,soft,nointr   C. retry=2,soft   D. retry=3,soft

564. Given a class B IP address of 171.25.33.0 and subnet mask of 255.255.224.0, how many subnets and hosts can you get?

    A. 8 / 8192   B. 4 / 16384   C. 16 / 4096   D. 32 / 2048

565. Which LVM command is used to detach a mirrored logical volume?

    A. lvsplit   B. lvmerge   C. lvdetach   D. lvattach

566. Which LVM command is used to attach a detached mirrored copy to its primary?

    A. lvsplit   B. lvmerge   C. lvdetach   D. lvattach

567. Which command would you use to synchronize a mirrored logical volume?

    A. lvsync   B. lvmerge   C. vgsync   D. vgmerge

568. Which software component must be installed on your system in order to take advantage of the HP-UX mirroring capabilities ?

    A. OnlineJFS   B. MirrorDisk/UX   C. Both A & B   D. None of these

569. What software product is needed to get enhanced security attributes added to a non-trusted system?

    A. SecExt   B. EnhancedSec C. TrustedSec   D. StdModSecExt

570. Which command identifies which hardware address is associated with which device file? Choose TWO.

    A. insf   B. lssf   C. ioscan   D. lanscan

571. What LVM command would you run to form a new volume group?

    A. vgform   B. vgmake   C. vgdo   D. vgcreate

572. What are the three areas that the Standard Mode Security Extensions target? Choose THREE.

    A. user login   B. user password   C. user auditing   D. user creation

573. Which command would you run to create a mirror of an existing logical volume?

    A. lvmirror   B. lvmir   C. lvcreate   D. lvextend

574. What would be the sequence of commads that you would execute on a mounted, busy file system to run fsck on it? You have to remount the file system.

    1. fsck   2. mount   3. umount   4. fuser

    A. 1,2,3,4   B. 4,1,3,2   C. 3.4,1,2   D. 4,3,1,2

575. The _____ command is used to display swap space information.

576. In a logical SCSI device file name cXtXdX, what does the "t" represent.

    A. target device B. logical unit number   C. controller number   D. None of the above

577. Bridges can perform translation up to and including which layer in the OSI reference model.

    A. network   B. transport   C. physical   D. data link

578. The _____ configuration file is referenced at system boot to configure IP address(es).

579. VAR=`pwd` is an example of:
    A. command aliasing   B. variable substitution   C. command substitution   D. function setting

580. Which protocol is used by Ignite-UX server to transfer files to the client?
    A. FTP   B. BootP   C. SFTP   D. TFTP

581. Which is the preferred and more secure tool to use in place of telnet?
    A. ssh   B. sftp   C. scp   D. rlogin

582. which combination of NFS mount options most likely prevent client system hangs?
    A. retry=4,soft,nointr   B. retry=4,soft   C. retry=1000   D. hard,intr

583. During the HP-UX system startup, which script executes the startup scripts at various run levls.
    A. /sbin/rc   B. /sbin/init.d   C. /sbin directory   D. /etc/rc

584. The anonymous user (nobody) is pre-configured to have UID:
    A. -1   B. -2   C. 64535   D. 0

585. A socket address is a concatenation of:
    A. port and IP address   B. IP address and port
    C. MAC address and IP address   D. IP address and protocol

586. The lpadmin command can be used to define a new printer when:
    A. scheduler is running   B. scheduler is not running
    C. does not matter   D. none of the above

587. What are the commands to commit superseded patches? Choose TWO.
    A. cleanup   B. swremove   C. swunreg   D. swmodify

588. What is the default priority of a child process?
    A. It gets an average priority   B. It gets the highest priority
    C. It inherits from parent process   D. It gets the lowest priority

589. Choose TWO. File system swap should be created on:
    A. slower disks   B. heavily utilized file systems   C. faster disks   D. less utilized file systems

590. You can view shared memory segment using which command.
    A. vmstat   B. ipcs   C. shstat   D. ioscan

591. Which TWO tools may be used for DNS queries?
    A. dig   B. nslookup   C. nsswitch   D. resolver

592. Which technology are the Intel Itanium2 processors are based on?
    A. Reduced Instruction Set Code   B. Complex Instruction Set Code
    C. Intel Pentium technology   D. Explicitly Parallel Instruction Computing

593. Which of the three components every Integrity server must have?
    A. PCI I/O card   B. Cell board   C. Itanium2 processor   D. Core I/O

594. Following is based on ioscan command. Match the following:

A. full listing   B. list only disk devices   C. listing with device files   D. short listing

1. ioscan –fC disk
2. ioscan
3. ioscan –f
4. ioscan –fn

595. Pluggable Authentication Module (PAM):
    A. enables system administrators to use an available service for NFS
    B. gives system administrators the flexibility of choosing an available authentication service
    C. must be configured, otherwise the system cannot use it
    D. none of the above

596. SSH enables:
    A. authentication based on standard 128-bit encryption
    B. authentication based on standard mode security extension
    C. authentication based on hidden keys
    D. authentication based on trusted mode security

597. Host Intrusion Detection System (HIDS) is used to:
    A. detect attacks on an HP-UX system   B. attack an HP-UX system
    C. monitor host utilization   D. improve HP-UX system utilization

598. Match the following:

A. make_tape_recovery	1.	used for online Oracle DB backup
B. fbackup	2.	byte for byte duplication
C. dd	3.	system recovery archive
D. cpio	4.	copy data using the find command
E. tar	5.	used complex criteria to backup data
F. Data Protector	6.	archives files

599. Choose THREE to view UP status of a LAN card.
    A. ioscan   B. ifconfig   C. lanadmin   D. netstat   E. lanscan   F. nslookup

600. Choose TWO methods to install HP-UX OE using Ignite server.
    A. boot lan.<IP address> install   B. boot net - install
    C. boot from local media and point to ignite server   D. boot <IP address>

601. What would the following do if dir1 is empty?
    ln -f file1 file2 dir1

    A.   links file1 with file2 under dir1   links file2 with file1 under dir1
    B.   creates file1 and file2 under dir1   creates file1 and file2 under dir1 and linked them back
          to file1 and file2

602. Select TWO to trim logfile.
    A. cat < /dev/trim > logfile   B. cat < /dev/null > logfile C. > logfile   D. trim logfile

603. What is the purpose of CIFS server on HP-UX?

A. share Windows file systems / directories with HP-UX
B. share HP-UX file systems / directories with Windows
C. share Windows file systems / directories with HP-UX and vice versa
D. share OpenVMS file systems / directories with HP-UX

604. Name four vxfs file system structure components:
     A. fragment   B. inode table   C. cylinder group
     D. intent log   E. allocation units   F. superblock

605. Select THREE advantages that VxVM has over LVM:
     A. online data migration
     B. support for RAID 0 and RAID 1
     C. load balancing and redundancy over multiple paths to storage device
     D. online conversion from one RAID level to another

606. Which one of the following would you use to check installed patches on your HP-UX system?
     A. check_patches   B. swlist -l product | grep -i ph
     C. swlist -l product | grep -i patch   D. patchinfo

607. Which THREE of the following would you use to software terminate a process with PID 123?
     A. kill -15 123   B. kill –SIGTERM 123   C. kill –s SIGTERM 123   D. kill –s 123

608. What two ways are available to you to fine tune an existing journaled file system?
     A. tunefs   B. mount options   C. vxtunefs   D. vxtune

609. Virtual Private Network (VPN) allows:
     A. data packets over public network   B. data packets over corporate LAN
     C. data packets over private network   D. data packets over corporate WAN

610. HP Data Protector enterprise backup software can be used for: CHOOSE THREE.
     A. online backup of oracle database   B. offline backup of oracle database
     C. Windows file system backups   D. none of the above

611. Which of the following is not a single point of failure (SPOF) in an HP ServiceGuard cluster?
     A. human error   B. application   C. electrical power   D. network card   E. none of the above

612. What are the THREE HP ServiceGuard cluster configurations?
     A. active/active   B. active/standby   C. rolling upgrade   D. passive/passive

613. What is the purpose of Virtual Private Network (VPN)? Choose TWO.
     A. transfer data over the internet securely and confidentially
     B. transfer data over the inetnet insecurely and non-confidentially
     C. transfer stream of packets over public network securely and confidentially
     D. transfer stream of packets over public network insecurely and non-confidentially

614. What are the advantages of HP Data Protector software? Choose TWO.
     A. supports backing up open files   B. allows online backup of Oracle database
     C. does not allow online backup or Oracle database   D. none of the above

615. Why do you have lost+found directory in a file system?
   A. used for JFS intent logging
   B. used to store orphan files
   C. used to store unnecessary files
   D. used to store unnecessary directories

616. To run fsck on a file system, what step-by-step procedure do you need to follow. List them in sequeunce.

Step 1	A. fsck
Step 2	B. umount
Step 3	C. mount
Step 4	D. Stop all processes using the file system

617. To install a CPU in a system, what step-by-step procedure do you need to follow. List them in sequeunce.

Step 1	A. shutdown the system to power off state
Step 2	B. stop all running applications
Step 3	C. boot the system
Step 4	D. install the CPU
Step 5	E. verify the install using the ioscan command
Step 6	F. open the box

618. What is the sequence to boot and clone a server using ignite-ux tape.

Step 1	A. search for the bootable tape
Step 2	B. Say No to Interact with IPL
Step 3	C. stop the boot process togo to BCH
Step 4	D. use the boot command and specify the tape device path

619. Which ones of the following are Berkeley services? Choose THREE.
   A. telnet   B. BIND   C. ftp   D. rlogin   E. remsh

620. What is the default physical extent size in LVM?
   A. 1MB   B. 2MB   C. 4MB   D. 8MB

621. What is the purpose of PV Links? Choose TWO.
   A. provide load balancing
   B. provide redundancy
   C. provide access to same disk via multiple channels
   D. provide access to different disks via one single channel

622. What is the default number of CDE workspaces?
   A. 2   B. 4   C. 6   D. 8

623. Paths defined in which variable are used for searching man page locations?
   A. PATH   B. ECHOPATH   C. MANPATH   D. PATHMAN

624. Which user's privileges a normal user gets if his/her UID is changed to 0 in the /etc/passwd file?
   A. bin   B. root   C. sysadm   D. lp

625. What are THREE benefits of using OnlineJFS?
   A. online resizing   B. fast resynchronization

C. automatic deletion of unused files   D. auto defragmentaiton

626. Which TWO statements are true about an LVM logical volume?
    A. not a file system   B. is a file system   C. may contain a file system
    D. is a swap device   E. contains a volume group   F. exists inside a volume group

627. When is information contained in VGRA loaded in memory?
    A. when vgsync is executed   B. when a volume group is activated
    C. when vgscan is executed   D. when a volume group is deactivated

628. Which THREE protocols are used by a PA-RISC client for OS install using an ignite-ux server?
    A. CIFS   B. NFS   C. TFTP   D. instl_bootd

629. What TWO methods can be used to install OS on a bran new client system using the ignite-ux server?
    A. boot the client using CD/DVD and point it to ignite-ux server
    B. boot the client from the ignite-ux server
    C. boot the client from the BCH prompt pointing to the ignite-ux server
    D. boot the client using any bootable CD and point it to ignite-ux server

630. Before installing a patch, how would you check if the patch requires a reboot following its installation.
    A. All patches require a reboot   B. No patches require a reboot
    C. Check the patch's readme file   D. None of the above

631. Which THREE are true for lanadmin command?
    A. can be used to reset a lan card   B. tells the status of a lan card
    C. displays lan card IP address   D. tells lan card I/O errors

632. Which of the following service provides you file sharing between HP-UX and Windows systems?
    A. LDAP   B. CIFS   C. NIS   D. NIS+

633. Which of the TWO enables you to end your login session?
    A. ctrl+d   B. logout   C. exit   D. quit

634. Which of the following can be used to secure an HP-UX system? Choose THREE.
    A. ssh   B. NIS   C. HIDS   D. PAM

635. How would you force users to change their passwords on a regular basis? Choose THREE.
    A. enable password aging   B. enable standard mode security extensions
    C. convert the system to trusted mode   D. use NIS

636. Anonymous user on HP-UX has UID -2 by default?
    A. True   B. False

637. Which THREE are normal user password requirements?
    A. has to be 6-8 characters in length
    B. has to start with a letter
    C. has to use both upper and lowercase letters
    D. has to contain at least one lowercase letter and one numeric or special character

638. When a new process is forked, which of the following statements about swap is true?
   A. kernel reserves memory for the process
   B. kernel creates a new swap space
   C. kernel deletes information about the process's parent process
   D. kernel reserves space for the process

639. What are the steps in the sequence to reboot a PA-RISC system gracefully from run level 3 to single user mode?

Step 1	A. ISL> hpux –is
Step 2	B. Interrupt the boot process
Step 3	C. stop all applications
Step 4	D. shutdown –ry
Step 5	E. BCH> boot

640. What are the steps in the sequence to reboot an Integrity system gracefully from run level 3 to single user mode?

Step 1	A. HPUX> boot –is
Step 2	B. interrupt the boot process
Step 3	C. stop all applications
Step 4	D. shutdown –ry

641. Which variable defines a user's default printer?
   A. PRNDEST   B. LPDEST   C. PRINT   D. DEFAULT

642. In which file the default system run level is defined ?
   A. /etc/profile   B. /etc/default/inittab   C. /etc/inittab   D. /sbin/inittab

643. What is the purpose of security patch check tool?
   A. reports on missing security patches   B. reports on missing recommended patches
   C. tightens system security   D. checks and installs missing security patches

644. What are the steps in the sequence to extend a busy HFS file system in an LVM logical volume?

Step 1	A. umount
Step 2	B. lvextend
Step 3	C. fuser –ck
Step 4	D. mount
Step 5	E. extendfs

645. Which of the following would run first and last when a system boots up? Choose TWO.
   A. /sbin/rc2.d/S99abc   B. /sbin/rc1.d/s98abc   C. /sbin/rc1.d/S98abc   D. /sbin/rc2.d/s99abc

646. How can a system administrator with root privileges determine a user's lost password?
   A. by decrypting from the /etc/passwd file   B. by decrypting from the /etc/shadow file
   C. by running a password crack tool   D. cannot determine

647. Which command is used to send a system-wide message to all logged in users?

A. wall   B. rwall   C. broadcast   D. send

648. Which ftp command enables you to upload multiple files?
    A. pull   B. mget   C. mput   D. mpull E. put

649. Which processor families support running HP-UX OE? Choose TWO.
    A. Intel Pentium   B. Intel Itanium   C. PA-RISC   D. SPARC   E. Alpha   F. Non-stop

650. What needs to be done after updating the /etc/mail/aliases file?
    A. restart Sendmail daemon   B. run newaliases command
    C. run alises command   D. reboot the system

651. What are the TWO steps in the sequence to extend a busy VxFS file system in an LVM logical volume?

Step 1	A. umount
Step 2	B. lvextend
Step 3	C. fuser –ck
Step 4	D. mount
Step 5	E. extendfs
Step 6	F. fsadm

652. What is the purpose of the break command in a looping construct?
    A. breaks out of the shell script   B. breaks out of the loop
    C. takes you to the start of the loop   D. no effect

653. Which of the following is not an entry in the /etc/passwd file?
    A. UID   B. username   C. shell   D. pwd

654. Available memory refers to:
    A. available shared memory   B. memory available after kernel is loaded
    C. total system memory   D. available memory for swapping

655. Which daemon responds to a client boot request on an Ignite-UX server?
    A. bootd   B. instl_bootd   C. inetd   D. tftpd

656. Which file is referenced when a client boot request arrives on an Ignite-UX server?
    A. /etc/boottab   B. /etc/opt/ignite/instl_bootd
    C. /etc/inetd.conf   D. /etc/rc.config.d/boottab

657. Which of the following is not a correct subnet mask ?
    A. 255.255.255.255   B. 255.255.255.192   C. 255.255.255.128   D. 255.255.255.160

658. Which IP subnet mask divides a class A IP address into 2000+ networks and 8000+ nodes per subnet?
    A. 255.255.192.0   B. 255.255.128.0   C. 255.255.255.128   D. 255.255. 224.0

659. If you have a value containing six space-separated fields defined in a variable VAR, how would you extract only the third field?

A. echo $VAR | cut –f2 –d" "   B. echo $VAR | cut –f3 –d" "
C. cut –f3 –d" " < echo $VAR   D. echo $VAR | grep –f3

660. To start automounter functionality at each system reboot, where would you define an entry.
    A. /etc/rc.config.d/netconf   B. /etc/rc.config.d/nfsconf
    C. /etc/rc.config.d/netdaemons   D. /etc/rc.config.d/automount

661. Match the following:
    A. to check slot usage information on HP-UX 11iv1   B. to check your system's name
    C. to check what HP-UX OE version you are running   D. to check slot usage information on
    HP-UX 11iv2

    1. olrad   2. uname   3. hostname   4. rad

662. Given an IP address of 192.168.1.200 and netmask 255.255.255.192, what is the subnet IP?
    A. 192.168.1.192   B. 192.168.1.200   C. 192.168.1.255   D. 192.168.1.0

663. Which command in HP-UX is used to determine the route a packet takes to reach the destination system
over the network?
    A. tracert   B. traceroute   C. route find   D. findroute

664. Which two are not advantages offered by HP Data Protector software? Choose TWO.
    A. automated backup and restore   B. Centralize management
    C. supports UNIX operating systems only D. online database backup
    E. open file backup   F. does not support data replication

665. Which command in HP-UX is used to report if there are any issues with installed patches?
    A. report_patches   B. find_patches   C. check_patches   D. test_patches

666. What is the boot sequence for a vPar on HP 9000 server? Choose FOUR in the order.
    A. hpux   B. ISL   C. /stand/vpmon   D. /stand/vmunix

667. What is the boot sequence for a non-vPar HP 9000 system? Choose THREE in the order.
    A. hpux   B. ISL   C. /stand/vpmon   D. /stand/vmunix

668. Which protocol is commonly used for network management and monitoring?
    A. SMTP   B. SNMP   C. DNS   D. LDAP

669. What is the boot sequence for a vPar on Integrity server? Choose FOUR in the order.
    A. EFI   B. hpux.efi   C. /stand/vpmon   D. /stand/vmunix

670. What is the boot sequence for a non-vPar Integrity system? Choose THREE in the order.
    A. EFI   B. hpux.efi   C. /stand/vpmon   D. /stand/vmunix

671. Which command is used to unshar a shar file?
    A. shar   B. unshar   C. sh   D. share

672. Which of the following commands are executed by the create_depot script? Choose THREE.
    A. swcopy   B. swinstall   C. sh   D. swpackage

HP Certified Systems Administrator

Answers to Sample CSA Exam Questions

1. C	2. D	3. A, D	4. C
5. C	6. C	7. E	8. D
9. C	10. B, C, D	11. C	12. A
13. B, C	14. A, B, C	15. D	16. A
17. A	18. B	19. C	20. D
21. B	22. B	23. C	24. B
25. C	26. B	27. C	28. D
29. C	30. C	31. D	32. C
33. B	34. D	35. C	36. A
37. A	38. A,B,C	39. A,B,C	40. E
41. C	42. B	43. B	44. B
45. A	46. B	47. B	48. B
49. D	50. C	51. A,C	52. D
53. B	54. A	55. C	56. A
57. B	58. A	59. C	60. D
61. D	62. D	63. C	64. A
65. B	66. A	67. A	68. B
69. A	70. B	71. A	72. B,D
73. B,D	74. A	75. C	76. B
77. B	78. A,B	79. D	80. A
81. B	82. A	83. A	84. C
85. A	86. A	87. C	88. A
89. C	90. D	91. A	92. B
93. D	94. C	95. B,D	96. D
97. B	98. A	99. C	100. A,D
101. D	102. B	103. D	104. C
105. C	106. C,D	107. C	108. C
109. A	110. D	111. C	112. A,C
113. D	114. B	115. A	116. A
117. A	118. B	119. A,B,D	120. A
121. A	122. B	123. B,C	124. A
125. D	126. D	127. A,B	128. B
129. A	130. A	131. A	132. B
133. D	134. C	135. A	136. A
137. A,C	138. C	139. A	140. A,D

141. A	142. D	143. A,C,D	144. D
145. A	146. C	147. A	148. B
149. A,B,D	150. B	151. C	152. A
153. B	154. C,D	155. D	156. D
157. A	158. A	159. C	160. B
161. C	162. B,D	163. A,B,D	164. A
165. C	166. A	167. B	168. C
169. A,C,D	170. B	171. A	172. A,B,D,F
173. E	174. C	175. A,C,D	176. C
177. B	178. B	179. B	180. E
181. C	182. D	183. B	184. A
185. A	186. C	187. B	188. A
189. A,D	190. B	191. A	192. B
193. B,C	194. D	195. B	196. A
197. A,B	198. D	199. C	200. C
201. B	202. B	203. A	204. C
205. B	206. D	207. C	208. A
209. D	210. B	211. D	212. C
213. D	214. C,D	215. A	216. B
217. A	218. C	219. A,C	220. B
221. B	222. C	223. D	224. C
225. A,B	226. B,C	227. D	228. A
229. C	230. D	231. B	232. C
233. D	234. A	235. A	236. B
237. A	238. D	239. A	240. D
241. A	242. D	243. A,D	244. C
245. D	246. A,C	247. A	248. B
249. D	250. A	251. C	252. B
253. D	254. A	255. D	256. C
257. D	258. B	259. A,B	260. C
261. A,D	262. B	263. C	264. B
265. A	266. D	267. A	268. B
269. B	270. C	271. D	272. C
273. B	274. C	275. A	276. B
277. D	278. B	279. B	280. B
281. A	282. B	283. C	284. A
285. A,B,C	286. D	287. B,D	288. B
289. C	290. B	291. D	292. B
293. A	294. B	295. C	296. B
297. C,D	298. C	299. A	300. B
301. A	302. A	303. C	304. B
305. D	306. D	307. B	308. C
309. A,B,D	310. A	311. B	312. A
313. C	314. A	315. B	316. B
317. C	318. C	319. C	320. B
321. D	322. A,C,D	323. A	324. A,B
325. C	326. B,C	327. C	328. A,C,D

329. B	330. B	331. B	332. A
333. D	334. A,B,D	335. A	336. A
337. A,B,C	338. B	339. D	340. A
341. D	342. B,D	343. B,C	344. D
345. A	346. C	347. B	348. A,C
349. D	350. C,D	351. A	352. C
353. A	354. C	355. A	356. C
357. B	358. B	359. C,D	360. C
361. A	362. A	363. C	364. D
365. B	366. D	367. C	368. A
369. C	370. B,D	371. C	372. B
373. A,B,C	374. C	375. A,B	376. B,D
377. A	378. A,B,C	379. B	380. C
381. B	382. B	383. A	384. C,D
385. B	386. B	387. C	388. A,C
389. D	390. B	391. A,B,D,E	392. A,D
393. B	394. A	395. C	396. B,C,D
397. D	398. C,E	399. B	400. A,B,D
401. C	402. A	403. C	404. A
405. B	406. D	407. C	408. B,C,D
409. B,C	410. C	411. B	412. A
413. B	414. A	415. B	416. D
417. B	418. C	419. D	420. A
421. D	422. B,D	423. D	424. C
425. B	426. A	427. A,D	428. B
429. A	430. B	431. D	432. D
433. A,B,C	434. A	435. C	436. B
437. A	438. C	439. C	440. C
441. C	442. D	443. D	444. A
445. B	446. A	447. D	448. C
449. B	450. B	451. C	452. D
453. A	454. A	455. B	456. C
457. B	458. C	459. D	460. B
461. C	462. D	463. C	464. A
465. B	466. A	467. C	468. D
469. B	470. B,D	471. B	472. C
473. A	474. A,B,C	475. B	476. A,B,C
477. C	478. B	479. B	480. C
481. B,C,D,E,F	482. B	483. C	484. A
485. A	486. C	487. D	488. B
489. C	490. D	491. A	492. C
493. A	494. B	495. D	496. B
497. A	498. B	499. B	500. D
501. C	502. A	503. B	504. A
505. D	506. A	507. B	508. D
509. C	510. B	511. C	512. A
513. B	514. C	515. D	516. A,D

517. B	518. C	519. D	520. B
521. A	522. C	523. A,B,D	524. A,C
525. B	526. C	527. B,C	528. B
529. B,C,D	530. B	531. C	532. A,C,D
533. D	534. B	535. B	536. B
537. B,C	538. B	539. A	540. A
541. B	542. C	543. D	544. A
545. B	546. C	547. B	548. B
549. B	550. D	551. B	552. A
553. D	554. A	555. D	556. B
557. A	558. C	559. D	560. C
561. A	562. A,B,C	563. D	564. A
565. A	566. B	567. A	568. B
569. D	570. B,C	571. D	572. A,B,C
573. D	574. D	575. swapinfo	576. A
577. D	578. netconf	579. C	580. D
581. A	582. A	583. A	584. B
585. B	586. B	587. A,D	588. C
589. C,D	590. B	591. A,B	592. D
593. A,C,D	594. A3,B1,C4,D2	595. B	596. C
597. A	598. A3,B5,C2,D4,E6,F1	599. B,C,E	600. A,C
601. D	602. B,C	603. B	604. B,D,E,F
605. A,C,D	606. B	607. A,B,C	608. B,C
609. A	610. A,B,C	611. A	612.A,B,D
613. A,C	614. A,B	615. B	616.D,B,A,C
617. B,A,F,D,C,E	618. C,A,D,B	619. B,D,E	620.C
621. B,C	622. B	623. C	624.B
625. A,B,D	626. C,F	627. B	628.B,C,D
629. A,C	630. C	631. A,B,D	632.B
633. A,C	634. A,C,D	635. A,B,C	636.A
637. A,B,D	638. D	639. C,D,B,E,A	640.C,D,B,A
641. B	642. C	643. A	644. C,A,B,E,D
645. C,A	646. D	647. A	648.C
649. B,C	650. B	651. B,F	652.B
653. D	654. B	655. C	656.C
657. A	658. D	659. B	660.B
661. 4,3,2,1	662. A	663. B	664.C,F
665. C	666. B,A,C,D	667. B,A,D	668. B
669. A,B,C,D	670. A,B,D	671. C	672. A,C,D

HP Certified Systems Administrator

Table of HP-UX Commands

This table provides a list of significant HP-UX commands and their short description. Although there are hundreds of commands available in the operating environment software, however only those are covered that are used more oftenly.

File and Directory	
cat	Creates a small file, joins two files, and displays contents of a file.
cd	Changes directory.
chacl	Adds/modifies/deletes/copies/summarizes ACLs on files.
compress/uncompress	Compresses/uncompresses files.
cp	Copies files or directories.
diff	Compares files or directories for differences.
file	Displays file type.
find	Searches for files in the directory structure.
getacl	Displays ACL information on a file or directory in a JFS file system.
grep/egrep/fgrep	Matches text within text files.
gzip/gunzip	Compresses/uncompresses files.
head/tail	Displays beginning/ending of a text file.
ln	Links files and directories.
ls/lsf/lsx/lsr/ll/l/lc	Lists files and directories in different formats.
lsacl	Displays ACLs on a file.
mkdir	Creates a directory.
more/pg	Displays a text file one screenful at a time.
mv	Moves and renames files and directories.
mvdir	Moves and renames directories.
pwd	Displays full path to the current working directory.
rcp	Copies files from one system to another.
rm	Removes files and directories.
rmdir	Removes an empty directory.
setacl	Sets ACL attributes on a file or directory in a JFS file system.
shar	Packs data into a bundle file. Unpacks the bundle file.
sort	Sorts text files or given input.
strings	Extracts and displays legible information out of a non-text file.
touch	Creates an empty file. Updates time stamp on an existing file.
vi/edit	Creates or modifies a text file.
view	Displays a text file.
wc	Displays number of lines, characters, words, and bytes in a file.
what	Gets SCCS identification information.

whereis	Displays full pathname to a program or command and its manual pages.
which/whence	Displays full pathname to a program or command.
zip/unzip	Compresses/uncompresses files.
Hardware and Devices	
dmesg	Gathers and displays system diagnostics messages.
insf/mknod/mksf	Creates device special files.
ioscan	Displays connected hardware devices.
lsdev	Displays device drivers in the kernel.
lssf	Lists special files.
model/getconf	Displays system hardware model.
mt	Performs tape operations.
olrad	Displays slot status information on select Integrity systems.
rad	Displays slot status information on select HP 9000 systems.
rmsf	Removes device special files.
stty	Displays or sets terminal port settings.
tset	Initializes a terminal based on its type.
tty	Displays full device path to the terminal session.
ttytype	Identifies a terminal.
Partitioning	
parcreate	Creates an nPar.
parmgr	GUI tool used to perform nPar operations.
parmodify	Modifies an nPar.
parremove	Removes an nPar.
parstatus	Displays status information about nPars.
vparboot	Boots a vPar.
vparcreate	Creates a vPar.
vparmodify	Modifies a vPar.
vparremove	Removes a vPar.
vparreset	Resets a vPar.
vparstatus	Displays status information about vPars.
Software and Patches	
check_patches	Checks for any problems with patches.
cleanup	Commits/removes superseded patches.
security_patch_check	Checks for security-related patches.
swacl	Displays or modifies ACLs that protect software products.
swagent	Starts by swagentd to perform software management tasks.
swconfig	Configures/reconfigures/unconfigures an installed software.
swcopy	Copies software from source to depot.
swinstall/swremove	Installs/removes software.
swlist	Lists installed software.
swmodify	Modifies software.
swpackage	Packages software into a depot.
swreg	Registers a software depot.
swverify	Verifies software.
Users and Groups	
chgrp	Changes group membership on a file or directory.

HP Certified Systems Administrator

chmod	Changes permissions on a file or directory.
chown	Changes ownership (and group membership) on a file or directory.
chsh	Changes a user's login shell permanently.
groupadd	Creates a group account.
groupdel	Deletes a group account.
groupmod	Modifies a group account.
groups	Displays a user's secondary group memberships.
grpck	Checks /etc/group for consistency.
id	Displays a user's username, UID, groups, and GIDs.
last	Displays history of successful user login/logout attempts.
lastb	Displays history of unsuccessful user login attempts.
login	Displays login prompt.
logname	Displays the login name.
mesg	Allows/disallows messages to terminal.
newgrp	Changes a user's primary group temporarily.
passwd	Changes user password.
pwck	Checks /etc/passwd for consistency.
quot	Displays which user is using how much disk space.
rsh/rksh/rcsh	Restricted Bourne, Korn, and C shells.
sh/ksh/csh	Bourne, Korn, and C shells.
su	Switch to a different user.
talk	Invokes an interactive chat session with another logged in user.
umask	Displays or sets file mode creation mask.
uptime	Displays how long the system is up for.
ulimit	Gets and sets user limits.
useradd	Creates a new user account.
userdel	Deletes a user account.
usermod	Modifies a user account.
users	Displays a list of currently logged in users.
vipw	Opens /etc/passwd file in vi and locks it.
w	Displays who is currently logged in, what he/she is doing, and how long the system has been up for.
wall	Broadcasts a system wide message.
who	Displays a list of currently logged in users.
whoami	Displays effective user name.
whodo	Displays who is doing what.
write	Chat with another user.
Disks and LVM	
diskinfo	Displays disk size and manufacturer information.
lvchange	changes the characteristics of a logical volume.
lvcreate/lvremove	Creates/removes a logical volume.
lvdisplay	Displays information about a logical volume.
lvextend/lvreduce	Increases/decreases the number of physical extents allocated to a logical volume.
lvlnboot/lvrmboot	Prepares/removes a logical volume to be a root, swap or dump volume.
lvmerge/lvsplit	Merges/splits mirrored volumes.

lvsync	synchronizes stale logical volume mirrors.
mediainit	Initializes a hard disk.
mkboot/rmboot	Installs/removes boot utilities on/from a disk.
mknod	Creates a device file.
pvchange	Changes characteristics of a physical volume.
pvck	Checks and repairs a physical volume.
pvcreate	Creates a physical volume.
pvdisplay	Displays information about one or more physical volumes.
pvmove	Moves allocated physical extents from one physical volume to another.
setboot	Displays and sets boot parameters.
vgcfgbackup/vgcfgrestore	Saves/restores LVM configuration for a volume group.
vgchange	Changes the status of a volume group.
vgcreate/vgremove	Creates/removes a volume group.
vgdisplay	Displays information about a volume group.
vgextend/vgreduce	Extends/reduces a volume group by adding/removing a physical volume.
vgimport/vgexport	Imports/exports a volume group.
vgscan	Scans physical volumes for volume groups.
vgsync	Synchronizes all stale logical volume mirrors within a volume group.
Veritas Volume Manager	
vea	Java-based GUI tool to perform VxVM administration tasks on one or more systems.
vxassist	Performs volume management tasks.
vxcp_lvmroot	Converts LVM root disk to VxVM root disk.
vxdctl	Manages the vxconfigd daemon.
vxdg	Performs disk group management tasks.
vxdisk	Performs disk management tasks.
vxdiskadm	Performs VxVM administration tasks.
vxdisksetup	Brings a disk under VxVM control.
vxdiskunsetup	Removes a disk from VxVM control.
vxdmpadm	Administers Dynamic MultiPathing (DMP).
vxedit	Creates, modifies, and removes VxVM records.
vxinfo	Displays information on volume usability.
vxinstall	Menu driven program run to setup VxVM initially.
vxlicense	Administers VxVM licenses.
vxmake	Creates records for volumes, plexes, and subdisks.
vxplex	Performs operations on plexes and/or volumes.
vxprint	Displays VxVM configuration.
vxrecover	Performs operations specific to volume recovery.
vxrelayout	Changes layout of a volume.
vxresize	Resizes a volume along with file system structures within it.
vxrootmir	Creates a mirror of a VxVM root disk.
vxtask	Performs basic administration tasks on running VxVM operations.
vxunreloc	Unrelocates a subdisk back to its original disk.
vxvmboot	Sets volumes to be root, boot, dump, or primary swap.
vxvmconvert	Converts an LVM volume group into a VxVM disk group.

vxvol	Performs volume-related operations, such as starting volumes, stopping volumes, changing volume characteristics, etc.

File Systems	
bdf	Displays disk utilization.
df	Displays disk utilization.
du	Displays directory or file system utilization.
extendfs	Extends an offline file system.
find	Searches for files/directories.
fsadm	Extends an online file system.
fsck	Checks and repairs a file system.
fstyp	Displays file system type.
fuser	Lists/kills processes using a file system.
mkfs	Backend for newfs. Used to create a new file system.
mklost+found	Creates a lost+found directory.
mount/umount	Connects/disconnects a file system to/from directory tree.
mountall/umountall	Connects/disconnects all unmounted file systems listed in /etc/fstab file to/from directory tree.
newfs	Creates file system structures.
tunefs	Tunes an HFS file system.
vxtunefs	Tunes a JFS file system.

Swap	
swapinfo	Displays information about configured swap spaces.
swapon	Enables a configured swap space.
vmstat	Displays virtual memory statistics.

Startup and Shutdown	
From OS Level:	
init	Changes run level of a running HP-UX system.
lifcp	Copies LIF files.
lifls	Displays LIF directory contents.
lifrm	Removes a LIF file.
reboot	Reboots a system.
shutdown	Shuts a system down gracefully.
who	Displays current system run level.
From BOOT_ADMIN Level:	
boot	Boots a system normally using default boot disk.
efi_cp	Copies AUTO file from EFI partition to local disk, and vice versa.
path	Displays path information for boot devices.
search	Searches for bootable devices.
From ISL Prompt:	
hpux	Loads the secondary system loader into memory.
hpux /stand/vmunix.prev	Boots a system using an alternate HP-UX kernel file.
hpux –is	Boots a system to single user state.
hpux –lm	Boots a system to LVM maintenance state.
hpux –lq	Boots a system ignoring LVM quorum.
hpux –vm	Boots a system to VxVM maintenance state.
hpux ls	Displays contents of /stand.
hpux set autofile	Sets AUTO file contents.

hpux show autofile	Displays AUTO file contents.
Kernel	
ioinit	Maintains consistency between kernel I/O structures and /etc/ioconfig.
kclog	Kernel log file.
kcmodule	Queries and modifies DLKMs.
kconfig	Performs kernel configuration administration.
kcpath	Displays location of currently running kernel.
kctune	Queries and modifies kernel parameters.
kcweb	Administers kernel.
kmadmin	Performs administration of kernel modules.
kmpath	Displays location of currently running kernel.
kmsystem	Queries and modifies DLKMs.
kmtune	Queries and modifies kernel parameters.
kmupdate	Updates default kernel and associated files.
mk_kernel	Regenerates a new kernel.
sysdef	Displays kernel parameters.
system_prep	Gathers running kernel configuration.
Backup, Restore, and Recovery	
check_net_recovery	Compares network-based system recovery archive contents to the running system.
check_recovery	Compares tape-based system recovery archive contents to the running system.
check_tape_recovery	Compares tape-based system recovery archive contents to the running system.
cpio	Creates file archives.
dd	Performs bit by bit copy.
dump/restore	Performs HFS file system backups/restores.
fbackup/frecover	Performs full and incremental file system backups/restores.
make_net_recovery	Creates a system recovery archive on a network directory.
make_recovery	Creates a system recovery archive on tape.
make_tape_recovery	Creates a system recovery archive on tape.
pax	Copies files and directories.
rdump	Performs a remote file system backup.
tar	Archives files.
vxdump/vxrestore	Performs VxFS (JFS) file system backups/restores.
LP Spooler	
accept/reject	Allows/disallows users to submit print requests.
addqueue	Creates queues for printers.
cancel	Cancels a submitted print request.
enable/disable	Enables/disables a printer.
hppi	Configures and manages network printers.
lp	Sends a print request to a printer.
lpadmin	Sets up LP spooler system.
lpalt	Alters a submitted print request.
lpfence	Sets minimum priority for printing.
lpmove	Moves one or more or all print jobs from one printer to another.
lpsched/lpshut	Starts/stops lpsched daemon.

lpstat	Displays printer status information.
Performance	
glance (gpm)	Runs HP GlancePus tool.
iostat	Displays I/O statistics.
ipcs	Displays IPC status.
nice	Executes a command at a non-default priority.
renice	Changes priority of a running command.
sar	Reports various system activities.
time/timex	Displays real, user, and system time spent on the execution of a command.
top	Displays information about running processes.
uptime	Displays how long a system has been up for.
Scripting and Variables	
awk	A programming language.
break	Breaks a loop.
case	A type of logical construct.
continue	Skips execution of the remaining part of a loop and gives the control back to the start of the loop.
echo	Displays variable values and echos arguments.
env	Displays or modifies current environment variables.
exit	Terminates a process or shell script.
export	Makes a variable a global variable.
expr	Evaluate supplied arguments as an expression.
if	A type of logical construct.
read	Prompts for user input.
sed	Stream editor.
set	Displays set variables.
sleep	Suspends execution of a loop for the specified time period.
test	Evaluates a condition.
trap	Ignores signals.
IP Connectivity and Routing	
arp	Displays and modifies MAC-IP address translation.
hostname	Displays or sets system name.
ifconfig	Displays or configures a LAN card/port.
lanadmin	Administers a LAN card/port.
lanscan	Displays installed LAN cards/ports.
linkloop	Checks physical level connectivity between two HP-UX machines.
ndd	Tunes network parameters.
netstat	Displays network status.
nettl	Controls network tracing and logging.
ping	Tests connectivity between two machines.
route	Manages routing table.
set_parms	Configures TCP/IP parameters.
traceroute	Displays all routes to destination host.
uname	Displays summary information about a system.
Internet Services	
bootpquery	Sends bootrequests to a BootP server.

finger	Displays user information.
ftp	Uploads and downloads files.
mail/rmail	Sends/reads mail.
mailx	Sends/receives/reads mail.
newaliases	Rebuilds mail aliases database.
ntpdate	Sets date/time via NTP.
ntpq	Queries NTP daemon.
ntptrace	Displays NTP server hierarchy.
rcp	Transfers files between two UNIX machines.
remsh/rexec	Runs a command on a remote UNIX system without logging in to it.
rlogin/remsh	Logs a user in to a remote UNIX machine.
ruptime/rup	Displays status of remote systems.
rusers	Displays logged in users on remote systems.
rwho	Displays who is logged in on remote systems.
sendmail	Sends mail over the internet.
telnet	Displays login prompt.
tftp	Transfers files to a BootP client.
NFS, AutoFS, and CIFS	
automount	Establishes automount mount points and associates automount maps to them.
cifslist	Displays CIFS-mounted resources.
cifslogin	Logs in to a CIFS share.
cifsmount	Mounts a CIFS share.
exportfs	Exports and unexports files, directories, or file systems to/from NFS client machines.
nfsstat	Displays NFS usage statistics.
rpcinfo	Displays RPC information.
showmount	Displays remote NFS mounts.
smbpasswd	Sets password for SAMBA users.
smbstatus	Displays the status of SAMBA shares.
testparm	Checks for any syntax errors in SAMBA configuration file.
NIS	
domainname	Displays and sets an NIS domain.
nsquery	Queries a specified name service.
ypcat	Displays contents of an NIS map.
ypinit	Sets up an NIS master, slave, or client.
ypmake	Builds NIS map files.
ypmatch	Greps for a pattern in an NIS map.
yppasswd	Changes a user password in NIS maps.
yppoll	Queries NIS server for NIS maps.
yppush	Pushes out NIS maps from master NIS server to slave servers.
ypset	Binds to an NIS server.
ypwhich	Displays which NIS domain the client is bound to.
ypxfr	Pulls NIS map files from master NIS server.
DNS	
dig	Lookup and troubleshooting utility.
hosts_to_named	Converts /etc/hosts file to DNS zone files.

HP Certified Systems Administrator

nslookup	Queries DNS/hosts for name resolution.
nsquery	Queries DNS/NIS/NIS+/hosts for name resolution.
sig_named	Terminates/restarts named daemon.
Ignite-UX	
bootsys	Reboots remote clients.
ignite	Configures, installs, and recovers HP-UX.
Instl_adm	Administers Ignite-UX configuration files.
make_config	Builds Ignite-UX configuration files from software depots.
make_depots	Builds Ignite-UX software depots.
manage_index	Manages the Ignite-UX INDEX file.
setup_server	Performs management tasks for an Ignite-UX server.
Security	
audevent	Displays and sets system events.
audisp	Displays audit records.
audomon	Sets audit file monitoring and size parameters.
audsys	Used for stopping and starting auditing, and displaying and setting audit file/directory information.
chroot	Changes root directory for the specified command.
modprpw	Unlocks a locked user account in trusted mode.
pwconv	Converts to shadow password.
ssh	Opens up a secure login session on a remote UNIX system.
ssh-keygen	Generates keys for ssh passwordless remote login.
tsconvert	Converts/unconverts a system to/from trusted mode.
userdbset	Sets user attributes.
userdbget	Displays user attributes.
userdbck	Verifies the integrity of per-user security file contents.
Miscellaneous	
alias/unalias	Sets/unsets shortcuts.
at	Executes a command at a later time.
banner	Displays letters in large format.
batch	Executes batched commands right away.
cal	Displays calendar.
catman	Creates a whatis database to facilitate keyword search on man pages.
clear	Clears a terminal screen.
crontab	Schedules user cron jobs.
cut	Extracts selected columns.
date	Displays or sets system date/time.
freedisk	Finds and removes filesets appeared to be not in use.
getty	Sets terminal type, modes, speed, and line discipline.
history	Displays previously executed commands.
kill	Sends a signal to a process.
killall	Kills all active processes.
man	Displays manual pages.
nohup	Executes a command immune to hangup signals.
pr	Prints a file on the display terminal.
ps	Displays running processes.

r	Repeats the last command executed.
sam	Administers HP-UX resources.
samlog_viewer	Displays SAM logs.
tee	Sends output to two locations.
tr	Translates characters.
uniq	Displays repeated lines in a file.

Appendix D

Table of Important HP-UX Files

This table contains a list of various significant HP-UX files including configuration, startup, log, and other important files along with their short description.

Hardware and Devices	
/etc/ioconfig	Maintains I/O configuration information.
/stand/ioconfig	A copy of /etc/ioconfig.
Software and Patches	
/var/adm/sw/swagent.log	Logs software agent activities.
/var/adm/sw/swagentd.log	Logs software daemon activities.
/var/adm/sw/swconfig.log	Logs software configuration activities.
/var/adm/sw/swcopy.log	Logs software copy activities.
/var/adm/sw/swinstall.log	Logs software installation activities.
/var/adm/sw/swmodify.log	Logs software modification activities.
/var/adm/sw/swpackage.log	Logs software packaging activities.
/var/adm/sw/swreg.log	Logs software depot registration activities.
/var/adm/sw/swremove.log	Logs software removal activities.
/var/adm/sw/swverify.log	Logs software verification activities.
Users and Groups	
$HOME/.cshrc	Shell initialization file for C shell users.
$HOME/.dtprofile	CDE user initialization file.
$HOME/.exrc	Startup configuration file for the vi editor.
$HOME/.login	User initialization file for C shell users.
$HOME/.profile	User initialization file for Bourne, Korn, and POSIX shells.
$HOME/.shrc	Shell initialization file for Bourne, Korn, and POSIX shells.
/etc/group	Maintains a database of all defined groups on the system.
/etc/logingroup	Contains default group access list for each user.
/etc/passwd	Maintains a database of all defined users on the system.
/etc/profile	System-wide initialization file for Bourne, Korn and POSIX users.
/etc/shadow	Stores passwords and password aging parameters.
/etc/skel/*	Location of user initialization file templates.
/etc/utmp	Contains a list of all currently logged in users.
/tcb/*	Stores passwords and password aging parameters on trusted mode systems.
/var/adm/btmp	Maintains a history of all failed user login attempts.
/var/adm/sulog	Logs switch user activities.
/var/adm/wtmp	Maintains a history of all successful user login attempts.
Disks and LVM	
/etc/lvmconf/*	Stores LVM information.

/etc/lvmtab	Maintains information about volume groups and physical volumes.
File Systems and Swap	
/*/lost+found	Resides in every file system to be used to hold orphan files.
/etc/fstab	Contains entries for file systems and swap spaces that are automatically mounted when system boots up.
/etc/mnttab	Maintains information about currently mounted file systems.
/var/adm/sbtab	Contains a list of all superblock location entries for the root file system.
Startup and Shutdown	
/etc/inittab	Source file for the init process.
/etc/issue	Contents of this file are printed as the login banner.
/etc/motd	Contains a message that you want all users to view when log in.
/etc/rc.config.d/*	Configuration files for startup scripts.
/etc/rc.log	Logs service startup status at system boot.
/etc/shutdownlog	Logs system shutdown activities.
/sbin/init.d/*	Location of all startup & shutdown scripts.
/sbin/rc*.d/*	Sequencer directories pointing to startup scripts located in /sbin/init.d directory.
Kernel	
/stand/build/*	Contains kernel-related files to generate a new kernel.
/stand/dlkm	Contains Dynamically Loadable Kernel Module information.
/stand/system	Contains drivers, tunable parameters, and subsystems whose support is included in the current kernel.
/stand/vmunix	Default HP-UX kernel file.
/stand/vmunix.prev	Old kernel file.
/stand/vpdb	Stores all vPar configuration information.
/stand/vpmon	Software piece that sits between the server firmware and HP-UX OE instances running in vPars.
Backup, Restore, and Recovery	
/var/adm/dumpdates	The vxdump and dump commands updates this file with backup time stamps if the –u option is used with the commands.
/var/adm/fbackupfiles/dates	The fbackup utility updates this file with backup time stamps if the –u option is used with the command.
LP Spooler	
/etc/lp/*	Contains print configuration information.
/var/adm/lp/*	Contains log files for the printing system.
/var/spool/lp/request/*	Holds print requests temporarily.
IP Connectivity and Routing	
/etc/hosts	Contains hostnames (and optionally aliases) and their corresponding IP addresses.
/etc/rc.config.d/netconf	Startup configuration file that defines hostname, routes, LAN card configuration information, etc.
/sbin/init.d/net	Startup script that sets hostname, routes, LAN card configuration as defined in the /etc/rc.config.d/netconf file.
Internet Services	
$HOME/.rhosts	Per user host equivalency file.
/etc/ftpd/ftpusers	Contains a list of disallowed ftp users.

HP Certified Systems Administrator

/etc/hosts.equiv	System-wide host equivalency file.
/etc/inetd.conf	Contains internet services information and used by the inetd daemon.
/etc/networks	Contains information about known networks.
/etc/ntp.conf	Configuration file for NTP.
/etc/rc.config.d/netdaemons	Startup configuration file for internet services including NTP.
/etc/rpc	Contains a list of RPC services along with their port numbers.
/etc/services	Contains various services and their corresponding port numbers.
/etc/shells	Contains a list of allowed login shells.
/var/adm/inetd.sec	Security file for the inetd daemon.
/etc/securetty	Disables direct telnet access into a system.
/etc/protocols	Lists available protocols.
/etc/ntp.drift	Helps xntpd keep track of local system clock accuracy.
/etc/ntp.key	Defines NTP encryption to be used.
/var/adm/syslog/mail.log	Logs mail transfer information.
NFS, AutoFS, and CIFS	
/etc/auto_master	Contains maps for direct, indirect, and special AutoFS maps.
/var/adm/automount.log	Log file for the automount daemon.
/etc/exports	Contains entries for file systems that are NFS exported.
/etc/fstab	Contains entries for file systems and swap spaces that are automatically mounted when system boots up.
/etc/rc.config.d/nfsconf	Startup script for NFS services.
/etc/rmtab	Maintains a list of exported resources.
/etc/xtab	Maintains a list of remotely mounted resources.
/sbin/init.d/nfs.client	Startup script for NFS client.
/sbin/init.d/nfs.core	Startup script for rpcbind daemon.
/sbin/init.d/nfs.server	Startup script for NFS server.
NIS	
/etc/nsswitch.conf	Name server switch file.
/etc/rc.config.d/namesvrs	Startup configuration file for NIS.
/var/yp/*	Default directory that holds all NIS maps and other related information.
DNS	
/etc/dns/*	Directory that holds DNS zone files.
/etc/named.conf	Boot file on DNS servers.
/etc/nsswitch.conf	Name server switch file.
/etc/rc.config.d/namesvrs	Startup configuration file for DNS .
/etc/resolv.conf	Client-side resolver file.
/sbin/init.d/named	The DNS daemon.
Ignite-UX	
/etc/bootptab	Stores configuration information for Itanium2 boot clients.
/etc/opt/ignite/instl_boottab	Stores IP address and MAC information for PA-RISC boot clients.
/var/opt/ignite/INDEX	Maintains available configurations for Ignite-UX clients.
Security	
$HOME/.ssh/*	Stores per-user files related to secure shell access into the system.
/etc/default/security	System-wide user security file.
/etc/pam.conf	System-wide PAM configuration file.

/etc/pam_user.conf	Per-user PAM configuration file.
/etc/security.dsc	System-wide security file that contains default security attributes.
/var/adm/userdb	Per-user user security file.
Miscellaneous	
/etc/syslog.conf	Configuration file for syslogd daemon.
/var/adm/at.allow	Allow file for at use.
/var/adm/at.deny	Deny file for at use.
/var/adm/cron.allow	Allow file for cron use.
/var/adm/cron.deny	Deny file for cron use.
/var/adm/cron/log	Logs cron activities.
/var/adm/syslog/syslog.log	Logs all system activities.
/var/spool/cron/atjobs	Spool area for at jobs.
/var/spool/cron/crontabs	Spool area for cron jobs.

Appendix E

Table of HP-UX System Daemons

This table lists several main HP-UX daemon programs and their short description. These daemons are critical to proper service operation.

Hardware and Devices	
ioconfigd	I/O configuration daemon.
Software and Patches	
swagent	Invoked by swagentd to perform software management tasks.
swagentd	Software management daemon.
Users and Groups	
pwgrd	Password and group caching and hashing daemon.
Disks, LVM, and VxVM	
lvmkd	Watches LVM queue.
vxconfigd	VxVM configuration daemon. Must be running in order to perform any configuration modifications.
vxiod	Starts, stops, and reports on VxVM kernel I/O daemons.
vxnotify	Displays VxVM configuration events.
vxrelocd	Monitors VxVM disks for failures and relocates failed disks.
Swap	
swapper	Works with vhand and handles paging and deactivation.
vhand	Works with swapper and handles paging and deactivation.
Startup and Shutdown	
init	Primary Initialization daemon.
LP Spooler	
lpsched	Local print scheduler daemon.
rlpdaemon	Remote print spooling daemon.
Internet Services	
bootpd	Boot server daemon.
ftpd	FTP server daemon.
inetd	Master internet services daemon.
rarpd	Provides a client with its IP address. Responds to ARP requests.
remshd	Remote shell daemon that serves rcp, rdist, and remsh.
rexecd	Responds to rexec and remsh commands.
rlogind	Remote login daemon to serve the rlogin client requests.

rpc.rusersd	Responds to rusers command and provides a list of users logged on users.
rwhod	Responds to queries to provide status of the system.
sendmail	Sends and receives mail.
telnetd	Remote login daemon to serve the telnet client requests.
tftpd	Trivial FTP server daemon.
xntpd	Runs on the NTP server where clients and peers have their clocks synchronized.
NFS	
biod	Manages buffer cache.
nfsd	Handles NFS client requests.
pcnfsd	Provides authentication and printing service to DOS and Mac clients.
rpc.lockd	Provides NFS file locking services.
rpc.mountd	Provides file handle for the file system resource requested to be mounted by a client.
rpc.statd	Works with rpc.lockd to provide crash and recovery services.
rpcbind	Maintains programs-to-address mappings.
NIS	
keyserv	Stores private encryption keys for users.
rpc.yppasswdd	Manages password change requests in NIS map files.
rpc.ypupdated	Modifies NIS maps based on the updated information.
rpcbind	Maintains programs-to-address mappings.
ypbind	Runs on all NIS servers and clients. Binds the client to an NIS server.
ypserv	Runs on both master and slave NIS servers. The daemon serves client requests.
ypxfrd	Runs on the master NIS server only. Transfers NIS maps over to the slave NIS server when the slave server executes the ypxfr command.
DNS	
named	Runs on DNS servers and clients.
Ignite-UX	
instl_bootd	Responds to boot client requests.
Security	
sshd	Secure shell daemon for ssh utilities.
Miscellaneous	
cron	Executes jobs at scheduled times.
syslogd	Logs system messages.

Glossary

. (single dot)	Represents current directory.
.. (double dots)	Represents parent directory of the current directory.
9000 systems	A family of HP UNIX systems based on PA-RISC processors.
Absolute mode	A way of giving permissions to a file or directory.
Absolute path	A pathname that begins with a /.
Access Control List	A method of allocating extended permissions to a specific user or group on a file.
Access mode	See file permissions.
ACL	See Access Control List.
Active node	The node where a package is configured to automatically start when cluster services are brought up.
Address Resolution Protocol	A protocol used to find a system's Ethernet address when its IP address is known.
Address space	Memory location that a process can refer.
Adoptive node	The node to which a package fails over.
Anonymous client	A client that gets any available IP address from the Ignite-UX server.
Archive	A file that contains one or more compressed files.
Argument	A value passed to a command or program.
ARP	Displays and changes IP to Ethernet translation mappings.
ASCII	An acronym for American Standard Code for Information Interchange.
Auditing	System and user activity record and analysis.
Authentication	The process of identifying a user to a system.
Autoboot	Enables or disables automatic boot of an HP-UX system.
AUTO file	The file that contains boot string.
AutoFS	The NFS client-side service that automatically mounts and unmounts an NFS resource on an as-needed basis.
Autosearch	Enables or disables automatic search for a bootable device.
Availability	A measure of overall system uptime minus any unplanned downtime.
Background process	A process that runs in the background.
Backup	The process of saving data on an alternate media, such as a tape.
Bastille	A security hardening and lockdown tool.
BCH	See Boot Console Handler.
Berkeley Internet Name Domain	A UC Berkeley implementation of DNS. See also DNS.
BIND	See Berkeley Internet Name Domain.
Block	A collection of bytes of data transmitted as a single unit.
Block device file	A device special file associated with devices that transfer data in blocks. For example, disk, CD, and DVD devices.
Boot	The process of starting up a system.

Boot area	A small portion on the boot disk that contains boot utilities necessary to boot the system.
Boot Console Handler	An interface for doing pre-boot tasks.
BootROM	Boot Read Only Memory. BootROM contains stable storage, PDC, and other code required to boot an HP-UX system.
Bridge	A network device that connects two LANs together provided they use the same data-link layer protocol.
Broadcast client	An NTP client that listens to time broadcasts over the network.
Broadcast server	An NTP server that broadcasts time over the network.
Bus	Data communication path among devices in a computer system.
CDE	Common Desktop Environment. A graphical windowing interface for UNIX users.
Cell board	A board that holds processors and memory in n-partitionable servers.
Character	A single letter, digit, or special symbol, such as a comma or a dot.
Character special file	A device special file associated with devices that transfer data serially. For example, disk, tape, serial, and other such devices.
Child process	A sub-process started by a process.
Chroot jail	Changes the directory specified at the command line to become the root directory for the specified command.
CIFS	Common Internet File System. Allows resources to be shared among UNIX and non-UNIX systems.
CIFS client	A system that accesses a resource shared by a CIFS server.
CIFS server	A system that shares a resource to be accessed by a CIFS client.
Cloning	Building systems with identical configuration.
Cluster	A group of 2 or more independent systems that work in conjunction with one another under the control of a management software to provide HA.
Command	An instruction given to the system to perform certain task(s).
Command aliasing	Allows creating command shortcuts.
Command history	A feature that maintains a log of all commands executed at the command line.
Command interpreter	See shell.
Command line editing	Allows editing at the command line.
Command prompt	The OS prompt where you type commands.
COPS	Computer Oracle and Password System. It gathers OS security weaknesses and generates reports for review.
Core cell board	The cell board in an nPar or server that contains a core I/O.
Core I/O	A card that provides console access into an nPar or a server.
Crack	Identifies easily crackable passwords in the /etc/passwd file.
Crash	An abnormal system shutdown caused by electrical outage or kernel malfunction, etc.
Current directory	The present working directory.
Daemon	A server process that runs in the background and responds to client requests.
Data Protector	HP's enterprise backup and restore software product.
De-encapsulation	The reverse of encapsulation. See encapsulation.
Defunct process	See zombie process.

Depot	See software depot.
Device	A peripheral, such as a printer, disk drive, and CD/DVD-ROM.
Device driver	The software that controls a device.
Device file	See special file.
Directory structure	Inverted tree-like UNIX directory structure.
Disk group	A logical container that holds VxVM disks, volumes, plexes, and file systems.
Disk partitioning	Creating multiple partitions on a given hard drive so as to access them as separate logical containers for data storage.
Distinguished name	A fully qualified object path in LDAP DIT.
DIT	Directory Information Tree. An LDAP directory hierarchy.
DLKM	See Dynamically Loadable Kernel Module.
DNS	Domain Name System. A widely used name resolution method on the internet.
Downtime	Time period during which a business application is unavailable or non-functional due to a failure.
Driver	See device driver.
DTKP	See Dynamically Tunable Kernel Parameter.
Dynamically Loadable Kernel Module	Modules that can be automatically loaded into (and unloaded from) memory as per need.
Dynamically Tunable Kernel Parameter	Parameters that can automatically become part of the running kernel.
EFI	Extensible Firmware Interface. It contains boot utilities.
Encapsulation	The process of forming a packet through the seven OSI layers.
Enterprise OE	HP-UX OE that contains basic HP-UX OE plus enhanced components.
EOF	Marks the End OF File.
EOL	Marks the End Of Line.
EPIC	See Explicitly Parallel Instruction Computing.
Explicitly Parallel Instruction Computing	A processor technology.
Export	Making a file, directory, or a file system available over the network as a share.
Extended PCI	A higher speed PCI bus.
Failback	Opposite of failover.
Failover	The process whereby a cluster management software transfers the control of a software package to another node in the cluster.
Fault tolerant	The ability of a computer system to survive and continue to function in the event a sudden hardware or software failure occurs.
FIFO file	First In First Out. A special file used to access data on a first-in-first-out basis.
File descriptor	A unique, per-process integer value used to refer to an open file.
File permissions	Read, write, execute, or no permissions assigned to a file or directory at the user, group, or public level.
File system	A grouping of files stored in special data structures.
Filename completion	Allows completing a filename by typing a partial filename at the command line and then hitting the Esc key twice.
Filename expansion	See filename completion.
Filter	A command that performs data transformation on the given input.

Floating IP address	The IP address not tied to a specific node in a cluster.
Foundation OE	HP-UX OE software that contains basic HP-UX OE.
Full path	See absolute path.
Gateway	A device that links two networks that run completely different protocols.
Genesis partition	The first nPar created on an n-partitionable server.
GID	See group ID.
Golden image	A complete system image that can be deployed on other machines with similar hardware.
Group	A collection of users that requires same permissions on a set of files.
Group ID	A unique identification number assigned to a group.
GSP	See management processor.
Guardian Service Processor	See management processor.
GUI	Graphical User Interface.
Hardening	See Security hardening.
Hard partition	See node partition.
HFS	High-Performance File System. A file system type supported by HP-UX.
HIDS	Host Intrusion Detection System. It monitors for unauthorized access and suspicious activities on one or more systems.
High availability	A design technique whereby a computer system is built in such a way that it recovers quickly from a hardware or software failure.
Home directory	A directory where a user lands when he or she logs into a system.
Host equivalency	Making a system trusted on a remote machine.
Hostname	A unique name assigned to a node on a network.
Hub	A network device that receives data from one or more directions and forwards it to one or more directions.
IA-64	See Itanium.
Ignite-UX	A set of tools and techniques that provide various ways of installing HP-UX.
Initial System Loader	Loads HP-UX after POST is complete.
Inode	An index node number holds a file properties including permissions, size, creation/modification time, etc. It also contains a pointer to the data blocks that actually store the file data.
Installed Product Database	Contains information about all software loaded on a system.
Integrity systems	A family of HP systems based on Itanium2 processors and capable of running HP-UX, Windows, and Linux operating systems.
Intent Log	An area within a JFS file system that holds file system structural information.
Interface card	A card that allows a system to communicate to external devices.
I/O chassis	Cage that holds I/O slots.
I/O redirection	A shell feature that gets input from a non-default location and sends output and error messages to non-default locations.
IP address	A unique 32-bit software address assigned to a node on a network.
IPD	See Installed Product Database.
IPL	See Initial System Loader.
IP multiplexing	Assigning multiple IP addresses to a single physical LAN card or port.
ISL	See Initial System Loader.

ISS	Internet Security Scan. It checks for known security holes.
Itanium2	A 64-bit Itanium2 processor used in HP Integrity systems. Formerly known as IA-64 and Itanium processor.
Job control	A shell feature that allows a process to be taken to background, brought to foreground, and to suspend its execution.
Job scheduling	Execution of commands, programs, or scripts at a later time in future.
Kernel	Software piece that controls an entire HP-UX system including all hardware and software.
LAN	See Local Area Network.
LDAP	Lightweight Directory Access Protocol.
LDIF	LDAP Data Interchange Format. A special format used by LDAP for importing and exporting LDAP data among LDAP servers.
LIF	See Logical Interchange Format.
Link	An object that associates a file name to any type of file.
Link count	Number of links that refer to a file.
Load balancing	A technique whereby more than one servers serve client requests.
Local Area Network	A campus-wide network of computers.
Local printer	A printer connected directly to a computer.
Logical construct	A statement in shell scripting whose output relies on a specified condition.
Logical Interchange Format	Helps transport media.
Logical volume	A logical container that holds one file system.
Login	A process that begins when a user enters his/her username and password correctly at the login prompt.
Login directory	See home directory.
Looping construct	A statement in shell scripting that continuously generates output until a specified condition is met.
LVM	Logical Volume Manager. A disk partitioning solution.
MAC address	A unique 48-bit hardware address of a network card or port. Also called physical address, station address, ethernet address, and hardware address.
Machine	A computer, a system, an HP-UX workstation, or an HP-UX server.
Major number	Points to a device driver.
Management processor	A hardware module installed on a server for system hardware management.
Metacharacters	Characters that have special meaning to the shell.
Minor number	Points to an individual device controlled by a specific device driver.
Mirror	An exact copy of original data.
Mirroring	The process of creating mirrors.
Mission Critical OE	HP-UX OE software that contains Enterprise HP-UX OE plus enhanced components.
Mounting	Attaching a device (a file system, a CD/DVD) to the directory structure.
MP	See Management Processor.
Multifunction card	An interface card that provides two or more different types of I/O connections.
Name resolution	The technique to determine IP address by providing hostname.
Network	Two or more computers joined together to share resources.
Network management	Monitoring, supporting, and administering of network devices.

Network printer	A printer connected to a network port and has an IP address and hostname.
Network Time Protocol	A protocol used to synchronize system clock.
NFS	Network File System. Allows UNIX systems to share files, directories and file systems.
NFS client	Enables mounting an exported UNIX resource.
NFS server	Makes available (exports) a resource for mounting by an NFS client.
NIS	Network Information Service.
NIS client	UNIX system that binds itself with an NIS server for accessing administrative files.
NIS server	Maintains and makes available shared administrative files.
NIS+	NIS Plus. An enhanced NIS software product.
Node	A device connected directly to a network port and has a hostname and an IP address associated with it. A node could be a computer, an HP-UX workstation, an HP-UX server, an X terminal, a printer, a router, a hub, a switch, a tape library, and so on.
Node name	A unique name assigned to a node.
Node partition	A physical partition within an HP UNIX system that can run either a dedicated, standalone HP-UX OE instance within it, or can house one or more vPars.
Npar	See node partition.
NTP	See Network Time Protocol.
Octal mode	A method of setting permissions on a file or directory using octal numbering system.
Octal numbering system	A 3 digit numbering system that represents values from 0 to 7.
OE	See operating environment.
OnlineJFS	Software product that allows to extend the size of a JFS file system online.
Open Systems Interconnection	A layered networking model that provides guidelines to networking equipment manufacturers to develop their products for multi-vendor interoperability.
Operating environment	A collection of core OS and additional tools and utilities including networking software, etc.
Operating system	The core HP-UX functionality.
Orphan process	An alive child process of a terminated parent process.
OS	See operating system.
OSI	See Open Systems Interconnection.
Owner	The user that creates a file or starts a process.
PAM	See Pluggable Authentication Module.
Parent directory	A directory one level above the current directory in the file system hierarchy.
Parent process ID	The ID of a process that starts a child process.
PA-RISC	Precision Architecture – Reduced Instruction Set Computing. A RISC-based microprocessor architecture used in HP 9000 systems.
Partitioning continuum	A family of server partitioning technologies.
Passive node	See adoptive node.
Password aging	Provides enhanced control on user passwords.
Patch attributes	Attributes associated with a patch.
PCI	See Peripheral Component Interconnect.

PCI-X	See extended PCI.
PDC	See Processor Dependent Code.
Performance monitoring	The process of acquiring data from system components for analysis and decision-making purposes.
Peripheral Component Interconnect	A local bus that connects various peripheral devices to the system.
Permission	Right to read, write, or execute.
Physical volume	A hard drive logically brought under LVM control.
PID	See process ID.
Pipe	Sends output from one command as input to the second command.
Plex	Represents one copy of data within a volume.
Pluggable Authentication Module	A set of library routines that allows using any authentication service available on a system for user authentication, password modification, and user account validation purposes.
Port	A number appended to an IP address. This number could be associated with a well-known service or is randomly generated.
POST	Power On Self Test. Runs by PDC at system boot time to test hardware.
PPID	See parent process ID.
Primary node	See active node.
Primary prompt	The symbol where commands and programs are typed for execution.
Process	Any command, program, or daemon that runs on an HP-UX system.
Process ID	An identification number assigned by kernel to each starting process.
Processor	A CPU. It may contain more than one cores.
Processor Dependant Code	Firmware code stored in BootROM and executed at system boot up for performing POST and other necessary boot related tasks.
Prompt	See primary prompt.
Protocol	A common language that two nodes understand to communicate.
RAID	Redundant Array of Independent Disks.
Reliability	The ability of a computer system to carry out and keep up its function in normal as well as abnormal circumstances.
RDN	Relative Distinguished Name. A relative location of an object in LDAP DIT.
Recovery	Recovering a crashed system back to normal using Ignite system recovery tape. This process may include restoring backed up data.
Redirection	Getting input from and sending output to non-default destinations.
Redundancy	A technique whereby an alternate device acts for a primary device should it fails. The device could be a server, a boot disk, a network card, and so on.
Referral	An entity defined on an LDAP server to forward a client request to some other LDAP server that contains the client requested information.
Registered client	A client that has a dedicated IP addresses defined on the Ignite-UX server.
Regular expression	A string of characters commonly used for pattern matching purposes.
Relative path	A path to a file relative to the current user location in the file system hierarchy.
Remote printer	A printer accessed by users on remote systems.
Repeater	A network device removes unwanted noise from incoming signals, and amplifies and regenerates the signals to cover extended distances.
Replica	A slave LDAP server that shares master LDAP server's load and provides HA.
Resource partition	A software partitioning technique.

Restore	The process of retrieving data from an offline media.
Rolling upgrade	In a cluster environment, rolling upgrade allows for application upgrades with minimal amount of downtime.
Root	See superuser.
Router	A device that routes data packets from one network to another.
Routing	The process of choosing a path over which to send a data packet.
Run control levels	Different levels of HP-UX operation.
SAM	See System Administration Manager.
Samba	See CIFS server.
SAN	See Storage Area Network.
SATAN	Security Administrators Tool for Analyzing Networks. It gathers network security weaknesses and generates reports for review.
Schema	A set of attributes and object classes.
Script	A text program written to perform a series of tasks.
SCSI	See Small Computer System Interface.
Search path	A list of directories where the system looks for the command specified at the command line.
Secondary prompt	A prompt indicating that the entered command needs more input.
Secure shell	A set of secure tools to gain access to an HP-UX system.
Security hardening	Implementation of security measures to enhance system security.
Server	A powerful system that runs HP-UX software.
Server complex	A complete physical hardware box including server expansion unit.
Server expansion unit	A hardware box that holds extended hardware components of a server.
Set Group ID	Sets real and effective group IDs.
Set User ID	Sets real and effective user IDs.
Setgid	See set group ID.
Setuid	See set user ID.
Shadow password	Mechanism to move passwords and password aging information to secure file.
Shared memory	A portion in memory created by a process to be shared with other processes that communicate with that process.
Shell	The UNIX command interpreter that sits between a user and UNIX kernel.
Shell program	See script.
Shell script	See script.
Shell scripting	Programming in a UNIX shell to automate a given task.
Signal	A software interrupt sent to a process.
Single-user mode	An OS state in which the system cannot be accessed over the network.
Slot	A receptable of an I/O card in a computer system.
Small Computer System Interface	A parallel interface used to connect peripheral devices to the system.
Socket	A combination of an IP address and the port number.
Software depot	A logical repository to store software.
Software distributor	A set of commands to perform software and patch management tasks.
Special characters	See metacharacters.
Special file	A file that points to a specific device.
SPOF	Single Point Of Failure.

Stable storage	A small non-volatile area in PDC that contains hardware paths of system console and boot devices, among other boot-related information.
Standard error	The location to send error messages generated by a command. The default is the terminal screen where the command is executed.
Standard input	The location to receive input from. The default is the keyboard.
Standard mode security	A set of advanced security features.
Standard output	The location to send output, other than error messages, generated by a command. The default is the terminal screen where the command is executed.
Standby node	See adoptive node.
Stderr	See standard error.
Stdin	See standard input.
Stdout	See standard output.
Sticky bit	Prevents deletion of files in a directory by non-owners.
Storage Area Netwrok	A network of computers that share storage device(s).
Stratum level	The categorization of NTP time sources based on reliability and accuracy.
String	A series of characters.
Subdisk	A logical, contiguous chunk of disk space.
Subnet	One of the smaller networks formed by dividing an IP address.
Subnetting	The process of dividing an IP address into several smaller subnetworks.
Superblock	A small portion in a file system that holds the file system's critical information.
Superuser	A user that has limitless powers on an HP-UX system.
Swap	Alternate disk location for demand paging.
Switch	A network device that looks at the MAC address and switches the packet to the correct destination port.
Symbolic link	A shortcut created to point to a file located somewhere in file system hierarchy.
Symbolic mode	A method of setting permissions on a file using non-decimal values.
System	A machine that runs HP-UX Operating Environment software.
System Administration Manager	A graphical, windowing tool for HP-UX system administration.
System call	A mechanism that applications use to request service from the kernel.
System console	A display device (usually a dumb terminal) connected directly to an HP-UX system.
System recovery	The process of recovering an unbootable system.
TCP/IP	Transmission Control Protocol / Internet Protocol. A stacked, standard, suite of protocols for computer communication.
Terminal	See system console.
Topology	Ways of connecting network nodes together.
Trusted mode security	A C2 level of security that implements strict password control policies among other restrictions on a UNIX system.
Tty	Refers to a terminal.
UID	See user ID.
Ultra high availability	Design that involes cluster nodes residing in distant data centers.
Unmounting	Detaching a mounted file system or a CD/DVD from the directory structure.

Uptime	The length of time during which a business application remains up and available for user access.
User equivalency	Making a user trusted on a remote machine.
User ID	A unique identification number assigned to a user.
Variable	A temporary storage of data in memory.
Virtual IP address	See floating IP address.
Virtual machine	A partitioning technique on HP Integrity machines.
Virtual partition	A logical partition within an HP-UX system complex that runs a dedicated, standalone HP-UX OE instance within it.
Virtual Private Network	A virtual network on the internet to transfer confidential information securely.
Volume group	A logical container that holds physical volumes, logical volumes, and file systems.
vPar	See virtual partition.
VPN	See Virtual Private Network.
VxVM	Veritas Volume Manager. A disk partitioning solution.
WAN	See Wide Area Network.
Wide Area Network	A network with systems located geographically apart.
Wildcard characters	See metacharacters.
Workstation	A system that runs HP-UX software. These are usually deskside machines used by individuals for specific tasks.
Zombie process	A child process that terminated abnormally and whose parent process still waits for it.

Index

/etc/hosts file, 498
/etc/services file, 477
/etc/shutdownlog, 345
/var/adm/btmp file, 235
Absolute path, 32
accept command, 411
Access Control List, 69
  Default ACLs, 73
Active node, 674
Address Resolution Protocol (ARP), 482
Adoptive node, 672, 674
alias command, 100
ARP cache, 483
arp command, 482
ARPA (See Internet services)
at command, 419
auddisplay command, 682
audevent command, 682
audomon command, 682
audsys command, 682
Authentication, 676
Authorization, 676
AutoFS
  Accessing user home directories, 576
  Benefits, 568
  Daemons, 569
  Defined, 568
  Features, 568
  How it works, 568
  Maps, 570
    Direct map, 572
    Indirect map, 574
    Master map, 570
    Special map, 571
  Replicated server access, 575
  Starting and stopping, 569
  Versus Automounter, 576
automount command, 569
Automounter, 576
Availability, 672, 765
awk command, 82
Backup, 390
  Differential, 390
  Full, 390
  Incremental, 390
  Levels, 390
  Tools, 392
banner command, 20
BDC (See Boot Console Handler)

bdf command, 324, 562
Berkeley services (See Internet services)
Block special device file (See File types)
Boot
  /etc/inittab file, 362
  /etc/ioconfig file, 363
  /sbin/bcheckrc script, 363
  /sbin/lvmrc script, 363
  /sbin/pre_init_rc script, 362
  /sbin/rc script, 364
  /var/adm/rc.log file, 367
  HP 9000, 346
    Autoboot flag, 350
    Autosearch flag, 350
    Booting from alternate kernel, 355
    Booting from device paths, 352
    Booting to single user state, 353
    Booting without quorum, 354
    LVM maintenance state, 354
    Setting boot device paths, 351
    Viewing and modifying AUTO file, 355
    VxVM maintenance state, 354
  HP Integrity, 356
    Autoboot and boot delay, 358
    Boot manager, 357
    Booting from alternate device, 359
    Booting from an alternate kernel, 361
    Booting to single user state, 359
    EFI, 357
    Setting boot paths, 359
    Viewing and modifying AUTO file, 360
  init process, 362
  Initialization, 362
  Kernel initialization, 362
  LVM maintenance state, 360
  Sequencer directories, 365
  Startup configuration files, 366
  Startup scripts, 367
  VxVM maintenance state, 360
Boot Console Handler, 349
BootP
  Adding and verifying, 640
  Defined, 638
  How it works, 638
bootpquery command, 640
break command, 462
Bridge, 478
cal command, 19
cancel command, 415
case command, 454
cat command, 37, 39

catman command, 25
cd command, 15
chacl command, 70
Character special device file (See File types)
check_patches command, 215
check_recovery command, 665
chgrp command, 66
chmod command, 62
chown command, 66
chroot command, 688
CIFS (See Common Internet File System)
cifslist command, 586
cifslogin command, 586
cifsmount command, 586
cleanup command, 217
clear command, 19
Cluster, 671, 673
Common Desktop Environment
    Application manager, 11
    Calendar manager, 8
    Clock, 8
    Exit, 10
    File manager, 8
    Front panel, 6
    Front Panel, 7
    Front panel lock, 9
    Mail manager, 9
    Personal applications, 9
    Printer manager, 11
    Style manager, 11
    Virtual workspaces, 9
Common Internet File System
    /etc/opt/samba/smb.conf configuration file, 582
    /etc/rc.config.d/samba server startup file, 582
    /sbin/init.d/cifsclient client startup script, 586
    /var/opt/samba/private/smbpasswd file, 584
    Accessing HP-UX share on Windows, 585
    Accessing Windows share on HP-UX, 585
    Defined, 580
    Features, 580
    Setting up, 582
    Testing, 586
Concatenation, 287
Console, 4
continue command, 462
cp command, 45
cpio command, 398
crontab command, 421
cut command, 105
Data Protector, 399
date command, 19
dd command, 399
Default gateway (See Default route)
Default route, 499
Device file
    Logical, 138
    Physical, 137
    Tape, 140
    Terminal and modem, 141

df command, 326
DHCP (See Dynamic Host Configuration Protocol)
diff command, 21
dig command, 626
Digital Security Algorithm, 685
disable command, 411
Disk partitioning
    Defined, 246
    LVM, 246
    VERITAS Volume Manager, 284
    Whole disk, 280
diskinfo command, 252
DLKM (See Dynamically Loadable Kernel
    Modules)
dmesg command, 144, 331
Domain Name System
    /etc/nsswitch.conf file, 622
    /etc/resolv.conf file, 624
    Defined, 608, 609
    Domain, 609
    FQDN, 610
    How DNS works, 613
    Name space, 609
    Roles, 611
        Caching-only, 611
        Client, 611
        Master, 611
        Slave, 611
    Setting up, 613
        Caching-only server, 622
        Client, 622
        Master server, 613
        Slave server, 621
    Updating, 626
    Verifying, 625
    Versions, 612
    Zone, 611
    Zone files, 611, 615
domainname command, 593
Downtime, 672
DSA (See Digital Security Algorithm), 685
DTKP (See Dynamically Tunable Kernel
    Parameters)
du command, 327
dump command, 395
Dynamic Host Configuration Protocol, 503
Dynamically Loadable Kernel Modules, 373, 380,
    382
Dynamically Tunable Kernel Parameters, 373
echo command, 439
EFI shell, 173
enable command, 411
exportfs command, 559, 563
Failback, 674
Failover, 672, 674
Fault tolerance, 672, 767
fbackup command, 392
File permissions
    Classes, 60
    Default, 65

Initial value, 64
Modes, 60
Octal notation, 62, 63
Special, 67
    setgid bit, 68
    setuid bit, 67
    Sticky bit, 69
Symbolic notation, 62
Types, 60
umask, 64, 65
File system
    /etc/fstab file, 319
    /etc/mnttab file, 312
    Creating, 309
    Defined, 304
    Defragmenting, 317
    Extending, 315
    Monitoring, 324
    Mounting, 312
    Mounting and unmounting CDFS, 323
    Mounting and unmounting LOFS, 324
    Reducing, 316
    Removing, 320
    Repairing, 321
    Tuning, 317
    Types, 304
        HFS, 305
            Cylinder group, 307
            Data block, 307
            Fragment, 307
            Inode, 307
            Superblock, 305
        JFS or VxFS, 247, 284, 307
            Allocation unit, 309
            Inode, 309
            Intent log, 309
            Superblock, 308
    Unmounting, 318
    Viewing, 313
File system tree
    /, 29
    /home, 32
    /opt, 32
    /stand, 31
    /tmp, 32
    /usr, 31
    /var, 31
    Defined, 28
File types, 33
    Block special device file, 29, 35
    Character special device file, 29, 35
    Directories, 34
    Executable files, 34
    Named pipe, 36
    Raw device file, 29, 35
    Regular files, 33
    Socket files, 36
    Symbolic links, 35
Files and directories
    Command summary, 48
    Copying, 45
    Moving and renaming, 46

Naming convention, 37
Removing, 47
find command, 51, 68
finger command, 532
Floating IP Address, 673
frecover command, 393
fsadm command, 316
fsck command, 321
FTP
    /etc/ftpusers file, 535
    Enable, 534
    Enabling anonymous ftp, 535
    Enabling *ftp* logging, 537
    Using anonymous ftp, 537
Full path (See Absolute path)
fuser command, 318, 563
Gateway, 475
getacl command, 70
getconf command, 18
glance command, 430, 434
Golden image, 661
gpm command, 431
grep command, 48
groupadd command, 236
groupdel command, 237
groupmod command, 236
Groups
    /etc/group file, 225
    Creating, 236
    Deleting, 237
    Modifying, 236
    Multiple group memberships, 238
groups command, 18
grpck command, 227
GSP (See Management Processor), 149
Guardian Service Processor (See Management
    Processor), 149
HA (See High Availability), 668
Hardware address (See MAC address)
Hardware components
    Bus, 131
    Bus converter, 131
    Cabinet, 133
    Cell board, 131
    Core I/O, 132
    EPIC processors, 131
    I/O Chassis, 132
    Interface card, 129
    Itanium2 processor, 131
    Multi-function card, 130
    Network Interface Card, 129
    PCI & PCI-X, 128
    Power supplies, 132
    Processor core, 131
    Processor module, 131
    SCSI Host Bus Adapter, 130
    Server complex, 133
    Server Expansion Unit, 132
    Slot, 127
head command, 42

High Availability, 668, 673
Home directory, 6
Host equivalency, 528
hostname, 483
hostname command, 18
hosts_to_named command, 614
HP-UX features, 4
Hub, 479
id command, 17
ifconfig command, 485, 495
Ignite-UX
    Anonymous client, 645
    Benefits, 644
    Booting clients and installing HP-UX, 655
    Cloning, 663
    Defined, 644
    Golden image, 661
    Registered client, 645
    Setting up, 644
init command, 344
init process, 362
Initialization files, 239
Input/Output/Error Redirection
    Defined, 95
    Standard error, 96
    Standard input, 96
    Standard output, 96
insf command, 143
Installation
    Local, 172
instl_adm command, 654
Inter Process Communication (IPC), 435
Internet services, 522
    /etc/inetd.conf file, 524
    /etc/rpc file, 525
    /etc/services file, 525
    /var/adm/inetd.sec file, 526
    Host equivalency, 528
    inetd daemon, 522
    inetd logging, 527
    User equivalency, 529
ioinit command, 142, 363
ioscan command, 137, 508
iostat command, 433
IP address, 6, 484, 485, 486, 487, 495, 498, 534
IP multiplexing, 491, 496
IP network classes, 485
    Class A, 486
    Class B, 486
    Class C, 487
ipcs command, 435
Job control, 115
Job scheduling, 418
    /var/adm/cron/log, 419
    Controlling access, 418
    cron daemon, 418
    cron startup configuration file, 418
    cron startup script, 418
    crontab file syntax, 421
    Listing and removing *at* jobs, 420

    Listing and removing *cron* jobs, 422
    Setting up *cron* jobs, 422
    Using *at* command, 419
    Using *crontab* command, 421
kclog command, 383
kcmodule command, 383
kconfig command, 383
kcpath command, 384
kctune command, 384
kcweb command, 384
Kernel, 2
    Reconfiguring HP-UX 11iv1, 373
    Reconfiguring HP-UX 11iv2, 383
    Why reconfigure kernel, 372
kill command, 114
kmadmin command, 380, 382
kmsystem command, 374
kmtune command, 374, 382
kmupdate command, 375
LAN (See Local Area Network)
LAN card
    Configuration file, 496
    Configuring IP multiplexing, 496
    Defined (See Hardware components)
    Detecting, 494
lanadmin command, 482, 511
lanscan command, 482, 495, 509
last command, 234
lastb command, 235
lc command, 12
LDAP (See Lightweight Directory Access Protocol)
ldapsearch command, 635
let command, 456
lifcp command, 269
lifls command, 347
Lightweight Directory Access Protocol
    Defined, 630
    Features and Benefits, 630
    Installing client, 635
    Netscape Directory Server, 634
    Roles
        Client, 633
        Referral, 634
        Replica, 633
        Server, 633
    Terminology
        Attribute, 631
        Directory, 631
        Distinguished name, 633
        Entry, 631
        LDIF, 632
        Matching rule, 632
        Object class, 632
        Relative distinguished name, 633
        Schema, 632
Link files, 55
    Hard link, 56
    Symbolic link, 55
linkloop command, 510
Load balancing, 673

Local Area Network, 468
Logical Volume Manager, 246
   /etc/lvmtab file, 259
   Backing up and recovering LVM configuration, 263
   Creating a logical volume, 256
   Creating a physical volume, 253
   Creating a Volume group, 254
   Data structures, 250
   Extending a logical volume, 260
   Extending a volume group, 259
   Logical extent, 249
   Logical volume, 248
   Major number, 250
   Minor number, 250
   Physical extent, 248
   Physical volume, 247
   Reducing a logical volume, 261
   Reducing a volume group, 262
   Removing a logical volume, 262
   Removing a volume group, 262
   Volume group, 247
logname command, 17
lp command, 414
lpadmin command, 406, 410
lpalt command, 415
lpfence command, 413
lpmove command, 415
lpsched daemon, 402
lpshut command, 403
lpstat command, 412
ls command, 12
lsacl command, 70
lsf command, 14
lsr command, 15
lssf command, 139
lvchange command, 268
lvcreate command, 256
lvdisplay command, 258
lvextend command, 257, 260
lvlnboot command, 267, 269
LVM / VxVM comparison, 301
LVM Mirroring, 264
   Allocation policies, 270
     /ec/lvmpvg file, 273
     Distributed allocation policy, 277
     PVG-Strict allocation policy, 273
     Strict allocation policy, 270
   Benefits, 264
   Extending mirrors, 278
   Merging mirrors, 280
   Mirroring non-*vg00*, 269
   Mirroring *vg00*, 264
   MWC, 267
   Reducing mirrors, 278
   Splitting mirrors, 279
   Synchronizing mirrors, 279
lvmerge command, 280
lvreduce command, 261, 278
lvremove command, 262
lvsplit command, 279
lvsync command, 279
MAC address, 482
mailq command, 539
mailx command, 539
Major number, 141
make_config command, 652
make_depots command, 652
make_net_recovery command, 662
make_recovery command, 665
make_sys_image command, 662
make_tape_recovery command, 661
man command, 23
manage_index command, 654
Management Processor, 148
mediainit command, 253
Minor number, 142
Mirroring, 287
mk_kernel command, 375
mkboot command, 160
mkdir command, 38
mkfs command, 310
mklost+found command, 30
mknod command, 144
mksf command, 144
model command, 18
modprpw command, 679
more command, 40
mount command, 312, 561
mountall command, 561
mv command, 46
Name resolution
   Defined, 608
   Methods, 608
ndd command, 516
netstat command, 485, 499, 500, 514
nettl command, 518
Network, 468
Network access methods, 472
Network File System
   Basic troubleshooting, 564
   Benefits, 552
   Commands, 553
   Daemons, 553
   Defined, 552
   Export options, 557
   How it works, 555
   Monitoring, 563
   Related files, 554
   Resource, 552
   Setting up
     NFS client, 559
     NFS server, 556
   Startup scripts, 555
   Unexporting a resource, 563
   Unmounting a resource, 563
   Versions, 553
   Viewing resources, 562
Network Information Service
   /etc/nsswitch.conf file, 598

Alternate passwd file, 604
Daemons, 592
Defined, 590
Displaying and searching maps, 601
Domain, 590
Maps, 590
Modifying user password, 602
Roles
   Client, 592
   Master server, 591
   Slave server, 591
Securing, 605
Setting up
   Client, 597
   Master server, 593
   Slave server, 596
Testing, 600
Updating maps on master, 602
Updating maps on slave, 603
Network management
   Agent, 519
   Managed device, 519
   Management station, 520
   MIB, 520
   Overview, 519
Network Time Protocol
   /etc/rc.config.d/netdaemons file, 545, 546
   Authentication, 547
   Basic troubleshooting, 549
   Daemon, 545, 546
   Defined, 542
   Querying, 548
   Roles
      Client, 543
      Peer, 543
      Primary server, 543
      Secondary server, 543
   Setting up
      Client, 546
      Server & peer, 544
   Stratum levels, 543, 773
   Time source
      Internet-based, 542
      Local system clock, 542
      Radio clock, 542
   Tracing roots, 549
   Updating manually, 548
Network topologies, 469
   Bus, 469
   Hybrid, 471
   Ring, 471
   Star, 470
newaliases command, 540
newfs command, 310
newgrp command, 238
NFS (See Network File System)
nfsstat command, 563
nice command, 112
NIS (See Network Information Service)
Node partition, 152
   Adding cell, 155
   Changing nPar name, 155

Creating genesis partition, 153
Creating nPar, 154
Removing cell, 156
Removing nPar, 156
Using Partition Manager GUI, 156
nohup command, 116
nPar (See Node partition), 152
nslookup command, 625
nsquery command, 601, 625, 636
NTP (See Network Time Protocol)
ntpdate command, 548
ntpq command, 548
ntptrace command, 549
OLA/R, 129
olrad command, 127
Online backup, 399
Operating environment
   Comparison, 170
Orphan file, 30
OSI Reference model
   Defined, 473
   Encapsulation & de-encapsulation, 480
   Layers, 474
   Peer to peer, 480
Outage, 672
PAM (See Pluggable Authentication Module)
parcreate command, 152, 154
parmgr command, 157
parmodify command, 152, 154, 155
parremove command, 152, 156
parstatus command, 152, 153, 154
Partition Manager, 156
Partitioning Continuum
   Benefits, 148
   Overview, 148
Passive node (See Adoptive node), 674
passwd command, 228, 602
Password aging, 676
Password requirements, 229
Passwordless user access, 684
Patches
   Acquiring
      Bundles, 211
      Individual, 208
   Ancestry, 205
   Category tags, 205
   Committing, 216
   Critical and non-critical, 204
   Dependency, 203
   Installing
      Bundles, 212
      From CD/DVD, 214
      From tape, 214
      Individual, 208
   Listing, 206
   Naming convention, 202
   Patch Assessment Tool, 217
   Patch types
      Common, 202
      Kernel, 202

Network, 202
   Subsystem, 202
Rating, 204
Rolling back, 216
Security Patch Check Tool, 219
Software Assistant, 220
State, 204
Status, 204
Suppression, 203
Verifying, 214
Why apply patches?, 202
Pattern matching, 48
PDC (See Processor Dependent Code)
Performance
   Areas
      CPU, 429
      Disk, 433
      Network, 436
      Physical memory, 431
      Swap, 431
   Fixing, 436
   Monitoring, 428, 771
   Tools, 428
pg command, 41
Physical partition (See Node partition)
Physical Point of Attachment, 491
ping command, 514
Pipe, 103
Planned downtime, 672
Pluggable Authentication Module, 686
   Account management, 687
   Authentication management, 687
   Password management, 687
   Session management, 687
Port, 477
PPA (See Physical Point of Attachment)
pr command, 105
Primary node, 674
Printers
   Adding
      Local, 406
      Network, 408
      Remote, 407
   Checking status, 412
   Defined, 402
   Directory structure, 402
   Enabling and disabling, 411
   Removing, 413
   Requests
      Accepting and rejecting, 411
      Cancelling, 415
      Modifying, 415
      Moving, 415
      Sending, 414
   Setting default, 410
   Setting fence level, 413
   Setting priority, 412
   Setting up, 405
   Setup types, 403
      Local, 404
      Network, 405
      Remote, 404

Starting and stopping daemon, 403
Process
   Daemon, 110
   Listing, 110
   PID, 110
   Priority, 112
   Signals, 113
   States, 112
Process Resource Manager, 166
Processor Dependent Code, 349
Protocol, 475
ps command, 110, 434
PuTTY software, 683
pvcreate command, 253
pvdisplay command, 255
pwck command, 227
pwconv command, 677
pwd command, 15
pwunconv command, 677
quot command, 328
rad command, 127
RAID levels, 287
RARP (See Reverse Address Resolution Protocol)
Raw device file (See File types)
rcp command, 523, 531
read command, 446
reboot command, 346
Recovery, 258, 271
Redundancy, 669
reject command, 411
Relative path, 33
Reliability, 672
remsh command, 523, 531
renice command, 113
Repeater, 479
Resource partitioning, 166
Restore, 390
restore command, 395
Reverse Address Resolution Protocol, 483
rlogin command, 6, 523, 530
rlpdaemon daemon, 402
rm command, 47
rmsf command, 144
Rolling upgrade, 673, 772
route command, 500
Router, 478
Routing, 498
   /etc/netconf file, 499
   Adding, 501
   Deleting, 502
   Flushing, 502
   Routing table, 499
   Setting default route, 502
rpcinfo command, 564, 600
Run control levels, 342
rup command, 531
ruptime command, 532
rwho command, 532

SAM (See System Administration Manager)
Samba, 580
samba_setup command, 585
samlog_viewer command, 125
SAN (See Storage Area Network), 672
sar command, 429
scp command, 682
SD-UX
  Commands, 182
  Daemons, 183
  Defined, 182
  Dependencies, 184
  Depot
    Catalog, 192
    Concepts, 192
    Copying to, 193
    Listing, 196
    Registering and uregistering, 195
    Removing, 199
    Removing from, 198
    Verifying, 197
  Installed Product Database, 184
  Installing, 187
  Listing, 184
  Protected software, 184
  Removing, 190
  Starting and stopping, 183
  Structure, 182
  Verifying, 190
Secure shell, 682
  authorized_keys file, 685
  Encryption, 683
Security
  Tools, 688
    Bastille, 689
    COPS, 688
    Crack, 688
    HIDS, 689
    ISS, 688
    SATAN, 689
sed command, 85
sendmail, 537
  Setting, 537
  Starting, 538
  Verifying, 539
Server hardening tasks, 689
Servers
  9000 series, 135
  Integrity series, 134
set_parms command, 178, 502, 504
setacl command, 70
setboot command, 252, 269, 291
sftp command, 682
Shadow password, 677
Shell
  Bourne, 90
  C shell, 91
  Command aliasing, 99
  Command history, 97
  Command line completion, 97
  Command line editing, 97

  Defined, 2, 90
  Features, 91
  Key, 91
  Korn, 90
  Masking special characters, 102
  Modifying command prompt, 95
  POSIX, 90
  Setting variable, 92
    Environment, 91
    Local, 91
  Special characters, 101
  Unsetting variable, 92
  Viewing, 92
Shell Scripting
  Benefits, 438
  Command line arguments, 444
  Debugging, 440
  Defined, 438
  Escape sequences, 447
  Executing, 440
  Exit codes, 448
  Ignoring signals, 464
  Logical construct
    case, 454
    Defined, 448
    if-then-elif-fi, 452
    if-then-else-fi, 451
    if-then-fi, 450
  Looping construct
    Controlling loop behavior, 462
    Defined, 455
    for-do-done, 457
    until-do-done, 460
    while-do-done, 459
  Parsing command output, 443
  Positional parameters (See Command line
    arguments)
  Shifting command line arguments, 445
  Testing conditions, 449
  Using environment variables, 442
  Using local variables, 441
  Writing interactive script, 446
showauto command, 361
showmount command, 559
shutdown command, 344
sig_named command, 626
Single Point Of Failure, 668
sleep command, 462
smbpasswd command, 584
smbstatus command, 584
SMSE (See Standard Mode Security Extensions,
  679, 773
Socket, 477
Software Assistant, 220
Software distributor (See SD-UX), 182
sort command, 53
SPOF (See Single Point Of Failure), 668
ssh command, 6, 685
ssh-keygen command, 684
Standard Mode Security Extensions
  Auditing, 680, 682

Authorization, 680
Defined, 679
Standby node (See Adoptive node), 674
startsmb command, 584
Startup configuration files, 366
Startup scripts, 367
Station address (See MAC address)
Storage Area Network, 671
strings command, 45
Striping, 287
su command, 67
Subnet mask, 488
Subnetting, 487
sudo command, 690
Swap
  Best practices, 337
  Creating, 332
  Defined, 330
  Demand paging, 331
  Device and file system, 332
  Enabling, 332
  Enabling at boot, 336
  Primary and secondary, 332
  Priority, 337
  Related kernel parameters, 338
  Viewing utilization, 336
swapinfo command, 333, 431
swapon command, 332
swcopy command, 192, 193
swinstall command, 187, 213
Switch, 478
swlist command, 184, 196, 203, 494
swpackage command, 192
swreg command, 195
swremove command, 198
swverify command, 190, 197
sysdef command, 376
System Administration Manager
  Defined, 122
  Log, 125
  Restricted, 126
System administrator
  Overview, 120
  Resources, 120
  Responsibilities, 120
System logging, 423
  /etc/syslog.conf file, 423
  /sbin/init.d/syslogd script, 423
  /var/adm/syslog/syslog.log file, 425
  syslogd daemon, 423
System recovery, 664
tail command, 43
talk command, 22
tar command, 397
TCP, 476
TCP window size, 476
TCP/IP
  Layers, 481
  Suite, 481

tee command, 104
telnet command, 4
telnet enable, 533
testparm command, 583
Text processors
  awk, 82
  sed, 85
TFTP
  Defined, 638
  How it works, 638
tilde, 15
time command, 434, 436
timex command, 434, 436
top command, 111, 430
touch command, 37
tr command, 107
traceroute command, 516
trap command, 464
Trusted mode, 677
tsconvert command, 678, 679
tty command, 16
UDP, 476
ulimit command, 235
Ultra High Availability, 671, 673
umount command, 317, 318
umountall command, 318
unalias command, 100
uname command, 18
UNIX directory structure, 2
Unplanned downtime, 670, 672
Uptime, 672
uptime command, 19, 429
User equivalency, 529
User login process, 238
useradd command, 227
userdbchk command, 681
userdbget command, 681
userdbset command, 681
userdel command, 233
usermod command, 232
Users
  /etc/group file, 225
  /etc/passwd file, 224
  Creating, 227
  Creating multiple, 231
  Deactivating, 233
  Deleting, 233
  Displaying logged in users, 235
  Displaying login history, 234, 235
  Locking */etc/passwd* file, 227
  Modifying, 232
  Reactivating, 233
  Setting limits, 235
VERITAS Volume Manager
  Benefits, 284
  Concepts and structure, 284
  Converting non-*vg00* to non-*rootdg*, 298
  Converting *vg00* to *rootdg*, 297
  Creating a disk group, 294

Creating a volume, 294
Deporting a disk group, 296
Destroying a disk group, 297
Disk, 286
Diskgroup, 286
Displaying disk groups, 294
Expanding a disk group, 295
Growing a volume, 295
Importing a disk group, 296
Initializing a disk, 293
Interfaces, 287
Making disk visible, 291
Plex, 286
Private region, 284
Public region, 284
Reducing a disk group, 296
Removing a volume, 296
Renaming a disk group, 297
Shrinking a volume, 295
Subdisk, 286
Virtual objects, 285
Volume, 286
vgcfgbackup command, 263
vgcfgrestore command, 263
vgchange command, 263, 268
vgcreate command, 254
vgdisplay command, 254
vgexport command, 263
vgextend command, 259
vgreduce command, 262
vgsync command, 279
vi editor, 76
  Changing text, 80
  Copying, moving, and pasting, 79
  Customizing, 80
  Deleting text, 78
  Importing, 80
  Inserting text, 77
  Modes, 76
    Command mode, 76
    Input mode, 76
    Last line mode, 76
  Navigating, 77
  Saving and quitting, 81
  Searching and replacing, 79
  Starting, 76
  Undoing and repeating, 78
view command, 44
vipw command, 227
Virtual Front Panel, 149
Virtual IP Address (See Floating IP Address), 673
Virtual machines partitioning, 165
Virtual partition, 158
  Adding CPU, 162
  Adding I/O, 163
  Adding memory, 164
  Bound processor, 159
  Creating, 161
  Rebooting vpmon, 164
  Removing CPU, 163
  Removing I/O, 163
  Removing vPar, 164

  Resetting vPar, 164
  Unbound processor, 159
  Using Virtual Partition Manager GUI, 165
  vPar database, 158
  vpmon, 158
Virtual Private Network, 491
vmstat command, 432
vPar (See Virtual partition), 158
vPar database, 160
vparboot command, 162
vparcreate command, 160
vparload command, 160
vparmodify command, 162
vparremove command, 164
vparstatus command, 161
vpmon, 158
VPN (See Virtual Private Network), 491
vxassist command, 294
vxcp_lvmroot command, 297
vxdctl command, 291
vxdg command, 294
vxdisk command, 291, 294
vxdisksetup command, 293
vxdump command, 396
vxprint command, 292
vxresize command, 295
vxrestore command, 396
vxrootmir command, 299
vxtunefs command, 317
VxVM Mirroring, 298
  Benefits, 299
  Growing mirrors, 301
  Mirroring non-*rootdg*, 301
  Mirroring *rootdg*, 299
  Shrinking mirrors, 301
vxvmconvert command, 298
w command, 17
wall command, 23
wc command, 20
what command, 612
whence command, 22
whereis command, 22
which command, 22
who command, 16, 235
whoami command, 17
Wide Area Network, 469
WorkLoad Manager, 166
write command, 22
ypcat command, 601
ypinit command, 594
ypmake command, 603
ypmatch command, 601
yppasswd command, 602
yppoll command, 601
yppush command, 602
ypset command, 604
ypwhich command, 600

Printed in the United States
117057LV00002B/11-12/A

9 781424 342310